JAPANESE
LEARNER'S DICTIONARY

JAPANESE-ENGLISH / ENGLISH-JAPANESE
Revised and updated

LIVING LANGUAGE®

JAPANESE
LEARNER'S
DICTIONARY
JAPANESE-ENGLISH / ENGLISH-JAPANESE
Revised and updated

Revised by Hiroko Storm, Ph.D.

University of Arizona

Assistant Professor of Japanese
Lafayette College

Based on the original by Ichiro Shirato

This work was previously published under the title *Living Language*™ *Common Usage Dictionary—Japanese* by Ichiro Shirato, based on the dictionary developed by Ralph Weiman.

Published in the United States by Living Language, an imprint of Random House, Inc.

www.livinglanguage.com

ISBN: 978-1-4000-2448-3

This book is available for special discounts for bulk purchases for sales promotions or premiums. Special editions, including personalized covers, excerpts of existing books, and corporate imprints, can be created in large quantities for special needs. For more information, write to Special Markets/ Premium Sales, 1745 Broadway, MD 6-2, New York, New York, 10019 or e-mail specialmarkets@randomhouse.com.

PRINTED IN THE UNITED STATES OF AMERICA

10 9 8 7 6 5 4 3 2 1

CONTENTS

CONTENTS

INTRODUCTION

The *Living Language® Japanese Dictionary* lists more than 15,000 of the most frequently used Japanese words, gives their most important meanings, and illustrates their uses. This revised edition contains updated phrases and expressions, as well as many new entries related to business, technology, and the media.

1. More than 1,000 of the most essential words are capitalized to make them easy to find.

2. Numerous definitions are illustrated with phrases, sentences, and idiomatic expressions. Where there is no close English equivalent for a Japanese word, or where the English equivalent has several meanings, the context of the illustrative sentences helps to clarify the meanings.

3. Because of these useful phrases, the *Living Language® Japanese Dictionary* also serves as a phrase book and conversation guide. The dictionary is helpful both to beginners who are building their vocabulary and to advanced students who want to perfect their command of colloquial Japanese.

4. The Japanese expressions (particularly the idiomatic and colloquial ones) have been translated to their English

equivalents. However, literal translations have been added to help the beginner. For example, under the entry **TE,** *hand,* you will find: "**te ga aite iru** to be free; to have no work on hand." This dual feature also makes the dictionary useful for translation work.

EXPLANATORY NOTES

NOUNS, VERBS, AND ADJECTIVES. The designation of nouns (*n.*), verbs (*v.*), adjectives (*adj.*), and adverbs (*adv.*) given in this dictionary refers to the word class (part of speech) of the English equivalent and *not* to the Japanese word.

Many nouns in Japanese can be converted into verbs simply by adding *suru*: (e.g., *benkyoo suru* = to study).

A verb that is translated in English in the infinitive form appears in the "plain present affirmative" in Japanese. Beginners are reminded that when such a verb is used as a predicate verb in sentences, it can be changed to the appropriate -*masu* (polite) form: -*masu, -mashita, -masen deshita, -mashoo,* etc.

Adjectives (*i* = adjectives) are listed in their "plain present affirmative" form. When they are used a predicate adjectives, an appropriate form of -*desu* (*desu, deshita, -ku arimasen, -ku arimasen deshita,* etc.) can be used.

PERSON AND NUMBER. An arbitrary choice has been made for the person (i.e., I, you, he, she, it, we, you, they) and number (singular or plural) used in the English translation of a Japanese sentence. Usually a Japanese sentence can be translated in several other ways.

HOMONYMS. In Japanese, there are many words that sound and are spelled alike but that have different meanings.

In the traditional Japanese writing system, however, such words may be written with different symbols (*kanji*).

COLLOQUIAL AND HONORIFICS. Very colloquial words, phrases, and sentences are marked either *colloq.* or *vulgar.* *Respect* and *humble* designate honorifics. *Respect* is an expression that can be used only in talking about someone else (not about oneself: speaker); and *humble* is used only in talking about oneself (the speaker or the speaker's in-group).

Japanese-English

A

a *(interj.)* O! oh! look! **a to iwaseru** to astonish, surprise. **A taihen.** Oh! heavens! Good Lord!

AA *(interj.)* O! oh! ah! alas! dear me! *(adv.)* in that way; like that; so; **aa suru** to do so (like that); **aa iu** to say so; like that; **aa iu hito** a person like that; **aa iu koto** a thing like that; **aa iu fuu na hito** that sort of person; **aa iu fuu ni** in that way; like that. **Aa kirei da!** Oh, how beautiful! **Aa omoshirokatta.** Oh, it was so interesting! **Aa soo?** Really? Is it? Did you?

aachi arch.

aa iu = aa yuu that sort of; **aa iu koto** that sort of thing; **aa iu hanashi** that sort of story.

aasu ground wire.

abaku to disclose, to reveal *(a secret);* to expose; to bring to light.

abara ribs; side; **abara bone** rib; side of the chest.

abaraya crumbling house; poor hut.

abare- prefix denoting: rough; rowdy; unruly; **abareuma** runaway horse.

abaredasu to get rowdy, riotous; to break loose; grow restive; to start to behave violently.

abaremawaru to rave, to riot.

abaremono *(n.)* rowdy; hooligan.

abareru to act (behave) violent; to rage; to be riotous.

abekobe being topsy-turvy; **abekobe no** opposite; inverse; **abekobe ni** in a contrary manner; upside down.

abiru to pour on oneself; to bathe in; to be under fire; **hitofuro abiru** to have a bath; **chuumoku o abiru** to receive attention.

abisekakeru See **abiseru.**

abiseru, abisekakeru to pour on; to shower; to lay (something) on; to heap reproaches on.

abu horsefly; gadfly.

abuku See **awa.**

abunage na insecure (in appearance).

ABUNAI dangerous, risky, precarious; critical; **abunai me ni au** to have a terrible experience. **Abunai!** Look out! Watch out!

abunakkashii insecure, unsteady; unstable; unreliable; **abunakkashii tetsuki de** in a clumsy manner.

ABUNAKU nearly; barely; **abunaku naru** to get dangerous. **Abunaku okureru tokoro deshita.** I almost missed the train.

abunasa danger, risk, peril.

abunasoo na dangerous-looking.

ABURA oil; fat; **aburadarake** covered with grease; oil-stained; **abura de ageru** to fry in oil; **abura ga noru** to become interested in; **aburaase** greasy sweat; **aburaase o nagashite** by the sweat of one's brow; **aburake no aru** oily, fatty, rich (food); **aburake no nai** lean; light; **aburakkoi** greasy, fatty, oily (food). **Aburakkoi mono ga suki desu.** I like greasy foods.

aburaage = age bean curd fried in oil (popular food item).

aburae oil painting; **aburae o kaku** to paint in oils.

aburagusuri liniment; ointment.

aburami fat; fatty part of meat.

aburamushi cockroach; aphid.

aburu to place over a fire; to grill; to warm; to dry; **te o aburu** to warm one's hands at a fire.

achikochi *(adv.),* **achira kochira** here and there; to and fro.

ACHIRA *(n.)* that direction; other side; over there; yonder; overseas; **achira no shuukan** customs of a foreign country. **Achira e ikimashoo.** Let's go that way.

ACHIRA KOCHIRA *(n., adv.)* here and there; various places; to and fro; up and down; **achira kochira kara** from far and near; **achira kochira o sagasu** to look for (something) here and there; **achira kochira inaka o ryokoo suru** to travel about the country.

ada enemy; revenge; vengeance; resentment; harm.

adana nickname.

adokenai innocent, artless; naïve *(used when speaking of a child)* **adokenai yoosu** naïve manner; innocent air.

aegi pant; gasp; **aegi aegi** gaspingly; out of breath.

aegu to pant; to gasp.

aen zinc.

aenai untimely; sad; pitiful; **aenai saigo** pitiful end (death); **aenai saigo o togeru** to come to a sad end.

aenaku sadly; unexpectedly; flatly; **aenaku kotowaru** to refuse flatly; **aenaku naru** to die.

aete *(adv.)* boldly; without hesitation; by any means; **aete suru** to dare, venture; **aete iu** I presume; I venture to say.

afureru to overflow, run over.

agaku to paw; to struggle.

agameru to revere; to worship; to respect; to glorify.

aganai atonement; redemption; compensation.

aganau to buy, purchase, atone, expiate, redeem.

AGARIGUCHI entranceway in a Japanese-style house.

agariori *(n.)* ascent and descent; **kaidan no agariori** going up and down the staircase.

agarisagari rise and fall; fluctuation; **nedan no agarisagari** fluctuation of prices.

AGARU to go up, come up; to rise; to ascend, climb (up); to rise in rank; to improve; to come to an end; to visit *(humble);* to go ashore; to eat, drink *(respect);* to become nervous; **chu ga agaru** to be promoted. **ude ga agaru** to become more skillful; **ame ga agaru** to stop raining; **riku ni agaru** to go ashore. **Mata agarimashoo.** I will call again. **Okashi o oagari kudasai.** Help yourself to a sweet, please. **Pitchas ga agaru.** The pitcher *(baseball)* is getting nervous.

age tuck (in Japanese clothes).

ageashi fault-finding; hypercriticism; **ageashi o toru** to trip (a person) up.

ageku *(adv.)* = **ageku ni; ageku no hate ni** the end; finally, at last; on top of all this; to make matters worse. **Shigoto o nakushita ageku ni by ooki ni natta.** He lost his job, and on top of that (to make matters worse), he became ill.

agemono fried food.

agenabe frying pan.

ageoroshi = **agesage** loading and unloading; raising and lowering; **hashi no ageoroshi ni mo kogoto o iu** to find fault with everything [to make comments even on how the chopsticks are handled].

AGERU to raise, elevate, lift (up); to give, present (honorific; used when the speaker gives something to someone else). **Okane o ageta.** I gave her some money.

agesage = **ageoroshi** raising and lowering; praise and blame; **hashi no agesage ni mo kogoto o iu** to be (too) particular about trifles.

ageshio flood (rising) tide.

AGO jaw; chin.

-agumu suffix denoting to grow tired of, get (become) weary; **machiagumu** to grow tired of waiting.

agura o kaku to sit cross-legged.

ahen opium.

ahiru duck, drake; **ahiru no ko** duckling.

ahoo fool; idiot; blockhead; **ahoo na** foolish; stupid; **ahorashii** foolish; silly; ridiculous; **ahoo na koto** foolish affair.

AI love; affection; attachment; **ai suru** to love; care for; **fukaku ai suru** to love tenderly (deeply).

ai indigo, blue; **ai-iro no** blue, bluish.

ai- prefix denoting: mutually; with each other; **ai-mukatte** face to face; **ai-narande tatsu** to stand shoulder to shoulder.

aibiki secret meeting (of lovers); rendezvous.

aiboo partner; accomplice.

aibu caress; fondling; **aibu suru** to caress, fondle, pet.

aichaku deep attachment; passion; **-ni aichaku suru** to love passionately.

AIDA space (between); time (between); distance; interval; **sono aida** in the meanwhile; **nagai aida** for a long time; **hitotsuki no aida ni** in the course of a month; **watakushi ga ikite iru aida wa** as long as I live; **roppun no aida o oite** at intervals of six minutes.

aidagara relationship; terms; **shitashii aidagara de aru** to be on very friendly terms.

aidoku suru to read for pleasure; **aidokusha** subscriber; reader; reading public; **aidokusho** one's favorite book.

aifuku, aigi lightweight suit.

aijin lover, sweetheart; **aijoo** love, affection; **aijoo no aru hito** affectionate, warmhearted person.

aikagi passkey.

AIKAWARAZU as usual; as always; **aikawarazu isogashii desu** as busy as ever.

aiko a tie, even game, draw; **aiko ni naru** to end in a tie. **Kore de aiko da.** This makes us even.

aikoku love for one's country, patriotism.

aikotoba password.

aikyoo charm; amiability; **aikyoo no aru hito** charming, amiable person; **aikyoo no nai hito** disagreeable person; **aikyoo o furimaku** to have a smile for everybody.

aima interval; leisure; **aima ni** at intervals; **shigoto no aima ni** in one's spare time.

aimai obscurity; ambiguity; **aimai na** obscure; ambiguous; vague.

AINIKU unluckily; unfortunately; **ainiku na** unfavorable; unfortunate. **Oainiku sama.** I am very sorry (that I do not have it). **Ainiku ame ga futte kimashita.** Unfortunately, it started to rain.

ainoko *(n.)* hybrid; Eurasian.

Ainu Ainus (a minority tribe of northern Japan).

airashii charming; amiable; sweet.

AIRON iron (for pressing); **airon o kakeru** to iron.

aisatsu greeting, salutation; **aisatsu suru** to greet, salute.

aiso sociability, cordiality; **aiso no yoi** sociable, cordial; **aiso no nai hito** cold, blunt person; **oaiso o iu** to flatter; **-ni aiso ga tsukiru** to be disgusted with. **Aiso yoku hanashimashita.** He spoke very pleasantly.

aisuhokkee ice hockey.

aisukuriimu ice cream.

aita empty, vacant; opened; **te ga aita toki** when he is free.

aitagai ni with each other.

AITE companion; partner; adversary; **-no aite ni naru** to keep company with; to become a partner of; **-o aite ni shinai** to pay no attention to; **-o aite ni suru** to challenge; to deal with.

aitsu that fellow; that rascal (derogatory).

aitsuide one after another; successively.

aizu signal; **aizu suru** to signal.

AJI taste, flavor; relish; **aji no aru** tasty; **aji no nai** tasteless; **-no aji ga suru** it tastes like; **aji ga kawaru** to become stale, turn sour; **aji o tsukeru** to flavor, season.

aji bluefin tuna.

AJIA Asia; **Ajia no** *(adj.)* Asian, Asiatic; **Ajiajin** *(n.)* Asian, Asiatic.

ajikenai irksome, wearisome; lonely; **ajikenaku kurasu** to lead a miserable life.

ajina dainty; clever; smart; **ajina koto o suru** to act cleverly; **ajina koto o iu** to say something clever.

ajisai hydrangea.

ajitsukenori seasoned seaweed (a popular food item).

ajiwau to taste; to experience; to enjoy; to appreciate.

AKA *(n.)* red, crimson, scarlet; communism; communist; **aka no tanin** utter stranger.

aka dirt, filth; **aka darake** dirty, filthy; **-ni aka ga tsuku** to become dirty; **aka o nagasu** to wash off dirt; to wash (oneself).

AKABOO redcap, porter (for luggage).

AKACHAN = **akago** baby, infant.

akagire chap, crack (in the skin); **akagire ga kireru** to become chapped.

akago See **akachan**.

akahaji disgrace; open shame; **akahaji o kakasareru** to be put to shame.

AKAI red, ruddy, flushed; **akai kao o suru** to blush.

akaji red figures, deficit; **akaji o dasu** to go into the red; to have a deficit.

akajimita soiled, dirty.

akaku ruddily; redly; **akaku naru** to redden; to flush; to glow.

akami redness; tinge of red.

akami lean meat.

Akamon Red Gate of Tokyo University; synonym for Tokyo University.

akanboo baby, infant. (See also **akachan**.)

akanuke polish, gloss; refinement; **akanuke no shita hito** polished person; **akanuke no shinai hito** unpolished, uncouth person.

akaramu to turn red; to glow; to ripen (fruit).

akarasama na plain, clear; frank, candid; **akarasama ni** plainly; frankly; without reserve; **akarasama ni ieba** to be frank; to tell the truth in plain terms.

akari light, lamp; **akari o tsukeru** to light a lamp.

AKARUI bright; light; knowing well; versed in; **akaruku naru** to grow light; **akarui heya** well-lighted room; **hooritsu ni akarui** to be familiar with the laws; **akarui uchi ni** while it is light; before it gets dark.

akarumi light place; light; **akarumi e dasu** to bring a thing to light; to expose (something).

akasu to spend the whole night; to sit up all night; to reveal the truth, to confess; to speak one's mind.

akasu to weary, tire; **kane ni akashite** regardless of the expense; regardless of the cost.

akatsuchi red earth (clay).

akatsuki = **akegata** dawn, daybreak; **akatsuki chikaku** toward daybreak; **-no akatsuki ni wa** when; in the event of; in case of.

akazatoo brown sugar.

akegata See **akatsuki**.

akehanasu to throw open (a window).

akekure morning and evening; day and night; all the time.

AKERU to open; to turn over (pages); to make room (for); to evacuate (a house, premises); to empty (a box); to expire; **ie o akeru** to stay out; **ana o akeru** to make a hole; **mizu o akeru** to pour out water. **Yo ga akeru.** The day is breaking.

AKI room; space; vacancy; **aki o fusagu** to fill a gap.

AKI autumn, fall; **akibare** a clear autumn day.

aki- prefix denoting: vacant, unoccupied; spare; **akibin** empty bottle; **akichi** vacant lot; **akidaru** empty barrel; **akima** vacant room.

akimekura illiterate (person).

akinai trade, business; **akinai suru** to do business; **akinai o shite iru** to be in business; to be engaged in a trade; **akinai joozu** good at trade; **akinai beta** poor at trade.

akinau to deal in, trade in.

AKIRAKA NA bright; clear; **akiraka ni suru** to make clear; to account for; **akiraka ni** brightly; clearly; undoubtedly; no doubt. **Akiraka desu.** It is clear.

akirame resignation; relinquishment; **akirameru** to give up; to resign oneself to; to submit to one's fate; to relinquish.

akireru to be amazed at; to be dumbfounded; be disgusted with; **akirete** with astonishment; in amazement; **akirete mono ga ienai** to be dumbfounded.

akiru to get tired of, be sick of; to have enough of; **akiru hodo taberu** to eat one's fill; **-ni akiyasui** to be soon tired of; **akiru hodo asobu** to play to one's heart's content.

akisu sneak thief.

AKIYA vacant house; unoccupied house; house for rent.

akkan rascal, rogue.

akka suru to go from bad to worse.

akke *(n.)* being dumfounded when an event has happened; **akke nai** too soon; too brief; too sudden; **akke ni torareru** to be taken aback; to be amazed. **Tsukihi ga akke naku tatte shimatta.** The days passed all too quickly. **Sore de wa amari akke nai.** That's too abrupt.

akkoo abuse, insulting remarks; **akkoo suru** to abuse, insult.

akogare longing, yearning; desire.

akogareru to long for, yearn for, yearn after.

aku evil, vice; wrong; wickedness; **aku ni mukuiru ni zen o motte suru** to return good for evil.

AKU to open; to be opened; to become empty, become vacant; **te ga aku** to be free, be disengaged. **Maku ga aku.** The curtain rises.

akubi yawn; **ooakubi** great yawn; **akubi suru** to yawn.

akudoi tedious; heavy (color or food); glaring.

akufuu evil practices; evil manners; evil habit.

akuheki bad habit; vice.

akuhitsu illegible handwriting; poor penmanship.

akui malice, ill will; malicious intent; **akui de** from malice; purposely; **akui no aru hito** malicious, evil-minded person.

akuji evil thing; evil deed; criminal action.

AKUKANJOO ill feeling; ill will.

akumade to the utmost; to the best of one's ability; persistently; **akumade mo** to the last; stubbornly; to the end; **akumade yaru** to do one's utmost.

akunin bad person, villain.

akuratsu na unscrupulous; sharp; crafty; wicked.

akurei bad precedent; bad example; **akurei o tsukuru** to set a bad precedent.

AKURU next, following (time); **akuru asa** the following morning; **akuru toshi** the following year.

akuseku diligently, industriously; busily; restlessly; **akuseku suru** to busy oneself; worry about; **-ni akuseku to suru** to be busy with; **akuseku to kasegu** to work hard (for a living).

akusento accent, stress; pitch (of the voice).

AKUSHU handshake; **akushu suru** to shake hands.

akushuu bad habit; evil practices; **akushuu ga tsuku** to develop a bad habit; **akushuu o dassuru** to get rid of a bad habit.

akutoo villain, scoundrel.

akuun ill luck; evil fate.

akuyoo misuse; improper use; abuse; **akuyoo suru** to misuse; abuse.

akuyuu bad friend; bad companion; **akuyuu to majiwaru** to keep bad company.

ama diving woman (professional pearl-diver).

AMA- prefix denoting: rain; of rain, for rain; **amadare** raindrops; **amado** rain door; **amagasa** umbrella; **amagoi** prayers for rain; **amagu** rain gear; **amagumo** rain cloud; **amamizu** rain water; **amagu o yooi shite deru** to go out prepared for rain; **amagu no yooi o suru** to provide oneself with rain gear.

amachua amateur.

amaeru, amattareru to behave like a spoiled child; to coax; to be coquettish; to take advantage of; **amaeru yoo ni** coaxingly. **Okotoba ni amaemashoo.** I'll take advantage of your kind offer.

amaguri roast chestnuts.

AMAI sweet, sugary; not salted enough; indulgent; not strict; **amaku suru** to sweeten; **amai mono** sweets, candy; **amai kotoba** sweet (soft) words; **amaku miru** to have little regard for a person. **Kono sake wa ama-jio da.** This salmon is not salted enough.

amajio slightly salted.

amakuchi fondness for sweet things; sweet tooth; honeyed words. **Kare wa amakuchi da.** He has a sweet tooth.

amami sweet flavor; sweetness; **amami no aru** sweetish; **amami o tsukeru** to sweeten. **Amami ga tarinai.** It is not sweet enough.

amamori leak in the roof.

amemoyoo signs of rain; **amamoyoo no sora** a threatening sky. **Amamoyoo desu.** It looks like rain.

AMANEKU widely, universally; far and wide; **amaneku aekai ni shirarete iru** to be known all over the world; **amaneku zenkoku o jun'yuu suru** to travel all over the country.

AMANJIRU, amanzuru to be content with, be satisfied with; to put up with; **amanjite** contentedly; willingly; **amanjite seisai o ukeru** to submit willingly to punishment. **Kare wa kore ni amanjite wa inai.** He is not content with this.

Amanogawa Milky Way; Galaxy.

amanzuru See **amanjiru**.

AMARI See **ANMARI**

AMARI remainder, rest; surplus, excess; remnants.

AMARU to remain, be left over; to be too much; to be in excess; to be beyond one's power; **mini amaru kooei** an undeserved honor; **chikara ni amaru** beyond one's power.

amasu to leave over; to save; **kane o amasazu tsukau** to spend all one's money. **Hitotsu mo amasanakatta.** I didn't leave even one.

amata (a great) many; many a; a number of; numerous.

amatsusae besides; moreover; what is more; into the bargain; to make matters worse.

amattareru See **amaeru**.

amattarui sweetish; sugary; **amattarui kotoba** honeyed words; **amattarui shibai** sentimental play (drama).

amayadori suru to take shelter from the rain.

amayakasu to pet; to indulge (a child) too much; to spoil.

amayoke shelter from the rain; protection against rain.

amazake sweet drink made from fermented rice.

amazarashi exposure to rain.

AME rain; rainy; wet; **ame no** rainy; wet; **ame tsuzuki** spell of rainy weather; **ame ni naru** to change to rain; to begin to rain; **ame ni au** to be caught in the rain. **Ame ga furisoo desu.** It looks like rain.

AME candy; wheat gluten.

AMEFURI rain; rainy weather; rainy day; **amefuri ni soto o aruku** to walk in the rain.

ameiro no light brown.

AMERIKA America; **Amerika no** (adj.) American; **AMERIKAJIN** (n.) American; **Amerika Gasshuukoku** United States of America.

ami net; fishing net; **ami no me** meshes (of a net).

amibari, amiboo knitting needles.

amidana rack (in a train or bus).

amimono (n.) knitting; crocheting; **amimono o suru** to knit.

aminome mesh.

amu to knit; to braid; **kutsushita o amu;** to knit socks.

an proposal; bill; draft; plan; opinion; idea; **an o dasu** to make a proposal; **an o tateru** to make a plan; **an o tsukuru** to make a draft; **an ni sooi shite** contrary to expectation; **an no gotoku** as was expected.

an bean paste, bean jam.

ANA hole; aperture; den, cave; pit; loss; shortage; fault; **ana o akeru** to make a hole, perforate; **zaisan ni ana o akeru** to cut into one's assets; **ana o fusagu** to fill up a hole; stop a gap.

anadori contempt; disdain; **anadoru** to despise; to slight; to make light of; to look down upon; **anadori o ukeru** to be despised; to be scorned; **anadorigatai** formidable. **Shooteki o anadoru na.** Don't despise a weak enemy.

anagachi necessarily, of necessity; always (used with a negative). **Sore wa anagachi muri de wa nai.** It's not altogether unreasonable.

anago sea eel.

an'anri ni tacitly; by tacit agreement; secretly; **an'anri ni shoodaku suru** to give tacit consent. **An'anri ni itchi shita.** It was tacitly agreed.

ANATA you, sweetheart.

ANATAGATA you (pl. formal).

ANATATACHI you (pl.).

anaunsaa announcer.

anbai seasoning; taste; state of health; condition; **anbai suru** to season; to arrange; **yoi anbai ni** fortunately.

anbaransu unbalance; **eiyoo no anbaransu** unbalance of diet.

anchaku safe arrival; **anchaku suru** to arrive safely.

anchoku na cheap, low-priced, inexpensive; **anchoku ni** cheaply, inexpensively.

anchuu mosaku suru to grope in the dark.

ANE older sister.

anemuko husband of an older sister.

ANGAI NA unexpected; unforeseen; surprising; **angai ni** unexpectedly; **angai muzukashii** more difficult than imagined.

ANI older brother.

aniyome elder brother's wife.

anji hint; suggestion; **anji suru** to hint; to suggest; **anji o tsutaeru** to give a hint; **anji ni tonda** suggestive; full of suggestions.

ANJIRU to be anxious, be concerned; to worry.

anka cheapness; low price; **anka na** cheap; inexpensive; **anka ni** cheaply; at a low price; **anka na seikatsu** cheap living; **anka na kairaku** cheap pleasure.

ankeeto questionnaire.

anki suru to learn by heart, memorize.

anma masseur; massage; **anma suru** to massage.

ANMARI, AMARI too much; excessively; too hard; cruel; unreasonable. **Sore wa anmari desu.** That's too hard. That's too cruel. **Anmari omoshiroku nai.** It's not too interesting.

ANMIN quiet sleep; sound sleep; **anmin suru** to sleep well; **anmin o boogai suru** to disturb someone else's sleep.

anmoku tacit consent, tacit understanding. **anmoku no uchi ni** by tacit consent.

ANNA that sort of; like that; such; **anna ni** like that; in that way; **anna utsukushii musume** such a pretty girl; a girl as pretty as that; **anna hito** a person like that; that sort of person.

ANNAI guidance; conduct; invitation; **annai suru** to usher, guide; to invite; **annaijoo** letter or card of invitation; **annaiki** guidebook; **annaisha** guide; usher; pilot; **annaisho** guidebook, handbook; **annai nashi ni** unannounced; without knowing; without a guide; **annai o kou** to ask to see. **Annai nashi ni haitte kita.** She entered the room without knocking.

annei public peace; public welfare.

an ni by hints; tacitly; in secret; implicitly; **an ni shiraseru** to hint; suggest; insinuate.

ANO that; those; **ano yoo na** like that; of that sort; that sort of; **ano kata** he; she; that person. **Ano ne.** You see! I say, Listen!

anoo well; I say; look here.

ano yo other world; next world; **ano yo de** in the world to come.

anpan bean-jam bun; bun.

ANPI safety; welfare; health; **anpi o tazuneru** to inquire after (someone's) health.

anpojooyaku the (Japan-U.S.) Security Pact.

ANRAKU comfort, ease; **anraku na** comfortable, easy; happy; **anraku isu** easy chair; **anraku na seikatsu o suru** to lead a life of ease; **anraku ni kurasu** to live comfortably.

ANSEI quietness, rest; **ansei ni** quietly; in quiet; **ansei o tamotsu** to keep quiet; to lie quietly.

ANSHIN peace of mind, freedom from anxiety; confidence; **anshin suru** to feel at ease; to feel relieved; **anshin saseru** to set (someone) at ease; **anshin no dekiru hito** reliable person; **anshin no dekinai hito** unreliable person; **anshin shite** with confidence; with peace of mind.

anshitsu dark room.

anshoo recitation; **anshoo suru** say by rote.

anshutsu invention; contrivance; **anshutsu suru** to think out; to contrive, devise; to invent.

ansoku rest, respose **ansoku suru** to rest; to take a rest.

ansokujitsu Sunday, Sabbath.

anta (colloq.) you.

antei stability; equilibrium; **antei suru** to be stabilized; to be settled; **antei o tamotsu** to keep one's balance; **antei o ushinau** to lose one's balance.

antena antenna.

ANZEN safety, security; **anzen na** safe; secure; **anzen ni** safely; securely; **anzen chitai** safety zone; **anzen kamisori** safety razor.

ANZU apricot.

anzuru to be anxious about, worry about. **Watakushi no koto o anjinaide kudasai.** Don't worry about me.

AO blue; green; **aoao shita** verdant; freshly green; **aoba** green leaves, foliage.

aodatami new or freshly renovated mat.

aogu to fan; to raise one's eyes; to ask for; to depend upon; **hojo o aogu** to ask for aid. **Sora o aoida.** He looked up at the sky.

AOI blue; green; pale; unripe; inexperienced; **aoku naru** to become blue (pale); **aoku someru** to dye (something) blue. **Aoi kao o shite iru.** He looks pale. **Sora ga aoku harete iru.** The sky is clear.

aoi hollyhock.

aoiki gasp; **aoiki o tsuku** to gasp; to heave a deep sigh; **aoiki toiki de** gaspingly; with greatest effort. **Aoiki toiki desu.** I am in great distress.

aojashin blueprint.

aojiroi pale, pallid; sickly.

aomi blueness; blue tint; greenness; **aomi gakatta** bluish; greenish.

aomono vegetables; **aomono ichiba** vegetable market; **aomonoya** greengrocer; vegetable seller.

aomuki ni on one's back. **aomuki ni taoreru** to fall on one's back; **aomuku** to look up, turn one's face up.

aonisai greenhorn; raw youth; stripling.

aonori seaweed processed for food.

aori flapping; bump; **aori o kurau** to feel the influence of; to be hit by; **aoru** to fan; to flap; to stir up, incite; **kaze ni aorarete iru** to flap in the wind. **Kaze ga kaen o aotta.** The strong wind fanned the flames.

aotenjoo (azure) heaven; vault of heaven; open sky.

aounabara blue expanse of water; ocean.

aozameru to turn pale. **Aozameta kao o shite iru.** His face is white as a sheet.

aozora blue sky.

APAATO apartment house.

appaku pressure; stress; oppression; **appaku suru** to oppress; bear down upon.

appare (n.) being splendid; bravo!; well done! **appare na** splendid! admirable; **appare na hataraki** splendid achievement; **appare na**

jinbutsu person of fine (admirable) character.

ara ah! oh! good gracious! oh, my! (used by women).

ara defect, fault, blemish; bony parts (of fish); **ara o sagasu** to look for defects (in others); find fault with others.

ara- prefix denoting: coarse; rough, harsh; **arashigoto** a rough work.

Arabia Arabia; **Arabia no** *(adj.)* Arabic; Arabian; **Arabiago** Arabic language; **Arabiajin** *(n.)* Arab; Arabian; **Arabia suuji** Arabic numerals.

aradateru to excite; to agitate; to exasperate; to inflame; to complicate; **koto o aradateru** to complicate matters; to aggravate the matter.

aragyoo asceticism.

ARAI rough; coarse; rude; wild; violent; **arai shima** a rough pattern; **araku** harshly; roughly. **Umi ga arai.** The sea is rough.

arai wash; washing; raw fish slices; **araigami** newly washed and untied hair; **araitate** just washed; **araitate no** newly washed; **arai ga kiku** to wash well; to be washable; **arai ga kikanai** not washable.

ARAKAJIME previously; in anticipation; **arakajime tsuuchi suru** to inform beforehand; **arakajime yooi suru** to prepare beforehand.

ARAKATA for the most part; mostly; most of. **Shigoto wa arakata dekiagari mashita.** The work is nearly completed.

arakezuri no roughly planned; rough-hewn.

arakure otoko *(n.)* rough; rowdy.

aramashi roughly; nearly, almost; practically; all but; briefly.

aramonoya kitchenware dealer.

arankagiri as much as possible; **arankagiri ni** every; all; utmost; **arankagiri no chikara o dashite** with the utmost exertion; **arankagiri no koe de** at the top of one's voice; as loudly as possible.

arappoi rough; rough-mannered; violent.

arare hail; hailstone; salty rice cracker (seasoned with soy sauce). **Arare ga futte iru.** It is hailing.

araryooji drastic treatment, drastic remedy; drastic measures.

arasagashi *(n.)* fault-finding; **arasagashi o suru** to find fault (with).

ARASHI storm; **arashi no** stormy.

arashigoto rough work; rough labor.

ARASOI quarrel; contention; **arasoi o okosu** to start a dispute; **uchiwa no arasoi** family quarrel; internal troubles.

ARASOU to quarrel; to dispute; to struggle, compete, vie; **saki o arasou** to scramble

for a seat; **arasou koto no dekinai** indisputable.

ARASU to ruin, to devastate.

arasuji outline, brief summary.

ARATAMARU to be changed, be altered; to be improved, be reformed; to take a turn for the worse (in illness); to stand on ceremony. **Soo aratamaranaide kudasai.** Don't stand on ceremony.

aratameru to renew; to renovate, alter, change, revise; to improve; to examine.

aratamete anew; another time; **aratamete tazuneru** to ask again. **Aratamete mairimasu.** I'll come another time. I'll come again.

arata na new, fresh, novel; **arata na sumai** a new house; **arata ni hajimeru** to begin anew.

arate fresh force; new hand.

ARAU to wash; to purify; to cleanse; **ashi o arau** to wash one's hands of a matter; to quit.

araumi rough sea, stormy sea.

arawareru to come out; to make an appearance, turn up, show oneself. **Kao ni arawarete iru.** It is written on your face.

ARAWASU to show, display; to bring to light, lay bare; to write (a book, novel, etc.); to publish; to make known; **udemae o arawasu** to show ability; **tookaku o arawasu** to stand head and shoulders above others; **ikari o kao ni arawasu** to show anger (in one's face); **na o arawasu** to win fame; to distinguish oneself.

ARAYURU all; every possible; all sorts of; **arayuru shurui no hito** all sorts of people; **arayuru shudan o kokoromiru** to try every known method.

ARE that; it; roughness, coarseness; **ARE!** listen! look! **are hodo** like that; that (so) much; that degree; **are hodo itta noni** in spite of all that I have said; **are hodo kane ga atte mo** with all his riches; **are ka kore ka** this or that; **are ya kore ya** this and that; with one thing or another; **are ya kore ya de ki o momu** to worry oneself with one thing or another. **Are! Nan daroo?** Listen! What can that be?

arebiyori stormy weather.

arechi wasteland; uncultivated land.

arehateru to be dilapidated; to be utterly ruined; **arehateta** dilapidated; ruined.

arekkiri since then; any more; all; last. **Arekkiri otosata ga arimasen.** I haven't heard from him since then. **Arekkiri yoshimashita.** After that I left off completely.

aremawaru to rush about furiously.

aremoyoo threatening sky; signs of approaching storm.

areno wildness; wilds; wild tract of land.

areru to fall into decay; to lie waste; to rush about furiously; to be rough. **Umi wa arete ita.** The sea was rough.

ari ant; **arizuka** an anthill.

ariamaru (*pronoun*) ample; abundant; **ariamaru hodo kane ga aru** to have money to spare.

ariari to vividly; distinctly; plainly.

ariawase potluck; **ariawase no** ready; on hand; **mise no ariawase no shinamono** articles in stock; **ariawase no mono o taberu** to take potluck; to eat what is available.

aribai alibi.

arifureta common; ordinary.

arigachi frequent occurrence; **arigachi no** common; frequent. **Konna koto wa arigachi desu.** Such things are apt to happen.

arigane cash on hand.

arigatagaru to be thankful, feel grateful; **arigata meiwaku** unappreciated favor; misplaced kindness; **arigata namida** tears of gratitude. **Ano hito wa watashi no okurimono o arigatagarimashita.** She was thankful for my gift.

ARIGATAI thankful; **arigatai koto ni wa** fortunately; **arigataku** with thanks.

arigatami gratefulness, sense of gratitude.

ARIGATOO many thanks; I am much obliged to you. **Arigatoo gozaimasu.** Thank you.

arika whereabouts; place where a thing is.

arikitari no customary; conventional; **arikitari no hoohoo** the customary method.

ari no mama exact truth; plain fact; **ari no mama o iu** to tell the exact truth; **ari no mama ni** just as it is; frankly.

arisama circumstances; state; condition. **Soo iu arisama desu.** That's the situation.

arisoo na seemingly possible; **arisoo mo nai** unlikely; improbable. **Arisoo na koto desu.** It's likely to happen.

aritei as it is; frankly (*colloq.*); **aritei ni iu** to speak the truth; state frankly.

aritsuku to come by, come upon; to find; to get, obtain; **shigoto ni aritsuku** to get work.

arittake all that there is; all that one has; **arittake no chikara o dasu** to put forth all one's efforts.

ariubekarazaru impossible; improbable; **ariubeki** possible; probable. **Sore wa ariubekarazaru koto desu.** That's impossible. That could never happen.

ARU certain; some; a; an; **aru tokoro de** at a certain place; **aru hi** one day; once; **aru hito** a certain person; a person; somebody; **aru toki** on a certain occasion; once upon a time.

ARU to be at; to exist, live; to be situated; to lie; to have; to take place; to experience; to find; to get. **Hon ga tsukue no ue ni arimasu.** The book is on the desk. **Oomori wa Tookyoo to Yokohama no aida ni aru.** Omori lies between Tokyo and Yokohama. **Tookyoo ni itta koto ga arimasu ka?** Have you ever been to Tokyo? **Kono hon wa doko ni arimashita ka?** Where did you find this book? **Taihen na koto ga atta no desu.** A dreadful thing happened.

ARUBAITO side job; **ARUBAITO SURU** to do a side job.

ARUBAMU album.

arufabetto alphabet.

ARUIWA or else; perhaps; probably; maybe. **Aruiwa soo ka mo shirenai.** It may be so. It is not impossible.

aruji master; host; head of the family.

arukaseru to make walk, let walk (said of a child, horse, etc.)

arukikata one's manner of walking.

arukimawaru to walk about; to wander about; to go around; to gad about.

arukooru alcohol.

ARUKU to walk, go on foot. **Aruku no wa karada ni taihen ii desu.** Walking is very good for your health.

arumajiki improper; unbecoming; improbable.

arumi, aruminyuumu aluminum.

aruto alto.

ASA morning; in the morning; **asa hayaku** early in the morning; **asa no aida** all morning; **asa kara ban made** from morning till evening; **asaban** every morning and evening.

asa hemp; flax; linen; **asaito** hemp yarn; **asanawa** hempen cord.

asa- prefix denoting: light; shallow; **asamidori** light green.

asagao morning glory.

asagi (*n.*) light blue.

ASAGOHAN breakfast. **Asagohan wa hachiji desu.** Breakfast is at eight.

asaguroi dark; dark-skinned; brown.

asahaka na shallow (of mind); superficial; half-witted.

asahi morning sun; rising sun.

ASAI shallow; superficial; short, brief; **asai kawa** shallow river; **asai kangae** shallow thought; **hi ga asai . . .** it is a short time (since).

asakusa nori dried seaweed (food).

asamashii mean, miserable; wretched; **asamashii yononaka** the wretched world; **asamashii kokoro no otoko** a mean-spirited man.

asamidori (*n.*) light green.

asanagi morning calm.

asane o suru to lie in bed late; to sleep late; **asaneboo** late riser, sleepyhead; **asaneboo o suru** to oversleep; to get up late.

asaru to fish for; to search for; to hunt for; **iro o asaru** to philander.

asase shoal; shallows; **asase ni noriageru** to run aground.

asatsuyu morning dew.

ASATTE day after tomorrow. **Asatte ome ni kakarimasu.** I will see you the day after tomorrow.

asayake morning glow; sky at dawn.

ASE sweat; perspiration; **asebamu** to become sweaty; to be wet with sweat; **asekaki** one who perspires profusely; **ase ga deru** to perspire; **ase o kaku** to perspire; to become sweaty; **asemidoro ni natte** in a sweat; soaked with sweat; **asemizu o nagashite hataraku** to sweat with hard work; work by the sweat of one's brow.

asemo prickly heat.

aseru to hurry; to get impatient; to be hasty.

aseru to fade, to discolor. **Iro ga aseru.** The color has faded.

ASHI foot; leg; paw; step; pace; **ashi no koo** instep; **ashi no ura** sole; **ashiato** footprint; **ashi ni makasete iku** to go without knowing where; **ashi ga tsuku** to be traced; leave a clue.

ashi reed; rush.

ashiba scaffolding; foothold.

ashibumi step; **ashibumi suru** to step; stamp one's feet.

ashibyooshi keeping time with the feet.

ashidamari stand; footing; **ashidamari o eru** to get a footing.

ashidematoi encumbrance, burden, nuisance; **ashidematoi ni naru** to become a nuisance; to get in the way.

ashidome confinement; **ashidome o suru** to keep (someone) indoors.

ashidori gait; manner of walking; tread.

ashikake foothold; pedal. **Kite kara ashikake gonen ni naru.** It is five [calendar] years since I came here.

ashikarazu. Please don't take it amiss.

ASHIKUBI ankle.

ashimoto place where one stands; **ashimoto ni** at (near) one's feet; **ashimoto no akarui uchi ni** before it gets dark; before getting caught; **ashimoto o miru** to take advantage of (someone else's) weakness.

ashinami pace; **ashinami o soroete** with measured steps; keeping pace with; **ashinami o soroete aruku** to walk in step.

ashioto footfall, sound of a footstep.

ashirai treatment; reception.

ashirau to treat, entertain; to receive; to handle; to deal with; to harmonize; to add.

ashi shigeku often, frequently (refers to visits); **ashi shigeku kayou** to visit frequently.

ASHITA, ASU tomorrow. **Ashita mata.** See you again tomorrow.

asobaseru to leave (something) idle; **kane o asobasete oku** to let money lie idle.

ASOBI play; sport; amusement; pleasure; recreation; sensual pleasure; dissipation; **asobi ni iku** to go out to play; to seek recreation; **asobi gatera** for amusement; half in play.

ASOBU to play; to be idle; to go on a spree; to amuse.

ASOKO that place; there; **asoko ni** over there, yonder.

assaku pressure; compression; **assaku suru** to press.

ASSARI simply; lightly; moderately; briefly; **assari shita** simple; light; plain; **assari katazukeru** to make short work of.

assen mediation; **assen suru** to help, to mediate; arbitrate; **assensha** mediator, arbitrator.

ASU See **ASHITA.**

asufaruto asphalt. **asufaruto no michi** asphalt road.

asupirin aspirin.

ataeru to give; to let have; to present, award; **shigoto o ataeru** to give work; **-ni songai o ataeru** to inflict damage on; **ataerareta shigoto** work assigned.

atafuta hurriedly; helter-skelter.

atai price; value; **atai suru** to be worth; to cost; to deserve.

ATAKAMO just as if, so to speak. **Atakamo Nihonjin no yooni.** Just as if she were Japanese.

ATAMA head; top; brains; **atama o sageru** to bow respectfully; **atama ga yoi** a clear head; **atama ga warui** stupid; **atama gonashi ni** unsparingly; cruelly; **atama kara ashi no saki made** from head to foot; **atamakabu** leader; leading member.

atamakazu number of persons.

atamawari equal division; **atamawari ni suru** to divide equally, allot equal shares.

ATARASHII new, fresh, novel; recent, latest; **atarashii sakana** fresh fish; **atarashiku** newly; anew; afresh; **atarashiku suru** to renovate; freshen; **atarashiku hajimeru** to begin anew.

11

atari neighborhood; vicinity; near; **-no atari ni** in the neighborhood of; near; about; **atari kamawazu** regardless of the people present.

atari success; hit; **atari doshi** fruitful (successful) year; **atari fuda** price-number ticket; **atari hazure** hit or miss; success or failure; **atari o toru** to make a hit.

ATARIMAE NO right, proper, reasonable; deserving; natural; usual; **atarimae no koto** a matter of course. **Okoru no wa atarimae desu.** She has good reason to get angry.

atarisawari consequence; **atarisawari no nai** neutral, noncommittal; **atarisawari no nai koto o iu** to talk so as not to hurt someone's feelings.

ataru to strike; to come true; to be exposed; to disagree with; to warm oneself; to succeed; to try; **soozoo ga ataru** to guess right; **ataru bekarazaru** irresistible; overpowering. **Keikaku ga atatta.** The plan succeeded. **Tonikaku atatte kudakero da.** Try anyhow.

ATATAKAI warm; genial; mild; **atatakai hito** warmhearted, genial person; **atatakai fuyu** warm winter; **atatakaku naru** to become warm; **atatakami** mildness; warmth; geniality; **atatakami no aru** warm, warmhearted.

atatakasoo ni snugly.

atatamaru to get warm; to warm oneself; **Yatto kore de atatamarimashita.** Now I'm warm.

atatameru to warm up, heat; **kyuukoo o atatameru** to renew an old friendship; **te o atatameru** to warm one's hands (over a brazier).

ate aim, object; **ate ni naranai** unreliable; **ate nashi ni** aimlessly; at random; **atedo naku** aimlessly, without an aim, at random; **ate ni suru** to depend on; **ate ga nai** to find no clue.

-ate addressed to; **watashiate no tegami** letter addressed to me.

ategai appointment; allotment; **ategaibuchi** rations; stipend (*colloq.*).

ategau to apportion; to allow; to give rations; to supply.

atehamaru to apply to; to hold good for; to conform to; **atehameru** to apply; to fit; to conform.

atekkosuri, atekosuri sly hint; insinuating remark.

atekomi anticipation; expectation.

atekomu to expect; to hope; **atekonde** in expectation of.

atekosuru to make an insinuating remark; to satirize.

atena address (place); **atena no hito** addressee; **atena o kaku** to address a letter.

ateru to hit; to touch; to guess; to expose to; to address to; to guess; to expose to; to address to; **mato ni ateru** to hit the mark. **Ano hito ni atete tegami dashimashita.** I sent a letter to her attention. **Hi ni atenaide kudasai.** Please do not expose it to the sun. **aterareru** to be hit; to be affected by; to disagree with. **Tabeta sakana ni ateraremashita.** The fish that I ate didn't agree with me.

atezuiryoo conjecture, random guess; **atezuiryoo o suru** to hazard a guess.

atezuppoo guess; guesswork; **atezuppoo ni** at random; **atezuppoo o iu** to hazard a guess.

ATO back, rear; results; **ato ni** behind; **ato de** later; **ato ni nokoru** to stay behind; **ato o ou** to chase after. **Ato ga warui daroo.** The results won't be good.

atogama successor; **atogama ni suwaru** to succeed (someone).

atokara atokara one after another, in rapid succession.

atokata trace, vestige; proof, evidence; **atokata mo nai** unfounded, groundless.

atokatazuke clearing up; **atokatazuke o suru** to put things in order after a work is completed.

atomawashi postponement, deferment; **atomawashi ni suru** to defer, postpone.

atomodori relapse; setback; **atomodori suru** to go back; to degenerate.

atooshi o suru to push from behind; to back up; to support; to abet.

atosaki fore and aft; first and last; both ends; **atosaki ni naru** to be mixed up; to be in the wrong order; **atosaki no kangae naku** regardless of the consequences; thoughtlessly.

atoshimatsu settlement (of an affair); **atoshimatsu o suru** to put in order.

atotori inheritor; successor.

atsugami pasteboard, cardboard.

atsugaru to be very sensitive to the heat. **Watashi wa atsugari desu.** I feel the heat.

atsugeshoo heavy makeup; **atsugeshoo shita** thickly made up; heavily powdered.

atsugi many layers of clothing; **atsugi suru** to be warmly dressed.

ATSUI very warm; hot; **atsuku naru** to become hotter; **atsuku suru** to warm; heat; **onna ni atsuku naru** to run madly after a woman.

ATSUI thick; heavy; **atsui kimono** heavy clothes; **atsui hon** bulky book.

atsukai management; handling, treatment; reception. **Shinsetsu na atsukai o ukemashita.** I received kind treatment.

atsukamashii impudent, brazen, shameless; **atsukamashiku suru** to act shamelessly; **atsukamashisa** impudence, shamelessness.

atsukau to handle, manage; to transact; **jimu o atsukau** to transact business; **kazoku ni shite atsukau** to treat as a member of the family.

atsukurushii close; sultry; sweltering.

ATSUMARI meeting, assembly; crowd, group.

atsumaru to meet, assemble. **Kuji ni atsumarimashoo.** Let's meet at nine. **Atsumare!** Line up!

atsumeru to gather, collect; to call together; **hitai o atsumeru** to put two heads together; to talk over something.

atsurae order (purchase); **atsurae no** custom made; **atsuraeru** to order from; to place an order; **atsurae muki no** just the thing; the very thing (person) for . . .

atsureki friction. **Atsureki ga shoojiru.** Friction arises.

atsuryoku pressure; stress; **atsuryoku o kuwaeru** to pressure.

ATSUSA heat, warmth; **atsusa atari** heat prostration; sunstroke; **atsusa ni ataru** to suffer from the (summer) heat.

ATSUSA thickness. **Atsusa wa ikura arimasu ka?** How thick is that?

attooteki na overwhelming; **attooteki daitasuu** overwhelming majority.

AU to meet; to see; to have an interview with, meet with; **hito ni au** to meet someone; **hidoi me ni au** to have a terrible time; **ame ni au** to be caught in the rain.

au to agree with; to fit in; to be in tune with; **pittari au** to fit perfectly. **Kono tabemono wa watakushi ni wa aimasen.** This food doesn't agree with me.

auto out; out of play (in baseball).

awa millet.

awa bubbles, foam, lather; **awa ga tatsu** to bubble, foam; to ferment; **awa o kuu** to be flustered.

awabi abalone.

aware pity; sadness; **aware na** pitiful, poor, sad, miserable; **awaremi** pity, compassion, mercy; **awaremu** to pity; **awaremubeki** poor, pitiable, miserable, wretched; **awareppoi** pitiful, poor, sad, miserable; **aware ni omou** to feel pity; **awaremi o kakeru** to treat with tenderness or compassion; **awaremi no fukai hito** person of great compassion.

awase lined lightweight garment.

awaseme joint; seam.

awaseru to put together, unite; **chikara o awaseru** to combine efforts; **hanashi no chooshi o awaseru** to chime in; **tokei o awaseru** to set a watch by; **genbun to awaseru** to compare with the original.

awatadashii restless; busy; hurried.

awatemono giddy (flighty) person.

AWATERU to be confused; to lose one's head; to hurry.

awaya exclamation of alarm, agitation, or surprise; **awaya to miru ma ri** in an instant; in the twinkling of an eye.

awayokuba if things go well.

aya figure, design; twill; damask; figure of speech.

ayabumu to fear; to doubt; to hesitate; to have misgivings.

ayadoru to interweave; to embellish; to make designs.

ayamachi fault; mistake; blunder.

ayamari mistake, error.

ayamaru to err. **Sentaku o ayamarimashita.** He made a mistake in his choice.

ayamaru to apologize.

ayame iris.

AYASHII suspicious; uncertain; **ayashii ningen** suspicious (shady) person; **ayashii eigo** poor English.

ayashimu to suspect; to doubt; to wonder at.

ayasu to amuse; to humor; to caress (an infant).

ayatsuri ningyoo puppet, marionette.

ayatsuru to handle; to control; to pull the wires; **hito o ayatsuru** to play on a person's weakness.

ayaui dangerous; very near; **ayauku** barely; narrowly; on the point of; **ayauku nogareru** to have a narrow escape; **ayauku suru** to imperil, jeopardize, endanger.

ayu sweetfish (fresh-water game fish).

aza birthmark.

azami thistle.

azamuku to deceive; to cheat; to impose upon; **azamuki yasui** gullible; **hana o azamuku bijin** a beautiful woman.

azawarai derisive laughter; contempt; ridicule; **azawarau** to laugh at, ridicule; to sneer at.

azayaka na clear; splendid; vivid; **azayaka ni** clearly; splendidly.

aze footpaths between rice fields; low dikes separating rice fields.

azukari taking charge (custody).

azukarimono something left in one's charge.

azukaru to be trusted with; to keep. **Sore o oazukari itashimashoo.** I will keep it for you.

azukaru to participate, to share; **soodan ni azukaru** to be consulted.

azukeru to deposit; to leave in someone's charge; **azukenushi** depositor; **okane o ginkoo ni azukeru** to deposit money in a bank. **Tomodachi ni kodomo o azukete Nihon e ikimasu.** I'm leaving my child with a friend as I'm going to Japan.

azuki red bean.

azusa catalpa tree.

baabekyuu barbecue.

baagen bargain sale.

BAAI occasion; time; moment; case; circumstances; **-no baai ni wa** when; in case; in the event that; on the occasion of; **baai ni yotte wa** according to circumstances; **hitsuyoo no baai ni wa** in case of need.

BAI double; twice (as large, as many, as much); **bai ni suru** to make twice as large; to double; times; -fold (a counter); **ni bai** twice; two times; **ni bai ni suru** to double.

baibai (n.) buying and selling; **baibai suru** to trade in; **baibai keiyaku** bargain; contract of sale.

baidoku syphilis.

baika selling price.

baikai mediation; matchmatching; **baikai suru** to mediate; to convey; **baikaibutsu** medium; agent; **baikaisha** go-between.

baikin bacillus.

baimei self-advertisement; **baimeika** publicity seeker.

baiorin violin.

baishaku (n.) matchmaking; **baishaku suru** to arrange marriages; **baishakunin** go-between; matchmaker.

baishoo compensation, indemnify, reparation; **baishoo suru** to indemnify, make reparation for a loss; **baishookin** money for reparations, damages.

baishuu purchase; bribe; **baishuu suru** to bribe, buy off.

BAITEN stand, stall, booth; store.

baiyaku contract of sale. **Baiyakuzumi!** Sold!

baji toofuu utter indifference; **baji toofuu to kikinagasu** to turn a deaf ear to.

BAKA fool, blockhead, idiot, folly, nonsense, absurdity; **baka o iu** to talk nonsense; **baka o miru** to be fooled; **baka o suru** to make a fool of oneself; **baka ni suru** to make fun of; make a fool of; **baka na hito** foolish person; **baka ni** awfully.

BAKABAKASHII foolish, silly; **bakabakashii koto** foolish matter. **Baka yaroo** You fool! Idiot! (vulgar).

BAKARI about; some; just; only; almost; on the point of; **-bakari de naku** not only . . . but. **Ima kita bakari desu.** I've just come. **Nakan bakari de atta.** She was ready to cry.

bakashoojiki stubborn honesty; simpleness. **Ano otoko wa bakashoojiki da.** That man is too honest.

bakawarai boisterous laughter; horse laugh.

bakazu experience; **bakazu o fumu** to gain experience; **bakazu o funda** experienced; veteran.

bakemono ghost, goblin.

baken pool ticket, pari-mutuel ticket; **bakenjoo** grandstand at a racetrack.

bake no kawa dissemblance; disguise; **bake no kawa ga arawareru** to reveal one's true colors.

BAKETSU bucket.

bakkin fine, penalty; **bakkin o kasu** to levy a fine.

bakku back; background; backer; **bakku suru** to back up (a vehicle); **bakku miraa** rearview mirror (in a car).

bakuchi gambling; **bakuchi o utsu** to gamble; **bakuchiba** gambling place; **bakuchiuchi** gambler.

bakudai na enormous, vast; immense, tremendous.

bakudan bomb; **bakudan tooka** (n.) bombing; **bakudan o tooka suru** to bomb.

bakuhatsu explosion, detonation; **bakuhatsu suru** to explode, blow up, burst.

bakuon explosive sound; roaring of an engine; buzzing.

bakuro exposure; disclosure; **bakuro suru** to expose; lay bare.

bakushin rush; dash; **bakushin suru** to rush; to dash forward.

bakuzen to shita vague, uncertain; ambiguous, indefinite. **Imi ga bakuzen to shite iru.** The meaning is vague.

BAN evening; night; **ban ni** in the evening; **Nichiyoo no ban ni** on Sunday evening.

BAN- prefix denoting: numerous; innumerable; all; every; **banji** everything.

ban watch, guard, lookout; number; order; turn; time; round; game; **ban o suru** to keep watch.

BANANA banana.

banbutsu all things (under the sun); creation; entire universe.

bancha coarse tea; green tea of poor quality; **bancha mo debana** everything in its season.

banchi lot number; address.

bandai all ages; eternity; **bandai ni** through all ages; forever; **bandai fueki no** immutable, eternal.

bando belt; band (music).

bangai *(n.)* extra; additional turn; **bangai no** *(adj.)* extra; additional.

bangata evening; nightfall; **bangata ni** in the evening; toward evening.

BANGOO number; **bangoo o utsu** to number.

BANGUMI program; list.

banji everything; all things. **Banji kootsugoo ni itte iru.** Everything is going well.

bankara Bohemianism; bohemian; **bankara no** unconventional; uncouth; rough and coarse.

banken watchdog.

bankuruwase surprise; expected result; **bankuruwase no** unexpected.

-BANME suffix denoting: ordinal number; **kado kara sanbanme no ie** the third house from the corner.

bannen ni in one's old age.

bannin watchman; caretaker.

banpaa bumper.

banpei sentry, sentinel, guard.

BANSAN supper; dinner; **bansankai** dinner party.

banshaku evening drink; **banshaku o yaru** to have a drink with supper.

bansoo accompaniment; **bansoo suru** to accompany; **bansoosha** accompanist.

bansookoo adhesive plaster; bandage strip.

bantoo head clerk.

banzai cheers; "long live"; **"banzai";** "viva"; **banzai o sanshoo suru** to give three cheers.

banzuke list; program, schedule; playbill.

bara rose; rosebush.

barabara *(n.)* being in pieces, drops; **barabara ni** in bits or pieces; **barabara ni suru** to break up.

barakku barracks; shack.

baramaku to scatter; **kane o baramaku** to spend money recklessly.

baransu balance; **baransu o toru** to keep in balance.

barasu to break into pieces; to lay bare (a secret); to dispose of; to kill.

baree ballet.

barikan hair clippers.

bariki horsepower; **bariki o kakeru** to get up steam; to make an effort.

basha carriage; coach.

basho space, place; seat; location; situation; room.

bashogara character (of a place); locality; neighborhood.

bassui extract; selection; **bassui suru** to extract; select.

bassuru to punish; to bring to justice.

BASU bus; **yuuran basu** sight-seeing bus; **basu de** by bus.

basu bath; **basu tsuki no heya** room with a bath.

basu bass (music).

basue outskirts, suburbs.

basuketto booru basketball.

BATAA butter; **batakusai** exotic, alien (lit: having the smell of butter). **Ano hito wa batakusai.** He acts like a Westerner.

batabata with a clatter (onomatopoetic); one after another; noisily; **batabata suru** to flap. **Kaze de to ga batabata suru.** The wind makes the doors rattle (clatter).

batoo abuse; denunciation; **batoo suru** to abuse; denounce.

-batsu clique, faction; clan.

batsu punishment, penalty; **bassuru** to punish; **batsu o ukeru** to be punished.

batsugun no distinguished; conspicuous.

batta grasshopper.

battaa batter (in baseball); **battaajun** batting order.

BATTARI suddenly; unexpectedly; with a thud. **battari yukiau** to come across, fall in with (a person); **battari butsukaru** to run against, bump into; **battari taoreru** to fall down with a thud; **battari tomaru** to come to an abrupt stop.

batteki selection, promotion; **batteki suru** to select, to promote.

batten demerit; black mark.

batto bat.

bazaa bazaar.

beddo bed.

Beekoku See **Bei.**

beeru veil.

beesubooru baseball.

Bei- prefix denoting: U.S.A. **Beigun** American Army; **Beijin, Beikokujin** *(n.)* American; **beika** American currency; **beikan** American warship; **BEIKOKU** = **Beekoku** America (U.S.A.).

bei- prefix denoting: of rice, pertaining to rice; **beika** the price of rice.

bekkoo tortoise shell; **bekkoo no kushi** tortoise-shell comb; **bekkoo buchi** tortoise-shell rims; **bekkoo buchi no megane** tortoise-shell glasses; **bekko iro** amber color; **bekkoo zaiku** tortoise-shell work.

bekkyo separation; **bekkyo suru** to be separated.

ben valve.

ben eloquence; **ben ga tatsu** to speak fluently.

ben feces.

ben convenience; **-no ben o hakatte** for the convenience of. **Basu no ben ga aru.** Buses are available.

benchi bench.

bengi convenience; facilities; **bengi o ataeru** to provide facilities; to give aid to; **bengijoo** for the sake of convenience.

bengo defense; **bengo suru** to plead; to defend; **bengonin** counsel (for the defense); lawyer; **bengoshi** lawyer; public attorney.

beni rouge; lipstick; **kuchibeni o tsukeru** to put on lipstick.

benimasu red trout.

benjo privy; toilet *(vulgar)*; **benjo ni iku** to go to the toilet; to wash one's hands.

benkai explanation; apology; **benkai suru** to explain; to apologize.

benkeijima checks, plaid (pattern).

benki chamber pot; bedpan.

BENKYOO study; diligence; industry; selling at a small profit; **benkyoo suru** to study; to work hard; **benkyoo suru mise** a shop where prices are cheap; **benkyooka** studious person; hard worker.

benpi constipation.

BENRI convenience; facilities; handiness; **benri na** convenient; handy; useful; **benri ni** conveniently; **benri na tokoro ni sunde iru** to live in a convenient location.

benshi orator, speaker.

benshoo reparation, compensation.

BENTOO box lunch; **bentoo o taberu** to eat a box lunch; **bentoobako** lunchbox; **bentoodai** lunch money; cost of lunch.

bentsuu bowel movement.

benzetsu eloquence; tongue; **benzetsu sawayaka na** eloquent; fluent; **benzetsu sawayaka ni** eloquently, fluently. **Benzetsu ga takumi da.** He speaks fluently.

beppuu separate cover; **beppuu no tegami** a letter under separate cover.

berabera continually; volubly; **berabera shaberu** to chatter unceasingly; to talk volubly.

beraboo (slang) blockhead; fool; **beraboo ni** awfully; **beraboo ni samui** awfully cold. **Beraboo me!** Confound it, you fool you! *(vulgar).*

beranda veranda, porch.

beru bell; doorbell; **beru o narasu** to ring a bell.

beso wry face; **beso o kaku** to be ready to cry.

BESUTO best; **besuto o tsukusu** to do one's best.

betabeta all over; thickly; sticky (referring to paint or powder); **betabeta oshiroi o nuru** to powder one's face thickly.

BETSU difference; discrimination; **betsu no** different; another; **betsu no hito** another person; **betsu naku** without discrimination; alike; **danjo no betsu naku** regardless of sex.

betsu atsurae special order; **betsu atsurae no** made to order; **betsu atsurae no kutsu** custom-made shoes.

BETSUBETSU NO separate; **betsubetsu ni** separately; **betsubetsu ni naru** to become separate; to be separated; **betsubetsu ni suru** to keep separate.

betsudan special; specially; particularly; in particular.

betsujitate specially made or equipped.

bi beauty; prettiness; grace; **bijin** beautiful woman; beautiful girl; **bidan** beautiful story; fine anecdote.

bideo video.

BIFUTEKI beefsteak.

biganjutsu facial (beauty treatment); **biganjutsushi** beautician.

biiru beer; ale; **nama biiru** draught beer, **chozoo biiru** lager beer.

bijinesuman businessman.

bijutsu fine arts; **bijutsu gakkoo** art school; **bijutsu tenrankai** art exhibition; **bijutsuhin** object (work) of art; **bijutsuka** artist; **bijutsukan** art museum; **bijutsuteki** artistic; **bijutsuteki ni** artistically.

bikko lameness; lame person; **bikko no** lame; crippled; wrongly paired; unsymmetrical; **bikko o hiku** to limp. **Kono tsukue no ashi wa bikko da.** The legs of this table are uneven.

BIKKURI SURU to start (with surprise); to be surprised; **bikkuri saseru** to startle; **bikkuri gyooten** astonishment, amazement; **bikkuri gyooten suru** to be frightened out of one's wits. **Aa bikkuri shita!** How you startled me!

bikoo incognito; **bikoo suru** to go incognito; to go in disguise.

bikubiku suru to tremble with fear, be afraid; to feel nervous.

biku to mo shinai to remain unmoved (calm, composed); to be unflinching; to be unperturbed.

bimyoo na delicate; nice; fine; **hijoo ni bimyoo na ten** a very delicate point.

BIN opportunity, occasion; message; news; mail; **tsugi no bin de** by the next mail; **kookuu bin de** by airmail.

bin bottle, jar, decanter; **momo no binzume** a jar of peaches.

BINBOO NA poor, destitute; **binboonin** poor person; poor (people).

biniiru vinyl.

binkan na susceptible; sensitive.

binkatsu na quick; alert; prompt; **binkatsu na shochi o toru** to take prompt measures; **binkatsu ni hataraku** to work rapidly.

BINSEN letter paper; pad of letter paper.

binshoo na quick, sharp, smart, shrewd;

binshoo ni quickly, etc.; **koodoo ga binshoo da** is quick in action.

binsoku na quick, prompt; **binsoku ni** quickly, promptly; **binsoku ni haitatsu suru** to deliver promptly.

binzume no bottled; in a jar; **binzume no sake** bottled sake.

biri *(n.)* last; bottom (of the class).

biriyaado billiards.

biroodo velvet.

BIRU, BIRUDINGU building.

biryoku slight ability; humble effort; **biryoku o tsukusu** to do one's best.

bishibishi rigorously; severely.

bishobisho thoroughly drenched, soaked to the skin; drizzling.

bishonure no dripping, drenched; **bishonure ni naru** to get wet through.

bishoo smile; **bishoo suru** to smile; **bishoo shite** with a smile.

bishoonen handsome youth; Adonis.

bisshori thoroughly; (wet) to the skin; **bisshori ase o kaku** to be soaked with sweat.

BISUKETTO cookies; tea biscuits.

bitamin vitamin.

biten, bitoku virtue; good quality.

biwa loquat (plumlike fruit).

biwa Japanese musical instrument with four strings; **biwa o hiku** to play the biwa.

biyoo beauty; **biyooin** beauty shop.

bochi graveyard, cemetery.

bodaiju linden tree.

bohyoo gravestone; tomb.

boikotto boycott.

boin vowel (sound).

bokashi gradation; shading, shade (of color); **bokasu** to shade, soften, blend colors.

boke Japanese quince.

bokeru to be senile; to be in one's dotage; to be weak-minded; to fade; to grow faint. **Kon ga boketa.** The indigo has faded. **Ano hito wa atama ga bokete iru.** He is senile.

boki bookkeeping; **bokichoo** account book.

bokkoo sudden rise; **bokkoo suru** to rise suddenly (in power); to spring into existence; **koogyoo no bokkoo** the growth of industry.

bokkooshoo *(n.)* independent; **-towa bokkooshoo de aru** to have no relation to; to have no connection (between).

bokkusu box.

bokoku mother country, homeland; **bokokugo** mother tongue.

bokoo alma mater.

BOKU I (used in men's talk).

bokuchiku stock farming; **bokuchikuka** stock farmer; **bokujoo** stock farm; pasture.

bokumetsu destruction, extermination; **bokumetsu suru** to destroy; stamp out.

bokushi pastor, minister.

bokushingu boxing.

bokutotsu honesty, artlessness, simplicity; **bokutotsu na** artless; simple; plain-spoken.

Bon Feast of Lanterns; Buddhist All Souls' Day in July.

bon, obon tray.

bonchi basin; valley.

bonjin ordinary, mediocre person.

bonnoo passion; lust.

bonsai dwarf tree; miniature garden set in a pot.

bonseki miniature landscape (on a tray).

bon'yari stupid person, blockhead; absentmindedly; vacantly; distractedly; **bon'yari kangaekomu** to be lost in reverie; **bon'yari ichinichi o kurasu** to idle away a whole day; **bon'yarimono** dull-witted, absent-minded person; **bon'yari shita** dull-witted, stupid; absent-minded; vacant; dim. **Imi ga bon'yari shite iru.** The meaning is vague. **Kesa wa atama ga bon'yari shite iru.** My head is not clear this morning.

BOO staff, club, rod, stick; **boo de utsu** to strike with a stick; **shindai o boo ni furu** to squander one's fortune; **ichinichi o boo ni furu** to waste a whole day.

boo- prefix denoting: one; certain (one); **boosho** (a certain) place; **booshi** (a certain) person.

boobaku taru vast, boundless, limitless; vague; obscure; **boobaku taru umi** a vast expanse of sea. **Zento wa boobaku taru mono da.** The prospects are very dim.

boobi defense; defensive preparations.

booboo taru extensive; boundless, vast; **booboo to** shaggily; thickly; **booboo to hige o nobashita otoko** a man with a shaggy beard.

boochoo attendance; sitting in conference; **boochooken** admission ticket (for a visitor to the Diet, a conference, etc.); **boochooryoo** admission fee.

boodoo disturbance; riot, insurrection.

BOOEKI trade; commerce; **booeki suru** to trade, carry on commerce; **booekifuu** trade wind; **booekishoo** merchant trader (importer or exporter); **booeki shookai** trading firm.

booenkyoo telescope.

boofuu storm; stormy weather; typhoon; **boofuu keihoo** storm warning; **boofuu no** stormy; **boofuu no chuushin** storm center.

boofuzai antiseptic; preservative.

boogai disturbance; obstruction, hindrance, obstacle; **boogai suru** to disturb, etc.

boogen violent language; **boogen o haku** to use violent (abusive) language.

boogyo defense; **boogyo no** defensive; **boogyo suru** to defend; **boogyosen** line of defense.

boohatei breakwater.

booka *(n.)* fireproof; fire prevention; **booka no** *(adj.)* fireproof; fire-resisting; **booka setsubi** fire protection; **bookaheki** fireproof walls.

bookan *(n.)* bully; rough; rowdy.

bookan sha spectator; onlooker; **bookan suru** to remain a spectator.

booken adventure; risk, hazard; **booken suru** to venture, hazard, run a risk; **bookendan** tale of adventure; adventure; **bookenka** adventurer; **bookenteki** risky, hazardous; adventurous.

bookoo violence, violent conduct; outrage; **bookoo suru** to use violence; **bookoo o kuwaeru** to assault.

bookoo bladder.

bookun tyrant, despot.

bookyo violence; violent conduct.

boomei flight; **boomei suru** to flee, take flight, seek refuge; **boomeisha** refugee; fugitive; exile.

boonasu bonus.

boonenkai social gathering at the end of the year.

boorei ghost.

boori excessive profit; **boori o musaboru** to profiteer, make excessive profit; **boori torishimari rei** ordinance to control excessive profits.

booru bowl; ball.

boorubako pasteboard box, carton.

boorugami cardboard, pasteboard.

booryoku brute force, violence; **booryokudan** gang of roughs.

boosatsu sareru to be hard-pressed with business.

booseki spinning; **booseki gaisha** fabric (spinning) company; **booseki koojoo** fabric mill.

BOOSHI hat, cap; bonnet; **boshi o kaburu** to put on one's hat; **boshi o kabutte miru** to try on a hat; **boshi o nugu** to take off one's hat; **booshikake** hat rack, hat peg; **booshiya** hatter; milliner; hat store.

booshi prevention.

booshokuzai antiseptic; anticorrosive.

boosui waterproof; protection against floods; **boosuifuku** waterproof cloth.

booto mob; insurgents; rioters.

booto rowboat; **booto o kogu** to row a boat.

bootoo abnormal rise; boom. **Satoo ga bootoo shita.** The price of sugar has gone up enormously.

booya (diminutive) my boy; my darling (said of a male infant).

boozu (derogatory) monk.

bora gray mullet.

boro rags, tatters; hidden fault; **boro no** ragged, threadbare; **boro o kita** in rags; **boro o dasu** to betray a weakness; show one's true colors; **boroboro no** tattered, ragged; **boroboro ni naru** to crumble, fall to pieces; **borogimono** old (threadbare) clothes; rags.

boru to charge exorbitant prices; to profiteer.

bosei motherhood, maternity; **boseiai** maternal love.

boseki tombstone.

boshuu levy; recruiting; **boshuu suru** to collect; recruit; raise.

bosshuu confiscation, forfeiture; **bosshuu suru** to confiscate, forfeit, seize.

bossuru to sink; to disappear; to die.

BOTAN button, stud; knob; **botan o kakeru** to button; **botan o hazusu** to unbutton; **botan o osu** to push a button.

botan tree peony.

botchan boy (someone else's son); green youth, young master.

botsuraku ruin, downfall, **botsuraku suru** to be ruined.

bottoo suru to be absorbed in; to devote oneself to; to be engrossed with; **shigoto ni bottoo suru** to bury oneself in work.

boya small fire.

bu rate, percentage; part, portion, section, division; **buai** rate, commission, royalty; **buai o dasu** to give (someone) a percentage. **Rishi wa san bu desu.** The interest rate is 3 percent.

bu department; **keiribu** accountant's department.

-bu copy (a counter for newspapers, pamphlets, etc.).

buaikyoo surliness; curtness; bluntness; **buaikyoo na** surly; blunt; unobliging.

buaisoo inhospitableness; curtness, unsociability; **buaisoo na** unsociable, curt, inhospitable; **buaisoo na henji** a curt reply; **hito ni buaisoo o suru** to be surly.

bubun part, portion, section; **bubunhin** parts (of machines); **bubunteki ni** partially; locally.

buchi spots, specks; patches; **buchi no** spotted, speckled; **buchi neko** tabby cat.

buchoo chief (head) of a department.

budoo grape; grapevine; **budoo no fusa** a bunch of grapes; **budooen** vineyard;

budooshu wine; claret; **shiro buddooshu** white wine; **aka budooshu** red wine.

buenryo rudeness; boldness; **buenryo na** unreserved; rude; bold; **buenryo ni** without reserve, boldly.

buji peace; safety; good health; **buji na** safe, sound; peaceful; **buji ni** safely; peacefully.

bujoku insult, affront; disgrace; **bujoku suru** to insult, disgrace; **bujoku o ukeru** to be insulted.

buka *(n.)* subordinate; under-officer.

bukakkoo clumsiness, awkwardness (in appearance); **bukakkoo na** clumsy, awkward; **bukakkoo ni** clumsily, bunglingly.

buki arms, weapons.

bukiyoo lack of skill, clumsiness; **bukiyoo na** unskillful.

bukka prices; **bukka o toosei suru** to control prices; **bukka choosetsu** price control. **Bukka ga geraku suru.** Prices are falling. **Bukka ga tooki suru.** Prices are rising.

bukkaku Buddhist temple.

bukkiraboo abruptness; curtness; **bukkiraboo na** curt. **bukkiraboo na kotae o suru** to make a curt reply; **bukkiraboo ni kotowaru** to refuse curtly.

Bukkyoo Buddhism; **Bukkyooto** Buddhist.

bukotsu bluntness; roughness; rusticity; **bukotsu na** blunt; rustic; clumsy.

bukubuku bubbling; baggy; bulging; **bukubuku futoru** to become very fat; **bukubuku awadatsu** to bubble up.

bumon class; branch; department; **bumon ni wakeru** to classify.

bun portion, share; social position, lot in life; **bun ni yasunzuru** to be contented with one's lot. **Kore wa watakshi no bun desu.** This is my share.

bun sentence, writing, composition. **Kono bun o yakushite kudasai.** Please translate this sentence.

bun- prefix denoting: writing, literature; civil life; **bundan** literary circles; **bungaku** literature; **bungaku no** literary; **bungei** literature; **bungo** literary expression; written language; classical Japanese; **bungoo** great writer.

buna beech tree.

bun'an draft, sketch; **bun'an o tsukuru** to make a draft; draw up (a deed, etc.)

bunan na safe, secure; **bunan ni** safely; tolerably well.

bunboogu stationery; **bunbooguya** stationer, one who sells paper, etc.

bunchoo rice (paddy) bird.

bundori capture, seizure; spoil, plunder; **bundorihin** trophy, booty, spoils.

bunjoo division; distribution; **bunjoo suru** to divide, distribute; **bunjoochi** land for sale in lots.

bunka culture, civilization; **bunkateki na** cultural.

bunkai analysis; decomposition; **bunkai suru** to analyze; to resolve; to decompose; to break up; to pull to pieces.

bunkan civil official.

bunke branch of a family.

bunken literature; documents, records.

bunko handbox; bookcase; library; collection of works.

bunkoojoo branch factory.

bunmei civilization; **bunmei no** civilized; **bunmeikoku** civilized country.

bunpai division, distribution; **bunpai suru** to divide, share; **rieki no bunpai** a division of profits.

bunpoo grammar. **Bunpoo o machigaeta.** I made a mistake in grammar.

bunpu distribution (geographical).

bunretsu split, rupture; **bunretsu suru** to break up; split.

bunri separation; isolation; **bunri suru** to separate; to isolate.

bunrui classification, assortment.

bunryoo quantity.

bunseki analysis, assay.

bunshi writer.

bunshi numerator, molecule.

bunshoo composition, writing; **bunshooka** good (clear) writer.

bunsuirei watershed.

buntan allotment, share; **buntan suru** to share; **buntankin** share of expenses.

buntsuu correspondence; **buntsuu suru** to write to.

buppin article; goods, commodities.

burabura idly, aimlessly; leisurely; **burabura aruku** to walk leisurely, take a stroll; **burabura suru** to loaf, be idle; **burabura shite hi o okuru** to while away one's time.

burakku risuto black list.

buraku community; village.

buranko swing.

burashi brush; **burashi o kakeru** to brush up; to brush.

buratsuku to wander about, walk aimlessly; **machi o buratsuku** to window-shop.

burausu blouse.

bureeki, bureiki brake. **Bureiki ga kikanai.** The brake does not work.

burei breach of etiquette; incivility, rudeness; **burei na** rude, insolent; **burei na koto o iu** to speak insultingly; **burei na koto o suru** to behave impolitely; to act insultingly.

buri yellowtail, yellowfish.

-buri suffix denoting: way, manner; after (a time); **gonenburi de** after a lapse of five years; **hanashiburi** way of talking.

burikaesu to relapse, have a relapse.

buriki tin plate; **burikikan** tin can.

buroochi brooch.

-buru suffix denoting: to give oneself airs.

buruburu suru to shiver, shudder.

burui class, order, sort, group; **burui o wakeru** to sort, classify; **burui wake** classification; **burui wake o suru** to catalogue.

burujoa (n.) bourgeois.

buryoku military power, armed force.

busahoo mono ill-mannered person, boor.

busata long silence; **gobusata suru** to neglect to write (or visit) for a long time.

bushi warrior, samurai.

busho appointed post; place of duty.

bushoo laziness, sloth, indolence; **bushoo na** lazy; **bushoo mono** lazy person; lazy-bones.

busoo arms, armaments; **busoo suru** to arm; **busoo kaijo** disarmament.

bussan products; produce.

busshi goods, commodities, raw materials, resources; **busshi no yutaka na** rich in natural resources.

busshitsu matter, substance; **busshitsuteki** material, physical; worldly; **busshitsuteki ni** materially, physically.

bussoo na unsafe, dangerous; suspicious; **bussoo na yononaka** restless times (days).

busui na unfashionable; in poor taste; inelegant.

BUTA pig, swine; pork; **buta no abura** lard; **butagoya** pigsty; **BUTANIKU** pork.

butai stage (theater); footlights; scene; sphere; **butai ni tatsu** to go on the stage; **butaigeki** theatrical drama.

butoo dance; dancing; **butoo suru** to dance; **butookai** ball, dance (party).

butsubutsu rash; **kao ni butsubutsu ga dekiru** to get a rash on the face.

butsubutsu murmuring; grumbling; **butsubutsu iu** to grumble; to murmur.

butsubutsu kookan barter.

Butsudan (household) Buddhist altar.

Butsudoo Buddhist teachings.

butsugi discussion; public censure.

butsukaru to collide with; to clash; to knock (run) against; to fall on; **konnan ni butsukaru** to encounter difficulties. **Saijitsu ga Nichiyoobi ni butsukaru.** The national holiday falls on Sunday.

butsukeru to throw at; to knock against. **Atama o hashira ni butsuketa.** I knocked my head against a post.

butsuri natural laws, physical laws, physics; **butsuriteki** physical.

butsurigaku physics; **butsurigakusha** physicist.

butsuyoku worldly desires.

Butsuzoo Buddhist image.

buttooshi ni throughout; all through; without a break; **tooka kan buttooshi ni** for ten days running.

buttsuke ni directly; personally; outright.

buyo gnat; sandfly.

buyoo ballet; dance; **buyoogeki** dance drama.

buyoojin insecurity. **buyoojin na** insecure, unsafe.

buyuuden heroic story.

buzama na ungainly; uncouth; clumsy.

BYOO second (of time); **byoo o kizamu** to tick away the time.

byoo tack, rivet; **byoo de tomeru** to tack down.

byoo ancestral shrine, mausoleum.

byoo- prefix denoting: disease, illness; **byoodoku** virus; disease germs; **byoogen** cause of a disease; **byoogenkin** germs; **byoogo** convalescence; **byoogo no hito** a convalescent; **BYOOIN** hospital; **byooin ni hairu** to be hospitalized; **BYOOKI** illness; **byooki ni kakaru** to fall ill; **byooki no** sick, ill; **atama no byooki** mental illness; **BYOONIN** sick person; **byoosei** condition (of a disease); **byooshin no** weak, sickly, delicate, in poor health; **byooshitsu** sickroom; ward; **byooshoo** sickbed. **Byoosei ga aratamarimashita.** He took a turn for the worse.

-byoo suffix denoting: disease, illness; **haibyoo** (lung) tuberculosis; **ganbyoo** eye disease.

byoobu folding screen; **byoobu o tateru** to set up a screen.

byoodoo equality; **byoodoo no** equal; **byoodoo ni** equally; without discrimination; **byoodoo ni suru** to make equal; **byoodoo no kenri** an equal right.

byoosha depiction; description; representation; **byoosha suru** to sketch, describe.

CH

CHA, OCHA tea; **ocha o ireru** to prepare tea; **ocha o irekaeru** to make fresh tea; **ocha o dasu** to serve (offer) a cup of tea; **ocha o tsugu** to pour tea; **cha no yu** tea ceremony; art of tea-making; **chabanashi** tea-talk, gossip, chat (over a bowl of tea); **chabashira** tea stalk floating erect in one's cup (foretelling something good, according to superstition); **chadansu** tea cabinet; **chadoogu** tea-things; tea set; **chagara** used tea leaves; **chagashi** cake, sweets (served with tea); **CHAKA = saka** tea and cake; light refreshment; **chamise** tea stall; refreshment house; **chaseki** place where the tea ceremony is held; **chasen** (bamboo) tea whisk; tea stirrer for powdered tea (used in the tea ceremony); **chashaku** tea ladle; tea scoop, **chataku** tea saucer. **CHAWAN** teacup; rice bowl; **CHAYA** teahouse; roadside snack bar. **Chabashira ga tatte imasu.** A tea stalk is floating erect in his cup.

chabudai low eating-table.

CHAIRO *(n.)* light brown; **chairo no** *(adj.)* light brown; brownish.

chakasshoku light-brown color.

chakasu to laugh, banter; to make fun of.

-chaku suffix denoting: a "counter" for a suit of clothes; **yoofuku itchaku** a suit of Western clothes.

-chaku arrival; **rokuji chaku** arriving at six o'clock.

chakuchaku *(adv.)* steadily; step by step; **chakuchaku shinkoo suru** to make steady progress.

chakuganten point aimed at; viewpoint.

chakujitsu sincerity; steadiness and honesty; **chakujitsu ni** honestly; faithfully.

chakuriku *(n.)* landing; **chakuriku suru** to land, alight; **chakurikuba, chakurikujoo** landing field; airstrip.

chakushoku *(n.)* coloring; **chakushoku suru** to color.

chakushu commencement, start; **chakushu suru** to commence, set about, start, begin.

chame playfulness, sportiness; playful fellow, urchin; **chame o hakki suru** to be jovial (jolly).

chanoma sitting room; living room; tearoom.

chanpon mixture; **chanpon ni** alternately.

CHAN TO *(adv.)* in good order, neatly; properly; thoroughly; fully, exactly, precisely, correctly; **chan to shita fukusoo** proper dress; **kimono o chan to kiru** to dress properly.

CHASAJI teaspoon.

chazuke rice steeped in hot tea (eaten as a simple meal or after rich food); **chazuke o kakikomu** to eat a hasty meal.

CHI blood; blood relation; **chi ga deru** to bleed; **chi o tomeru** to stop bleeding; **chi no meguri no yoi** quick-witted; sensible; **chi no meguri no warui** dull-witted; not sensible; **chi o waketa** related by blood; **chibashiru** to become bloodshot;

chibashitta me bloodshot eyes; **chidarake no** bloody.

chi intellect; **chiteki** intellectual.

chibi dwarf, pygmy.

chibusa breast.

CHICHI father; **chichikata no** paternal. **Chichikata no shinseki ga aru.** I have relatives on my father's side.

chichi milk.

chichuu ground, earth; **chichuu ni** in the ground; underground.

Chichuukai Mediterranean Sea.

chie wisdom, intelligence; sense; advice, counsel; **chie no aru** wise; **chie no nai** unwise; **chie o kasu** to advise; **chie o shiboru** to rack one's brains; **chie o tsukeru** to suggest.

chifusu typhoid fever, typhus.

chigaeru to change, alter; to make a mistake; to dislocate, put out of joint; **yakusoku o chigaeru** to break a promise.

CHIGAI difference, disparity; distinction; mistake, error; **CHIGAI NAKU** certainly, surely; without doubt; **-ni chigai nai** there is no mistake about it (that); . . . **undei no chigai ga aru** to be as different as heaven and earth. **Chigai ga aru.** There is a difference. **Kimi wa kare ni atta ni chigai nai.** You must have seen him.

CHIGAU to be different, differ (from); to be unlike; to disagree, not be in accordance with, to be wrong, be mistaken. **Ano hito wa chotto hito to chigau.** He is a little different from other people.

chigireru to be torn off; to come off. **Sode ga chigireta.** A sleeve was torn off.

chigiru to tear off, to pluck, to pick.

chiguhagu no odd, uneven, unequal.

chiheisen horizon; **chiheisen joo ni** above (on) the horizon.

chihoo locality; country (rural area); **chihoo no** local; provincial; **chihooshoku** local color.

chii rank, social status, position.

chiiki tract of land; area.

chiimu team.

CHIISAI small, trifling; **chiisaku naru** to dwindle; to cringe, shrink.

CHIIZU cheese.

chijimaru = chijimu to shrink. **Keorimono wa nettoo ni irereba chijimimasu.** Woolen fabric shrinks in hot water.

chijimeru to shorten, to reduce, to draw in; **kimono o chijimeru** to shorten a dress.

chijimi cotton crepe.

chijimiagaru to tremble with fear, to cringe.

chijimu See **chijimaru**.

chijin acquaintance; friend.

chijirege frizzled, wavy hair.

chijireru to be wavy; to become curly.

chijoku disgrace, dishonor, shame.

CHIJOO surface of the earth; earth; world; **chijoo no** earthly, terrestrial; on the earth; **chijoo ni** on the ground, on the earth.

chika subterranean, underground; **chika ni** under the ground; **chikadoo** underground passage.

CHIKAGORO recently, lately; nowadays, in these days, **chikagoro made** till recent times; until lately.

CHIKAI near; intimate; verging on; akin to; **chikai miyori** a near relation; **chikai uchi ni** before long; one of these days; **kanzen ni chikai.** It is nearly perfect. It is close to perfection.

chikai oath, vow; **chikai o tateru** to make a vow, swear an oath, give a pledge; **chikai o mamoru** to keep an oath; **chikai o yaburu** to break an oath (vow). See also **chikau.**

CHIKAKU nearby place; nearly; in the neighborhood of; shortly, in a short time; **shoogo chikaku ni kaeru** to go home close to noon. **Sugu kono chikaku ni sunde imasu.** I live near here.

chikamichi shortcut; **chikamichi o suru** to take a shortcut.

CHIKARA strength, might, power, force; spirit; vigor; efforts, exertions; ability, talent; authority; **chikara ga yowai** weak; **chikara ga tsuyoi** strong; **chikara no aru** strong, powerful; **chikara no nai** powerless, incapable; **chikara ga tsukiru** to get exhausted; **chikara ni oyobanai** to be beyond one's power; **chikara o otosu** to be discouraged; **chikara o tsukeru** to cheer up, encourage; **chikarazuku** to recover one's strength or health; to be cheered up.

chikashii close, intimate; familiar; **chikashii aida de** between friends.

chikashitsu basement, cellar.

CHIKATETSU subway.

chikatte upon my word, upon my honor.

chikau to swear, vow, pledge one's word.

chikayoru to draw near, approach.

chikazukeru to keep company with, to allow to come close to; to allow.

chikazuki acquaintance; **chikazuki ni naru** to get acquainted with.

chikazukigatai to be inaccessible, be difficult of access.

chikazukiyasui to be accessible.

chikazuku to draw near, approach; **chikazukanai yooni suru** to keep away from.

chikei topography; lay of the land.

chiki acquaintance; friend.

chikki luggage receipt, baggage check; **chikki suru** to check one's baggage.

chikkyo confinement in one's house; **chikkyo suru** to stay indoors.

chikoku *(n.)* being late; **chikoku suru** to be late.

chikubi teat; nipple.

chikuchiku prickle; tingle; sharp pain.

chikudenchi storage battery.

chikushoo birds and beasts; beast; brute (of a man); **Chikushoo!** Damn it! Hang it! *(vulgar);* **Kon chikushoo me!** You brute! *(vulgar).*

CHIKYUU earth; **chikyuugi** globe.

chimayou to go mad, be crazed.

chimei place name.

chimidoro ni natte strenuously; desperately.

chin Japanese spaniel.

-chin suffix denoting: charge, price; **denshachin** train fare; **yachin** house rent.

chinamu to be associated with; to call (or name) after.

chinba lameness; odd pair.

chinbotsu sinking; floundering; shipwreck.

chingin wages; **chingin seikatsusha** wage-earner.

chinka sinking, submersion; subsidence; **chinka suru** to sink to the bottom; to be put out; to be brought under control; to be extinguished.

chinkyaku rare guest; welcome visitor.

chinmi dainty (thing); delicacy.

chinmoku silence, reticence; **chinmoku suru** to be silent; to hold one's tongue; **chinmoku saseru** to silence.

chinomigo suckling, infant.

chinpu na stale; old-fashioned commonplace; hackneyed.

chinretsu exhibition, display, arrangement; **chinretsu suru** to exhibit, display, show; **chinretsubako** showcase; **chinretsukan** museum; gallery; exhibition; **chinretsumado** show window; **chinretsushitsu** showroom. **Sore wa chinretsu shite aru.** It is on view.

chin shigoto piecework; **chin shigoto o suru** to do piecework.

CHIPPU tip; **chippu o harau** to tip (a waiter, etc.).

chirabaru to be scattered, be in disorder. **Hon ga chirabatte ita.** Books were scattered about.

chirachira flutteringly; flickeringly; gleamingly. **Yuki ga chirachira futte ita.** The snowflakes were falling lightly. **Ki no aida kara hikari ga chirachira shite ita.** The light gleamed through the trees.

Hikari de me ga chirachira suru. The light dazzles my eyes.

chirahora here and there. **Sakura ga chirahora sakidashita.** The cherry trees have started to bloom here and there.

chirakasu to scatter; to disarrange.

chirari to at a glance; by accident; **chirari to kikikomu** to hear by accident; **chirari to miru** to catch a glimpse of; glance at (a thing).

chirashi handbill, leaflet.

chirasu to scatter, disperse; **ki o chirasu** to distract (someone's) attention; to divert. (See also **chirabaru**.)

chiri geography; topography.

chiri dust; **chiriharai** duster; **chiritori** dustpan. **chiri hodo mo nai.** There isn't a bit.

chiribameru to inlay; to set; **shinju o chiribameta yubiwa** a ring set with pearls.

CHIRIGAMI toilet paper; facial tissue.

chirijiri ni in all directions; separately; **chirijiri ni naru** to disperse in all directions, scatter; **chirijiri ni natte iru** to be scattered about, be dispersed.

chirimen crepe; **chirimengami** crepe paper.

chirin chirin tingling; jingle-jangle; **chirin chirin naru** to ring.

CHIRU to fall; to disperse; to be scattered; to be distracted; **ki ga chiru** to be distracted (mentally). **Kumo ga chitte iru.** The clouds are dispersing.

chiryoo medical treatment; cure; **chiryoo suru** to treat; to cure; **chiryoo o ukeru** to receive treatment.

chisei geographical features; topography.

chishiki knowledge, information, learning; **chishikijin** learned person; intellectual.

chissoku suffocation; **chissoku suru** to suffocate.

chisuji blood; lineage; descent.

chitsujo order; **chitsujo no aru** orderly; **chitsujo no nai** disorderly; **chitsujo ga midarete iru** to be out of order; **chitsujo tadashii** to be in good order; **chitsujo tadashiku** in an orderly manner; systematically.

CHITTOMO (used with a negative) not at all; not a bit. **Gohan ga chittomo oishikunai.** I don't have any appetite at all. **Chitto mo kamawanai.** He doesn't care a bit.

chizu map; topographical chart; atlas.

chochiku savings; **chochiku suru** to save up, store, lay by; **chochiku ginkoo** savings bank; **chochikushin no aru** thrifty; **chochikushin no nai** extravagant, prodigal.

chokin savings; **chokin suru** to save money.

chokkaku right angle; **chokkaku ni** at right angles.

chokkei diameter.

chokkoo nonstop trip; direct voyage; **chokkoo suru** to go direct to.

chokkyuu straight ball; line drive.

choko sake cup.

chokochoko at a trot; with short, mincing steps; **chokochoko komata ni aruku** to walk with short steps; to mince along.

CHOKOREETO chocolate.

chokuchoku now and then. **Chokuchoku hanashi ni kuru.** He comes to see us now and then.

chokumen suru to face, confront.

chokuritsu suru to stand up.

chokusen straight line.

chokusetsu directly; **chokusetsu no** direct; immediate; personal; **chokusetsu ni** directly; personally.

chokutsuu direct communication; through traffic; **chokutsuu ressha** through train.

chokuyaku literal translation.

chomei na well-known, famous, noted.

CHOO- prefix denoting: town; street; **choonai de** in the town.

choo intestines, bowels.

-choo suffix denoting: government office; **Kikakuchoo** Planning Board.

-choo suffix denoting: chief, director; **shachoo** company president.

chooba counter for Japanese-style establishment (hotel, etc.).

choobatsu discipline; punishment.

choobo account book; register; **choobo o tsukeru** to keep accounts.

choochin paper lantern; **-no choochin o motsu** to sing someone's praises; boast; **choochin ni tsurigane** an ill-assorted couple (in a marriage); an ill-matched pair.

CHOOCHOO butterfly; **Choochoo san** Madame Butterfly.

choodai suru (humble) to receive; to drink; to eat. **Koohii no kawari ni ocha o choodai itashimashoo.** I will take tea instead of coffee.

CHOODO just; right; exactly; **choodo goji ni** exactly at five o'clock; **choodo yoi toki ni** just at the right time; **choodo mannaka ni** right in the middle.

chooetsu superiority, excellence; **chooetsu suru** to surpass; to be superior to.

choogoo (n.) compounding, mixing, preparation; **choogoo suru** to mix, concoct, prepare; **choogoozai** compound, mixture.

choohatsu suru to requisition.

choohonnin ringleader; leader.

choohoogaru to find a thing useful.

choohoo na convenient; handy, useful; **choohoo na hito** handy man. **Kuchi wa choohoo na mono da.** The mouth is a convenient thing (You can say what you please).

choohookei rectangle; **choohookei no** rectangular, oblong.

chooji words of condolence; funeral address, eulogy.

choojin superman; **choojinteki** superhuman.

choojo oldest daughter.

CHOOJOO top, summit; **choojoo kaigi** summit conference.

chooka excess; **chooka suru** to exceed.

chookan morning edition (of a newspaper).

chookeshi cancellation; writing off; **chookeshi ni suru** to square accounts. **Kore de chookeshi da.** Now we're quits.

chookoku engraving; sculpture; **chookokuka** engraver; sculptor.

chookoo sign(s); symptom; **jidai no chookoo** a sign of the times.

chookoo attendance at a lecture; **chookooryoo** admission fee.

chookyori long distance; **chookyori denwa** long-distance telephone; **chookyori hikoo** long-distance flight.

-CHOOME suffix denoting: street (employed when an ordinal number is used to name a thoroughfare or section of town). **Itchoome** First Street; **Nichoome** Second Street.

choomei long life; longevity; **choomei no** long-lived.

choomen notebook.

choomi seasoning, flavor; **choomiryoo** seasoning, condiments, spices.

choomusubi rosette; bow.

choonan oldest son.

chooryoku (power of) hearing.

chooryuu tidal current, tide; tendency, trend.

choosa examination, investigation, inquiry; **choosa suru** to investigate, examine.

choosei regulation; adjustment; preparation, drafting, drawing up; **choosei suru** to regulate; to put in order; to prepare, draft, draw up.

CHOOSEN Korea; **Choosenjin** Korean people; **Choosengo** Korean language. (See also **Kankoku.**)

choosen challenge; defiance; **choosen suru** to challenge; **choosen ni oozuru** to accept a challenge; **choosenteki** challenging, aggressive; defiant.

choosetsu regulation, control; adjustment; **choosetsu suru** to regulate, control; **bukka o choosetsu suru** to regulate prices.

chooshi tune; pitch; key; rate of stroke; **chooshi ga atte iru** to be in tune; **chooshi ga atte inai** out of tune; **chooshi no yoi** harmonious; melodious.

chooshinki stethoscope.

choosho strong point; one's forte; merit.

chooshu suru to hear; to listen in.

chooshuu audience; (people in) attendance. **Chooshuu ga ooi.** There is a large audience.

chooshuu collection; levy, assessment; **chooshuu suru** to collect; levy; **zei o chooshuu suru** to collect taxes.

chooteisha arbitrator, mediator.

chooten highest point, apex, zenith.

chooto long distance; long journey. **Chooto no ryokoo ni tsuita.** He started on a long journey.

chootsugai hinge.

choowa harmony, accord, agreement; **choowa suru** to harmonize; to agree with; **iro no choowa** harmony of colors.

choozen to aloof; above the world.

choozoo sculpture; statue.

chorochoro trickling (of a brook).

chosaku literary work; **chosakuken** copyright; **chosakusha, chosha** writer, author.

chosho work (literary); production; publication.

chosuichi reservoir.

CHOTTO just for a moment; a few minutes; a little; a bit; **chotto no ma ni** in a moment; in no time. **Chotto matte kudasai.** Just a moment, please. Wait a bit, please. **Chotto dekinai.** It's no easy thing. **Chotto shita koto de kenka shita.** They quarreled over a trifle. **Chotto shita ie ga aru.** There's a nice-looking house.

chozoomai stored rice.

chuu comment; annotation; footnote.

chuubu central part; center; **Chuubu chihoo** Central Japan.

chuucho hesitation; indecision; **chuucho suru** to hesitate; waver; **chuucho shite** hesitatingly.

chuudan interruption; break; **chuudan suru** to cut in two, break in the middle.

chuudoku (n.) poisoning; ptomaine; **chuudoku suru** to be poisoned; **chuudokusei no** poisonous, toxic.

chuugaeri somersault.

chuugakkoo junior high school.

chuugata medium size; **chuugata no** medium-sized; medium.

chuugen midyear present.

CHUUGOKU China; **Chuugokujin** Chinese people; **Chuugokugo** Chinese language.

chuui attention, care; warning, caution; advice; hint; **chuui suru** to pay attention to; to attend to; to warn, etc.; **chuui shite** with care; **hito no chuui o hiku** to attract someone's attention; **chuui o ukeru** to be warned; **chuui o unagasu** to call attention to; **chuuibukai** cautious, careful; attentive; **chuui jinbutsu** marked person; suspicious character; **chuui ryoku** attentiveness; **chuuisubeki** noteworthy, worthy of notice.

chuujitsu faithfulness; honesty; **chuujitsu na** faithful; honest; **chuujitsu ni** faithfully; honestly.

chuujun middle ten days of a month; **Gogatsu no chuujun ni** about (in) the middle of May.

CHUUKA China; **chuuka ryoori** Chinese food; **Chuuka Minkoku** Chinese Republic (Nationalist China); **Chuuka Jinmin Kyoowa koku** People's Republic of China (Communist China).

chuukan the middle; midway; **chuukan no** middle, intermediate; **-no chuukan ni** halfway between.

chuuken main body; backbone; center field (in baseball).

chuukoku advice, counsel; warning; **chuukoku suru** to advise; to warn; **chuukoku o ireru** to follow advice; **chuukoku ni somuku** to act against advice.

chuumoku notice, observation; attention; **chuumoku suru** to pay attention to; to watch, keep an eye on.

CHUUMON order; command(s); request; **chuumon suru** to order; **chuumon o toru** to take an order.

chuumon tori traveling salesman; canvasser.

chuunen middle age; **chuunen no** middle-aged.

chuuniku chuuzei medium build.

chuunyuu injection, pouring into; cramming; **chuunyuu suru** to pour into.

chuuoo center, middle; **chuuoo shijoo** central market.

chuuritsu neutrality; **chuuritsu chitai** neutral zone.

chuuryuu midstream; middle class; **chuuryuu kaikyuu** middle class.

chuusai mediation, arbitration; **chuusai nin** mediator, peacemaker; **chuusai suru** to mediate, arbitrate.

chuusan moderate means (wealth); **chuusan kaikyuu** middle class.

chuusei neuter gender.

chuusei Middle Ages; **chuusei no** medieval.

chuusen lottery, drawing; **chuusen suru** to draw lots; **chuusen de sadameru** to decide by lots; **chuusenken** lottery ticket.

chuushi suspension, stoppage; steady gaze; close observation; **chuushi suru** to stop, suspend, discontinue; to gaze steadily at; to watch closely; **jigyoo no chuushi** work stoppage; **shiai o chuushi suru** to call off a game.

chuushin center, core, heart; balance; **chuushin o toru** to balance; **machi no chuushin ni** in the center of the city; **chuushin jinbutsu** central figure; leader.

chuushoo defamation, slander.

CHUUTO midway, halfway; in the middle; unfinished; **chuuto de yameru** to stop in the middle of; to drop out of; **chuuto hanpa** (*n.*) halfway; **chuuto hanpa no** (*adj.*) unfinished; **chuuto hanpa ni** (*adv.*) halfway; **chuuto hanpa na koto o suru** to do things by halves.

chuutongun army of occupation.

chuutoo medium quality; **chuutoo no** middle grade; medium; **chuutoo no shinamono** goods of medium quality.

chuuya day and night; **chuuya yasumazu hataraku** to work day and night without rest.

chuuyoo moderation; **chuuyoo o mamoru** to take the middle course; **chuuyoo o eta** moderate; **chuuyoo o enai** immoderate; one-sided.

chuuzai residence; **chuuzai no** (*adj.*) resident; **chuuzai suru** to reside.

chuuzaisho police station.

chuuzetsu interruption; suspension; **chuuzetsu suru** to be interrupted; to be suspended; discontinued. **Shigoto wa chuuzetsu shita.** The work has been held up. **Chuuzetsu shite iru.** It is in abeyance.

DA plain present of **desu**, it is. **Kore wa nan da?** What is this? **Fude da.** It is a writing brush. **Are wa dare da?** Who is he? **Boku wa iku no wa iya da.** I don't want to go.

DAASU dozen; **ichi daasu** one dozen; **daasu de uru** to sell by the dozen.

dabi cremation.

dabokushoo bruise.

dabora (*colloq.*) big talk; **dabora o fuku** to boast.

dabudabu loose; baggy; **dabudabu no zubon** baggy trousers.

dachin reward; tip; small consideration; **dachin ni** in payment for. **Kore wa otsukai no dachin da.** This is your reward for doing the errand.

dadakko spoiled child; cross, fretful child.

daden (*n.*) telegraphing; **daden suru** to telegraph, to wire.

daeki saliva, spittle.

DAGA but; for all that; all the same; at the same time; on the other hand.

dagashi coarse (cheap) confectionery (candy).

dageki blow; hit; shock; hitting, batting (in baseball); **dageki o kuwaeru** to deal a blow; **dageki o ukeru** to receive a blow.

daha *(n.)* overthrow; **daha suru** to break down; to overthrow; to frustrate.

DAI time, period, age, generation; reign, dynasty; (one's) lifetime; pedestal, block; stand; rest; table; bench.

DAI title, heading, theme, subject, topic; question, problem; **dai o tsukeru** entitle.

dai pedestal, block, stand, rest, table.

dai- prefix which makes an ordinal from a cardinal number; **daiichi** the first; **daini** the second.

dai- prefix denoting: big, large, great; grand, high; colossal; **daitokai** a big city; **daibubun** greater part, for the most part.

-dai money given in exchange; cost, price; **gasudai** gas bill.

-dai counter for vehicles (machines); **kuruma ichidai** one car.

DAIBU, DAIBUN greatly, considerably, remarkably, rather, much, many. **Daibu atsui.** It is pretty hot. **Kesa wa daibu yoi.** I am much better this morning. **Daibu son o shita.** He suffered a big loss. **Daibu kane ga kakaru.** It takes a lot of money.

daichi earth; ground.

daichoo large intestines; colon.

daidai bitter orange.

daidai successive generations; from generation to generation; **daidai no** successive; hereditary.

daidaiteki big, grand; splendid; wholesale; **daidaiteki ni** on a large (grand) scale; splendidly; **daidaiteki ni kookoku suru** to advertise extensively.

DAIDOKORO kitchen; **daidokoro doogu** kitchen utensils.

daidoo enzetsu soap-box oration; street speaker.

daidoo shooi general similarity; **daidoo shooi de aru** to be nearly the same. **Yoo suru ni daidoo shooi de aru.** In short, there is no choice between them.

DAIGAKU university, college; **daigakusei** college student.

daigakuin graduate school.

daigishi member of the House of Representatives.

daihon text of a play; libretto.

daihyoo representation; type; **daihyoo suru** to represent; **daihyoosha** *(n.)* representative,

deputy; delegate; **daihyooteki** *(adj.)* representative, typical.

DAIICHI NI in the first place, first of all, firstly; **daiichi no** first, foremost, primary.

DAIJI great enterprise; great thing; serious affair; emergency; **daiji na** important; serious; precious; **daiji na yooji** an important matter; **daiji ni suru** to take care of; **daiji o toru** to be cautious; **Kimi wa daiji o torisugiru.** You are overcautious. **Odaiji ni.** Take care of yourself.

DAIJOOBU safe, secure, certain; strong; certainly, undoubtedly, without fail; I am sure; I assure you. **Sono hako wa daijoobu desu ka?** Is that box safe? **Moo daijoobu desu.** I am quite out of danger now. **Daijoobu naorimasu.** You will surely get well.

daika, daikin price, charge; purchase money; **daikin hikikae** cash on delivery; C.O.D.; **daikin hikikae yuubin** C.O.D. **Daika wa ikura desu ka?** What is the price?

daikin See **daika**.

daikirai hateful, loathsome; abominable, detestable; **daikirai da** to hate, loathe, have an antipathy to, have a strong aversion to. **Watakushi wa hebi ga daikirai desu.** I loathe snakes.

daikon white radish; **daikon oroshi** radish grater; grated radish.

daiku carpenter; carpentry.

daimeishi pronoun.

daimoku title (of a book); heading.

dainamaito dynamite.

dainashi spoiled, ruined; dirty; **dainashi ni suru** to spoil, ruin; to soil; **dainashi ni naru** to become spoiled, ruined. **Kimono ga dainashi ni natta.** The garment is ruined. **Booshi o dainashi ni shita.** You've ruined your hat.

dairi deputation; agency; **dairi o suru** to act for, take the place of; **dairi no** acting; deputy; **dairinin** proxy; representative, agent; **dairiten** agency.

dairiseki marble.

DAIROKU sixth; **dairokujuu** sixtieth; **dairokkan** sixth sense.

DAISAN third; **DAISANJUU** thirtieth; **DAISANSHA** third person; bystander; **daisansha no tachiba kara kangaeru** to put yourself in a third person's position.

daisharin big wheel, giant swing.

DAISHI fourth.

daishi pasteboard, board-mounting; **shashin o daishi ni haru** to mount a photograph.

DAISHICHI seventh. **DAISHICHIJUU** the seventieth.

daishin doctor's assistant.

daishonin scribe, notary.

daishoo compensation, recompense; -no daishoo to shite in compensation for; in recompense for.

daisoreta audacious, bold, insolent; atrocious; daisoreta mane o suru to behave atrociously.

daisuki *(adj.)* favorite, pet; daisuki de aru to have a great liking (for), be extremely fond of; watakushi no daisuki na hon my favorite book.

daisuu, daisuugaku algebra.

DAITAI main points, gist; outline, mainly; on the whole; daitai ni oite on the whole, in general; taking all things together; daitai no mitsumori rough estimate; jiken no daitai o hanasu to give an outline of the case.

daitan bravery; boldness, audacity; daitan na brave, fearless; bold, daring; daitan ni fearlessly; boldly, audaciously.

daitooryoo president (of a republic).

daiyamondo diamond.

daiyaru dial.

daiyoo substitution; daiyoo suru to substitute for, use in place of; to serve as, serve the purpose of; -no daiyoo ni naru to be used as a substitute; to serve the purpose of; daiyoobutsu substitute.

daizai subject matter, theme.

daizainin great (criminal) offender.

DAIZU soya bean.

dajare poor joke; cheap jest; dajare o iu to crack a joke.

DAKARA accordingly, therefore, so; and so. Dakara sonna koto o shite wa ikenai. That's why you must not do such a thing.

DAKE only; alone; by; as much (many) as; as . . . as; worth; ni inchi dake nagai to be two inches too long; dekiru dake hayaku as fast (soon) as one can. Onegai wa sore dake. That's all I ask. Boku hitori dake de atta. I was all by myself.

DAKEDO, DAKEDOMO, DAKEREDOMO See DAGA.

dakiageru to lift up in one's arms.

dakiau to embrace (each other).

dakikomu to bring over to one's side, win over; to buy off; to entice.

dakishimeru to embrace closely, hug.

dakitomeru to stop by throwing one's arms round another; to hold (a person) back.

dakitsuku to fly into (someone's) arms; to cling, to embrace affectionately.

dakiyoseru to draw (someone) close to one's breast.

daku to embrace, to hug; to hatch (eggs).

dakudaku in stream; dakudaku deru to gush out, spout forth.

dakuon voiced consonant (such as b, d, g, or z).

dakuryuu, dakusui muddy stream or river; turbid water.

dakyoo compromise; agreement; dakyoo suru to compromise; to come to an agreement.

DAMARU to be silent. Damatte kudasai. Please stop talking.

damasu to deceive, cheat, defraud; to impose upon; to bewitch; to soothe, humor (a crying child).

damatte silently, in silence; without telling; without leave; damatte kiite iru to be listening in silence; damatte hito no mono o tsukau to use someone else's things without permission.

DAME NA fruitless; hopeless; futile; dame de aru to be useless; to be hopeless; to be futile; to be all over (with someone); dame ni naru to fail; dame ni suru to render useless; spoil.

damu dam.

dan platform, rostrum, dais; steps, stairs; flight of stairs; grade, class; act; scene; saidan altar.

dan talk, conversation; ryokoodan account of one's travels.

-dan suffix denoting: group, body, party, team; ichidan o nashite in a group; jitsugyoodan party of businessmen.

dan'an decision; conclusion; dan'an o kudasu to make a decision.

dan'atsu suppression; oppression.

danboo heating; danboo soochi heating apparatus.

danchi housing-development apartment.

danchigai de aru to be no match for; to outclass.

danchoo leader of a party.

DANDAN gradually, little by little; by and by. Dandan kuraku natte kimashita. By and by it became dark.

dandori plan, program, design.

dangai precipice, cliff.

dangan bullet, shot; shell.

dangen assertion; affirmation; dangen suru to assert, to declare.

dango dumpling.

dangoku warm country; warm climate.

dangoo consultation, conference; dangoo suru to consult, confer with.

DANJITE absolutely; decidedly; on my word; never; by no means. Danjite ikenai! Positively no!

danjo man and woman; both sexes; **danjo kyoogaku** coeducation.

dankai steps, grade, gradation.

dankoo resolute action; **dankoo suru** to take decisive steps, act resolutely.

danko taru decisive, resolute, determined, positive; **danko to shite** decisively, positively.

danmari dumb show; silence; reticence; man of few words.

danna (colloq.) master; husband; sir; gentleman; **dannasama** master (of the house).

dannen suru to abandon (an idea, hope, desire).

danpan negotiation; parley. **Danpan ga haretsu suru.** There is a breakdown in the negotiations.

danpatsu bobbed hair.

danpen fragment, piece; odds and ends; **danpenteki** fragmentary.

danran circle; harmony; **danran suru** to sit (around) together.

danro heating stove; fireplace.

danryoku elasticity; **danryoku aru** elastic, springy.

dansaa dancer; taxi dancer.

DANSEI male; man; masculinity; **danseiteki** masculine, manly.

dansen disconnection (of a wire). **Dansen suru.** A wire breaks.

DANSHI boy; man; **danshirashii** manly; **danshirashikunai** unmanly. **Danshi.** Men's Room.

dansu dance, dancing (occidental style).

dantai party, body; group.

dantei decision; conclusion; **dantei suru** to decide; to conclude.

danwa conversation, talk; **danwa suru** to talk, chat; **danwatai** colloquial, conversational style.

danzetsu disconnection, rupture; **danzetsu suru** to be cut off; to become extinct, be disconnected.

danzoku intermission; **danzokuteki no** intermittent; **danzokuteki ni** intermittently, on and off.

daradara in drops; lazily, sluggishly; leisurely; sloppily; **daradara suru** to work sloppily; **ase ga daradara nagareru** to sweat profusely; **daradara zaka** a gentle slope.

-darake suffix denoting: full of; covered with; **asedarake no** covered with sweat.

darakeru to feel dull, languid.

daraku depravity, corruption.

darari to loosely; languidly.

darashi nai loose; careless; untidy; **darashi nai fuu o suru** to dress sloppily.

DARE who; **dare no** whose; **dare de mo** anyone, anybody; whoever; **dare de mo mina** everyone, everybody; **dare ka** someone, somebody; anyone, anybody. **Dare ga shimashita ka?** Who did it? **Kore wa dare no desu ka?** Whose is this? **Dare ni agemashoo ka?** Who should I give it to? **Dare ka anata o yonde iru.** Someone is calling you.

dareru to grow listless; to get bored; to relax; to be dull. **Hanashi ga dareta.** The conversation lagged.

-DAROO I speculate, I guess. **Ashita ame ga furudaroo.** I guess it will rain tomorrow.

DARUI to be dull; to feel languid; to feel heavy; **Ashi ga darui desu.** My legs feel heavy.

daruma Dharma; toy image of Dharma.

daryoku See dasei.

dasan calculation; **dasan suru** to calculate, count; **dasanteki** calculating, mercenary.

dasei, daryoku inertia; **ima made no dasei** by force of habit.

dashimono program; repertoire.

dashin suru to tap, sound.

DASHINUKE suddenness, abruptness; **dashinuke ni** suddenly; abruptly; unexpectedly; without warning; **dashinuke o kurau** to be taken by surprise.

dashinuku to forestall; to get ahead of.

dashishiburu to begrudge.

dassen derailment, digression; **dassen suru** to digress; to deviate.

dasshimen absorbent cotton.

dassoo desertion; flight; escape; **dassoo suru** to desert, run away; **dassoosha** fugitive, runaway.

dassuru to get out; to escape from; to omit, leave out; to get rid of; **akushuu o dassuru** to get rid of a bad habit.

DASU to put forth; to take out; to produce; to turn on; to turn away; to lay bare; to serve (a meal, tea, etc.); **tegami o dasu** to mail a letter; **shigoto ni te o dasu** to throw oneself into the job.

datai abortion.

datchoo hernia, rupture.

DATTA -ta form (past) of **da.**

datte (colloq.) but, still; because; for. **Naze gakkoo e ikanai no desu ka? Datte atama ga itai n desu mono.** Why don't you go to school? Because I have a headache.

DE in; at; start; in the matter of; **mikka de** in three days; **jikan de** by the hour; **Tookyoo de wa ichiban ii mise desu.** In Tokyo, it's the best store. **Amerika de kaimashita.** I bought it in America. **Mizu de arau.** I wash it in water.

de flow; going out; rise; birth; origin; outset, start; turnout. **Kyoo wa hito no de ga ii.** There's a large turnout today.

de aru See **desu.**

dearuku to go out; to gad about.

DEAU to meet, come across; to happen to meet.

debaboocho big kitchen knife.

debudebu no fat, plump.

debushoo one who prefers to stay at home.

dedokoro source; origin.

degarashi tea leaves; coffee grounds.

DEGUCHI exit.

deiri entrance and exit; **deiri suru** to go in and out; to frequent, visit regularly; **deiriguchi** entrance, doorway.

deisui intoxication; **deisui suru** to be dead drunk; **deisuisha** drunkard.

DEKAKERU to go out; to start, set out; **degake ni** on the point of going, on one's way; **ryokoo ni dekakeru** to start on a trip. **Degake ni denwa ga kakatta.** Just as I was on the point of going out, I received a phone call.

dekasegi emigration; working in another country; **dekasegi suru** to work away from home; **dekaseginin** worker away from home.

dekata attitude, move.

deki workmanship; make; tailoring; cut; result, effect; crop, yield; **deki no yoi** of fine workmanship; **deki no warui** of poor workmanship; **deki fudeki** success and failure. **Deki fudeki ga arimasu.** It is not always successful.

dekiagaru to be finished, be completed, be ready.

dekiai no ready made.

dekibae effect, result; manner of execution. **Rippa na dekibae deshita.** It was a fine performance.

dekigokoro sudden impulse; passing fancy; **dekigokoro de** on the spur of the moment.

dekigoto event, incident; **hibi no dekigoto** daily occurrence; everyday event; **saikin no dekigoto** recent event.

dekimono boil; sore; tumor; ulcer.

DEKINAI cannot do; poor. **Nihongo ga yoku dekinai.** I can't speak Japanese well.

DEKIRU can, may; to be able; to be possible, to be capable of; be done; be completed; **dekiru koto nara** if possible [it is a thing that I can do]. **Shokuji ga dekita.** Dinner is ready.

DEKIRU DAKE to the best of one's ability; as . . . as possible; **dekiru dake hayaku** as soon as possible; as early as possible; **dekiru dake no koto o suru** to do what one can, to do everything one can.

dekishi drowning; **dekishi suru** to drown; **dekishisha** a drowned person.

dekisokonai failure; **dekisokonai no** defective; bungled; half-baked; clumsy; deformed.

dekisokonau to fail; to be a failure; to be badly done, be botched, be bungled. **Shigoto wa dekisokonatta.** The job was bungled.

dekitate brand-new; just made; fresh.

dekki deck.

dekoboko unevenness; **dekoboko no** uneven, bumpy; rough; jagged.

demado bay window.

demae catering. **Demae o suru.** They do catering.

deme protruding eyes; **deme no** goggle-eyed.

demise branch (store); **demise o dasu** to open a branch.

DEMO even, though; even if; as well, also; but, still. **Watakushi demo dekimasu.** Even I can do it. **Donna pen demo ii desu.** Any pen will do.

demodori divorced woman.

demukae meeting; reception; **demukae o ukeru** to be met (by someone).

DEMUKAERU to go to meet (on arrival).

denaosu to come again; to go again; to call again.

den'atsu voltage.

denbun telegram, telegraphic message.

denchi electric cell; battery.

denchuu telegraph or telephone pole; electric-light pole.

dendoo missionary work; **dendooshi** evangelist, missionary.

den'en country, farms; rural districts; **den'en no** rural, countrified.

denka electrification; **denka suru** to put in electricity; to operate by electricity.

DENKI electricity; **denki no** electric(al); **denkidokei** electric clock; **denkijikake no** operated by electricity.

denki biography.

DENKYUU electric bulb.

denpoo telegram; cable; **denpoo de** by wire, by cable; **denpoo o utsu** to send a telegram (wire, cable); **denpooryoo** telegraph fee. (See also **denshin.**)

denryuu electric current.

densen infection, contagion; **densen suru** to be infectious; to be infected with; **densenbyoo** infectious, contagious disease; epidemic.

densetsu tradition; legend; **densetsuteki** traditional, legendary.

DENSHA streetcar, train; **densha de iku** to go by streetcar; **densha ni noru** to take a streetcar; **denshachin** streetcar fare; **denshadoori** street with a trolley line.

denshi renji microwave oven.

denshin telegram; **denshin bashira** telegraph pole; **denshinkyoku** telegraph office. (See also **denpoo**.)

denshin gawase wire transfer.

DENTOO electric light; **dentoo o tsukeru** to turn on the lights; **dentoo o kesu** to turn off the lights.

dentoo tradition; convention; **dentooteki** conventional; traditional.

DENWA telephone; **denwa choo** telephone directory; **denwa de** by telephone; **denwa shitsu** telephone booth; **kooshuu denwa** public telephone; **denwa o kakeru** to call, make a phone call; **denwa o kiru** to hang up; **denwa o hiku** to have a phone installed.

DEPAATO department store.

DERU to come out; to appear; to rise; to be up; to go out; to attend; to flow out; to break out; **soto e deru** to go out (outside); **uchi o deru** to leave the house; **shiki ni deru** to attend a ceremony. **Mizu ga deru.** There is a flood.

desakari height of the season.

desaki place to which someone has gone. **Desaki ga wakaranai.** I don't know where he has gone.

deshabaru to meddle, interfere.

deshi pupil, disciple, apprentice.

deshita See **desu**.

deshoo See **desu**.

desorou to come out fully; to be all out.

DESU, de aru, da be; it is; equals. **Watakushi wa gakusei desu.** I am a student. **Amerikasei deshita.** It was an American make (product). **Eikokujin deshoo.** Probably he is British.

desugiru to protrude (stick out) too much; to be too far out; to be too strong.

DESUKARA, DAKARA that is why; therefore. **Desukara minna ni sukaremasu.** That is why she is liked by everyone.

detarame irresponsible remark; nonsense; **detarame o iu** to speak nonsense.

DEWA then, in that case, if so. **Dewa sayoonara.** Good-bye now. **Dewa mata.** I'll be seeing you. **Dewa soo shite kudasai.** If that is the case, please do so.

DEZAATO dessert.

dezain design.

do degree, measure, extent; times; **ichi ni do** once or twice; **do o sugosu** to go to extremes.

DOA door (Western style).

dobin earthen teapot.

doboku public works; engineering; **doboku gishi** civil engineer.

dobu ditch.

dobunezumi water rat.

doburoku raw (unrefined) sake.

DOCHIRA which way; which (of the two); where; what place; **dochira e?** where? **dochira demo** whichever; either; both.

dodai foundation, basis.

dogimagi in confusion; **dogimagi suru** to act confused, act flustered.

dohyoo sandbag; Japanese wrestling ring, arena. **dohyoo giwa de** at the last possible moment; at the eleventh hour.

DOITSU Germany; **Doitsu no** (*adj.*) German; **Doitsujin** (*n.*) German; **Doitsugo** German language.

dojoo earth, soil.

dokadoka in rapid succession; in crowds; **dokadoka haitte kuru** to come in crowds, to rush in.

dokan to See **dokkari**.

dokata laborer; coolie.

dokeru to remove; to get out of the way.

doki earthenware.

doki anger, resentment; **doki o obite** in anger.

dokidoki suru to throb violently. **Mune ga dokidoki shimasu.** My heart is beating rapidly.

dokitto suru to be startled, get a shock.

dokkari to = **dokan to** heavily; with a thud.

dokku dock; **dokku ni hairu** to dock (as a ship).

DOKO where, what place; **doko e itte mo** wherever you go; **doko ka** somewhere; **doko kara** from where; **doko made** how far; **doko mo** everywhere.

dokoro ka far from; to say nothing of; anything but. **Hikooki dokoro ka kuruma mo motte imasen.** He doesn't even own a car, let alone an airplane.

doku poison; harm; **doku no aru** poisonous; **doku ni naru** to be bad for; **doku suru** to harm; to poison. **Oki no doku sama.** I'm sorry for you.

doku to get out of the way; to move aside. **Doite kure.** Clear the way! Get out of my way! (rough).

dokudan arbitrary decision; **dokudanteki** dogmatic, arbitrary.

dokudokushii malicious, spiteful; poisonous-looking; **dokudokushii koto o iu** to say malicious things.

dokuen solo performance, recital.

dokugaku studying by oneself, without a teacher.

dokuja poisonous snake.

dokuji no original; personal; individual; **dokujisei** originality; **dokuji no kangae** personal opinion.

dokukeshi antidote.

DOKURITSU independence; self-support; **dokuritsu suru** to be independent, stand on one's own feet; **dokuritsu no** independent; **dokuritsu de** independently; **dokuritsukoku** independent state; **dokuritsushin** independent spirit. **Dokuritsu Kinenbi** Independence Day (Fourth of July).

dokuryoku de on one's own, by oneself, singlehanded; **dokuryoku de yaru** to do something on one's own.

dokusai dictatorship; **dokusai seiji** dictatorship; **dekusaisha** dictator.

dokusatsu suru to poison.

dokusen monopoly; **dokusen jigyoo** monopolistic enterprise, monopoly; **dokusenteki** monopolistic, exclusive.

dokusha reader; subscriber; reading public; **dokushoka** book-lover; great reader.

dokusho reading.

dokusho suru to read (books).

dokushoo vocal solo.

dokushuu, dokugaku studying without a teacher; **dokushuusho** book for self-teaching; "do-it-yourself" book.

dokusoo originality; **dokusooteki na** original; creative; **dokusoo no sai** creative ability; talent.

dokuyaku poison.

dokyoo spirit; courage; **dokyoo no aru** daring, courageous; **dokyoo no nai** timid, cowardly.

doma earthen floor.

donabe earthen pot.

donaru to shout, thunder at.

DONATA who *(respect)*, **donata de mo** anybody. **Donata desu ka?** Who are you? **Donata ka ome ni kakaritai soo desu.** Someone wishes to see you.

donburi deep bowl, **donburi meshi** boiled rice served in a deep bowl; **oyako donburi** chicken, eggs, and rice in a deep bowl.

dondon rub-a-rub, rat-a-rat; **dondon susumu** to advance rapidly; **dondon mookeru** to make money rapidly.

DONNA what; what sort of, kind of; **donna ni** how much; however. **Donna hon desu ka?** What kind of a book is it?

DONO which; what; **dono kurai** to what degree?; how long?; how far?; **dono hito** which person?

donzoko rock bottom; **donzoko seikatsu** poverty-stricken life.

DOO how; what; **doo atte mo** in any case. **Doo itashimashite.** Don't mention it! Not at all! **Sore wa doo ni mo narimasen.** It can't be helped.

doo copper.

doo torso.

doo temple, shrine, hall; **doo ni iru** to attain proficiency, to become an expert.

doo (can also be prefix) the same; the said (aforementioned); corresponding; equal; **doo banchi** the same street number; **doodan** same, ditto; **dooyoo** the same, ditto; **doo mikka** the third day of the same month.

DOOBUTSU animal; living creature; **doobutsuen** zoo; **doobutsugaku** zoology.

DOO DE MO in any way; **doo de mo koo de mo** by any means, at any cost; **doo de mo ii koto** a trivial matter. **Doo de mo ii desu.** It doesn't matter one way or the other.

doodoo suru to go with, accompany.

doofuu enclosure(s); **doofuu no tegami** the enclosed letter.

doogi morality, morals, principles, ethics.

doogi motion made during a meeting.

DOOGU tools, implements, utensils; sets; property; household goods; **doogubako** toolbox; **dooguya** secondhand dealer; curio shop; furniture shop.

doohai equal colleague.

doohan suru to accompany.

dooi consent, approval, agreement; **dooi suru** to consent to, approve.

DOO ITASHIMASHITE! Don't mention it. Not at all. The pleasure is mine.

dooitsu equality; **dooitsu no** same; identical, equal.

dooji same time; **dooji no** simultaneous, concurrent; **dooji ni** at the same time; **doojidai** same age; **doojidai no** contemporary; **doojitsu** same (very) day.

doojoo exercise hall (for Judo, fencing, etc.); arena; Buddhist seminary.

doojoo sympathy, compassion; **doojoo aru** sympathetic, warmhearted; **doojoo no nai** unsympathetic.

DOOKA, DOOZO please; somehow or other; **DOOKA KOOKA** somehow or other; some way or other; barely; with difficulty; **dooka shite** somehow, in one way or another.

dooka assimilation.

dooka copper coin.

dookaku same rank, status, etc.

dookan same sentiment, same feeling; same opinion; **dookan de aru** to be of the same opinion; to feel the same way.

dooke *(n.)* clowning; **dooke shibai** farce; **dooke yakusha** clown; **dooketa** comic, foolish; **dookeru** to clown.

dookei aspiration, longing; worship.

dooki motive, incentive.

dooki palpitation; **dooki ga suru** to throb, to palpitate.

dooki same period; same class; **dooki no** of the same year; **dookisei, dookyuusei** classmate.

dookokujin fellow countryman.

dookoo pupil of the eye.

dookoo suru to go together; **dookoosha** traveling companion.

doomei alliance; league; **doomei koku** ally.

DOOMO very; much; rather; quite. **Doomo arigatoo gozaimasu.** I'm much obliged.

doonen same year; same age; **doonen de aru** to be the same age.

DOO NI KA somehow or other; **doo ni ka suru** to manage somehow, try one's best.

DOORO road.

dooryoku motor power; power.

DOOSE anyway; after all, at best; of course; at all. **Doose yaranakereba naranai desu.** I must do it anyway.

dooseiai homosexuality.

DOO SHITE why; how; **DOO SHITE MO** in any case; by any means; whatever may happen. **Doo shite sore o gozonji desu ka?** How do you know that? **Doo shite mo ikanakereba narimasen.** Whatever may happen (in any case, no matter what happens), I have to go.

dootoo equality; parity; **dootoo no** equal, equivalent; **dootoo ni** equally; **dootoo ni suru** to make equal, equalize.

DOOZO please; if you please. **Doozo moo ichido itte kudasai.** Please say it again.

doozoo bronze statue.

dora gong.

dorama drama.

doramu drum (musical); **doramu kan** drum (for storage).

DORE which one? **Dore ga ichiban ii desu ka?** Which is the best?

doro mud; **doro darake no** muddy; **doromizu** muddy water.

doroboo thief.

DORU dollar; **doru sooba** exchange rate of the dollar.

doryoku effort, exertion; **doryoku suru** to exert oneself; to endeavor.

dosakusa confusion; tumult; trouble.

doshidoshi in large numbers; rapidly; in rapid succession.

DOSSARI in great quantity or numbers. **Tegami ga dossari kita.** Many letters came.

DOTTO all of a sudden; suddenly; with a rush.

DOYOOBI Saturday.

dozoo storehouse with earthen walls.

E

E particle denoting: to, toward, in the direction of; **Kyooto e ikimasu.** I'm going to Kyoto.

E picture, painting; drawing, illustration, sketch; **e o kaku** to make (draw, paint) a picture; **e no yoo na** like a picture; picturesque.

e handle, crank, haft, shaft.

ebi lobster; shrimp; prawn.

ebicha maroon; brownish red.

eda branch, bough; twig; **edaburi** spread of branches; **edaha** branches; ramifications; digressions; **hanashi ga edaha ni hairu** to digress; **edaha no giron** side issue; digression.

EE, HAI yes. **Ee, soo desu.** Yes, that is so. Correct.

eeteru ether.

ee to let me see; well (used when stalling for time). **Ee to, sore wa nan deshita ka?** Let me see, what was it?

egao smiling face; smile; **egao ni naru** to smile; **egao de** with a smile.

egatai hard to get; not easily obtainable; **mata to egatai kikai** a rare opportunity.

EHAGAKI picture postcard.

ehon picture book for children; illustrated book.

Ei- prefix denoting: Anglo-, English, British; **Eitaishi kan** British Embassy; **Eibungaku** English Literature.

Ei-Bei England and America; **Ei-Bei no** Anglo-American; **Ei-Beijin** the English and the Americans.

eibin na keen, sharp, smart, clever, quick-witted; **eibin na kansatsu** keen observation; **eibin na mimi** sharp ears.

EIBUN English; English sentence; English composition; English-language text; **Eibun wayaku** translation from English into Japanese.

eien eternity; permanence; **eien no** eternal; permanent; everlasting; **eien ni** forever, perpetually.

EIGA movie; motion pictures; **eigagaisha** film-producing company; **eigakai no meiyuu** movie star; **EIGAKAN** movie theater.

EIGO English language; English; **Eigo no** *(adj.)* English; written in English; **Eigo ga dekiru, Eigo de hanasu** to speak in

English; **Eigo ga wakaru** to understand English.

EIGYOO business, trade; trading; **eigyoo suru** to engage in business; trade in; **eigyoohi** business expenses; **eigyoo jikan** business (office) hours; **eigyoozei** business tax.

eijuu permanent residence; **eijuu no** settled; resident; **eijuu suru** to reside permanently.

Eika English currency; sterling; British-made goods.

eikan crown of glory; laurels.

eiki high spirits; vigor; energy. **eiki o sogu** to dampen one's enthusiasm.

EIKOKU England, Great Britain; **Eikoku no** (*adj.*) English; **Eikokujin** English person (See also **Eigo.**)

EIKYOO influence; effect; **eikyoo suru** to influence; to affect; **eikyoo o ukeru** to be influenced, be affected.

eikyuu permanence; eternity; **eikyuuteki** permanent; perpetual, eternal; **eikyuu ni** permanently, forever.

eimin death (human only); **eimin suru** to die.

eiri gain, profit; **eiriteki no** money-making; commercial; **eiri jigyoo** commercial undertaking; **eiri gaisha** commercial concern.

eiri na sharp, keen; sharp-edged.

Eiryoo British dominion.

eisei hygiene, sanitation; health; **eisei ni yoi** healthful; wholesome; **eisei ni warui** bad for the health; **eiseitekina** hygienic; sanitary.

eisei satellite; **eiseikoku** satellite nation; **jinkoo eisei** man-made satellite; **eisei chuukei** satellite telecast.

eishaki film projector.

eishashitsu projection room.

eiten transfer on promotion.

EI-WA JISHO English-Japanese dictionary.

Eiyaku English translation.

eiyo honor; glory.

eiyoo nutrition; nourishment; **eiyoo aru** nutritious, nourishing; **eiyoo furyoo** malnutrition; **eiyoobutsu** nutritious food.

eizoku permanence; continuation; **eizokuteki** lasting, permanent; **eizoku suru** to last long, remain permanently.

eizuru to be reflected (as in a mirror in water); to impress.

EKI use; good; benefit; advantage, profit; **eki no aru** beneficial, profitable; **eki no nai** useless; unprofitable; **eki suru** to benefit, do good to.

EKI = **teishajoo** railway station; **ekichoo** stationmaster; **ekiin** porter; station employee; **Tokyooeki** Tokyo Station.

eki sap, liquid, fluid.

ekibyoo epidemic, pestilence, plague.

ekiri dysentery; children's summer diarrhea.

ekisu extract, essence.

ekitai liquid, fluid.

ekkususen X rays.

ekohiiki partiality, favoritism; **ekohiiki no** partial, unfair; **ekohiiki no nai** impartial, fair; **ekohiiki suru** to show partiality to; be partial to.

ekoji na stubborn, perverse, obstinate; **ekoji ni natte** in spite; out of spite.

ekubo dimple.

emono game, a catch; trophy; prize, spoils.

EN yen (Japanese money); **hyaku en** 100 yen **hyaku en satsu** 100-yen note.

en circle.

en affinity; fate; blood relation, blood connection; **en o musubu** to marry.

en feast, dinner party; **en o haru** to give a dinner party.

enban disk, discus.

enbifuku (male) evening dress.

enboo vista; distant view.

enchaku delayed arrival; **enchaku suru** to arrive late; to be delayed.

enchoo continuation, extension; **enchoo suru** to extend, prolong, lengthen.

endan proposal (of marriage).

endan rostrum, platform.

endoo route; road; **endoo ni** en route; along the road.

en'en in a blaze; **en'en taru** blazing, flaming; **en'en to shite** in (fierce) flames.

enerugii energy.

engan coast; **engan no** on the shore along the coast.

ENGAWA veranda, porch.

engei dramatic performance; entertainment, **engeisha** performer, artist; **engeijoo** variety theater; an entertainment hall; **engeikai** variety show; **engei mokuroku** program; repertoire.

engeki play; theatrical performance.

engi luck; omen; history; legend; **engi no yoi** lucky, auspicious; **engi no warui** unlucky, ominous, ill-omened.

engi playacting, performance.

engo support; backing.

engumi marriage; alliance; adoption (of a son); **engumi suru** to marry; to adopt.

enja relative, kinsman.

enjo assistance; help, aid; **enjo suru** to assist, help; to support.

enjuku maturity; mellowness; perfection; **enjuku suru** to grow ripe, mature; to mellow; **enjuku shita** mature; mellow; perfect.

enka exchange rate, value of the yen.

enkai social gathering; feast, banquet; dinner party; **enkai o hiraku** to give a dinner party.

enkai coast, sea (near land); **enkai gyogyoo** inshore fishery.

enkei distant view; perspective; circle; **enkei no** round, circular.

enki postponement; adjournment; **enki suru** to postpone, put off.

enkin distance; far and near; **enkin kara** from far and near.

enko connection; relation; affinity.

enkyori far distance, great distance; **enkyori de** at a great distance.

enmachoo black list; teacher's record book.

enman perfection; harmony; **enman na** perfect; harmonious; peaceful; **enman ni** harmoniously, smoothly; peacefully; **enman na katei** happy home; **enman ni koto o osameru** to settle the matter smoothly.

ennetsu burning (scorching) heat; heat of the sun.

ennichi fete day (of a local deity); fair; festival.

en no shita ground or space under the veranda or floor in a Japanese house; **en no shita no chikaramochi o suru** to be engaged in a thankless task; to labor in the background.

enogu paints, oils; colors, pigments; **enoguzara** dish for blending colors.

ENPITSU pencil; **iro-enpitsu** colored pencils; **enpitsu kezuri** pencil sharpener.

enpoo great distance; distant place.

enrai no kyaku visitor (guest) from a distant place.

enro long way; great distance; long journey. **Enro go-sokuroo o wazurawashimashite sumimasen.** I thank you for coming all the way.

ENRYO reserve; modesty; respect; **enryo suru** to be reserved; to refrain from; to withhold; **enryo naku** without reserve, freely; **enryo bukai** modest; shy; **-ni enryo shite** out of respect for (someone); **enryo eshaku mo naku** without the least reserve.

ensaki edge of a veranda.

ensei, enseikan pessimism; **enseiteki** pessimistic; **enseika** pessimist.

enshoo inflammation; spread of a fire; **enshoo suru** to catch fire.

enshutsu performance (of a play, an opera, a film); **enshutsu suru** to play, perform, to execute.

ensoku excursion (on foot), hike; picnic; **ensoku ni iku** to go on a hike; to take a long walk.

ensoo musical performance; recital; **ensoosha** performer, player; **ensookai** concert, recital.

entaku round table.

enten blazing (burning) sun; heat of the day.

ENTOTSU chimney; chimney stack; funnel.

en'yoo gyogyoo deep-sea fishing.

en'yoo kookai ocean voyage.

en'yuukai garden party.

enzetsu speech, address; **enzetsu suru** to make a speech; **enzetsukai** speech meeting.

enzuku to get married.

episoodo episode.

ERABU to choose, select, elect, single out; to sort; **hon o erabu** to select a book. **Ii no dake o erabimashoo.** Let's choose only a good one.

ERAI great; extraordinary; worthy; eminent; wonderful; serious; heavy. **Erai koto ni natta.** It looks bad.

EREBEETAA elevator.

ERI neck; neckband; collar; **erikubi** nape of the neck; **erimaki** muffler, scarf; **eri o tadasu** to adjust one's dress; to sit up straight.

eru to gain; to get.

eshaku greeting, salutation; **eshaku suru** to greet; to bow slightly.

esukareetaa escalator.

etai form, shape; nature; **etai no shirenu** unfamiliar, strange; nondescript; **etai no shirenu hito** a perfect stranger.

ete skill; specialty, one's forte; **ete ni ho o ageru** to sail before the wind; to give scope to one's skill; **-ga ete da** to be a good hand at; **-wa ete de nai** to be a poor hand at.

etoku understanding, comprehension; **etoku suru** to understand, grasp; **etoku shiyoi** easy to understand; **etoku shinikui** difficult to understand.

F

FAAMASHII pharmacy.

faindaa finder.

fan fan, enthusiast; **eiga fan** movie fan.

fassho fascist.

fauru foul ball (in baseball).

feruto See **fueruto.**

fiito = **fuiito** feet (a measure).

Firipin Philippine Islands; **Firipinjin** Filipino.

firumu = **fuirumu** film.

firutaa filter.

fooku fork.

-fu suffix denoting: urban prefecture (used only with Kyoto and Osaka); **Kyooto fu** Kyoto prefecture.

fuan insecurity; anxiety; **fuan na** unsafe; insecure; anxious.

fuan ni omou to feel insecure (uncertain, anxious) about. **Fuan de atta.** I felt uneasy.

fuannai unfamiliarity; ignorance; **fuannai na** unfamiliar; ignorant; **fuannai na tochi** strange place; **tochi ni fuannai na hito** stranger, person who is not familiar with a place. **Watakushi wa koko wa fuannai desu.** I am pretty much of a stranger here.

fuantei instability; **fuantei na** unstable; unsteady; insecure.

FUBEN inconvenience; **fuben na** inconvenient; **fuben o shoozuru** to cause inconvenience; **fuben o shinobu** to put up with inconvenience; **fuben o kanzuru** to be put to inconvenience.

fubi deficiency; defect, imperfection; **fubi no** defective; incomplete; imperfect; **fubi no ten** defects; imperfections.

fubin na pitiful; poor; **fubin ni omou** to pity, take pity on.

FUBO parents.

fubuki snowstorm, blizzard.

fuchakuriku hikoo non-stop flight.

fuchaku suru to stick to; to attach.

fuchi edge, brink, rim; margin, border; **fuchi o toru** to hem; to fringe; etc.; **fuchi o tsukeru** to frame, border.

fuchi deep pool, deep water; abyss.

fuchin ups and downs; rise and fall; **isshoo no fuchin ni kansuru daiji** a matter affecting one's whole life.

fuchoo disagreement; rupture; failure; **fuchoo ni owaru** to end in failure.

fuchoowa discord; incongruity; **fuchoowa na** unharmonious, discordant; **fuchoowa de aru** to clash.

FUCHUUI carelessness; inattention; **fuchuui na** careless; inattentive; **fuchuui ni** carelessly.

fuchuujitsu unfaithfulness, disloyalty; **fuchuujitsu na** unfaithful, disloyal.

FUDA card; label, tag; placard; **fuda o tsukeru** to attach a card (or label); to tag.

FUDAN usually, ordinarily; habitually; **fudan no** usual; habitual; common; **fudan no toori** as usual.

fudangi everyday clothes.

fude writing brush.

fudeki failure; poor work; **fudeki na** badly made (done); clumsy. **Kono hako wa fudeki desu.** This box is badly made. **Ine ga fudeki desu.** The rice crop is poor.

fudoo difference, diversity, dissimilarity; inequality; **fudoo de aru** to be unequal; to differ; to be irregular.

fudooi disagreement, difference of opinion.

fudoosan immovable property; real estate.

fudootoku immorality; **fudootoku na** immoral, unprincipled.

fue flute, whistle.

fueisei na unsanitary; unhealthy.

FUERU to increase (in number or quantity), multiply. **Mizu ga fuete kita.** The river is rising. **Okane ga fueta.** His income has increased.

fueruto = **feruto** felt.

fuete weak point; unskillfulness; **fuete na** unskillful, inexpert. **Sono hoo wa fuete desu.** I'm a poor hand at it. It's not in my line.

fufuku dissatisfaction, discontent; disapproval; objection; **fufuku ga aru** to be dissatisfied, etc.; **fufuku o iu** to express dissatisfaction.

fugai nai unmanly, effeminate; poor-spirited; cowardly.

fugi immorality; injustice; adultery; **fugi no** immoral; improper.

fugiri ingratitude; dishonesty; **fugiri no** unjust; dishonest; ungrateful; **fugiri ga aru** to owe a debt.

fugoo millionaire.

fugoo mark, sign, symbol, cipher.

fugookaku failure; elimination; rejection; **figookaku to naru** to fail.

fugoori absurdity; **fugoori na** absurd; irrational, illogical.

fugu deformity; **fugu no** deformed, disfigured, crippled; **fugu ni naru** to become disfigured.

fuguu misfortune, adversity; **fuguu no** unfortunate.

fugyooseki loose conduct; dissipation.

fuhai decomposition; decay; **fuhai suru** to rot; to be corrupted.

fuhei discontent; dissatisfaction; **fuhei o iu** to grumble, complain; **fuhei de aru** to be discontented; **fuhei o motte iru** to have a complaint; **fuheika** grumbler, malcontent.

fuheikin inequality, disproportion; **fuheikin no** unequal; disproportionate.

fuhen unchangeability; **fuhen no** unchangeable, constant; invariable.

fuhinkoo immoral conduct; dissipation; **fuhinkoo na** loose, immoral.

fuhitsuyoo na needless, unnecessary.

fuhon'i unwillingness, reluctance; **fuhon'i no** unwilling, reluctant; **fuhon'i nagara** against one's will.

fuhoo na unlawful, violent; illegal.

fui unexpectedness; suddenness; **fui no** unexpected; sudden; unlooked for; **fui o utsu** to take by surprise; **fui o kurau** to be taken by surprise.

fuichoo announcement; advertisement; recommendation; **fuichoo suru** to announce; to advertise; to make known.

fuiito See **fiito.**

fuirumu See **firumu.**

fuiuchi unexpected blow, surprise attack.

fujichaku, fujichakuriku forced landing, emergency landing.

FUJIN woman; lady; **fujinrashii** womanly; ladylike.

fuji no incurable; fatal.

fujitsu insincerity; faithlessness; lack of feeling; **fujitsu no** faithless; insincere; unfeeling.

fujiyuu inconvenience; want; discomfort; **fujiyuu na** uncomfortable; inconvenient; **fujiyuu o suru** to be short (wanting).

fujo assistance, aid; support; **fujo suru** to assist, aid.

fujoori unreasonableness, irrationality; **fujoori na** unreasonable, irrational.

fujun impurity; **fujun no** impure.

fujun unseasonability, irregularity; **fujun na** unseasonable, irregular.

fujuubun insufficiency; **fujuubun na** insufficient; incomplete.

fuka addition, supplement; **fuka suru** to add, supplement.

fukagen slight illness, indisposition; unsavoriness; **fukagen na** unsavory; indisposed, unwell.

FUKAI deep, profound; thick, dense; **fukai kangae** deep thought; **fukai kiri** dense fog; **fukai naka ni naru** to form a close relationship.

fukai unpleasantness. See **fuyukai.**

fukairi (*n.*) going too far; addiction; **fukairi suru** to go deeply into; to be taken up too much with.

fukakai mystery; **fukakai na** mysterious; insoluble; **fukakai na koto** mystery, mysterious affair.

fukakooryoku act of God; **fukakooryoku no** unavoidable; inevitable; irresistible.

fukaku negligence, fault; **fukaku o toru** to be beaten. **Sore wa watakushi no fukaku deshita.** It was my fault.

fukakujitsu uncertainty; unreliability; **fukakujitsu no** uncertain; unreliable.

fukami depth; deep place; **fukami no aru** deep, profound; **fukami ni hairu** to get beyond one's depth.

fukanoo impossibility; **fukanoo na** impossible; impractical. **Hotondo fukanoo de aru.** It is almost impossible.

fukanzen imperfection; incompleteness; **fukanzen na** defective; incomplete.

fukkappatsu inactivity; stagnation; dullness; **fukappatsu na** dull; inactive; stagnant.

fukasa depth. **Fukasa ga go fiito desu.** It is five feet deep.

fukeiki depression; dullness; hard times; **fukeiki na** dull; depressed, gloomy, dismal.

fukeizai na uneconomical; wasteful.

fukenkoo unhealthiness; poor health; **fukenkoo na** unhealthy, unwholesome.

fukenshiki lack of proper judgment; **fukenshiki na** disgraceful, shameful.

fukenzen na morbid, unwholesome.

FUKERU to grow old, age; to grow late, advance; **yo ga fukeru made hataraku** to work late into the night. **Yo wa dandan fuketa.** The night wore away. It grew late.

fuketsu dirtiness; **fuketsu na** dirty, filthy; **fuketsubutsu** dirt, filth.

fuki appendix; **fuki suru** to add.

fukiageru to blow up; to spout; to throw up.

fukichirasu to scatter about; to blow away.

fukidasu to spout, gush out; to burst out laughing.

fukidemono (body) rash.

fukikakeru to pick (a quarrel); to breathe on. **Kimi wa boku ni kenka o fukikakeru no ka?** Do you want to pick a fight with me?

fukikesu to blow out a light.

fukikomu to blow into (a house, room, etc.); to inspire; to instill in one's mind; to record (make a sound recording); to polish, rub bright.

fukimakuru to blow about; to sweep along.

FUKIN a napkin; dish towel, dishcloth.

fukin neighborhood; **fukin ni** in the neighborhood; **fukin no** neighboring, adjacent.

fukinshin na indiscreet; immodest.

fukiorosu to blow down.

fukiritsu lack of discipline; irregularity; **fukiritsu na** disorderly; undisciplined; irregular.

fukisoku irregularity; **fukisoku na** unsystematic; irregular.

fukisooji wiping; cleaning; **fukisooji o suru** to mop.

fukisusamu to blow furiously.

fukitoru to wipe away; to wipe out.

fukitsu ill omen; ill luck; **fukitsu na** unlucky, ill-omened; ominous.

fukitsukeru to blow against; to beat against. **Ame ga mado ni fukitsukeru.** The rain beats against the window.

fukiyoseru to drift; to blow together.

fukkatsu revival; **fukkatsu suru** to revive.

Fukkatsusai, Fukkatsusetsu Easter.

fukkoo revival, renaissance; restoration; **fukkoo suru** to revive, be restored.

fukkyuu restoration; **fukkyuu suru** to restore to the original state; to be restored to normalcy.

fukokoroe indiscretion; misconduct; **fukokoroe na** unwise, indiscreet; **fukokoroe na koto o suru** to behave badly; to act indiscreetly.

fukoku decree, proclamation; notification; **fukoku suru** to notify; to decree, proclaim.

FUKOO misery; unhappiness; disaster; mishap; disobedience to parents; **fukoo na** unhappy, unfortunate; miserable; undutiful, unfilial; **fukoo ni mo** unfortunately; **fukoo ni au** to have a misfortune.

fukoohei unfairness, partiality; **fukoohei na** unfair, partial, unjust; **fukoohei ni** unjustly, unfairly.

FUKU to wipe; to dry; to mop, to rub off; **tenugui de te o fuku** to wipe the hands with a towel.

fuku to blow; to breathe; to whistle. **Hidoku fuite iru.** It's blowing hard. **me o fuku** to send out a new shoot; **fue o fuku** to play a flute; **hora o fuku** (colloq.) to boast.

fuku- prefix denoting: assistant, vice-; **fukugichoo** vice-chairman; **Fukudaitooryoo** Vice-President (of the U.S.A.).

fuku- sub, double, composite; **fukuri** compound interest.

-fuku suffix denoting: clothes, dress; garment; **yoofuku** European clothes; **fujinfuku** women's clothes.

fukuan plan, idea; scheme. **Watakushi ni fukuan ga arimasu.** I have a good plan.

fukubiki lottery; distribution of prizes.

fukubukushii happy-looking; radiant.

fukugyoo subsidiary business; side job.

fukumuu to have (hold) in the mouth; to bear in mind; to include; to imply. **Doozo kono koto o ofukumioki kudasai.** Please keep this in mind.

fukurahagi calf (of the leg).

fukuramasu to swell, expand, puff out.

fukurami bulge, swelling.

fukureru to swell, puff out; to be sulky; to become sore.

fukurettsura (colloq.) sulky, sullen look.

FUKURO bag, sack, pouch.

fukurodataki sound thrashing, drubbing.

fukuryooji vice-consul.

fukusanbutsu by-product.

fukusayoo ill effect; secondary reaction; harmful side effects; **fukusayoo no nai** harmless.

fukusei reproduction; duplication.

fukusha copying; **fukusha suru** to copy, reproduce; **fukushaki** duplicator.

fukushachoo vice-president (of a company).

fukushi adverb.

fukushi welfare.

fukushin devotion; confidence; **fukushin no** devoted; confidential; faithful; **fukushin no tomo** devoted friend.

fukushoku reappointment; **fukushoku suru** to resume office.

fukushuu review; **fukushuu suru** to review, go over.

fukushuu revenge, vengeance; **fukushuu suru** to be revenged.

fukusuu (n.) plural (number); **fukusuu no** (adj.) plural.

fukutsu no inflexible; indomitable.

fukutsuu stomachache; bellyache.

fukuyoo suru to take a dose of medicine.

fukuzatsu na complex, complicated, intricate; **fukuzatsu ni suru** to complicate.

fukuzoo reserve; **fukuzoo naku** without reserve, frankly; **fukuzoo no nai** frank, candid, unreserved; **fukuzoo naku ieba** to be frank with you; **fukuzoo naku iken o noberu** to express one's views freely, without reserve.

fukyoo business depression, slump, inactivity, slackness, displeasure; ill-humor, disfavor, **fukyoo no** inactive; depressed; weak; in a slump.

fukyuu diffusion, propagation, spread; **fukyuu suru** to diffuse, propagate, spread.

fukyuu immortality, eternity; **fukyuu no** eternal, immortal, undying.

fuman, fumanzoku discontent, dissatisfaction; **fuman na** discontented, dissatisfied; **fuman ni omou** to be displeased with, dissatisfied with.

fumei obscurity, uncertainty; ignorance; **fumei no** obscure, indistinct, vague; **fumeiryoo** not clear, indistinct. **Yukisaki wa fumei da.** His destination is unknown.

fumeiyo disgrace, dishonor; discredit; **fumeiyo na** disgraceful, dishonorable.

fumetsu immortality; indestructibility.

fumidai step; footstool.

fumidan step; steps, stairs.

fumidasu to step forward.

fumihazusu to miss (lose) one's footing.

fumikatameru to tread; to stamp down.

fumikiri railway crossing; grade crossing.

fumikoeru to step over (a thing).

fumikomu to step into; to make a raid; to rush in; to trespass; to force an entrance.

fumikudaku to trample.

fumimochi dissipation; immoral conduct.

fuminarasu to stamp (one's feet) noisily; to tread; to level by treading.

fumin fukyuu without sleep or rest.

fuminijiru to trample, crush with the feet.

fuminshoo insomnia, sleeplessness.

fumitaosu to kick down; to evade payment; to bargain.

fumitodomaru to stand one's ground, remain.

fumitsukeru to trample; to treat with contempt; **hito o fumitsuke ni shita koto o iu** to make an insulting remark.

fumoto foot of a hill or mountain.

fumu to step; to tread on; to go through; to value at; **jitchi o fumu** to experience; **tetsuzuki o fumu** to go through the formalities; **shinamono no ne o fumu** to put a price on something.

fumuki unfit for, unsuitable for.

FUN, pun minute; **ippun** one minute; **gofun kan** for five minutes.

funaashi speed, draft, headway (of a ship); **funaashi no hayai fune** fast boat.

funaasobi boat excursion; **funaasobi ni yuku** to go boating.

funachin passage fare; shipping freight; freightage.

funade ship departure; sailing; **funade suru** to set sail.

funani shooken bill of lading.

funanori sailor, seaman.

funare unfamiliarity; inexperience; **funare na** unfamiliar; inexperienced; **roodoo ni funare de aru** to be unaccustomed to labor.

funayoi seasickness.

funbaru to stretch one's legs; to straddle; to make an effort; to persevere; **saigo made funbaru** to hold fast to the end.

funbetsu discretion, good sense; discernment; **funbetsu no aru** discreet, prudent; thoughtful; **funbetsu no nai** indiscreet etc.; **funbetsu zakari no hito** mature person.

fundan ni in plenty, fully. **Tabemono ga fundan ni aru.** There is plenty to eat.

FUNE ship, boat, vessel; **fune ni noru** to board a ship; to go to sea; **fune ni you** to get seasick.

funesshin indifference; **funesshin na** halfhearted, indifferent, lukewarm.

fungai resentment, indignation; **fungai shite** indignantly; **fungai suru** to be indignant, resent.

funiai unbecoming (to), unsuitable; ill-matched; **funiai no fuufu** ill-matched couple.

fun'iki atmosphere.

funinjoo na unfeeling, coldhearted.

funka eruption, volcanic activity; **funkazan** volcano.

funki suru to be stirred up, be inspired by; to rouse oneself to action.

funmatsu powder; **funmatsu ni suru** to pulverize.

funoo impossibility; incompetency; impotency; **funoo no** impossible.

funpatsu exertion, endeavor(s); **funpatsu suru** to exert oneself; to rouse; to make a great effort.

funsai suru to shatter (smash) to pieces.

funshitsu loss; **funshitsu suru** to lose; to miss; to be missing; **funshitu butsu** lost article.

funshutsu spout, gush, jet; **funshutsu suru** to gush out.

funsoo trouble; dispute; difficulties.

funsoo disguise; **funsoo suru = funsuru** to disguise, to impersonate.

funsui fountain; jet.

funsuru See **funsoo suru**.

funtoo hard struggle, desperate fight; **funtoo suru** to struggle, fight desperately.

funzen resolutely; plucking up one's courage; indignantly; in a fit of anger.

fuon unrest; **fuon na** threatening; disquieting; improper; riotous; **fuon na nyuusu** unsettling news. **Keisei ga fuon de aru.** The situation is quite disturbing.

fuontoo impropriety, inappropriateness; **fuontoo no, fuontoo na** improper, inappropriate; unjust.

furachi outrageousness; insolence; misconduct; **furachi na** outrageous, insolent; vicious; **furachi na koto o suru** to misconduct oneself; to act viciously.

furafura to dizzy, unsteady; **furafura suru** to feel dizzy; to reel, stagger. **Atama ga furafura suru.** My head is swimming.

furai fry **sakana no furai** fried fish; **furaipan** frying pan.

furanneru flannel.

FURANSU France; **Furansugo** French language; **Furansujin** French person.

furareru to be jilted.

furasshu flashlight.

furekomi announcement, proclamation.

furekomu to announce; to represent oneself as.

furemawasu to broadcast, to spread news.

fureru to touch; to strike against; to refer to; to conflict with; **hooritsu ni fureru** to be contrary to the law; **mondai ni fureru** to refer to the question.

furi disadvantage, drawback; **furi na** disadvantageous, unfavorable; unprofitable.

furi appearance; air; pretension; **shiranai furi o suru** to pretend ignorance.

furi- prefix denoting: to shake; to brandish, wave, flourish.

furidashi drawing; start, starting point; issue.

furidasu to begin to fall (as rain or snow). **Ame ga furidashita.** It began to rain.

furieki disadvantage; handicap.

furigana Kana (Japanese syllabic sign) attached to *Kanji* to show the pronunciation.

furihanasu to shake free from; to break away.

furiharau to shake from.

furikae change; transfer.

furikaeru, furimuku to turn around; to look back over one's shoulder.

furikakaru to fall on; to befall, happen.

furikakeru to sprinkle over.

furikazasu to hold aloft; to brandish.

furikiru break away from.

furiko pendulum.

furimawasu to brandish, flourish.

furimuku See **furikaeru.**

furiotosu to shake off.

furishikiru to rain or snow incessantly.

furisuteru to leave, abandon, to shake off.

furitateru to shake; to toss; to raise one's voice.

furitsuke dance composition; choreography.

furitsuzuku to rain or snow continuously.

FURO bath, hot bath; **furo ni hairu** to take a bath; **furoba** bathroom; **furoya** bathhouse.

furoku supplement, appendix.

furoonin wanderer; tramp.

FUROSHIKI wrapping cloth (square piece of cotton or silk used to wrap and carry something); **furoshiki de tsutsumu** to wrap in a wrapping cloth.

FURU to fall, to come down (rain, etc.). **Hidoku ame ga futte iru.** Rain is falling heavily. **Yuki ga futta.** There was a snowfall.

furu to shake; to wave, wag; **kubi o tate ni furu** to nod, assent to.

furu- prefix denoting: old; **furuhon** old book; **furuhonya** secondhand book store; **furubiru** to be worn out; to be aged; **furubita** old, worn-out; **furumono** secondhand goods; **furudoogu** old furniture; secondhand household utensils; **furudooguya** secondhand dealer; curio shop; **furugi** old clothes; secondhand clothes; **furugi ya** secondhand-clothes dealer.

furue *(n.)* shaking, trembling, shivering; **furueagaru** to tremble with fear; **furuegoe** trembling voice; timid voice.

furueru to shake, shudder, tremble.

furui sieve; **furui ni kakeru** to sift (out) sieve.

furui old (used when speaking of things); ancient; antique.

furuiokosu to stir up, rouse, awaken; **yuuki o furuiokosu** to summon up courage.

furuitatsu to stir up; to be roused to action.

furukizu old wound; scar; former misdeed.

furukusai stale; old-fashioned; hackneyed.

furumai behavior, conduct, action.

furumau to behave, act; to treat, behave toward (a person).

furutte energetically; voluntarily; willingly. **Furutte goshusseki kudasai.** Please make every effort to attend.

furuuto flute (Western style).

furyo no unexpected, accidental; **furyo no dekigoto** accident; unforeseen event, an emergency.

furyoo no bad; poor; unsatisfactory; deliquent; **furyoo shoonen** bad boy(s); **furyoohin** inferior goods.

furyooken indiscretion; rash act; **furyooken na** rash; ill-advised.

fusa tassel; tuft; fringe; bunch; cluster.

fusagaru to get blocked; to become choked; to be occupied, engaged; to be filled. **Kono michi wa saki ga fusagatte iru.** This road is blocked. **Sono ie wa fusagatte iru.** That house is occupied. **Kono seki wa fusagatte iru.** This seat is taken. **Ima te ga fusagatte imasu.** I am tied up just now. I am busy now.

fusagikomu to be in low spirits; to mope.

fusagu to close, shut up; to stand in the way; to be dejected, depressed; **basho o fusagu** to take up room; **jikan o fusagu** to fill up the time; **michi o fusagu** to stand in the way.

fusai debt; loan.

fusansei disapproval; dissent; **fusansei de aru** to dissent; disapprove; **fusansei o tonaeru** to raise objections to; to express disapproval. **Kimi wa sansei ka fusansei ka?** Are you for or against it?

FUSAWASHII suitable, becoming.

fusegu to defend, protect, guard against; to prevent; to resist.

fusei dishonesty; injustice; unlawfulness; **fusei na** dishonest; wrong; corrupt; unlawful; **fuseihin** sham (fraudulent article).

fuseijitsu insincerity, dishonesty; **fuseijitsu na** dishonest; false.

fuseikaku uncertainty; inaccuracy.

fuseikoo failure; fiasco; miscarriage; **fuseikoo no** unsuccessful, abortive.

fuseiseki poor (unsatisfactory) result; bad record; poor performance; failure; **fuseiseki de aru** to be unsuccessful, be a failure; **fuseiseki ni owaru** to end in failure.

fusen tag, label; slip.

fuseru to put upside down; to turn over; to be down; to take cover.

fusessei neglect of health.

fushi joint; knuckle; knot; **fushi ana** knothole.

fushiawase unhappiness; misfortune, **fushiawase na** unhappy; unfortunate; unlucky; **fushiawase ni mo** unfortunately.

fushidara untidiness; looseness, laxity; **fushidara na** untidy; sloppy; irregular; loose; dissipated.

FUSHIGI wonder, miracle; **fushigi na** wonderful; marvelous; mysterious; miraculous; strange; **fushigi ni** wonderfully, miraculously.

fushimatsu mismanagement; carelessness; misconduct; prodigality; **fushimatsu na** lax; wasteful; irregular.

fushin doubt, suspicion; question; **fushin no** doubtful, suspicious, questionable; **fushin ni omou** to wonder; to think strange.

fushinjin unbelief; impiety; **fushinjin na** unbelieving, irreligious.

fushinjitsu insincerity; faithlessness; **fushinjitsu na** faithless, insincere.

fushinkoo unbelief; **fushinkoo no** unbelieving; freethinking.

fushinsetsu unkindness; **fushinsetsu na** unkind; unobliging.

fushin'yoo distrust, lack of confidence.

fushizen na unnatural, artificial; affected.

fushoo injury, wound; **fushoo suru** to be injured, get hurt; **fushoo sha** injured person.

fushoo bushoo ni reluctantly, unwillingly.

fushoochi dissent; disapproval; **fushoochi o iu** to dissent; to disapprove.

fushoojiki dishonesty; **fushoojiki na** dishonest.

fushooka indigestion.

fushubi failure; fiasco; displeasure; **fushubi ni naru** to fall into disfavor; **fushubi ni owaru** to end in failure.

fusoku shortage, deficiency; dissatisfaction; **fushoku suru** to want, lack, be short; **fusoku o iu** to grumble, complain; **fusoku gaku** shortage, deficit.

fusoooo na unsuitable, unfitting, unbecoming; undue; **mibun fusoooo na seikatsu o suru** to live above one's means.

FUSUMA sliding screen door covered with paper.

FUTA lid, cover; **futatsuki no** covered; **futa o suru, futa o shimeru** to cover, put on a lid; **futa o toru** to lift the lid.

futae double, twofold.

futago twins.

futaoya one's parents.

FUTARI couple, two persons.

futashika uncertainty; **futashika na** uncertain; doubtful.

FUTATABI again.

FUTATSU two; **futatsu henji de** ready enough; most willingly; **futatsu to nai** matchless, unique; **futatsu tomo** both; **futatsu ni wakeru** to divide in two.

futei na uncertain, indefinite; inconstant.

futeisai na unseemly, indecent; unsightly; clumsy.

futeki na bold, daring, fearless.

futekinin unfitness, incompetency; **futekinin de aru** to be unfit (for a task), be unsuitable for, be unqualified for; **futekininsha** a misfit.

futettei imperfect; inconsistent; unconvincing; not thoroughgoing.

FUTO suddenly; by chance, by accident; **futo omoidasu** to remember in a flash.

futodoki na insolent, rude.

FUTOI big; thick; deep; sonorous.

futokoro bosom; purse; pocket; **futokoro ga sabishii** to be short (of money); **futokoro ni suru** to put in one's pocket.

futokusaku poor plan; unwise course; disadvantage; **futokusaku na** unwise, inadvisable, inexpedient.

futomomo thigh.

FUTON mattress; quilt; cushion; bedding, **futon o shiku** to make a bed.

futoo injustice; **futoo na** unjust, unfair; unreasonable; **futoo ritoku** unreasonable profits.

futoppara generosity; broad-mindedness; **futoppara no** generous; broad-minded.

futoraseru to fatten; **FUTORU** to grow fat; **shindai ga futoru** to prosper.

futosa thickness; bulk.

FUTOTTA fat; plump; **futotta hito** fat person.

futsugoo inconvenience; misconduct; **futsugoo na** wrong; improper, objectionable; inconvenient; **futsugoo na koto o suru** to behave wrongly.

FUTSUKA two days; second day (of the month); **Sangatsu futsuka** March 2.

futsukayoi hangover; **futsukayoi o suru** to have a hangover.

futsuriai incongruity; imbalance, disproportion; **futsuriai no** disproportionate; ill-matched.

FUTSUU usually, normally.

futsuu ni naru to be suspended, cut off, interrupted.

futtei scarcity, shortage; **futtei de aru** to be scarce; **futtei suru** to run short.

futtemo tettemo rain or shine; no matter what the weather.

futtoo boiling; bubbling; agitation; **futtoo suru** to boil up; to bubble; **futtoo ten**

boiling point. **Giron ga futtoo shita.** The discussion became heated.

futtsuri utterly, entirely. **Ito ga futtsuri kireta.** The string snapped.

fuu appearance; customs; manners; way; seal; closing.

fuu seal; **fuu o suru** to seal, to fasten.

fuubun rumor.

fuubutsu scenery; nature; landscape.

fuuchoo trend of the times; fashion, tendency.

FUUFU husband and wife; married couple; **fuufu ni naru** to marry; **fuufu wakare** divorce; **fuufunaka** married life.

fuuga elegance; refinement; **fuuga na** elegant; refined.

fuugetsu scenery; (beauties of) nature.

fuugi manners; customs; **fuugi no yoi** well-mannered; well-bred; **fuugi no warui** ill-mannered; ill-bred.

fuuha wind and waves; storm; heavy sea; discord; trouble.

fuuhyoo current rumor; report.

FUUKEI landscape; scenery; **fuukeiga** landscape; seascape (painting); **fuukeigaka** landscape painter.

fuukiri release; **fuukiri suru** to break a seal; to release (a film, etc.).

fuumi flavor; taste; **fuumi no yoi** tasty, delicious.

fuun misfortune; ill luck; **fuun na** unfortunate, unlucky.

fuurin wind bell (tiny bell that tinkles in the wind).

fuuryuu elegance; taste; **fuuryuu na** elegant.

fuusa blockade.

fuusen balloon.

fuusetsu snowstorm, blizzard.

FUUSHUU manners; custom, usage, practice.

fuusoku wind velocity.

fuutei appearance, looks; dress.

FUUTOO envelope. **Fuutoo ni irete kudasai.** Please put it in an envelope.

fuuu wind and rain; rainstorm; **fuuu ni sarasareta** weather-beaten; **fuuu ni sarasu** to expose to the weather; **fuuu o okashite iku** go in spite of the storm.

fuuzoku customs; manners; public morals.

fuwa discord; strife; **fuwa de aru** to be on bad terms; **fuwa ni naru** to become estranged.

fuwafuwa light; thin; soft; spongy; lightly; softly.

fuwari lightly; softly; buoyantly.

fuyakasu to steep, soak.

fuyakeru to swell up; to get soaked; to be saturated.

fuyasu to increase; to add to; to raise.

fuyoo ni naru to be out of use; to fall into disuse.

fuyooi na unprepared, careless; thoughtless.

fuyoojoo neglect of health; intemperance; **fuyoojoo na** careless of one's health.

FUYU winter; **fuyu no** wintry; winter, **fuyufuku, fuyu mo no** winter clothes; **fuyuyasumi** winter vacation.

fuyukai, fukai unpleasantness; discomfort; **fuyukai na** unpleasant; uncomfortable; **fuyukai ni** unpleasantly, uncomfortably.

fuyukitodoki carelessness; neglect; **fuyukitodoki na** careless, negligent.

fuzai absence; **fuzai de aru** to be absent.

fuzoku attached to; belonging to; **fuzoku suru** to be attached to; to belong to; **fuzokuhin** accessories.

G

GA particle marking an emphatic subject; but; and yet; however; although. **Sumisu san ni denwa o kakemashita ga rusu deshita.** I phoned Mr. Smith, but he was not in.

ga self, ego; self-will, selfishness; **ga o oru** to give in, to yield; **ga o toosu** to have one's way; **ga no tsuyoi** self-willed, obstinate.

gaarusukauto girl scout.

gaaze cheesecloth; surgical gauze.

gaba to all of a sudden; **gaba to okiagaru** to spring out of bed; to spring to one's feet.

gabugabu used only with **nomu** to take long draughts; to swill.

gaburi to used only with **nomu, kuitsuku; gaburi to nomu** to drain at one gulp; to gulp down; **gaburi to kuitsuku** to bite (snap) at.

gachagacha clattering, rattling; **gachagacha saseru** to clatter, rattle.

-GACHI suffix denoting: apt to, prone to; prevailing; of frequent occurrence; **okotarigachi no** prone to neglect; **byookigachi no** prone to illness; ill most of the time; **kumorigachi no** cloudy; gloomy.

gahaku great painter.

gai injury, harm, damage; **gai suru** to injure, harm, hurt; **gai ni naru** to be injurious or harmful.

gaibu outside, exterior; **gaibu no** external, outer; **gaibu no hito** outsiders.

gaibun reputation; honor.

gaichuu harmful insect; blight; vermin.

GAIDO tourist guide.

gaihaku suru to stay out, stay away from home (at night).

gaijin foreigner.

gaikai outside world.

gaikan external appearance; outside view; general view; outline.

gaikei external form.

gaiken outward appearance.

GAIKOKU foreign country; **gaikoku no** foreign; exotic; alien; **gaikoku e iku** to go abroad; **gaikoku sei** foreign (product); **gaikoku booeki** foreign trade; **gaikoku kawase** foreign exchange (rate); **gaikoku shijoo** foreign market; **gaikokusen** foreign ships; **GAIKOKUGO** foreign language; **GAIKOKUJIN** foreigner; **gaikokujin machi** section where many foreigners live.

gaikoo diplomacy; **gaikooka, gaikookan** diplomat; **gaikooteki** diplomatic; **gaikoodan** diplomatic corps.

gaikooin canvasser.

gaikotsu skeleton; bones.

gaimen *(n.)* outside; surface; **gaimen no** exterior, external; outside.

gaimu foreign affairs.

gainen concept, general idea; conception.

gairai foreign; exotic; imported.

GAISHITE in general; generally speaking; on the whole.

gaishutsu suru to go out; **gaishutsugi** street dress.

gaitoo street lamp.

gaitoo street; **gaitoo enzetsu** soapbox oratory; **gaitoo ni tatsu** to go out (in the street).

gaitoo suru to fall under, to correspond to.

gaiyuu suru to travel abroad.

gaka painter; artist.

gake cliff, precipice; **gakekuzure** landslide.

-gake suffix denoting: being on the way to; **toorigake ni** in passing; **negake ni** just before going to bed.

gakka lesson; course of study, subject.

GAKKARI SURU to be disappointed; to lose heart; to be tired out, be exhausted. **Kabuki ni ikenakute gakkari shita.** I was disappointed because I could not get to the Kabuki theater.

gakki musical instrument.

gakki school term, semester.

GAKKOO school; college; **gakkoo e yuku** to go to school; **gakkoo tomodachi** schoolmate.

gakkyoku musical piece.

gakkyuu class, grade.

gaku prefix or suffix denoting: learning, studies; science.

gaku amount, sum, denomination.

gaku framed picture; **gaku buchi** picture frame.

gakuha school; academic group.

gakui academic degree.

gakumen face value; par; **gakumen ika ni sagaru** to fall below par.

gakumon learning; study; **gakumon suru** to study.

GAKUSEI student; schoolboy (-girl); **gakusei jidai** schooldays.

gakusetsu theory; doctrine.

gakusha learned man; scholar.

gakushiki scholarship; learning.

gakushuu study; **gakushuu suru** to study.

gakutai (musical) band.

gakuto students; scholars.

gakuya dressing room; **gakuya guchi** stage door.

gakuyuu fellow student; classmate.

gakuzen in amazement; amazed; aghast; **gakuzen to suru** to strike with horror; to shock.

GAMAN patience, endurance; pardon; **gaman zuyoi** patient; having great endurance; **gaman suru** to bear, endure. **Kare ni wa gaman ga dekinai.** I'm out of patience with him.

gan invocation, prayer.

gan cancer.

gan- prefix denoting: pertaining to the eye; **ganbyoo** eye disease; sore eyes.

ganbaru to persist in; to stand firm, refuse to give in.

ganboo desire, wish.

ganchuu ni in one's eyes; **ganchuu ni nai** beneath one's notice; **ganchuu ni okanai** to take no notice of; to ignore; to think nothing of.

gangan dingdong; clang; **gangan naru** to clang, ring noisily. **Mimi ga gangan suru.** My ears are ringing. **Atama ga gangan suru.** My head aches.

GANJITSU New Year's Day.

ganjoo na solid; robust; strongly built.

ganko stubbornness, obstinacy; **ganko na** stubborn, obstinate.

gankyoo stubbornness; persistence; **gankyoo na** obstinate, stubborn; persistent; **gankyoo ni** stubbornly, obstinately.

ganpeki quay, wharf, pier.

ganrai originally; from the first; by nature.

ganseki rock; crag; stones.

ganshiki discernment, insight; critical eye.

gansho written application.

ganso originator, founder, father of.

GANTAN New Year's Day; morning of New Year's Day.

gan'yaku pill; pellet.

ganze nai innocent, artless; helpless.

ganzoo forgery.

gappei union; combination; amalgamation; **gappei suru** to amalgamate; incorporate.

GARA pattern, design; build; nature (character); **iegara** the family standing.

garagara clattering; rattling; rattle (toy).

garakuta rubbish; worn-out articles.

garandoo empty, vacant; hollow.

garan to suru to appear empty; to seem deserted.

garari to completely; with a clatter; suddenly **garari to kawaru** to change completely.

GARASU (*n.*) glass; **garasu no** (*adj.*) glass; glazed; **garasu ita** (glass) pane; plate glass; **garasu kooba** glass factory.

GAREEJI garage.

garigari noisily, with noise; **garigari kajiru** to munch; **garigari hikkaku** to scrape; to scratch.

garon gallon.

-garu suffix denoting: to wish, want; to be inclined to; **mitagaru** to want to see; **ikitagaru** to want to go; **ureshigaru** to feel glad.

garyoo generosity; tolerance; **garyoo no aru** tolerant; generous; broad-minded; **garyoo no nai** intolerant; ungenerous.

garyuu de in one's own way.

gasagasa suru to rustle; **gasagasa no** rough; loose.

gasatsu na rude, rough, unmannerly; **gasatsu na otoko** unmannerly (rude) man.

gashi suru to starve to death.

gashitsu studio.

GASORIN gasoline; **gasorin sutando** gas station.

gassaku collaboration; **gassaku suru** to collaborate, work jointly; **gassakusha** a collaborator.

gasshiri to tightly; closely; **gasshiri shita** massive; well built; sturdy; **gasshiri shite iru** to be massive, etc.

gasshoo chorus; **gasshoo suru** to sing together; **gasshootai** chorus; choir.

gasshuku lodging together; **gasshuku suru** to lodge together.

gasshukusho training camp.

Gasshuukoku United States.

gassoo playing music together; **nibu gassoo** duet.

gassuru to add (join) together; to unite.

GASU gas; **gasu o tsukeru** to light the gas; **gasu o tomeru** to turn off the gas; **gasu sutoobu** gas heater; **gasugaisha** gas company.

gatagata rattling (clattering) sound; **gatagata furueru** to shake, shiver, tremble; **gatagata iu** to rattle, to shake.

-gatai suffix denoting: cannot; hard, difficult; impossible; **egatai** hard to get; unobtainable; **shinjigatai** difficult to believe; incredible.

gatapishi noisily; roughly; with a bang.

gaten comprehension, understanding; consent; agreement; **gaten suru** to understand, grasp the meaning; to be convinced of; to agree, consent; **gaten no ikanai** puzzling; doubtful.

-GATSU counter denoting: month of; **Ichigatsu** January.

gatsugatsu greedily; ravenously; **gatsugatsu taberu** to eat greedily.

-gawa suffix denoting: side; **soto gawa** outside; **uchi gawa** inside; **minami gawa** south side.

gayagaya noisily; **gayagaya sawagu** to make noise, clamor.

gebita vulgar; low; mean.

geemu game; **geemu o yaru** to play a game.

gehin meanness; vulgarity; **gehin na** mean; vulgar; low.

gei arts; accomplishments; feats; tricks; performance; **gei no aru hito** accomplished person.

geijutsu art; fine arts; **geijutsuteki** artistic; **geijutsuka** artist.

geinin professional entertainer.

geisha geisha (girl).

GEJUN latter part of a month; last ten days of a month.

geka surgery; **gekai** surgeon.

gekai this world; earth.

geki play, drama; **gekiteki** dramatic; **gekidan** theatrical world; dramatic company; **gekihyoo** theatrical criticism; **gekihyooka** theater critic; **GEKIJOO** theater, playhouse; **gekisakka** dramatist; playwright. (See also **gikyoku**.)

gekiha suru to defeat, rout.

gekirei encouragement; **gekirei suru** to encourage.

gekiron heated discussion; **gekiron suru** to argue hotly.

gekiryuu rapid stream; swift current.

gekishin severe earthquake. **Sakuban gekishin ga atta.** There was a severe earthquake last night.

gekiyaku powerful medicine; violent poison.

gekizoo sudden increase.

gekkan monthly publication; **gekkan zasshi** monthly magazine.

gekkei menstruation.

gekken fencing (Japanese style).

GEKKOO moonlight; moonbeams.

GEKKYUU monthly salary; **gekkyuu bi** payday; **gekkyuu bukuro** pay envelope; **gekkyuu tori** a salaried man.

gen words; speech; **gen o sayuu ni takushite** on one pretext or another.

gen- prefix denoting: original; primary; fundamental; **genbun** original text; **genga** original picture.

genan manservant.

genba the actual place, scene; **genba de** on the spot.

genbaku atomic bomb.

genbatsu severe punishment.

GENDAI present time; modern times; **gendaiteki na** modern; **gendaika suru** to modernize.

gengai unexpressed; between the lines; **gengai no imi o toru** to read between the lines.

gengakki stringed instrument.

gengaku reduction, discount; **gengaku suru** to reduce, cut down, curtail.

GENGO language, speech; words; **gengo ni zessuru** to be unspeakable; to be beyond description.

gen'in cause; origin; **-ni gen'in suru** to be due to, attributable to; **gen'in fumei** unaccountable; unknown.

genjitsu reality, actuality; **genjitsu no** real, actual; **genjitsu bakuro** disillusionment; **genjitsu shugi** realism.

genjoo status quo, existing state of things; **genjoo iji** maintenance of the status quo.

genjuu severity, strictness; **genjuu na** severe, strict; **genjuu ni** severely.

genkai limit, boundary.

genkaku strictness; sternness; **genkaku na** strict; rigorous; stern; **genkaku ni** rigorously.

GENKAN, genkanguchi entrance hall.

GENKI spirits; courage; vigor; energy; **genki no yoi** cheerful; healthy; **genki yoku** in high spirits; cheerfully; **genki no nai** in poor (low) spirits; **genki o dasu** to brace up; **genki o tsukeru** to encourage; to cheer up; **genki na** healthy, spirited.

GENKIN cash; **genkin de kau** to buy for cash; **genkin barai** cash payment; **genkin gakari** cashier; **genkin torihiki** cash transaction.

genkin strict prohibition, ban; **genkin suru** to ban.

genko fist; **genko o katameru** to clench a fist.

genkoku plaintiff; accuser.

genkoo words and deeds; **genkooroku** memoirs; **genkoo itchi suru** to live up to one's words.

genkoo manuscript; draft; **genkoo yooshi** copy paper; writing pad.

genkoohan flagrant offense. **Genkoohan de kare wa taihosareta.** He was caught red-handed.

genmai unpolished rice, unhulled rice (eaten for high nutritive value).

genmei declaration, statement; announcement; **genmei suru** to make a statement.

genmetsu disillusionment.

genmitsu strictness; precision; **genmitsu na** strict; precise; exact; **genmitsu ni** strictly;

closely; **genmitsu ni ieba** strictly speaking.

gen ni actually; before one's eyes. **Watakushi wa gen ni sore o mita no desu.** I saw it with my own eyes.

genpin goods; thing.

genri See **gensoku.**

genryoo raw materials.

gensanchi country of origin; habitat; home.

genshi atom; beginning; origin; **genshi no** atomic; **genshi bakudan** atomic bomb; **genshiro** nuclear reactor; **genshiryoku** nuclear energy.

gensho original (work); **Eigo no gensho de yomu** to read in the original English.

genshoku primary color(s).

genshoo decrease; **genshoo suru** to decrease, diminish.

genshoo phenomenon.

genshu strict observance; **genshu suru** to observe strictly; **jikan o genshuu suru** to be punctual.

genshuku gravity, solemnity; **genshuku na** solemn; grave.

genshutsu appearance; disclosure; **genshutsu suru** to appear; to be disclosed.

genso element (chem.).

gensoku, genri principle; fundamental law; **gensoku to shite** as a general rule.

genson no existing, in existence.

gentoo lantern slide.

GENZAI (n., adv.) present time; at present; actually; at the present moment.

genzei tax reduction.

genzoo (n.) developing; **genzoo suru** to develop (photography).

geppoo monthly salary.

geppu monthly installment; **geppu de** by monthly payments.

geragera warau to cackle; to give a horselaugh.

geraku fall; decline; depreciation; **geraku suru** to fall; decline; depreciate.

geri diarrhea.

gesha suru to dismount.

GESHUKU (n.) lodging; boarding; lodging house; **geshuku suru** to lodge; to board; **geshukunin** lodger; **geshukuya** lodging house; **geshukuryoo** lodging charge (rate).

geshunin murderer; criminal.

gessha monthly fee; tuition fee.

gesui sewer; drain; sewage.

geta wooden clogs; **geta o haku** to put on clogs; **geta o nugu** to take off clogs; **getaya** clog shop.

getsugaku monthly sum (amount).

getsumatsu end of a month; **getsumatsu kanjoo** end-of-the month payment.

GETSUYOOBI Monday.

gezai laxative.

gichoo chairperson.

gidai subject for discussion.

gidayuu ballad drama.

gihitsu forgery (handwriting or picture).

giin member of assembly or Diet.

giji proceedings.

gijoo assembly hall; chamber; conference site.

GIJUTSU art; useful art; technique; skill; **sentan gijutsu** advanced technology; **gijutsujoo no** technical.

gikai Diet; assembly.

gikan chief engineer; technical offical.

gikei older brother-in-law.

giketsu decision, resolution.

gikochinai stiff-mannered; awkward.

gikoo artistic excellence; technical skill.

gikyoku drama; **gikyoku sakusha** dramatist, playwright. (See also **geki**.)

gikyoodai brother-in-law; sister-in-law.

gimei assumed name, false name.

GIMON question; doubt; **gimonfu** question mark.

gimu duty; obligation; **gimu o hatasu** to perform one's duty.

GIN silver, **gin no** silvered; silver; **gin iro no** silvery; **gingami** silver paper; tin foil; **ginka** silver coin; **ginkonshiki** silver wedding anniversary; **genmekki no** (adj.) silver-plated; **ginpai** silver medal; silver cup.

GINKOO bank; **ginkooka** banker; **ginkoo'in** bank employee; **ginkoo yokin** bank deposit; **ginkoo yokin kooza** bank account; **ginkoo yokin zandaka** bank balance; **ginkoo kawase tegata** bank exchange; **ginkoo kanjoo hookoku sho** bank statement.

ginmi examination, trial.

ginnan fruit of the gingko; gingko nut.

ginoo ability, capacity; skill; **ginoo no aru** able; skillful; talented.

giragira glittering; dazzling; **giragira suru** to glitter, to dazzle; to glare.

giri obligation; duty; honor; courtesy; **giri no** adoptive; step-; -in-law; **giri no kyoodai** brother-in-law, sister-in-law; **giri o kaku** to fail to do one's duty; **girigatai** having a high sense of duty.

Girisha Greece; **Girishajin** (n.) Greek; **Girishago** Greek language.

giron argument; discussion; debate; dispute; **giron suru** to argue, etc.; **gironzuki na** argumentative.

giryoo ability; talent, skill; **giryoo no aru** talented.

gisei sacrifice; victim; scapegoat.

gishi engineer; technical expert; **gishi choo** chief engineer.

gishiki ceremony, rite; **gishiki no** (adj.) ritual.

gishu artificial arm.

gisoku artificial leg.

gisshiri closely; compactly; **gisshiri tsumekomu** to pack, jam, cram.

gitaa guitar.

gitei younger brother-in-law.

gizagiza notches.

gizen hypocrisy; **gizensha** hypocrite; **gizenteki** hypocritical.

gizoo forgery. (See also **gihitsu**.)

GO word, term; language; **Eigo** (an) English word; English language; **go o tsuyomete iu** to speak emphatically; **gobi** ending (of a word); end (of a sentence); **gobi henka** inflection.

GO five; **DAIGO** fifth; **GOJUU** fifty; **GOJI** five o'clock; **gojuu no too** five-story pagoda.

go game resembling checkers; **go o utsu** to play "go"; **goban** "go" board; checkerboard; **goban gata no** checkered; **goishi** pieces used in playing "go."

-go suffix denoting: after; **sonogo** after that; since then; **sensoogo** postwar.

gobugari short haircut, crew cut.

gobugobu equally well matched; equal; **gobugobu ni naru** to end in a draw (tie); **gobugobu no tachiba de** on equal terms.

GOBUSATA SURU to neglect to write or call. **Gobusata itashimashita.** I am sorry I didn't write you. I am sorry I didn't call you earlier.

gochagocha no mixed up, confused; **gochagocha suru** to mix up, jumble; **gochagocha ni naru** to be confused.

GOCHISOO treat; feast. **Kyoo wa watashi ga gochisoo shimashoo.** Let me treat you to dinner today. Be my guest at dinner today. **Gochisoosama.** Thanks for the fine dinner.

gochoo tone of voice; accent.

goei guard; escort; **goei suru** to guard; to escort.

gofuku kimono fabric; **gofukuya** fabric dealer.

gogaku study of languages, linguistics.

GOGATSU May.

GOGO afternoon; **gogo niji** two p.m.

GOHAN boiled rice; meal; **gohan o taberu** to eat a meal; **gohan o taku** to cook rice.

gohoo false report.

gojitsu some other day; in the future.

gojuunensai semi-centennial; jubilee.

gojuuon Japanese syllabary.

gokai misunderstanding; **gokai suru** to misunderstand; to take amiss.

goke widow; widowhood.

goki tone; manner of speaking; **goki surudoku** sharply, in a sharp tone; **goki o tsuyomete hanasu** to speak emphatically.

gokoo halo; glory.

GOKU very; extremely; **goku mezurashii** extremely rare; **goku chiisai** very small.

gokui secret; secret principles.

gokuin stamp; hallmark.

gokujoo (n.) first-rate; best quality; **gokujoo no** (adj.) best; first-rate; first-class.

gokuraku paradise; Eden.

goma sesame seed; **goma o suru** to grind sesame seed; to flatter; to fawn upon; **gomaabura** sesame oil.

gomakashi trickery; hocus-pocus; deception; **gomakashi no** fraudulent; sham; **gomakasu** to deceive; to cheat; to cover up; to tamper with.

GOMEN pardon, permission; **GOMEN NASAI.** Pardon me. Excuse me. **Chotto gomen kudasai.** Excuse me a minute.

GOMI rubbish, refuse; dirt; **gomitori** dustpan; **gomibako** garbage (rubbish) can.

GOMU gum; rubber; **gomubando** rubber band; **gomuhimo** elastic tape; **gomumari** rubber ball; **gomunori** mucilage; **gomuwa** rubber tire.

gongo doodan unspeakable; outrageous; absurd.

goo district. **Goo ni itte wa goo ni shitagae.** When in Rome, do as the Romans do.

goo fate; **goo no fukai** sinful; **goo o niyasu** to be greatly aggravated.

-goo number; issue; **dai san goo** issue no. 3; **sono zasshi no Gogatsugoo** the May issue of the magazine.

goodatsu seizure; extortion; plunder; **goodatsu suru** to plunder.

goodoo combination; union; **goodoo suru** to amalgamate; to incorporate; **goodoo no** united; incorporated.

googai "extra"; special issue of a newspaper.

gooi agreement; mutual understanding; **gooi de** by mutual agreement.

goojoo obstinacy, stubbornness; **goojoo na** stubborn, obstinate; **goojoo o haru** to be obstinate.

gookaban deluxe edition.

gookaku eligibility; success; **gookaku suru** to be eligible for; to pass; to be successful in.

gookan rape; assault.

gookasen luxury liner.

GOOKEI sum, total, total amount; **gookei suru** to sum up; **gookei . . . ni naru** to amount to . . . in all; to add up to.

gooketsu hero; great man.

gookin metallic compound; alloy.

gooman haughtiness, arrogance; **gooman na** haughty, arrogant.

goomon torture; **goomon ni kakeru** to torture.

goorei command, order; **goorei suru** to

command, order; to rule; **goorei o kakeru** to give a command or order.

gooriki great strength; mountain guide.

gooru goal.

goosha luxury; magnificence; **goosha na** luxurious; magnificent; **goosha o kiwameru** to live in magnificent style.

gootan fearlessness; boldness; **gootan na** fearless; daring; bold.

gootoo burglar, thief.

goou heavy rain.

gooyoku avarice, greed.

gooyuu extravagant pleasures; spree; **gooyuu suru** to go on a spree.

goozen haughtily, arrogantly; proudly.

goraku pleasure; pastime; amusement; recreation; **gorakuyoo no** for amusement; **gorakushitsu** recreation room.

goran (n.) seeing, viewing (used only in reference to the second or third person); **goran ni ireru** to present something for inspection. **Goran kudasai.** Please take a look. **Goran no toori.** As you see. **Chotto kore o goran nasai.** Just look at this. **Maa kangaete goran nasai.** Think it over, anyway.

gorira gorilla.

-GORO suffix denoting: about (in point of time); around; toward; **nijigoro** about two o'clock; **yoakegoro** toward dawn.

goro sound; **goro ga ii** euphonic.

goro grounder (in baseball).

gorogoro rumbling; rolling; gurgling; lying idle; **gorogoro korobu** to roll about; **me ga gorogoro suru** to have a sore (an irritated) eye. **Kare wa mainichi gorogoro shite iru.** He idles away his time every day. **Neko ga nodo o gorogoro narasu.** The cat purrs.

gorufu golf; **gorufu o suru** to play golf; **gorufujoo** gold links.

gosai second wife; **gosai o mukaeru** (for a man) to marry again.

gosan miscalculation; **gosan suru** to miscalculate.

goshin suru to diagnose wrongly.

Gosho Imperial Palace.

goshoo daiji ni with the greatest possible care; most carefully; **goshoo daijin ni suru** to take care of; **goshoo daiji ni tsutomeru** to serve most faithfully.

gosoo escort; convoy; **gosoo suru** to escort, to accompany.

gotagota trouble; difficulties; confusion; disorder; **gotagota suru** to be in confusion; to be disordered. **Gotagota ga okorikakete iru.** Trouble is brewing.

gotamaze jumble; muddle.

gotatsuku to quarrel; to be agitated; to be in disorder.

gotcha in confusion.

-GOTO NI every; every time; at intervals of; **ni mairu goto ni** every two miles; **hi goto ni** every day; **mikka goto ni** every three days.

gotsugotsu rough; rugged; harsh; stiff; **gotsugotsu iu** to speak harshly; **gotsugotsu shite iru** to be stiff, rough.

goza mat; matting; **goza o shiku** to spread a mat (on the floor).

GOZAIMASU there is, there are *(humble)*.

GOZEN forenoon; **gozen ni** in the morning.

guai condition; fitness; manner; working order; **guai ga warui** to feel indisposed, be unwell; to be out of order. **Kono hikidashi wa guai ga warui.** This drawer does not work smoothly. **Banji guai yoku itta.** Everything went very well.

guchi idle complaints; **guchi o kobosu** to grumble; complain; **guchippoi** grumbling; complaining.

-gumi company, firm; gang; **Fujita gumi** Fujita Company.

gun district; county.

gun crowd; **gun o nasu** to crowd; to flock; **gun o nuku** to be far above the crowd (to distinguish oneself); **gunshuu** crowd of people, multitude.

gun *(n.)* military; **gunbi** arms; **gunbi shukushoo** disarmament; **guntai** armed forces.

guntoo archipelago, group of islands.

gunyagunya flabby; limp.

guragura suru to be shaky; to totter, waver.

-GURAI = **kurai** suffix denoting: about; almost; some; something like; or so. **Ano hito wa sanjuu-gurai deshoo.** She must be about 30 years old.

guramu gram.

guratsuku to totter; to be shaky.

guretsu na stupid; ridiculous; absurd; silly.

guron foolish argument; absurd opinion.

guru conspiracy; collusion; accomplice, conspirator; **guru ni naru** to conspire with, plot together; **-to guru ni natte** in collusion with (someone).

GURUGURU round and round; **guruguru mawaru** to whirl; spin round and round.

gururi circumference; surroundings; **gururi to** round.

-gurushii suffix denoting: to be unpleasant to, repulsive to; **negurushii** to be sleepless; to sleep badly.

guruupu group.

gutto considerably; firmly; with great strength; **gutto nomu** to gulp down; **gutto fueru** to increase markedly.

guusuu even number; **guusuu no** even-numbered.

GUUZEN by chance; accidentally; **guuzen no** accidental; unexpected; casual; **guuzen no dekigoto** an accident; **guuzen desu** to come across, meet by chance.

guuzoo image, idol, statue.

guzu imbecile; weak-minded person.

guzuguzu lazily; idly; tardily; **guzuguzu suru** to hesitate; to loiter; **guzuguzu iu** to complain; to murmur.

guzuru to be peevish; to be fretful.

gyakkoo retrogression; **gyakkoo suru** to move back; to run counter to; to retrogress.

gyaku opposite, contrary, reverse, **gyaku ni** contrarily, conversely; **gyaku ni suru** to reverse; to invert; **gyaku ni mawasu** to turn (something) the other way; **gyakumodori** retrogression; reversal; **gyakumodori suru** to go (turn) backward; to have a relapse; to lapse into; **gyakuten** sudden change; reversal; **gyakuten suru** to retrogress.

gyakusatsu slaughter; massacre.

gyakutai ill-treatment; **gyakutai suru** to ill-treat.

gyangu gang.

gyogyoo fishery; fishing industry.

gyokuro sweet green tea (the best and most expensive type).

gyoo line; verse.

gyoogi behavior; manners; **gyoogi no yoi** well behaved; well mannered; **gyoogi no warui** poorly behaved; **gyoogi sahoo** etiquette.

gyooja devotee; pilgrim; ascetic.

gyooji observances; functions; proceedings.

gyooji referee (of Japanese wrestling, sumoo).

gyoojoo behavior, conduct.

gyooketsu coagulation, congealing.

gyoomu business; affairs; duties.

gyooretsu procession, parade; **gyooretsu o nashite** in procession.

gyoosei administration; **gyooseikan** administrator.

gyooshoo peddling; peddler.

gyooten suru to be surprised, amazed, astounded.

gyoozui *(n.)* taking a shower (Japanese style: pouring water over the body from a small tub); bathing; **gyoozui suru** to take a Japanese-style shower.

gyosen fishing boat.

gyoson fishing village.

gyotto suru to be startled, alarmed.

gyuuba oxen and horses; horses and cattle.

GYUUNIKU beef; **gyuunikuya** butcher shop.

GYUUNYUU cow's milk; **gyuunyuu ya** milkman; **gyuunyuu bin** milk bottle.

gyuutto hard; violently; firmly; **gyuutto osu** to push violently (with force); **gyuutto hiku** to pull with a jerk.

H

HA tooth; cog; **ha no aru** toothed; cogged; **ha no nai** toothless; blunt; **ha no tsuita** sharp-edged; **ha ga uku** to set the teeth on edge; **ha o migaku** to brush the teeth; **ha ga itamu** to have a toothache.

ha leaf (of a plant).

haamonika harmonica.

haapu harp.

haato heart (in a card game).

HABA width, breadth; **haba ga kiku** to have great influence over; **haba o kikasu** to exert great influence; **haba go inchi aru** five inches wide.

habakiki influential person.

habataki suru to flutter, flap wings.

habikoru to spread; to grow thick; to become powerful.

habuku to curtail; to save; to leave out; **jikan o habuku** to save time; **hiyoo o habuku** to cut expenses.

HABURASHI toothbrush.

haburi influence; power; **haburi ga yoi** to be influential.

habutae glossy silk.

HACHI eight; **dai hachi** eighth.

HACHI bowl, basin; pot.

hachi bee; **hachi no su** beehive; **hachimitsu** honey.

hachiawase suru to be brought face to face (bump heads together).

HACHIGATSU August.

HACHIJUU eighty; **dai hachijuu** eightieth.

hachimaki headband; hand towel tied around the head.

hachiue potted plant.

hada skin; body; disposition; character; **shiroi hada** fair skin; **hada ga au** to get on well (with).

HADAGI underwear.

hadaka nakedness, nudity; **hadaka no** naked, nude, bare; **hadaka ni naru** to strip off one's clothes.

hadashi bare feet; **hadashi de aruku** to walk barefoot; **kurooto hadashi da** to put even a professional to shame.

hadazawari touch. **Biroodo wa hadazawari ga yoi.** Velvet feels soft [is agreeable to touch].

HADE gaiety; flashiness; display; **hade na** gay; bright; flashy; **hade na iro** bright

(gay) color; **hade zuki de aru** to be fond of display.

HAE fly.

haegiwa hairline.

haeru to grow; to sprout; to spring up. **Hana no me ga haeta.** The flower seeds sprouted.

haetataki flyswatter.

haetori flytrap.

HAGAKI postcard; **hagaki o dasu** to drop (send) a card.

hagami suru to gnash one's teeth.

hagane steel.

hagasu to strip; to tear off.

hagayui to feel impatient; to feel irritated. **Kare no guzuguzu shite iru no ga hagayukatta.** I was irritated by his dawdling.

hage bald spot; bald head; **hageatama** bald head.

hagemasu to encourage; to cheer up; to stimulate.

hagemi stimulation; encouragement; diligence; **hagemi ga tsuku** to be stimulated; to be encouraged; **hagemi o tsukeru** to stimulate; to encourage.

HAGEMU to endeavor; to exert onself; to be diligent.

hageru to grow bald; to come off; to fade; **iro no hageta** discolored; faded.

hageshii violent, severe, intense; furious; **hageshiku** violently; **hageshii seishitsu** violent nature (referring to a person); **hageshii atsusa** intensely hot weather.

hagishiri suru to grit one's teeth.

hagitoru to strip off; to deprive; to tear off.

hagu to strip; to strip off clothes; **ki no kawa o hagu** to strip the bark off a tree.

haguki gums (of the mouth).

hagureru to stray; to be separated from (one's companions).

haguruma cog, gear (of a wheel); toothed wheel.

HAHA, HAHAOYA mother, motherhood; **haha rashii** motherly; maternal; **Haha no hi** Mother's Day; **hahakata** maternal (side); **hahakata no shinseki** maternal relative.

HAI yes; yes, sir.

hai lungs; **haibyoo** consumption; **haigan** lung cancer; **haien** pneumonia.

hai ashes; cinder; **hai ni naru** to be reduced to ashes; lungs.

haiagaru to creep (crawl) up; to climb up.

haichi arrangement; **haichi suru** to dispose; to arrange; to station.

haidasu to crawl out, creep out.

haigamai rice with embryo buds.

haigo rear; back (of a person); **-no haigo ni** at the rear of; behind. **Kare no haigo ni shisanka ga hikaete iru.** He has a wealthy supporter behind him.

haigoo harmony; combination; arrangement; **haigoo suru** to harmonize; to combine; to match. **Iro no haigoo ga warui.** These colors do not match.

haigyoo suru to close up shop; to give up one's practice; to quit business.

haihiiru high heel.

haiiro ash-gray (color).

haikan discontinuance of publication; **haikan suru** to discontinue publication.

haikara na stylish; foppish; fashionable. **Haikara na yoofuku o kite imashita.** He was wearing a high-styled suit.

haikei background; background scenery.

haikei Dear Sir or Madam (as used in a formal letter).

HAIKEN looking at; inspection *(humble)*; **haiken suru** to see; to look at. **Chotto haiken.** Please let me see it. **Haiken shimashita.** I saw it.

haikingu hiking.

haikomu to crawl (creep) in.

haiku seventeen-syllable poem.

haikyuu distribution; supply; **haikyuu suru** to distribute; supply.

hainichi anti-Japanese.

hairetsu arrangement; distribution; **hairetsu suru** to arrange in order.

hairikomu to get in; to force one's way in.

HAIRU to enter; to go in; to break into; to join; to hold; to accommodate; **kurabu ni hairu** to join a club; **oyu ni hairu** to take a bath. **O hairi.** Come in! Walk in! **Hi ga nishi ni hairu.** The sun sets in the west.

haiseki expulsion; exclusion; **haiseki suru** to exclude; to ostracize.

HAISHA dentist.

haishaku suru to borrow *(humble)*. **Haishaku itashimasu.** I'll borrow it.

haishi abolition; **haishi suru** to abolish, discontinue.

haishutsu suru to discharge; to exhaust; **haishutsuguchi** outlet; issue; **haishutsukan** exhaust pipe.

haisui drainage; sewerage; supply of water; **haisui suru** to drain; to pump out.

HAITATSU delivery; distribution; **haitatsu suru** to deliver; to distribute; **haitatsu ryoo** delivery charge; **haitatsunin** distributor; carrier; **haitatsusaki** receiver; destination (of a delivery).

haitoo allotment; dividend; **haitoo suru** to pay a dividend; to allot to; **haitookin** dividend.

haiyuu actor; actress.

haizara ashtray.

haji shame; disgrace; dishonor; **haji o kaku** to be put to shame; **haji o kakaseru** to put to shame; **haji shirazu** without a sense of shame; shameless.

hajikeru to split open; to pop.

hajiku to flip; to snap; to repeal; to repel; **yubi o hajiku** to snap one's fingers.

HAJIMARU to begin, commence; to be opened; to originate from.

HAJIME commencement, beginning; outset; origin; **hajime no** first; original; initial; **hajime kara owari made** from beginning to end; **hajime wa** at first.

HAJIMERU to begin; commence; to open; **shoobai o hajimeru** to open a business; **benkyoo o hajimeru** to begin studying.

HAJIMETE first; for the first time; for once. **Hajimete ome ni kakarimasu.** How do you do. Glad to meet you [I meet you for the first time]. **Hajimete ikimashita.** I went there for the first time.

hajiru to be ashamed of.

haka grave, tomb; **hakaba** graveyard, cemetery.

hakadoru to progress rapidly; to make good progress.

hakai destruction; demolition; **hakai suru** to destroy, demolish, wreck; **hakaiteki** destructive; **hakairyoku** destructive power.

hakaku no exceptional; unprecedented; special.

hakama loose Japanese trousers; pleated skirt.

hakanai transient, passing; uncertain; vain; hopeless; **hakanai saigo o togeru** to meet with an untimely death; **hakanai nozomi** vain hope.

hakarai management; arrangement; disposal; **Kono hen wa anata no ohakarai ni omakaseshimasu.** I'll leave the matter to your discretion.

hakarau to manage; to arrange; to take measures; **Sore ni tsuite wa anata ga yoi yoo ni hakaratte ii desu.** You can do about it as you think best.

HAKARAZU MO unexpectedly; by chance.

hakari balance, scales; **hakari ni kakeru** to weigh on a scale.

hakarigoto stratagem, ruse; artifice; plan, scheme; **hakarigoto ni ochiru** to fall for a trick; **hakarigoto o megurasu** to devise a stratagem; to form plans.

HAKARU to measure; to weigh; to survey; to sound; to judge (a person's mind); **mekata o hakaru** to check a weight; **nagasa o hakaru** to measure a length. **Ano hito no kimochi o hakaru koto wa muzukashii.** It is hard to understand his mind.

hakase See **hakushi.**

hake drainage; flow; sale; demand; **hake ga yoi** to flow freely; to sell well.

hake brush.

haken dispatch; **haken suru** to dispatch, send; **hakengun** expeditionary force.

hakeru to drain off; to sell.

haki breach; annulment; **haki suru** to break and throw away; to annul.

hakichigaeru to wear someone else's shoes by mistake; to mistake; to misunderstand.

hakidame rubbish heap.

hakidasu to spit out; to emit; to breathe out.

hakidasu to sweep out.

hakike nausea; **hakike o moyoosu** to feel sick; to be nauseous.

HAKIMONO footgear; clogs.

hakiyoseru to sweep up, gather up with a broom.

hakka peppermint; mint.

hakka firing; ignition; **hakka suru** to catch fire, ignite.

hakken discovery; **hakken suru** to discover; **hakkensha** discover.

hakkin platinum.

HAKKIRI clearly; distinctly; positively; definitely; exactly; **hakkiri shita** clear, distinct, positive; **hakkiri shita koe** clear voice; **hakkiri shita henji** definite answer. **Hakkiri zonjimasen.** I don't know exactly.

hakkoo publication; issue; **hakkoo suru** to publish; to issue.

hakkoo fermentation; **hakkoo suru** to ferment.

hakkotsu skeleton; bleached bones.

hakkutsu excavation; **hakkutsu suru** to excavate.

hakkyuu low (small) salary.

HAKO box; case; chest. **Hako ni irete kudasai.** Please put it in the box.

hakobi progress; arrangement; **ashi no hakobi** walking pace.

HAKOBU to carry, convey, transport; to go on; to progress; **nimotsu o hakobu** to carry the baggage; **shibashiba ashi o hakobu** to make frequent calls. **Subete umaku hakobimashita.** Everything went all right. Everything turned out all right.

hakoniwa miniature garden.

hakozume packed in a box; boxed; **hakozume ni suru** to pack in a box.

HAKU to put on (from waist down; clogs, sandals, shoes, socks, pants, skirts, etc.); **kutsu o haku** to put on shoes.

haku to sweep; **heya o haku** to sweep the room.

hakubutsukan museum.

hakuchi idiot; imbecile.

hakuchoo swan.

hakuchuu broad daylight.

hakugai persecution; **hakugai suru** to persecute.

hakugaku erudition, learning; **hakugaku no** erudite; learned.

hakuhatsu white hair; gray hair; **hakuhatsu no roojin** white-haired old person.

hakujaku feebleness, weakness; **hakujaku na** feeble, weak; fragile; **seishin hakujaku jidoo** mentally handicapped child.

hakujin white person; white race (Occidental).

hakujoo confession; **hakujoo suru** to confess, make a clean breast of.

hakujoo coldheartedness; **hakujoo na** unfeeling, heartless. **Ano hito wa hakujoo na hito desu.** She is a coldhearted woman.

hakumai hulled (cleaned) rice.

hakumei misfortune; sad fate; **hakumei na** unfortunate; ill-fated.

hakurai imported; **hakuraihin** imported merchandise. **Hakuraihin wa takai kara kaemasen.** I can't buy imported goods because they are expensive.

hakurankai exposition; fair; **hakurankaijoo** fair grounds.

hakushi, hakase doctor; doctorate degree, Ph.D.; **hakushigoo** doctorate degree; **Yamada Hakushi** Dr. Yamada.

hakushi blank sheet of paper; white paper; clean slate.

hakushiki wide knowledge, erudition.

hakushu applause; **hakushu suru** to clap hands, applaud; to cheer; **hakushu kassai** applause and cheers.

hakyuu propagation, spread; **hakyuu suru** to extend, spread, propagate; to influence; to effect; **zenkoku ni hakyuu suru** to extend over the whole country.

hama seashore, beach; **hama zutai ni** along the beach; **hamabe** seashore; beach.

hamaguri clam.

hamaki cigar.

hamarikomu to fall (sink) into; to become infatuated with; to be addicted to; **onna ni hamarikomu** to be infatuated with a woman.

hamaru to be fixed; to fit; to fall into.

hameru to put in, insert; to fix in; to set; to have (wear) on (one's finger or hand).

hametsu ruin, destruction; **hametsu suru** to be ruined, destroyed.

hamidasu to protrude, stick out.

HAMIGAKI toothpaste.

hamon suru to excommunicate; to expel.

hamono edged tool; cutlery.

HAMU ham; **hamu sarada** ham salad.

HAN stamp; personal seal (used in place of a signature); **han o osu** to stamp; to seal; **han de oshita yoo na** stereotyped, cut-and-dried.

HAN- prefix denoting: half; **hantoshi** half a year; **hantsuki** half a month.

han edition; **han o kasaneru** to go through many editions; **shohan** first edition.

han- prefix denoting: opposition; **hankyoo** anti-communism.

HANA flower, blossom; essence, spirit; belle; **hana no** floral; **hana o kiru** to cut flowers; **hana o ikeru** to arrange flowers; **hanabasami** flower scissors; pruning shears; **hanaike** flower vase; **hanataba** bunch of flowers, bouquet; **hanawa** wreath, garland; **hanaya** florist, flower shop; **hanayaka na** flowery; showy; gay. **Wakai uchi ga hana.** Youth is the springtime of life. **Giron ni hana ga saite kita.** The discussion is becoming heated.

HANA nose, nasal mucus; **hana o susuru** to sniff; **hana o kamu** to blow one's nose; **hana o tarasu** to have a runny nose; **hana ga kiku** to have a good sense of smell; **hana ni kakeru** to be vain; **hana o akasu** to take the conceit out of someone; **hana o takaku suru** to be proud; **hanasaki ni** under one's very nose; **hanagoe** nasal sound; twang; **hanaiki** *(n.)* breathing through the nose; snoring; **hanaiki ga arai** to be arrogant; to swagger; **hito no hanaiki o ukagau** to curry favor with someone; **hanaji** nosebleed; **hanaji o dasu** to have a nosebleed; **hanakaze** head cold. **Hanakaze o hiita.** I have a cold in the head. **hanabashira, hanappashira, hanasuji** bridge of the nose. **Hanabashira ga tsuyoi desu.** He is haughty.

hanabanashii brilliant; splendid; glorious; **hanabanashiku** brilliantly; splendidly.

hanabi fireworks display; **hanabi o ageru** to set off fireworks.

hanagata floral pattern; star; **eiga no hanagata yakusha** screen star; **hanagata senshu** star player.

hanagumori springtime cloudy weather.

hanahadashii excessive, extreme, exceeding.

hanami *(n.)* flower-viewing; **hanami ni iku** to visit places well known for their flower displays (such as cherry blossoms).

hanamuko bridegroom.

hanao clog thong; straps.

hanare detached room; **hanareya** detached house; **hanarezashiki** detached guest room.

hanarebanare separation; **hanarebanare ni** separately, apart from each other; **hanarebanare ni naru** to become separated.

HANARERU to separate; part from; to come off; **hanareta** separated, detached, isolated, distant, far off; **hanareta tokoro kara miru** to watch from a distance; **hanareta tochi** distant place; **hanarete iru** be distant, live apart from. **Ima shoku o hanarete iru.** He is now out of work.

HANASHI talk, conversation, chat; gossip, story; **hanashi joozu** good speaker; **hanashibeta** poor speaker; **hanashi aite** companion to talk with; **hanashi o suru** to talk, chat; **hanashiburi** way (manner) of speaking; **hanashichuu** busy signal (telephone); **hanashiai** conference, consultation; **hanashiau** to talk with, consult with; **hanashigoe** voices (in conversation); **hanashi no tane** topic for conversation; **hanashi ga tsuku** to arrive at an understanding; **hanashi o soraseru** to change the subject; **hanashika** professional storyteller; **hanashikomu** to chat for hours; **hanashizuki na** talkative.

HANASU to speak, talk, converse; to tell, state. **Eigo de hanashite kudasai.** Please speak English. **Anata ni hanashitai koto ga aru.** I have something I'd like to tell you.

hanasu to separate, to part, to set free; **te o hanasu** to loosen one's hold, to let go of someone's hand.

hanauta humming; **hanauta o utau** to hum a song or tune.

hanayome bride.

hanazakari full bloom.

hanazono flower garden.

hanbai sale; **hanbai suru** to sell, deal in; **hanbainin** dealer, **hanbaigakari** salesman, saleswoman; **hanbaiten** distributor.

HANBUN half; **hanbun ni suru** to divide into halves.

handan judgment, interpretation.

handobaggu handbag.

handon half-holiday.

handoo reaction; **handoo suru** to react upon; **handooteki** reactionary.

handoru handle; steering wheel.

hane feather; plumage; wing; shuttlecock; **hane buton** feather quilt.

hane *(n.)* splashes of mud, close; **hane ga agatte iru** to be splashed with mud; **Shibai no hane wa juuji desu.** The theater closes at ten.

hanekaeru to rebound, spring back.

hanemawaru to bounce about, leap about; to romp.

han'enkei semicircle; **han'enkei no** semicircular.

haneru to leap, spring, bound; to splash, splatter. **Sooba ga haneta.** Prices jumped. **Abura ga hanete yakedo o shita.** The cooking oil splashed and I got burnt.

haneru to reject, to throw out, to exclude.

hanetsukeru to refuse; to reject; to repel.

hangaku half (amount); half the sum (price, fare, etc.); **hangaku de** at half-price, half-fare. **Kodomo no jooshachin wa hangaku desu.** Children can travel for half-price. **Kodomo no nyuujoo ryoo wa hangaku desu.** Children are admitted for half-price.

hangen reduction by half; **hangen suru** to reduce by half.

han'i scope, sphere; limit, bounds.

hanikamu to be shy, bashful.

hanji judge.

HANJIKAN half an hour.

hanjoo good business; prosperity; **hanjoo suru** to prosper, flourish, do a good business.

hanjuku half-cooked; soft-boiled; half-ripe; **hanjuku no tamago** soft-boiled egg.

HANKACHI handkerchief.

hankan antipathy, ill-feeling; **hankan o idaku** to provoke ill-feeling.

hankechi See **HANKACHI.**

hankei radius.

hanko seal.

hankoo resistance, opposition; defiance; **hankooteki** defiant, rebellious.

hankyoo echo; response; anti-communism; **hankyoo suru** to echo, resound.

hankyuu half-holiday.

hanmen profile, silhouette; one side; **hanmen no shinri** half truth; **kao no hanmen** one side of the face; **hanmenzoo** profile.

hanmoku hostility, antagonism.

hanmon anguish; agony; mortification; **hanmon suru** to be in agony; to feel anguish; to be mortified.

hanne half the price; **hanne de uru** to sell at half the price.

hannichi half a day.

hannin offender, criminal.

hannoo reaction, response; **hannoo suru** to react, respond; to act upon.

hanpa odds; odds and ends; fragments; **hanpa no** odd; half-done; incomplete; **hanpa mono** a broken set. **Ano hito wa hanpa na shigoto shika dekimasen.** He never finishes his tasks.

hanran rebellion, revolt.

hantai opposition; contradiction; **hantai suru** to oppose; to object to; **hantai no** opposite; opposed; **hantai ni** on the contrary; in the opposite direction; **hantai undoo** opposition movement, counter movement; **hantaisha** opponent; objector; **hantaitoo** opposition party.

hantei judgment, decision.

hanten spot; speck, dot.

hantoo peninsula.

hantoshi half a year.

hantsuki half a month.

han'yake partly burned; half-roasted, half-baked.

hanzai crime, offense; **hanzai nin** criminal, culprit; **hanzai kooi** criminal act.

hanzatsu complication; **hanzatsu na** complex, complicated.

hanzen to clearly, distinctly; definitely; **hanzen to shita** clear, distinct; definite. **Sono hanashi o kiite hanzen to simashita.** Now that I've heard that explanation, the whole story has become clear.

haori Japanese coat.

happoo all directions; all sides; **happoo ni** in all directions; on all sides; all around; **happoo bijin** everybody's friend.

happun suru to be roused to action.

happyoo announcement; publication; **happyoo suru** to announce; to publish; to make known.

hara field; plain; moor; prairie; wild region.

hara *(colloq.)* belly, bowels; abdomen; stomach; **hara no ookii** magnanimous; **hara no suwatta** resolute, firm; **hara ga tatsu** to be offended; **hara o kakaete warau** to split with laughter; **harabai ni naru** to lie on one's stomach; **haramaki** belt.

harachigai half brother, half sister.

harahara suru to feel uneasy; to be in suspense. **Namida o harahara to nagashita.** The tears fell in big drops. **Mite ite mo harahara shita.** I felt nervous just looking at it.

harai payment; account **haraikomi** payment; installment payment; **haraikomu** to pay in, pay up; **haraimodoshi** repayment; refund; **haraimodosu** to pay back, repay.

haraisage government surplus sale.

harasu to clear away; to divert; **urami o harasu** to pay off old scores.

HARAU to pay (a bill, etc.); to brush off, to clear away; **shakkin o harau** to pay off a debt. **Namida o haratte shigoto o tsuzuketa.** She brushed away her tears and resumed her task.

harawata *(colloq.)* intestines; bowels; heart; character; **harawata o tatsu** to break (someone's) heart.

hare *(n.)* swelling; **hareru** to swell, **haremono** swelling, boil.

hare fine (fair) weather; **hare no kimono** holiday (Sunday) clothes; **haregi** holiday clothes.

HARERU to clear up (weather); to clear away; to be dispelled; **kengi ga hareru** to be cleared of a charge. **Sora ga hareta.** The sky has cleared.

haretsu explosion; eruption; **haretsu suru** to explode, burst, blow up; to be broken off.

HARI needle; pin; hand (of a watch); fishhook; sting (of a bee); **hari no me** eye of a needle; **haribako** needlecase; workbox; **harisashi** pincushion; **harishigoto** needlework; **harishigoto o suru** to sew.

haridasu to post (on a bulletin board); **keiji o haridasu** to post a notice.

harifuda bill; poster; **harifuda o suru** to put up a poster.

harigami label; poster.

harigane wire.

haritsukeru to stick on, paste on; to paste over.

HARU spring (season). **Haru ni Amerika e kaerimasu.** I am returning to the United States in the spring.

haru to stick; **kitte o haru** to paste on a stamp.

hasamaru to get in between; to lie between. **Niku ga ha no aida ni hasamarimashita.** A piece of meat got stuck between his teeth.

HASAMI scissors, shears; **niwaki ni hasami o ireru** to prune bushes.

hasamu to place; to hold between; to pinch; to pick up; **hibashi de mono o hasamu** to pick up something with tongs.

HASHI pair of chopsticks; **hashi o tsukeru** to start eating.

HASHI bridge; **hashi o wataru** to cross a bridge.

hashi edge, border; end; **hashi kara hashi made** from end to end; **dooro no hashi no hoo o tooru** to keep to the side of the road.

hashigo ladder; flight of stairs; **hashigodan** staircase.

hashika measles.

hashikkoi smart, shrewd, sharp.

HASHIRA pillar, post, column; pole; prop; **hashira dokei** wall clock; **daikoku hashira** main pillar; main support (a person).

hashiri *(n.)* running; movement; first (of something); **hashiri mawaru** to run about; **cha no hashiri** the first supply of tea; **hashirigaki suru** to write hurriedly; to scribble; **hashiriyomi o suru** to read hurriedly; to skim; **hashirizukai** running

an errand. **Kono to no hashiri ga yoi.** This sliding door moves easily.

HASHIRU to run; to sail; to move fast. **Kare wa ya no yoo ni hashitte itta.** He was off like a shot.

hashita fraction; fragment; odds and ends.

hashutsufu daily houseworker (female).

hashutsusho branch station; police box.

hassha starting (of a train, bus, etc.); **hassha suru** to start; to depart.

hasshin suru to dispatch a message; to send a letter.

hassoo suru to send off; to forward (a letter or package).

hassuru to emit; to radiate; to fire; to discharge (a gun); to issue.

hata flag, banner, standard; **hatazao** flagstaff.

hata side; neighborhood; **hata de** nearby; beside; **hata no mono** bystanders; outsiders.

HATACHI twenty years old (said of a person). **Watakushi wa hatachi desu.** I am twenty years old.

hatairo outlook, circumstances; **hatairo o miru** to see how things go.

hatake field; kitchen garden; farm.

hataki duster (made of pieces of cloth attached to a stick).

hataku to dust; to beat; to slap; to empty; to use up; **saifu no soko o hataku** to spend every penny one has.

hataori weaver, weaving; **hataori kikai** power loom; **hataori kooba** mill.

HATARAKI action; motion; work, labor; ability; talent; merits; **hataraki no aru hito** an able person; **hataraki mono** a hard worker.

HATARAKU to work, toil, labor; to commit; to do. **Ichinichi juu soto de hatarakimashita.** I worked outside all day long.

HATASHITE sure enough; just as I expected.

hatasu to accomplish, achieve; to fulfill; **yakusoku o hatasu** to fulfill one's promise; **mokuteki o hatasu** to achieve one's purpose; **gimu o hatasu** to do one's duty.

hata to suddenly; completely.

HATE end, termination; consequence, result; limit; **hate wa** finally; in the end; **hate ga nai** limitless, endless.

hatenkoo record-breaking; unprecedented; unheard of.

hateshi end; limits; **hateshi nai** endless, boundless; **hateshi nai giron** an endless argument.

hato dove, pigeon.

hatoba wharf, dock, pier.

hatsu first, beginning; **hatsu no** first; initial; new.

hatsuan suggestion, proposal; **hatsuan suru** to suggest, propose.

hatsubai for sale; **hatsubai suru** to offer for sale, put on sale.

hatsubutai debut; first public performance.

hatsubyoo suru to fall ill.

hatsudooki engine; motor.

hatsufuyu early winter.

hatsugen speech; **hatsugen suru** to open one's mouth; to speak (at a conference); **hatsugensha** speaker.

hatsugi proposal, motion.

hatsui suggestion; instance; proposal; original idea; **jibun no hatsui de** on one's own initiative.

HATSUKA the twentieth (of the month); (for) twenty days.

hatsukookai maiden voyage.

hatsumei invention; **hatsumeisha** inventor.

hatsumimi news (to a person). **Kore wa hatsumimi da.** This is news to me.

hatsunetsu suru to have a fever.

HATSUON pronunciation; **hatsuon suru** to pronounce. **Ano hito no Nihongo no hatsuon wa taihen ii desu.** His pronunciation of Japanese words is very good.

hatsuratsu to shita lively; keen; animated.

hattatsu development, progress, growth; **hattatsu suru** to develop, make progress, grow.

hatten development, expansion, growth; **hatten suru** to develop, expand, extend.

hau to crawl, creep.

haya- prefix denoting: quick; fast; swift; early; **hayaashi** quick steps; trot; **hayagaten** hasty conclusion; **hayagaten suru** to jump to a conclusion; **hayagawari** quick change (of costume); **hayagawari suru** to make a quick change.

HAYAI quick, fast, rapid, swift; early; **hayaku** quickly, promptly, early, etc.; **ki no hayai** excitable (person).

hayaku breach of contract; **hayaku suru** to break a contract.

hayakuchi rapid speech; **hayakuchi de hanasu** to jabber; to speak rapidly; **hayakuchi no** glib-tongued; **hayakuchi kotoba** tongue twister.

hayamaru to be overhasty, be rash; to act hastily; **hayamatta** rash; hasty; **hayamatta koto o suru** to act rashly. **Sonna ni hayamatte wa ikemasen.** Don't be so hasty. **Nan to iu hayamatta koto o shite kureta.** What a rash thing you've done!

hayame ni somewhat early, before time; **uchi o hayame ni deru** to leave home a little early.

hayameru to quicken, hasten, accelerate; **ashi o hayameru** to quicken one's steps.

hayane o suru to go to bed early; **hayane hayaoki** early to bed and early to rise.

hayanomikomi o suru to jump to a conclusion.

hayaoki suru to get up early.

hayari fashion, mode, vogue; **hayari no** fashionable, popular; **hayari no shingata** new style.

hayariuta popular song.

HAYARU to be in fashion; to prevail; to rage; to prosper; to be hasty; to be impetuous; **hayaranaku naru** to go out of fashion; to lose popularity. **Ano mise wa yoku hayatte iru.** That store is doing a good business.

hayasa quickness, swiftness, rapidity, speed, velocity.

HAYASHI forest, wood, grove.

hayasu to cut into small fragments; to slice up; to hash; to grow; to let grow; **hige o hayasu** to grow a beard; to grow a mustache.

hayawakari quick understanding; **hayawakari no suru** to be quick of understanding; to be intelligent; to be easy to understand.

hayawaza clever trick; sleight of hand.

HAZU ought to; is to be; **-hazu wa nai** cannot be; must not be; there is no reason to believe that . . . **Kare wa kesa shuppatsu suru hazu deshita.** He was to start this morning. **Ano hito wa kyoo kuru hazu desu.** He is expected here today. **Ano hito ga kyoo kuru hazu wa nai.** There is no reason to believe that he would come here today.

hazukashigaru to be shy, be bashful.

Hazukashii to be ashamed; to be shameful; to be dishonorable; to be bashful. **Ohazukashii koto desu ga . . .** To my shame I must confess that . . .

hazukashime shame, disgrace; insult; **hito kara hazukashime o ukeru** to be humiliated by someone; **hazukashimeru** to put to shame; to outrage.

hazumi momentum, impetus; **hazumi o tsukeru** to give impetus to; **hazumi ga tsuku** to be encouraged; to be stimulated; **toki no hazumi de** on the spur of the moment.

hazumu to bounce; to rebound; to get lively; to treat oneself to; **iki ga hazumu** to be out of breath; to pant.

hazure end, edge; outskirts; miss; disappointment; failure (of crops); poor harvest; **machi no hazure** the end of a street.

hazureru to be disconnected, to be dislocated; to come off; to be out of joint; to fail; to miss; **ate ga hazureru** to be disappointed in one's expectations.

hazusu to remove; to unfasten; to lose; to avoid; **megane o hazusu** to take off one's glasses; **kikai o hazusu** to lose an opportunity; **seki o hazusu** to slip out of the room; to leave the table.

hebi snake, serpent.

hedatari distance; difference; gap.

hedataru to be distant; to become estranged.

hedate distinction; discrimination; reserve; estrangement; barrier; **hedate no aru** distant; discriminating; **hedate no nai** candid; openhearted; **hedate naku hanasu** to speak without reserve.

hedateru to part from; separate by; to intervene, come between; to alienate; **hedatete** apart; at a distance; at intervals of; **juunen o hedatete** after an interval of ten years.

heddofoon headphones.

heddoraito headlight.

hei wall; fence; **hei o megurasu** to surround with a wall.

heian peace, tranquility; **heian ni** peacefully, in peace.

heibon commonness; mediocrity; **heibon na** commonplace, mediocre; tame; uneventful; **heibon na tsuki** an uneventful month.

heigai evils; evil influence, evil effect.

heihei bonbon commonplace, mediocre.

Heika His (Her) Majesty.

heikai closing, adjournment; **heikai suru** to adjourn.

heiki coolness, calmness, composure; **heiki na** cool, calm, composed; indifferent; unconcerned; **heiki de** calmly; with composure. **Heiki na kao o shite imashita.** He looked unconcerned.

heikin average; balance; equilibrium; **heikin shite** on the average.

heikoo suru to be defeated; to be silenced; to be annoyed; to be embarrassed.

heion tranquility; peace and quiet; **heion no, heion na** quiet; tranquil; **heion ni naru** to become quiet.

Heisei present era (counted from ascent of present emperor to throne in 1989); **Heisei 4 nen** the year 1992.

heisei composure; **kokoro no heisei o tamotsu** to keep one's presence of mind.

heitai soldier.

heiten *(n.)* closing of a shop or business; **heiten suru** to close up shop.

HEIWA peace; **heiwa no, heiwa na** peaceful, peaceable; **heiwa ni** peacefully; **heiwaronsha** pacifist.

heiya plain; moor; prairie.

heizei at ordinary times; usually. **Heizei wa yoru uchi ni imasu.** I am usually at home at night.

heizen to shite calmly, composedly.

hekieki suru to shrink from; to flinch; to be nonplussed.

hekomasu to hollow, to depress; to defeat; to silence.

hekomu to become hollow; to become depressed; to be humiliated; to give in, yield.

hekotareru to be discouraged; to be exhausted.

hen neighborhood; region; side; **kono hen ni** in this neighborhood.

-hen chapter; book, volume.

henden telegram (in reply); **henden suru** to reply by telegram.

hendoo change, alteration; fluctuations; **hendoo suru** to change; to fluctuate.

HENJI, hentoo reply, answer; **henji suru** to reply, answer; **tegami no henji o dasu** to answer a letter.

henjin eccentric person, odd fish.

henka change, variation; **henka suru** to change, alter.

henken prejudice; prejudiced view.

henkin repayment; refund; **henkin suru** to pay back, repay.

henkoo alteration, making changes.

henkutsu eccentricity; obstinacy; narrow-mindedness; **henkutsu na** eccentric; narrow-minded; cranky; obstinate. **Ano hito wa henkutsu na hito desu.** He is an eccentric person.

henmei alias; assumed name.

HEN NA odd, strange, queer; **hen na me ni au** to have an odd experience; **hen na kokochi ga suru** to have a strange sensation; **hen ni omou** to think (something) to be strange.

hennyuu admission; assignment.

henrei return (of a present or call); **-no henrei ni** in return for.

hensai repayment; **hensai suru** to repay.

hensan compilation; editing.

hensei organization; formation.

hensen change; vicissitudes; **hensen suru** to change, undergo a change.

henshi unnatural death.

henshin change of mind; unfaithfulness; **henshin suru** to change one's mind.

henshoku partiality (weakness) for a particular kind of food.

hensoo disguise.

hentai abnormality.

hentoo See **HENJI.**

hentoosen tonsils; **hentoosen en** tonsillitis.

herasu to decrease, lessen, reduce.

heri border, edge, brim, brink; **heri o toru** to hem, border.

herikoputaa helicopter.

herikudaru to be modest; to humble oneself; **herikudatte** modestly, humbly.

herikutsu o iu to quibble; to argue for the sake of arguing.

HERU to decrease, lessen; to be reduced. **Ame de hitode ga hetta.** Because of the rain, the crowds have thinned out.

heru to pass; to elapse; to pass through; to go by way of.

herumetto helmet.

hesokurigane secret savings; pin money.

HETA unskillfulness, awkwardness; **heta na** unskillful, awkward, clumsy. **Watakushi wa Nihongo ga heta desu.** My Japanese is poor.

heta calyx.

hete after; through; by way of; **ichinen o hete** after a year; **yuujin no te o hete** through a friend; **Rondon o hete** by way of London.

hetoheto ni naru to be reduced to a pulp; to be tired out; to be exhausted.

hetsurai flattery; **hetsurai mono** flatterer; **hetsurau** to flatter; to fawn on.

hetto beef fat.

HEYA room, chamber.

HI sun; day; time; date; **hi no de** sunrise; **hi no iri** sunset; **aru hi** one day; **hiatari** exposure to sun; **hiatari ga yoi** to be sunny, have plenty of sunshine; **hiatari ga warui** to be dark and gloomy; **hi ni yakeru** to be sunburnt; **hi ni sarasu** to expose to the sun; **hi no me o miru** to see the light of day; **hi no me o minai** to lack sun. **Hi ga nagaku natte kita.** The days are getting longer. **Hi wa rokuji ni deta.** The sun rose at six.

HI fire, flame; spark; light; **hi ga tsuku** to catch fire; **hi ni ataru** to warm oneself by a fire; **hi no ko** flying sparks; **hi no te** flames; blaze; **hi no te ga agaru** to burst into flames; **hi no yoo na** fiery, blazing.

hi error, fault; **hi o narasu** to attack, to declaim against; **hi no uchidokoro ga nai** impeccable, unimpeachable.

hi tombstone, monument.

hi- prefix denoting: un-; anti-; non-; **hikinzoku** non-metal.

hiagaru to dry up; to be parched; to starve to death.

hiai sadness; sorrow.

hibachi brazier; charcoal brazier; **hibachi ni ataru** to warm oneself at a brazier.

hiban off duty; **hiban de aru** to be off duty.

hibana sparks; **hibana o tobasu** to shoot out sparks. (See also **kasai.**)

hibi crack; fissure; flaw; **hibi ga iru** to be cracked; to have a flaw; **hibi ga kireru** to be chapped.

hibiki sound; echo, reverberation; **hibiki wataru** to resound, reverberate.

hibiku to sound; to echo; to affect; to influence; **myoo ni hibiku** to sound strange.

hibon na, hibon no out of the ordinary, extraordinary; uncommon.

hiboshi drying in the sun.

hibukure blister caused by a burn.

hibunmei uncivilized; uncultured.

hida fold; tuck; plait; **hida o toru** to tuck; to fold; crease.

hidachi growth; recovery; convalescence.

HIDARI left; **hidari no** left; left side; **hidari ni** to the left; on the left; **hidari kiki** left-handedness; left-handed person; winelover, a heavy drinker; **hidari kiki no** left-handed.

hidarimae adversity; downward course. **Shinshoo ga hidarimae ni naru.** His luck is failing. Luck is deserting him.

hiden secret; trade secret.

hideri drought, dry weather.

HIDOI severe; excessive; intense; violent; awful; terrible; **hidoi me ni au** to have a bad time of it.

hidoku severely; intensely; violently; hard.

hidori o kimeru to fix a date, fix on a day; to name a day.

hieru to grow cold, get chilly.

HIFU skin.

higaeri return trip made in one day; **higaeri suru, higaeri ni suru** to go and return in one day.

higai damage, injury; **higaisha** sufferer; victim.

higami jaundice; warp.

higamu to be jealous; to be prejudiced.

higan other shore (side); goal.

HIGASHI east. **Taiyoo wa higashi kara deru.** The sun rises in the east.

higashi confectionery.

hige mustache; beard; whiskers; **hige o hayasu** to grow a mustache (or beard); **hige moja no** heavily bearded.

higeki tragedy, tragic event.

HIGORO always; for a long time; **higoro no** usual; long-cherished. **Kare wa higoro kara kinben da.** He has always been industrious. **Higoro no negai ga kanatta.** My long-cherished dream has been fulfilled.

higoto ni everyday; day by day.

HIGURE twilight; nightfall; **higure ni** toward evening; at dusk.

hihan comment; criticism; **hihan suru** to criticize; to censure.

hihoo sad news.

hihyoo critique; comment; **hihyoo suru** to criticize, comment, review; **hihyooteki** critical; **hihyooka** critic, reviewer.

hiiki favor; patronage; partiality; **hiiki o suru** to favor, be partial to; **hiiki no** favorite; **hiikikyaku** patron.

HIJI elbow; **hijikake isu** armchair.

hijideppoo rebuff; cold shoulder; **hijideppoo o kuwaseru** to give (someone) the cold shoulder.

hijoo extraordinary occasion; emergency; **hijoo na** extraordinary; uncommon; **HIJOO NI** extraordinarily; exceedingly; **hijoo no sai ni wa** in case of emergency; **hijooguchi** emergency exit; **hijooji** emergency, crisis; **hijooshudan** exceptional measures.

hijooshiki lack of common sense; **hijooshiki na** eccentric; nonsensical. **Hijooshiki na hito desu.** He lacks common sense.

hikae note, memorandum; duplicate.

hikaeme moderation; modesty; temperance; **hikaeme ni** moderately; with reserve; **hikaeme ni suru** to be moderate; **banji hikaeme ni suru** to do all things with moderation.

hikaeru to jot down, note down; to wait; to be moderate, to stop.

hikage shade; shadow; shady spot.

hikaku comparison; **hikaku suru** to compare; **hikakuteki** comparatively.

hikan pessimism; **hikan suru** to be pessimistic; **hikan ronsha** pessimist.

hikarabiru to dry up, shrivel, wither.

hikaraseru to brighten; to polish; to cause to shine; to glimmer.

HIKARI light, brightness, brilliancy; glimmer, twinkle, luster, gloss; **hikari tsuushin** fiber-optic communication.

hikaru to shine; to be bright, sparkle; etc.

hikazu number of days; **hikazu ga kakaru** to take many days.

hike weak point; **hike o toru** to be defeated, be inferior to.

hikeru to be closed; to close; to lose courage; to feel small. **Yakusho ga goji ni hikeru.** The office closes at five. **Watakushi wa sore o kangaeru to ki ga hikeru.** I feel small when I think of it; **hikedoki** closing hour.

hiketsu secret; **seikoo no hiketsu** secret of success.

-HIKI counter head denoting (for fish or four-legged animals); **ippiki no ushi** one head of cattle; **nihiki no ushi** two head of cattle.

hiki joy and sorrow; **hiki komogomo** a mixed feeling of joy and sorrow.

hiki (n.) pulling; help, backing; influence. **Ano hito wa yoi hiki ga aru.** He has good connections.

hiki- prefix denoting: pulling; drawing; **hikishio** ebb tide; low tide.

hikiage pulling up; evacuation; withdrawal.

hikiageru to pull up, draw up; to evacuate; to withdraw.

hikiai witness; instance; example; **hikiai ni dasu** to use as an example.

hikiau to pay (off) well; to make a good return. **Sono shigoto wa hikiawanai.** The work does not pay.

hikiawase introduction; bringing together; comparison; **hikiawaseru** to introduce; to compare with; to check up.

hikicha powdered tea.

hikichigiru to pull off; to tear off.

hikidashi drawer; **hikidashi o akeru** to open a drawer.

hikidasu to draw out; to pull out; **yokin o hikidasu** to draw money from a bank.

hikifune towboat; tugboat.

hikigeki tragicomedy.

hikiharau to vacate; to remove; **ie o hikiharau** to move from a house.

hikiireru to draw into; to pull into; to win over; **mikata ni hikiireru** to win a person (over) to one's side.

hikiiru to lead; to head; to control; to manage.

hikikae exchange; conversion; **-to hikikae ni** in exchange for.

hikikaeru to exchange; to convert; **sore ni hikikaete** on the contrary; on the other hand.

hikikaesu to come back; to turn back; to return.

hikikomisen railway siding, service wire.

hikikomoru to shut oneself in; to be confined.

hikikomu to retire.

hikimodosu to bring back; to revert to; to restore.

HIKINIKU chopped meat; **hikinikuki** meat grinder.

hikin na familiar; common; popular; **hikin na rei** familiar example.

hikinobasu to stretch; to draw out; to enlarge (a photo); to postpone; to put off.

hikinobashi shashin enlarged photograph.

hikiokosu to raise up; to lift up; to cause; to give rise to; to awaken.

hikiorosu to pull down.

hikisagaru to withdraw; to retire.

hikisaku to tear up, tear to pieces.

hikishimaru to tighten; to tie harder; to brace; to be tightened up; to grow tight; to be braced up; **hikishimatta** firm; tight; tense;

fukuro no himo o hikishimeru to draw the strings of a bag together.

hikitaosu to pull down.

hikitate favor; patronage.

hikitateru to favor; to patronize; to set off (beauty); to set off to advantage; **ki o hikitateru** to encourage.

hikitatsu to look well (better); to improve; to become active; **ki ga hikitatsu** to cheer up; to be inspired with hope.

hikite catch; knob.

hikitomeru to detain; to stop.

hikitoru to withdraw; to take back; to take over.

hikitsugu to succeed in; to take over.

hikitsuke convulsion.

hikitsukeru to draw toward me; to attract.

HIKITSUZUITE continually; successively; **gonen hikitsuzuite** for five years running.

hikitsuzuki continuation; succession; sequel.

hikitsuzuku to continue; to last.

hikiuke undertaking. **Ano ginkoo wa kono tegata no hikiuke o kobanda.** That bank didn't honor this check.

hikiukeru to undertake; to accept; to take over; to assume; to shoulder the responsibility for.

hikiwake draw, tie; **hikiwake ni naru** to end in a draw.

hikiwakeru to part; to pull apart; to separate.

hikiwatashi delivery; transfer; surrender. **Shoohin no hikiwatashi wa yokka ni sunda.** The delivery of merchandise was completed on the fourth.

hikiwatasu to deliver; to hand over; to surrender.

hikiyoseru to draw near; to bring close; to pull near.

hikizan subtraction.

hikizuru to drag, pull along; **ashi o hikizutte aruku** to drag one's feet; **hikizuridasu** to pull out, drag out; **hikizurikomu** to drag in; to bring in.

hikkaburu to pull (draw) over one's head.

hikkakaru to be caught (on a nail, tree, etc.); to be hooked; to be entangled; to be cheated.

hikkakeru to hook; to hang on; to cheat; to seduce; to evade payment; **ippai hikkakeru** to have drink.

hikkaku to scratch; to claw.

hikki transcript; **hikki suru** to write down; to copy; to take notes; **hikkisha** stenographer; **hikkichoo** notebook; **hikkishiken** written examination.

hikkomeru to pull (draw) in; to draw back; to move back.

hikkomu to retire, withdraw; to disappear; **hikkomigachi no, hikkomijian no** retiring

(in disposition); **inaka e hikkomu** to retire to the country. **Ie wa dooro kara hikkonde iru.** The house stands back from the road.

hikkonda secluded; sunken; hollow; **hikkonda basho** secluded place.

HIKKOSU to move (into another house); **hikkoshi no torrakku** moving van. **Tookyoo e hikkoshimasu.** I am going to move to Tokyo.

hikkurikaeru to tumble down; to be upset; to tip over; to be overturned.

hikkurikaeshi topsy-turvy; upside down; wrong side up; inside out. **Uchi no naka wa hikkurikaeshi ni natte imasu.** The house is upside down.

hikkurikaesu to overturn, upset; to topple over; to knock down.

hikkurumeru to bundle (together); to include.

hikoku defendant; prisoner.

HIKOO flight; aviation; **hikoo suru** to fly; **HIKOOJOO** airport; **HIKOOKI** airplane; **hikoosen** blimp; dirigible.

hikooshiki no informal, not official; **hikooshiki ni** unofficially; informally.

HIKU to draw; to attract; to lead; to install; to quote; to consult; to subtract; **kuji o hiku** to draw lots; **sode o hiku** to pull (someone) by the sleeve; **kuruma o hiku** to draw a cart; **chuui o hiku** to attract attention; **doojoo o hiku** to win sympathy; **kaze o hiku** to catch a cold; **denwa o hiku** to install a telephone; **jisho o hiku** to refer to a dictionary; **nedan o hiku** to cut the price; **chisuji o hiku** to descend from.

hiku to play (an instrument); **piano a hiku** to play the piano.

hiku to resign, to retire; recede, ebb. **Hare ga hikimashita.** The swelling has gone down. **Netsu ga hikimashita.** The fever has dropped.

HIKUI low; humble; short; flat; **hikui hana** a flat nose; **hikui koe** a low voice. **Sei ga hikui.** She is short (in stature).

hikutsu meanness; servility; **hikutsu na** servile; mean.

hikyoo cowardice; **hikyoo na** cowardly; **hikyoo mono** coward.

HIMA leisure; (spare) time; dismissal; leave; interval; recess; **hima de aru** to be free, be at leisure; **hima ga iru** to require (more) time; **hima ga nai** to have no time; **hima o dasu** to dismiss (a servant); **hima o toru** to resign; **himadoru** to take (much) time; to delay; **himajin** leisured or unemployed person. **Shoobai ga hima de aru.** Business is slack.

himashi ni more and more each day; **himashi**

ni byooki ga yoku naru to get better day by day.

himei cry of distress; shriek; **himei o ageru** to utter a groan.

himitsu secret; secrecy; **himitsu no** secret, confidential, private; **himitsu ni** secretly, privately; **himitsu ni suru** to keep secret; **himitsu o abaku** to divulge a secret.

HIMO string, cord; braid; tape; ribbon; thong; **himo o musubu** to tie a string. **himo de musubu** to tie (something) with string. .

himojii to be starved. **Taihen himojii omoi o shimashita.** I was very hungry.

himono dried fish.

hin poverty; **hin suru** to be poor.

hin elegance; grace; refinement; **hin ga tsuku** to be refined; **hin no yoi** refined; elegant; **hin no warui** vulgar; uncouth; coarse; **hin o sageru** to disgrace oneself.

hinaka broad daylight; daytime.

hinan blame, censure, reproach; **hinan suru** to blame.

hinan refuge, shelter; **hinan suru** to take shelter; **hinansha** refugee; **hinansho** refugee shelter.

hinata sunny place; sunshine; **hinata ni hosu** to dry in the sun; **hinata bokko o suru** to take a sunbath.

hinekureru to become crooked; **hinekureta** distorted, crooked; perverse; **hinekureta onna** perverse woman; **hinekureta kangae** distorted view.

hinekuru to twirl; to finger; to toy with.

hineru to twirl; to turn on (or off); **gasu o hineru** to turn on the gas (in a stove).

hiniku sarcasm; caustic remark; **hiniku na** sarcastic; cynical, ironic; **hiniku o iu** to speak sarcastically or ironically.

hinin birth control, contraception.

hinjaku meagerness; poverty; **hinjaku na** meager; shelter.

hinketsu anemia.

hinkoo behavior, conduct; **hinkoo no yoi** well-behaved.

hinminkutsu slums.

hinobe postponement; extension of time; reprieve; **hinobe suru** to postpone, etc.

hinoki butai (theater) stage (of cypress); (= first-class stage).

hi no kuruma extreme poverty; **hi no kuruma de aru** to be in great financial difficulty.

hi no maru national flag of Japan; disk of the sun; red circle.

hinpan frequency, **hinpan na** frequent; incessant; **hinpan ni, hinpan to** frequently, incessantly.

hinshi dying; **hinshi no jootai ni aru** to be on the verge of death.

hinshitsu quality.

hinsoo poor appearance; **hinsoo na nari o shite iru** to be poorly dressed.

hippaku pressure (for money); tightness (of money). **Ano hito wa shikin ni hippaku shite iru.** She is pressed for funds.

hipparidako de aru to be sought for eagerly; to be in great demand.

HIPPARU to pull, draw, drag, tug; to stretch; to entice; to solicit; **mikata ni hipparu** to win over to our side.

hira- prefix denoting: flat, level; plain, simple; common; **hiraya** one-story house; **hirachi** level land, flat ground.

HIRAGANA one of the two sets of Japanese syllabary called **kana.**

hirashira fluttering; flapping. **Ki no ha ga hirashira to chitta.** The leaves fluttered down.

hiraishin lightning rod.

hirakeru to become civilized; to become modernized; to be cultivated; to develop; to grow; **hiraketa** modernized; up-to-date; civilized; **hiraketa hito** person of the world.

hiraki opening; closet; difference; distance; gap.

HIRAKU to open; to lift (a lid); to unfold; to commence; to set up; to cultivate; to bloom; **tenrankai o hiraku** to open an exhibit. **Hana ga hiraite iru.** The flower is blooming.

hiramekasu to flash; to brandish.

hirameki flash; flashing; gleam.

hirameku to flash; to gleam; to wave.

hira ni humbly; earnestly; intently. **Hira ni goyoosha o kou.** I sincerely hope you will pardon me (used in letters).

hirari to nimbly; lightly.

hiratai, hirattai flat, level; simple, plain; **hirataku** flatly; evenly; easily; simply, plainly; **hirataku suru** to flatten; **hirataku ieba** to speak plainly.

hirate palm of the hand; open hand; **hirate de utsu** to slap.

hiraya one-story house.

hire fin.

hireniku steak; filet mignon.

hiretsu meanness; baseness.

hirihiri suru to be pungent; to have a burning taste; to smart.

hiroba open space; square (of a town).

hirobiro to shita spacious; roomy; open; extensive.

hirogari extension; expansion; spread.

hirogaru to extend; to expand; to spread.

HIROGERU to spread; to extend; to widen; to open; to unfold; to unroll. **Michi o hirogemashita.** They widened the road.

Mise o hirogeru tsumori desu. I intend to expand (enlarge) the store.

HIROI wide, broad; extensive; roomy; **hiroi heya** spacious (big) room.

hiroiageru to pick up.

hiroiatsumeru to gather, collect; to select.

hiroimono piece of good luck; find; **hiroimono o suru** to find (pick up) (something); to make a rare find.

hiroiyomi o suru to read here and there; to skim; to skip over (details); to pick up the chief points.

hiroku widely, extensively; generally; universally; **hiroku suru** to widen; to enlarge.

hiroma spacious room; hall.

hiromaru to circulate; to be circulated; to be diffused.

hirome announcement; debut.

hiromeru to spread, propagate.

hiroo fatigue; exhaustion; **hiroo suru** to get weary, to be exhausted.

hiroo announcement; introduction; **hiroo suru** to announce; to introduce.

hirosa width, breadth; area; dimension. **Kono kooen no hirosa wa dore hodo arimasu ka?** How large is this park?

HIROU to pick up; to find; to gather. **Michi de sen en satsu o hirotta.** I found a thousand-yen bill on the road.

HIRU daytime; noon, midday; **hiru hinaka** in broad daylight.

HIRUGOHAN lunch, midday meal; **hirugohan o taberu** to have lunch.

hirugaeru to wave; to fly; to float; to flap; **hirugaesu** to wave; to fly; to change.

hiruhan See hirugohan.

HIRUMA daytime; **hiruma ni** in the daytime.

hirumae forenoon; **hirumae ni** in the morning.

hirumu to flinch; to shrink.

hirune midday nap; siesta; **hirune o suru** to take a nap.

hirusugi shortly after noon.

HIRUYASUMI midday recess; lunch hour.

hiryoo manure; fertilizer.

hisan misery; distress; **hisan na** tragic; miserable, wretched.

hisashi visor (of a cap); eaves; canopy.

HISASHIBURI DE after a long time; for the first time in many days (weeks, years, etc.); **hisashiburi de au** to see after a long interval. **Hisashiburi desu nee!** It's a long time since I last saw you.

hisashii long; long continued; of long standing; **hisashii aida** for a long time.

HISASHIKU for a long time. **Kare ni wa hisashiku awanai.** I haven't seen him for a long time.

hisenron pacifism; **hisenronsha** pacifist.

hishaku ladle, dipper.

hishihishi to firmly; tightly; densely; deeply.

hishimeku to clamor, make a noise.

hishochi summer resort.

hisohiso in whispers; secretly; **hisohiso banashi** whispered conversation.

hisomeru to raise or knit (one's brows); **mayu o hisometa** with a frown.

hisoo na touching, pathetic.

hisshi desperation; **hisshi no** desperate; **hisshi ni** desperately; **hisshi to natte** in desperation; **hisshi no doryoku o suru** to make desperate efforts.

hisuterii hysteria, hysterics; **hisuterii o okosu** to go into hysterics.

HITAI forehead; brow.

hitasu to steep; to dip; to soak.

HITO person; people; others; nature; disposition; **hito no yoi** good-natured; **hito no warui** ill-natured; **hito no ooi jikoku** rush hour.

hito- prefix denoting: one; **hitoban** one night (evening); all night; whole night; **hitohako** one box.

HITOBITO people.

hitochigai mistaken identity.

hitodanomi o suru to depend on someone else.

hitode helping hand; help; **hitode ga tarinai** short of hands; short of help; **hitode o kariru** to ask for help; **hitode ni wataru** to change hands.

hitode, hitogomi crowd; throng. **Taihen na hitode de atta.** There was a large crowd.

hitodenashi inhuman wretch; ungrateful person.

hitodoori pedestrian traffic; **hitodoori no ooi machi** a busy street. **Koko wa hitodoori ga ooi.** It is very crowded here.

hitoemono summer clothes.

hitofude line; stroke; **hitofude de** with one stroke of the brush.

hitogara personal character; personal appearance.

hitogoe voice.

hitogomi (See also **hitode.**) **hitogomi no naka o oshiwakete iku** to push through a crowd of people.

hitogoroshi murder; murderer.

hitogoto other people's affairs. **Hitogoto to wa omoenai.** I feel as if it were my own concern.

hitohada nugu to lend a helping hand; to give every assistance possible.

hitoiki one breath; **hitoiki tsuite** after a pause; **hitoiki de** in one breath; at a stretch.

hitokata naranu unusual, uncommon; great, immense.

hitokata narazu not a little; extremely; immensely.

HITOKIWA especially, particularly; conspicuously; in a high degree; still more.

hitokoto single word; **hitokoto mo iwanai** to be silent; not to say a single word.

hitokuchi mouthful; bite; morsel; **hitokuchi ni taberu** to eat in one bite.

hitokuse peculiarity; uncommon trait.

hitomae de in public.

hitomaku act; scene; **hitomaku mono** one-act play.

hitomane imitation; mimicry.

hitomatome ni in a lump; in a bunch; **hitomatome ni suru** to put together.

hitomawari turn; round; **hitomawari suru** to go on one's rounds; **kooen o hitomawari sanpo suru** to take a walk through the park.

HITOMAZU for the present; for the time being; for a while; anyhow.

hitome notice; attention; **hitome o shinobu** to avoid the public eye; **hitome o shinonde** in secret; secretly; **hitome o hiku** to attract attention.

hitome look; glance; **hitome de** at a glance; **hitome miru** to glance at.

hitomishiri suru to be afraid of strangers; to be bashful.

hitomukashi age; decade.

hitonaka crowd of people; **hitonaka de** in the presence of others.

hitonami no average; common; ordinary; **hitonami ni** like other people; **hitonami hazureta** uncommon; eccentric.

hitonemuri nap; short sleep.

hitonigiri handful; **hitonigiri no kome** handful of rice.

hitoomoi ni without further hesitation; instantly; at once; without further ado.

HITORI (single) person; **hitori de** alone; unaided; **hitorimono** bachelor. **Hitori de shimashita.** I did it myself.

hitori bitori, hitori hitori one by one; one after another (person). **Hitori bitori de kangae ga chigau.** Each person has his or her own opinion.

hitoride ni spontaneously.

hitorigaten one's own judgment; hasty conclusion.

hitorigoto soliloquy; **hitorigoto o iu** to talk to oneself.

hitorigurashi living alone; bachelorhood.

hitori hitori (See **hitori bitori.**) one by one; one at a time. **Hitori hitori no kangae o itte kudasai.** Will each of you express your opinion?

hitorikko only child.

hitorimusuko only son.

hitorimusume only daughter.

hitori nokorazu everyone.

hitoritabi (n.) traveling alone.

hitoriyogari self-satisfaction; self-complacency; **hitoriyogari no** self-satisfied.

hitosarai abduction, kidnapping; kidnapper.

HITOSASHIYUBI forefinger.

hitosawagase scare; false alarm.

hitoshii equal to, equivalent to.

hitosoroi set; suit; **hitosoroi no chadoogu** tea set; **fuyugi hitosoroi** winter suit.

hitosuji line; **hitosuji michi** straight road; **hitosuji ni** straight, in a straight line; intently.

HITOTONARI personality; character.

hitotoori in a general way; **hitotoori no** general; common; **hitotoori naranu** unusual, uncommon; **hitotoori hanashite kikaseru** to give a short account.

HITOTSU one; same; identical; **hitotsu no** one; single; **hitotsu ni suru** to unite, join, combine; **hitotsu bitotsu** one by one; separately; **hitotsu oki ni** alternately.

hitotsubu grain; **hitotsubu no kome** grain of rice.

hitotsukami handful; fistful.

hitouchi blow; stroke; **hitouchi ni** at one blow.

hitozuki attractiveness; amiability; **hitozuki no suru** attractive; pleasing; amiable; charming; **hitozuki no shinai** unprepossessing; unattractive.

hitozute hearsay; **hitozute ni** secondhand; by hearsay. **Hitozute ni kiite shitte imasu.** I know it through hearsay. **Sore wa hitozute ni kiita no desu.** It came to me secondhand.

HITSUYOO necessity; need; **HITSUYOO NA** necessary; requisite, required; **hitsuyoo no sai wa** in case of need. **Ano hon ga zehi hitsuyoo desu.** I must have that book.

hittakuru to snatch, take by force.

hiwari daily rate; schedule; program; **hiwari de harau** to pay by the day; **hiwari o kimeru** to fix the dates.

hiyaase o kaku to be in a cold sweat.

hiyahiya suru to be chilly; to be in great fear.

hiyakashi banter; jeering; ridicule; (mere) inspection.

hiyakasu to make fun of; just to look at. **Chotto hiyakashi ni iku dake desu.** I'll just go and look at the things. **Ano hito wa anata o hiyakashite iru no da.** She is making fun of you.

hiyari to suru to feel chilled; to be startled, be alarmed at.

hiyasu to cool; to refrigerate; **hiyashite oku** to keep (something) cool.

hiyayaka coldness; coldheartedness; **hiyayaka ni** coldheartedly; coolly; **hiyayaka na hito** coldhearted person; **hiyayaka na kaze** chilly wind.

hiyoke screen (against sun); awning; **hiyoke o suru** to screen from the sun.

HIYOO cost, expense, expenditure; **hiyoo ga kakaru** to be expensive. **Dore hodo hiyoo ga kakarimashita ka?** How much did it cost you?

HIYORI weather; fine weather; condition; state of affairs; **hiryori o miru** to watch which way the wind blows; to sit on the fence. **Hiyori ga kawatta.** The weather has changed.

HIZA knee; lap; **hiza o tsuku** to kneel; **hizagashira** kneecap; **hizakake** lap robe (rug); **hizamazuku** to kneel; to fall on one's knees.

hizoo treasure, valuable possession; **hizoo no** treasured, valued; dearest; **hizoo suru** to treasure, cherish, keep with great care; **hizoohin** valued possession.

hizuke date.

hobashira mast.

HOBO almost, nearly; about.

HOBO kindergarten teacher.

hochoo pace, step; **hochoo o soroeru** to keep pace with.

HODO degree; limit; moderation; some; about; the more . . . the more; as; **hodo yoku** moderately; properly; modestly; **kore hodo** this much; so much; **sore hodo** that much. **Joodan ni mo hodo ga aru.** There is a limit even to a joke. **Hayakereba hayai hodo yoi desu.** The sooner the better.

hodoai moderation; golden mean.

hodokeru to come loose; to get untied.

hodokoshi alms, charity.

hodokosu to give; to give alms; to practice; to try; **arayuru shudan o hodokosu** to try every means.

HODOKU to untie, unfasten; to loosen; to disentangle; **nimotsu o hodoku** to unpack (luggage); **himo o hodoku** to untie a knot.

HODONAKU shortly; before long; by and by.

hodoo footpath; sidewalk; pavement; paved road.

hoeru to bark; to howl; to roar. **Ano inu wa yoku hoeru.** That dog is noisy.

hogaraka melodiousness; cheerfulness; **hogaraka na** sonorous; cheerful, bright; **hogaraka na koe** in a clear voice; **hogaraka ni** cheerfully.

hogo protection; **hogo suru** to protect; **hogosha** protector, guardian.

hogu, hogo wastepaper; **hogu ni suru** to annul, invalidate.

hogusu to unfasten, untie; to disentangle; to unravel.

hojiru, hojikuru to pick; to dig; to ferret out.

hojo assistance, aid, subsidy; **hojo no** subsidiary, auxiliary; **hojo suru** to aid, subsidize; **hojo o ukeru** to be subsidized; **hojokin** subsidy, grant-in-aid.

hojuu suru to supplement; to replenish.

HOKA others; rest; besides; another phase; **hoka ni** besides; **hoka no** another; the other; **-no hoka wa** except; **hoka no tokoro** another place; elsewhere; **hoka no hitotachi** other people.

hokan suru to take custody of; to take in charge; **hokannin** custodian.

hoken insurance; **hoken o kakeru** to insure (against accidents); **seimei hoken** life insurance; **kasai hoken** fire insurance.

hoketsu substitute, filling a vacancy; **hoketsu senshu** substitute player.

hokki promotion; proposal, suggestion.

hokku hook.

HOKORI dust; **hokori darake** dusty; **hokori ga tatsu** to be dusty; **hokori o harau** to dust.

hokori pride. **Kodomo o hokori ni shite imasu.** She takes pride in her children.

hokorobi rip; run (ravel).

hokorobiru to get ripped; to be torn open; to unravel, run.

hokoru to boast of; to be proud.

hokuro mole (body).

hokyuu supply; replenishment; **hokyuu suru** to supply; to make up the lack.

HOMERU to praise, commend; to admire. **Mina anata o homete imasu.** Everybody speaks well of you.

HON book, volume; **hon'ya** bookstore; bookdealer; **honbako** bookcase; **hondana** bookshelf.

HON- prefix denoting: original; natural; proper; main; head; chief; true; real; regular; genuine; this; present; our; **honbun** body (of a letter); text; **hondo** mainland; **honkan** main building; **honke** head (main) family; originator; original manufacturer; head house.

-hon counter denoting: things which have length, such as pencils, sticks, and poles; **enpitsu nihon** two pencils.

honba home; best place for.

honbu home office; headquarters.

honburi downpour. **Ame ga iyoiyo honburi ni narimashita.** The rain was coming down in earnest.

hone bone; frame (of a sliding door); spirit; **hone to kawa bakari** (only) skin and bones; **hone o oru** to take the trouble to; **hone ga oreru** to be troublesome; to require great effort; **hone no aru otoko** man of courage; **honedarake na** bony; full of bones; **honegumi** build; physique; framework.

honeori exertion; labor; foil; **honeorizon** *(n.)* working for nothing. **Honeroizon no kutabire mooke.** It was so much useless labor.

honeoshimi laziness; **honeoshimi suru** to spare oneself.

honki seriousness, earnestness; **honki no** serious, earnest; **honki de** seriously, in earnest. **Anata wa honki desu ka?** Are you serious?

honkyoku head (main) office.

honmono real thing; genuine article; original article; **honmono no** real, genuine.

honnin person in question.

HONNO mere; just; little; few; **honno sukoshi** just a little. **Mada honno kodomo desu.** He is a mere child.

honnoo instinct.

honomekasu to allude, hint, suggest.

honoo flame.

honpoo principal salary.

honsai (legal) wife.

honseki permanent residence.

honshiki regular (orthodox) way; **honshiki no** regular; formal; orthodox.

honshoku one's regular occupation; **honshoku no** professional.

honsoo suru to run about (in pursuit of something); to busy oneself about.

HONTOO truth; reality; fact; **hontoo no** true, real, genuine; regular; **hontoo ni** truly, really; **hontoo ni suru** to accept as fact; to take seriously.

hon'yaku translation; **hon'yaku suru** to translate; **hon'yakusha** translator.

HOO direction; quarter; side; **migi no hoo ni** on the right side. **Kono hoo ga ii desu.** This is better. **Iku hoo ga ii desu.** It's better to go.

HOO cheek; **hoobone** cheekbone; **hoobeni** rouge; **hoohige** whiskers.

hoo law.

hoobaru to stuff one's mouth; to eat in one mouthful.

hoobi prize; reward; **hoobi o morau** to win a prize.

hooboo everywhere, in all directions. **Hooboo anata o sagashimashita.** I looked all over for you.

hoochiku dismissal; banishment; **hoochiku suru** to expel, dismiss; to banish; to turn out.

HOOCHOO kitchen knife.

-hoodai suffix denoting: as one pleases; to one's heart's content; **iitaihoodai o iu** to talk as one likes; **shitaihoodai o suru** to act as one pleases.

hoodoo information; report.

hoofu abundance; **hoofu na** rich; abundant.

hoofu ambition, aspiration.

hoogai na exorbitant; **hoogai no takane** exorbitant price.

hoogaku direction; bearing; **hoogaku ga wakaranaku naru** to lose one's bearings; be unable to find one's way.

hoogen dialect; provincialism.

hoohoo no tei de precipitately, hurriedly; sneakingly; **hoohoo no tei de nigedasu** to beat a hasty retreat.

hooka arson.

HOOKI broom; **hooki no e** broomstick.

hookoku report; information, direction, course; **hookoku suru** to report; to inform.

hookoo public duty; service; apprenticeship; **hookoonin** servant; domestic; **hookooguchi** domestic position; **hookoo suru** to enter (domestic) service.

hookyuu salary; **hookyuubi** payday; **hookyuu seikatsusha** salaried person.

hooman laxity, looseness; **hooman na** lax, loose; reckless; wild.

hoomen release; acquittal; **hoomen suru** to release, liberate, release from custody; to acquit.

hoomen direction; quarter, district; **Shizuoka hoomen** the Shizuoka district.

HOOMON call; visit; **hoomon suru** to call on, visit; **hoomon kyaku** visitor; **hoomon o ukeru** to receive a visit.

hoomotsu treasure; heirloom.

hoomuran home run (in baseball).

hoomushikku homesick.

hooriageru to furl up; to throw up.

hooridasu to throw away, cast away, cast out.

hoorikomu to throw in, into.

hooritsu law. **Sore wa hooritsu ihan da.** It's against the law.

hooritsukeru to throw at, against.

hooroku baking pan; earthen pan used for parching tea, etc., at high temperatures.

hooru to throw, fling.

hooshin course, aim; plan; principle; policy; **hooshin o sadameru** to shape one's course; to decide on a policy.

hoosoo = **shutoo** vaccination.

hoosoo (radio) broadcasting; **hoosookyoku** broadcasting station.

hoosu hose.

hootai bandage.

hora boast; brag; tall (big) talk; **hora o fuku** to blow one's own horn; to boast; **horafuki** braggart.

horaana cave, cavern; natural cavity.

horebore suru to be charmed; to be fascinated.

horeru *(colloq.)* to fall in love; to be enamored of.

horidasu to dig out; to unearth, excavate.

horikaesu to dig (turn over the soil).

horu to dig; to excavate; to burrow; to scoop out; to sink (a well).

HOSHI star. **Sora ni hoshi ga kagayaite iru.** Stars are glittering in the sky. **Kotoshi wa hoshimawari ga yoi.** I am lucky this year.

hoshigaru to wish for; to long for; to crave; to covet.

HOSHII to be desirous of having (something); to want. **Ano hon ga hoshii.** I want that book.

hoshimono laundered clothes.

hoshoo guarantee; **hoshoonin** guarantor; certifier.

hosobiki cord, rope.

HOSOI slender; fine; narrow; thin; **hosome ni** slightly; narrowly; **hosome ni kiru** to cut fine; **hosomichi** narrow path; lane; **hosonagai** long and slender; lanky.

hosu to dry (in the air); to sun; to empty a liquid; to draw off; to pump dry; **sakazuki o hosu** to drink up.

hoteru to feel hot; to burn. **Kao ga hoteru.** My face burns.

HOTERU hotel.

hotoke Buddha; deceased (person); departed soul.

HOTONDO almost, very nearly, all but; approximately; hardly, scarcely. **Ano biru wa hotondo kanseishite iru.** That building is near completion.

hotsureru to become loose; to be frayed.

hotto suru to sigh with relief; **hotto iki o tsuku** to heave a deep sigh.

hoyoo preservation of health; recreation; relaxation; **hoyoo suru** to take care of oneself; to recuperate; to relax.

HYAKU *(n.)* hundred; **hyaku mo shoochishite iru** to know too well; to be well aware of.

hyakushoo peasant, farmer.

hyoo table, chart; **jikanhyoo** timetable.

hyooban reputation; fame; popularity; report; rumor; **hyooban no** famed; notorious; **hyooban no yoi** popular; of good reputation; **hyooban no warui** unpopular; **hyooban ni naru** to be much talked about.

hyoomen *(n.)* surface; outside; **hyoomen no** *(adj.)* outside, external.

hyoosatsu doorplate; name plate.

HYOOSHI binding; **kami hyooshi** paper cover, paper binding.

hyooshi time, rhythm; chance; **hyooshi o toru** to beat time.

hyorohyoro staggeringly; slimly; **hyorohyoro shita** staggering, reeling; slim; lanky.

HYOTTO by chance, by accident; **hyotto shitara** possibly, maybe.

hyuuhyuu whistling; whizzing. **Kaze ga hyuuhyuu fuku.** The wind whistles.

I

I stomach.

iawaseru to happen to be present.

ibaru to be haughty; to brag; to give oneself airs.

ibiki snoring; **ibiki o kaku** to snore.

iburu to smolder, smoke. **Kono sumi wa iburu.** This charcoal smokes.

ibusu to smoke; to fumigate.

ICHI one; **ICHIBAN** first; number one; game, round; **ichiban ato de** last of all; at the very end; **ichiban saki no** first, foremost; **ichiban osoi** slowest.

ichi position; situation; location.

ICHIBA marketplace, market; **aomono ichiba** vegetable market; **uo ichiba** fish market.

ichibu part, portion; some part; **ichibu shijuu** the whole, all the details; from beginning to end.

ichidaiji serious affair.

ICHIDO once, one time.

ICHIDOO all; all (the persons) present; **kanai ichidoo** all the members of the family.

ICHIGATSU January.

ICHIICHI in every single case; in detail. **Ichiichi monku o iwanaide kudasai.** Please don't complain all the time.

ICHIJI one o'clock; for the present; for a while; **ichijiteki no** temporary.

ICHIMAI one (sheet, leaf, card).

ICHIMEN entire area, whole surface; one side; other hand; first page (of a newspaper); **ichimenkiji** front-page news; **-no ichimen ni wa . . .** on the other hand . . . **Ichimen ni hana ga saite iru.** Everything is in bloom.

ichimoku glance, look; **ichimoku ryoozen to** be clear at a glance; **ichimokusan ni** at full speed.

ICHINEN one year; **ichinen juu** all year round.

ICHINICHI one day; whole day through; all day; **ichinichi oki ni** every other day.

ICHIOO once; for the time being; in the first place; first; in outline. **Ichioo soo shite okimashoo.** We will leave it that way, at least for the time being.

ICHIRYOOJITSU day or two; **ichiryoojitsu chuu ni** in a day or two.

ichiryuu first class; **ichiryuu no** first rate.

ichiyaku at a single bound.

iden heredity.

ido well (for water); **idobata** side of a well. **idobata kaigi** gossiping.

IDOKORO address; residence; whereabouts.

IE house; dwelling; cottage; home; family; **ie o tateru** to build a house; **ie ni kaeru** to go home.

iegara birth, lineage.

igai na unexpected; unlooked for; **igai ni** unexpectedly.

igen dignity; prestige; **igen aru fuusai** dignified appearance.

IGIRISU = **Eikoku** the United Kingdom; **Igirisu no** *(adj.)* British.

igokochi comfortableness; **igokochi ga yoi** snug; comfortable; **igokochi ga warui** uncomfortable.

ihan violation; infringement; **ihan suru** to act against; to infringe upon.

II = **yoi** good; pretty; likable; **ii hito** nice person. **Ii kimi da.** It serves you right.

iiarasou to dispute, quarrel.

iiateru to guess correctly.

IIE no. **Iie, moo kekko desu.** No, thank you. (I've had enough.)

iifurasu to spread a story, circulate a tale.

iiharu to insist on; to persist in; to assert positively.

iihiraki vindication.

iikaeru to express in another word; **iikaereba** that is to say.

iikaneru to hesitate to say; to be unable to speak out.

iikata way of speaking; expression.

iikiru to speak positively; to assert.

iimorasu to neglect to tell; to forget to tell.

iin committee; committee member.

iinazuke fiancé; fiancée.

iine de at the price asked.

iinuke excuse; evasive answer.

iisokonai slip of the tongue; misstatement.

iisugi exaggeration.

iisugiru to say too much; to exaggerate.

iitsuke order, command; instruction.

iitsukeru to order, command; to bid.

iitsutae tradition; legend; hearsay.

IIWAKE apology; excuse; pretext; **iiwake o suru** to make an excuse; **iiwake ga tatanai** to be inexcusable.

iiwatasu to tell; to pass judgment; to sentence.

iji temper; disposition; **iji o haru** to be obstinate, be stubborn; **soko iji ga aru** strong-willed.

ijikeru to cower.

ijikitanai greedy.

ijimeru to tease; to treat badly; to torment.

ijipparu to persist in; to be obstinate.

ijirashii pitiable; pathetic; touching.

ijiru to finger; to play with.

IJIWARU ill-natured person; **ijiwaru na** nasty, mean.

ijiwarui ill-natured, ill-tempered; **ijiwaruku** spitefully.

IJOO more than; above-mentioned; above; upward of, beyond; since, now that; **yottsu ijoo** more than four.

ijoo something unusual; abnormal symptoms; deformity; **ijoo na** unusual, abnormal. **Betsu ni ijoo wa arimasen.** There is nothing unusual.

ijuu suru to move to; to migrate.

IKA *(n.)* following; less than, under. **Juunisai ika wa tada desu.** There is no charge for children under twelve. **Sore wa gosen en ika desu.** It costs less than 5000 yen.

IKAGA how; what *(pol.).* **Kyoo wa okagen wa ikaga desu ka?** How do you feel today? **Goiken wa ikaga desu ka?** What is your opinion?

ikagawashii questionable, doubtful.

ikahodo how much; how many.

ikameshii solemn, grave; stern; authoritative.

IKANIMO very; truly; indeed.

ikasu to make good use of; to spare one's life; to keep alive; **kane o ikashite tsukau** to make good use of money.

ike pond.

ikedoru to capture.

iken opinion; view; **iken o noberu** to give an opinion; **iken suru** to admonish; to give advice.

IKENAI be of no use; will not do. **Kore wa ikenai.** This will not do. **Ame ga furu to ikenai kara.** Lest it rain. **Ikanakereba ikenai.** I must go. [It won't do if I don't go.]

ikeru to arrange flowers.

iki breath; spirit; **iki ga kireru** to be out of breath; **iki o tsuku** to breathe; to heave a sigh of relief; **iki yoo yoo to** triumphantly.

iki smartness, stylishness; **iki na** smart, stylish, fashionable.

ikidooru to be angry, be enraged; to be indignant.

ikigomi eagerness; ardor, zeal.

ikigomu to set one's heart on.

ikigurushii suffocating, stifling, choking.

iki iki shita lively; active; spirited; vivid; fresh; **iki iki shita sakana** fresh-looking fish.

ikimono living thing, creature; animal.

IKINARI suddenly; all at once.

ikinokoru to survive, to outlive.

ikioi power, force, energy; **ikioi no nai** spiritless, lifeless; **ikioi no yoi** lively; vigorous; **ikioi yoku** vigorously.

IKIRU to live.

ikiutsushi exact copy; **ikiutsushi no** lifelike, true to life.

ikka whole family.

IKKAI first floor; one floor, one story; **ikkai date no uchi** one-story house. **Kutsu wa ikkai de utte imasu.** Shoes are sold on the first floor.

ikken affair; matter.

ikkoku moment; second; **ikkoku mo hayaku** as soon as possible.

ikkoo party (of tourists); suite.

ikoo intention; **ikoo o saguru** to sound; to speak one's mind.

IKU = yuku to go; **machi e iku** to go to town. **Hayaku itte kudasai.** Please go quickly.

IKU- prefix denoting: now many; **IKUDO** how often; how many times; **ikudo to naku** countless times; **ikue** manyfold; **ikue ni mo** many times over; repeatedly; earnestly; on bended knee; **ikunichi** how many days; **IKURA** how many; how much; **ikura ka** somewhat; to some extent; **ikura demo** as many (much) as one pleases; any amount; **IKUTSU** how many; how old. **Ikura desu ka?** How much? **Kyoo wa ikura ka kibun ga yoi.** I feel a little better today. **Nihongo ga ikura ka hanasemasu.** I can speak Japanese to some extent. **Ikutsu desu ka?** How old are you? **Ikutsu arimasu ka?** How many are there?

IKUBUN partly; somewhat. **Anata mo ikubun ka sekinin ga aru.** You, too, are responsible for it.

iku dooon ni unanimously.

ikuji spirit; backbone; **ikuji no nai** spiritless; weak.

IMA now; **ima motte** as yet. **Ima ni kimasu.** She will soon come.

imada yet (used only with a negative verb). **Imada ni konai.** It hasn't come yet.

IMADOKI now; nowadays; these days.

IMAGORO about this time. **Imagoro nani o shite iru daroo.** What would she be doing at this time?

imaimashii provoking; mortifying; disgusting.

imani very soon; before long; by and by. **Imani kuru deshoo.** He will probably come very soon.

imasara now; at this time (in a negative sense). **Imasara sonna koto mo iemasen.** How can you say such a thing now!

imashime instruction; warning, admonition, rebuke, reprimand; **imashimeru** to instruct; to caution, admonish; to warn against; to reprimand, rebuke.

IMASU (form of **iru**) there is.

imawashii offensive; abominable.

IMI meaning, sense, significance; **imi arige na** significant, meaningful; **imi shinchoo** profound meaning. **Sore wa doo iu imi desu ka?** What do you mean by that?

IMOOTO younger sister.

-in suffix denoting: one who; member of; **jimuin** clerk; **kaishain** businessman.

inagara without any effort; without stirring.

INAI within; less than; not exceeding. **Gofun inai ni ome ni kakarimasu.** I will see you within five minutes.

inaka countryside, country; **inaka no** rural, rustic. **Inaka ni sunde imasu.** I live in the country.

inbai prostitution; **imbaifu** prostitute.

inchi inch.

inchiki na fraudulent; sham; feigned.

Indo India; **Indoyoo** Indian Ocean; **Indojin** Indian; Hindu.

ine rice plant.

inemuri nap; **inemuri suru** to nap; to doze.

infure inflation.

infuruenza influenza.

inga cause and effect; misfortune; **inga na** unlucky; **inga to akirameru** to resign oneself to fate.

ingin politeness, courtesy; **ingin na** polite, courteous.

ingoo na stubborn; merciless.

inki gloominess; melancholy; **inki na** cheerless, gloomy, dismal.

INKU = INKI ink.

innen affinity; relation; fate; objection.

INOCHI life; **inochi biroi o suru** to have a narrow escape.

inokoru to remain behind; stay behind.

inoru to pray; **seikoo o inoru** to wish someone every success.

insatsu *(n.)* printing; **insatsubutsu** printed matter; **insatsujo** printing house; press.

inseki relative by marriage.

inshoo impression; **inshoo o ataeru** to impress; to make an impression.

insotsu suru to lead, conduct, command.

intai retirement; **intai suru** to retire; to resign.

interi intelligentsia; intellectuals.

INU dog; **inugoya** kennel.

in'utsu gloom, gloominess; **in'utsu na** gloomy.

inwai obscenity; indecency; **inwai na** obscene, lewd, indecent.

inzei royalty (on a literary work).

ioo sulphur.

ippa religious sect; school; party; faction.

IPPAI cupful, bowlful; full of. **Mizu o ippai kudasai.** May I have a glass of water?

ippaku night's lodging; **ippaku suru** to put up for the night.

IPPAN generality; outline; **ippan no** general; common; **ippan ni** generally.

ippen once.

ippen suru to change completely, to undergo a complete change.

ippon chooshi monotone; **ippon chooshi no** monotonous; simpleminded.

ippondachi independence; **ippondachi de** independently.

ippoo one side; one party; **ippoo ni oite wa** on the one hand.

ippuu kawatta curious; funny; queer.

iradatsu to be irritated; to be excited.

IRAI since; since then.

irai dependence; reliance; request; **irai suru** to rely on; to request; **irai ni oozuru** to comply with a request.

ira ira suru to be irritated; to be fretful.

IRASSHARU to come, go, be at *(respect)*. **Yamada-san wa Tookyoo ni irasshaimasu.** Mr. Yamada is in Tokyo. **Tanaka-san wa Kyooto e irasshaimashita.** Ms. Tanaka went to Kyoto.

ireba artificial tooth.

irechigaeru to misplace, put in the wrong place.

irechigau to come just as someone else leaves; to leave just as someone else comes in. **Yamada-san wa Tanaka-san to irechigai ni dete itta.** Mr. Yamada had just gone out when Ms. Tanaka came in.

irekaeru to replace; to change; to make (tea, coffee) afresh.

irekawaru to change places; **sekio irekawaru** to change seats with someone else; **irekawari tachikawari** in rapid succession, one after another.

iremono receptacle; vessel; case.

IRERU to put in; to let in; to hold; to comply with; to listen to; **hito no setsu o ireru** to take advice; **ocha o ireru** to make tea.

irezumi tattoo.

iri attendance, audience; contents; **ooiri** full house.

iribitaru to be a constant guest; to stay all the time.

irie inlet; creek.

IRIGUCHI entrance; door.

irihi twilight, sunset.

irikomu to enter; to force an entrance.

irikumu to be complicated.

irimidareru to be mixed up; to be in confusion.

iritsukeru to parch; to sizzle.

IRO color, tint, hue; lover *(colloq.)*; **iro age** *(n.)* redying; restoring a color; **iro otoko** lover; **iro onna** mistress; **iroke** coloring; shade; tone; sexual passion; tender passion; **irozuri** color print; **iroke no aru** seductive; amorous; **iroke no nai** unromantic; innocent; **kaoiro** complexion (facial); **iro age suru** to redye; **iro o nasu** to turn red with anger; **irodoru** to color; to paint.

iroha 47-syllable poem containing all of the 47 syllables in the traditional table of Japanese syllabaries. **Iroha mo shiranai.** He doesn't know even the simplest things (not even the ABC's).

IROIRO NA various; many; diverse; (all) kinds of. **Iroiro shitsumon sareta.** I was asked several questions.

iromeku to be alive; to be stirred; to show signs of uneasiness; to become animated.

irori hearth; fireplace.

irotsuya gloss; luster; complexion; **irotsuya no yoi** ruddy; healthy.

irozuku to color; to be tinged; to turn red (as foliage).

IRU to require, want, need. **Watakushi wa kore ga irimasu.** I need this. **Soko e hairu ni wa okane ga irimasu.** You have to pay [money] to enter. **Sore wa iranai deshoo.** It would not be necessary.

IRU to be at, exist *(animate objects);* to be present; to live; to stay. Following a *-te* form verb, it makes a progressive or stative form (describing a state resulting from an action that has taken place). **Sono hito wa heya ni imasu.** He is in the room. **Ame ga futte imasu.** It is raining. **Yamada-san wa kite imasu.** Yamada is here (as a result of having come). **Tookyoo ni imasu.** He is in Tokyo. **Kyooto ni mikka imashita.** I was in Kyoto for three days. **Nihongo o benkyoo shite imasu.** I'm studying Japanese. **Tegami ga kite imasu.** There is [has come and is here] a letter for you.

iru to toast; to parch.

irui clothes, garments.

iryoo medical treatment.

iryuuhin lost article; (thing) left behind.

isagiyoi clean; pure; upright; brave; manly.

isai particulars, details.

isakai quarrel.

isamashii courageous, brave.

isame admonition; advice, counsel.

isamu to be encouraged; to be in high spirits; to take heart.

isan legacy, inheritance; **isan soozokunin** heir, heiress.

isasaka little; bit, slightly; rather. **Isasaka odorokimashita.** I was a bit surprised.

iseebi lobster.

isei other (opposite) sex. **Ano hito wa isei no aida ni koosai ga hiroi desu.** He has a large acquaintance among the opposite sex.

isei power, influence.

iseisha statesman.

iseki ruins, remains, relics.

isetsu different view(s); conflicting opinion.

ISHA doctor, physician; M.D. **isha ni kakaru** to go to a doctor; **isha ni mite morau** to consult a doctor. **Isha ni kakaru to nakanaka kane ga irimasu.** Medical expenses are very high.

isha comfort, consolation; **isharyoo** consolation money.

ishi stone; rock; **ishi dooroo** stone lantern (in front of a shrine); **ishidan** stone steps; **ishigaki** stone wall; **ishiya** stonecutter.

ishi will, intention; **ishi ga tsuyoi** to have a strong will; **ishi ga sotsuu suru** to come to an understanding.

ishiki consciousness; **ishikiteki ni** consciously; **ishiki suru** to be conscious of.

ishin restoration; renovation.

ishin denshin tacit understanding; telepathy.

ishiwata asbestos.

ishizue foundation; basis; groundwork.

isho will, testament.

ishoku food and clothing; means of support; **ishokujuu** food, clothes, and shelter.

ishoku commission; request; charge.

ishoo design; idea.

ishoo clothes, dress, garments.

isobe beach, shore.

isogaseru to hurry up, urge on.

ISOGASHII busy, occupied, engaged. **Shiken de taihen isogashii desu.** I am very busy with my exams.

ISOGI hurry, haste; **isogi no** hasty; urgent, pressing.

ISOGU to hurry, hasten; to be in a hurry. **Isogu hitsuyoo wa arimasen.** There is no rush.

isoiso to cheerfully; lightheartedly.

isooroo hanger-on.

issai all; altogether, every; wholly.

issakuban evening before last.

issakujitsu day before yesterday.

issakunen year before last.

issakuya night before last.

issei ni simultaneously; all at once.

issha senri rush; **issha senri ni** in a rush; in a hurry; at full speed.

isshiki complete set (of).

isshinfuran whole mind; single heart; **isshinfuran ni** wholeheartedly; intently; with undivided attention.

ISSHO together; at the same time; all at once; **ISSHO NI** together with; simultaneously. **Issho ni ikimashoo.** Let's go together.

isshoo laugh; smile; **isshoo shite** with a laugh; with a smile; **isshoo ni fusu** to dismiss with a laugh; to laugh one's troubles away.

isshoo lifetime, all through one's life; **isshoo ho nozomi** life-long desire.

ISSHOOKENMEI as hard as one can; with all one's might (efforts); with one's whole heart. **Isshookenmei benkyoo shite imasu.** He is studying hard.

isshu kind, type, variety.

isshuu one round, lap; **isshuu suru** to go round; to make a tour; **sekai isshuu ryokoo** round-the-world trip.

ISSHUUKAN one week.

isso rather; sooner; preferably.

issoku pair (of shoes or other footgear).

ISSOO much more; all the more.

ISSUN one *sun* (Japanese unit of length, one tenth of a *shaku*); **issun saki mo mienai** pitch dark.

issuru to miss; to lose; **kooki o issuru** to miss a good opportunity.

ISU chair; sofa; couch; **isu ni kakeru** to take a seat.

Isuraeru Israel.

isuwaru to remain in the same position (in office); to remain in power.

ita board; plank; plate; sheet; **itabei** wooden wall; board fence.

itabasami fix; predicament; **itabasami ni naru** to be in a fix.

itachi weasel.

ITADAKU to receive; to be presented with; to be given; to accept with gratitude *(humble)*. **Juubun itadakimashita.** I've had enough, thank you.

itade hard blow; severe wound.

itagane sheet metal.

itagarasu plate glass.

ITAI painful; sore. **Atama ga itai desu.** I have a headache. **Onaka ga itai desu.** I have a stomachache.

itaitashii pathetic, sad, pitiful.

itamashii miserable; touching, sad, pathetic.

itameru to hurt, injure; to worry; **kokoro o itameru** to be worried about (something).

itami pain, ache; sore, bruise.

itami iru to be greatly obliged; to feel grateful. **Doomo itamiirimasu.** I'm much obliged to you.

itamu to ache, feel a pain.

ITARII = ITARIYA Italy.

itaru to arrive, reach; to result in; to come to; **itaru tokoro** everywhere; throughout; **haru kara aki ni itaru made** from spring to autumn.

itasa pain.

itashikata nai it can't be helped; **itashikata naku** necessarily; of necessity.

ITASU to do, make *(humble).* **Soo itashimashoo.** Let's do so. **Doo itashimashite.** Don't mention it.

itatte exceedingly, extremely, very.

itawaru to pity, sympathize with, console.

itazura mischief; prank; **itazura hanbun** for fun; **itazura na** naughty; mischievous; **itazura ni** needlessly; to no purpose.

itchaku first (in a race); one suit of clothes.

itchi agreement; harmony; **itchi suru** to agree with; harmonize.

itchokusen straight line; **itchokusen ni** in a straight line.

itchoo once; one day *(literary usage);* **itchoo isseki ni** in a single day; in a short space of time.

iten transfer, removal; **iten suru** to transfer; to move. **Inaka kara machi e iten shimashita.** We moved from the country to the city.

ITO thread; yarn; twine; string; **momen ito** cotton thread; **kinu ito** silk thread.

itoguchi clue; beginning; **itoguchi o hiraku** to make a start.

itoguruma spinning wheel.

ITOKO cousin.

itoma leisure; time to spare; leave of absence; **yasumu itoma mo nai** to have no time to rest.

itomaki spool, bobbin, reel.

itonamu to carry on; to conduct (business); to run, operate; **seikei o itonamu** to earn a living.

itoosu to shoot through; to pierce.

ITSU when; at what time; how soon; **itsu demo** at any time; at a moment's notice; **itsu kara** how long; since when; **itsu made** how long; till when; **itsu ka** some day; **itsu mo** always.

itsukushimi love; affection; compassion *(literary usage);* **itsukushimu** to love; to treat with tenderness.

itsu ni solely, entirely.

ITSUTSU five.

itsuu one letter.

itsuwa anecdote.

itsuwari lie; **itsuwari no** false, untrue.

itsuwaru to lie, tell a lie.

ittai zentai on earth; in the world. **Ittai zentai dare daroo.** I wonder who in the world it can be.

ittan part; outline; one end.

ittan once, if. **Ittan kankyuu areba . . .** Should an emergency arise . . .

itte hanbai sole agency; monopoly; **itte hanbainin** sole agent; sole distributor.

ittei no fixed, immovable, set; definite; regular.

itten point; dot; spot.

ittenbari persistency; **ittenbari de** sticking to; solely by.

ITTOO first class; **ittoo ni noru** to travel first class; **ittoo no kippu** first-class ticket; **nitoo sha** second-class car. **Ittoo ii mono desu.** It is the best.

IU = YUU to say, speak, tell, relate, mention; **ookiku iu** to exaggerate; **iu made mo naku** of course, naturally. **Iu made mo nai.** It goes without saying.

iwa rock; **iwa no ooi** rocky.

iwaba in a word; so to speak.

iwai celebration; feast; festival.

iwaku reason; **iwaku ga atte** for certain reasons; **iwaku o tsukeru** to find fault with.

iware reason, cause; origin; **iware mo naku** without any cause; **iware no nai** unreasonable; unwarranted.

iwashi sardine.

iwau to congratulate; to celebrate.

IWAYURU so-called; what you call. **Kare wa iwayuru jiyuu shugisha desu.** He is a so-called liberal.

IYA, IIE no.

iyafoon earphone.

iyagaru to dislike, to hate.

iya iya reluctantly; **iya iya nagara** unwillingly; with reluctance.

iyaku medicine; physic.

iyami offensiveness, bad taste, sarcasm; **iyami no aru** offensive, disagreeable.

iya na disagreeable, unpleasant; **iya na kao o suru** to frown.

iyashii low; humble; vulgar.

iyashikumo at all; in the least.

iyashimu to despise, to look down on, to scorn.

iyoiyo still more; all the more; certainly; positively; no doubt.

iza come now; now then; **iza to nareba** at the last moment; when the time comes; at a pinch. **Iza saraba.** Farewell *(archaic).*

izakaya tavern, saloon, bar.

izen ago; before; prior to; formerly. **Tooka izen ni kite kudasai.** Please come before the tenth.

izen as before; as it was.

izon objection; **izon nai** to have no objection; **izon ga aru** to have an objection.

izumi spring; fountain.

IZURE which; someday; sometime; sooner or later; **izure mo** any; all; either; every; both; **izure ni shite mo** in either case; **izure sono uchi ni** one of these days.

J

JA, JAA well; then; in that case. **Ja, sayonara.** Well, so long.

jaanarisuto journalist.

JAGAIMO potato.

jaguchi faucet, tap; spout.

jaken meanness, unkindness; **jaken na** cruel, unkind.

jaketto sweater.

jakkan some; little; number of.

-jaku suffix denoting: little less than, little short of. **Yokohama made wa nijuu mairujaku desu.** It is a little less than twenty miles to Yokohama.

JAMA obstruction, obstacle, hindrance; **jama suru** to obstruct, hinder; **jama ni naru** to stand (be) in the way; **jama o nozoku** to remove an obstacle. **Ojama shimashita.** Excuse me for disturbing you. **Ojama de wa arimasen ka.** I hope I'm not disturbing you.

jamu jam, jelly.

janen vicious mind; evil thought.

jan jan jingle jingle; dingdong; profusely; a lot (slang).

janken Japanese equivalent of toss-up. **Janken de kimemashoo.** Let's toss for it.

jaratsuku to flirt with.

jareru to be playful.

jari gravel; pebbles.

jasui distrust; groundless suspicion; **jasui suru** to distrust; suspect without reason. **jasui bukai** suspicious, distrustful.

jazu jazz.

JI character, letter, ideograph; **ji o kaku** to write. **ji o oboeru** to learn how to read and write (characters); **kanji** Chinese characters (used in Japanese writing system).

ji piles, hemorrhoids.

ji ground, earth, soil; **jimoto** local.

ji- prefix denoting: next; second; vice-; **jikai** next session.

-JI counter denoting: o'clock; hour; time; **ichiji** one o'clock. **Ichiji wa soo omoimashita.** Once I thought that way but now I have a different opinion.

jiban base, foundation.

jibara o kiru to pay out of one's own pocket.

JIBIKI dictionary; lexicon; **jibiki o hiku** to look something up in the dictionary; to use a dictionary.

jiboojiki desperation; despair; **jiboojiki ni naru** to become desperate.

JIBUN oneself; **jibun no** my/his/her/their own, your own, mine/yours/his/hers/theirs; personal; **jibun hitori de** by oneself; **jibun to shite wa** for my part.

jibyoo chronic disease.

jichi self-government.

jichoo self-respect; self-love; caution; **jichooshin** self-respect. **Jichoo shite kudasai.** Take good care of yourself.

jidai time, period, epoch, era; **jidai sakugo** anachronism; **jidaimono** old-fashioned article (furniture, etc.); historical drama; **jidaiokure** one who is old-fashioned; **jidaiokure no** old-fashioned, antiquated.

jidan private settlement; compromise.

jidaraku sloppiness, untidiness; **jidaraku na** sloppy, untidy.

jiden autobiography.

jidoo child; boys and girls; **jidoo no** juvenile.

jidoo automatic action; **jidoo no** automatic; **jidoo hanbaiki** slot machine; **jidoo tobira** automatic door.

JIDOOSHA automobile, car; **jidoosha ni noru** to ride in a car.

jiei self-defense.

jifushin pride; self-confidence.

jigane metal, ore; true character.

jigoku hell.

jigyoo enterprise, undertaking; achievement; deed; work; **jigyookai** the business (industrial) world.

jihaku confession; **jihaku suru** to confess.

jihatsuteki voluntary; spontaneous; **jihatsuteki ni** voluntarily.

jihen emergency; disaster; incident.

jihi mercy; benevolence; pity; **jihi bukai** benevolent; charitable.

jihitsu handwriting; autograph.

jihoo time signal; current news.

jii intention to resign.

jiin Buddhist temple.

jiji current events.

jijii (*colloq.*) grandfather; old man (derogatory).

jijitsu fact; truth; **jijitsujoo** practically, virtually; in reality, actually.

jijitsu time; date.

jijoo circumstances; reasons; state of affairs; **koo iu jijoo da kara** under these circumstances.

jika current price.

jikaku self-consciousness; **jikaku suru** to be conscious, aware of; to realize.

JIKAN time; hour; **jikan ni ma ni au** to be on time; **jikan ni ma ni awanai** to be late. **Mada daibu jikan ga aru.** There is still plenty of time.

jikanhyoo timetable; schedule.

jikani personally; at firsthand; directly.

jikatsu suru to support oneself.

jiken affair; matter; scandal.

jiketsu self-determination; resignation; suicide.

JIKI time; period; season.

jiki- prefix denoting: direct; **jikideshi** one's immediate apprentice.

JIKI NI immediately; at once; presently.

jikken experiment; test.

jikkoo practice; action; execution; **jikkoo suru** to carry out; to put into practice; **jikkoo shigatai** impractical; difficult to put into practice.

jiko self; ego; **jiko chuushin no** egocentric.

jiko accident, incident; **kootsuu jiko** traffic accident.

jikoku time; hour; **jikokuhyoo** transportation schedule.

JIKOO season; weather; current fashion; latest style, vogue; **jikoo hazure no** unseasonable.

jiku phraseology; expressions; wording.

jiku axis; axle; pivot; shaft; stem; stalk.

jikyoku situation, state of affairs; political situation.

jikyuu self-support; independence.

jiman pride, boast; **jiman suru** to boast; to be conceited.

jime jime shita damp; wet; moist; humid.

jimen ground; surface of the earth; plot of land.

jimi na simple; modest; unpretentious; **jimi na hito** unpretentious person; quiet person.

jimu business; duties; **jimuin** clerk; office worker; **jimusho** office; **jimuchoo** chief clerk; head official; purser (of a ship).

-JIN suffix denoting: people; **Nihonjin** Japanese; **Amerikajin** American.

jinan second son.

jinboo popularity; **jinboo aru hito** idol (of the people).

jinbutsu person; personality; portrait.

jinchooge sweet-smelling daphne (common garden plant in Japan).

jindai na extraordinary; enormous, huge,

great. **Songai wa jindai na mono deshita.** The damage was very great.

jindoo sidewalk, pavement; **jindoo o aruku** to walk on the pavement.

jindoo humanity; morality.

jinguu Shinto shrine (a national monument).

jinja Shinto shrine.

jinji fusei unconsciousness; **jinji fusei ni naru** to faint; **jinji fusei no** unconscious.

jinjoo commonness; **jinjoo no** common, ordinary; **jinjoo ni** commonly.

jinkaku personality, character.

jinken artificial silk; rayon.

jinken juurin infringement of personal rights.

JINKOO population, **jinkoo chuumitsu na** thickly populated.

jinkoo artificiality; **jinkoo no** artificial; **jinkoo kokyuu** artificial respiration.

jinmei the name of a person; **jinmeibo** list of names of persons; directory; **jinmeijisho** biographical dictionary.

jinmin people; public.

jinmon inquiry; examination.

jinrin moral law; human relations.

jinrui human race.

jinryoku human power, human strength; effort, endeavor; help; **jinryoku suru** to make an effort; to work on someone's behalf.

jinsei human existence; life.

jinshu (human) race; **jinshuteki henken** racial prejudice.

jinsoku swiftness, rapidity; **jinsoku na** swift, rapid, quick.

jintai human body.

jinushi landlord.

jinzoo artificial, synthetic; **jinzoo gomu** synthetic rubber.

jinzoo kidney.

jippa hitokarage ni in a wholesale way; sweepingly.

jippi actual expenses; cost of production; **jippi de** at cost.

jippu one's natural father.

jirasu to provoke, irritate; to tease.

jirei government order; written order; manner of speaking.

jirenma dilemma.

jireru to be irritated; to fret and fume; to become impatient.

jirettai irritating, provoking; irritated.

JIRIJIRI slowly; gradually; little by little. **Jirijiri tsume yorimashita** He edged up to me.

jiriki de by oneself.

jiritsu independence; self-support; **jiritsu suru** to stand on one's own feet.

jiro jiro miru to stare at.

jiron personal opinion; pet theory.

jirori to with a glance; **jirori to miru** to glance at.

jiryoku magnetism.

jisan *(n.)* bringing; carrying; **jisan suru** to bring; to carry along.

jisatsu suicide (the act); **jisatsusha** suicide (person).

jisei times; mood of the times; **jisei ni okureru** to fall behind the times.

jisei self-control; **jisei suru** to control oneself.

jisetsu season; times; age; **jisetsu hazure no** out of season; **jisetsu toorai** the time has come.

jishaku magnet; compass.

JISHIN earthquake. **Nihon wa jishin ga ooi.** Earthquakes occur frequently in Japan.

JISHO dictionary.

jisho land, plot of ground, estate.

jishoku resignation.

jison self-respect; pride; **jison shin o kizutsukeru** to hurt one's pride.

jishoo self-styled, would-be; **jishoo shijin.** A would-be poet.

jissai truth; reality; **jissai wa** in reality; in fact; **jissai no** actual; practical.

jisshi enforcement; **jisshi suru** to put into effect; to enforce.

jisshi one's natural child.

jisshin hoo decimal system.

jisshitsu substance, essence.

jisuberi landslide.

jisui suru to cook one's meals.

jisuru to decline; to refuse; to resign.

jitai situation; state of affairs.

jitaku house, residence; **jitaku e kaeru** to go home.

jiten, jisho dictionary.

JITENSHA bicycle; **jitensha ni noru** to ride a bicycle.

JITSU truth; reality; **JITSU NI** really; truly; very, exceedingly; in fact; surely; exceedingly; **jitsu no** true; real; **jitsu wa** in reality; to tell the truth.

jitsubo one's natural mother.

jitsubutsu real thing; actual object; **jitsubutsu dai no** life-size.

jitsugen realization; **jitsugen suru** to realize; to materialize.

jitsugyoo business, industry; **jitsugyoo no** commercial, industrial; **jitsugyookai** business world.

jitsujoo actual condition; true state of affairs. **Jitsujoo wa koo desu.** The fact is this.

jitsuyoo utility; practical use; **jitsuyoo ni tekisuru** to be of practical use. **jitsuyoo muki no** serviceable; practical; **jitsuyoohin** necessity; article having practical use.

jitsuzuki adjoining land.

jitto fixedly; firmly; steadily; **jitto mitsumeru** to stare at, look fixedly at; **jitto shite iru** to keep still.

jiyoo nourishment; **jiyoo butsu** nourishing food; **jiyoo aru** nourishing, nutritious.

jiyuu liberty, freedom; **jiyuu booeki** free trade; **jiyuu kyoosoo** open (free) competition; **jiyuu na** free; **jiyuu ni suru** to do as one pleases. **Gojiyuu ni.** Help yourself.

jizen philanthropic work; **jizen ka** philanthropist; **jizen jigyoo** philanthropic work.

jobun preface, foreword, introduction.

jochoo promotion; advancement; **jochoo suru** to promote, foster, encourage.

jodooshi auxiliary verb; inflected particle, i.e., *-(r)areru* (passive) and *-(s)aseru* (causative).

jogai exception; **jogai suru** to make an exception of; to exclude; to exempt from.

jogen advice, counsel; suggestion, hint; **jogen suru** to give advice; to suggest.

joi female doctor.

jojo ni slowly; gradually.

jojooshi lyrical poem, ballad.

jojutsu description; **jojutsu no** descriptive; **jojutsu suru** to describe; to narrate; **jojutsubun** description.

jokoo slow pace; **jokoo suru** to go slowly. **jokoo.** Go slow. Drive slowly.

joo feeling, emotion, sentiment; affection, love; sympathy; **joo ga fukai** affectionate; warmhearted; **joo ga nai** cold, heartless; **joo ni moroi** emotional, sentimental.

joo lock; **joo o kakeru** to lock; **joo o hazusu** to unlock.

-joo article; **Dai Kyuujoo** Article IX.

-joo floor mat (Japanese rooms are measured by the number of **joo** mats they contain); **juujoo no ma** 10-mat room.

-joo suffix denoting: letter; **shookaijoo** letter of introduction; **annaijoo** (letter of) invitation; **shookanjoo** warrant.

jooai affection, love; **jooai no fukai** loving, affectionate.

jooba horseback riding.

JOOBU good health; soundness of body; **joobu na** durable; robust, strong; **joobu soo na** strong-looking, healthy-looking; **joobu ni naru** to grow strong.

joobu top, upper part, upper surface.

joocho mood; atmosphere.

joodan joke, prank; fun; **joodan o iu** to joke; **joodan o suru** to take as a joke.

joodeki good performance; success; good work; **joodeki no** well-done; excellent. **Joodeki!** Well done! Bravo!

jooen suru to put on, perform (a play); to put on the stage.

jooge top and bottom, upper and lower.

joogi ruler; square; standard; norm.

joogo drinker, sake-lover.

joogo funnel.

joohatsu evaporation; **joohatsu suru** to evaporate.

joohin elegance; refinement; **joohin na** refined; elegant; graceful.

jooho concession, compromise.

joohoo report; information.

joojiru = **joozuru** to multiply; to take advantage of.

joojitsu personal feelings (considerations).

jooju accomplishment, achievement; **jooju suru** to achieve, realize, accomplish.

JOOJUN first ten days of the month; **Ichigatsu joojun** early in January.

jooken condition, term; **jooken zuki** conditional; qualified.

jooki regular (normal) course; **jooki o issuru** to deviate, depart from the normal course.

jooki steam, vapor; **jooki kikan** steam engine.

jookigen good humor; **jookigen de** in a good humor.

jookyaku passenger.

jookyoo state of affairs; conditions.

joomae lock.

joomuin crew.

joomu torishimari managing director.

joomyaku vein.

joonetsu passion.

joooo queen.

jooriku suru to disembark, go ashore; **jooriku chiten** point of embarkation.

jooro watering can.

jooruri Japanese ballad-drama.

jooryokuju evergreen (tree or shrub).

joosei state of affairs; **genka no joosei de wa** under the present circumstances.

joosha (n.) taking a train, bus, etc.; **joosha suru** to take a train; to board a train; **jooshachin** carfare, train fare; **jooshaken** ticket (for a train, streetcar, or bus).

jooshiki common sense; **jooshiki o kaku** to lack common sense; **jooshikiteki na** sensible; practical.

jooshubi success; happy result; **jooshubi no** successful. **Jooshubi da.** It's all right.

joosoo upper layer; upper stories (of a building); (top) social class.

jootai condition, state; circumstances; **mokka no jootai de wa** as matters now stand.

jootatsu suru to improve; advance; progress.

jootenki fine (splendid) weather.

JOOTOO (n.) best; first class; **jootoo hin** first-class article; **jootoo no** (adj.) best, superior.

jootoogo hackneyed expression, trite saying.

jooyaku treaty, pact, agreement.

jooyoku lust.

jooyoo kanji ideographic characters included in the Japanese Government's 1945 list of basic symbols for writing.

joozai tablet (medicinal).

JOOZU skill, dexterity, proficiency; **JOOZU NA** skillful, expert, proficient. **Joozu desu.** He is skillful. **Ano hito wa hanashi ga joozu desu.** He/she is a good speaker.

joozuru See **joojiru.**

joryoku aid, assistance; **joryoku suru** to aid, help.

joryuu sakka female author.

josainai shrewd, clever, smart.

josanpu midwife.

josei womanhood, femininity; **joseiteki** feminine.

josei aid, assistance; **josei suru** to aid, to assist (financially); to subsidize; **joseikin** subsidy.

joshi particle (grammar) e.g., **wa, ga, o,** etc. (used in postposition).

joshi woman; girl; daughter; female.

JOYA New Year's Eve.

joyaku assistant official.

joyuu actress.

jugaku = **jukyoo** Confucianism.

JUGYOO teaching, instruction; **jugyoo o suru** to teach; **jugyoo o ukeru** to take lessons.

jukkoo reflection; careful consideration; **jukkoo suru** to consider carefully; to reflect; to deliberate. **Sono mondai wa jukkoo chuu desu.** That matter is receiving careful consideration.

jukuchi suru to have full knowledge of; to be familiar with. **Watakushi wa sono koto o jukuchi shite imasu.** I'm fully aware of that.

jukuren skill, dexterity; **jukuren suru** to become skilled; **jukuren o kaku** to lack skill.

jukusui suru to sleep soundly.

juku suru to ripen, mature, become ripe.

jukyoo See **jugaku.**

jumoku trees. **Sono kooen ni wa jumoku ga ooi desu.** There are many trees in that park.

jumyoo life; life span.

jun pureness, purity; **jun na** pure; genuine; innocent; **junkin** pure gold.

jun, junban regular order; turn; **jun ni, junban ni** in regular order; in turn; **jun ni naraberu** to arrange in order. **Junban o matte kudasai.** Please wait your turn.

junbi preparation, arrangements; **junbi suru** to prepare, arrange; to get ready for; **junbi ga dekite iru** to be prepared.

junchoo favorable, satisfactory condition; **junchoo ni** smoothly; favorably, without a hitch; **junchoo ni iku** to go well; **junchoo ni mukau** to improve.

jun'eki net profit. **jun'eki o eru** to earn a net profit, to clear.

junjo order, sequence; **junjo tadashiku** in good order.

junkan suru to circulate; recur.

junkesshoo semifinals.

junketsu purity; cleanliness; **junketsu na** pure, chaste; clean.

junrei pilgrim; pilgrimage.

junsa policeman; **junsa hashutsujo** police box; **junsa buchoo** police sergeant. **Keisatsusho de junsa ni hanashimashita.** I told it to a policeman at the police station.

junshi inspection tour; **junshi suru** to make the rounds.

junshin pureness; genuineness; **junshin na** pure; unsophisticated.

junsui purity, genuineness. **Kore wa junsui no Nihon no kinu desu.** This is genuine Japanese silk.

juntoo natural; regular; appropriate; normal. **Juntoo ni ikeba tooka ni dekimasu.** If all goes well, it will be done on the tenth.

jushin suru to receive a letter or message.

jutai suru to conceive, become pregnant.

jutsu art; technique; means; way; trick.

JUU ten, tenth; **juu ga juu made** in every case.

-JUU suffix denoting: all through the course of; during; all over; throughout. **Tookyoojuu** throughout Tokyo. **Uchijuu de dekakemasu.** The entire family goes out together.

juubako pile (nest) of lacquered boxes used as picnic boxes or as containers for foods at festivals.

juuban undergarment worn with Japanese clothing.

JUUBUN plenty; enough; **juubun na** full; sufficient; enough; **juubun ni taberu** to eat enough.

juubyoo serious illness.

juudai importance; seriousness; **juudai na** important; **juudaishi suru** to take seriously.

JUUGATSU October.

JUUGO fifteen; **juugoya no tsuki** harvest moon.

JUUHACHI eighteen; **juuhachiban** one's forte; hobby; favorite trick.

JUUICHI eleven.

JUUICHIGATSU November.

juuji *(n.)* cross; **juuji ni** crosswise; **juuji no** cross-shaped; **juujigun** crusade.

juujika (See also **juuji.**) **juujika zoo** crucifix.

juuji suru to engage in, practice, pursue.

juujitsu perfection; enrichment; fullness.

juujun gentleness; obedience; **juujun na** gentle, meek; obedient.

juuketsu congestion (medical). **Me ga juuketsu shite imasu.** His eyes are bloodshot.

JUUKU nineteen; **dai juuku** nineteenth.

juukyo dwelling, residence; **juukyonin** resident.

juuman suru to be filled with; to be replete with.

juumin residents, inhabitants.

juumonji cross; **juumonji ni** crosswise. (See also **juuji.**)

juunen decade.

JUUNI twelve, dozen; **juunibun ni** more than enough.

JUUNIGATSU December.

juunin ten persons; **juunin nami no** ordinary, average, normal; mediocre.

juurai heretofore; so far; up to now; **juurai no** old, traditional; **juurai no toori** as in the past.

JUUROKU sixteen.

juurui beast, animals.

juuryoo weight; **juuryoo busoku** short weight.

juuryoo hunting (with a gun); **juuryooka** sportsman.

JUUSAN thirteen.

JUUSHI fourteen.

JUUSHICHI seventeen.

juushimatsu lovebird.

juushoku high office; responsible position.

JUUSHO dwelling, residence; address; **juusho seimei** name and address. **Gojuusho wa dochira desu ka?** What's your address?

juushoo serious wound, injury.

juusoo bicarbonate of soda.

JUUSU juice; **orenji juusu** orange juice.

juutai critical stage; serious condition.

juutaku house, residence; **juutakuchi** residential section.

juuyaku director; board of directors.

juuyoo importance; **juuyoo na** important; **juuyoo de nai** unimportant.

juuzai felony; capital offense.

juuzei heavy taxation; heavy tax.

juwaki telephone receiver.

juyo suru to award (a prize); to confer (a degree).

juyoo demand; **juyoo ga aru** to be in demand; **juyoo o mitasu** to meet the demand.

juzu rosary (mainly Buddhist).

K

kabu turnip.

kabu stock, share; **kabunushi** shareholder.

kabuki classic Japanese play.

kabun superfluous; **kabun no** excessive; undue.

kabureru to be poisoned; to be influenced.

KABURU to put on or over one's head; to be covered with; to take upon oneself; **booshi o kaburu** to put on a hat.

kabusaru to get covered; to overlap.

kabuseru to cover with; to put a thing on.

kabuto helmet; **kabuto o nugu** to admit defeat; to throw in the sponge; **kabuto mushi** beetle.

kachi victory, conquest; success.

kachi value, worth, merit; **kachi ga aru** valuable.

kachiau to clash with; to knock against; to collide with.

kachiki na unyielding; strong-minded; resolute.

kachiku domestic animals; livestock.

kadai *(n.)* being too big; **kadai no** too big; exaggerated; too much; too heavy.

kadai subject; theme.

kadan garden; flower bed.

KADO corner; turn; angle; edge; **kado no mise** corner store. **Soo iu to kado ga tatsu.** That sounds harsh.

kado excess, immoderateness.

kado charge; suspicion; grounded; **-no kado de** on the grounds of, on account of, for the reason that.

kadode departure; **kadode suru** to set out; to leave home.

kaede maple tree.

kaerigake ni on the way back; upon one's return.

kaeri michi return road; way home.

kaerimiru to look back; to reflect upon; to think of.

KAERU to return, come back; to go back. **Okaeri nasai.** Welcome back!

KAERU to change, alter; to exchange; to replace; to convert; **setsu o kaeru** to change one's opinion; **michi o kaeru** to take another road; **kane o kaeru** to change money.

kaeru to be hatched.

kaeru frog.

KAESU to give back, restore, return; to pay back; **okane o kaesu** to repay money.

kaesu to hatch (eggs).

KAETTE on the contrary; instead; on the other hand; all the more.

kafun pollen.

kafusu cuff(s).

kafuu family customs (tradition).

kagaisha assailant.

kagaku science; **kagaku no** scientific; **kagakusha** scientist.

kagaku chemistry; **kagakusha** chemist; **kagaku koogyoo** chemical industry.

kagameru to bend; to bow; **koshi o kagameru** to stoop, bend down.

KAGAMI mirror; **kagami o miru** to look in a mirror.

kagamu to bend, bow; to crouch.

kagaribi campfire; bonfire.

kagayakasu to light up; to make shine; to brighten.

kagayaki luster; brilliance; glitter.

kagayaku to shine, glitter, sparkle, glisten.

kage shadow; silhouette; image; reflection, shade; **kage ni naru** to be shaded; **kage ni** in the shade; **kage ga sasu** to cast a shadow.

kageguchi malicious gossip; **kageguchi o iu** to gossip maliciously.

kagehinata two-faced; faithless; **kagehinata no nai** faithful; conscientious.

kageki opera; operetta; **kageki dan** opera company; **kagekijoo** opera house.

kageki excessive; extreme; violent; radical; **kagekiha** radicals (political); **kageki shisoo** radical ideas; dangerous thoughts. **Kageki na undoo o shite wa ikemasen.** You must not engage in strenuous physical exercise.

kagemusha man who pulls strings or exerts influence behind the scenes.

kagen degree, proportion, extent.

kageroo fly living only one day; **kageroo no yoo na** short-lived, ephemeral.

kageru to become shady; to get dark; to darken.

-KAGETSU counter denoting: (one) month's duration; **ikkagetsu** one month; **nikagetsu** two months; **sankagetsu** three months.

KAGI key; **kagi ana** keyhole; **kagi de akeru** to unlock; **kagi o kakeru** to lock.

kagi hook.

kagiri limit, bounds; **kagiri no aru** limited, restricted. **Watakushi no shiru kagiri.** As far as I know.

kagiru to limit, restrict.

kago basket; cage; sedan chair; **kago ni noru** to ride in a sedan chair.

kagoo suru to combine.

KAGU furniture, furnishings; **kaguya** furniture store.

kagu to smell; to scent; to sniff; **kagitsukeru** to get wind of.

kagura sacred music and dancing in front of a shrine (Shinto).

kahei money; currency.

kahi right or wrong; good or bad; propriety. **Sono kahi wa toohyoo de kimemashoo.** Let's decide the matter by vote.

kahoo ancestral treasure; heirloom.

kahoo luck; good fortune; **kahoo na** lucky.

kai avail, effect, use; **kai ga nai** of no effect; **kai naku** without avail; **kai no nai** useless; fruitless.

kai meeting, assembly; association; society; (society) member; **kai hi** membership fee; subscription; admission fee.

kai time, cycle; **nikai** two times, twice.

kai oar, paddle; **kai de kogu** to row.

kai shellfish.

-kai suffix denoting: stairs; story (of a building); **ikkai** first floor; **nikai-date** two-story house.

-kai suffix denoting: sea, **Nihonkai** Japan Sea.

kaiageru to purchase, buy; to requisition.

kaibatsu above sea level.

kaiboo autopsy; dissection; analysis.

kaibutsu monster.

kaichiku rebuilding, reconstruction.

kaichuu pocket; **kaichuu mono** purse; **kaichuudokei** pocket watch.

kaidaku willing consent; **kaidaku suru** to give ready consent; to consent readily.

KAIDAN stairway, staircase; flight of steps. **Heya wa kaidan o agatte hidari no hoo desu.** My room is to the left of the stairway.

kaidashi marketing, shopping; daily needs.

kaidasu to drain off; to ladle; to scoop out.

kaifuku recovery; restoration; re-establishment; **kaifuku suru** to recover; restore.

kaifuu suru to open a letter; break a seal.

kaiga pictures; painting(s); **kaiga tenrankai** art exhibition.

kaigai (n.) abroad; foreign country; **kaigai kara** from abroad; **kaigai ni iku** to go abroad.

kaigaishii prompt; brisk; faithful; **kaigaishiku** promptly; briskly; willingly.

kaigan seashore, coast; **kaigansen** coastline.

kaigi council; conference; convention.

kaigoo meeting, assembly.

kaigun navy; **kaigun no** naval.

kaigyoo suru to open a shop; to open a business.

kaihan revised edition.

kaihatsu suru to develop; to exploit; to cultivate; to open up.

kaihen seashore, seaside, beach.

kaihi suru to avoid, shun, evade.

kaihoo liberation, release; **kaihoo suru** to set free.

kaihoo good news.

kaihoo opening; **kaihoo suru** to open to the public.

kaihoo suru to nurse (tend) a sick person.

kaihyoo suru to count votes.

kaiin shiki opening ceremony of the Diet (Japanese Parliament).

kaijin ashes; **kaijin ni kisuru** to be reduced to ashes.

kaijo cancellation; release, discharge; **kaijo suru** to cancel, rescind, etc.

kaijoo sea; **kaijoo no** marine, maritime.

kaijoo circular (letter); **kaijoo o mawasu** to send out a circular.

kaijoo ni upstairs; **kaijoo e iku** to go upstairs.

kaikaburu to pay too much; to overestimate; overrate.

kaikaku reformation; reorganization; **kaikaku suru** to reform; reorganize; innovate.

kaikan hall; assembly hall.

kaikata buyer.

kaikatsu cheerfulness; **kaikatsu na** cheerful, gay; jovial.

kaikei accounts; **kaikeibo** account book; **kaikei gakari** accountant; cashier; **kaikei hookoku** financial report.

kaiken interview, audience; **kaiken o mooshikomu** to ask for an interview; **kaiken suru** to interview.

kaiketsu settlement; solution; **kaiketsu suru** to settle; to solve; to fix up; **kaiketsu ga tsuku** to come to a settlement; to arrive at a solution.

kaiko retrospection; reflection; review; **kaiko suru** to look back; to reflect.

kaiko discharge; dismissal; **kaiko suru** to discharge, dismiss.

kaiko silkworm.

kaikomu to hold (carry) under one's arm.

kaikon development; clearing.

kaikoojoo open port.

kaikyoo strait; sound.

kaikyuu class; rank; order; grade.

kaimen surface of the sea.

kaimetsu destruction, ruin.

kaimodosu to buy back, repurchase.

kaimoku entirely, utterly, altogether (used with a negative). **Kaimoku wakarimasen.** I don't understand it at all.

KAIMONO shopping; marketing; purchase; **kaimono o suru** to buy, shop; **kaimono ni iku** to go shopping.

kaimu (n.) having nothing; having none at all;

nil. **Okane wa kaimu desu.** I have no money at all.

kain Lower House of the Diet.

kainarasu to tame, domesticate.

kainushi owner of an animal; keeper; master.

kainushi buyer; purchaser. **Watakushi no ie no kainushi ga mitsukarimashita.** We found a buyer for our house.

kairi nautical mile.

kairiki superhuman strength.

kairo sea route; **kairo o iku** to go by sea.

kairo circuit.

kairoo corridor; passageway; gallery.

kairyoo improvement; reform; **kairyoo suru** to reform; to improve.

kairyuu tide; tidal current; trend.

kaisaku adaptation.

kaisan dispersion; liquidation; breakup; **kaisan suru** to break up; to dissolve; to liquidate.

kaisanbutsu marine products.

kaisangyoo marine products industry (processing and selling fish, lobsters, shellfish, and edible seaweeds).

kaisatsuguchi ticket gate.

kaisei fine weather; clear sky.

kaisetsu explanation; interpretation; **kaisetsu suru** to explain; to interpret; to comment on.

KAISHA company; corporation; firm; **kaishain** employee of a business firm; businessperson. **Ano kaisha ni tsutomete imasu.** I am working for that firm.

kaishaku interpretation; construction; explanation.

kaishimeru to buy up; to corner (the market).

kaishi suru to begin.

kaishoo dissolution; extinction; cancellation.

kaishuu withdrawal; collection; **kaishuu suru** to withdraw; to call in.

kaisoku regulations, rules of an organization.

kaisoo shipping; forwarding; **kaisoo suru** to forward; to transport; **kaisoogyoosha** shipping agency.

kaisoo seaweed.

kaisoo recollection, reminiscence; **kaisoo suru** to recollect, to reminisce.

kaisui seawater; salt water; **kaisuiyokujoo** seaside resort; beach; **kaisuiyoku o suru** to go bathing in the sea.

kaisuu frequency; **kaisuu o kasaneru** to repeat many times.

kaitai dissection; dismemberment.

kaite buyer, purchaser.

kaiten revolution, rotation; **kaiten suru** to revolve, rotate; **kaitengi** gyroscope.

kaitoo solution; reply; answer; **kaitoo suru** to solve; to reply, answer.

kaitoo president (of an organization).

kaitsumande to make a long story short; in a word. **Kaitsumande ohanashi shimashoo.** I will tell you briefly.

kaiungyoo marine shipping. (See also **kaisoo.**)

KAIWA conversation.

kaiwai neighborhood; **kaiwai ni** in the neighborhood.

kaizoku pirate.

KAJI fire. **Watakushi wa kyonen kaji ni aimashita.** I experienced a fire last year.

kajikamu to be numb with cold; to be numbed.

kajiritsuku to hold on to; to clutch.

kajiru to gnaw; to nibble; to bite; to get a smattering of.

kajitsu fruit; berry; nut.

kajoo article, item; clause; **kajoo o ageru** to itemize.

kajoo excess, surplus.

kajuu overweight.

kakae embrace; employ.

kakaeru to hold under one's arms, to embrace; to employ, to hire.

kakageru to hold up; to raise, hoist.

KAKAKU price; value; **kakaku o tsukeru** to set a price; to fix the value of.

KAKARI charge(s); duty; **kakariin** official in charge.

kakariai implication; involvement; **kakariai ni naru** to be involved in.

KAKARU to hang; to stand; to rest (against); to set about; to be dependent on; to concern; to catch; to be caught; to begin, start; to take; to need; to cost; **byooki ni kakaru** to become ill; **isha ni kakaru** to consult a doctor. **Soko e iku no ni ichijikan kakarimasu.** It takes an hour to get there. **Ikura kakarimasu ka?** How much does it cost? **Kono uchi ni wa okane ga kakatte iru.** This house cost a lot of money.

kakasazu regularly, consistently; without missing; constantly.

kakashi scarecrow.

KAKATO heel.

KAKAWARAZU in spite of, despite; no matter (how, what); regardless of; **ame ni mo kakawarazu** in spite of the rain.

kakawaru to take part, participate in; to concern; to affect; to be at stake.

kake betting; **kakegoto** gambling; **kake o suru** to make a bet, wager.

kakeai negotiation; consultation; **kakeai o suru** to negotiate (with).

kakeau to negotiate; to bargain with.

kakeashi run; double time; gallop; **kakeashi de** on the double; at a run; **kakeashi ni naru** to break into a run; to gallop.

kakebuton quilt; bed-coverlet.

kakedasu to start running; to run out.

kakegae substitute; spare; **kakegae no nai** irreplaceable (most precious) thing.

kakegoe yell, shout; **kakegoe o kakeru** to yell, shout.

kakehi waterpipe, drainpipe.

kakehiki bargaining; tactics; tact, diplomacy; **kakehiki o suru** to bargain (with a person).

kakei lineage, genealogy.

kakekin installment; premium; **kakekin o suru** to pay in installments.

kakekko race; **kakekko o suru** to run a race.

kakemochi part-time job; working at two or more jobs at one time.

kakemono hanging picture-scroll.

kakene overcharge; high price; **kakene o iu** to overcharge.

kakeochi elopement.

KAKERU to sit, take a seat; to spend; to invest; to gallop; to run; to hang; to suspend; to cover; to spread on; to put on; to pour on; **isu ni kakeru** to sit on a chair; **kane o kakeru** to spend money; **koshi o kakeru** to sit down; **kugi ni kakeru** to hang (something) on a peg; **megane o kakeru** to wear glasses.

kakeru run, gallop.

-kakeru to begin to; **yomikakeru** to begin to read.

kakeru to be broken; to be cracked; to be short of.

kaketsu approval; adoption; passage; **kaketsu suru** to pass, be approved.

kakezu map, chart.

kaki oyster; **kaki furai** fried oysters.

kakiarawasu to put in writing.

kakiatsumeru to collect; to rake together; to gather up.

kakiawaseru to adjust, arrange.

kakiire entry; notes; insertion; **kakiireru** to insert; to write in.

kakikae rewriting; transfer; **kakikaeru** to rewrite; to transfer.

kakimawasu to stir (coffee, etc.); to beat; to rummage; to ransack.

kakimidasu to confuse, throw into confusion; to disturb.

kakimono written document; writing.

kakimushiru to tear; to scratch off.

kakine hedge.

kakinokeru to push aside.

kakinuki extract; abstract.

kakioki will; posthumous letter.

kakiorosu to write down.

kakiotosu to scrape off.

kakisoeru to add a postscript.

kakitateru to play up; to write up; to make a big story of.

kakitome = **kakitome yuubin** registered mail. **Kono tegami o kakitome ni shite kudasai.** Please register this letter.

kakitomeru to make notes of; to make a memo.

kakitome yuubin See **kakitome.**

kakitoru to dictate.

kakitsuke document; bill.

kakiwakeru to push (elbow) aside, to force oneself through.

kakka Your (His) Excellency.

kakke beriberi.

kakki animation; spirit; **kakki no aru** animated; **kakki no nai** lifeless; dull.

kakko parentheses, brackets.

kakkoo shape, form; appearance; style; **kakkoo na** suitable; moderate; **kakkoo no yoi** well-formed; stylish.

kako *(n.)* past; bygone days; previous existence; **kako ni oite** in the past.

kakoi enclosure; fence; **kakoi o suru** to enclose; to fence in.

kakomi siege.

kakomu to surround; to enclose; to close in on.

kakotsuke pretense, pretext.

kakotsukeru to make a pretense of; **kakotsukete** under the pretext (pretense) of.

kakou to keep; to store; to preserve.

KAKU to write; to draw; to paint; **tegami o kaku** to write a letter; **e o kaku** to draw (paint) a picture.

kaku to rake, to scratch; **yuki o kaku** to clear away snow.

kaku each, every.

kaku angle; **chokkaku** right angle.

kaku nucleus; **kaku sensoo** nuclear war.

KAKUBETSU especially, particularly. **kakubetsu no** particular, special.

kakuchoo suru to extend, expand, enlarge.

kakudai suru to magnify; **kakudai kyoo** magnifying glass.

kakugen maxim, saying.

kakugetsu every other month.

kakugo preparedness; resolution; resignation; **kakugo suru** to be prepared; to be resolved.

kakuhoo authentic news, definite report.

kakuhoomen in every direction; in all directions.

kakujitsu reliability; authenticity; certainty; **kakujitsu na** reliable; sure; authentic; **kakujitsu ni** certainly.

kakujitsu every other day.

kakumau to shelter; to protect.

kakumei revolution; **kakumeiteki** revolutionary.

kakunin confirmation; **kakunin suru** to confirm, affirm.

kakunooko airplane hangar.

kakuran disturbance.

kakurega hiding place; den.

KAKURERU to hide oneself; to take shelter; to disappear. **Tsuki ga kumo ni kakureta.** The moon disappeared in the cloud.

kakuri isolation; **kakurishitsu** isolation ward.

kakuritsu suru to establish; to fix; to settle.

kakusaku plan, scheme; project; **kakusaku suru** to plan, scheme.

kakusei disillusionment; **kakusei suru** to awake; be awakened; to be disillusioned.

kakuseiki loudspeaker.

kakushidate concealment; **kakushidate o suru** to conceal a fact.

kakushiki social status.

kakushin reform, renovation; **kakushin suru** to believe strongly, to be confident of.

kakusho every place; various places; **kakusho ni** everywhere; in several places.

kakushoo conclusive evidence; proof.

KAKUSHU every kind; **kakushu no** of every kind.

KAKUSU to hide, conceal.

kakutei decision; settlement; **kakutei suru** to decide; to settle.

KAKUTERU cocktail.

kakutoku acquisition; possession; **kakutoku suru** to acquire, obtain, secure.

kakutoo suru to give a definite answer.

kakuu no imaginary; fanciful.

KAKUYASU NA cheap; **kakuyasu ni** cheaply; at a moderate price.

kakuzatoo lump (cube) sugar.

kakuzuke classification, grading; **kakuzuke suru** to classify, grade.

kakyoku melody, tune.

kakyuu no petty; low-grade; low-class; inferior; subordinate.

kakyuu no pressing, urgent; imminent.

kama kettle; iron pot; kiln.

kama scythe.

kamae structure; appearance.

kamaeru to build, construct; to set up house; to take an attitude.

KAMAU to care, mind, be concerned about; to trouble oneself about; to give attention to; **kamawazu** regardless of. **Kamawanaide kudasai.** Please don't trouble yourself on my account. Don't bother me.

kame turtle.

kame jar; jug; vase; urn.

kamei family name; family honor.

kamei alliance, affiliation.

kamen mask; disguise.

KAMERA camera.

KAMI paper; **kami byooshi** paper cover; **kami kuzu** wastepaper; scraps of paper;

kamibasami paper clip; **kamiyasuri** sandpaper.

kami god, deity; **kami dana** family shrine (a shelf in a Japanese house for Shinto tablets).

kami hair; **kami o toku** to comb one's hair.

KAMINARI thunder. **Kaminari ga natte imasu.** It is thundering.

KAMISORI razor; **kamisori o ateru** to shave.

kamite upstage (in a theater).

KAMOKU course, subject, lesson.

kamosu to stir up, arouse.

kamotsu freight, cargo; merchandise; **kamotsusen** freighter (ship).

KAMU = **kami-** to chew; to bite; to gnaw. **Kande fukumeru yoo ni setsumei shimashita.** He explained it, taking great pains to make it clear.

kamufuraaju camouflage, disguise.

kan perception; feeling, sentiment, emotion; **kan kiwamaru** to be filled with emotion; to be deeply moved.

kan tin can; **kanzume** canned goods.

kan temper; irritability; **kan o okosu** to become impatient; **kan ga tsuyoi** to be hot-tempered; **kan o osaeru** to control one's temper.

-kan counter for volume; reel (motion picture); **dai ikkan** the first volume.

-kan suffix denoting: duration or space between; **isshuukan** one week; **Tookyoo Oosaka kan** between Tokyo and Osaka; **ikkagetsukan** during one month.

kana Japanese syllabary.

kanaboo crowbar; metal rod; horizontal bar.

kanadarai metal basin; washbowl.

kanaeru to grant; to comply with; **negai o kanaeru** to grant one's wishes; to answer one's prayers.

kanagu metal ornaments or fittings.

KANAI family; household; wife; **kanaijuu** the whole family.

kanakirigoe shrill, voice; **kanakirigoe o dasu** to scream.

kanamono hardware; ironware; **kanamonoya** hardware store or dealer.

KANARAZU certainly; no doubt, by all means; without fail; invariably. **Kanarazu kite kudasai.** Please be sure to come. Please come without fail.

KANARI fairly; pretty; considerably; **kanari no** considerable; **kanari yoi** fairly well.

kanariya canary.

KANASHII sad, sorrowful.

kanashimi sorrow, grief.

kanashimu to lament; to mourn; to regret.

kanau to suit; to be suitable; to conform to; to accomplish; to agree with. **Mokuteki ni kanau.** It answers the purpose.

kanazuchi iron hammer.

kanban signboard, billboard.

kanbashii sweet; fragrant.

kanbashitta shrill, piercing; sharp.

kanbatsu drought.

kanben na handy; convenient; **kanben ni** simply; easily.

kanben suru to pardon, forgive. **Kanben shite kudasai.** Please excuse me.

kanbi completion; perfection.

kanboo cold; flu.

kanbotsu suru to sink, subside; to cave in.

kanbu staff; management.

kanbutsuya grocery specializing in dried vegetables and fruits.

kanbyoo = kango *(n.)* nursing; **kanbyoonin** nurse.

kanchoo spy.

kanchoo government office.

kandai generosity; leniency; tolerance; **kandai na** generous; lenient; tolerant.

kandankei thermometer.

kandan nai continual, incessant, endless; **kandan naku** continually.

kandoo emotion; impression; excitement; **kandoo suru** to be moved, be affected; to disown; **kandoo saseru** to move; to impress; to inspire; to appeal to.

kandoo disinheritance; **kandoo suru** to disinherit.

KANE, OKANE money; **kane ga nai** to have no money; **kaneire** money box; purse; **kanekashi** moneylender; **kanemochi** rich person; **kanezukai** manner of spending money; **kane banare no yoi** generous with money; **kane ga kakaru** to be costly; **kanekashi suru** to lend money; **ooganemochi** very rich man; **kanezukai no arai hito** a free spender.

kane bell; **kanetsukidoo** bell tower.

kanegane previously; beforehand.

kanete already; previously; lately; some time ago.

kangae thought, idea, opinion.

kangaechigai misunderstanding; mistake; mistaken ideal; **kangaechigai suru** to misunderstand.

KANGAERU to think, consider, deliberate, believe, be of the opinion; **kangae bukai** thoughtful; **kangaenaosu** to reconsider. **Sore wa kangaeru no mo iya desu.** I dislike the very thought of it.

kangei welcome; reception; **kangei suru** to welcome; **kangei o ukeru** to be received warmly.

kangeki *(n.)* theatergoing; **kangeki ni dekakeru** to go to the theater; **kangekikai** theater party.

kangeki emotion; excitement; inspiration. **Sono hanashi o kiite kangeki shimashita.** I was very much moved when I heard the story.

kango See **kanbyoo**; **kangofu** nurse.

kani crab.

kan'i simplicity; **kan'i na** simple; **kan'i ni** simply.

kan'in adultery.

kanja *(n.)* patient.

KANJI sense, feeling; **kanji no nibui** insensitive; **kanjiyasui** sensitive; sentimental.

KANJI Chinese character (ideograph) used in Japanese writing system.

kanji manager; staff secretary; executive committee.

kanjin na important; essential, vital.

KANJIRU = KANZURU to feel; **atsusa o kanjiru** to feel the heat; **konnan o kanjiru** to find difficulty.

KANJOO calculation, counting; **kanjoo ni ireru** to take into account; **kanjoogaki** check, bill. **Hayaku kanjoo shite kudasai.** Please count it quickly. **Kanjoo o machigaeta.** I miscalculated.

kanjoo feeling, sentiment, passion; **kanjooteki** emotional.

kanjusei susceptibility; receptivity.

kanka influence.

kankaku space, distance, interval.

kankaku sensation, sense.

kankei relation, connection; concern, interest; relationship; **-to kankei ga aru** to have a relation to, be connected with.

KANKOKU South Korea.

kankoo sight-seeing; **kankoo kyaku** sightseer; **kankoo ni iku** to go sight-seeing; **kankoodan** tourist party.

kankoo publication; **kankoo suru** to publish; **teiki kankoobutsu** periodical.

kankyoo environment, surroundings.

kankyuu emergency.

kankyuu suru to be moved to tears.

kanmei deep impression; **kanmei suru** to impress deeply; to be deeply impressed; to be deeply moved.

kanmei terseness; **kanmei na** terse, concise, simple and brief.

kanmuri crown.

kannen idea, sense, concept, notion.

kannin patience; forgiveness.

kannuki bolt, bar (of a gate or door); **kannuki o kakeru** to bolt; **kannuki o hazusu** to unbolt.

kanoo suppuration; infection; **kanoo suru** to be infected.

kanoo possibility; **kanoo na** possible.

kanpai toast; **kanpai suru** to drink a toast.

kanpan deck; **jookanpan** upper deck; **chuukanpan** main deck.

kanraku fall; cave in; **kanraku suru** to fall; to sink; to collapse; to cave in.

kanri management, administration, control; **kanrisha** superintendent; manager.

kanryaku simplicity; brevity; **kanryaku na** simple; brief; **kanryaku ni** simply; briefly. **Kanryaku ni shite kudasai.** Please make it very brief.

kanryoo completion; conclusion.

kansatsu observation.

kansen infection; contagion.

kansen trunk line; main line.

kansetsu indirectness; **kansetsu no** roundabout, indirect; **kansetsu ni** at second hand, indirectly.

kansetsu joint; **kansetsu o kujiku** to dislocate.

kansha thanks, gratitude. **Kansha no kotoba mo arimasen.** I can't thank you enough.

kansha official residence.

kanshaku passion; temper; impatience; **kanshaku no tsuyoi** hot-tempered; irritable; **kanshaku o okosu** to lose one's temper.

kanshi watch, lookout, vigil; **kanshi suru** to watch, keep an eye on.

kanshin concern, interest; **kanshin o motsu** to be concerned about, be interested in.

kanshin admiration; **kanshin na** admirable, praiseworthy; **kanshin ni** admirably; **kanshin suru** to admire, to be impressed.

kanshoku suru to eat between meals.

kanshoo appreciation; **kanshoo suru** to appreciate; **kanshooteki** appreciative.

kanshoo sentimentality; **kanshoo shugi** sentimentalism; **kanshooteki** sentimental.

kanshuu spectators.

kansoku observation; survey; **kansokusho** observatory (weather, etc.).

kansoo impression(s); thoughts; **kansoo o noberu** to give one's impression.

kansoo aridity; **kansoo suru** to dry.

kan suru to be concerned with; to relate to, bear on; to be connected with: **-ni kan shite** in regard to.

kanjoo account.

KANTAN brevity; simplicity; **KANTAN NA** simple, brief; **kantan ni** briefly; in a few words; simply, easily. **Soko e wa kantan ni ikemasu.** You can go there very easily.

kantan suru to admire.

kantei judgment; expert opinion; appraisal.

kantei official residence.

kantoku supervision; control; superintendent; inspector; **kantoku suru** to supervise; control.

kantsuu penetration; **kantsuu suru** to penetrate, pierce.

kan'yoo na important; necessary.

kanyuu entry; joining; admission; **kanyuu suru** to join; to subscribe; to enter; **kanyuusha** member; subscriber.

kanzei customs (duty); **kanzei no kakaru** dutiable; **kanzei no kakaranai** duty free.

KANZEN perfection; completeness; **kanzen na** perfect; complete; integral; **kanzen ni** perfectly.

kanzuku to get wind of; to have an inkling of; to suspect.

KANZURU See **KANJIRU.**

KAO face; looks; complexion; **kao ga urete iru** to be well known.

kaoru to smell; to be fragrant.

kappa old-fashioned raincoat; oilskin; water spirit.

kapparai shoplifter; pilfering, thieving.

kappatsu activity; briskness; **kappatsu na** active, lively; brisk.

kappu cup (trophy). (See also **koppu.**)

KARA (n.) being empty; vacant (adj.) **kara no** empty; **kara ni suru** to empty. **Kara desu.** It is empty.

KARA from; out of; since; on; in; and so; because; as; for (following a sentence-ending form of a verb, the copula, or adjective); **kore kara nochi** from now on; **Tookyoo kara Oosaka made** from Tokyo to Osaka. **Byooki deshita kara ikimasen deshita.** I was sick so I didn't go.

kara husks, hulls, shells.

KARADA body; **karada no** physical; bodily; **karada no tame ni naru** to be good for one's health. **Karada ga warui.** She is sick. I am sick.

karageru to tie up, bind; to tuck in.

KARAI hot; acrid; salty; pungent. **Kono otsuyu wa karai desu.** This soup is too salty.

karaibari bluff; empty boast.

karakau to tease; to make fun of; to play a joke on.

karakaze dry wind.

karamaru, karamu to twine around; to coil; to be entangled.

karari to completely, fully, entirely. **Sora ga karari to haremashita.** The sky has cleared.

kara sawagi much ado about nothing; **kara sawagi suru** to make a big fuss about nothing.

karasu to let wither; to dry up. (See also **KARERU.**)

karatto carat.

karazeki dry (hacking) cough.

KARE he; **kare no** his; **kare ni** to him; **kare o** him; **karera** they.

kare- prefix denoting: dry; withered; hoarse; **karegoe** hoarse voice.

karee curry; **raisu karee** curried rice; **kareiko** curry powder.

KAREKORE this and that; one thing and another; some; about; **karekore ninen bakari** two years or so.

karendaa calendar.

KARERU to wither, dry up; to die; to get hoarse. **Koe ga karete kimashita.** My voice is hoarse. **Ido ga karemashita.** The well has dried up. **Ki ga karemashita.** The tree has died. (See also **karasu.**)

KARI (n.) loan; debt; borrowing.

kari hunting.

kariatsumeru to gather together, muster.

karidasu to hunt out; to round up.

kariireru to harvest, gather in.

karikomi (n.) cutting, pruning.

karikomu to cut, trim, prune.

karikoshi outstanding debt; overdraft.

kari no temporary; **kari ni** temporarily; tentatively.

karinui (n.) basting, sewing loosely; **karinui suru** to baste.

kariru to borrow; **karikata** debtor; **kariukenin** borrower. **Yamada-san ni okane o karimashita.** I borrowed some money from Mr. Yamada.

KAROOJITE with much difficulty; barely, hardly.

karu to reap; to cut; to trim; to hunt; to chase; **kusa o karu** to cut grass; **ine o karu** to harvest rice.

karuhazumi rashness; hastiness; **karuhazumi na** rash; hasty; thoughtless.

KARUI light, not heavy, slight, trifling; not serious; simple; insignificant; **karui shigoto** light work; **karui nimotsu** light baggage; **karuku** lightly; slightly; **karuku suru** to lighten, ease; **karuku utsu** to tap; to pat.

karyoku heating power.

karyuu downstream.

KASA umbrella; parasol.

kasa bulk, volume; size; quantity; **kasabatta** bulky.

kasabuta scab.

kasai fire, blaze; **kasai o okosu** to start a fire; **kasai hoochiki** fire alarm; **kasai hoken** fire insurance. (See also **hi.**)

kasamu to swell, increase in volume.

kasanaru to be piled up; to lie one on top of another.

kasanegasane repeatedly, again and again, over and over.

kasaneru to pile up, put one on top of the other; to repeat; **kasanete** in layers; one on the other; repeatedly.

Kasei Mars.

kasei (n.) keeping house; **kaseigaku** home economics.

kasetsu construction; **kasetsu suru** to construct, erect; to lay; **denwa o kasetsu suru** to have a telephone installed; **kasetsuchuu de aru** to be under construction.

kasetsu hypothesis.

kasetsu no temporary, provisional.

kasetto cassette.

kasha freight car.

kashi lending; **kashikata** creditor, **kashikin** loan.

kashi, OKASHI cake; confectionery; sweets; candy; **kashiya** confectionery store.

kashigeru to incline; **kubi o kashigeru** to tilt one's head.

Kashi kandankei Fahrenheit thermometer.

kashikiri charted (bus, etc.).

KASHIKOI wise, clever, intelligent.

kashikomaru to obey; to assent to; to sit straight. **Kashikomarimashita.** Yes, sir. I'll follow your instructions.

KASHIMA room to let; apartment; **kashiya** house for rent.

kashimashii noisy, boisterous.

kashira (n.) head, chief; ringleader; **kashira datta** (adj.) chief, leading, principal.

kashu singer.

kassai ovation.

KASU to lend; **kane o kasu** to lend money.

kasu refuse, dregs, scum; sediment.

KASUKA NA faint, dim, vague, indistinct; **kasuka ni** faintly, etc.; **kasuka ni kioku suru** to have a faint recollection.

kasumi haze; mist; **kasumi no kakatta** hazy; misty.

kasumu to grow hazy, grow dim.

kasureru to get hoarse.

kasurikizu scratch; bruise.

kasuru to graze, scrape, scratch.

KATA shoulder; **katakake** shawl; **kata o motsu** to take sides. **Kata ga koru.** I have a stiff neck.

kata form, shape; pattern, model, figure; design, mold.

kata- prefix denoting: single; **katahoo** one of a pair; **kataashi de tatsu** to stand on one leg.

-kata suffix denoting: person (respect); **kono kata** this person; **ano kata** that person.

KATACHI form, shape; figure; personal appearance; **mime katachi no ii**

handsome; shapely. **Sore wa donna katachi o shite imasu ka?** What kind of shape does it have?

katachinba odd; mismatched.

katagata by way of; at the same time; partly; combined with. **Sanpo katagata ikimashita.** I went there both to take a walk and [at the same time] pay a visit.

katagawa one side; **katagawa tsuuko** one-way street.

katagi no honest; honorable; decent.

KATAI hard; tough; stiff; upright; strong; firm; conscientious; **kataku** strongly; firmly; tightly; strictly; resolutely; stubbornly; **katakurushii** strict; stiff-mannered; formal; **kataku suru** to harden; stiffen. **Ano hito wa katai hito desu.** He is a conscientious person. **Kono niku wa taihen katai desu.** This meat is very tough.

KATAKANA one of the two sets of Japanese syllabary called **kana. Sore wa katakana de kaite kudasai.** Please write it in **katakana.**

katamari lump; clod; mass.

katamaru (intrans.) to coagulate; congeal; to group together.

katameru (trans.) to harden; to solidify; to stiffen; to consolidate.

katami memento, souvenir; **katami to suru** to keep as a memento.

KATAMICHI one way; one trip; **katamichi jooshaken** one-way ticket.

katamukeru to incline, bend, tilt.

katamuki trend; slant; slope; **-no katamuki ga aru** to be apt to, to be inclined to.

katamuku to incline, lean; to decline.

katan ito cotton thread.

katana sword.

katappashi (colloq.) one by one; one and all; wholesale.

katasa hardness; toughness; solidity.

katasumi corner; nook; **heya no katasumi ni** in a corner of the room.

kataware fragment, piece.

katazukeru to put in order; to clear; to put away; to dispose of; to settle.

katazuku to be put in order; to be settled; to come to an end.

KATEI home; family; household; **katei no** domestic; household; house.

katei assumption, supposition; **katei suru** to assume, to suppose.

katoo inferiority; **katoo no** low; coarse; vulgar.

katsu to conquer, be victorious, win.

katsudoo, katsuyaku activity; **katsudooteki** active; energetic; **katsudooka** active person; **katsudooryoku** vitality; energy.

katsugu to shoulder, carry; to carry on the shoulder.

katsuyaku, katsudoo activity; action; boom (rapid, expanding growth); **katsuyaku suru** to be active in; to play an active part.

KATTE one's own way; selfishness; condition; circumstances; **KATTE NA** selfish; willful; **temae katte ni** selfishly; **katte ni furumau** to have one's own way; **katte no yoi** handy, convenient.

KAU to buy, purchase; to incur; to provoke; **kenka o kau** to pick a quarrel. **Kono hon o hyakuen de kaimashita.** I bought this book for one hundred yen.

KAU to keep, raise (an animal or bird). **Watakushi wa inu o katte imasu.** I have a dog.

KAWA skin, hide; leather; bark; peel; etc.; **kawa o hagu** to peel off (skin or bark); **kawazuki no** unpeeled.

KAWA river, stream; **kawa o wataru** to cross a river.

KAWAIGARU to love; to pet, fondle, caress. **Kare wa muyami to neko o kawaigatta.** He made a great pet of a cat.

KAWAII dear; darling; loving; tiny; **kawaii akanboo** precious baby; **kawaii koe** sweet voice; **kawairashii** sweet; lovely; pretty; charming; amiable; pathetic. **Ano hito ni wa kawairashii akanboo ga arimasu.** She has a cute baby.

KAWAISOO NA poor, pitiful, pathetic. **Kawaisoo ha koto o shita.** That was a pity.

KAWAKASU to dry.

KAWAKI thirst.

KAWAKU to dry; to get dry; to feel thirsty; **nodo ga kawaku** to be thirsty. **Kuchi ga kawaita.** My mouth felt dry.

kawara tile; **kawarabuki no** tile-roofed.

KAWARI substitute, proxy; compensation; **kawari ni** on behalf of; in place of; **kawari o suru** to substitute, take someone's place. **Kawari ga nai.** Nothing is the matter.

kawaru to replace, **kawarugawaru** in turn, by turns.

kawaru to change; **yoku kawaru** changeable. **Ame ga yuki ni kawarmashita.** The rain changed into snow.

KAWASE money order; exchange; **kawase sooba** rate of exchange. **Kawase de gosenen okutta.** I sent a money order for 5,000 yen.

KAYOOBI Tuesday.

kayou to pass to and fro; to frequent; to go regularly; **gakkoo e kayou** to attend school.

kayowai weak; tender; delicate, fragile.

kayui itchy.

KAZARU to adorn, decorate, embellish; to display; kikazaru dress up.

KAZE wind; breeze; kasuka na kaze breath of air; light breeze. Kaze ga fuite imasu. The wind is blowing.

KAZE cold; kaze o hiku to catch a cold.

kazei taxation; kazeihin taxable item; kazeiritsu tax rate.

KAZOERU to count, calculate; to number; hi o kazoeru to count the days.

KAZOKU family; household.

KAZU number; kazu kagiri nai innumerable, countless; kazu no ooi many; numerous.

KE hair ke darake no hairy; ke no nai bald, hairless.

-KE suffix denoting: house, family; Fujiwarake the Fujiwaras.

-KE suffix denoting: temper, feeling; nature; hinoke signs of fire.

kebakebashii gaudy, showy.

kechi fault; stinginess; poor quality; kechi na stingy, miserly; kechi o tsukeru to find fault with.

kechirasu to kick about.

kedakai dignified; noble.

kedamono beast.

KEGA wound, injury; accident; KEGA O SURU to get hurt; kega o saseru to injure, hurt; kega no koomyoo lucky mistake; lucky hit.

kegare pollution, contamination; stain.

kegareru to be polluted.

kegasu to stain; to soil; to pollute; to disgrace.

kegirai prejudice; kegirai suru to be prejudiced against.

keiba horse race; keibajoo racetrack.

keibetsu contempt; slight; insult; keibetsu suru to despise; to sneer at.

keiei management, conduct.

keifuku suru to respect; to admire; to look up to.

keiji notice, notification; keijiban bulletin board.

keika progress; development; course; jiken no keika the course of an event.

keikai watch; guard; keikai shingoo warning signal; keikai suru to watch for; guard against.

keikaku plan, project, scheme; keikaku suru to plan, etc.

KEIKEN experience; keiken aru experienced; keiken no nai inexperienced; keiken suru to experience; keikensha experienced person.

keiken na pious, devout.

keiki condition, state; times; kookeiki business boom. Keiki ga yoi desu. Trade is brisk.

keiko exercise, practice, drill; study; keiko suru to practice; to take lessons.

keikoku warning; advice; keikoku suru to warn, admonish.

keikoo tendency, inclination; trend.

keimusho prison.

keiniku chicken (as food).

keiran (chicken) egg.

keirei salute, salutation.

keiren convulsions; spasm.

keiryaku stratagem, artifice.

keisan calculation, reckoning; estimation; keisangakari accountant; keisanki adding machine, calculator.

KEISATSU police station; keisatsukan police officer.

keisha slant, incline, slope.

keishiki forms; formality; keishikiteki formal; conventional; keishikiteki ni formally.

keiteki foghorn; police whistle; alarm whistle.

keito worsted; woolen yarn.

keitoo system; lineage; keitoo o tateru to systematize; keitooteki systematic.

keitoo suru to exhaust; to concentrate.

keiyaku contract; agreement; promise; keiyaku suru to make a contract; keiyakusho written contract.

keizai economy; finance; keizaiteki economical; keizaijoo financially.

KEKKA result, outcome, consequence, effect; sono kekka consequently.

kekkan blood vessel.

KEKKIN absence (from work); kekkin suru to be absent; kekkinsha absentee.

kekkon marriage; wedding; KEKKON SURU to marry; kekkonshiki marriage ceremony.

kekkoo na splendid; fine; good; beautiful; kekkoo na niku delicious meat.

kekkoo suru to take decisive action; to carry out (something) decisively.

KEKKYOKU eventually, finally, ultimately, in the end; kekkyoku no final, ultimate.

kemono beast, brute.

kemui smoky.

KEMURI smoke; fumes.

KEN prefecture; kenchoo prefectural office; kenchiji prefectural governor; Chibaken Chiba prefecture.

ken sword, saber.

-ken house (used as a counter). Kado kara sangenme no ie desu. It is the third house from the corner. (In sangenme, "g" takes the place of "k.")

kenage na brave, heroic; manly; kenage ni bravely; heroically; nobly.

ken'aku na dangerous; serious; stormy; rough; ken'aku na sora stormy (threatening) sky.

kenasu to abuse, slander.

kenbikyoo microscope.

KENBUTSU sight-seeing; **kenbutsunin** sight-seer; visitor; **kenbutsu suru** to see, look at; to pay a visit to; **kenbutsu ni iku** to go sight-seeing.

kenchiku construction, erection; building; architecture; **kenchiku yooshiki** architectural style; **kenchiku suru** to build.

ken'etsu censorship.

kengaku observation; inspection; **kengaku suru** to visit (a factory, etc.) for study.

kengi suspicion; **kengi o kakeru** to suspect; **kengi ga kakaru** to be under suspicion.

kengo na strong; stable; firm, solid; **kengo ni** firmly; strongly.

kenka quarrel, dispute, brawl; **kenka suru** to quarrel, fight; **kenka o shikakeru** to pick a fight.

KENKOO health; **kenkoo na** healthy.

KENKYUU research, study, investigation; **kenkyuu suru** to study; to do research; **kenkyuukai** learned society; society for scientific research; **kenkyuujo** laboratory; research institute.

ken mo hororo no aisatsu curt, blunt, or brusque reply; rebuff.

kenpoo constitution; constitutional law.

kenpu silk cloth.

kenri right, privilege; **kenri o shuchoo suru** to insist on one's rights.

kenryoku power, authority, influence; **kenryoku no aru** powerful, influential.

kensa inspection; investigation; **kensa suru** to inspect, examine.

kensetsu construction; establishment; building; **kensetsu suru** to construct; to found; to establish.

kensoku arrest, restraint; surveillance; **kensoku suru** to restrain, check.

kenson modesty, humility; **kenson na** modest, humble; **kenson suru** to be modest.

kentoo boxing; **kentoo suru** to box; **kentooka** boxer, fighter.

kentoo aim; anticipation; **kentoo o tsukeru** to anticipate; to take aim at; **kentoo ga hazureru** to miss one's aim.

ken'yaku economy; thrift; **ken'yaku suru** to economize; **ken'yaku no** economical, thrifty.

keorimono woolen fabric.

keppaku purity, innocence; **keppaku na** pure, innocent, spotless, clean.

KEREDOMO but, however, although, yet. **Kyoo wa hidoku atsui keredomo ikimashoo.** It is hot today, but let's go anyway.

KERU to kick.

KESA this morning. **Kesa wa ikaga desu ka?** How are you feeling this morning?

keshikaran outrageous; rude; insulting; insolent.

KESHIKI view, sight, scenery, landscape. **Taihen keshiki ga yoi.** The scenery is very good.

keshitomeru to put out (a fire).

kessaku masterpiece.

kesseki absence (from school or a meeting); **mukesseki** regular attendance.

kesshin resolution, determination; **kesshin suru** to be resolute, to make up one's mind.

KESSHITE never, by no means; not at all; not in the least. **Kesshite sonna koto wa itashimasen.** I wouldn't do it for anything. **Kesshite sawatte wa ikemasen.** Don't touch it under any circumstances.

KESU to put out, extinguish; to blow out; to switch off, to erase; to cancel; **sugata o kesu** to vanish, to disappear; **akari o kesu** to switch off the light; to put out the light.

ketatamashii noisy, loud; piercing; alarming; **ketatamashiku** frantically; noisily, loudly.

ketsuron conclusion; **ketsuron suru** to conclude; **ketsuron to shite** in conclusion.

kettei determination; decision; conclusion; **ketteiteki** decisive; conclusive; **kettei suru** to decide upon; to be decided.

ketten flaw, defect, blemish; **ketten no aru** defective, imperfect; **ketten no nai** flawless; perfect.

kewashii steep, precipitous.

KEZURU to shave; to sharpen; **enpitsu o kezuru** to sharpen a pencil; **namae o kezuru** to remove a name from a list. **Honemi o kezutte shigoto ni hagenda.** He worked hard without sparing himself.

ki- prefix denoting: air; vapor; atmosphere; **kiatsu** atmospheric pressure; **kion** temperature (of the air).

kibarashi diversion, pastime; **kibarashi o suru** to amuse oneself.

kibaru to exert oneself; to bear down.

kibatsu na original; extraordinary; novel; unusual.

kibikibi shita vivacious, full of life.

kibin smartness; **kibin na** smart, clever, quick-witted; **kibin ni** cleverly.

kibishii severe, strict, stern; **kibishiku** severely, strictly.

kibone care, worry; **kibone no oreru** to be troublesome.

KIBOO wish, desire, hope; **kiboo suru** to hope, wish, desire.

KIBUN feeling, frame of mind, mood; **kibun ga yoi** to feel better. **Kibun ga warui desu.** I feel sick.

kichi dangerous situation; **kichi o dassuru** to have a close shave; to have a narrow escape.

kichigai madness, insanity; insane person; **kichigai ni naru** to go mad.

kichin to precisely; neatly; **kichin to shita** orderly, tidy; **kichin to shite iru** to be in good order.

kichoomen na orderly; precise; **kichoomen na hito** one who works in an orderly manner.

kidate disposition, temper; **kidate no yoi** good-tempered.

kidoru to assume airs, be conceited; **kidotte** affectedly.

kien tall talk; **kien o ageru** to talk big; to boast.

KIERU to go out; to be put out, be extinguished; **sugata ga kieru** to disappear. **Hi ga kieta.** The fire has gone out.

kifu contribution, donation; subscription; **kifu suru** to contribute; to subscribe; **kifusha** contributor; subscriber.

kigae change of clothes.

kigakari anxiety, worry; misgivings.

KIGARU NA cheerful, lighthearted; pleasant, agreeable.

KIGEN state of health; temper; mood; **kigen no yoi** good-humored; cheerful; **kigen o sokonau** to offend.

KIGEN term, period, time; **kigen ga kuru** to come due; **kigen ga keikasuru** to be overdue.

kigoo sign, symbol, mark, emblem.

kigurai pride; **kigurai no takai** proud.

kihon foundation, basis; standard; **kihonteki** fundamental, basic.

KIIROI yellow; **kiiroi booshi** yellow cap; **kiiroi koe** shrill voice.

kiji description; account (in a newspaper or magazine).

kiji grain (of wood), color (of wood).

kijitsu appointed date; fixed date.

KIKAI machine; implement; apparatus; machinery; **kikaiteki** mechanical; **kikaigaku** mechanics.

KIKAI opportunity, chance; **kikai no arishidai** at the first chance; **kikai o toraeru** to seize the opportunity.

kikiawaseru to inquire, make inquiries.

KIKIDASU to hear; to find out; to get wind of.

kikiireru to comply with, assent to, consent to.

kikiiru to listen to.

kikikajiri smattering (of information).

kikikajiru to get a smattering of.

kikikomu to be informed of, get wind of.

kikime effect; efficacy; benefit; **kikime no aru** effective; **kikime no nai** ineffective.

KIKIMORASU to fail to hear; not to hear (catch) what is said.

kikin famine.

kikinagasu to pay no heed (to what is said).

kikinaosu to ask someone to repeat (something).

kikinareru to get used to hearing, be accustomed to hearing.

kikinikui difficult to hear.

kikioboe recollection (feeling) that one has heard (something) before.

kikisokonai mishearing; misunderstanding.

kikitadasu to ascertain, confirm.

kikitagaru to be inquisitive, be curious.

kikitoru to hear; to get wind of.

kikitsutae hearsay.

kikitsutaeru to hear from others, hear at second hand.

KIKKARI punctually; exactly, precisely.

KIKOERU to hear; to be able to hear; to be audible. **Watakushi wa mimi ga yoku kikoemasen.** I'm hard of hearing. **Uta ga kikoemasu.** I hear a song.

KIKOO climate, season; weather; **onwa na kikoo** mild climate.

KIKU to hear, listen to; to ask; to accept; **kiku tokoro ni yoreba . . .** I hear that . . . it is said that . . .

kimae generosity; **kimae no yoi** generous; openhanded; **kimae yoku kane o tsukau** to be generous with one's money.

kimagure caprice; **kimagure na** capricious, whimsical; **kimagure ni** capriciously.

kimama willfulness; waywardness; selfishness; **kimama na** selfish, etc.

kimari settlement; conclusion; rule; custom; **kimari o tsukeru** to settle, arrange.

kimaru to be settled, to come to an agreement, to be fixed. **Hanashi ga kimaru.** The matter is settled. **kimatta** regular, fixed, routine.

KIMERU to settle, decide; to arrange; to determine; **hi o kimeru** to set the day; **kimeta jikan ni** at the appointed time; **hara o kimeru** to make up one's mind.

kimazui disagreeable, unpleasant.

kimetsukeru to scold, reprimand.

kimi you (used colloq. by men).

kimi egg yolk.

kimijika na short-tempered, touchy.

kimochi feeling, sensation; **kimochi no yoi** pleasant; refreshing; **kimochi ga warui** to feel uncomfortable.

KIMONO Japanese clothing, garment; **kimono o kiru** to get dressed; **kimono o nugu** to get undressed; **kimono o kikaeru** to change one's clothes.

kimuzukashii hard to please; moody.

KIN gold; **kin'iro no** golden; **kinpatsu** blond hair.

kinchoku conscientiousness; **kinchoku na** conscientious; scrupulous; discreet; honest.

kinchoo tension, strain; **kinchoo suru** to strain; to become tense.

kindai modern times; **kindai shisoo** modern ideas; **kindaika suru** to modernize.

kin'en prohibition against smoking; **kin'ensha** nonsmoker.

kinen commemoration, remembrance; memory; **kinen suru** to commemorate; **kinen no tame ni** in memory of; **kinenhi** monument.

kingan nearsightedness; **kingankyoo** eyeglasses for a nearsighted person. (See also **kinshigan**.)

KINJO neighborhood; **kinjo no** neighboring; **kinjo no hito** neighbor.

kinkan kumquat.

kinko safe; cashbox.

kinniku muscles; **kinniku roodoo** physical labor; **kinniku no** muscular.

kinomi kinomama de in the clothes one is wearing; without changing clothes; **kinomi kinomama de neru** to go to sleep without changing into pajamas.

KINOO = **sakujitsu** yesterday; **kinoo no hiru** yesterday at noon. **Kinoo gakkoo o yasuminashita.** I was absent from school yesterday.

kinshi prohibition, ban, embargo; **kinshi suru** to prohibit, forbid; **kinshi o toku** to lift an embargo. **Kitsuen kinshi.** No smoking.

kinshigan = **kingan** nearsightedness; **kinshigan no** nearsighted.

kinshu abstinence, teetotalism; **kinshu suru** to abstain from drinking alcoholic beverages.

KINU silk; **kinu ito** silk thread; **kinu orimono** silk fabric; **kinu ura** silk lining.

kinuke *(n.)* being dejected; **kinuke no shita** dejected, spiritless; absentminded; **kinuke suru** to be dejected.

KIN'YOOBI Friday.

kinzoku metal; **kinzoku no** metallic; **kinzoku seihin** metal goods; hardware.

kinzuru to forbid, prohibit; to suppress.

kioku memory, recollection; **kioku suru** to remember, recollect; **kioku subeki** memorable, noteworthy; **kioku ryoku ga yoi** to have a good memory; **kioku ryoku ga warui** to have a poor memory.

kippari to explicitly, distinctly; definitely, decidedly; **kippari to kotowaru** to refuse flatly.

KIPPU ticket, pass; **kippu o kiru** to punch a ticket; **kippu uriba** ticket window.

KIRAI dislike, distaste, aversion; **kirai na** distasteful; abominable. **Kirai desu.** I dislike it. I don't like it.

kirakira brilliantly; glitteringly; **kirakira suru** to glitter, to dazzle.

KIRAKU NA easygoing, easy, carefree, happy-go-lucky; **kiraku na mono** easygoing person; **kiraku ni kurasu** to take things easy; to lead a relaxed life. **Doozo okiraku ni.** Make yourself comfortable!

kirameku to glitter, sparkle.

kirasu to run out of, be short of; **iki o kirasu** to be short of breath.

kirau to dislike, to hate, detest.

-kire counter for: piece, bit, scrap, fragment; slice. **Pan o hitokire kudasai.** Please give me a piece of bread.

KIREI NA beautiful, lovely, pretty; handsome, good-looking; clean; clear; **kirei na onna no hito** a beautiful (good-looking) woman; **kirei na mizu** clear water; **kirei ni suru** to clean; to tidy up; to put in order.

kireme gap, break; pause, intermission; **kireme o tsunagu** to close a gap.

kiremono cutlery, knives.

kireru to cut (well), to be sharp; to run out; to be worn out; to wear out. **Kimono ga kireta.** The clothes have worn out. **Naifu ga yoku kireru.** The knife cuts well. **Kigen ga kireta.** The term has expired.

kiri fog, mist; **kiribue** foghorn. **Kiri ga fukai.** It is foggy.

kiri end; limit; **kiri ga nai** unlimited.

-kiri suffix denoting: all (there is); only; sole; no more. **Korekkiri desu.** This is all I have.

kiriageru to stop; to close; to cut short; to wind up; **hanashi o kiriageru** to end a talk; cut a conversation short.

kiridasu to quarry; to cut down (timber) to break ice; **hanashi o kiridasu** to broach a subject; to break the ice (conversationally).

kirihanasu to cut off; to separate.

kiriharau to cut and clear away; prune.

kirihiraku to cut open; to clear (land).

kirikabu tree stump.

kirikuchi cut end; opening; slit; section.

kirikuzusu to cut down; to demolish.

kirimi fish slices, fillets.

kirinukeru to cut one's way through; to find the way out of (a difficulty); to struggle through.

kirinuki cutting, clipping, scrap; excerpt.

kirinuku to cut out, clip.

kirisame drizzle.

KIRISUTO Christ.

KIRISUTOKYOO Christianity;
  Kirisutokyoo Seinenkai Y.M.C.A.,
  Kirisuto kyookai Christian church.
kiritsu order, discipline; rule, regulations; *(n.)*
  standing up; **kiritsu aru** orderly,
  disciplined; **kiritsu o mamoru** to obey the
  rules; **kiritsu suru** to stand up, get to one's
  feet; **kiritsu o yaburu** to break the rules.
kiritsumeru to shorten, reduce, curtail; **hiyoo**
  o kiritsumeru to cut down on expenses.
-KIRO counter denoting: kilometer; kilogram;
  kiloliter; kilowatt.
kiroku annals; archives; minutes, record;
  kiroku suru to record, write down, keep
  records.
KIRU to cut; to chop; to carve; to break off
  (relations); **yubi o kiru** to cut one's finger;
  denwa o kiru to hang up (the telephone
  receiver). **Kare to wa te o kitta.** I am
  through with him.
KIRU to wear; to put on; **kimono o kiru** to
  put on clothes, dress; **kite iru** to be
  dressed in; to have on. **Nani o kite ikoo**
  ka? What shall I wear (in going there)?
kiryoku energy, vigor; virility; **kiryoku ga nai**
  to be languid, lacking in energy; **kiryoku**
  ga otoroeru to lose one's vigor; to have
  less energy.
kiryoo personal appearance, looks, features
  (usually used when speaking of women);
  kiryoo no yoi pretty, beautiful, handsome.
KISEN steamship, steamer; **kisen de** by ship;
  kisen de iku to go by ship; **kisen gaisha**
  steamship company.
kiseru to dress, clothe; to plate, gild, coat; to
  impute; **tsumi o hito ni kiseru** to put the
  blame on someone else.
KISETSU season; **kisetsu no** in season,
  seasonal; **kisetsu hazure no** out of season;
  kisetsu fuu monsoon season; **sakura no**
  kisetsu cherry blossom season.
KISHA railroad train; **kisha ni noru** to get on
  a train; **kisha de iku** to go by train; **kisha**
  o oriru to get off a train; **kishachin** train
  fare; **yogisha** night train.
kisha journalist; **tsuushin kisha**
  correspondent; **kishaseki** press gallery.
KISHI shore, coast; bank; **mukoo gishi** other
  side of the river.
kishitsu disposition, temperament; **yoi**
  kishitsu no hito person of good
  disposition.
kishoku mood, feeling; **kishoku ga yoi** to be
  in a good mood; to feel well; **kishoku ga**
  warui to be in a bad mood.
kishoo weather; weather conditions;
  kishoodai weather bureau.
kishu horseman, jockey, rider.

kishuku lodging; room and board;
  kishukunin a boarder; **kishuku suru** to
  board at; **kishukusha** dormitory.
KISOKU rule, regulations; **kisoku tadashii**
  regular; systematic; orderly; **kisoku**
  tadashiku regularly, systematically;
  kisoku o mamoru to observe the rules.
KISSATEN tearoom; coffee shop.
kissui no pure; genuine.
kisuu odd number.
KITA north; **kita no** northerly; northern.
kitaeru to forge; to drill, train; to discipline; to
  harden.
kitai expectation, anticipation; **kitai suru** to
  expect, hope for; to look forward to; to
  count on; **kitai ni sou** to meet
  expectations.
kitaku suru to go home; to come home.
KITANAI dirty; filthy; nasty; shabby;
  kitanaku suru to soil, make dirty.
kitchiri punctually, sharp; exactly; **kitchiri**
  niji ni at two o'clock sharp; at two on the
  dot.
kiteki siren; steam whistle; **kiteki o narasu** to
  blow a whistle; to sound a siren.
kiten ready wit; tact; **kiten no kiita** tactful;
  quick-witted; **kiten o kikasu** to be on the
  alert.
kitoku serious, critical. **Seimei kitoku desu.**
  He/she is seriously ill.
kitsuen smoking; **kitsuen suru** to smoke;
  kitsuenshitsu smoking room; **kitsuensha**
  smoking car (on a train).
kitsui brave; strong; intense; severe.
KITTE postage stamp; **kitte o haru** to put a
  stamp on (a letter). **Kono tegami ni wa**
  ikura no kitte o haru n desu ka? How
  much is the postage for this letter?
KITTO certainly, without fail; undoubtedly,
  surely. **Kitto kite kudasai.** Please be sure
  to come. **Kitto mairimasu.** Certainly I'll
  come.
kiwadatsu to stand out, be conspicuous; to be
  in contrast with.
kiwadoi critical; dangerous, risky; **kiwadoi**
  shoobu a close game (match); **kiwadoi**
  tokoro de in the nick of time; at the last
  minute.
kiwameru to exhaust; to get to the bottom of;
  to carry to an extreme; **shinsoo o**
  kiwameru to get at the truth.
kiwamete extremely, exceedingly;
  excessively.
kiyoo na clever, skillful; ingenious; **kiyoo na**
  hito jack-of-all-trades; handy person.
kiyowai timid, shy.
kiza na offensive; conceited.
kizetsu *(n.)* fainting; **kizetsu suru** to faint.

KIZU wound, injury, bruise; flaw, defect; **kizuato** scar; **kizugusuri** ointment for a bruise or wound.

kizukai fear; anxiety.

kizukare worry; mental fatigue; **kizukare ga suru** to be worried.

kizuku to become aware of.

kizutsukeru to hurt, injure, wound.

kizutsuku to be wounded, hurt.

kizuyoi resolute; brave; **kizuyoku omou** to be reassured; to be confident.

KO child; infant, baby; cub of an animal.

ko- prefix denoting: little, small; **koburi** light rain; light fall of snow; **kozakana** small fish; **kojima** small island.

-ko suffix denoting: lake; **Biwako** Lake Biwa.

kobiritsuku to stick fast, cling.

kobore overflow; droppings; **koboredane** fallen seed.

KOBORERU to run over, overflow; to drop; to spill; to be scattered.

kobosu to spill; to drop; to pour out; **namida o kobosu** to shed tears; **mizu o kobosu** to spill water.

kobu bump, swelling, protuberance.

KOCHIRA this place, here; this one; **KOCHIRAGAWA** this side. **Doozo kochira e.** This way, please. **Tabakoya wa toori no kochiragawa desu.** The cigar store is on this side of the street.

kodachi grove, clump of trees.

KODOMO child; **kodomo rashii** childish; **kodomoppoi** childlike; childish. **Watakushi wa kodomo ga sannin arimasu.** I have three children. **Kodomoatsukai ni suru na.** Don't treat me like a child.

KOE voice; **koedaka ni** in a loud voice; **koe o kagiri ni** at the top of one's voice; **chiisai koe de** in a low voice; softly; **kogoe** low voice; whisper; **kogoe de** in a low voice; in a whisper.

koeda twig, sprig, small branch.

koeru to cross; go across; to pass; to go beyond; exceed.

kogasu to burn; to scorch, singe.

kogatana small knife; pocketknife.

kogawase postal money order.

kogechairo dark brown, umber.

kogeru to get scorched, to get burned.

KOGITTE (bank) check; **kogitte o kiru** to issue a check; **kogitte de shiharau** to pay by check.

kogoeru to be frozen; to be chilled to the bone, be numb with cold.

kogoto scolding; blame; **kogoto o iu** to scold; **kogoto o iwareru** to be scolded; to be blamed.

kogu to row; **kogiwataru** to row across.

kohaku amber.

KOI (n.) love; **koi suru** to love; to fall in love; **koibito** lover; **koishii** dear; beloved; **koishigaru** to yearn for.

koi evil intention; evil will; **koi no** intentional, deliberate; **koi ni** on purpose, intentionally. **Koi no koto de wa arimasen.** It isn't anything that was done intentionally.

koi dark, deep, thick, strong (as tea).

koishi pebble.

koitsu this man (vulgar). **Koitsu!** You rat!

kojiakeru to wrench open.

kojiki beggar.

kojin individual; private citizen; **kojinteki** personal, private individual; **kojinsei** individually.

kojinmari to cozily; **kojinmari to shita** snug, cozy.

kojireru to go wrong; to get complicated.

kojitsuke distortion; forced meaning; **kojitsuke no** distorted; farfetched.

kojitsukeru to distort, (twist) the meaning.

kokage shade of a tree.

kokiorosu to disparage; to abuse.

kokitsukau to work like a horse; to drive (someone) hard.

kokka state, country, nation; **kokka shugi** nationalism.

kokkai parliament, national assembly, Diet.

kokkan severe cold; intense cold.

kokkei na comical; **kokkei na hanashi** funny (comical) story.

kokki national flag.

kokkoo diplomatic relations.

kokkyoo frontier, border; boundaries.

KOKO this place; here; **koko ni** here, in this place; **koko kara** from here; **koko shibaraku** for the present; for some time to come. **Koko da, koko da.** Here we are. This is the place.

kokoku one's native land.

KOKONOKA ninth day of the month.

KOKONOTSU nine.

KOKORO heart; mind; spirit; **kokoro aru hito** thoughtful person; **kokoro yuku** made as one pleases; to one's heart's content; **kokoro ni kakaru** to be anxious; **kokoro ni ukabu** to occur to one; **kokoro ni tomeru** to bear in mind; **kokoro ga kawaru** to change one's mind; **kokoro yasuku naru** to become intimate; **kokoro no ookii** broadminded; **kokoro atari** clue; **kokoro atari ga nai** to have no idea of; **KOKORO BOSOI** helpless; uneasy; **kokoro bosoku omou** to feel helpless.

kokoroe understanding; knowledge; **kokoroe chigai** misbehavior, misapprehension.

KOKOROERU to know; to think; to consider.

kokorogakari care; anxiety; concern; **kokorogakari ni naru** feel uneasy; to be anxious.

kokorogake purpose, intention, aim; attention; **kokorogake no yoi** careful; conscientious.

kokorogakeru to keep in mind; to think about.

kokorogamae preparedness.

kokorogawari change of mind; caprice; **kokorogawari no suru** fickle; faithless; capricious.

kokorogurushii to be uneasy.

kokoromi trial; experiment; attempt; **kokoromi ni** tentatively.

kokoromiru to try, attempt, make an attempt.

kokoromochi feeling, sensation; mood; idea; shade; **ii kokoromochi ga suru** to feel comfortable; **kokoromochi yoku** willingly; **kokoromochi o waruku suru** to hurt (someone's) feelings; to displease.

kokoromotonai insecure; apprehensive.

kokoronaki thoughtless; heartless.

kokorone feelings; heart.

kokoroyoi pleasant, agreeable, nice; delightful.

kokorozashi will; intention; motive.

kokorozasu to intend; to aim at, aspire to.

kokorozukai worry, anxiety, concern.

kokorozuke tip, gratuity.

kokorozuyoi assuring.

koku- prefix denoting; pertaining to a country, nation, or state; **kokuboo** national defense; **kokufu** national wealth; **kokuhoo** law of the land; **kokugai** abroad; overseas; outside the country; **kokugo** national language; Japanese language; **KOKUMIN** nation; people; **kokumin keizai** national economy; **kokumin seikatsu** national life; **kokuseki** nationality, citizenship.

kokuban blackboard; **kokuban fuki** blackboard eraser.

kokubyaku black and white; right and wrong; **kokubyaku o tsukeru** to tell right from wrong; to discriminate between good and bad; **kokubyaku o arasou** argue the merits (of something).

kokuhatsu prosecution; indictment; accusation.

Kokujin black person; **Kokujinshu** black race.

kokumotsu cereals, grain, corn; **kokumotsugura** granary.

kokunai *(n.)* interior; **kokunai no** domestic; internal; home; **kokunai shoogyoo** domestic commerce.

kokyuu breath; breathing; **kokyuu suru** to breathe.

KOMAKA NA, KOMAKAI small, minute; fine, detailed; delicate, thrifty; **komaka na koto** trifling matter; **komakaku chuui suru** to pay close attention.

komaraseru to annoy; to trouble; to muzzle.

KOMARU to be distressed; to be embarrassed; to be in trouble; to have a hard time, be hard up.

KOME rice; **kome o tsukuru** to grow (cultivate) rice.

komiau to be crowded; to be full; to swarm.

KOMU to be crowded; to be jammed; to be full up. **Kono kisha wa komu deshoo.** This train will probably be crowded.

komichi path, lane.

komiiru to be complicated; to get entangled.

komogomo alternately, by turns; reciprocally.

komugi wheat; corn; **komugiko** wheat flour.

kon- prefix denoting: present, current; **KONBAN** this evening; tonight; **KONGETSU** this month; **kongetsu tooka** on the tenth of this month; **KONNICHI** today; nowadays; the present time; **konnichi igo** from now on; from today on. **KONBAN WA.** Good evening. **KONNICHI WA!** Good afternoon! Good day!

kona flour; powder; **konagona ni kudaku** to break into pieces; pulverize.

konasu to grind, reduce to powder; to digest; to handle; **joozu ni konasu** to handle with skill.

konboo club, cudgel.

KONDATE menu.

KONDO now; this time; next time; new; **kondo no** this; next; coming; **kondo iku toki** the next time I go. **Kondo no densha de ikimashoo.** Let's take the next train. **Kondo wa yurushite agemasu.** I'll forgive you this time.

kongaragaru to get entangled, become involved; to get confused.

kon'i acquaintance; friendship; **kon'i na** intimate, familiar; **kon'i ni shite iru** to be on friendly terms.

konimotsu baggage, luggage.

konki energy; perseverance; patience; **konki no yoi** energetic.

konmori densely; thickly; **konmori shigetta** densely wooded.

KONNA such; this sort of; **konna fuu ni** in this manner; **konna toki ni** at a time like this.

konnan difficulty; difficulties; troubles; **konnan na** difficult; troublesome.

KONO this; these; **kono hen ni** in this neighborhood; **kono tsugi** next time; **kono mae** before this; the last time; **kono saki** hereafter; in the future; **kono yo** this world; this life; **kono yo no** worldly; mundane; **kono yoo na** such; of this sort.

KONOAIDA the other day; recently; not too long ago; **konoaida no ban** the other evening.

KONOGORO these days. **Konogoro wa ikaga desu ka?** How have you been lately?

KONOKATA since; **juunen konokata** these ten years; in the past ten years.

konomi liking, preference, choice.

konomu to like, be fond of; to prefer.

KONPYUUTAA computer. **dejitaru konpyuutaa** digital computer; **konpyuutaa gengo** computer language; **konpyuutaa puroguramu** computer program; **pasokon** personal computer.

konran commotion, confusion, disorder; **konran suru** to be confused, be in confusion.

KONSHUU this week. **Konshuu no Kin'yoobi ni kite kudasai.** Please come to see me this week on Friday.

konton chaos; **konton taru** chaotic.

kon'yaku (marriage) engagement, betrothal; **kon'yaku suru** to be engaged. **kon'yaku o haki suru** to break an engagement.

konzatsu disorder; complication; **konzatsu suru** to be in disorder, to be confused; to be complicated.

KOO this way. **Koo shite kudasai.** Please do it this way. **Koo natte wa shikata ga nai.** We can't do much when things go this way.

kooan design, plan; **kooan suru** to design, scheme, plan.

KOOBA = **KOOJOO** factory, mill. **Watakushi wa ano kooba de hataraite imasu.** I am working at that factory.

koobashii fragrant; savory; favorable.

KOOCHA Western black tea.

koochoo school principal.

koochoo high tide, climax.

koodan platform, pulpit, rostrum.

koodoo lecture hall, auditorium.

koodoo action, movement; conduct, behavior; **koodoo suru** to act, conduct oneself; to move.

KOOEN park, public garden.

KOOEN lecture, address; **kooen suru** to give a lecture; **kooensha** lecturer.

kooen support, aid, backing; **kooen suru** to back up, support; **kooensha** supporter.

koofu workman.

koofuku happiness; well-being; bliss; good fortune; **koofuku na** happy; fortunate; **koofuku ni kurasu** to live a happy life.

koofun stimulation; excitement; **koofun suru** to be stimulated; to be excited.

KOOGAI suburbs.

KOOGAI public hazard.

koogen plateau.

koogi lecture, discourse.

koogyoo industry; manufacturing; **koogyoochi** manufacturing district; **koogyooka** manufacturer; **koogyoo no** industrial.

koohei impartiality; fair play; **koohei na** fair, just, impartial.

KOOHII coffee.

koohyoo favorable criticism; **koohyoo de aru** to be popular, win popularity; to receive favorable criticism.

kooi kind intentions; kindness.

KOO IU such; this sort of; **koo iu fuu ni** in this way; **koo iu koto** such a thing as this.

kooji construction; works; **kooji chuu** under construction.

kooji alley, lane, narrow street.

koojiru to grow worse, change for the worse.

koojitsu excuse, pretext.

KOOJOO See **KOOBA.**

kooka effect, result; **kooka ga nai** not to take effect; to have no result or effect; **kooka ga aru** to be effective.

kookai voyage, crossing; **kookai suru** to sail; navigate.

KOOKAN exchange; **iken kookan** exchange of views; **kookan kakaku** exchange value; **kookandai** telephone switchboard; **kookanshu** telephone operator.

kookan favorable impression, good feeling.

kookei spectacle, sight; scene.

kooken suru to contribute, make a contribution toward; to be conducive to; to go far toward.

kookishin curiosity; **kookishin no tsuyoi** curious.

KOOKOKU advertisement; notice, announcement; **kookoku bira** poster, placard; **kookoku suru** to advertise; **sangyoo kookoku** classified advertisement.

kookoo so and so; such and such; **kookoo iu wake de** under such (these) circumstances.

kookoo filial piety, obedience to parents.

kookotsu rapture, ecstasy; **kookotsu to suru** to be in ecstasy; to be enraptured; to be enchanted.

kookuubin airmail.

kookuuki aircraft.

kookyoo (*n.*) public; society; **kookyoo no** public; common; **kookyooshin no aru** community-minded.

kookyoo prosperity, business boom.

kookyoogaku symphony; **kookyoogakudan** symphony orchestra.

koonoo effect, efficacy; virtue; **koonoo no nai** ineffective; **koonoo no aru** effective; useful; **koonoo ga aru** to be good for; to be effective, be useful.

KOORI ice; **koori no hatta** frozen, covered with ice; **koorizume no** refrigerated; iced.

kooron dispute; **kooron suru** to dispute, quarrel.

kooroo merits, meritorious deed; **kooroo aru** meritorious.

kooru to freeze.

kooryoku effect, efficacy; **kooryoku no aru** valid; effective.

koosa intersection, crossing; **koosa suru** to intersect, cross; **koosaten** intersection, crossroad.

koosai intercourse; association; society; company; fellowship; **koosaika** sociable person; good mixer.

koosan surrender, capitulation; **koosan suru** to surrender, submit; **koosan saseru** to make someone surrender.

koosatsu consideration; contemplation; **koosatsu suru** to consider; weight; to examine; to contemplate.

kooseki distinguished service.

koosen light; beam (ray) of light; **koosen o ireru** to let in the light.

koosetsu public; municipal **koosetsu shijoo** public market.

kooshi lecturer.

kooshi minister (diplomatic service); **kooshikan** legation.

kooshiki formula; formality; **kooshiki no** formal; state; official; **kooshiki de arawasu** to formulate.

kooshoo negotiation; **kooshoo chuu** under negotiation; **kooshoo suru** to negotiate; **nanra no kooshoo mo nai** to have nothing to do with.

kooshuu (n.) public; **kooshuu toire** restroom, public lavatory; **kooshuu yokujoo** public bath; **kooshuu no** public; common.

koosoku confinement; restraint; detention; **koosoku suru** to confine, detain; **koosoku o ukete inai** to be free from restraint.

koosokudo high speed; rapid transit.

koosui perfume, cologne, scent; **koosui o tsukeru** to use perfume.

kootai relief; substitution; **kootai ni** alternately; in turn; **kootai suru** to relieve; take turns.

Kootaishi Crown Prince.

kootei affirmation; **kootei suru** to affirm; to acknowledge; **kooteiteki** affirmative.

kootei fluctuation, high and low, unevenness, undulations; **kootei aru** fluctuating, undulating.

kootoo oral, verbal; **kootoo de** orally, verbally.

kootoo gakkoo senior high school.

kootsugoo favorable circumstances; **kootsugoo no** convenient; **kootsugoo na** favorable; fortunate; **kootsugoo ni**

conveniently, etc.; **kootsugoo de aru** to suit one's convenience.

KOOTSUU communication; traffic; **kootsuu kikan** means of communication; **kootsuu o seiri suru** to control traffic; **kootsuu no ben o hakaru** to facilitate communications.

kooun good luck, stroke of luck; **kooun na** lucky, fortunate; **kooun ni mo** fortunately; luckily.

kooza (university) chair, professorship; university course.

koozan mine; **koozan gishi** mining engineer; **koozangyoo** mining industry.

koozen openly; in public; **koozen no** open; public; official.

koozoo construction; structure; formation.

koozui flood, inundation.

KOPPU glass (for drinking). **Koppu ni mizu o ippai kudasai.** May I have a glass of water? (See also **kappu**.)

koraeru to bear, endure; to control; to restrain; **itasa o koraeru** to endure the pain.

KORE this; these; **kore hodo** this much; so much, so many; **kore kagiri** this is all; once and for all.

korigori suru, koriru to take warning from; to learn by experience.

korikatamaru to coagulate; to be absorbed in, to be bigoted.

koroai suitable; adequate, handy; **koroai o hakatte** just in time.

korobu to fall to the ground.

korogaru to roll; to tumble; to fall; to lie down.

korogasu to roll; to tumble down.

korosu to kill, put to death; **iki o koroshite** with bated breath, breathlessly.

koru to be absorbed in; to be devoted to; to get stiff; **kenkyuu ni koru** to be absorbed in one's studies; **tabemono ni koru** to be fussy about eating.

kosame light rain, drizzle.

kosei individuality; personality; idiosyncrasy.

KOSHI hip(s); waist; loin; **koshi o sueru** to settle down; **koshikake** seat, stool, etc.

KOSHIKAKERU to sit on a chair.

KOSHIRAERU to make, manufacture; to prepare; to build; to raise; **hako o koshiraeru** to make a box; **kane o koshiraeru** to raise funds; to make a fortune.

KOSHOO pepper.

koshoo obstacle, hitch; defect; accident; protest, objection; mechanical trouble; **koshoo naku** without a hitch; without any trouble. **Koshoo ga nai.** Nothing is wrong. Nothing is the matter.

kosokoso stealthily, secretly, sneakingly; **kosokoso dete iku** to sneak out.

kosu to go over, go across; to outrun; to move; to pass; **yama o kosu** to go over the top; to pass the most difficult point.

kosui lake; **kosui no soba** lakeside.

kosuru to rub; to scrub; to scrape; **me o kosuru** to rub one's eyes.

kotae answer, reply, response; solution.

KOTAERU to answer, reply, respond; **-ni kotaete** in reply (answer) to; **soo da to kotaeru** to answer in the affirmative; **shitsumon ni kotaeru** to answer a question.

kotaeru to come home, to strike home, to have an effect on; to be a strain on. **Ano hito no kotoba wa mi ni kotaemashita.** Her words came home to me.

kote iron (for clothes); soldering iron; trowel; **kote o ateru** to iron clothes; to solder; to curl with tongs.

KOTO thing; matter; affair; account; event, occurrence; duty, task; **koto naku** without a hitch; uneventfully, peacefully. **Sore wa nan no koto desu ka?** What does it mean? What do you mean? **Sore wa koto to baai ni yoru.** That depends on the circumstances.

KOTOBA language; word; term; speech; expression; **kotoba o kakeru** to speak; to call to; **kotoba o kawasu** to exchange words with; **kotoba o nigosu** to give a vague answer; **kotoba takumi ni** persuasively, convincingly. **Kono kotoba no imi wa nan desu ka?** What is the meaning of this word?

KOTOGOTOKU wholly, entirely; completely; without exception, in every case. **Koko ni aru hon wa kotogotoku yomimashita.** I have read all the books here.

KOTO NI especially; above all; moreover.

koto no hoka remarkably, extremely, unusually.

kotosara ni intentionally, on purpose, purposely.

KOTOSHI this year; present year. **Kotoshi no natsu wa taihen atsui desu.** It is very hot this summer.

kotowari excuse; denial; refusal; warning; notice; **kotowari mo naku** without permission, without one's knowledge.

KOTOWARU to make excuses; to refuse, decline; to ask permission; **tei yoku kotowaru** to decline politely.

kotowaza saying, maxim, proverb.

kotsukotsu to untiringly; laboriously; **kotsukotsu to aruku** to plod; **kotsukotsu to shigoto o suru** to work untiringly.

kowabaru to stiffen; to get stiff.

kowagaru to fear, be afraid of; to be frightened; **kowagowa** timidly, fearfully. **Nani mo kowagaru koto wa nai.** You have nothing to be afraid of.

kowai fearful, frightful, terrible, horrible; **kowai kao** angry look; grim face; **kowai me ni au** to have a terrible experience.

koware breakage; fragment; **kowaremono** fragile thing.

KOWARERU to break; to be broken; to be ruined; **Mado ga kowarete imasu.** The window is broken. **kowareyasui** fragile.

KOWASU to break down; to destroy, demolish, smash, wreck; **ie o kowasu** to pull down a house; **karada o kowasu** to ruin one's health.

koya hut, shed, cabin; pen.

koyashi manure; fertilizer.

koyomi calendar; almanac.

KOZUTSUMI parcel; small package; **kozutsumi yuubin de** by parcel post.

KU pain; suffering; bitterness; **ku ni naru** become worried about; bother; to cause anxiety; **ku ni suru** take seriously; be concerned about, be worried about. **Ame wa sukoshi mo ku ni narimasen.** The rain doesn't bother me at all. **Sonna koto o ku ni suru na.** Don't trouble yourself about such a matter.

KU = KYUU nine; **daiku** ninth.

kubaru to distribute; to deal out; to dispose (of); **shinbun o kubaru** to deliver a newspaper.

kubetsu distinction; classification, division; **kubetsu suru** to distribute, to differentiate (between good and bad); **kubetsu o tsukeru** to make a distinction.

KUBI neck; head; **kubi ni suru** to dismiss; discharge; **kubi ni naru** to be dismissed; **kubi o nagaku shite matsu** to wait impatiently; **kubimaki** scarf, muffler; **kubiwa** (dog) collar.

kubomi cavity; hollow; dent.

kubomu to become hollow; to be depressed; to sink.

KUBU DOORI nearly; in all probability; ten to one. **Kubu doori dekimashita.** It is nearly done.

kubun division; **kubun suru** to divide, partition.

KUCHI mouth; door, aperture; hole; post; kind; share; **kuchi no tassha na** fluent; **kuchi no karui** talkative; **kuchi ga aku** to open; burst open; **kuchi o kiru** to break a seal; to open the mouth; **KUCHIBIRU** lips; **kuchibue** whistle; **kuchibue o fuku** to whistle.

kuchidashi meddling, interference; **kuchidashi suru** to meddle; to poke one's nose in someone else's business.

kuchidome suru to hush up (a matter); to stop (someone) from speaking.

kuchigotae retort; **kuchigotae suru** to answer back.

kuchiurusai See **kuchiyakamashii.**

kuchiyakamashii = **kuchiurusai** nagging; critical.

KUDAMONO fruit; **kudamonoya** fruit-seller. **Kudamono ga hoshii desu.** I want some fruit.

KUDARANAI stupid, foolish; absurd; useless, insignificant; **kudaranai koto o iu** to talk foolishly.

kudari (*n.*) going down, down; **kudarizaka** downgrade, downhill.

KUDASAI please give me. **Sore o kudasai.** Please give it to me.

KUDASARU to offer; to give (respect). **Kore o watakushi ni kudasaru no desu ka?** Is this for me? **Hitotsu kudasaru wake ni wa ikimasen ka?** Can't you spare me one of these?

kudoi tedious; long-winded.

kudoku to make love to; to attempt to seduce; to entreat; to solicit.

kufuu device; contrivance; plan; scheme; means; expedient; **kufuu suru** to scheme, etc.

KUGATSU September.

kugi nail; **kugi o utsu** to nail; **kugi o sasu** to remind someone of what he or she must do.

kugiri full stop; pause; period; **kugiri o tsukeru** to settle; to put an end to.

kuguru to pass through; **mon o kuguru** to go through a gate.

kui post; stake; pile.

kuiki limit; boundary; **kuiki no** inside the boundary.

kuikomi loss; deficit.

kuikomu to eat into; to encroach upon; to leave a deficit; to go into one's capital. **Sengetsu wa ichi man en kuikomimashita.** Last month there was a deficit of ten thousand yen.

kuiru to regret; be sorry for.

kuitomeru to check; hold in check; arrest.

kuitsuku to bite; to snap; to take the bait. **Inu ni ashi o kuitsukaremashita.** I was bitten by a dog.

kuitsumeru to have no means of subsistence.

kujikeru to be disheartened; to lose heart.

kujiku to sprain; wrench; break; crush; discourage; **ude o kujiku** to break an arm; **ashikubi o kujiku** to sprain an ankle.

KUKKIRI clearly; distinctly; plainly; strikingly.

kukyoo adversity; awkward situation; **kukyoo ni ochiiru** to be put in an awkward situation.

kumen contrivance; makeshift; **kumen suru** to devise; to contrive; to manage.

KUMI class; gang; band; company; team; crew; set, pack; **kumigashira** head of a group; boss; **kumiawaseru** to combine, join together; to match; **kumiai** association; guild; partnership; **kumiaiin** member (of an association); **kumiai keisan** joint account.

kumidasu to dip out; to bail out.

kumitate structure, framework; system, organization.

KUMO cloud(s); **kumo o tsuku yoo na** lofty; towering; **kumo o tsukamu yoo na** vague; visionary; **kumogire** break in the clouds; **kumo yuki o miru** to see how the wind blows; to wait for the results.

kumori cloudy, overcast; **kumori naki** clean; clear; cloudless; spotless; **kumoribi** cloudy day; **kumori garasu** frosted glass.

KUMORU to get cloudy. **Sora ga kumotte kimashita.** The sky is getting cloudy. **Kare wa kao ga kumorimashita.** His face became clouded.

kumu to unite; to associate with; to be in a partnership with; to braid; to fit together; to pair with; **hiza o kumu** to cross one's legs; **ude o kumu** to fold one's arms.

-kun suffix denoting: Mr. (same as **san** but usually used for and by men); **Yamada-kun** Mr. Yamada.

KUNI country, land, state, nation; province; territory; **kunimoto** native (home) province; **kuni namari** dialect. **Dono kuni kara irasshaimashita ka?** From which country have you come?

kura warehouse; storehouse; granary; **kurabarai** clearance sale.

KURABERU to compare; to contrast; to match; **ookisa o kuraberu** to compare the size.

kuragari darkness; dark place; **kuragari de** in the dark.

KURAI dark, dim, gloomy, obscure; **kuraku naru** to become dark. **Totemo kurai desu.** It's very dark.

kurai grade, rank; **kurai suru** to stand; to be situated, be located; to lie; **kurai ga tsuku** to gain in dignity.

-kurai See **-GURAI.**

kurashi living, livelihood; **kurashikata** one's manner of living; **kurashi o tateru** to make one's living.

KURASU to live; to make a living; **rippa ni kurasu** to live well.

kurayami dark, darkness; **kurayami de** in the dark.

Kureguremo repeatedly; earnestly.

KURERU to give; to grant. **Ano hito ga watakushi ni sore o kureta.** He/she gave it to me.

kureru to grow dark. **Hi ga kurete kimashita.** The day is growing dark.

kureyon crayon.

kuriageru to move up; advance; **kijitsu o kuriageru** to move up a date.

kuriawase arrangement.

kuriawaseru, kuriawasu to make time; to arrange the time.

KURIKAESU to repeat; reiterate. **Moo ichido kurikaeshite kudasai.** Please repeat it.

kurikomu to carry over; to carry into.

kurikosu to transfer; to carry forward; to bring over.

kurireru to transfer; to carry forward.

KURISUMASU Christmas.

KURO black; **kuro nuri no** black-lacquered; painted black; **kuro kumo** dark clouds.

KUROI black; tanned; dusky; **kuroi kami** black hair. **Ano hito wa iro ga kuroi.** He has a dark complexion.

kuroo hardship; suffering; care, concern; **kuroo shoo no** nervous; worrisome; **kuroo suru** to work hard.

kurooto expert; professional; specialist; connoisseur.

KURU to come; to come over; to arrive. **Haru ga kimashita.** Spring has come. **Otegami ga kimashita.** Here is a letter for you. **Ashita kuru deshoo.** It will probably come tomorrow.

kurui disorder, confusion; madness; **kurui ga kuru** to get out of order.

KURUMA car, vehicle, carriage, cart, wagon; wheel; **kuruma de iku** to go by car.

kurumaru to be wrapped up in; to tuck oneself into or wrap oneself in; **kurumu** to wrap up; to cover up; to coat, gild.

KURUSHII painful; hard; trying; distressing; **kurushii me ni au** to undergo great suffering; **kurushii tachiba ni iru** to be in an awkward position.

kurushimeru to torment, torture; to persecute; **kokoro o kurushimeru** to worry; **doobutsu o kurushimeru** to be cruel to (an) animal(s).

kurushimi pain, suffering; hardship; agony; torture.

KURUSHIMU to feel pain; to suffer from; to be worried; **hin ni kurushimu** to be poverty-stricken. **Nani o sonna ni kurushinde iru no desu ka?** What are you suffering so much from? What makes you suffer so?

kuruu to go mad; to get out of order; to go wrong; to fluctuate. **Kono tokei wa doko ka kurutte iru.** There is something wrong with this watch.

kusa grass; herb; weed; **kusa o karu** to mow grass; **niwa no kusa o toru** to weed a garden.

kusai stinking, bad-smelling.

kusami stink, offensive odor.

kusarasu to corrupt; to cause to decay; to spoil.

kusari chain; tether.

kusaru to rot, decay; to turn sour; to corrode; **kusatta** rotten, sour. **ki ga kusaru** to feel low.

kuse habit, way; characteristic, peculiarity; **kuse ga tsuku** to get into a habit; **kuse o tsukeru** to form a habit; **kuse o naosu** to break a habit.

kushakusha na creased; wrinkled.

kushami sneezing; sneeze; **kushami ga deru** to sneeze.

KUSHI comb; **kushi** skewer, spit; **kushi de kami o toku** to comb hair.

kushin care; anxiety; struggle; **kushin suru** to take pains; to do one's best.

kushoo bitter smile; forced smile.

kusuburu to smoke, smolder; **uchi ni kusubutte iru** to remain indoors.

KUSURI medicine, drug; remedy; cure; physic; **kusuri o kau** to buy a medicine; **kusuri o nomu** to take a medicine; **kusuriya** pharmacist; druggist; drugstore.

KUTABIRERU, TSUKARERU to get tired; to be exhausted; **machikutabireru** to be tired of waiting.

KUTSU shoes; boots; **kutsu zure ga dekiru** to have one's feet hurt from wearing shoes; **kutsunugui** doormat; **kutsu himo** shoelace; **kutsuzumi** shoe polish; **KUTSUYA** shoe store; shoe-repair shop.

kutsurogu to be at ease; to relax; to make oneself comfortable; **kutsuroide hanasu** to have a heart-to-heart talk.

KUTSUSHITA socks; stockings; **kutsushitadome** garters.

kuttsukeru to join; to attach; to glue; to stick.

KUUKI air; atmosphere; **shinsen na kuuki** fresh air; **kuuku no ryuutsuu** the ventilation of air.

kuusoo fancy; vision; fantasy; **kuusooka** dreamer; **kuusooteki** visionary; imaginary; **kuusoo o egaku** to build castles in the sky.

kuuzen no unprecedented; unequaled; record-breaking. **Sore wa kuuzen no dekigoto desu.** That is an unprecedented event.

kuwadate plan, scheme; attempt, undertaking; **kuwadateru** to plan, scheme; to devise; to attempt, undertake.

kuwaeru to add (up); to give; to deliver; to offer; **bujoku o kuwaeru** to insult someone. **Ni ni ni o kuwaeru to yon desu.** Two and two are four.

kuwaeru to hold in the mouth; to bite; **yubi o kuwaete** looking wistfully [with finger in the mouth].

KUWASHII to be well versed; detailed; minute; particular; familiar with; **kuwashiku** minutely; to detail; at length; particularly; **kuwashiku noberu** to explain in detail; to give full particulars. **Kuwashii hanashi wa ato de hanashimashoo.** Later we shall talk about it in detail. **Ano hito wa rekishi ni kuwashii desu.** He is well versed in history.

KUWAWARU to join; to enter; to participate, take part in; **ikko ni kuwawaru** to join the party; **kyoogi ni kuwawaru** to take part in the game.

kuyami condolence; repentance; regret; **kuyamijoo** letter of condolence; **kuyami o noberu** to offer one's condolences.

kuyamu to regret; to repent of; to lament.

kuyashii regrettable; vexing.

kuyashisa regret.

kuyokuyo suru to worry about; to worry (oneself); to take to heart; to brood over.

kuzu waste, refuse, trash; **kuzukago** wastepaper basket; **kuzutetsu** scrap iron.

kuzureru to go to pieces, collapse, give away; to get out of shape.

KUZUSU to pull down; to break down; to destroy; to change. **Kono sen en satsu o kuzushite kudasai.** Please break this one-thousand-yen bill.

KYAKU visitor; guest; customer; patron; passenger; **kyakusha** passenger train; **kyakusen** passenger boat; **okyaku sama** personal guest; customer *(respect).*

kyakuhon script, scenario; **kyakuhonka** playwright.

kyakushoku dramatization; adaptation; plot.

kyohi suru to deny, refuse; to reject.

kyoka permission; leave; admission; license; **kyoka suru** to permit, allow; to admit; to authorize.

kyoku office; department; bureau; **yuubinkyoku** post office.

KYOKUTOO Far East.

KYONEN = sakunen last year; **kyonen no Ichigatsu** January of last year.

KYOO today. **Kyoo wa nan'yoobi desu ka?** What day of the week is today?

kyoo interest; amusement; **kyoo o samasu** to spoil the fun; **kyoo o soeru** to add to the fun; **kyoo ga noru** to become interested.

kyooboo collusion, complicity; **kyooboo suru** to conspire; plot together; **kyooboosha** accomplice.

kyoochoo cooperation; **kyoochoo suru** to cooperate; to act harmoniously.

KYOODAI brothers and sisters. **Kyoodai wa nan nin in arimasu ka?** How many brothers and sisters do you have?

kyoodan teacher's platform; pulpit.

kyoodoo cooperation; collaboration; partnership; association; union; **kyoodoo doosa** united action; **kyoodoo kanri** joint control; **kyoodoo no** common, joint.

kyoofu fear, fright, dread; **kyoofu o kanjiru** to fear, etc.

kyoogaku coeducation.

kyoogi game, match; **kyoogijoo** arena; **kyoogikai** tournament, meet; **kyoogisha** contestant.

kyoogi conference; discussion; **kyoogi suru** to consult; to confer with.

kyooguu condition; situation; circumstance.

kyoohaku compulsion; threat, menace; **kyoohaku suru** to compel; to threaten, intimidate.

kyoohan complicity; **kyoohansha** accomplice.

kyooi astonishment, wonder; **kyooiteki** surprising; wonderful.

kyooiku education; training; **kyooiku suru** to educate; to train; to bring up.

kyooin schoolteacher.

kyooju teaching; instruction; professor; faculty; **kyoojuhoo** methods of teaching.

kyookai association.

kyookai church; religious association; **kyookaidoo** church building; cathedral.

kyookai border, boundary.

kyoomei resonance; sympathy; response; **kyoomei suru** to sympathize with; to echo; respond to.

kyoomi interest, appeal; **kyoomi no aru** interesting; attractive; **kyoomi no nai** dull, uninteresting; lacking in appeal.

kyooshi teacher, tutor; professor; master. (See also **KYOOIKU.**)

kyooshitsu schoolroom, classroom.

kyooshuku obligation; humiliation; **kyooshuku suru** to be much obliged, be grateful to, appreciate deeply; to be sorry for, regret. **Osokunatte kyooshuku desu.** I am sorry to be late.

kyoosoo competition, rivalry; footrace; sprint; **kyoosoo shiken** competitive examination; **kyoosoo suru** to compete, contest; to run a race; **kyoosoosha** rival, competitor.

kyootaku kin securities deposit.

kyootei agreement, pact; **kyootei suru** to agree; to agree upon; **kyootei nedan** stipulated price.

kyootsuu no common.

kyootsuuten common feature; thing in common.

kyooyaku agreement, pact.

kyooyoo extortion; exaction; **kyooyoo suru** to extort.

kyooyoo no for common use; **kyooyoo suru** to use something in common.

kyooyuu co-ownership; **kyooyuu suru** to hold jointly; **kyooyuusha** co-owner, joint owner; **kyooyuuzaisan** common property.

kyoozai teaching materials.

kyori distance; range; radius; **kyori ga aru** to be far, distant.

kyozetsu refusal; rejection; **kyozetsu suru** to refuse; reject.

KYUU = KU (see **KOKONOTSU**) nine.

KYUU urgency; emergency; **kyuu ni** suddenly; **kyuu ni sonaeru** to provide for an emergency; **kyuu o tsugeru** to be urgent; to become critical; **kyuu o yoosuru** urgent; **kyuuba** critical moment; **kyuuba no shochi** emergency measure.

kyuu class; grade (in a school); **ikkyuu** first grade; **nikyuu** second grade.

kyuu- prefix denoting: quick, sudden, abrupt; steep; **kyuubyoo** sudden illness; **kyuuhen** sudden change.

kyuuchi difficult situation; fix.

kyuuen rescue; help; **kyuuen suru** to relieve; rescue; to reinforce.

kyuugyoo vacation; suspension of operation; **kyuugyoo suru** to close; to take a holiday; to suspend one's business.

kyuujo relief, help **kyuujo suru** to rescue, save; to help; **kyuujoami** safety net; **kyuujosen** lifeboat.

KYUUJUU ninety.

kyuuka holidays, vacation; leave of absence.

kyuukai adjournment; **kyuukai suru** to adjourn.

KYUUKOO express (train); **kyuukoo suru** to rush; to dash; to go like an express; **kyuukooressha** express train. **tokubetsu kyuukooressha** special express train; **kyuukooryookin** express charges.

M

ma space; room; apartment; time, interval, spare moments; **ma ga aru** to have time; **ma mo naku** before long, in a little while;

magashi suru to rent out a room; **ma ga waruku** unfortunately.

ma truth; **ma ni ukeru** to accept as truth, to believe what one hears.

MAA 1. Indeed! Dear me! **Maa dooshita no?** Dear me! What happened? 2. I should say, well. **Maa soo desu.** Well, it's something like that. 3. Just. **Maa matte kudasai.** Just wait, please.

maaketingu marketing.

maatarashii brand-new.

mabara sparsity; **mabara na** sparse, thin, scattered; **mabara ni** sparsely, thinly; here and there.

mabataki wink, blink; **mabataki suru** to wink, blink; **mabataki suru ma ni** in the twinkling of an eye.

mabayui dazzling, glaring.

mabiku to thin out; to eliminate.

maboroshi phantom; apparition; vision; illusion.

mabusu to cover with, sprinkle with.

MABUTA eyelid.

MACHI town, city; street; **machi hazure** outskirts of town; **machi e iku** to go to town.

MACHIAISHITSU waiting room.

machiawaseru to meet, rendezvous (with); to wait for.

machibooke waiting in vain; **machibooke o kuu** to wait for someone in vain; **machibooke o kuwasu** to keep someone waiting in vain.

machidooshii to be impatient; to be long in coming.

MACHIGAERU = MACHIGAU to mistake, err, make a mistake, blunder; **hatsuon o machigaeru** to pronounce incorrectly; **michi o machigaeru** to take the wrong road; **machigaete** by mistake, in error. **Futatsu machigaemashita.** I made two mistakes.

MACHIGAI mistake, error; fault; accident; **machigai naku** without fail; certainly; **machigai o shoozuru** to cause an accident.

MACHIGAU, MACHIGAERU

machikamaeru to await eagerly; to wait anxiously.

machikaneru to wait impatiently for. **Omachikane no nimotsu ga todokimashita.** The baggage that you have been waiting for so long has arrived.

machimachi diversity; variety; **machimachi no** diverse, various; divergent, conflicting.

MADA as yet; not yet (when used with a negative); still; so far. **Ano ko wa mada honno kodomo desu.** She (he) is still a mere child. **Mada futatsu arimasu.** We still have two.

MADE till, until, up to; to; as far as; **Tookyoo made** as far as Tokyo; **asa kara ban made** from morning till night.

MADO window; **mado garasu** windowpane; **mado o akeru** to open a window; **mado o shimeru** to close a window.

MAE time before; past; front; since; **mae no** previous, former; **mae ni** formerly, prior; **mae motte** beforehand; **mae kara** previously; from the front.

maeba front tooth.

maebarai prepayment; **maebarai no** prepaid; **maebarai suru** to pay in advance.

maebure announcement; preliminary notice.

maekake apron.

maekoojoo prologue; preamble.

maeoki preliminary statement, introduction.

magari crook, bend, turn.

MAGARU to bend, to yield; to turn; to wind; **magatta** bent, crooked, etc.; **magarikunetta michi** winding (rambling) road.

MAGERU to bend, curve. **Soko o magete onegai itashimasu.** Please say yes. [Please bring yourself to consent (against your will).]

magirasu to turn away, divert; **ki o magirasu** to divert (someone's) attention.

magirawashii confusing; ambiguous; misleading.

magire confusion; **magire no nai** evident, unmistakable; **magire mo naku** undoubtedly.

magirekomu to get mixed with; lost among; **gunshuu ni magirekomu** to get lost in the crowd; to be hidden in the crowd.

magireru to be mistaken for; to become confused.

magiwa verge, brink; **magiwa ni** on the verge of; **magiwa ni natte** at the last minute.

MAGO grandchild.

magokoro sincerity; devotion; **magokoro no aru** sincere.

magomago suru to be at a loss; to be bewildered.

magureatari lucky hit, lucky shot; fluke.

MAGURO tuna fish.

mahi paralysis; numbness; **mahi suru** to be paralyzed; **mahi shita** paralyzed.

MAI- prefix denoting: every, each; **maido** every time, each time; **maigetsu** every month; **mainen** every year; **maiasa** every morning; **maiban** every evening.

-MAI counter denoting: sheet; piece; page; leaf (a counter); **kami sanmai** three sheets of paper.

majiwari association; relations.

majiwaru to associate with; to mingle with. **Ano hito wa hito to majiwaru koto o kiraimasu.** She dislikes mingling with people.

makaseru to entrust (something to someone); to leave a person with some matter or business; **nariyuki ni makaseru** to let the matter take its course. **Banji kimi ni makasemasu.** I leave everything to you.

makasu to beat; to overpower; to beat down (a price), to bargain; **hyaku yen ni makasu** to beat down the price to 100 yen. **Kare o iimakasu koto ga dekinai.** I can't beat him in an argument.

make defeat, loss; lost game.

makeru to lose, be defeated; to concede, yield; to be outdone; to reduce (the price); **makezu otorazu** closely matched. **Makete kuremasen ka?** Can't you make it cheaper?

makijaku tape measure.

makikomu to roll up; to wrap up, enfold in.

makitabako cigarette; **makitabako ikko** pack of cigarettes; **makitabakoire** cigarette case.

MAKKA NA crimson, deep red; **makka na uso** outright lie; **makka ni naru** to turn red, blush deeply.

makkura pitch darkness; **makkura na** pitch dark.

MAKKURO NA deep black, ebony; **makkuro na kami no ke** jet-black hair.

MAKOTO truth; sincerity; honesty; faithfulness; **makoto no** genuine; real; sincere; **MAKOTO NI** truthfully; sincerely; really; greatly, exceedingly.

MAKU to wind, roll, coil, reel; **tokei no neji o maku** to wind up a clock.

MAKU to scatter, strew, sprinkle; to sow; **shibafu ni mizu o maku** to sprinkle the lawn with water.

maku curtain, hanging screen, drapery; act; **shomaku** opening act, first act; **maku o hikishiboru** to pull a curtain aside. **Maku ga aku.** The curtain rises.

MAKURA pillow, cushion; **makura o suru** to rest one's head on a pillow.

makuru to turn (roll, tuck) up; **ude o makuru** to roll up one's sleeves.

makushitateru to argue furiously.

MAMA as; as is; as it stands; intact; **sono mama** just as it is; **sono mama ni shite oku** to leave (something, or someone) as is. **Mama yo.** I don't care. Never mind.

mame beans; peas; soybeans; midget; tiny; **mame jidoosha** midget car.

mame na healthy, robust; brisk, active; faithful; **mame ni hataraku** to work briskly.

mamireru to be covered, stained with; **doro ni mamireru** to be covered with mud.

MAMORU to protect, defend, guard; to obey; **hoo o mamoru** to obey the laws; **yakusoku o mamoru** to keep a promise.

MAMUKOO just opposite; just in front of; **mamukoo no** just opposite; **mamukoo ni** right (just) in front of.

MAN ten thousand; myriad; **man ni hitotsu** one in ten thousand.

manabu to learn, study.

manben naku without exception; equally; uniformly.

mane imitation, mimicry; **maneru** to imitate; copy, mimic, simulate; **manete** in imitation of.

maneki invitation; beckoning.

MANEKU to invite; to call in; to bring upon oneself.

maniawase (n.) makeshift, expedient; **maniawase no** temporary.

maniawaseru to manage with, make do, serve the purpose.

MAN'ICHI by any chance; by any possibility; even though; **man'ichi no baai ni wa** if anything should happen; in case of emergency.

MAN'IN no vacancy; full house; crowded; **man'in fuda** "sold out" notice; "SRO" notice.

manjoo whole house, hall, assembly; **manjoo ittchi de** unanimously; with one accord.

manki expiration (of a contract); maturity; **manki ni naru** to fall due; to expire; to serve a full term.

manmaru na, manmarui perfectly round.

MANNAKA center, middle; heart; **mannaka ni** in the center; right in the middle.

mannenhitsu fountain pen.

mansei no chronic, confirmed.

manukareru to escape; to get rid of, be freed from; to be exempt; **ayauku manugareru** to have a narrow escape.

manuke (colloq.) stupid person, ass; half-wit; **manuke na** stupid, foolish.

manzara not wholly; not altogether. **Manzara baka de wa nai.** He is not a complete fool.

manzen at random, aimlessly; vaguely.

MANZOKU satisfaction, gratification; **manzoku na** satisfactory; complete; **manzoku ni** satisfactorily; **manzoku shite** contentedly; **manzoku suru** to be satisfied. **Manzoku shimashita.** I am satisfied.

mappadaka nakedness, nudity; **mappadaka no** stark naked.

mappira not by any means; not for anything. **Sonna koto wa mappira desu.** I wouldn't do it for anything.

mapputatsu ni right in two; **mapputatsu ni suru** to cut right in two.

marason marathon (race).

MARE NA rare, unusual, uncommon; **mare ni** rarely, seldom.

mari ball; **mari o tsuku** to play (with a) ball.

maru circle, ring.

MARUI circular, round, spherical. **marui kao (marugao)** round face; **MARUKU** round; in a circle; peacefully; smoothly; **me o maruku shite** wide-eyed; with the eyes wide open; **maruku osameru** to smooth over (a quarrel); to patch up.

MARUDE quite; thoroughly; almost like. **Marude natte inai.** It's quite hopeless. **Marude Nihonjin no yoo ni hanashimasu.** He speaks almost like a Japanese.

marukiri = marukkiri completely, entirely.

marumeru to make round.

marumooke clear profit; cleanup; **marumooke o suru** make a clear profit.

MASAKA by no means, on no account; surely not; you don't say; **masaka no toki ni** in time of need; in an emergency. **Masaka sonna koto wa arumai.** It's not at all likely.

masa ni just, exactly. **Masa ni sono toori desu.** It's exactly true.

masaru to surpass, excel.

masashiku certainly, no doubt. **Masashiku ano hito no yatta koto desu.** There is no question that he has done it.

masatsu rubbing, chafing, friction; **masatsu suru** to rub (against or with), chafe.

maseta precocious; **maseta kodomo** precocious child; **masete iru** to be precocious.

mashi increase; addition; extra; **mashi jikan** overtime; extra time; **ichi wari mashi** a 10 percent increase.

-MASHITA verb ending; past of **masu** (marks ordinary pol. verbs). **Kinoo gakkoo e ikimashita.** I went to school yesterday. **Tsukue no ue ni hon ga arimashita.** There was a book on the table.

mashitani right under, directly below; **mado no mashita ni** right beneath the window.

mashite much more; how much more. **Hawai ni itta koto mo nai no desu. Mashite Nihon ni wa ichido mo ikimasen.** I haven't been to Hawaii, let alone Japan.

massaichuu in the midst of; at the height of.

massakari height; prime; full bloom; **massakari de aru** to be at the height of; to be in full bloom.

massakasama ni headfirst; headlong; head over heels.

massaki *(n.)* foremost; head; **massaki no** first; foremost; **massaki ni** at the very beginning; first of all.

massao na deep blue; deadly pale; white as a sheet; **massao ni naru** to turn as white as a sheet.

masshigura ni impetuously; at full speed; full tilt.

MASSHIRO NA pure white; snow white; **masshiro na kimono** pure white clothes.

MASSHOOMEN direct, front; **masshoomen ni** directly in front of; directly opposite; full in the face; **masshoomen no tatemono** the building directly opposite.

MASSUGU NA straight; direct; upright; **massugu ni** directly; in a straight line.

MASU to increase; to swell; to raise; to rise. **Jinkoo ga kyonen yori niwari mashimashita.** The population increased by 20 percent over last year.

MASUMASU more and more; still more; increasingly. **Masumasu muzukashiku naru deshoo.** It will probably get increasingly difficult.

MATA and; besides; again; too; also; indirect; another; **MATA WA** or else; **mata aru toki wa** on another occasion; **matagiki** indirect information; hearsay; **mata tanomisuru** to ask something (of someone) indirectly (through someone else). **Watakushi mo mata motte iru.** I have it, too. So have I. **Mata dekakeru n desu ka?** Are you going out again?

matagaru to mount (a horse); to extend over, stretch over, span; **uma ni matagaru** to ride horseback; **sannen ni matagaru** extending over three years.

matagu to step over; to straddle.

mataseru to keep a person waiting.

matataku to wink, blink.

MATCHI match; matches; **matchibako** matchbox; **matchi o suru** to light a match; **matchibako no yoo na ie** tiny house (like a matchbox).

mato target, mark; point; **mato ga hazurete iru** to be wide of the mark; miss the point.

matomari conclusion; settlement; unity; coherence.

matomaru to be settled, decided; to come to a conclusion; to be completed.

matomeru to adjust, settle; to decide; to finish.

matomo ni right in front.

MATSU to wait; to await; to watch for, be on the lookout for; to expect; **mate!** wait!; hold on!; **nezu ni matsu** to sit up and wait for (someone).

matsu pine (tree); **matsukasa** pine cone; **matsubayashi** pine forest, grove.

matsubazue crutches.

matsuri festival; memorial services for one's ancestors.

matsuru to deify; to worship; to enshrine.

MATTAKU completely, entirely, totally; quite; perfectly; **mattaku no** entire, complete. **Mattaku soo desu.** You're quite right! **Makkaku fushigi desu!** How strange! **Mattaku wakarimasen.** I don't get it at all.

mattoo suru to accomplish; to fulfill; to complete.

mau to dance.

maue just above, right above; **atama no maue ni** directly overhead. **Ano hito no heya wa kono maue ni arimasu.** His room is right over this room.

MAWARI circumference; surroundings; neighborhood; **mawaridooi** roundabout; **mawarimichi** detour; roundabout road, roundabout way. **Ie no mawari wa hatake desu.** The farmland surrounds my house. **Mawari wa roku mairu arimasu.** The circumference is six miles.

mawari awase luck; chance.

MAWARU to turn (around); to go round; to come around, revolve, rotate; to spin. **Ichinen ni nido mawatte kimasu.** He comes around twice a year.

MAWASU to turn; to revolve, rotate; to roll; to whirl; to forward; to pass around; **kuruma o mawasu** to turn a wheel; to dispatch a car; **tsugi e mawasu** to pass on to the next.

mayaku drug, narcotic; **mayaku chuudoku** drug addiction.

mayoi delusion; superstition; illusion; infatuation.

mayonaka dead of night.

mayou to be puzzled; to waver, hesitate; to go astray; to lose one's way.

mayowasu to puzzle, bewilder; to mislead, misguide; to fascinate, captivate; to seduce.

MAYU eyebrows; **mayu o hisomeru** to frown; **mayuzumi** eyebrow pencil.

mazamaza to clearly, distinctly, vividly.

mazarimono mixture; compound.

mazaru to mingle.

mazeru to mix, adulterate.

mazekaesu to interrupt, butt in; to ridicule, sneer at.

MAZU first; in the first place; to begin with; about; almost; nearly; anyway; anyhow. **Mazu!** Well! **Mazu joodeki da.** It is fairly successful.

MAZUI tasteless, untasty, insipid; plain, homely; poor; awkward, clumsy; **mazusoo na** unappetizing. **Gohan ga mazui desu.** I don't enjoy eating.

ME eye; sight, look, glance; eyesight, vision; notice, observation; point of view; discrimination; insight; bud, sprout, shoot; **me no todoku kagiri** as far as one can see; as far as the eye can see; **me ga tsubureru** to lose one's sight; to become blind; **me ni amaru** to be innumerable; to be too much for; to be unpardonable; **me ni mienai** to be invisible, be unseen; **me ni tsuku** to attract (someone's) attention; to catch the eye; **me ga warui** to have poor eyesight; **me ga sameru** to wake up; to be awakened; to have one's eyes opened; **me o ageru** to lift one's eyes, look up; **me o maruku shite odoroku** to stare in wonder; **me o muku** to stare; to glare at; **me to me o miawasu** to exchange glances; **me ni hairu** to come into sight; to come into view; **me ni tatsu** to be conspicuous; **me ga kiku** to have an eye for; to be a good judge of. **Nagai me de mite ite kudasai.** Time will tell.

me bud, sprout, shoot; **me ga deru** to bud, to sprout; **me o tsumu** to nip (something) in the bud.

-me suffix denoting; order in which things are arranged; **sandome** the third time.

meate aim, object, end; **meate ni suru** to aim at, aim for.

meboshi objective, aim.

mebunryoo rough estimation (done by the eye).

mechamecha ni in disorder, in confusion; **mechamecha ni suru** to make a mess of, upset; to ruin, wreck; **mechamecha ni naru** to go to pieces; to be spoiled; to get mixed up.

medatsu to be conspicuous; to stand out; **medatsu iro** a loud, gay color; **medatta** striking, remarkable.

medetai happy; auspicious; successful; **medetai koto** happy event; matter for congratulations; **medetaku** happily, auspiciously; **medetaku owaru** to end happily. **Omedetoo!** Congratulations!

meetoru meter (measure); gauge; **meetoruboo** metric system.

MEGANE eyeglasses; insight; judgment; **meganeya** optician. **Megane nashi de yomemasen.** I can't read without glasses; **megane ni kanau** to find favorable.

megurasu to enclose with; surround.

meguri circumference, a tour; round; circulation; flow; **meisho meguri o suru** to make a tour of famous places.

meguriau to come across; to happen to meet.

meguru to go around; circulate.

MEI niece.

meian good idea, good suggestion; bright (brilliant) plan.

meibo register, roll of names, roster.

meibutsu specialty; noted product; attraction; feature. **Koko no meibutsu wa nan desu ka?** What is this place noted for?

meichuu hit; **meichuu suru** to hit the mark; to tell; **meichuu shinai** to miss, go wide (of the mark).

meigetsu full moon; **chuushuu no meigetsu** harvest moon.

MEIGI name; **meigijoo no** nominal, titular; **meigijoo wa** nominally; ostensibly.

meihaku na clear, distinct, explicit.

meii famous physician.

meijin expert; master.

meijiru, meizuru to command, to give orders.

meikaku na clear; definite; distinct; clear-cut; **meiki suru** to state clearly; to specify.

meimei christening, naming; **meimeishiki** christening ceremony; **meimei suru** to christen, name.

meirei command, order, injunction; **meireiteki na** imperative, peremptory; **meirei ni yotte** by order of; **meirei suru** to order, command, decree; to give orders to.

meisai particulars, details; **meisai na** detailed, minute; **meisai ni** minutely, in detail; fully; **meisaigaki** detailed description, statement, account.

meisaku masterpiece; fine piece of work.

meisan noted product.

meisei fame, reputation; **meisei aru** noted, renowned.

meishi calling card, visiting card; business card.

meishin superstition; **meishinteki na** superstitious.

meisho famous place; famous sight; **meisho o mawaru** to see the sights.

meishoo place of scenic beauty.

meisoo meditation, contemplation; dream, illusion; fallacy, erroneous idea; **meisoo suru** to meditate.

meitei drunkenness; **meiteisha** drunkard; **meitei suru** to get drunk.

MEIWAKU trouble; bother; nuisance; **meiwaku na** troublesome, annoying; **meiwaku suru** to be troubled; to have trouble; to get into trouble; **meiwaku o kakeru** to bother, annoy. **Gomeiwaku de wa arimasen ka?** (Are you sure) I'm not bothering you?

meiyo honor; glory; fame; **meiyo o hakusuru** to attain an honor; to attain a reputation; **meiyo o omonzuru** to have a sense of honor; **meiyoshin** ambition; desire for fame.

meizuru See meijiru.

mejiri corner of the eye.

mejirushi mark; landmark; sign; guide.

mekakushi blindfold; screen; blind.

mekasu to primp; deck oneself out; to dress elaborately; to dress up.

MEKATA weight; **mekata de uru** to sell by weight; **mekata o hakaru** to weigh (a thing).

mekimeki more and more; visibly; rapidly. **Nihongo ga mekimeki jootatsu shite imasu.** You are making rapid progress in Japanese.

mekkiri considerably, noticeably.

mekubase suru to wink meaningfully at.

mekura blindness; blind person; **mekura meppoo ni** recklessly; **mekura saguri o suru** to fumble; to grope. **Mekura hebi ni ojizu.** Fools rush in where angels fear to tread.

memai dizziness; **memai ga suru** to be dizzy.

memeshii effeminate, unmanly.

memori graduations (on a thermometer, etc.); graduations; markings.

men face; mask; surface; facet, aspect, phase, side; **men to mukatte** face to face; **men suru** to face, front on; to border on; to look out on. **Heya wa toori ni men shimasu.** The room looks out on the street; **menboku (menmoku)** face, countenance; honor; **menboku (menmoku) o isshin suru** to undergo a complete change.

men cotton (fabric); **menka** raw cotton; **menshi** cotton thread.

mendoo trouble, difficulty; troubles; complications; **mendoo na** complicated; troublesome; **mendoo o kakeru** to give trouble; **mendoo o miru** to take the trouble; to look after; **mendookusai** troublesome. **Mattaku mendookusai desu.** It's a great deal of trouble.

men'eki immunity (to disease); **men'eki ni natte iru** to be immune to; **men'eki chuusha** inoculation.

menjo exemption; excuse; discharge; **menjo suru** to exempt (from a tax); to release; to excuse.

menjoo diploma.

menkai interview; **menkai suru** to have an interview; **menkaibi** reception; visitors' day; office day.

menkurau to be confused; to be upset; to be at a loss.

menkyo = **menkyojoo** license; certificate; **menkyoryoo** license fee; **menkyojoo o motte iru** to hold a license.

menmitsu na detailed, minute; close; nice; meticulous; **menmitsu ni** minutely, etc.

menshiki acquaintance; **menshiki no aru hito** acquaintance; **ichi menshiki mo nai hito** complete stranger.

menshoku discharge, dismissal; **menshoku suru** to dismiss, discharge.

menuki no principal, main; **menuki no basho** busiest section; business center; **menuki no oodoori** main thoroughfare; busy street.

merikomu to cave in; to sink.

mesaki foresight; **mesaki ni** before one's eyes; under one's nose; **mesaki no mienai** stupid; **mesaki no** at hand; immediate.

meshi *(vulgar)* boiled rice; meal; food; **meshi o taku** to cook rice.

MESHIAGARU to eat; to drink *(respect)*. **Meshiagatte kudasai.** Please help yourself.

meshita inferior, subordinate.

meshitsukai servant.

mesu female (animal); **mesu neko** she-cat.

metsuboo downfall; ruin, destruction.

metsuki expression of the eyes; **kowai metsuki** menacing look.

metta na reckless; inconsiderate; **metta ni** rarely, seldom; recklessly; thoughtlessly.

meue superior, senior; **meue no hito o uyamau** to respect one's superiors.

mezamashi dokei alarm clock.

mezamashii remarkable; brilliant; admirable.

mezawari eyesore; offense to the eye.

MEZURASHII rare, unusual; new; curious; **mezurashii mono** novelty, curio.

mi body; person; self; oneself; **mi mo kokoro mo** body and soul; **mi o ayamaru** to lead a dissipated life; **mi no ue** one's station in life; **mi no mawari no mono** personal belongings.

mi fruit, nut, berry.

miageta admirable, praiseworthy; respectable.

miawaseru to exchange glances; to look at each other, to put off, postpone, defer; to abandon.

miboojin widow.

mibun social position, social standing; identity; **mibun o akasu** to reveal one's identity.

miburi gesture, motion; **miburi o suru** to gesture; make a motion.

miburui shivering, trembling; shiver; shudder; **miburui suru** to shiver (with cold), to tremble (with fear); to shudder (with horror). **Omotta dake de mo miburui ga suru.** The mere thought of it makes me shudder.

MICHI way, road, route, course; highway; **komichi** path, lane; **michi ni mayou** to lose one's way; **michi o kiku** to ask directions; **michibata** roadside, wayside; **michisuji** route, course.

michibiju to lead, guide.

michigaeru to mistake (by sight) one thing for another; **michigaeru hodo kawaru** to change beyond recognition.

michi no unknown, strange.

michinori distance, journey; **kisha de ichijikan hodo no michinori** about an hour's ride by train.

michishirube guidepost; street sign.

michizure fellow traveler, companion on a trip.

midara na indecent, obscene, lewd.

midare disorder; disturbance; irregularity.

midareru to be disordered; to go out of order.

midashi index; title; headline; heading.

midasu to put out of order; to turn upside down; to agitate, disturb; to demoralize.

MIDORI, MIDORIIRO green color; **midorigakatta** greenish; **midori no** green, verdant.

mie appearance, show, display; **mie no tame ni** for show; **mie ni suru** to do (something) for show or for the sake of appearance; **mie o haru** to show off.

MIERU to be visible; to see, catch sight of; to be in sight; to look like; to seem, appear; to be found; **mienaku naru** to disappear, become missing, become invisible. **Toshi no wari ni wakaku mieru.** He looks young for his age. **Me ga mieru yoo ni natta.** Now I can see things.

miesuita transparent; obvious, plain.

migaki polish; burnishing; **nihongo ni migaki o kakeru** to brush up one's Japanese.

MIGAKU to polish; to rub; to brush; to improve; to refine; **kutsu o migaku** to polish shoes; **ha o migaku** to brush one's teeth; **migakiageru** to polish (silver, etc.).

migamae attitude (posture) of being ready for action; **migamae o suru** to stand ready; to brace oneself.

migawari substitution; substitute; scapegoat; stand-in; **migawari o tateru** to put in one's place.

MIGI right, right-hand side; **migi e magaru** to turn to the right; **migi ni deru** to surpass, outdo. **Migigawa kootsuu.** Keep to the right.

migiwa waterside, water's edge.

MIGOTO NA beautiful; fine; pretty; brilliant; excellent; superb; **migoto ni** beautifully, etc. **Migoto migoto!** Well done!

migurushii ugly, unsightly; dishonorable, disgraceful.

mihakarai choice (at one's discretion). **Sore wa anata no omihakarai ni makasemasu.** I leave the choice to you.

mihakarau to choose (at one's discretion); to select (something) on one's own.

miharai outstanding (unpaid) account; **miharai no** outstanding, unpaid, unsettled.

miharashi view, prospect, outlook; **maharashi ga yoi** to have a fine view.

mihari watch, vigil, lookout, observation.

miharu to watch, keep watch, stand guard; **me o miharu** to open one's eyes wide; **me o mihatte** with wide-open eyes.

mihon sample, swatch, specimen.

MIJIKAI short, brief; **mijikaku suru** to curtail, shorten, abbreviate.

mijime misery; sadness; **mijime na** sad, miserable, pitiful.

mijin atoms; particles; **mijin ni naru** to be smashed to atoms.

MIJITAKU dress; equipment; preparation; **mijitaku o suru** to dress, get dressed; to equip; to prepare oneself.

mijuku immaturity, unripeness; **mijuku na** unripe, green, immature, inexperienced. **Watakushi no Eigo wa mijuku desu.** My English is far from perfect.

mikai no uncivilized, savage.

mikake daoshi no deceptive. **Sore wa mikake daoshi desu.** It's not as good as it looks.

mikaku sense of taste; palate; **mikaku o sosoru** to tempt the taste; **mikaku ni au** to suit one's taste.

MIKAN tangerine (popular fruit in Japan).

mikan no incomplete, unfinished.

mikata way of looking at things; point of view, viewpoint; **atarshii mikata o suru** to look at something in a new light; to see from a new point of view.

mikawasu to exchange looks.

mikazuki new, crescent moon.

miki trunk, stem.

mikiri abandonment; **mikiri o tsukeru** to wash one's hands of; to have nothing to do with; to give up; to desert.

mikiru to give up, abandon.

MIKKA three days; third day of the month; **mikkakan** three days; **Sangatsu mikka** March 3; **mikka ni agezu** almost every other day.

mikkai secret meeting, rendezvous.

mikkoku suru to inform against, betray; **mikkokusha** informer.

MIKOMI promise, hope, anticipation, prospect; **mikomi no aru** promising; **mikomi ga hazureru** to prove contrary to expectations.

mikonsha unmarried person.

mikosu to anticipate, foresee; to speculate (financially).

mikubiru to make light of; to think meanly of.

mikudasu to look down on; to despise.

mimai sympathy visit; **mimai ni iku** to visit a sick person.

miman under; below; less than; not more than; **hyakuen miman** less than one hundred yen; **jissai miman** under ten years of age; ten years and under.

mimau to visit a sick person.

mime features; face; looks; **mime yoi** good-looking; **mime uruwashii** beautiful, fair, pretty.

MIMI ear; hearing; **mimi ga yoi** to have a good ear; **mimi ni ireru** to inform; **mimi ni hairu** to reach one's ears; **mimi o katamukeru** to listen; **mimi o sobatateru** to strain one's ears; **mimi ni tako ga dekiru** to din into one's ears; **miminari** ringing in the ears; **mimi zawari no** grating, jarring (to the ears). **Miminari ga suru.** My ears are ringing.

mimochi conduct, behavior; **mimochi ga yoi** well-behaved, of good conduct; **mimochi ga warui** to lead a fast life, be of loose morals.

mimono sight, spectacle; attraction.

mimoto one's birth, parentage; identity; history; career.

mimuki mo sezu without looking around; without a look at; straight ahead.

MINA, MINNA all; everyone; everything; **mina de** in all; in a body; all told. **Mina de ikura desu ka?** How much for them all together? How much for the lot?

minage suru to drown oneself.

minagoroshi massacre, extermination, wholesale murder.

minakami source of a river or stream; headwaters.

MINAMI south; **minami no** southerly; southern; **minami ni** to the south; on the south.

minamoto source, fountainhead, origin, root.

minaosu to look at again; to have another look; to take a turn for the better, improve, look up.

minarai apprenticeship; apprentice; **minarau** to receive training, practice as an apprentice; to follow suit, copy; to learn from another.

MINARI dress, attire; personal appearance.

minashigo orphan.

minasu to regard as; to consider, think of; to suppose.

minato harbor, port.

mine peak, summit, top; back.

minikui indistinct, obscure; illegible; difficult to see.

minikui ugly.

minji civil affairs; civil case; **minji saibansho** civil court.

minogasu to neglect; to overlook; to forgive.

minoo nonpayment; default in payment; **minoo no** unpaid; in arrears.

minoru to bear fruit; to ripen.

minu furi o suru to pretend not to see; to wink at; to connive.

min'yoo ballad, folksong, popular song.

MIOBOE recognition; remembrance; **mioboe ga aru** to remember seeing before; to recollect; to recognize.

MIOKURU seeing someone off; **hito o miokuri ni iku** to go to see a person off. **Hikoojoo e tomodachi o miokuri ni ikimasu.** I am going to the airport to see a friend off.

miosame last look, farewell look.

miotori unfavorable comparison; **miotori ga suru** to compare unfavorably with; to suffer by comparison; to be eclipsed by.

miotoshi oversight, omission.

MIRAI (n.) future, time to come; future life; **mirai no** (adj.) future, prospective.

miren cowardice, attachment; regret; **miren ga aru** to be still attached to.

MIRU to see, look at, glance at, observe; to judge; to read; to look after, etc.; **yoku miru** to have a good look at; **chotto miru to** at first glance; **shinbun o miru** to read (look at) a newspaper. **Ima ni miro!** You'll soon see!

miryoku charm, fascination; (glamour) appeal; **miryoku ga nai** to have no appeal for; to have nothing attractive about.

miryoo suru to fascinate, charm.

misadameru to make sure of.

misagehateta mean, contemptible.

misaki cape, headland, promontory.

MISE store, shop; booth; **mise o hiraku** to open a store, to start a business.

misekake pretense, make-believe; appearance.

misekakeru to pretend, make a show of.

MISERU to show, let see, exhibit, display; to make something look like; to give an air of; **isha ni miseru** to consult a doctor, to be examined. **Anata no nooto o misete kudasai.** Please let me see your notebook.

miseshime lesson, object lesson, warning, example; **miseshime ni naru** to serve as a warning (lesson) to.

mishimishi iu to creak.

MISO soybean paste (food used in daily diet); **miso o tsukeru** to make a mess of; to make a poor showing; **miso shiru** soybean soup. **Soko ga miso da.** That's the beauty of it.

misoka last day of the month; **oomisoka** New Year's Eve.

misokonai misjudgment, mistaken impression.

misokonau to misjudge, make a mistake, make a wrong estimation.

missetsu na close, intimate; **missetsu na kankei ga aru** to be closely related to; to be in close connection with.

misshiri, mitchiri severely, seriously; closely, diligently; in earnest.

misuborashii shabby, ragged, seedy.

misumisu before one's very eyes; in full knowledge of the situation.

mitasu to fill, satisfy, appease, gratify; **kiboo o mitasu** to gratify a desire; **juyoo o mitasu** to meet a demand; to supply a need.

mitate diagnosis (medical); choice; **mitate chigai** wrong diagnosis; mistaken judgment.

mitateru to diagnose; to choose, select.

mitchaku suru to stick, adhere to; to be close together; to be interlocked.

mitchiri See **misshiri.**

mitei no unsettled, undecided.

mitodokeru to verify, make sure of; to satisfy oneself that.

mitomein private seal.

MITOMERU to see, witness; to catch sight of; to observe; to recognize; to admit.

mitooshi perspective, outlook; prospect; unobstructed view.

mitoosu to get an unobstructed view; to see through; to see into.

mitsu honey; **mitsubachi** honeybee; **mitsubachi no su** beehive; **mitsuzuki ryokoo** honeymoon.

mitsudan secret conversation, confidential talk; **mitsudan suru** to have a private (confidential) talk.

mitsugi secret; closed conference.

MITSUKERU to find out, discover; to detect; to sight, locate. **Uwagi o mitsukeru koto ga dekinai.** I can't find my coat.

mitsumeru to stare at, fix one's eyes on.

mitsumori estimate; assessment; evaluation.

mitsumoru to estimate; calculate; evaluate.

mitsurin thick forest, dense woods.

mitsu yunyuu smuggling; **mitsu yunyuusha** smuggler; **mitsu yunyuu suru** to smuggle.

mittomonai indecent; disgraceful; unsightly; ugly; plain-looking; **mittomonai otoko** poorly dressed man. **Mittomonai koto o shite wa ikemasen.** Don't behave so disgracefully.

MITTSU, SAN three. (See also **mikka.**)

miuchi relations; relative; friends; followers.

miwake discrimination; judgment.

miwakeru to discriminate; to discern; to judge.

miwatasu to look over; to gaze out on; **miwatasu kagiri** as far as one can see.

miyage, omiyage souvenir; gift, present; **miyagebanashi** account of interesting or unusual things seen or heard on a trip.

miyako capital; metropolis.

miyasui evident, easily seen, clear.

mizen ni beforehand; before something happens; **mizen ni fusegu** to prevent (keep from) occurring; to take preventive action.

mizo ditch, drain, gutter; groove.

mizore sleet. **Mizore ga furimasu.** It's sleeting.

mizou no unheard of; unprecedented.

MIZU water; cold water; **mizu no tooranai** waterproof; watertight; **mizu de yusugu** to rinse with water; **mizu o waru** to dilute; **mizuirazu de kurasu** to live alone (without outsiders in the same house); **mizubukure** water blister; **MIZUGI** swimsuit; **mizugiwa** water's edge; **mizugiwadatte** splendidly; brilliantly; **mizugiwadatta** splendid; striking; beautiful; wheel; **mizugusuri** liquid medicine; **mizuhake** drainage; drain; **MIZUKE** dampness; moisture; **mizuke no aru** juicy; watery; **mizuke no nai** dry; parched; **mizukemuri** spray; **mizukoshi** filter; strainer; **mizukasai** watery; **mizusashi** water pitcher; **mizutame** reservoir; water tank; **mizutori** waterfowl.

mizuhiki colored paper cord used for tying up formal presents (red and white are chosen for ceremonious occasions).

mizuiro (n.) light blue; **muzuiro no** (adj.) light blue.

mizukakeron fruitless argument; endless dispute.

mizumizushii fresh-looking; ruddy.

mizusaki annai, mizusaki annainin pilot (of a boat).

mizuumi lake.

MO particle denoting: as well as; too; also; as many (much) as; no less (fewer) than; neither . . . nor; even; even if; although; in spite of; **donna ni ame ga hidokute mo** no matter how hard it may rain; **futte no tette mo** rain or shine. **Watakushi mo ikimasu.** I'll go too. **Hitori mo imasen.** There isn't even one person.

mochi durability; wear; **mochi ga yoi** to wear well, be durable.

mochi rice cake.

mochiagaru to be lifted, raised up; to arise; to take place; **MOCHIAGERU** to raise, lift up; to hold up; to praise; to flatter. **Kono hako wa omokute mochiageru koto ga dekimasen.** This box is too heavy for me to lift up. **Mochiagenaide kudasai.** Please don't lift it up.

mochiau to balance, keep balanced; to remain steady; to share; to pool (expenses).

mochiawase things on hand, in stock. **Mochiawase ga nai.** There isn't any on hand.

mochiawaseru to have on hand; to have in stock.

mochiba post, station; duty; round, beat, route.

mochidasu to take out, bring out; to carry out; to carry away; to remove; to save; to propose; to introduce.

mochiiru to use; to make use of, employ; to adopt; to apply.

mochikaeru to pass from one (hand or person) to another.

mochikakeru to propose; to court.

mochikomi delivery to the door.

mochikomu to carry in, bring in.

mochikotaeru to endure; to hold out; to stand.

mochimono property, possessions, belongings. **Kono hon wa Tanaka-san no mochimono desu.** This book is Mr. Tanaka's. This book belongs to Mr. Tanaka.

mochinaosu to improve; to pick up; to recover (usually used when speaking of illness).

mochinige suru to make off with, run away with.

mochinushi owner, proprietor, possessor.

MOCHIRON, muron of course; naturally; to be sure; certainly; no doubt; needless to say. **Mochiron suki desu.** Of course I like it! Certainly, I like it.

mochiyoru to contribute one's share; to bring one's quota.

modaeru to be in agony; to be worried; to suffer great agony.

modokashigaru to lose patience.

modokashii irritating; slow; slow-moving; not quick enough; unsatisfactory.

modori return; temporary recovery.

modoru to return, come back; to go back; to turn back; to recede.

MODOSU to return; to give; to send back; to throw up, vomit.

moeagaru to burst into flames, blaze up; **moegara** embers; cinders.

moekiru to burn out, be burned up.

MOERU to burn, blaze, be in flames; **moetsuku** to catch fire; to ignite; **moesashi** embers; half-burnt stump; **moeyasui** combustible, inflammable; **moenai** noncombustible; **moeru omoi** burning passion. **Ie ga moeru.** The house is on fire. **Hi ga yoku moete imasu.** The fire is burning briskly. (See also **hi**.)

moeru to sprout, to bud.

mofuku mourning clothes.

mogaku to struggle; to writhe; to wriggle.

mogu to break off; to tear off.

moguri diving; diver; unlicensed practitioner.

moguru to dive (into water); to dip; to creep (into bed); **toko ni moguru** to get into bed; to crawl into bed.

moji letter, character, ideograph; **moji doori no** literal; **moji no wakaru** literate, educated; **moji ni akarui** to be learned.

mojimoji suru to hesitate.

mojiru to twist, distort; to parody, mimic.

mokei model, pattern.

MOKKA now, at present, for the present, currently; **mokka no** present; existing; **mokka no tokoro** for the time being.

mokkyo tacit permission; **mokkyo suru** to give tacit permission.

mokugeki observation; **mokugeki suru** to observe, witness; **mokugekisha** eyewitness.

MOKUHYOO mark, sign; goal, target, objective; **-o mokuhyoo ni suru** to aim at; to have (something) as one's objective.

mokuji table of contents.

mokumoku to silently, in silence.

mokumokutaru silent, dumb; implicit.

mokunin tacit approval; passive consent; **mokunin suru** to tolerate; to give tacit approval; to connive.

mokurei nod; **mokurei suru** to nod; to greet with a nod.

mokuroku table of contents; list; catalogue.

mokuromi plan.

mokusan expectation; calculation; estimate; **mokusan ga hazureru** to be disappointed in one's expectations; to fail to come up to one's estimate.

mokushi revelation.

mokushi suru to overlook; to pass unnoticed.

mokusoku suru to measure with the eye.

mokusoo meditation.

MOKUTEKI aim, purpose, intention; **mokutekichi** destination, end of the journey.

MOKUYOOBI Thursday.

mokuzai wood, lumber, timber.

mokuzen before one's eyes; immediate; **mokuzen ni** before one's eyes; in the presence of; **mokuzen ni semaru** to be close at hand; to be right in front of one's eyes; to be imminent.

momareru to be tried; to be knocked around, tossed about.

momegoto trouble; dissension.

MOMEN cotton; cotton cloth; **momen ito** cotton thread; **momen mono** cotton goods; cotton clothes.

momeru to get into a dispute; to get into trouble; to have trouble; to feel discord; to be rumpled.

momiau to shove and push, jostle, to struggle with a person.

momikesu to rub out; to crush out; to smother; to hush up; to stifle.

momiryooji massage; **momiryooji suru** to massage.

MOMO peach.

momohiki underwear (shorts), drawers, trunks.

momoiro *(n.)* pink; **momoiro no** *(adj.)* pink, pinkish.

momu to rub, massage; to crumple up, to wrinkle.

MON gate; gateway; **mon'ei** gatekeeper.

mon crest.

MONDAI question, problem; subject, topic; **mondai to naru** to give rise to discussion; to be criticized; **mondai ni naranai** to be out of the question; to be insignificant; **roodoo mondai** labor problem.

mondori utsu to turn a somersault.

mongen closing time, lockup time.

monjin pupil, disciple, follower(s).

monku wording, words, terms, expression, complaint, grievance; objection; excuse; **monku o iu** to make a complaint; to grumble; **monku o iwazu ni** without question.

MONO thing, object; substance, matter; stuff, article; goods; possession; something; **mono ni suru** to secure; to take possession of; to make something of; **mono ni naru** to come to (anything) good; **mono ni naranai** to come to nothing; to get nowhere; to end in failure.

mono person, somebody.

monohoshiba place for drying clothes.

monohoshizao clothes pole.

monomonoshii showy, ostentatious; pretentious, pompous.

MONO NO though; although; only; but; about; some; **to wa iu mono no** for all that; in spite of all that is said; **mono no nifun to tatanu uchi ni** in less than two minutes.

monooki storeroom, storehouse.

monoreeru monorail.

monosashi ruler; footrule; yardstick.

monoshiri well-informed person; man of great knowledge; scholar.

monosugoi dreary, dismal; ghastly, grim, gruesome, terrible; **monosugoi arisama** horrible scene; **monosugoi hitode** a terribly large crowd of people.

MOO already; not any longer; by now; now;

soon, before long; presently; **moo sukoshi** a little more, a few more; **moo ichido** once more. **Moo fuyu desu.** It's already winter. **Moo arimasen.** I haven't any more.

moo another. **Mizu o moo ippai kudasai.** May I have another cup of water?

mooderu to visit (a temple): to worship (at a temple or shrine).

moofu blanket.

moojuu wild beast; beast of prey.

mooka raging fire.

mookaru to be profitable; to make a profit; to pay; to be paying.

mooke profit, gains, earnings; **mooke ni naranai** to be unprofitable; **mookeguchi** profitable job, work, undertaking.

mookeru to make, earn profits; to make money; to set up, establish; to frame.

moomoo to dense, thick; dim; **moomoo to shite** thickly, in clouds.

mooretsu violence, fierceness; **mooretsu na** violent, fierce, furious, stormy; strong, intense; **mooretsu ni** violently, strongly, etc.; **mooretsu ni furu** to rain hard (furiously).

mooshiawase agreement; understanding; appointment.

mooshiawaseru to arrange; to agree upon; **mooshiawasete** by arrangement; **mooshiawaseta jikan ni** at the appointed (agreed-upon) hour.

mooshideru to make a proposal, make an offer.

mooshikomi offer, proposal; **mooshikomi yooshi** application form.

mooshikomu to apply for; to propose.

mooshitate statement, declaration; allegation; testimony; plea.

mooshitateru to state, declare; to testify.

mooshon motion; **mooshon o kakeru** to motion for (a person to do something); to make eyes at; to encourage.

MOOSU to say, tell *(humble)*. **Hai, soo mooshimasu.** Yes, I'll tell him so. **Watakushi wa Yamada to mooshimasu.** My name is Yamada.

MOPPARA chiefly, mostly, principally; solely, exclusively; entirely. **Kare wa moppara shigoto ni seidashite imasu.** He devotes himself to his business.

moraigo adopted child.

moraimono present, gift (that is received).

morasu to let leak; to reveal, disclose; to let out, omit, leave out.

MORAU to receive; to get, obtain; to be given; to be presented with; to get a person to do, have a person do (following a **-te**

form). **Kono hon o morau koto ga dekimasen ka?** Can't I get this book? Couldn't you give me this book? **Tanaka-san ni katte moraimashita.** I had Mr. Tanaka buy it.

more leak, leakage, omission; oversight; **more o fusagu** to stop a leak.

moreru to leak; to escape; to come through; to get out; to get wind of; to be omitted; to be excluded.

mori leak.

mori nursemaid; taking care of a baby.

mori forest; wood.

morikaesu to regain, recover.

MOSHI MO in case of; if; provided that; **moshi mo no koto ga attara** if anything should happen; in case of emergency.

MOSHI MOSHI I say; say; if you please; please. **Moshi moshi.** Hello! Are you there (in a telephone conversation)?

MOSHIYA by any chance; by some possibility. **Moshiya to omotte kiite mita.** I chanced asking her.

mosu, moyasu to burn (transitive).

mosurin muslin.

motareru to lean on, lean against; to rest against; to recline on; to sit heavily on; to lie heavily on.

motaseru to let (someone) have, let (someone) take; to get (someone) to carry.

moteamasu to be embarrassed at, by; not to know what to do with.

moteru to be welcomed, made much of; to be popular; to receive attention.

MOTO origin, source, cause, root; investment price; cost price; **moto wa** originally, at first; **moto kara** from the beginning; **moto yori** from the first; originally; **motomoto** from the beginning, originally; **motone** original price; cost price; **motone de uru** to sell at cost.

moto under; **oya no moto de** under parental supervision; **-no shusai no moto de** under the auspices of.

motode capital, funds; stock; **motode o orosu** to invest capital.

MOTOMERU to ask for, request, demand; to look for, search for.

MOTSU to hold; to carry; to have in hand; to possess, own; **shikkari to motsu** to grasp firmly; to take firm hold of.

motsure tangle; entanglement; trouble; complications.

motsureru to get entangled, be in a knot; to become complicated.

mottai artificial importance; **mottai o tsukeru** to exaggerate the importance of.

mottaiburu to put on airs.

mottainai wasteful; extravagant; impious; sacrilegious; gracious; more than one deserves. **Maa, mottainai!** What a waste! **Kare ni wa mottainai hodo no chii da.** The position is too good for him.

MOTTE with; by means of; by, through, because, on account of; **tegami de motte toiawaseru** to inquire by letter.

motte iku to take, carry (away).

motte kuru to bring; to fetch; to take along.

motte no hoka out of the question; outrageous; unpardonable.

MOTTO more; much; still more. **Motto kudasai.** Give me some more.

MOTTOMO most, exceedingly, extremely. **Mottomo juuyoo desu.** It is most important.

MOTTOMO indeed; it is true; but; **mottomo na** reasonable; right; rational; natural.

mottomorashii plausible.

moya haze, mist.

moyasu See **mosu.**

moyoo pattern; design; appearance, aspect.

moyooshi meeting; gathering.

moyoosu to organize, arrange; to hold (a meeting); to feel; to show signs of; to look like.

MOYORI NO nearest; adjacent, nearby. **Moyori no keisatsusho e shirasete kudasai.** Please notify any police station in your neighborhood.

mozoo imitation; **mozoo suru** to imitate, copy; **mozoohin** imitation, counterfeit.

muboo recklessness; thoughtlessness; **muboo na** reckless, rash; thoughtless, inconsiderate, ill-advised.

mucha nonsense; disorder; **mucha na** disorderly, confused; absurd, unreasonable; thoughtless; **mucha ni** recklessly; excessively, blindly; **muchakucha** unreasonable, absurd; mixed up, jumbled.

muchi ignorance; stupidity; **muchi na** ignorant, illiterate, etc.

muchuu unconsciousness; ecstasy; **muchuu ni naru** to become unconscious; to be carried away; to become ecstatic; **muchuu de** as in a dream; unknowingly; wildly, madly.

muda futility, uselessness; **muda na** fruitless, futile, no good, of no use; **muda ni naru** to get wasted; to be thrown away; to be in vain; **muda ni suru** to waste, throw away, etc.; **mudaashi** to go for nothing; **mudaashi o suru** to go in vain; to go on a fool's errand.

mudabanashi idle talk, gossip.

mudan without warning; without permission.

muden wireless communication.

mueki no useless, futile.

MUGI barley, oats, rye, wheat (general term for grain); **mugicha** barley tea; **komugiko** wheat flour; **mugimeshi** rice cooked with barley; **mugiwara booshi** straw hat.

mugon silence, muteness; **mugon no** silent, speechless, dumb; **mugon de** silently, in silence.

muhi uniqueness; **muhi no** unequaled, matchless, unique.

muhon rebellion, revolt, insurrection; treason; **muhon suru** to rebel, revolt; **muhonnin** rebel, insurgent; traitor.

muhoo na unlawful, unjust, outrageous.

muhooshuu without remuneration; **muhooshuu no** free; **muhooshuu de** free of charge, without recompense; **muhooshuu de hataraku** to work without pay.

muigi, muimi senselessness; **muigi na** senseless, absurd, meaningless.

MUIKA sixth day of the month; six days.

muimi See **muigi**.

muishiki unconsciousness; **muishiki ni** unconsciously; mechanically, automatically.

mujaki innocence, naïveté; **mujaki na** naive, innocent.

mujin See **mujinzoo**.

muji no plain, unfigured.

mujinzoo, mujin limitlessness.

mujoo heartlessness; **mujoo no** heartless, inhuman; highest; best; supreme.

mujooken de unconditionally; **mujooken no** unconditional; absolute.

mujun contradiction; inconsistency; **mujun no** contradictory; conflicting, inconsistent; **mujun suru** to be inconsistent.

mukae meeting (someone).

MUKAERU to meet, go to meet; to greet, welcome, receive; to invite, call for, send for; **Tookyoo eki de hito o mukaeru** to meet a person at the Tokyo station.

mukaiau to confront someone, to face each other.

mukaikaze head wind, adverse wind.

mukamuka suru to feel sick (nauseous); to feel offended; to get angry.

mukankaku insensibility; unconsciousness; lack of feeling; **mukankaku no** insensible; numb; unconscious.

mukankei no unrelated; unconcerned, disinterested.

mukanshoo non-intervention.

mukashi ancient times, old days, long ago, remote antiquity; **mukashibanashi** an old tale.

MUKAU to face, look out on; to be opposite; to meet, confront; to get toward; to turn toward; **kagami ni mukau** to look in a mirror; **Beikoku ni mukau** to head for (leave for, go to) America.

mukeiken inexperience; **mukeiken no** green, inexperienced.

mukeru to point at; to turn; to face; **me o mukeru** to turn one's eyes to.

mukeru to peel, to come off.

muki direction; quarter; situation; aspect; exposure; suitability; **kaze no muki** direction of the wind.

muki without limit in time; **muki no** unlimited, indefinite (service); **muki enki** indefinite postponement.

mukidashi nakedness; **mukidashi no** naked, uncovered, bare; **mukidashi ni** frankly, openly; **mukidashi ni suru** to expose.

mukimi shellfish stripped of their shells; hulled shellfish.

muki ni naru to become spirited.

mukiryoku enervation, lethargy.

mukizu spotlessness; **mukizu no** blameless; flawless; spotless; sound, perfect.

MUKO son-in-law; bridegroom.

MUKOO yonder; opposite direction; next to come; other party; **mukoo no** opposite, over there; **mukoo ni** on the opposite side, across; **MUKOOGAWA** the opposite side.

mukoo ineffectiveness; **mukoo no** invalid, ineffective, void; **mukoo ni naru** to become void.

mukoomizu recklessness; **mukoomizu no** reckless, foolhardy, rash; **mukoomizu ni** recklessly, head over heels.

muku to face, turn (one's face to); to look, look out on; to point to; to tend toward.

muku to suit, to be fit for.

muku to skin, to peel, to pare, to strip.

mukuchi reticence; **mukuchi no** reticent, closemouthed.

mukui retribution, punishment; reward, compensation.

mukuiru to reward, repay; to revenge; to retaliate.

mukumu to swell; to become swollen.

mukyoka de without permission.

mukyooiku illiteracy, lack of education; **mukyooiku na** uneducated.

mukyuu without salary; without pay; **mukyuu de** gratuitously, freely, without pay, for nothing; **mukyuu no** unpaid, unsalaried.

mumenkyo no unlicensed; without a license.

MUNE breast, chest; heart; mind; **mune ni ukabu** to occur, come to mind; **mune o uchiakeru** to open one's heart (or mind); to unburden oneself.

mune effect, purport, intention, principle. **Ashita kuru mune shirase ga arimashita.** There was a report that she intended to arrive tomorrow.

munoo, munooryoku incompetency, lack of ability; **munoo na** incapable, incompetent; **munoo na hito** a good-for-nothing.

MURA village, hamlet, rural community; **mura yakuba** village (municipal) office; **mura hazure de** on the outskirts of the village.

mura unevenness, capriciousness; cluster, clump; **mura no aru** uneven, irregular, lacking in uniformity; capricious, fickle.

muragaru to crowd, swarm, flock.

muragi caprice; **muragi na hito** fickle person.

MURASAKI *(n.)* purple; **murasaki no** *(adj.)* purple.

murasu to steam; to cook by steam; **gohan o murasu** to steam boiled rice.

mure group; crowd; herd; flock.

murekusai stuffy, musty, moldy.

mureru to be steamed; to be stuffy, to get musty, get moldy; **mureta** moldy, musty; stuffy.

MURI compulsion; coercion; unjustness, unreasonableness; **muri na** unreasonable, unjustifiable; unnatural; **muri ni** by force, forcibly; compulsorily; **muri yari ni** by force; **muri no nai** reasonable; natural; **muri na onegai** unreasonable request.

murikai lack of understanding; **murikai na** unsympathetic, unfeeling, heartless.

murishi de without interest, interest-free (money).

muron See **mochiron.**

murui matchlessness; **murui no** matchless, unique; unsurpassable.

muryoku weakness; debility, helplessness; **muryoku na** powerless, helpless, impotent; incompetent.

muryoo without charge; **muryoo no** free of charge, gratis; **muryoo de** free, for nothing, without charge; **muryoo shinryoojo** free clinic or infirmary.

musabetsu making no distinction; indifference; **musabetsu no** indiscriminate; equal; **musabetsu ni** indiscriminately; indifferently; equally.

musaboru to covet, be greedy for; **boori o musaboru** to profiteer, make an excess profit.

musakurushii filthy, dirty; shabby.

musan no having no property, unpropertied; **musansha** a proletarian; person without property; the "have-nots"; **musan kaikyuu** proletariat.

musebu to get choked (with tears).

museifu anarchy; **museifu shugi** anarchism; **museifu shugisha** anarchist.

museigen limitlessness; boundlessness; **museigen no** unlimited, limitless; free, unrestricted; **museigen ni** freely.

musekinin irresponsibility; **musekinan na** irresponsible.

musendenshin wireless telegraph; radiogram; **musendenshin de** by radiogram; **musendenshinkyoku** wireless telegraph office; wireless station; **musendenwa** radio-telephone.

museru to be choked (with).

musessoo inconstancy; **musessoo na** unprincipled; inconstant; unchaste.

mushaburitsuku to seize violently, pounce on; to grapple with.

mushakusha suru to be irritated; to be in an ugly mood; **mushakusha shita** irritated; shaggy, bushy; ragged.

musha musha munching, gobbling; **musha musha taberu** to munch, to eat greedily.

MUSHI insect, bug; worm; moth, caterpillar; temper; feeling; **mushi no sukanu** disagreeable; **mushi o korosu** to keep one's temper; **mushi no shirase** hunch, premonition; **mushi ni sasareru** to be bitten by an insect.

mushi disregard; **mushi suru** to disregard, ignore, take no account of, close one's eyes to; **-o mushi shite** in defiance of; disregarding.

mushiatsui hot and close, sultry.

mushikaku disqualification; incompetence; **mushikaku no** disqualified; uncertified; unlicensed.

mushin innocence; request; **mushin no** innocent; involuntary; mechanical; **mushin suru** to make a request; to beg for.

mushinkei apathy; **mushinkei na** dull, apathetic; insensible; **mushinkei de aru** to be insensible to; to be apathetic.

mushiro rather (than); better (than); sooner (than).

mushiru to pull off; to take off; to pluck.

mushoku lack of color; **mushoku no** colorless; transparent.

mushoku no unemployed, out of work.

mushozoku independence; being unattached; **mushozoku no** independent; unaffiliated, unattached; neutral.

mushuu no odorless.

musoo dream; dreaming; daydream; **musoo suru** to dream of; to fancy.

musu to steam; to heat with steam; to be sultry.

musubi knot, tie; end, conclusion, close; **musubi no kotoba** closing remarks; **mushubime** knot, tie.

MUSUBU to tie, knot; to close (a bargain); to conclude; to enter into; to join, link; to form; **himo de musubu** to tie with a cord.

MUSUKO son.

MUSUME daughter; young woman; girl.

musuu countless number; **musuu no** numberless, countless, innumerable; **musuu ni** without number; innumerably.

muteikoo nonresistance.

muteppoo recklessness; **muteppoo na** reckless, rash.

mutsumajii harmonious; intimate, friendly, on good terms; **mutsumajiku** harmoniously; happily.

mutto suru to get offended, take offense; to be stuffy, muggy.

MUTTSU, ROKU six.

muttsuri moodiness; moody person; **muttsuri shita** moody; sullen; grim.

muyami na excessive; indiscreet, thoughtless; rash; unreasonable.

muyoku unselfishness, **muyoku na** unselfish.

muyoo no unnecessary, needless; useless.

muzai innocence (of a crime); **muzai hoomen** acquittal; **muzai no** guiltless, innocent; **muzai ni naru** to be found innocent; to be acquitted.

muzamuza helplessly; recklessly; without much fuss; without regret.

muzei no tax free, duty free, untaxed; **muzeihin** duty-free goods.

muzukaru to fret; to be peevish (said of an infant).

MUZUKASHII hard, difficult, troublesome; delicate; doubtful; **muzukashii mondai** tough (touchy) question; hard problem; **muzukashii byooki** illness difficult to cure; **muzukashii tachiba** difficult situation.

muzumuzu suru to be itchy; to be irritated; to be impatient.

MYOO strangeness; cleverness; **myoo na** strange, queer, curious; miraculous; mysterious; **myoo na hito** strange person; **myoo na koto o iu** to say strange things; **myoo ni kikoeru** to sound funny.

myooasa, myoochoo tomorrow morning. **Myooasa mairimasu.** I will come tomorrow morning.

myooban tomorrow evening, tomorrow night.

MYOOGONICHI the day after tomorrow.

myooji surname, family name.

myoonichi tomorrow. (See also **ASHITA**.)

N

NA, NAMAE name; title; designation; surname; personal name; reputation; fame; pretext, pretense; **na bakari no** nominal, in name only; **na mo nai** nameless, unknown; **na no aru** famous, celebrated; **na ga nai** to be nameless; **na ga shirete iru** to be well known, to be famous; to be popular; **na o kataru** to impersonate; **na o otosu** to lose one's reputation; **na o tsukeru** to name; **nadakai** famous, well known; **nafuda** nameplate; name card.

na green, leafy vegetables.

NABE pot, pan.

nadameru to soothe, calm.

naderu to pat; to smooth.

nadetsukeru to comb (hair); **kami o nadetsukeru** to smooth down one's hair.

NADO and so forth; and the like, etc.; **watakushi nado** the like of me; a person like myself.

nae seedling, shoot, sapling; **naedoko** seedbed; nursery.

nagabiku to be prolonged; to drag on. **Ano hito no byooki wa nagabiite iru.** Her illness is dragging on.

nagagutsu high boots.

NAGAI long, lengthy; **nagai aida ni wa** in the long run; **nagai aida** for a long time; **nagaku** for a long time; for many years; **nagaiki** longevity, long life; **nagaiki suru** to live to a great age.

nagame view, scenery, landscape.

NAGAMERU to look at; to watch; **keshiki o nagameru** to gaze at the landscape; **sora o nagameru** to look up at the sky; **hito no kao o nagameru** to gaze into someone's face.

nagamochi oblong Japanese chest.

nagamochi endurance, durability; **nagamochi suru** to last long, endure.

naganaga very long; **naganaga to kataru** to speak at great length.

NAGANEN many years; **naganen no** long; long standing; **naganen no tomodachi** a friend of long standing.

-NAGARA suffix denoting: while; as; at the same time that; during. **Asagohan o tabenagara rajio o kiita.** I listened to the radio while eating breakfast. **Nenagara hon o yonde wa ikemasen.** Don't read books [while] in bed.

NAGARAKU for a long time.

nagare stream, current; lineage.

nagarekomu to flow into.

nagareru to flow; to run.

nagasa length; measure. **Nagasa wa dono gurai desu ka?** How long is it? What is its length?

nagasareru to drift; to be swept away; **umi e nagasareru** to be washed out to sea.

nagashi kitchen sink.

nagashime sidelong glance; **nagashime ni miru** to look askance at; to look at (someone) out of the corner of one's eyes.

NAGASU to let flow; to drain; to wash away; **mizu o nagasu** to pour water; to drain off; **se o nagasu** to wash one's back.

nagatarashii lengthy; tedious.

nagawazurai lingering illness.

nagaya house of Edo period.

nagedasu to throw out, discard; **ashi o nagedasu** to stretch one's legs.

nagekawashii sad, lamentable.

nageki grief, sorrow; **nageki o kakeru** to be a source of constant trouble to others.

nagekomu to throw into.

nageku to weep; to grieve.

NAGERU to throw, fling, toss.

nagetsukeru to throw at.

nageyari neglect, negligence; **nageyari ni suru** to neglect; **shigoto o nageyari ni suru** to do sloppy work.

nagi lull, calm.

nagori traces, remains; parting; **mukashi no nagori** remains of the past; **nagori o oshimu** to grieve at parting.

naguriai fight, scuffle; **naguriai ni naru** to come to blows; **naguriai o suru** to fight.

naguriau to fight.

naguru to strike; to beat.

nagusame comfort, consolation.

naguasameru to comfort; **mizukara nagusameru** to comfort oneself.

nagusami amusement, sport, diversion, recreation; **nagusami ni** for fun.

NAI there is not; does not exist; be gone, missing; not to be found; have not (no); lack, be devoid of. **Nani mo nai.** There is nothing. **Okane ga nai.** I've no money.

-NAI suffix denoting; not; negative ending. **Shinaide kudasai.** Please don't do it. **Konaide kudasai.** Please don't come.

naibu (n.) inside, interior.

naichi homeland; mainland; interior.

NAIFU knife; penknife.

naigai inside and outside; domestic and foreign; home and abroad.

naijoo internal conditions; real state of affairs. **Ano hito wa sono kaisha no naijoo o yoku shitte imasu.** He knows the internal conditions of that company very well.

naika internal medicine; **naikai** physician.

naikaku cabinet; ministry; **Naikaku Sooridaijin** Premier; Prime Minister.

naimen (n.) inside, interior.

nainai de secretly; privately; **nainai no** secret; confidential; **nainai ni suru** to keep something secret.

naishi from . . . to; between . . . and . . . **Sore wa sen en naishi ni sen en shimasu.** It costs from one to two thousand yen.

naishin inner feelings; **naishin de wa** at heart; inwardly. **Naishin wa goku ii hito desu.** He is a good man at heart.

naisho secrecy; privacy; secret; **naisho de** in private; **naishobanashi** confidential talk.

naishoku private occupation; outside work; sideline.

naishukketsu hemorrhage.

naitei unofficial decision; **naitei suru** to decide unofficially; to arrange tentatively.

naiyoo contents.

najimi familiarity; acquaintance; intimate friend; **najimi no** familiar; **najimi ni naru** to make friends with.

najimu to become familiar with; to become attached to.

najiru to reprove, rebuke.

NAKA interior; inside; center; **naka ni** within; **ie no naka ni** in the house, indoors; **hako no naka e ireru** to put in a box.

naka relations; relationship; **naka no ii** to be on good terms; to be friendly; **naka no warui** to be on bad terms; to be unfriendly; **naka yoku suru** to keep on good terms with.

nakaba half; middle; **natsu no nakaba ni** in the middle of summer.

nakadachinin broker.

nakagai, nakagaigyoo brokerage; **nakagainin** broker; commission merchant; **nakagaiten** brokerage house.

nakairi recess, intermission.

nakama companion; member; (social) set; circle; **nakama ni hairu** to take part (join) in.

nakamahazure ni sareru to be shunned, to be left out.

nakami inside, interior; contents.

NAKANAKA very; considerably; rather, quite; easily; **nakanaka juudai na koto** (thing) of no small importance; **nakanaka dooshite** on the contrary.

nakanaori reconciliation; **nakanaori o suru** to become reconciled; to settle differences; **kenka no nakanaori o saseru** to patch up a quarrel.

nakaniwa courtyard.

nakaore booshi man's felt hat.

nakaseru to move to tears; to make someone cry.

nakayasumi rest, respite (in the middle of

work); **nakayasumi suru** to take a rest; to take a coffee break.

nakayoshi good friend, pal, chum; **nakayoshi de aru** to be good friends with.

NAKAYUBI middle finger.

nakenashi no small amount (of money) one has. **Nakenashi no kane o yarimashita.** I gave her what little money I had.

naki deceased; late (lately deceased); **naki haha** my late mother; **ima wa naki Tanaka-shi** the late Mr. Tanaka.

nakigara remains, corpse.

nakigoe cry; scream; **nakigoe de iu** to talk while sobbing.

nakigoto complaint; whimper; **nakigoto o lu** to grumble.

nakitsuku to implore, entreat.

nakoodo matchmaker.

NAKU to weep, cry; **nakunaku** tearfully; **naite me o harasu** to cry one's eyes out; **nakitai dake naku** to have a good cry.

NAKUNARU to get used up; to run out of. **Moo kane ga nakunarimashita.** I am short of funds. My money ran out. **Watakushi no tokei ga nakunarimashita.** My watch is missing.

NAMAE, NA name. **Onamae wa?** What is your name?

namahanka incomplete; superficial; **namahanka no Eigo** superficial knowledge of English.

namahenji vague reply; **namahenji o suru** to give an evasive reply.

namaiki conceit; **namaiki na** conceited; affected.

namajii halfheartedly; indifferently; rashly; **namajii na** halfhearted.

namajikka ni thoughtlessly; rashly; halfheartedly; **namajikka na koto o suru** to leave something half done.

namakemono lazy person.

NAMAKERU to be lazy. **Kyoo wa ichinichi namakete shimatta.** I've loafed all day.

namakizu fresh bruise.

namamekashii charming; coquettish.

namanamashii vivid.

NAMA NO fresh; raw; unripe; **namazakana** raw fish.

namanurui lukewarm; **namanurui henji** halfhearted answer.

namari lead (metal).

namari dialect, provincial speech.

NAMATAMAGO raw egg.

namauo raw fish.

NAMERAKA smoothness; **nameraka na** smooth, glassy; **nameraka ni** smoothly.

NAMERU to lick; to lap up; to experience; **nameru yoo ni kawaigaru** to dote on; **kuroo o nameru** to experience a hardship.

NAMI wave; sea; **nami no oto** roar of the waves. **Nami ga takai.** The sea is rough.

nami average; **nami no** average, common; **namihazurete** out of the ordinary, uncommon.

namida tears; **namida o nagasu** to weep; **namida ni musebu** to be choked with tears; **namidagumu** to be moved to tears.

namiutsu to undulate, wave.

NAN, NANI prefix or pronoun denoting: what, which, how many. **Nannin imasu ka?** How many persons are there?

nan difficulty; trouble; accident, defect; **nan naku** easily, without difficulty; **nan ni au** to have difficulty.

naname no diagonal; **naname ni** diagonally.

NANATSU, SHICHI seven.

NANBAN what number; what size. **Nanban desu ka?** What is your (telephone) number? **Nanban?** Number, please (asked by a telephone operator).

NANBEN how often, how many times; **nanben mo** often; many times; over and over.

nanbutsu tough customer; difficult person.

NANDAKA somehow or other; somewhat. **Nandaka tsukareta.** I don't know why, but I'm somewhat tired.

NAN DE why; how.

nan de mo any; whatever; anything, everything, by all means; probably; **nani ga nan de mo** at any rate; **nan de mo ka de mo** anything and everything. **Nan de mo soo iu uwasa desu.** So they say. So I hear.

NANDO how many times.

NANDOKI, ITSU when; **nandoki demo** whenever.

nando mo many times, often.

NANGATSU what month.

nangi trouble; hardship; **nangi na** difficult, troublesome; **nangi suru** to suffer hardship; **nangi o kakeru** to cause trouble.

NANI what? why? which, some, any, something; what!; well!; **nani wa tomo are** at all events, in any case; **nani ka ni tsukete** in one way or another; **nani yori** more than anything else; **nani yori na** the most desirable; the nicest; **nani ka taberu mono** something to eat. **Nani kuso.** Damn it! (See also **NAN.**)

nanige naku unintentionally; accidentally; **nanige naku yosoou** to look innocent; to look unconcerned.

NANIGOTO what; **nanigoto ni mo** in everything; **nanigoto ga aroo to** no matter what happens. **Nanigoto desu ka?** What's the matter? **Nanigoto mo nai** [Nothing has happened.] It's O.K.

NANISHIRO anyhow; at any rate, for. **Nanishiro taihen isogashii desu.** I am really very busy.

nanitozo please *(formal)*.

NANJI what time. **Nanji desu ka?** What time is it?

nankinmame peanut.

nankuse fault; **nankuse o tsukeru** to find fault with.

Nankyoku South Pole.

nankyoku crisis, difficult situation; **nankyoku ni ataru** to deal with the situation.

Nankyokukai Antarctic Ocean.

nanmon difficult problem; puzzle; ticklish question.

NANNEN what year; how many years. **Nan nen koko ni sunde imasu ka?** How many years have you lived here?

NANNICHI what day; how many days. **Kyoo wa nannichi desu ka?** What date is it?

NAN NO what; what kind; no; not at all; **nan no tame ni** why; **nan no yooji de** on what business. **Nan no koto mo nakatta.** Nothing has happened.

NANOKA seventh day of the month; seven days.

nanpa shipwreck.

nanpasen wrecked ship; **nansen** shipwreck; **nansen suru** to be shipwrecked.

NAN TO how; what; **nan to itte mo** after all; when all is said and done; **nan to shite mo** at any cost. **Nan to maa!** What! **Nihongo de sore o nan to iimasu ka?** How do you say it in Japanese?

nanushi village head.

nao more; still; yet; all the more; less; **nao ichido** once again; **nao mata** furthermore; in addition. **Nao machigatte imasu.** It is still wrong.

NAORU to be repaired; to be corrected; to recover, get well; **byooki ga naoru** to recover from an illness. **Kono tokei wa sugu naorimasu.** This watch can be repaired easily.

NAOSARA more; still more; less; still less; **naosara ii** to be so much better.

naoshi correction; mending, repair.

NAOSU to repair, mend; to correct; to cure. **Kono kutsu o naoshite kudasai.** I want these shoes repaired.

napukin napkin.

NARA if; in case; provided. **Hitsuyoo nara sugu mairimasu.** I will come if necessary. **Hoshii nara agemasu.** If you want it. I will give it to you.

NARABERU to arrange, put in order; to line up; to compare with; **kata o naraberu** to be (someone's) equal; **mihon o naraberu** to show samples.

narabi row, line; equal; **narabi naki** unequaled; **narabi ni** together with; besides.

NARABU to be in a row, stand side by side; **itchokusen ni narabu** to stand in a straight line.

narai custom, habit; **narai to naru** to form a habit.

narasu to ring; to blow; to sound; to complain; to be famous.

narasu to level; to smooth out; to tame; to domesticate; to train; to get used to; **inu o narasu** to train a dog; **konnan ni narasu** to inure (someone) to trouble.

NARAU to learn; to take lessons; to imitate, copy; **ikebana o narau** to take lessons in flower arrangement. **Anata wa okaasan ni naratte ryoori ga joozu desu ne.** You are following in your mother's steps as a good cook, aren't you?

narazumono rascal.

NARERU to become familiar with; to get used to; to become overly familiar; to become tame; **nareta** domestic; familiar. **Tookyoo no kuuki ni nareru koto wa muzukashii.** It is hard for me to adjust myself to the atmosphere of Tokyo.

nari sound; ring; **nari o shizumeru** to be silent, to watch breathlessly.

nari form, shape; size; personal appearance; **nari ga ookii** to be tall.

naritachi origin; organization.

naritatsu to consist of, be composed of.

nariyuki result, consequence; course (of events); **nariyuki ni makaseru** to let (something) take its own course; **koto no nariyuki** course of events.

NARU to become; to make; to get; to grow; to come; to set in; to pass; to attain; to begin to; to come to; to get to; to consist of; to be made of; to result in; to turn out; **byooki ga waruku naru** to take a turn for the worse (in an illness); **byooki ni naru** to fall ill; **hontoo ni naru** to come true; **suki ni naru** to begin to like; to develop a fondness for; **toshi ni naru** to come of age. **Samuku narimashita.** It is getting cold. **Naru yoo ni shika naranai yo.** Let things go their own way. Take things as they come.

NARU to sound; to ring; to roar; to strike; to resound; to be famous; **mimi ga naru** to have a ringing in one's ears.

naru to bear fruit, to grow (on a tree). **Ie no ringo ga yoku narimashita.** My apple tree is laden with apples.

NARUBEKU, narutake as . . . as possible; if possible; as . . . as one can; **narubeku hayaku** as quickly as possible; at the first opportunity. **Narubeku kuru yoo ni shimasu.** I'll try my best to come.

NARUHODO really; indeed; I see; certainly. **Naruhodo hontoo desu.** I see it is true. Indeed, you are right.

narutake See **narubeku.**

nasake sympathy; compassion; benevolence; affection; **nasake aru hito** charitable person; **nasake o kakeru** to show sympathy for; **nasakebukai** compassionate; benevolent; charitable.

NASAKENAI unsympathetic; heartless; cruel; miserable; pitiful; shameful; deplorable; **nasakenai arisama** a wretched condition. **Nan to iu nasakenai koto da!** What a shame!

nasaru to do *(respect).*

nasu to do, accomplish; to perform; to achieve; to form; to constitute; to make; to practice; to commit; **aku o nasu** to do wrong; **kokorozashi o nasu** to accomplish one's purpose; **en o nasu** to form a circle. (See also **suru.**)

nasuru to smear; to rub on; to blame.

nata hatchet.

NATSU summer; **natsubooshi** summer hat; **natsufuku, natsumono** summer clothes; **natsuyasumi** summer vacation.

natsukashigaru to long for; to pine for; to languish; **mukashi o natsukashigaru** to think fondly of the past.

natsukashii dear; beloved; longed for; **natsukashiku** longingly; fondly; **natsukashii kokyoo** one's beloved home; one's dear native place; **natsukashii omoide** fond memories; **natsukashisooni** longingly; yearningly. **Watakushi wa kokyoo ga natsukashii.** I long for home. I'm homesick.

natsumikan Chinese citron; bitter orange (similar to grapefruit).

nawa rope, cord; **nawa ni kakaru** to be arrested; **nawabari** roping off; **nawabari o suru** to rope off; **nawabari shita zaseki** roped-off seats; **nawabari o arasu** to trespass upon; to encroach upon; **nawatobi o suru** to jump (skip) rope.

naya outbuildings; shed; barn.

nayami suffering, pain, anguish, distress, trouble; **nayami ga aru** to have troubles; **nayami ga nai** to have no troubles; to be carefree.

nayamu to be worried about; to be troubled with; to suffer from; **nayande iru** to be in pain, to be in distress.

nazashi designation; calling by name.

nazasu to name; to call by name.

NAZE why; for what reason; **naze da ka** somehow; without knowing why. **Naze soo ka?** Why so? **Naze ka shiranai.** I don't know why.

nazo puzzle; riddle; **nazo o kakeru** to drop a hint; **nazo o satoru** to take a hint; **nazo o toku** to solve a riddle.

nazukeru to tame; to domesticate; to win over.

nazukeru to name; to call.

nazuku to be tamed; to become attached to; to take kindly to.

NE root, origin, source, base, foundation, nature; **ne mo nai uwasa** a groundless rumor; **ne mo ha mo nai koto** a pure fabrication; **ne ga tsuku** to take root; **ne ni motsu** to bear a grudge; **ne o haru** to spread roots.

NE, NEDAN price, cost; value; **ne ga deru** to increase in price; **ne o kiku** to ask the price; **ne o tsukeru** to set a price on. **Ne ga takai.** The price is high. It is high priced. **Ne ga yasui.** The price is low. It is moderately priced.

ne sound, tone; **fue no ne** tone of a flute; **kane no ne** sound of a bell.

ne *(n.)* sleep; **ne ga tarinai** to not get enough sleep.

neage price rise; price hike; **neage suru** to raise prices.

nebaneba suru sticky, gluey, gummy, clammy.

nebari stickiness, adhesiveness, perseverance; tenacity; **nebarizuyoi** persistent, tenacious; **nebarizuyosa** perseverance, stick-to-itiveness. **Ano hito wa nebari ga nai.** He lacks perseverance. He doesn't stick to it.

nebaru to be sticky, be adhesive; to persevere, to stick to a job.

neboo oversleeping; late riser, sleepyhead; **neboo suru** to oversleep, to get up late.

nebumi appraisal; estimation; **nebumi suru** to appraise, assess, value.

NEDAN price, cost, terms. **Nedan wa ikura desu ka?** What is the price? (See also **NE.**)

nedaru to tease; to coax; to extort; to demand.

nedoko bed; **nedoko ni hairu** to go to bed, to get into bed; **nedoko o koshiraeru** to make a bed.

neesan older sister.

NEGAI desire, wish; request; **negai ni yori** at one's request; **negai ga kanau** to receive a wish, to have a desire fulfilled.

negaideru to apply for; to send in (make) a petition.

negaisage withdrawal (of a petition or application); **negaisage ni suru** to withdraw a petition or application.

negau to petition, to beg, to wish; to hope for. **Onegai shitai koto ga aru.** I have a favor to ask of you. **Sore wa negatte mo nai**

koto desu. Nothing suits (pleases) me more than your proposal.

negawashii desirable.

negi leek, green onion.

negiru to haggle, beat down the price.

neiro tone; tone quality (of music).

neji screw; **neji de shimeru** to screw down.

nejiau to contend; to struggle with someone.

nejifuseru to get (someone) down, to overpower (someone).

nejikeru to be crooked, twisted; to become perverse; **nejiketa** perverse, twisted.

nejikiru to twist; to wrench off.

nejikomu to screw in; to stuff into, to demand an apology.

NEJIMAWASHI screwdriver.

nejiru to twist; to screw; to distort.

nejitoru to wrench off; to twist (someone's) arm (and take something from him).

nekasu, nekaseru to put to sleep; to send to bed; to make (someone) lie down; to lay (something) on the side; to let (something) lie idle; to keep idle; **nekashimono** unsold goods; merchandise that does not sell.

nekkyoo enthusiasm; fanaticism; craze; rage; passion; **nekkyoo shite** frantically, mad with excitement; **nekkyoo saseru** to create excitement, stir up enthusiasm; to thrill; **nekkyoo suru** to go wild over, go crazy over; to grow excited; **nekkyooteki** wild; enthusiastic; mad; hotheaded.

NEKO cat, kitten; **neko zuki** cat lover; **neko mo shakushi mo** everyone; anybody and everybody.

nekoze hunchback; **nekoze no** stooping, hunchbacked.

NEKUTAI necktie; **nekutai o shimeru** to tie a necktie; **nekutai o toku** to untie a necktie.

nema bedroom.

nemaki sleeping apparel, nightgown, pajamas.

NEMUI, nemutai sleepy, drowsy; **nemuku naru** to feel sleepy.

nemuke sleepiness, drowsiness.

nemuri sleep, nap; **fukai nemuri** deep sleep.

NEMURU to sleep; to fall asleep; **yoku nemutte iru** to be fast asleep. (See also **neru.**)

nemutai, See **NEMUI.**

nen sense, feeling; idea, notion, thought, desire, wish; concern; **fuan no nen** feeling of uneasiness; **nen o irete** carefully; **nen o osu** to call one's attention to; to remind one of something.

NEN year; **nen ni** yearly; per annum; **nen ni ichido** once a year; **nen ni ichido no** yearly, annual; **nenjuu** all year round, every day of the year; the whole year, the year through; **nengara nenjuu** all year

round; year after year; **nendo** business year, fiscal year; school year; **nenmatsu** at the end of the year; **nenpoo** annual salary.

nendaijun chronological order; **nendaijun no** chronological; **nendaijun ni** chronologically.

nenga New Year's greetings; **nenga ni iku** to make a New Year's call; **nengajoo** New Year's card.

nen'iri carefulness; **nen'iri ni** carefully, scrupulously, minutely; **nen'iri na** careful, conscientious, attentive.

nenjiru = **nenzuru** to pray.

nenpyoo chronology, chronological table.

nenryoo fuel; **ekitai nenryoo** liquid fuel; **nenryoo kiki** energy crisis.

nenshi New Year's Day; **nenshikyaku** New Year's caller; **nenshi mawari** New Year's calls.

nenzuru See **nenjiru.**

neon neon; **neonsain** neon sign.

nerai aim, objective; **nerai o sadameru** to take careful aim. **neraidokoro** one's objective, point aimed at.

nerau to aim at; to watch for.

neri (n.) kneading; **neru** to knead; to soften; to train.

NERU to sleep; to go to sleep; fall asleep; to take a nap; to lie down; **nerarenai** to lie awake, to sleep poorly; **yoku neru** to sleep well. **Neru jikan da.** It's time to go to bed. It's time to go to sleep. (See also **NEMURU.**)

nesage price reduction.

nesshin zeal, enthusiasm; **nesshin na** enthusiastic; **nesshin ni** eagerly, enthusiastically; earnestly.

nessuru to heat, make hot; to ignite; to get excited.

netamu to be jealous; to be envious of.

netchuu enthusiasm, zeal; **netchuu suru** to be enthusiastic about; **netchuu shite iru** to be devoted to, to be immersed in.

netsu heat; fever, temperature; craze, fad; enthusiasm; **netsu ga deru** to become feverish; **netsu ga aru** to be feverish; to be enthusiastic; **-ni netsu o ageru** to be deeply involved in; **netsuai** passionate love; **netsuai suru** to be madly in love; **netsujoo** fervor, zeal.

nettai tropics; **nettai koku** tropical country; **nettai no** tropical.

netto (tennis) net.

nettoo boiling water; **nettoo o abiru** to be scalded.

NEUCHI value, worth; price; estimation; **neuchi no aru** valuable; **neuchi no nai** worthless; **neuchi ga agaru** to rise in value; to rise in one's estimation; **neuchi**

ga ochiru to fall in value; **neuchi ga aru** to be worthy of; to be worth.

nezumi rat; mouse; **nezumitori** mousetrap.

NEZUMIIRO *(n.)* gray; **nezumiiro no** *(adj.)* gray.

nezumizan geometrical progression. **Jinkoo ga nezumizan de fueru.** The population increases by geometrical progression.

NI particle denoting: in; at; on; into; for; to; by; and; with; of; **asa ni** in the morning; **gozen sanji ni** at 3:00 A.M.; **hako ni ireru** to put into a box; **hito ni hanashikakeru** to speak to a person; **inu ni kamareru** to be bitten by a dog; **mado ni** at the window; in the window: **-ni chiyahoya suru** to make much of; **tana ni noseru** to put on the shelf; **Tookyoo ni iku** to go to Tokyo.

NI, FUTATSU two. (See also **FUTSUKA.**)

ni load, burden; package; luggage; freight; **ni ni naru** to be a burden to; **ni o tsumu** to load; **ni o orosu** to unload; **ni o koshiraeru** to pack; **ni o toku** to unpack.

niau to suit; to become; to match; **niawanai** unsuitable, unbecoming. **Kono kimono wa kimi ni niau.** This dress (suit) is becoming to you. **Sono tebukuro wa booshi ni niau.** Those gloves match the hat.

nibui dull; dense; slow; thickheaded.

niburu to become dull, become blunt; to weaken; **kesshin ga niburu** to weaken in one's resolve.

nichanicha suru to be slimy; to be sticky; to be greasy.

nichibotsu sunset; **nichibotsu ni** at sunset; **nichibotsu no nochi** after sunset; after dark.

NICHIJOO every day; usually; always; **nichijoo no** daily; usual; ordinary; **nichijoo no koto** everyday occurrence; **nichijoo no shigoto** daily routine; everyday work; **nichijoo go** everyday speech; ordinary language.

NICHIYOO, NICHIYOOBI Sunday; **Nichiyoo gakkoo** Sunday school.

nichiyoohin everyday necessity; articles used daily.

nidashi broth.

NIDO twice, two times; second time; **nido to shinai** never again; **nidome** second time; **nidome no** second.

nieagaru well done (cooking).

niekiranai vague; undetermined; indecisive; irresolute; **niekiranai henji** vague answer; noncommittal reply; **niekiranai hito** irresolute (undecided) person.

NIERU to boil; to cook; to be boiled; to be cooked. **Yoku niete imasu ka?** Is it well done? **Kono niku wa yoku niete inai**

desu. This meat is not well done. This meat is half cooked.

nietatsu to boil.

nieyu boiling water; **nieyu o nomaseru** to betray; to deceive; **nieyu o nomasareru** to be betrayed.

NIGAI bitter; **nigai keiken** bitter experience; **nigai keiken o shite me ga sameru** to learn by bitter experience; to have one's eyes opened; **nigai kao o suru** to make a (sour) face; to frown.

nigami bitterness, bitter taste. **Nigami ga aru.** It is bitter. It tastes bitter.

niganigashii bitter; painful; unpleasant; disgusting; shameful. **Niganigashii koto da!** What a shame!

nigao portrait; likeness.

nigasu to release, set free; to let escape; to miss; **tomodachi o nigasu** to miss a friend. (See also **nigeru.**)

nigate tough customer; difficult person, weak point.

NIGATSU February.

nige escape; retreat; **nige o utsu** to try to escape; to prepare an escape; to excuse oneself from; to shirk, evade; **nigeshi** flight; retreat; **nigeashi ni naru** to be ready to quit; to be inclined to run away. **Ano hito wa itsumo nigeashi ni natte iru.** He is always ready to quit. **Nige o utte mo dame desu.** Such an excuse is no good.

NIGERU to run away, flee; to escape; **motte nigeru** to make off with something.

nigiru to grasp, take hold of; to grip, seize.

nigiwai prosperity; bustle, activity, stir.

nigiwashii to be flourishing, prosperous; to be bustling; to be animated.

NIGIWAU to flourish, be prosperous; to be lively, be astir; to be crowded. **Tookyoo no machi wa nigiwatte iru.** The streets of Tokyo are crowded. **Mise wa minna nigiwatte iru.** All the stores are doing good business. All the stores are prospering.

NIGIYAKA NA prosperous, flourishing, animated, lively; cheerful, gay; **nigiyaka na hito** happy fellow; **nigiyaka na basho** bustling section (place); **nigiyaka ni** gaily; animatedly; **nigiyaka ni asobu** to make merry.

nigori muddiness; impurity; voiced consonant; **nigori mizu** muddy water.

nigoru to become muddy; to become impure; **nigotta** muddy; cloudy; voiced. **Ame ga futta no de ike ga nigorimashita.** The rain has made the pond muddy.

nigosu to make muddy; to answer vaguely, to speak ambiguously; **kotoba o nigosu** to say something ambiguously.

niguruma cart, wagon.

NIHON Japan; **NIHONGO** Japanese (language); **NIHONJIN** Japanese (person). (See also **NIPPON**.)

niisan older brother.

nijimu to blot; to run; to spread; to smudge; **inki no nijinde iru** ink-stained. **Arau to iro ga nijimu.** If you wash it, the color will run.

nijinda blurred, smudged, smeared; stained.

NIJUU twenty. (See also **HATSUKA**.)

nijuu duplication; **nijuu no** double, duplicate; **nijuu no imi** double meaning; **nijuu ni** doubly; twice; **nijuu ni sakusei suru** to make out in duplicate.

NIKAI second floor; twice, two times; **nikai ni** upstairs; **nikai ni agaru** to go upstairs; **nikaidate** two-story house.

NIKKI diary, journal; **nikki ni tsukeru** to record in a diary, make an entry in a diary; **nikki o tsukeru** to keep a diary.

nikkoo sunshine, sunlight.

nikkyuu daily wage; **nikkyuu de hataraku** to work by the day; **nikkyuu de harau** to pay by the day; to hire someone by the day.

NIKU meat; flesh; muscle; **niku no atsui** thick; **niku no usui** thin; **niku ga tsuku** to get fat; to gain weight; **niku ga ochiru** to get thin; to lose weight; **niku o kiru** to carve meat; **nikuya** butcher shop; **nikurui** meat; **nikushoku** meat-eating; meat diet.

-NIKUI suffix denoting: difficult; troublesome; awkward. **Nihongo de wa omou koto o iiarawashinikui.** It is difficult to express my thought in Japanese.

nikui hateful, detestable; abominable.

nikumu to hate, abhor, detest; **nikumu beki** hateful, detestable.

NIMOTSU baggage, luggage; load; belongings, personal effects; **nimotsu no mekata o hakaru** to weigh one's baggage; **nimotsu o azukeru** to check one's baggage.

-NIN suffix used as a counter for people; **sanjuunin** thirty people.

nin duty; responsibility; task; office; post; **nin ni ataru** to undertake a responsibility; to take on a duty; **nin ni taenai** to be unequal to the task; to be incompetent; **nin ni tsuku** to assume one's post; take up one's duties; **nin o mattoo suru** to fulfill one's duty.

NINGEN, HITO human being; **ningen no** human, mortal.

ningyoo doll; puppet; **ningyoo no yoo ni** like a doll (charming, beautiful, handsome);

ningyooshibai puppet show; **ningyootsukai** puppeteer.

NINJIN carrot.

ninjoo humanity; humaneness; kindness; sympathy; **ninjoo no aru hito** humane person, kindhearted person; **ninjoo ga aru** to be humane; to be sympathetic; **ninjoo ga nai** to be inhuman, be heartless.

ninki popular feeling, popular sentiment; popularity; business (conditions); **ninki ni joojiru** to catch the popular fancy; **ninki no aru** popular; **ninki no nai** unpopular; **ninki o toru** to win popularity; to gain favor. **Ninki ga yoi** Business is brisk. **Ninki ga warui.** Business is slack.

ninpu laborer; **ninpugashira** foreman.

ninshiki recognition; **ninshiki suru** to recognize; to perceive.

nintai patience; endurance; perseverance; **nintai suru** to be patient; to persevere; **nintai ga dekinai** to have no patience with; to be impatient with; **nintai shite** patiently.

nintei recognition; conclusion; presumption; authorization, sanction; **nintei suru** to admit; to presume; to authorize.

nin'yoo appointment; employment; **nin'yoo suru** to appoint to a post.

ninzuu number of persons; **ninzuu no ooi ie** large family.

NIOI smell, odor, scent; perfume, fragrance; **ii nioi** sweet smell; fragrant odor; **nioi ga ii** to be sweet smelling, be fragrant; **warui nioi** bad smell; foul odor; **nioi ga warui** to be foul smelling.

niou to smell; to be fragrant. **Gasu ga niou.** I smell gas.

NIPPON Japan; **Nippon no** *(adj.)* Japanese; of Japan; **Nippongo** Japanese (language); **Nipponjin** Japanese (person). **Nippongo ga dekimasu ka?** Can you speak Japanese? (See also **NIHON**.)

nirami glare; sharp look; influence; authority; **nirami ga kiku** to have authority over; to have influence over; **nirami ga kikanai** to have no authority over; to have no influence over.

niramu to glare at, scowl; **jitto niramu** to stare fixedly.

NIRU to boil; to cook. **Watakushi wa niku wa yoku nita hoo ga ii désu.** I like my meat well done.

niru resemble, be like, be similar to; **totemo yoku nite iru** to be very similar to; to resemble closely; **nite inai** to have no resemblance to; to be dissimilar.

nise *(n.)* imitation, sham; counterfeit, forgery; **nise no** *(adj.)* counterfeit, forged, false;

nisemono imitation, fake, counterfeit article.

NISHI west; **nishi no** western; **nishi ni** in the west; **nishi gawa ni** on the west (side).

nita like; similar.

NI TSUITE of; about; with; on; over; as to; concerning; regarding; on the subject of; in connection with; relating to; in the case of; **kono koto ni tsuite** about this; with regard to this matter; **kono ten ni tsuite** on this point.

nittei daily routine; day's agenda.

NITTOO daily wages; **nittoo o harau** to pay daily wages.

NIWA garden; yard; courtyard; **niwashi** gardener.

niwakaame sudden shower, downpour.

niwaka no sudden; abrupt; unexpected; **niwaka ni** suddenly, abruptly; unexpectedly; all at once.

NIWATORI chicken, hen; cock.

nizukuri packing; crating; **nizukuri suru** to pack; to crate; **nizukuri ga yoku dekite iru** to be well packed; **nizukuri ga fukanzen da** to be badly packed.

NO particle denoting: pertaining to: —'s; of—; —'s own; in; at; on; for; by; **eigo no sensei** teacher of English; English teacher; **Goya no e** a painting by Goya; **ie no iriguchi** entrance to the house; **ishi no hashi** stone bridge; bridge made of stone; **kawa no hashi** bridge over the river; **kyoo no shinbun** today's newspaper; **mondai no hito** man in question; **otooto no hon** my brother's book; **yuki no hi** snowy day.

no field, plain.

nobasu to extend, lengthen, stretch, draw out, prolong; to postpone; to straighten; **kanjoo o nobasu** to defer (payment) on a bill.

noberu to express, state; to explain; **iken o noberu** to express an opinion; **kansoo o noberu** to give one's impression; **riyuu o noberu** to state one's reason.

nobetsu ni ceaselessly, perpetually, continuously.

nobi postponement; spread, growth; **nobi o suru** to stretch oneself.

nobiru to extend, stretch; to be prolonged; to be deferred; to increase, grow, develop. **Watakushi no shuppatsu ga nobita.** My departure has been delayed.

nobori rise, ascent; uphill road.

nobori streamer, banner.

NOBORU to climb; to go up, rise; to be prompted; **yama ni noboru** to climb a mountain. **Taiyoo ga noboru.** The sun rises.

nobose dizziness, vertigo.

noboseru to be dizzy; to get excited; to be infatuated with; to be absorbed in; **nobosete** in the excitement. **Ano hito wa nobosete iru.** The blood has rushed to his head.

NOCHI future time; forthcoming time; **sono nochi** thereafter, since then; **mikka nochi** three days later; **nochi no** subsequent; future; **nochi ni** later on; afterward.

-NODE because of. **Kaze o hiita node atama ga itai desu.** My headache is due to my cold. [I have a headache because of a cold.]

NODO throat voice; **nodo ga yoi** to have a sweet voice; **nodo o itameru** to have a sore throat. **Nodo ga kawakimashita.** I'm thirsty.

nodoka na quiet, calm; pleasant; **nodoka na tenki** mild weather; **nodoka na kokoro** peace of mind; **nodoka ni** quietly; peacefully.

nogareru to escape; to flee, get away; to avoid, evade; **abunai tokoro o nogareru** to have a narrow escape; **nogarerarenai** unavoidable, inevitable. **Watakushi wa nogareru koto ga dekinai.** I'm in for it; it's inevitable.

nohara field, plain.

nojuku camping outdoors; **nojuku suru** to camp out.

noki eaves (of a house); **noki o naraberu** to stand side by side; to stand in a row.

nokogiri saw; **nokogiri de hiku** to saw.

nokorazu all, entirely, wholly, without exception; **issen mo nokorazu** to the last cent.

NOKORI remainder, rest, balance; **nokori no** remaining; **nokori naku** all, entirely; **nokorimono** remains, leavings, leftovers, remnants, scraps (of food).

NOKORU to be left, to remain, to linger. **Okane ga ikura ka nokotte iru.** I have some money left.

NOKOSU to leave behind; to keep in; to leave over; to save; **kane o nokosu** to save money; **shigoto o nokosu** to leave the work (partly done).

nomareru to be swallowed up, to be drunk up; to be awed by; to cower.

nomaseru to give a drink, serve a drink; to let (someone) drink, to treat (someone) to a drink; **ippai nomaseru** to entertain with liquor. **Doozo mizu o ippai nomasete kudasai.** Please give me a drink of water.

nomikomu to swallow; to drink, to gulp; to understand; to take in, to know. **Anata no iu koto ga yoku nomikomenai.** I can't grasp your meaning. I don't follow what you say.

nomimizu drinking water.

NOMIMONO beverage; **tsumetai nomimono** cold beverage.

nominikui distasteful, disagreeable (to drink), undrinkable.

NOMU to drink; to take (in); to swallow; to smoke; **ocha o nomu** to drink tea; **tabako o nomu** to smoke.

NONBIRI easily; **nonbiri to shita** carefree; easy; quiet; **nonbiri to shita seikatsu** carefree life, quiet life; **nonbiri suru** to feel at leisure, to be at ease.

-NONI particle denoting: although, though; in spite of, despite. **Wakai noni yoku hatarakimasu.** He works hard despite his young age.

nonki na carefree; easygoing; happy-go-lucky; **nonki ni** leisurely; **nonki ni kurasu** to take life easy.

noo brain; talent; ability; skill; **noo o itameru** to rack one's brains; **noo nashi no** good for nothing.

noo Noh play (also spelled No).

nooen, noojoo farm; **nooen ni kurasu** to live on a farm.

nooen na charming; engaging; bewitching; voluptuous.

noofu farmer; farmhand.

noogu farm equipment.

noogyoo farming, agriculture; **noogyoo no** agricultural.

nooikketsu cerebral hemorrhage.

noojoo See **hooen.**

nooka farmhouse; farmer.

nookoo density, thickness; **nookoo na** thick, dense; heavy; rich; **nookoo ni** thickly, densely; richly; **nookoo na tabemono** rich food.

noomu dense fog.

nooritsu efficiency; capability; **nooritsu no aru** efficient; capable; **nooritsu no agaranai** inefficient; **nooritsu o ageru** to increase efficiency, raise efficiency.

nooryoku ability; facility; competency; capability; faculty.

noosakubutsu, noosanbutsu crops, farm produce, agricultural products.

nooson rural area; farm village; agricultural district; **nooson no** rural; agricultural.

nootan shading; tinting; light and shade.

nooten scalp; crown of the head.

noozei tax payment; **noozei suru** to pay taxes; **noozeisha** taxpayer.

nori dried seaweed (a food).

nori paste; glue; starch; **nori de haru** to paste; to glue; **nori o tsukeru** to starch. **Kore ni nori o tsukete hoshii.** I'd like this starched.

norikae transfer; change; changing; **norikaeeki** junction, transfer point; **norikaeba** transfer point; **norikaekippu** transfer ticket. **Oosaka iki wa koko de norikae desu.** You must transfer here for Osaka.

NORIKAERU transfer; change (for a train, car, ship, etc.). **Shinjuku de basu ni norikaeru hoo ga yoi deshoo.** It will be better to transfer to a bus at Shinjuku.

NORIMONO vehicle, conveyance.

noroi (n.) curse.

noroi slow; lagging; tardy; dull; dense; **noroi kisha** slow train; **shigoto ga noroi** to be slow at one's work. **Ano hito wa banji ni noroi otoko da.** He is dense about everything.

norou to curse; to wish (someone) ill.

NORU to ride (in, on); to get (in, on); to go on board; to join; to take part in; to be taken in; to be recorded; **kisha ni notte iku** to go by train; **shinbun ni noru** to appear (be reported) in the newspaper; **soodan ni noru** to take part in a consultation; **uma ni noru** to mount a horse.

noseru to put on top of; to place on, set on; to carry; to load; to take on board; to impose upon; to publish; to record; **jidoosha ni hito o nosete yaru** to give (someone) a lift in a car; **jookyaku o noseru** to take on passengers.

notto nautical mile, knot.

nottoru to follow; to conform to; to go by; to be in accord with.

NOZOITE except, excepting; with the exception of; but; **hitotsu nozoite minna** all but one; **-o nozoite** with the exception of; excluding; **shoosuu o nozoite** with a few exceptions. **Nichiyoobi o nozoite mainichi benkyoo suru.** I study every day, except Sunday.

nozoku to eliminate, remove, exclude; to abolish; to omit.

nozoku to peep in, to look in.

nozomi wish, desire, hope; expectation, aspiration, ambition; **nozomi o kakeru** to set one's heart on.

nozomu face; to meet; to attend; to be present; **shiki ni nozomu** to attend a ceremony. **Niwa wa yama ni nozonde iru.** The garden faces the mountains.

nozomu to wish, to desire, to hope for, to aspire to; to expect; to look out on.

nugeru to come off; to slip down.

NUGU to take off; to pull off; to undress. **Kutsu o nugu no desu ka?** Shall I take off my shoes?

nuibari needle.

nuka rice bran; **nukamiso** salt and rice bran paste (for pickling).

nukaru to be muddy; to be slushy; to blunder, make a mistake.

nukarumi mud; mud puddle.

nukasu to omit, exclude, leave out; to overlook.

nukedasu to get loose; to sneak out, steal out.

nukigaki selection; excerpt.

nukitoru to pull out, extract; to abstract; to steal.

NUKU to pull out, take out, draw out; to extract (a tooth); to uncork; to unscrew; to select; to leave out, omit.

numa swamp, bog; **numachi** swampy place.

nurasu to wet; to dampen; to soak; to drench. **Ashi o nurasu na.** Don't get your feet wet!

NURERU to become wet, get wet. **Kao ga namida ni nurete iru.** Her face is wet with tears.

nuri coating; varnishing; lacquering; painting; plastering.

NURU to apply; to spread on; to paint; to plaster; to coat; **pan ni bataa o nuru** to spread butter on bread.

nurui lukewarm; dull; sluggish.

nurumayu lukewarm water.

nusumimiru to steal looks at, look furtively at.

nusumu to steal; to rob; to snatch a minute's rest; to elude the eyes of others; **hitome o nusunde au** to meet (someone) secretly; **nusubito** thief. **Okane o nusumareta.** My money has been stolen.

NUU to sew; **hitogomi o nuu** to go through a crowd; **kimono o nuu** to sew clothes.

nyooboo (colloq.) wife.

nyuubai beginning of the rainy season.

nyuuden telegram (cable) received; **-no mune nyuuden ga atta.** A telegram has been received to the effect that.

NYUUGAKU (school) admission, matriculation; **nyuugaku suru** to enter school; to matriculate; **nyuugakushiken** entrance examination.

nyuugoku imprisonment.

nyuuhi cost; expenditure; expenses.

nyuuin suru to enter a hospital; to be hospitalized.

NYUUJOO entrance; admission; **nyuujoo suru** to enter; to be admitted; **nyuujoo muryoo** free admission; **nyuujooken** admission ticket; **nyuujooryoo** admission fee.

nyuukai joining (an organization); admission; **nyuukai suru** to become a member (in an organization); **nyuukai o mooshikomu** to apply for membership.

nyuukoo entry (into port); docking; **nyuukoo suru** to enter port; to dock.

nyuumon entering private school; primer; **Nippongo nyuumon** Japanese (language) primer.

nyuusatsu bid; bidding; **nyuusatsu suru** to bid, make a bid.

nyuusen suru to be selected; be accepted.

nyuusha suru to enter a firm.

NYUUSU news; **kaigai nyuusu** foreign news.

nyuutoo suru to join a political party.

nyuuwa na gentle; tender.

nyuuyoku bath; bathing; **nyuuyoku suru** to bathe.

nyuuyoo need, necessity; requirement; **nyuuyoo na** necessary; required; **nyuuyoo de aru** to be in need of; to want.

O

o tail, brush; **o o furu** to wag the tail; **o hire o tsukete hanasu** to exaggerate.

oashisu oasis.

OBA aunt; **obachan** auntie.

OBAASAN grandmother; old woman.

OBI belt, sash (worn with a kimono); **obi o shimeru** to do up a sash; **obi o toku** to take off an obi; **obiage** sash-bustle; **obidome** sashband.

obieru to become frightened; to have a nightmare.

obikidasu to lure, entice.

obitadashii immense, vast; **obitadashiku** abundantly, profusely, in large numbers.

obiyakasu to threaten, intimidate; to scare.

oboe learning; memory; feeling; recollection; experience; **oboe ga yoi** to have a good memory; to be quick to learn.

OBOERU to remember; to keep in mind; to memorize; to learn; to recollect; **samusa o oboeru** to feel chilly. **Yoku oboete imasu.** I remember it well.

obon See **bon.**

oboreru to drown; to be drowned; to indulge in, to be addicted to.

obotsukanai uncertain, doubtful, almost hopeless; uneasy, weak.

obusaru to ride on someone's shoulders; to ride piggyback; to rely on.

obuu to take (carry) on one's back; **kodomo o obuu** to carry a child on one's back.

OCHA, CHA tea (usually Japanese). (See also **koocha.**)

ochiau to meet, rendezvous; to come (across) someone.

ochibureru to be ruined, to be reduced to poverty.

ochido fault, error; blame; **ochido ga nai** to be blameless; **hito no ochido ni suru** to lay the blame on someone else.

ochiiru to fall; to be reduced. **kiken ni ochiiru** to be in danger. **kukyoo ni ochiiru** to get into trouble.

ochikomu to fall in, fall into; to be depressed. **Kare wa kawa ni ochikonda.** He fell into the river. **Shiken ni ochite ochikonda.** I was depressed when I failed the exam.

OCHIRU to fall; to drop; to come down; to collapse; to be left out; to fall short of. **Yane kara ochite ashi o otta.** I fell from the roof and broke my leg. **Seiseki ga ochite kimashita.** My marks are going down.

ochitsuki composure, self-possession. **ochitsuki no aru** calm, self-composed; **ochitsuki no nai** fidgety, restless; **ochitsuki haratte** calmly.

ochitsuku to settle down, become quiet; **ki ga ochitsuku** to feel relieved; to recover one's composure.

odayaka na quiet, calm, peaceful, gentle; moderate; **odayaka de nai** alarming, threatening; upsetting, serious. **odayaka ni naru** to calm down, become calm.

odokashi threat, menace.

odokasu to threaten, menace; to browbeat; to scare.

odori dance; dancing; **odoriagaru** to jump; to dance for joy.

odoroite in astonishment, in amazement.

odorokasu to astonish, surprise, amaze; to startle, frighten.

odoroki amazement, wonder, surprise.

ODOROKU to be surprised, be amazed, to be frightened. **Kare wa odoroite tobiagatta.** He jumped up in surprise. **Odoroku koto wa nai.** Nothing is surprising about it. Don't be surprised.

odoru to dance; to step; **bando ni awasete odoru** to dance to a band.

odoshi threat, menace.

odosu to frighten, intimidate; to browbeat.

oeru to end, conclude, finish; **kai o oeru** to bring a meeting to a close; **gyoo o oeru** to finish a course.

ogamu to worship, venerate; to pray for.

ogawa brook, stream.

oginau to make good, make up for, supplement; **ketsuin o oginau** to fill a vacancy; **sonshitsu o oginau** to make up a loss.

ogosoka na grave, solemn, austere; **ogosoka ni** with solemnity.

OHAYOO Good morning! **OHAYOO GOZAIMASU.** Good morning (vulgar).

OI nephew.

oi (colloq.) hello! hey! look here!

oichirasu to drive out; to scatter.

oidasu to drive out, expel, turn out, evict.

oihagi highway robber.

oiharau to drive away; to send away.

OIKAKERU to chase, run after. **Inu ga neko o oikakete iru.** A dog is chasing a cat.

oikomu to corner; to drive in.

oikosu to outrun; to pass, to outdistance. **Hoka no kuruma o oikoshimashita.** She passed another car.

oimawasu to run after; to chase around.

oioi gradually, little by little; step by step; eventually.

OISHII delicious, tasty, sweet. **Aa oishii!** It tastes good! **Gohan wa oishikatta.** The meal was good.

oitateru to evict; to urge; to drive away.

oitsuku to overtake, catch up with.

oitsumeru to corner, get into a corner.

OJI uncle.

ojigi bow (inclination of the head or body); **ojigi o suru** to bow.

OJIISAN grandfather; old man.

ojike fear, fright; **ojike ga tsuku** to be seized with fear, be frightened.

OJOOSAN miss; daughter (respect).

OKA hill, mound; land; shore.

OKAASAN mother, mama (used by children in the family); mother (somebody else's).

OKAGE indebtedness, favor. **Okage sama de.** Thanks to your kindness.

okami landlady; mistress; hostess (at a restaurant).

OKANE, kane money.

OKASHI, kashi cake.

OKASHII amusing, laughable, funny; ridiculous; strange. **Nani mo okashii koto wa nai.** There is nothing funny. **Okashii hanashi da.** The story is strange.

okashiya, kashiya cake shop, candy shop.

okasu to commit; to violate; to rape; to infringe on; to desecrate; **kokuhoo o okasu** to break the laws of the land.

okasu to defy; to risk; to damage.

okawari second helping; another cup; **okawari suru** to ask for a second helping.

oke tub, tank, pail; **oke ippai no mizu** pailful of water.

oki open sea.

okiagaru to get up; to sit up; **toko no ue ni okiagaru** to sit up in bed.

okidokei table clock.

okikaeru to rearrange; to displace.

okimono small, decorative ornament.

okinaoru to sit up, sit erect.

okinaosu to replace; to rearrange.

-OKI NI at intervals of; **gofun oki ni** at five-minute intervals; **ichinichi oki ni** every other day.

OKIRU to get up; to rise; to raise oneself; **asa hayaku oki ni** to get up early in the morning; **kan ga okiru** to have hysterics.

okite law, regulation, decree.

okizari desertion; **okizari ni suru** to desert; to leave behind.

okkuu na troublesome.

okonai act, deed; conduct; **okonai no yoi** well-behaved.

okonau to act, perform; to carry out; to conduct. **Kekkonshiki wa mikka ni okonaimasu.** We will hold the wedding on the third.

okoraseru to offend; to anger; to irritate (someone).

okori origin, source, cause, root.

okorippoi touchy, peevish, short-tempered.

OKORU to happen, occur, come about; to take place; to arise in; to originate. **Sensoo ga okoru ka mo shirenai.** A war may break out.

okoru to get angry; to lose one's temper; **okotte iru** to be angry. **Tanaka-san wa sono hanashi o kiite taihen okorimashita.** Ms. Tanaka got very angry at hearing that story. **Yamada-san ga konai node okotte imasu.** She is mad because Mr. Yamada hasn't come. **Sonna ni okotte wa ikemasen.** Don't be angry so much.

OKOSU to start, begin; to bring about; to establish; to promote; to improve; to awaken; to raise up, lift; to cause; to give rise to; **byooki o okosu** to fall ill; **shindai o okosu** to make a fortune. **Nanji ni anata o okoshimashoo ka?** When shall I wake you?

okotari negligence; **okotarigachi no** negligent, neglectful; **okotari naku** diligently, carefully.

okotaru to neglect; to fail to do.

OKU to put, place, lay, set; to keep; to establish, set up; to open; **fude o oku** to lay down a pen; **otetsudai o hitori oku** to hire domestic help; **nokoshite oku** to leave; **sono mama ni shite oku** to leave alone. **Kasa wa koko ni oite kudasai.** Please leave your umbrella here.

OKU back part; inner part; back; inner room; **oku e toosu** to show a person to the guest room; **yamaoku** the heart of (that part deep inside) a mountain.

OKU one hundred million.

okubyoo cowardice, timidity; **okubyoomono** coward.

okufukai deep, profound; of great depth.

okugai outdoors, in the open air.

okujoo rooftop.

okunai interior of a house, indoors.

okurasu to delay; to put off.

okure lag; **okure o toru** to be beaten; to be outstripped; **ki okure ga suru** to feel shy; to lose heart.

OKURERU to be late for; to be behind time; to get (fall) behind; to be left behind; **densha ni okureru** to miss a train.

okuridasu to send out; to forward; to see (someone) off; to show a person to the door.

okurikomu to see a person home; to escort (someone).

OKURIMONO present, gift; **okurimono o suru** to give (send) a gift.

OKURU to send; to see off; to send off; to escort; to spend, pass (time); **nimotsu o okuru** to send a package; **tanoshii seikatsu o okuru** to live a happy life. **Eki made ookuri shimashoo.** I will escort you to the station.

OKURU to present, to bestow; **gakui o okuru** to confer an academic degree. **Kare no sotsugyooiwai ni tokei o okurimashoo.** Let's give him a watch for a graduation gift.

OKUSAMA, OKUSAN madam, Mrs.

okusoko depth, bottom; **kokoro no okusoko de wa** in the back of one's mind; in the depths of one's heart.

okusoku guess, supposition; **okusoku suru** to guess, suppose.

okusuru to fear; to shrink; to hesitate; to be shy.

okuyukashii graceful; refined.

okuyuki depth; length.

okuzashiki inner room; back parlor.

Omachidoo sama. I'm sorry to have kept you waiting.

omae you *(impolite)*.

omedeta happy event.

Omedetoo. Congratulations!

omei slur; bad name; **omei o kiru** to get a bad name; to be dishonored; to have a bad name.

omiyage, miyage souvenir; parting present; gift.

OMOCHA toy; **omocha ni suru** to trifle with, toy with.

OMOI heavy; wealthy; serious, severe; important; **omoi byooki** serious illness; **ki ga omoi** to have a heavy heart.

OMOI thought, idea, mind; sense; heart; feeling; love; care, worry; will, wish; **omoi o kakeru** to take a fancy to; **omoi o kogasu** to burn with love; **omoi o korasu** to tax one's brain.

omoiataru to occur to; to call to mind.

omoiawaseru to consider (together); put two and two together. **Karekore omoiawasete yamemashita.** Taking everything into consideration, I gave up the idea.

omoichigai misunderstanding; **omoichigai o suru** to misunderstand.

OMOIDASU to recall, bring to mind, remember. **Dooshitemo omoidasenai.** Try as I may, I can't recall it.

omoide recollections, memories.

omoigakenai unexpected, unforeseen; least expected; chance, accidental; **omoigakenaku** unexpectedly.

omoikiri resolution.

omoikiru to resign oneself to; to give up; **omoikitte** boldly, resolutely.

omoikitta radical, bold, daring.

omoikomu to be under the impression that, to be possessed with (an idea).

omoinokosu to leave with regret.

omoiomoi each in one's own way; as one pleases.

omoishiraseru to teach someone (make someone learn) a lesson.

omoitsuki plan, suggestion. **Yoi omoitsuki desu.** That's a great idea.

omoitsuku to recall; to think of, to hit on. **Umai shukoo o omoitsuita.** I got a brilliant idea.

omoitsumeru to brood over; to love passionately.

omoiyari sympathy, consideration; **omoiyari no aru** sympathetic; considerate, kind.

omoiyaru to sympathize with.

omokage features, looks; image, likeness.

omokurushii heavy, ponderous; clumsy, oppressed.

omomi weight, emphasis, importance.

omomuki effect; taste, elegance, air, appearance; **omomuki no aru** refined, elegant; **omomuki no nai** tasteless, vulgar.

omomuku to go; to proceed to; to grow, to get.

omomuro ni slowly; gently; softly.

OMO NA chief, major, leading; **omo na hitobito** important persons; **omo na sangyoo** principal industries.

omoni heavy load.

omonjiru See **omonzuru.**

omonzuru, omonjiru to honor, respect, think much of.

omoomoshii serious; imposing; dignified; **omoomoshiku** solemnly, seriously.

omori weight, plumb, sinker.

omosa weight, heaviness.

omoshi weight (heavy object used to put pressure on something); **omoshi o oku** to place a weight on.

omoshirogaru to amuse oneself, to be amused; to think (something) funny.

omoshirohanbun half in fun.

OMOSHIROI interesting; pleasant, diverting; funny, odd; amusing; **omoshiroku** pleasantly; interestingly, delightfully, etc.; **omoshiroku nai** uninteresting, dull, stupid; unpleasant; unsatisfactory; undesirable.

omoshiromi interest; enjoyment; fun.

omoshirosoo ni with seeming (apparent) interest, enjoyment; like fun. **Kodomotachi wa omoshirosoo ni asonde imasu.** The children are playing, apparently enjoying themselves.

OMOTE face; obverse; right side; exterior; front; first half; **omote ni** outdoors; **omote no to** front door; **omote o dashite** right side up; **Omote Nihon** the Pacific side of Japan.

omotemon front gate.

omotemuki openly, publicly; officially; **omotemuki no** public, open.

omotezashiki front parlor.

OMOU to think; to consider; to believe; to wish, desire; to yearn for; to feel; to feel like; to regard (as); to expect; to hope; to imagine; **yoku omou** to think well of. **Kimi ga koko ni iru to wa omowanakkatta.** I had no idea you were here. **Maa omotte mo minasai.** Just think of it!

omowareru to seem, appear; to look; to be thought of (as). **Ame ga furisoo ni omowareru.** It looks like rain.

omowaseburi suggestive manner, coquetry; **omowaseburi na** suggestive, coquettish.

omowaseru to make (one) think; to remind (one) of; to be suggestive of.

omowashii satisfactory, desirable; **omowashiku nai** unsatisfactory.

omowazu unexpectedly; unconsciously, unintentionally.

omoya main house.

on kindness, goodness; favor; obligation; **on ni kanjiru** to feel indebted to; **on ni kiru** to be deeply grateful to; **on o kaesu** to repay a kindness.

on sound; tone; voice.

onaidoshi same age; **onaidoshi de aru** to be the same age.

ONAJI same, identical; equal, equivalent to, similar, like; **onaji yoo na** of the same kind; **onaji yoo ni** alike; **onaji ni** equally, etc.

ONAKA stomach, belly, abdomen. **Onaka ga suita.** I'm hungry. **Onaka ga itai.** I have a stomachache.

ONDO temperature.

ongaeshi repayment of a favor; **ongaeshi o suru** to repay a kindness (or favor).

ONGAKU music; **ongakuteki** musical; **ongaku no sensei** music teacher; **ongaku zuki** music lover.

ongi favor, obligation.

oni fiend, devil; ghost; **oni no yoo na** fiendish, inhuman.

onjin patron, benefactor.

onjoo warm heart, warm feeling; **onjoo aru** warmhearted.

onjooshugi paternalism.

onjun na gentle, meek.

onkei favor.

onken moderation; **onken na** moderate, temperate; sensible; **onken na setsu** a sensible opinion.

onkoo na gentle, courteous.

onkyoo sound, noise.

onkyuu pension; **onkyuu o ukeru** to receive a pension.

ONNA woman, female; female sex; mistress; **onna no** woman's; feminine; **onnarashii** womanly; ladylike; **ONNA NO KO** young girl; daughter; **onnashujin** landlady.

ono ax.

onoono each, everyone; all; respectively.

onsen, onsenba hot springs, spa; **onsenyado** hot springs inn.

onshi (highly respected) teacher (to whom a special indebtedness is felt).

onshin correspondence; **onshin suru** to correspond with.

onshirazu ingratitude; **onshirazu na** ungrateful.

onshitsu hothouse, greenhouse.

onsu ounce.

onwa na mild, gentle; genial.

oo oh! how!

ooame heavy rain, downpour.

ooarashi, ooare severe storm.

oobo subscription; application; **oobo suru** to subscribe to; to apply, make application; **oobosha** applicant; subscriber.

ooboo oppression, tyranny; **ooboo na** arbitrary; tyrannical; **ooboo o kiwameru** to tyrannize; to be high-handed.

oobun English or any Occidental written language or alphabet; **oobundenpoo** telegram written in the English (or any Occidental) alphabet.

oobun no appropriate, suitable; reasonable.

ooburi heavy downpour.

oochaku dishonesty; cunning; laziness; **oochaku na** dishonest; cunning; selfish; lazy.

ooda assault and battery; **ooda suru** to assault.

oodan crossing, intersection; **oodan suru** to cross, run across.

oodeki triumph, great success.

ooen aid, assistance; **ooen suru** to aid, support.

OOFUKU going and returning, round trip; **oofuku ryokoo** round trip; **oofuku suru** to go and return; **oofukuhagaki** return (post) card; **oofukukippu** round-trip ticket.

oogesa exaggeration; **oogesa na** exaggerated; **oogesa na hanashi** tall story, exaggeration; **oogesa na koto o iu** to exaggerate.

oogi folding fan; **oogi o tsukau** to fan oneself.

oogoe loud voice; **oogoe de** in a loud voice, loudly.

oohei arrogance; **oohei na** arrogant; **oohei ni** arrogantly.

oohiroma large, grand hall.

OOI lots of, heaps of, plenty, many, numerous, much. **Nihon ni wa yama ga ooi.** There are many mountains in Japan. **Nihonjin ni wa Eigo o hanasu hito ga ooi.** There are lots of Japanese who speak English. **Ano hito wa kodomo ga ooi.** He has many children.

ooi cover, covering; shade; screen; **ooi o suru** to cover, to wrap.

ooi yoo hoo!, hello!

ooisogi urgency; **ooisogi de** in great haste, hurriedly; **ooisogi de iku** to hurry to, rush to.

oojikake large scale; **oojikake de** on a large scale.

oojiru See **oozuru.**

oojite in proportion to; according to; in reply to; **hitsuyoo ni oojite** according to the need; according to the demand.

oojoo death; **oojoo suru** to die; to submit to, give in.

OOKATA probably, perhaps, maybe, almost, in general.

OOKEI O.K.

OOKII, OOKINA big, large, great; heavy; powerful; huge, massive; **hijoo ni ookii** huge, of great proportions; **ookina koto o iu** to talk big, brag, **ookiku naru** to grow larger, be enlarged; **ookiku suru** to enlarge, make larger.

ookina See **ookii.**

ookisa size, dimension, volume, bulk; **ookisa ga onaji** to be the same size; **ookisa ga chigau** to differ in size; **-kurai no ookisa de aru** to be about the size of.

ookoo being rampant; **ookoo suru** to overrun; to be rampant; to swagger; to go sideways.

ooku in many cases, in numerous cases; **ooku wa** mostly; for the most part; largely; **ooku no** a great many; plenty of; lots of; **ooku tomo** at most; generally.

Ookura Daijin Finance Minister; **Ookurashoo** Finance Ministry.

ookyuu emergency; first aid; **ookyuu teate** first-aid treatment.

oomata big strides; **oomata ni aruku** to stride; to walk with long steps.

oome overlooking; **oome ni miru** to overlook; to close one's eyes to; to let (something) pass.

oomisoka New Year's Eve.

oomizu heavy flood.

oomukashi remote antiquity; primitive ages; **oomukashi kara** from time immemorial.

oonoo anguish, agony; worry; **oonoo suru** to suffer anguish; to be in agony.

oo-oo often, frequently; sometimes.

ooppira ni openly, publicly.

oorai (street) traffic, comings and goings; **oorai suru** to come and go; to rise and fall. **Oorai ga ooi.** Traffic is heavy.

ooryoo usurpation, embezzlement; **ooryoo suru** to appropriate unlawfully; **ooryoosha** embezzler; **ooryoozai** embezzlement.

oosen response; acceptance; **oosen suru** to accept the challenge.

oosetsu reception; **oosetsu suru** to receive visitors; **oosetsuma** reception room, drawing room.

ooshin doctor's visit to a patient; house call.

ooshuu seizure, confiscation; **ooshuu suru** to seize.

ooshuu answer, reply; **ooshuu suru** to answer.

oosooji general cleaning; **oosooji o suru** to give a general cleaning.

ootai reception; **ootai suru** to receive, to wait on (a customer).

ooto vomiting; **ooto suru** to vomit.

ootobai motorcycle.

ootome automation.

ootoo answer, reply.

oou to reply; to veil; to wrap; to envelop, to hide, conceal; to shelter.

oouridashi large bargain sale.

ooutsushi close-up (in a movie).

ooyake (n.) public; government, **ooyake no** (adj.) public, open; official; **ooyake ni suru** to publish; to make known. **ooyake ni naru** to be made known.

ooyasuuri bargain sale.

ooyoo generosity; **ooyoo na** bighearted, generous.

ooyoo practical application; **ooyoo dekiru** applicable; **ooyoo suru** to put into use, to apply; to put to practical use.

oozappa na rough, loose, **oozappa na hanashi** rough, outline of a story.

OOZEI crowd, large number of people; **oozei de** in large numbers; **oozei no** many, large crowd of; **oozei no kazoku** large family.

oozora sky; heavens.

oozuru, oojiru to respond, reply, to comply with; to apply for.

opera opera.

Oranda Holland; **Orandago** Dutch (language); **Orandajin** Dutch (person).

OREI, REI etiquette, thanks, appreciation; remuneration.

oreru to break, snap, give way, yield; to be folded; **orete deru** to meet halfway. **Tsue ga oreta** The stick was broken.

ori cage, pen.

origami paper folding (popular Japanese pastime).

origamitsuki no certified, guaranteed.

oriibu olive.

orikasanaru to overlap; to lie one on another; **orikasanatte** overlapped; (stacked) in piles.

orimono cloth, textile.

ORIRU to go down; to come down; to get down; get off; to leave; to get out of; to alight, land; **densha o oriru** to get off a streetcar; **kaidan o oriru** to descend the staircase.

oroka not to mention; to say nothing of.

oroshi wholesale business; **oroshi de uru** to sell wholesale, at wholesale price; **oroshine** wholesale price(s).

orosoka careless, negligent; **orosoka ni suru** to neglect.

OROSU to take down; to lower; to bring down, to drop, let fall; to hand down; to unload; to let (someone) get off; to sell at wholesale. **Koko de oroshite kudasai.** Please let me get off here.

ORU to break; to bend, fold; to pick; **hana o oru** to pick a flower.

oru to weave.

orugan organ.

osaeru to stop; to curb, check, hold down, suppress.

osamaru to be at peace; to be calmed down, be pacified. **Kaze ga osamarismashita.** The wind has died down.

osameru to govern, rule; **ie o osameru** to manage a household.

osanai infant; young; childish; **osanai koro ni** in childhood.

osen pollution; **taiki osen** air pollution.

oshaberi chattering; gossip; gossiper; **oshaberi na** gossipy, talkative; **oshaberi suru** to chatter; to gossip.

oshi deaf-mute.

oshi weight; influence; **oshi no tsuyoi** overbearing, brazen; **oshi ga kiku** to have influence.

oshiageru to push; to thrust up.

oshiau to push, jostle.

oshidashi presence, appearance, look; **oshidashi no yoi** of fine appearance.

oshidasu to push out; to press forward; to force out.

oshie teaching, instruction; lesson; **oshiego** pupil.

OSHIERU to teach, give lessons; to show; to tell; **Nihongo o oshieru** to teach Japanese.

oshihiromeru to extend, expand, spread.

OSHII regrettable; precious, valuable; wasteful. **Sore wa oshii koto desu.** That's a pity! **Suteru no wa oshii desu.** It's too good to throw away.

OSHIIRE closet.

oshikakeru to force oneself into; to go uninvited.

oshikomeru, oshikomu to force in; to stuff into.

oshimazu liberally, freely.

oshime diaper.

oshimu to value, prize; to spare; to grudge; to be stingy of; to regret; **kane o oshimu** to be stingy with money; **wakare o oshimu** to be reluctant to leave.

oshinabete generally, in general.

oshinokeru to push away, to push aside.

oshiroi face powder.

oshitaosu to fell; to push down.

oshitateru to raise; set up, erect.

oshitoosu to push through; to persist to the end.

oshitsubusu to crush, smash, squash.

oshitsukeru to press, push against; to compel.

oshitsumaru to be jammed; to get near the end of the year. **Kotoshi mo oshitsumatte mairimashita.** It's getting near the end of the year.

oshiuri forcing a sale; **oshiuri suru** to force a person to buy.

oshiwakeru to push apart; to push through.

oshiyaru to push aside.

oshiyoseru to push to one side; to advance on.

OSOI late, tardy; behind time; slow; **ashi ga osoi** to walk slowly; **kaeri ga osoi** to be late in returning.

OSORAKU perhaps, maybe; in all probability; I'm afraid. **Osoraku moo Amerika e kaetta no deshoo.** I suppose he has already returned to the United States.

osore fear, terror; horror; awe, reverence; **osore o idaku** to be afraid of.

osoreiru to be overwhelmed, be awed. **Osoreirimasu.** I'm much obliged to you. **Osoreirimasu ga, kore o doko ni okimashoo ka?** Excuse me—where shall I put this?

osoreooi gracious, awe-inspiring; **osoreooku mo** graciously.

OSOROSHII fearful, awful, terrible, tremendous; **osoroshiku** terribly, etc; **osoroshiku atsui** terribly hot; **osoroshisa** fear, terror, horror.

osou to attack, assault.

osowaru to be taught.

ossharu to say, to speak, to tell, to relay, to mention (respect).

OSU to push, shove, press; to infer, deduce, guess; to recommend. **Yamada-san o oshimashita.** I recommended Mr. Yamada.

osu (n.) male (animal); **osu no** male (adj.); **osu neko** tomcat.

osui sewage; filthy water.

otafukukaze mumps.

otaku your house.

OTEARAI See **TEARAI.**

oten stain; blot; blemish; **oten o tsukeru** to stain; to spot; **oten no nai** spotless.

OTO sound, noise; roar; tone, note; fame; **oto ni kikoeta** celebrated, noted; **oto o tatete** noisily; **oto o tateru** to make a sound; to make noise.

OTOKO man, male; male adult; manly person; **otokorashii** manly; **otokorashiku** like a man; **otoko ni naru** to come of age; to become a man; **OTOKO NO KO** boy; **otokoyamome** widower.

OTONA adult (male or female).

OTONASHII gentle, good, quiet; **otonashiku suru** to keep quiet.

OTOOSAN father (used as term of address by the wife as well as children in the family); father (somebody else's).

OTOOTO younger brother.

otoroeru to decline; to fall.

otoru to be inferior; to fall behind.

otoshiireru to trap, capture.

OTOSU to drop, let fall; to lose; to dump; to remove; to take; to omit; to depreciate; **chikara o otosu** to lose strength, weaken. **Koppu o otoshite watta.** I dropped a cup and broke it.

OTOTOI day before yesterday.

OTOTOSHI year before last.

otozureru to call on, visit.

OTSURI = tsurisen small change (money).

otte later on; afterward.

OTTO husband.

OU to drive away, shoo; to pursue, to run after; **hi o otte** day by day; **jun o otte** gradually, in order; **hae o ou** to shoo flies.

ou to bear; to carry on one's back; to owe; to be due. **Watakushi wa ano hito ni ou tokoro ga ooi desu.** I owe him a lot. **Kodomo o senaka ni otte ikimashita.** She went there, carrying her child on her back.

OWARI end, termination, conclusion; **owari made** to the last; **owari ni** in the end; **owari no** final, last; **owari o tsugeru** to come to an end.

OWARU to end, come to an end, finish, complete. **Shigoto ga owatta.** The job is done.

owaseru to make carry; to lay a burden on.

OYA parent(s); dealer (of cards); **oya no** parental; **oya o uyamau** to respect one's parents.

OYA oh!; oh dear!; my!

oyabun boss; master.

OYAJI (vulgar) old man; chap, father.

oyakata boss, chief.

oyako parent and child.

oyama female impersonator (actor).

oyashiro Shinto shrine.

OYAYUBI thumb; big toe.

oyayuzuri inheritance; **oyayuzuri no** inherited (from one's parents).

oyobosu to influence, affect; exert; **kooeikyoo o oyobosu** to have a good influence on, to produce a good effect.

oyobu to reach; to amount to; to come up to; to extend; to cover; to match, equal; **oyobanai** to be no match (for); to be inferior (to); **oyobi mo tsukanai** not to begin to compare (to). **Sore ni wa oyobimasen.** Don't bother about that. **Watakushi wa kare ni oyobanai.** I'm no match for him.

oyogi (n.) swimming; swim; **oyogi ni iku** to go swimming.

OYOGU to swim; **yoku oyogu** to swim well. **Hitotsu oyogoo.** Let's go for a swim.

OYOSO about; roughly; as a rule; generally speaking; **oyoso gojuu en** approximately 50 yen. **Oyoso kare hodo atama no yoi mono wa nai.** It's not too much to say that there is no one as sharp as he.

OYU, YU hot water; warm water; bath; **oyu ni hairu** to take a bath.

paatonaa partner.

PAN bread; **panko** bread crumbs; **pan o eru** to earn one's living (bread); **pan o yaku** to bake bread; **pan'ya** bakery.

panama boo panama hat.

panku puncture; **panku suru** to puncture.

panorama panorama.

parapara with a clatter; scattering as it falls; pitapat.

pasokon personal computer.

pasu pass, free ticket.

patapata with a pattering sound; **patapata suru** to patter; to flutter.

patchi Japanese-style close-fitting trousers (worn by workmen).

pachiri with a click.

pattari suddenly; all of a sudden.

patto suddenly; **patto suru** to be gay; to be showy; **patto moeru** to flare up.

pechanko flattened; crushed; **pechanako ni naru** to be flattened or crushed.

peeji page.

pekopeko cringing; **pekopeko suru** to cringe; to fawn upon.

pekopeko hungry. **Onaka ga pekopeko desu.** I'm awfully hungry.

PEN fountain pen; pen; **penga** pen-and-ink drawing; **penjiku** penholder; **pensaki** pen point; **pen shuuji** penmanship.

pengin penguin.

penki paint; **penki o nuru** to paint; **penkiya** painter.

perapera fluently, glibly; **perapera hanasu** to speak fluently; **perapera shaberu** to chatter, jabber.

perori to with a quick motion of the tongue; **perori to nameru** to lick; **shita o perori to dasu** to stick out the tongue; **perori to taberu** to eat rapidly; to make short work of a meal.

pesuto pest; black plague.

PIANO piano; **piano o hiku** to play the piano.

piipii whistling; piping; **piipii naku** to cheep, chirp (said of birds); **piipii shite iru** to be hard up (for money).

pikaichi number one. (colloq.) ace, star.

pikapika glitteringly; **pikapika suru** to glitter, sparkle, flash, twinkle.

PIN pin; hairpin; **anzenpin** safety pin.

pinpin in a lively manner; **pinpin shite iru** to be full of life, to be in the pink, to be well and sound.

pinsetto tweezers.

pinto focus; **pinto o awaseru** to focus, adjust the focus of (a camera).

pirapira flapping.

piripiri smarting; **piripiri suru** to smart, sting, burn.

pishari with a bang; **pishari to to o shimeru** to slam the door shut.

pisutoru pistol, revolver.

pitari, pittari suddenly, closely, flatly; **pittari goji ni** at (five o'clock) sharp; **pittari to au** to fit to a T; **pitari to tomaru** to come to a dead stop, to stop suddenly.

pitchaa pitcher (in a ball game).

pitchi pitch (vocal or in a game).

pointo point; decimal point; (railroad) switch.

pokan to vacantly; absentmindedly; **pokan to shite iru** to look blank.

pokapoka growing warmer; **pokapoka shite kuru** to grow warmer; **pokapoka suru** to feel warm.

POKETTO pocket; **poketto manee** pocket money.

pondo pound.

ponpu pump; **ponpu de mizu o kumiageru** to pump up water (from a well).

pooru pole.

poroporo in drops, tricklingly.

POSUTO postbox, mailbox; **posuto ni ireru** to mail.

potapota drop by drop; **potapota to tareru** to fall in drops; to trickle; to drip.

potsupotsu little by little; in drops; bit by bit. **Potsupotsu furu.** It rains in small drops.

potto in a glow; **potto kao o akarameru** to blush.

punpun piquantly; **punpun niou** to smell piquant; to smell fragrant; to stink, reek; **punpun okoru** to be in a huff; to fume.

puremiamu premium; **puremiamu o tsukeru** to place a premium (on); **puremiamu ga tsuite iru** to be at a premium.

puro pro, professional athlete.

puropaganda propaganda; **puropaganda o suru** to publicize; to spread propaganda.

puropera propeller.

puroretaria proletariat; proletarians.

pyuu to whizzing, whistling; **pyuu to fuku** to whistle; **pyuu to tobu** to whiz through the air.

R

-RA suffix denoting: and others; and the like, etc. **Kimira ni wa ienai desu.** I can't tell it to you people.

rachi picket-fence; limit; **rachi mo nai** foolish, silly; **rachi ga aku** to reach a settlement; **rachi ga akanai** to make little headway, remain unsettled; **rachigai ni deru** to go beyond bounds.

ragubii rugby.

-rai suffix denoting: since, the past; **sakunenrai** since last year.

raichoo suru to arrive in Japan.

RAIGETSU next month; **saraigetsu** the month after next.

raiharu = raishun next spring.

raihin guest; **raihinseki** visitor's seats.

raihoo visit, call; **raihoo suru** to visit.

raikai attendance; **raikai suru** to attend a meeting; **raikaisha** audience; attendance.

raikyaku visitor, guest.

raimei thunderclap.

RAINEN next year; **sarainen** the year after next.

raion lion.

rairaku frankness; **rairaku na** frank; openhearted; broad-minded.

raireki career, history, origin (personal); **raireki o tadasu** to inquire into one's past.

raishun = raiharu next spring.

RAISHUU next week; **saraishuu** the week after next.

raisukaree curried rice.

raiu thunderstorm. **Raiu ga aru daroo.** There will be a thunderstorm.

raiyuu visit (from abroad); **raiyuusha** visitor; **raiyuu gaijin** foreign visitor.

RAJIO radio; **rajio hoosoo** radio broadcasting; **rajio o kiku** to listen to the radio; **rajio o tomeru** to turn off the radio; **keitai rajio** portable radio.

raketto racket (tennis, etc.).

rakka falling; **rakka suru** to fall; to drop.

rakkan optimism; **rakkanteki** optimistic; **rakkan suru** to be optimistic.

rakkasan parachute.

rakkasei peanut.

RAKU comfort, ease; pleasure; **raku na** comfortable, easy; **raku o suru** to take it easy. **Oraku ni nasatte kudasai.** Make yourself comfortable.

rakuchaku settlement; **rakuchaku saseru** to settle, bring to a conclusion; **rakuchaku suru** to be settled.

rakudai rejection; failure in an exam; **rakudai suru** to fail (flunk) an exam; to be rejected.

rakuen paradise.

rakugaki scribbling.

rakugo comic story.

rakugosha straggler.

rakuseishiki inauguration ceremony; completion ceremony.

rakusen defeat in an election; failure; rejection; **rakusensha** defeated candidate.

rakutan discouragement; despair; **rakutan saseru** to discourage; **rakutan suru** to be discouraged; to be disappointed.

rakutenka optimist; **rakutenshugi** optimism.

ranboo violence, outrage; **ranboo na** violent; rude; rowdy; disorderly; **ranboo suru** to behave rudely; **ranboomono** ruffian, rowdy.

RANCHI lunch; **ranchi o taberu** to have lunch.

randoku desultory reading.

rankan railing, handrail.

ranpu lamp.

ran'yoo abuse; misuse; **ran'yoo suru** to abuse.

ranzatsu disorder, confusion; **ranzatsu na** disorderly, untidy; **ranzatsu ni naru** to get confused; to be in disorder.

ranzoo overproduction; **ranzoo suru** to overproduce.

rappa trumpet, cornet, horn; **rappa o fuku** to blow a horn; **rappa nomi o yaru** to drink (something) directly from the bottle.

rasen screw; spiral spring; **rasenkei** spiral form; **rasenkei no** spiral-shaped.

rasha woolen cloth.

-RASHII -like; becoming; looking (like); appear, seem; it seems to me; probably; **kodomorashii** childlike. **Soo rashii.** I guess so. **Ame rashii.** It looks like rain. **Kuru rashii desu.** It seems he is coming.

rashinban compass.

rasshu awaa rush hour.

reesu lace; race.

REI custom, usage, habit, precedent; instance, case, example; **rei ni yotte** as usual; **rei no** usual, customary; **rei o ageru to** for instance; **rei o ageru** to give an instance; **rei ni naru** to set a precedent.

REI zero.

REI, OREI thanks, appreciation; **rei o noberu** to express thankfulness.

rei soul, spirit.

rei salutation; **rei o suru** to bow.

reidai example; exercise.

reido zero; freezing point (Centigrade); **reido ika** below zero.

reifuku evening dress.

reigai exception; **reigai no** exceptional; **reigai ni suru** to except, make an exception of.

reigi courtesy, etiquette; **reigi tadashii** courteous. **Kare wa reigi ga tadashii.** He has good manners.

reihai worship; **reihai suru** to worship; **reihaidoo** chapel; church.

reijoo letter of thanks; **reijoo o dasu** to send a letter of thanks.

reikai regular meeting.

reikoku cruelty; **reikoku na** cruel; coldhearted.

reikoo strict enforcement; **reikoo suru** to enforce strictly.

reikyaku refrigeration; cooling; **reikyaku suru** to cool; to refrigerate.

reimeiki dawn of a new age.

reinen ordinary year, average year; annually, every year; **reinen matsuri** annual festival; **reinen no toori** as usual; as every year.

reiraku ruin, downfall; **reiraku suru** to be ruined, go to ruin.

reisei coolness, calmness; **reisei na** cool, calm; **reisei na hito** coldhearted person; **reisei ni kangaeru** to think about something calmly.

reishoo cold smile, sneer; **reishoo suru** to sneer at; to mock; to give a mocking laugh.

reisoo formal wear; ceremonial dress.

reisui cold water; **reisuimasatsu** rubdown with a cold wet towel; **reisuiyoku** cold bath; **reisuiyoku o suru** to take a cold bath.

reitan indifference, coolness; **reitan na** cool; cold; indifferent; **seiji ni reitan de aru** to be indifferent to politics.

reiten zero, zero point; **reiten o toru** to get a zero.

reitooniku frozen meat.

reizen offering to the spirits of the dead.

reizoo cold storage; refrigeration; **reizoo suru** to refrigerate; **reizooko** refrigerator; **reizoosha** refrigerated freight car.

rekidai successive generations.

rekishi history; **Nippon no rekishi** Japanese history; **rekishijoo yuumei na tokoro** place of historical interest; **rekishijoo no jinbutsu** historical personage; **rekishika** historian.

rekizen to clearly, plainly; **rekizen to shite akiraka desu.** It's as plain as day.

rekkoku nations (of the world).

rekkyo enumeration; **rekkyo suru** to enumerate, list.

rekkyoo great (world) powers (countries).

rekoodo phonograph record; **rekoodo o kakeru** to play a record (on a phonograph).

REN'AI love; **ren'ai jiken** love affair; **ren'ai kankei ni naru** to fall in love; to have a love affair.

renchuu party, company.

renga brick(s).

rengoo combination, union, confederation, amalgamation; alliance, coalition; **rengoo suru** to combine, etc.; **rengoo no** allied, associated, etc.; **rengookoku** allied countries; **Kokusai Rengoo** United Nations.

renketsu suru to couple, join, connect.

renmei joint signature; **renmei suru** to sign jointly.

renpoo federation (of states); union; commonwealth; **renpoo no** united, federated, etc.

renraku connection; traffic; communication; **renraku suru** to make contact; **renraku o toru** to get in touch with; **renraku o ushinau** to lose touch, lose contact; **renrakusen** ferryboat (connected with a train).

renshuu practice, training, drill, rehearsal; **renshuu o tsunda** well-trained; **renshuu suru** to practice, etc.

rensoo association (of ideas); **rensoo suru** to be reminded of; to associate (one) with (another).

rentaisekinin joint responsibility.

Rentogen X-ray; **Rentogen ni kakaru** to be X-rayed.

renzoku continuity; succession; **renzoku suru** to continue; to last; **renzoku teki** continuous; consecutive; **renzokuteki ni** continuously.

renzu lens.

reppuu heavy wind, hurricane. **Reppuu ga fuite iru.** There's a heavy wind blowing.

resseki attendance; **-ni resseki suru** to attend, be present at.

resserareru to be ranked with.

ressha railway train.

ressuru to attend, to present; to rank with, take one's place among.

retsu row, rank, tier, column, line; **retsu o tsukuru** to form a row, line up.

rettoo archipelago, chain of islands; **Chishima rettoo** the Kuriles.

rettoo inferiority; **rettoo na otoko** man of bad moral character; **rettoo no** inferior, of poor quality; **rettoohin** low-quality goods.

rezubian lesbian

ri advantage; benefit; interest; **rokubu no ri** 6 percent interest; **ri no aru** advantageous, beneficial; **ri ga aru** to be profitable; **ri o eru** to profit from, gain by.

ri reason, right, truth, principle; **ri no aru** reasonable, justifiable; **ri ni somuku** to be against reason.

ribon ribbon; **ribon de musubu** to tie with a ribbon.

richi intellect; **richiteki na** intellectual.

richigimono upright person.

rieki benefit, gain, profit; **rieki no aru** profitable, lucrative; **rieki o hogo suru** to protect one's interests; **riekikin** profits, proceeds.

rien, RIKON divorce; **rien suru** to divorce.

rifujin unreasonableness; **rifujin na** unreasonable, unjust.

rigai advantages and disadvantages; interests; **rigai ni kankei ga aru** to have an effect on one's interests; to have an interest in.

rigaku hakushi Doctor of Science.

rigakushi Bachelor of Science.

rihatsu haircutting; hairdressing; **RIHATSUTEN** barber shop; **rihatsushi** barber.

riido *(n.)* leading; **riido suru** to lead.

riji director; manager; **rijichoo** chairman of a board of directors; **rijikai** board of directors.

rika science.

rikai understanding, comprehension; **rikai dekiru** understandable. comprehensible; **rikai no nai** without understanding; **rikai**

no aru hito sensible person; **rikai suru** to understand; to grasp; to appreciate; **rikairyoku** understanding, comprehension.

rikimu to strain oneself; to brag; to swagger.

rikisaku masterpiece; elaborate work.

rikisetsu suru to emphasize, to lay stress on; to be emphatic.

rikkooho candidacy (for an election); **rikkooho suru** to run as a candidate; **rikkooho o happyoo suru** to announce one's candidacy; **rikkoohosha** candidate.

RIKON, rien divorce; **rikon suru** to divorce.

rikoo cleverness, smartness; **rikoo na** clever, shrewd, bright, intelligent; **rikoo soo na** bright, intelligent looking.

rikoo suru to carry out, to fulfill.

rikoshugi egoism.

rikoteki egoistic, selfish.

riku, rikuchi land; **riku o iku** to go by land; **rikuro** land journey, land road (route). (See also **rikujoo**.)

rikugun army.

rikujoo land, ground; **rikujoo de** on land. (See also **riku**.)

rikutsu theory; argument; pretext; reason, logic; **rikutsu ni au** to stand to reason; **rikutsu ga tatanai** to be unreasonable, be illogical; **rikutsuppoi** argumentative; **rikutsuzeme** persuasive reasoning; **nan toka kan toka rikutsu o tsukete** on one pretext or another; **rikutsuzeme ni suru** to persuade (someone) by reason.

rikuzoku in succession, one after another.

rimen back, reverse, other side; **rimen de** behind the scenes, in secret; **rimen de ayatsuru** to pull strings; **rimen o kansatsu suru** to look at the other side.

rimokon remote control.

RINGO apple; **ringo no ki** apple tree.

ringoku neighboring country.

rinjin neighbor; **rinjin no yoshimi** neighborliness.

rinjuu one's last (deathbed) moment; **rinjuu no kotoba** dying words.

rinka neighboring house, house next door.

rinkaku contours, outline; **rinkaku o noberu** to give an outline, sketch.

rinri ethics, morality.

rinyuu suru to wean.

RIPPA fineness, richness; **rippa na** fine, splendid, good, nice, excellent, stately; **rippa ni** superbly, admirably, sufficiently; **rippa ni seikatsu suru** to make a decent living. **Rippa desu.** It's splendid.

rippoo legislation; **rippoo no** legislative.

rippuku anger, rage; **rippuku suru** to get angry; **rippuku saseru** to make angry.

rirei relay race.

rireki personal history, career; **rireki ga yoi** to have a good record of service; **rireki ga warui** to have a poor record of service; **rirekisho** personal history, record of one's life.

ririku takeoff; **ririku suru** to take off; to get afloat.

ririshii imposing; majestic.

riron theory.

riroseizen logical, valid.

risaichi stricken locality.

risaisha victim, sufferer.

risan dispersion; **risan suru** to be dispersed.

rishi interest; **yasui rishi** low interest; **takai rishi** high interest; **rishi o toru** to charge interest; **rishi o shoo zuru** to accrue.

risoo ideal; **takai risoo** high ideal; **risoo shugi** idealism; **risooteki** ideal; idealistic.

risookyoo utopia.

risshoo proof; **risshoo suru** to prove, demonstrate, bear out.

risshun first day of spring.

risurin glycerine.

ritei mileage, distance; **riteihyoo** milestone.

ritsu rate, proportion; **ritsu o ageru** to raise the rate.

ritsuan plan, device; **ritsuan suru** to plan, design, devise.

riyoo utilization; **riyoo suru** to use; to make use of, utilize; to take advantage of; **kikai o riyoo suru** to take advantage of an opportunity.

riyuu reason, cause; **riyuu de** for reasons of; **riyuu naku** without cause, without provocation; **riyuu no aru** reasonable; **riyuu no nai** groundless; **riyuu o noberu** to state one's reason.

rizai finance, economy.

ro hearth, fireplace; **robata** fireside.

ro oar.

roboo roadside, wayside; **roboo no chaya** wayside teahouse; **roboo no hito** passerby; **roboo ni tatsu** to stand by the roadside.

robotto robot.

rodai balcony (outdoor).

roji alley, lane.

roken discovery, exposure; **roken suru** to be found out; to be detected.

rokotsu frankness; **rokotsu na** frank, candid; plain; naked; **rokotsu na atekosuri** broad hint; **rokotsu ni ieba** frankly speaking.

ROKU, MUTTSU six; **dai roku** the sixth; **ROKUJUU** sixty; **rokumai byoobu** sixfold screen.

rokudenashi (n.) good-for-nothing.

ROKUGATSU June.

rokuon recording, transcription; **rokuonki** recorder (sound recording machine);

rokuon suru to record; to make a recording.

ron argument; discussion; essay; opinion; **ron o matanu** to be beyond argument; **ronbun** essay, article; thesis; **rongai** out of the question; irrelevant; **ronri** logic; **ronriteki** logical; **ronriteki ni** logically; **ronri ni awanai** to be illogical; **ronsetsu** essay; editorial, dissertation; **ronsetsu kisha** editorial writer.

ronjiru, ronzuru to discuss; to argue.

ronkoku prosecution; **ronkoku suru** to prosecute.

ronzuru See **ronjiru.**

roo wax; **roo o hiku** to wax; **roobiki** waxing; **roobiki no** waxed; **roogami** wax paper.

rooa deaf and dumb.

rooba old woman.

roobo aged mother.

roobai confusion, panic; **roobai suru** to be confused; to be in a panic.

rooden short circuit.

roodoku recitation; **roodoku suru** to recite, read aloud.

roodoo manual labor, work; **jikangai roodoo** overtime work; **roodoo jikan** working hours; **roodoo kaikyuu** laboring class; **roodoo kumiai** labor union; **roodoo kumiai yakuin** labor leader; **roodoo mondai** labor problem; **roodosha** laborer; **roodoo soogi** labor dispute; **roodoo undoo** labor movement; **roodoo suru** to labor, work. (See also **rooryoku.**)

roogo old age.

roohi waste (of time, energy); extravagance; **roohi suru** to waste, squander; **jikan o roohi suru** to waste time.

ROOJIN aged person.

rooka corridor, passageway, hall.

ROOMAJI Roman letters; romanization (anglicization); **roomaji de tsuzuru** to spell in Roman letters.

romansu romance.

ROOMA SUUJI Roman numerals.

roonen old age.

roonin unemployed person; **roonin shite iru** to be out of work; to be studying for an entrance examination to a college.

rooren expert; **rooren na** experienced.

rooryoku labor, effort; **rooryoku busoku** labor shortage. (See also **roodoo.**)

roosoku candle, **roosokutate** candlestick.

roosu sirloin.

rootai old person's body.

Rootarii Kurabu Rotary Club.

rooya, keimusho prison, jail.

ROSHIA. Roshia no (adj.) Russian; **Roshiago** Russian language. **Roshiajin** Russian (person).

roten open air; **roten no** outdoor.

rui kind, sort, variety; description; similar case; parallel. **rui no nai** unique; unparalleled; **ano rui no hito** people of that sort.

ruibetsu classification; **ruibetsu suru** to classify.

ruiji resemblance, similarity, likeness; **ruiji no** similar, analogous; **ruijiten** point of resemblance. **-ni ruiji suru** to be like, be similar to.

ruikei total sum. **ruikei suru** to total.

ruirei similar case, analogy; **ruirei no nai** unique; exceptional.

runpen tramp, hobo.

RUSU absence; **rusuchuu ni** during (one's) absence; **rusu ni suru** to be out (not at home); **rusu o tsukau** to pretend not to be in. **Sanpo ni itte rusu desu.** She has gone out for a walk.

rusuban temporary caretaker (while a person is away from home).

ryaku abbreviation; abridgment; **ryaku sazu ni** in detail (without abbreviating); **ryaku shite** in short; **ryaku suru** to abridge; to abbreviate; **ryakugo** abbreviation; **ryakuji** simplified character; simpler substitute; abbreviation.

ryakudatsu suru to loot; to plunder.

ryakushiki informal way; **ryakushiki no** informal; **ryakushiki de, ryakushiki ni** informally.

ryakuzu rough sketch; **ryakuzu o toru** to make a rough sketch of.

ryohi traveling expenses.

RYOKAKU traveler; passenger; tourist; **ryokaku annaijo** travelers' aid.

RYOKAN Japanese-style hotel or inn.

ryoken passport; **ryoken o hakko suru** to issue a passport; **ryoken o shinsei suru** to apply for a passport.

RYOKOO travel; trip; tour; **ryokoo suru** to travel; **ryokoo ni dekakeru** to start on a journey; **RYOKOO ANNAI** guidebook; **ryokoo annaisho** travel agency.

ryoo- prefix denoting: both, two; **ryooashi** both legs; both feet; **RYOOGAWA** both sides; **RYOOHOO** both; both sides; **ryoogan** both banks of a river; **ryoomen** both sides; **ryoomen o kansatsu suru** to examine both sides; **ryooshin** both parents; **ryootan** both ends; **ryoote** both hands; **ryoote de motsu** to hold in both hands. **Ryoohoo tomo shitte iru.** I know both of them.

ryoo hunting; shooting; game; fishing; **ryoo ni iku** to go hunting; to go fishing.

ryoo quantity, volume.

ryoodo territory, possession.

ryoogae money-changing, exchange of money; **Beika o Nihon no okane ni ryoogae suru** to change American money into Japanese money.

ryoohoo remedy; method of treatment.

ryooji consul; **ryoojikan** consulate; **soo ryoojikan** consulate general.

ryooji medical treatment.

ryookai comprehension; **ryookai suru** to comprehend, grasp; to see. **Sore wa watakushi ni wa ryookai dekinai.** It's beyond my comprehension.

ryooken idea, thought, notion; intention; view; direction; **ryooken o kiku** to ask (someone) his intention; **ryooken o sueru** to make up one's mind. **Doo iu ryooken de sonna koto o shita no desu ka?** What made you do such a thing?

RYOOKIN charge, fee; fare; **ryookin o torazu ni** free of charge; **ryookin o toru** to charge.

ryookoo na successful; favorable.

RYOORI cooking, cuisine; dish; food; **ryoori suru** to cook; to prepare food; **Nippon ryoori o taberu** to have a Japanese meal.

ryooritsu compatibility; coexistence; **ryooritsu suru** to be compatible with; to be consistent with; **ryooritsu shigatai** to be incompatible with, to be inconsistent with.

ryooriya restaurant (Japanese-style).

ryooshin conscience; **ryooshinteki** conscientious. **Ryooshin ga togameru.** My conscience bothers me.

ryooshuusho receipt.

ryooyoo convalescence; **ryooyoo suru** to convalesce.

ryuuchoo fluency; **ryuuchoo na** fluent; **ryuuchoo ni** fluently, eloquently; **ryuuchoo ni Nihongo o hanasu** to speak Japanese fluently.

ryuudoobutsu liquid diet.

ryuugakusei student studying abroad.

ryuugaku suru to study abroad.

ryuugi style; method.

ryuukan influenza.

RYUUKOO fashion, fad; popularity; **ryuukoo no** fashionable, in fashion; **ryuukoo suru** to be in fashion; to come into fashion; **ryuukoo ni okureru** to be out of fashion, out of style.

ryuumachi rheumatism.

-SA suffix added to the stem of an adjective to make a noun (comparable to English -ty, -ness); **bakabakashisa** stupidity, stupidness; **shitashisa** familiarity.

sa difference; margin. **Sa ga aru.** There is a difference.

SAA come; now; well; let me see. **Saa taihen na koto o shita.** Oh, what have I done! **Saa ikimashoo.** Let's go now.

saabisu service (at a restaurant, store, etc.). **Saabisu ga yoi.** The service is good.

saachiraito searchlight.

saakasu circus.

sabaketa sensible; frank; **sabaketa hito** person of the world.

sabaku desert.

sabaku to judge; to decide; to settle. **Hito o sabaku na.** Don't judge others.

sabaku to sell, to deal with.

sabasaba shita refreshing; agreeable.

saaberu Occidental-style sword; saber.

sabetsu distinction; discrimination; differentiation; difference; **sabetsu no aru** discriminating; **sabetsu naku** without discrimination; **sabetsu o suru** to discriminate.

sabi rust; patina; antique look; maturity; **sabi ga tsuku** to become rusty.

sabireru to cease to flourish.

SABISHII lonely, lonesome; deserted, desolate.

saboru to go slow; to sabotage; to cut classes.

sabotaaju sabotage; going slow.

sadamaru to fix; to become settled; to be determined; to be subjugated; **sadamatta** regular, fixed, definite. **Hi ga sadamarimashita.** The date is fixed. **Sadamatta jikan ni kimasu.** He comes at a regular time.

sadameru to establish, to lay down; to decide, to settle; **Shuppatsu no hi o sadamemashita.** I decided on a date of departure.

sadamete surely; to be sure.

SAE even; only. **Ano hito sae shitte imasu.** Even he knows it. **Okane sae areba kaimasu.** I'll buy it if only I have the money for it.

saegiru to cut off; to stop; to interrupt; to hinder, to obstruct, block; **me o saegiru** to obstruct a view; **hito no hanashi o saegiru** to cut in; to interrupt (someone's) conversation.

saeru to be bright, be clear; to attain a rare skill; **me ga saeru** to be wakeful. **Tsuki ga saeru.** The moon shines clearly. **Nakanaka saeta ude desu.** She is quite expert in it.

saezuru to sing, warble (a bird).

safuran saffron.

sagaku balance; difference.

SAGARU to hang down; to fall; to go down (in price); to leave; to retire. **Nichiyoohin**

no ne ga sagarimashita. The prices of ordinary commodities have come down.

sagashidasu to find out, discover.

SAGASU to seek, search for.

SAGERU to hang down; to lower, let down; to clear away; to wear (a sword); **akari o sageru** to lower a lamp; **nedan o sageru** to lower a price; **ozen o sageru** to clear a table.

sagi fraud; imposture; deceit, cheating; **sagi o hataraku** to defraud; **sagishi** swindler.

saguri probe; **saguri o ireru** to probe.

saguru to search for; to grope for; to probe; **iken o saguru** to feel out (someone's) view; **poketto o saguru** to fumble in one's pocket.

sagyoo work, operation; **sagyoo chuu** while working; **sagyoo o hajimeru** to begin work; **sagyooshitsu** workroom.

sahodo so; so much; much *(often used in the negative sense);* **sahodo ni mo nai** not so much as you think.

sahoo good manners, etiquette; **sahoo o shiranai** ill-mannered.

SAI talent; ability; difference; **sai no aru** talented; **gogaku no sai ga aru** to have an aptitude for languages; **sai o tanomu** to put too much confidence in one's own talents.

-sai year (as a counter for age); **san sai** three years old; **juugo sai** fifteen years old.

saiai no dearest, beloved.

saibai cultivation (of plants); **saibai suru** to cultivate.

SAIBAN judgment; trial; **saiban suru** to judge; **saibanchoo** chief judge; **saibankan** judge, bench (legal); **saibansho** court of justice, law court; **Saikoo Saibansho** Supreme Court.

saiboo cell.

saichi wit and intellect.

SAICHUU in the midst of; in the course of; at the height of; **shokuji no saichuu ni** in the middle of the meal. **Ima ga atsui saichuu da.** The summer heat is now at its height.

saidaa soda pop, soda water.

saidai greatest; maximum; **saidai no koofuku** to greatest happiness; **saidai sokuryoku** the maximum speed.

saidan altar.

saien talented woman.

SAIFU purse; wallet.

saigai calamity; **saigai o koomuru** to suffer a disaster.

saigen reappearance; **saigen suru** to reappear.

saigen limitation; **saigen ga nai** to be endless.

saigetsu time; years. **Saigetsu hito o matazu.** Time and tide wait for no man.

SAIGO last; **saigo no** last, closing; **saigo ni** lastly; **saigo no toshi** the last year; **saigo tsuuchoo** an ultimatum.

saigo one's last moment in life; **hisan na saigo o togeru** to die a sad death.

saihai (baton of) command; direction, leadership. **saihai o furu** to command.

saihan reprinting, second edition; **saihan suru** to reprint; **saihan ni naru** to run into a second edition.

saihatsu reappearance, **saihatsu suru** to appear again, have a second attack (of a disease).

saihi adoption or rejection; **saihi o kimeru** to decide on the adoption or rejection.

saihoo sewing; needlework; **saihoo suru** to sew; **saihooshi** tailor.

saijin sharp-witted person.

SAIJITSU national holiday.

SAIJOO (n.) best, highest; superlative; **saijoo no** (adj.) best, highest; **saijoohin** article of the best quality; **saijookyuu** the superlative degree.

saikai meeting again; **saikai o yakusuru** to promise to meet again.

saikasoo lowest layer.

saiken debenture; **saikensha** creditor.

saiketsu verdict, decision; **saiketsu suru** to bring in a verdict; to decide.

saiki pressing creditor.

SAIKIN latest; **saikin no joohoo** latest information.

saikin bacterium.

saikon second marriage; **saikon suru** to marry again.

saikoo maximum, **saikoo no** highest; supreme; **Saikoo Saibansho** Supreme Court.

saikoo revival, restoration; **saikoo suru** to reestablish, to renew.

saikoo reconsideration; **saikoo suru** to reconsider; **saikoo no ue de** on reflection.

saikooten highest point.

saikoro dice.

saiku workmanship; **saiku o suru** to work; to make; to patch up; to manipulate.

saikuru cycle.

saikutsu mining; **saikutsu suru** to work a mine.

saimatsu close of the year; **saimatsu no uridashi** year-end bargain.

saiminjutsu hypnotism; **saiminjutsu o kakeru** to hypnotize (someone).

saimitsu smallness; minuteness; **saimitsu na** minute; detailed; **saimitsu ni** in detail.

saimoku details; items; **saimoku ni wataru** to go into detail.

saimu debt; **saimu o hatasu** to settle one's debts; **saimusha** debtor.

sain signature; **sain suru** to sign.

sainan misfortune, calamity, accident; **sainan ni au** to meet with an accident (mishap); **sainan o manugareru** to escape a disaster.

sainin reappointment.

sairai second coming; reincarnation.

sairei festival.

saisai again and again; **saisai no** repeated; frequent.

saisan over and over again.

saisei regeneration; resuscitation; **saisei suru** to come to life again.

saisen offertory; sacred pennies; **saisen bako** offertory box (at a Shinto shrine).

saishi one's wife and children.

saishiki coloring; painting; **saishiki shita** colored; **saishiki suru** to paint.

saishin rehearing, retrial; **saishin suru** to rehear; to reexamine.

saishin no latest; **saishinshiki** latest model.

saishin no careful, prudent; **saishin no chuui o haratte** most carefully.

SAISHO beginning; **saisho no** first, original; **saisho wa** at first; **saisho ni** at the outset; in the first place; **saisho kara** from the very first.

saishoku living on vegetables only; vegetarian diet; **saishoku suru** to live on vegetables; **saishokushugisha** vegetarian.

saishoo (n.) minimum; smallest; **saishoo no** (adj.) smallest; least.

saishuu (n.) last, final; collection; **saishuu no** (adj.) last, final; **saishuu ressha** last train of the day.

saishuu collection; **saishuu suru** to collect, to gather samples.

saisoku urging; calling upon; **saisoku suru** to urge, press; **kane o saisoku suru** to call upon a person in order to pay off one's debts.

saisoku detailed rules.

saitei no lowest, minimum.

saiten marking, scoring.

saiwai good fortune; happiness; **saiwai na** happy, fortunate; **saiwai ni** happily, fortunately.

saiyoo adoption; appointment; **saiyoo suru** to adopt; to use, employ.

saizen (n.) best; one's best; **saizen no** (adj.) best; utmost; **saizen o tsukusu** to do one's best.

SAJI spoon; **saji de sukuu** to spoon up; **saji o nageru** to give up.

sajiki stand; gallery; upper boxes (in a theater).

SAKA sloping hill; slope; ascent; **saka ni naru** to slope; **saka o noboru** to go up a slope; **saka o kudaru** to go down a slope.

sakadachi o suru to stand on one's head.

sakaeru to prosper, flourish.

sakai boundary, border, frontier.

sakamichi a sloping way (road); sloping grade.

SAKANA fish; **sakana tsuri ni iku** to go fishing; **sakanaya** fishmonger; fish dealer.

sakan na prosperous; splendid; vigorous; **sakan ni** actively; vigorously; **sakan ni naru** to become active.

sakanoboru to go up; to go back, retrace.

sakaratte against; in the face of.

sakarau to oppose, go against.

sakari height, climax; rut, heat; **sakari de aru** to be in full bloom; to be in the prime of.

sakasa, sakasama inversion, inverted order; **sakasa no** inverted; **sakasa ni** wrong side up; upside down; **sakasa ni naru** to be inverted.

sakasama See **sakasa**.

sakaya sake shop.

sakazuki cup; wine cup; **sakazuki o sasu** to offer a cup (of wine); **sakazuki o hosu** to drink up (a cup of wine or sake); **sakazuki o mawasu** to pass around a cup.

SAKE Japanese liquor, wine.

sake salmon.

sakebi shout; cry.

sakebu to shout; to cry.

sakei leaning toward the left; **sakei suru** to lean toward the left; to become communistic.

sakeme crack.

sakenomi drinker.

sakeru to split; to be torn. **Kinomo ga sakemashita.** My dress was torn.

sakeru to avoid, to keep away.

SAKI point; tip; future; destination; front; **saki e itte** later on; **saki no** (*adj.*) future; coming; former; **saki ni** beyond; previously; **saki ga nagai** to have a long future; **yubi no saki** tip of the finger. **Saki ni itte kudasai.** Please go ahead.

sakidatsu to precede.

sakigake pioneer; **sakigake no** foremost; **sakigake o suru** to lead.

SAKIHODO, SAKKI little while ago; **sakihodo kara** for some time.

sakimawari preoccupation, forestallment; **sakimawari o suru** to get ahead of.

sakiototoi three days back, three days ago.

sakiototoshi three years ago.

sakisohon saxophone.

sakka writer, author; literary person.

sakkaku illusion.

SAKKI See **SAKIHODO**.

sakki thirst for blood; menace; **sakki datsu** to look menacing.

sakku sack; case.

sakkyoku musical composition, musical piece; **sakkyoku suru** to set to music; **sakkyokuka** composer of music.

SAKU to rend, split, tear; **naka o saku** to sever the two.

saku device; plan; **saku o megurasu** to devise a scheme; **saku ga tsukiru** to be at wit's end.

saku to bloom.

SAKUBAN last evening, last night. (See also **YUUBE**.)

sakubun composition.

sakudoo maneuvers; artful management.

sakugen curtailment; retrenchment; **sakugen suru** to cut down.

sakuhin work (literary, musical, etc.).

sakui design; motif.

sakuin index; **sakuin o tsukuru** to provide with an index.

sakujitsu See **KINOO**.

sakujo omission; **sakujo suru** to strike out; to omit.

SAKUNEN See **KYONEN**.

SAKURA cherry tree.

sakuranbo cherry (fruit).

sakurasoo Japanese primrose.

sakuryaku artifice; device; stratagem; scheme; **sakuryaku ni tomu** to be resourceful in scheming.

sakusei manufacture, production.

sakusen military or naval operation; strategy.

sakusha author; dramatist; poet; composer; maker.

SAKUYA last night.

sakyuu sandhill, dune.

-SAMA See **-SAN**.

samasu to wake up, awaken; to make sober; to cool; to bring down. **Kono ocha wa moo sukoshi samashite kara nomimashoo.** I will drink this tea after it has cooled a bit.

samatage disturbance; hindrance.

samatageru to obstruct, hinder.

samayou to wander about; to stray.

samazama various; **samazama na hito** all sorts of people; **samazama ni** in many ways.

SAMERU to wake up; to come to oneself; to become sober; **me ga sameru** to be awakened; **yoi ga sameru** to become sober.

samezame to bitterly; without restraint; **samezame to naku** to weep bitterly.

SAMO as though, as if; **samo manzoku soo ni** with evident satisfaction. **Samo ureshisoo desu.** She looks quite pleased.

samon inquisition, inquiry; **samon suru** to interrogate; **samon kai** court of inquiry.

samugari person who is oversensitive to cold.

samugaru to complain of the cold; to be sensitive to the cold.

SAMUI cold, chilly.

samuke chill, fit of cold, cold shiver.

samurai knight.

SAMUSA coldness. **Samusa ga kibishiku narimashita.** The cold has worsened.

SAN, MITTSU three.

-SAN Mr., Ms. **Yamada-san** Mr. (Mrs., Miss) Yamada.

sanba midwife.

sanbashi landing pier.

sanbi praise; adoration; **sanbi suru** to praise.

sanbika hymn; **sanbika o utau** to sing a hymn.

sanbun prose.

sanbutsu product.

sanchi mountainous region; highlands.

sanchi place of production.

sanchoo summit (peak) of a mountain.

sandan devising ways and means; **sandan suru** to find a means; **kane o sandan suru** to manage to raise money.

sandoitchi sandwiches.

sangai three stories, third floor.

sangai damage; disaster; **sensoo no sangai** the evils of war.

SANGATSU March.

sangyoo (manufacturing) industry; **sangyoo no** industrial.

sangyoo kookoku classified advertisement.

SANJUU thirty.

sanjuu no threefold, triple; **sanjuu no hako** nest (set) of three boxes.

sanjutsu arithmetic; **sanjutsu o suru** to do sums.

sanka participation. **-ni sanka suru** to take part in.

sankaku triangle; **sankaku no** triangular.

sankan visit; **sankan suru** to visit and see.

sankei visiting a temple; **sankei suru** to go and worship (at a Buddhist temple or a Shinto shrine); **sankeinin** visitor to a temple, worshiper; pilgrim.

sankoo reference; comparison; **sankoo ni suru** to refer to; **sankoo ni naru** to serve as a reference; **sankoo no tame ni** for reference; **sankoonin** witness; **sankoosho** book of reference.

sanmai three sheets (of paper, or anything flat and thin); **sakana o sanmai ni orosu** to fillet fish (to make three pieces, i.e., 2 pieces of fish and the bone).

sanmenkiji third-page items of a newspaper; general news.

sanmyaku mountain range.

sanpai worship; **sanpai suru** to visit and worship (at a Shinto shrine).

SANPO a walk; **sanpo suru** to take a walk; **sanpo ni iku** to go for a walk.

sanpu scattering; **sanpu suru** to spread, scatter.

sanpuku side of a mountain.

sanretsu attendance; **sanretsu suru** to attend, be present at.

sanrin forest.

sanrinsha tricycle.

sansei seconding, approval; **-ni sansei suru** to support; to approve of.

sanseiken suffrage; political right.

sanseisha supporter; seconder.

sanshoo comparison; reference; **sanshoo suru** to refer to.

sanshutsu production, output; **sanshutsu suru** to produce.

sanso oxygen.

sanson mountain village.

sansui hills and streams; landscape; landscape painting of mountains and rivers.

santan pitifulness; **santan taru** pitiful; tragic.

santoo third class.

san'yaku powdered medicine.

sanzai (n.) spending (money); squandering; **sanzai suru** to spend money.

sanzai lying scattered; **sanzai suru** to lie scattered.

SANZAN severely; terribly; **sanzan matsu** to wait a long time; **sanzan na me ni au** to have a bitter experience.

sao pole, rod; **saodake** bamboo pole.

SAPPARI at all; quite; entirely; **sappari shita** refreshing. **Sappari wakarimasen.** I don't understand at all.

sappuukei tastelessness; **sappuukei na** tasteless; dry.

SARA dish, plate.

sarada salad; **saradayu** salad oil.

SARAIGETSU month after next.

SARAINEN year after next.

SARAISHUU week after next.

sarakedasu to reveal; to bring shamelessly into view; to lay bare; **muchi o sarake dasu** to expose one's ignorance.

sara ni anew, afresh; once more, again; furthermore.

sararii salary; **saraiiman** salaried man.

sarasara in the least; smoothly; rustling; murmuring.

sarashi bleaching; refining; exposure; **sarashiko** bleaching powder; **sarashimomen** bleached cotton.

sarasu to bleach.

sarasu to expose; **haji o sarasu** to be put to shame.

sarau dredge; to clean; to sweep away; **ninki o sarau** to win (popularity) by a clean sweep.

sarau to kidnap, to spirit away, to snatch.

sarau (colloq.) to review; to repeat; to practice; **piano o sarau** to practice the piano.

saru to go away, to leave; to take off; to

divorce; **gakkoo o saru** to leave school; **shoku o saru** to retire from a post.

saru monkey.

sasaeru to support, maintain; **ikka o sasaeru** to support one's family.

sasageru to offer; to sacrifice; to lift up.

sasai na trifling; small; **sasai na koto** trivial matter.

sasayaki whispering.

sasayaku to whisper.

sasen degradation; **sasen suru** to degrade; demote.

saseru to make; to let; to force; to cause; to get; **kodomo ni benkyoo o saseru** to make a child study.

-(S)ASERU causative ending denoting; cause to, make to, force to, allow to, let; **ikaseru** to make (someone) go; **tabesaseru** to make eat; to allow to eat; to let eat; to force to eat.

SASHIAGERU to present, offer *(humble)*.

sashiatari for the present.

sashidashinin sender (of mail, etc.).

sashidasu to present, offer; to send.

sashidegamashii impertinent.

sashie illustration; cut.

sashigane instigation; carpenter's square; **-no sashigane de** at the instigation of.

sashihiki deduction; balance; excess; ebb and flow; **sashihiki suru** to balance; to deduct.

sashihiku to subtract, take away.

sashikakaru to come upon; to approach.

sashikomu to insert; to push in; to have a fit of acute pain. **Tsuki no hikari ga mado kara sashikomu.** The moonlight floods through the window.

SASHIMI sliced raw fish (popular Japanese food).

sashimukai face to face; facing each other; **sashimukai de** sitting face to face; **sashimukai ni naru** to sit face to face.

sashimukeru to send, dispatch.

sashioku to set aside; to leave; to leave out of consideration.

sashiosae attachment; seizure; **sashiosaeru** to seize; to attach. **Zaisan ga sashiosaerarete iru.** Her property is under attachment.

sashisematta pressing, urgent; imminent; **sashisematta yooji ga aru** to have urgent business.

sashitomeru to prohibit, place a ban on.

sashitsukae engagement; hindrance; trouble; inconvenience; objection; **sashitsukae ga nakereba** if you have no objection; **sashitsukae ga nai** to be disengaged.

sashitsukaeru to be hindered.

sashiwatashi diameter.

SASHIZU direction; instruction; **sashizu suru** to direct; to instruct; **sashizu no moto ni** under (someone's) direction.

sasoi invitation; temptation; **sasoi ni yoru** to call for; **sasoi o kakeru** to sound out (someone) on a subject.

SASOU to invite (someone) to call for; to tempt.

sassato quickly; promptly.

sasshi sympathy; consideration; **sasshi ga tsuku** to make out; to guess; **sasshi no aru** sympathetic.

SASSOKU immediately; directly; **sassoku no henji** quick answer.

sassuru to perceive; to surmise; to sympathize with.

SASU to point at; to pour in; to put in; to hold over one's head; to wear; to measure; to rise; to stream in; to play; to be tinged; to offer a cup (of sake); to stick; to put in; **kita o sasu** to point to the north; **kabin ni mizu o sasu** to pour water into a vase; **kabin ni hana o sasu** to put flowers in a vase; **higasa o sasu** to hold a parasol over one's head; **katana o sasu** to wear a sword; **sake o sasu** to offer a cup of sake.

sasu to stab, to stitch, to sting. **Hachi ga sashimashita.** A bee has stung me.

sasuga ni indeed; as one might have expected; true to one's reputation. **Ano hito wa sasuga ni erai desu.** He is indeed a great man.

sasuru to rub; to pat; to strike.

sata notice; news; report; instruction; order; **sata ga aru** to get news from; **sata o suru** to give notice.

sate well; now; **sate mata** again; **nani wa sate oki** first of all.

sato village; parent's home (of a married woman); **sato ni kaeru** to come back to one's home village; to come back home.

SATOO sugar (often used with prefix o-); **satoo o ireru** to sugar; **satoo de katameta** candied. **Osatoo o kudasai.** Please give me some sugar.

satori comprehension; understanding; spiritual awakening (Buddhist term). **satori o hiraku** to be enlightened.

satoru to comprehend; to perceive; **hi o satoru** to be convinced of one's error.

satosu to admonish; to counsel.

-SATSU (counter for books) volume; copy.

satsu, osatsu paper money.

satsubatsu na rough; warlike; violent; bloody.

satsuei taking a photograph; **satsuei suru** to take a photograph of.

satsui murderous intent; **satsui o okosu** to seek to kill a person.

satsujin homicide.

SATTO in a quick motion; **satto yuderu** to boil briefly in hot water.

sattoo pouring in; **sattoo suru** to rush in; **mooshikomi ga sattoo suru** to have a crowd of applicants.

sawagashii noisy, unquiet; **seken ga sawagashii** things look dark and ominous.

sawagasu to disturb, agitate.

sawagi noise; shouts.

SAWAGU to get noisy; to become agitated; **chiisai koto ni sawagu** to make a fuss over trifles.

sawari hindrance; impediment; affection; harm.

SAWARU to hinder; to be injurious to; **jikoo ga sawaru** to be affected by the weather; to touch; to feel; **kenkoo ni sawaru** to affect one's health; **hito no ki ni sawaru** to hurt (someone's) feelings.

sawaru to touch.

sawayaka delightful; refreshing; clear; sweet; fluent, eloquent; **benzetsu sawayaka na hito** a fluent speaker; **kibun ga sawayaka ni naru** to feel refreshed.

sayoku left wing.

SAYONARA, SAYOONARA good-bye.

sayoo action, process, operation; **-ni sayoo suru** to act upon.

SAYOONARA See **SAYONARA**.

sayuu (*n.*) right and left; **sayuu suru** to influence; **sayuu ni** from side to side; on the right and left.

SAZO surely; indeed; how; **sazo otsukare deshoo.** You must be tired.

sazukaru to receive; to be granted; to be taught.

sazukeru to grant; to confer on; **hiden o sazukeru** to teach the secrets.

se back; ridge. **Se ni hara wa kaerarenu.** Necessity is a hard master.

se, sei height (of the body). **Se ga takai desu.** She is tall.

sebameru to narrow; to reduce; **seken o sebameru** to be humiliated.

sebiro man's suit.

sebiru to importune, to tease into.

sebone backbone, spine.

sechigarai stern; hard; **sechigarai yononaka** hard life.

SEETAA sweater.

segamu to importune.

segare my son, our son.

sehyoo public opinion, popular judgment; **sehyoo ni noboru** to be talked about.

SEI essence; spirit; vital power; **sei ga deru** to work hard; **sei o dasu** to work hard; **Sei ga tsukiru.** His energy is gone.

sei See **se** (height).

sei family name, surname.

sei sex, gender.

sei cause, effect; **-no sei de** owing to, because of.

sei life, existence; **sei o ukeru** to be born.

-sei suffix denoting: student; **ichinensei** first-year student; **bunkasei** student of literature.

seibo present given at the end of the year (as a token of thanks for favors).

seibun ingredient; a component.

seibutsu living things.

seichoo growth; growing; **seichoo shita** grown-up; **seichoo suru** to grow up; to be brought up.

seidai splendor; prosperity; **seidai na** prosperous; **seidai ni** splendidly; on a grand scale.

seido system; institution; **seido no ue no** institutional.

seien encouragement; **seien suru** to encourage.

SEIFU government.

seifuku conquest; **seifuku suru** to subjugate.

seifuku uniform.

seigaku vocal music.

seigan petition; application.

seigen restriction; limit; **seigen suru** to restrict; **seigen naku** without limitations.

seigi righteousness; justice; **seigi no** righteous.

seigo correction of (typographical) errors in printing.

seigyo control; **seigyo suru** to control.

seigyoo occupation; livelihood.

seihantai direct opposition; **seihantai no** diametrically opposed; **seihantai ni** in direct opposition; conversely.

seiheki predisposition; inclination.

seihen political change.

seihi success or failure; result.

seihin manufactured goods; products.

SEIHOKU northwest; **seihoku no** northwesterly.

seihon bookbinding; **seihon suru** to bind a book.

seihoo method of manufacture.

seihoo west; **seihoo no** western. (See also **NISHI**.)

seihookei (*n.*) square; **seihookei no** (*adj.*) square.

seii sincerity; faith; **seii aru** sincere; faithful.

seiippai to the best of one's ability; as hard as possible.

seija right and wrong; good and evil; **seija o wakeru** to discriminate between right and wrong.

SEIJI government; politics; **seijigaku** politics;

the study of politics; **seijika** statesman; politician.

seijin adult; attaining the age of maturity; **seijin shita** grown-up; **seijin suru** to grow up.

seijin sage, saint; **seijin buru** to give oneself a sanctimonious air.

seijitsu sincerity; faithfulness; **seijitsu na** sincere, honest; **seijitsu ni** sincerely.

seijuku ripeness; maturity; **seijuku shita** ripe; mature; **seijuku suru** to ripen.

seika parental home.

seikai political world; **seikai ni hairu** to enter upon a political career.

seikaku accuracy; **seikaku na** correct, accurate.

seikaku character, personality.

SEIKATSU life; livelihood; **seikatsu ga yutaka de aru** to be well off; **seikatsu o tateru** to earn one's living; **seikatsu suru** to live; to support oneself.

seiken political power; **seiken o nigiru** to take the reins of government.

seiken political view; **seiken o happyoo suru** to announce one's political views.

seiketsu cleanliness; purity; **seiketsu na** clean; pure; **seiketsu ni** cleanly; **seiketsu ni suru** to clean.

seiki vitality, vigor, life; **seiki ga michite iru** to be full of life.

seiki century.

seikoo success; exquisiteness.

seikoo na fine.

seikoo shita successful; prosperous.

seikoo suru to succeed in.

seikyoo prosperity, boom.

seikyuu claim; demand; **seikyuu suru** to claim; to demand.

SEIMEI life; **seimei hoken** life insurance; **seimei hoken o kakeru** to insure one's life. **Kono byooki wa seimei ni kakawaru koto wa arimasen.** This disease will never prove fatal.

seimei declaration, statement; **seimei suru** to declare.

seimitsu precision; minuteness; **seimitsu na** minute, detailed; **seimitsu ni** minutely, in detail.

seimon front gate.

seimu government business; administration.

SEINAN southwest; **seinan no** southwestern.

seinen youth, young man; young manhood; **seinen no** young, youthful.

seinen full age; **seinen ni tassuru** to come of age.

seinengappi date of one's birth.

seirai by birth, by nature; **seirai no** natural, innate.

seirei diligence; **seirei suru** to be diligent.

SEIREKI Christian era; year according to the Christian calendar; A.D. **Kotoshi wa seireki sen kyuuhyaku kyuujuu ninen desu.** This year is 1992.

seiri adjustment; readjustment; putting things into order; **seiri suru** to adjust; to regulate.

seiritsu completion, conclusion; coming into existence; **seiritsu saseru** to bring into existence; **seiritsu suru** to come into being.

seiryaku policy; state policy.

seiryoku energy, vigor; influence, power; **seiryoku no aru** influential, powerful; **seiryoku no nai** uninfluential, powerless; **seiryoku no oosei na** energetic, vigorous; **seiryoku o furuu** to wield power; **seiryoku o ushinau** to lose power; **seiryokuka** energetic person.

seisai restraint; sanctions; **seisai o kuwaeru** to restrain, punish.

seisaku policy; fabrication, manufacture; **seisaku suru** to fabricate, manufacture, produce, make.

seisan feasible plan; **juubun seisan ga aru** to be confident of success.

seisan liquidation; **seisan suru** to liquidate.

seisan production; **seisan suru** to produce; **seisan kajoo** overproduction; **seisan-ryoku** productive power.

seisei doodoo with dignity and impartiality; fair and square.

seisei suru to be refreshed; to feel revived.

seiseki results; marks; **seiseki ga yoi** to be successful.

seishi life and death; life or death; **seishi fumei no** missing; **seishi no sakai ni aru** to hover between life and death.

seishi rest, repose; stillness; **seishi no** stationary, static, still.

seishi restraint, repression; **seishi suru** to restrain, to check.

seishi paper manufacturer.

seishiki due form; formality; **seishiki no** formal; regular; **seishiki ni** formally; duly.

seishin soul, spirit; mind; will; **seishin shinkei anteizai** tranquilizer; **seishinbyoo** mental disease.

seishin seii with sincerity; with faithfulness.

seishitsu nature, character; property, quality.

seisho fair copy; **seisho suru** to make a fair copy of.

seisho Holy Bible.

seishuku silence, quiet; **seishuku na** silent; **seishuku ni** silently; in an orderly manner.

SEISHUN youth; **seishun jidai** youthful days.

seisoo formal dress; **seisoo suru** to dress up.

seisoo political strife.

seisuru to control; to restrain.

seitai system of administration.

seitei enactment; establishment by law; **seitei suru** to pass a law; to establish.

seiten fine weather; clear sky.

SEITO student, pupil.

seiton arrangement; regulation; **seiton shita** orderly; well-organized; **seiton suru** to put in order; arrange; **seiton yoku shite iru** to be in good order.

seitoo justice; **seitoo booei** legal defense; reasonable self-defense; **seitoo na** proper; legal; fair and proper; **seitoo ni** legally.

seitoo political party.

seitsuu suru to have a thorough knowledge of.

seiyaku oath; covenant; **seiyaku suru** to swear; **seiyakusho** written oath.

Seiyoo Western (Occidental) countries; **Seiyoo no** Occidental; **Seiyoojin** (n.) Westerner; European; Occidental.

seizei to the best of one's power; at most.

seizen taru orderly; regular; well-organized; **seizen to** in good order.

seizon existence; **seizon suru** to exist.

seizoo manufacture, fabrication; **seizoo suru** to make, manufacture.

seizu drawing; cartography.

seji, oseji compliments; **seji no yoi, oseji no yoi,** affable.

SEKAI world, earth; **sekaiteki** being worldwide, international.

sekaseka suru to bustle; to hustle.

seken public; people; world.

sekennami commonness; **sekennami no** common, ordinary; **sekennami ni** according to custom.

SEKI seat; **seki ni tsuku** to sit down, take a seat.

seki census register, domicile.

seki dam, weir, barrier.

seki cough; **seki o suru,** to cough; **seki ga deru** to suffer from a cough; **sekibarai** cough for clearing the throat; **sekibarai o suru** to clear one's throat.

sekidoo equator; **sekidoo no** equatorial.

sekihi tombstone; stone tablet.

sekihin extreme poverty; **sekihin no** very poor.

sekiji seating order, seniority; precedence.

sekijitsu former days; old times.

sekikomu to be excited; to be agitated.

sekikonde impatiently; in haste.

sekimen blush (of embarrassment); **sekimen saseru** to make a person blush; **sekimen suru** to blush; to be ashamed.

sekinin responsibility; duty; obligation; **sekinin ga aru** to be responsible for; **sekinin o hatasu** to discharge one's duty; **sekinin o ou** to take the responsibility.

sekiryoo lonesomeness; desolation.

sekisetsu accumulated snow.

sekitan coal.

sekitateru to hurry; to press.

sekitomeru to dam up; to check.

sekiyu petroleum; kerosene.

sekizui spine.

sekkachi impetuosity; impetuousness; **sekkachi na** hasty; impetuous.

sekkai incision; operation; **sekkai suru** to incise.

SEKKAKU with much trouble; with great pains; especially; kindly. **Sekkaku kita noni.** I came in vain.

sekkei plan, design; **sekkei suru** to plan, lay out; to draw up plans for the construction of.

SEKKEN soap.

sekkin approach; proximity; **sekkin suru** to approach.

sekkyokuteki positive; **sekkyokuteki ni** positively.

sekkyoo sermon; preaching; **sekkyoo suru** to preach; to admonish.

SEMAI narrow; limited.

semakurushii narrow and close.

semaru to press; to urge.

semento cement.

semeru to attack; to torture; to call to account.

SEMETE at least; at best. **Semete moo ichinichi otomari kudasai.** Please stay at least one more day.

SEN line; route; **sen ni natte** in a line; **Tookaidoosen** Tookaidoo Railroad (line); **sen o hiku** to draw a line.

SEN thousand; **sanzen** three thousand.

sen stopper, plug; **sen o suru** to stop with a cork; **mimi ni sen o suru** to stuff (something) in one's ears.

sen choice, selection; **sen ni hairu** to be selected; **sen ni moreru** to be left out.

SENAKA back (of the body).

senbai monopoly (of sales); **senbai suru** to monopolize (business).

senbatsu selection, choice; **senbatsu suru** to select; **senbatsu sareta** selected. (See also **sentei.**)

senbetsu parting present; farewell gift.

senboo envy; **senboo suru** to feel envy; **senboo no mato to naru** to become the envy of.

sencha green tea.

senchaku first arrival.

senchimeetoru centimeter.

senchoo captain; master of a ship.

sendan arbitrary action; **sendan de** arbitrarily; at one's own discretion.

SENDEN publicity; propaganda; advertisement; **senden suru** to propagandize; to publicize.

sendoo guidance, leadership.

SENGETSU last month.

senkyooshi missionary.

SENMENJO washroom.

senmon no special; profession; **-o senmon ni atsukau** to specialize in.

senmu torishimari yaku managing director.

senpai *(n.)* senior; superior.

senpatsu starting out in advance of someone else; **senpatsu suru** to start in advance; **senpatsutai** advance party.

senpoo other person; one's destination.

senpuku concealment; state of being latent; **senpuku suru** to lie hidden; to go into hiding. (See also **senzai**.)

senpukuki period of incubation; latent period.

senpuu whirlwind; cyclone, tornado.

senpuuki electric fan.

senrei previous instance; precedence; **senrei no nai** unprecedented.

senrei baptism; christening; **senrei o hodokosu** to baptize; **senrei o ukeru** to be baptized.

senren polish; refinement; **senren sareta** refined; **senren suru** to refine.

senritsu melody; rhythm.

senro railway line; railroad track.

senryaku strategy; **senryakuka** strategist.

senryoo capture; occupancy; **senryoo suru** to take a position; to occupy.

senryoo dyestuff, dye.

sensai one's former wife.

sensaku search; investigation; **sensaku suru** to search into.

SENSEI teacher; an instructor; honorific for professional people (doctors, lawyers, etc.).

sensei oath; **sensei suru** to swear; to take an oath.

SENSENGETSU month before last.

sensen kyookyoo with great fear, with fear and trembling; **sensen kyookyoo to shite** living in constant fear.

SENSENSHUU week before last.

senshi death in military action; death on the battlefield.

senshinkoku advanced nation (in technology).

senshitsu cabin.

senshu champion; (sports) player.

senshutsu election; **senshutsu suru** to elect.

SENSHUU last week.

sensoo war; battle; **sensoo ni iku** to go to the front; **sensoo ni katsu** to win a battle; **sensoo suru** to make war; to fight.

sensu fan; folding fan.

sensui diving into water; submergence; **sensui suru** to dive; to submerge; **sensuikan** submarine.

SENTAKU wash, washing; laundry; **sentaku suru** to wash; **sentaku ni dasu** to send to

be washed; **sentaku ga kiku** to stand and wash; **sentakuya** laundry (shop); laundryman.

sentaku selection, choice; **sentaku ni makaseru** to leave it a matter of choice.

sentan extreme point; extremity.

sente forestalling; the first move (in a game); **sente o utsu** to take the initiative; have the first move.

sentei selection, choice; **sentei suru** to select, choose.

sententeki inherent, congenital.

sentoo head, lead; **sentoo ni tatsu** to head, lead.

sen'ya other night; few nights ago.

sen'yaku previous engagement; **sen'yaku no tame** owing to a previous engagement.

sen'yoo exclusive use; private use; **sen'yoo no** exclusive, private.

sen'yuu exclusive possession; **sen'yuu suru** to enjoy sole possession of.

senzai being latent; **senzai ishiki** subconscious; **senzai no** latent, dormant; **senzai suru** to be latent.

senzo ancestor, forefather; **senzo no** ancestral, hereditary.

senzoku specially attached; **-ni senzoku suru** to belong exclusively to.

seou to carry on one's back; to bear; to shoulder; **omoni o seou** to be burdened with a grave duty; **sekinin o seou** to take a responsibility on one's own shoulders.

seppaku pressure; urgency; imminence; **seppaku shita** urgent, imminent; **seppaku suru** to draw near; to be pressed.

seppun kiss; kissing; **seppun o nageru** to send a kiss; **seppun suru** to kiss, press one's lips upon.

serifu speech, dialogue (in a play).

sero cello, violoncello.

serori celery.

seru light serge.

serufutaimaa self-timer.

sessei temperance, moderation; **sessei suru** to be temperate.

sessen fighting at close quarters; **sessen suru** to fight hand to hand.

SESSE TO as much as one can; diligently; **sesse to hataraku** to be busy at work.

sesshi Centigrade thermometer.

SESSHOKU contact, touch; **sesshoku suru** to touch; to come in contact with; **sesshoku o tamotsu** to keep in touch with.

sesshoo negotiation; **sesshoo suru** to negotiate with.

sessuru to touch; to have a contract with.

setchi establishment; **setchi suru** to establish.

setchuu compromise; **setchuu suru** to compromise.

setomono porcelain; chinaware.

setsu opinion, view; theory, doctrine.

setsubi equipment, arrangement; **setsubi o suru** to equip; to provide for.

setsudan cutting off, trimming; **setsudan suru** to cut off; to trim.

SETSUMEI explanation, elucidation; **setsumei suru** to explain; **setsumeisho** instruction booklet.

setsuna moment, instant; **setsuna no** momentary; **sono setsuna** at the very moment.

setsu ni eagerly, earnestly.

setsuretsu poorness; clumsiness; **setsuretsu na** poor; clumsy; unskillful.

setsuritsu establishment, foundation; **setsuritsu suru** to establish, institute, found.

setsuyaku economy; saving; thrift; **setsuyaku suru** to save; to economize.

setsuyu admonition, reproof; **setsuyu suru** to admonish, warn, reprove.

setsuzoku connection, joining; **setsuzoku suru** to join, connect, link.

settai reception; entertainment; **settai suru** to receive; to entertain.

settei establishment, creation; **settei suru** to found, institute (a corporation, etc.).

setto set.

settoku persuasion; **settoku suru** to persuade, convince.

settoo theft, larceny; **settoo o hataraku** to commit a theft.

SEWA help, aid, assistance; good offices; service, care; trouble; **sewa no yakeru** troublesome; **-no sewa ni naru** to be under the care of; **yokei na sewa o yaku** to poke one's nose where one is not wanted; **sewa suru** to help, aid; to do a kind office; to take care of. **Osewani narimashita.** Thank you for all your kindness.

sewashii busy; busily engaged.

shaba this world.

shaberu shovel.

shaberu to chatter; to prattle.

shabon, SEKKEN soap.

shaburu to suck; to chew.

shachoo president of a company.

shadan interception; isolation; **shadan suru** to cut off from.

shadoo roadway.

shagamu to squat; to crouch.

shagareta hoarse (voice); grating (laugh).

shageki suru to shoot, fire at; **shagekijoo** rifle-range.

shain member of a company.

shajitsuteki realistic, true to life.

shakai society; **shaki no tame ni** for the good of the public; **shakaigaku** sociology, social science; **shakai-shugi** socialism; **shakai-shugisha** socialist.

shakkin debt; loan; **shakkin o kaesu** to pay a debt; **shakkin o koshiraeru** to fall into debt; **shakkin suru** to borrow money; **shakkintori** creditor.

shakkuri hiccup, hiccough; **shakkuri suru** to hiccup.

shakoo social life.

shaku Japanese foot; unit of measure corresponding to 3.30 cm. or 1.287 (American) foot. (No longer used.)

shakuchi leased land; rented ground.

shakudo measure, gauge, scale.

shakushi wooden spoon.

shakuya rented house; **shakuya suru** to rent a house; **shakuyanin** tenant.

shamen slanting surface; slope.

shanpen champagne.

share play upon words, pun; joke; **share o iu** to crack jokes.

sharei remuneration, reward; thanks; **sharei suru** to reward; to remunerate.

shareru to adorn oneself, to try to look pretty.

shareta stylish, tasteful.

sharin wheel.

sharyoo vehicles, cars.

shasai debentures; bond.

shasei sketching; **shasei suru** to sketch; to make a sketch.

shasetsu editorial, leading article.

shashi cross-eye.

SHASHIN photograph, **shashin no** photographic; **shashin ni toru** to take a photograph of; **shashin o hikinobasu** to enlarge a photograph; **shashin o toru** to have a photograph taken; to take a photograph; **shashin o yakitsukeru** to print a photograph; **SHASHINKI** camera.

SHASHOO conductor.

shatai body of a car.

SHATSU shirt, undershirt.

shattaa shutter.

shazai apology, **shazai suru** to acknowledge being at fault, apologize.

shazetsu refusal, denial; **shazetsu suru** to refuse, decline.

SHI city, municipality; **shi no** city, municipal; **shiyakusho** municipal building; City Hall.

SHI four (see also **YO, YON, YOTTSU**).

shi death; **shi ni hinshite iru** to be at the point of death; **shi o osorenai** to face death with calmness.

shi poetry, verse.

-SHI particle denoting: in addition to it. **Kane mo aru shi chii mo aru.** He has wealth and, in addition, high position.

-shi Mr., Ms. *(used mostly in writing).*

shiage finish, finishing; **shiage o suru** to give the finishing touches to.

shiageru to finish, complete.

shiai contest of skill, match; **shiai o suru** to play a match; **shiai o mooshikomu** to challenge to a game; **shiai o shoodaku suru** to accept a challenge (to a game).

shian meditation, consideration; **shian suru** to think; to consider.

SHIASATTE two days after tomorrow.

shiawase good fortune, happiness.

shibafu lawn; turf.

shibai play, drama; theater; **shibai ni iku** to go to the theater; **shibai o utsu** to give a performance; to trick someone.

SHIBARAKU for a while, for some time; **shibaraku shite** after a while.

shibaru to bind; to tie up; **kizu o shibaru** to bind up a wound; **kisoku de shibaru** to restrict (someone) by a rule.

SHIBASHIBA often, many times, repeatedly.

shibataku to blink.

shibire numbness; insensibility.

shibireru to numb; to be numbed.

shibomu to fade, wither.

SHIBOO death; **shiboo suru** to die.

shiboo wish, desire; **shiboo suru** to wish, to desire.

shiboo fat, grease, suet.

shiboosha applicant, candidate.

shiboru to press out, wring out, squeeze; **chie o shiboru** to rack one's brains; **namida ni sode o shiboru** to weep bitterly; **ushi no chichi o shiboru** to milk a cow.

shibu branch; subdivision.

shibui astringent; austere; glum; sullen; chaste; simple yet refined (in taste); quiet, sober; **shibui kao** glum face; **shibui konomi** quiet taste.

shibuki spray; **shibuki o tobasu** to spray, to splash.

shiburu to be reluctant, be unwilling; to become loose with gripping pain (of bowels); not to go smoothly.

shibushibu reluctantly, unwillingly.

shibutoi churlish; stubborn.

SHICHI, NANATSU seven.

shichi fatal position; **shichi o dassuru** to have a hairbreadth escape.

shichi pawn; **-o shichi ni ireru** o to pawn personal property.

SHICHIGATSU July.

SHICHIJUU seventy.

shichiya pawnbroker, pawnshop.

shichoo city administration building.

shichoo mayor.

shichuu inside a city or town; **shichuu o neriaruku** to walk the streets in a procession.

shichuu stew.

shichuu support.

shida fern.

SHIDAI order; the state of things; as soon as; **shidai ni** gradually; **shidai ni yotte wa** according to circumstances; **tsuki shidai ni** as soon as it comes. **Tenki shidai desu.** It depends upon the state of the weather.

shidoo guidance, leading; **shidoo suru** to guide; to lead.

shidoosha leader, director.

shiei private management; **shiei no** private.

shiei municipal management.

shieki employment; service; **shieki suru** to employ.

shifuku private clothes.

shigai outskirts of a city, suburbs.

shigai streets.

shigai dead body, corpse.

shigaisen ultraviolet rays.

shigamitsuku to clasp, cling to.

shigan desire; application; volunteering; **shiganhei** volunteer; enlisted soldier; **shigansha** applicant; **shigan suru** to apply for.

SHIGATSU April.

shigeki stimulus, stimulation; **shigeki suru** to stimulate.

shigemi thicket, bush.

shigeru to become dense; to grow thick and rank.

shigo after death.

shigoku very, extremely.

shigoku to draw through the hand; to stroke (as a beard).

SHIGOTO work, task; job; **shigoto o suru** to work; **shigoto o toru** to get a job; **shigotoba** workshop.

shigure wintertime rain; wintry shower.

shigusa manners, behaviors; gesture.

shihai rule, control, management; **shihai suru** to govern, rule, manage; **kanjoo ni shihai sareru** to be influenced by personal feelings; **shihaikaikyuu** governing class; **shihainin** manager, director.

SHIHARAI payment; **shiharai suru** to pay; **shiharai o seikyuu suru** to ask for payment; **shiharainin** payer (one who pays); **shiharaisaki** payee.

shiharau to pay; to discharge; **shiharau beki** payable.

shihei paper currency.

shihen volume of poems; Book of Psalms.

shihoo four sides; **shihoo ni** on all sides; **shihoo happoo** all directions; **shihoo happoo e** in all directions.

shihooken jurisdiction; judicial authority.

shihon capital; fund; **shihon o toozuru** to

invest one's capital in; **shihonka** capitalist; **shihonkin** capital; **shihonshugi** capitalism.

shiin cause of death.

shiin scene.

shiire stocking; laying in, buying up (of goods); **shiire o suru** to stock goods.

shiireru to stock goods, lay in (goods), to buy up (goods).

shiiru to compel; to force upon.

shiitageru to oppress, tyrannize.

shiite against one's will, by force.

shiitsu bed sheets, linen.

shiji support, maintenance; **shiji suru** to support; to maintain.

shijin poet, poetess.

shijitsu historical facts.

shijoo market, fair; **shijoo ni deru** to appear in a market; **shijoo ni dasu** to bring to market; **shijoo dookoo** market trends; **shijoo kakaku** market value; **shijoo no jissei** market forces; **shijoo shisuu** market index; **shika** market price.

SHIJUU the whole time, all the time, always.

shijuu forty. (See also **YONJUU**.)

SHIKA only *(used with a negative)*. **Osakana shika arimasen.** We have only fish. **Eigo shika hanasemasen.** I can speak only English.

shika market price.

shikaeshi tit for tat; revenge; **shikaeshi o suru** to take revenge.

shikai municipal assembly; town assembly.

shikai chairmanship.

shikake device, mechanism.

shikakeru to begin; to set to work; to fasten upon; to make advances.

SHIKAKU *(n.)* square; **shikaku na** *(adj.)* square; **shikakui hako** square box.

shikaku (sense of) sight, eyesight; **shikaku** qualification; capacity; **shikaku no aru** qualified; **-no shikaku de** in the capacity of; **shikaku o ushinau** to be disqualified for.

shikaku assassin.

shikakubaru to be formal; to stand on ceremony.

shikamo moreover, furthermore.

shikaru to scold; to reprove.

shikaruni however, nevertheless, but, yet *(formal);* **shikaruni mata** on the other hand.

SHIKASHI however, nevertheless.

SHIKATA method, way, means; **shikata ga naku** (**shikata nashi ni**) having no other choice. **Shikata ga nai desu.** I cannot help it.

shike stormy weather; scarcity of fish; **shike o kuu** to be overtaken by a storm.

shikei death penalty, capital punishment;

shikei o senkoku suru to pass sentence of death; **shikei o shikkoo suru** to execute.

SHIKEN examination, test; trial; **shiken ni tooru** to pass the examination; **shiken o okonau** to give an examination; **shiken suru** to examine, test; **shiken o ukeru** to take an examination.

shiki command, order; **shiki suru** to command, give an order; **-no shiki no moto ni** under the command of.

shiki ceremony; **shiki o ageru** to celebrate.

shiki four seasons.

-shiki suffix denoting: style; **seiyooshiki** Western style; Occidental style; **suisenshiki** flush style (toilet).

shikibetsu discrimination; discernment; **shikibetsu suru** to discern, distinguish.

shikibuton quiltlike mattress; bedding.

shikichi site, ground.

shikifu bed sheet.

shikii threshold, sill; **shikii o matagu** to cross the threshold.

shikiishi paving stone; pavement.

shikikan commander.

shikikin deposit, key money (for renting a house); **shikikin o ireru** to make a deposit on a house; to give key money.

shikimono matting; carpet; **shikimono o shiku** to lay a carpet.

shikin fund.

shikiri partition; settlement of accounts.

SHIKIRI NI frequently; continually; eagerly.

shikisai color, tint.

shikisha intelligent people; persons of good sense.

shikitsumeru to spread all over.

shikka at one's lap *(honorific address to parents, mostly used in letters);* **-no shikka ni** under the care of.

SHIKKARI firmly, tightly; strongly; exactly; **shikkari shita** strong; substantial.

shikkei disrespect; impoliteness; **shikkei na** impolite, rude; **shikkei suru** to say good-bye. **Shikkei shimashita.** I beg your pardon *(in men's talk).*

shikki damp; moisture; **shikki no aru** wet, damp, moist.

shikki lacquerware.

shikkoo execution, enforcement; **shikkoo suru** to execute, carry out, enforce; **shikkoo yuuyo** probation; suspension of execution; **shikkoo yuuyo to naru** to be released on probation.

shikkoo losing effect; invalidation.

shikkui mortar; plaster; **shikkui de nuru** to plaster.

shikomi training; teaching.

shikomu to train, to teach.

shikoo enforcement, carrying out; **shikoo**

sareru to take effect; **shikoo suru** to enforce.

shikoo taste; **shikoo ni tekisuru** to suit one's taste.

shikooryoku contemplative faculty, power to think.

shikori stiffness; bump.

shiku to spread, lay; to pave; to issue; to proclaim.

shikujiru to fail; to make a blunder; to be cashiered.

shikyo death.

shikyoku branch office.

shikyoo condition of the market.

shikyoo bishop.

shikyuu urgency; **shikyuu no** urgent; **shikyuu ni** at once, promptly.

shikyuu supply, allowance; **shikyuu suru** to provide; to supply.

SHIMA island.

shima stripes.

SHIMAI end, termination; **shimai ni** at last; **shimai ni naru** to come to an end; **shimai ni suru** to finish.

SHIMAI sisters.

shimai informal No dance (performed without wearing the formal standard costume).

SHIMARI tightness; locking, fastening, prudence; **shimari no aru** firm, locked; prudent; **shimari no nai** loose, impudent; stupid.

SHIMARU to shut, to close; to grow tight; to tighten, to sober down.

shimatsu management; circumstances, result, economy; **shimatsu no oenai** unmanageable; **shimatsu suru** to manage; to put in order.

shimatta compact; firm, well set.

shimau to close; to finish; to put away.

shimedasu to shut out, exclude.

SHIMEI full name.

shimei naming; nomination; **shimei suru** to name; to nominate.

shimei mission; errand; **shimei o mattoo suru** to fulfill a duty.

shimekiri close; closed; deadline.

shimekomu to lock in, shut in.

shimekorosu to strangle to death.

shimen space (in a magazine or newspaper).

shimeppoi damp; wet; **shimeppoi hanashi** tearful story.

SHIMERU to tie, to bind; to close, to shut.

shimeru to occupy; **jooseki o shimeru** to occupy the top seat.

shimeru to get damp; to get wet.

shimesu to point out; to show; to indicate.

shimesu to wet, moisten.

shimete altogether; in all.

shimi stain, blot; **shimi no aru** stained; **shimi**

darake no spotty. **Shimi ga demashita.** There is a stain.

shimijimi carefully; fully; heartily; **shimijimi kao o miru** to look searchingly into (someone's) face; **shimijimi kiku** to listen attentively to.

shimin citizen.

shiminken citizenship.

shimiru to penetrate; to soak into; to smart; to be touched with; **shinsetsu ga mi ni shimiru** to appreciate (someone's) kindness fully. **Kaze ga mi ni shimiru.** The wind is penetrating. **Kono rooshon wa shimiru.** This lotion smarts.

shimizu spring water.

SHIMO frost; **shimo de kareru** to be nipped by frost; **shimoyake** frostbite.

shimon trial; inquiry; examination; **shimon suru** to try (hear) a case.

shimon fingerprints; **shimon o toru** to take (someone's) fingerprints.

shimuke one's behavior toward; one's attitude.

shimukeru to act toward; to treat; to send.

SHIN heart; mind; core; **shin kara** heartily, sincerely; **shin made** to the core.

shin truth, reality; **shin ni** truly, really, actually; **shin no** true, real; **shin ni semaru** to be true to one's nature.

shina coquetry; **shina o tsukuru** to be coquettish.

shina article; goods, stuff.

shinabiru to wither; to droop.

shinagire out of stock; sold out.

shinai city; inside the city.

shin'ai affection, love; **shin'ai naru** dear, beloved.

shinamono article; goods.

shin'an new idea; new design.

shinario scenario.

shinayaka na pliant, flexible, supple.

shinboku friendship, intimacy; **shinboku o hakaru** to cultivate a friendship.

shinboo patience, endurance, forbearance; **shinboo no nai** impatient; **shinboo no yoi** patient; **shinboo suru** to endure; to be patient.

shinboo axle, shaft.

SHINBUN newspaper; journal; **shinbundane** news matter; **shinbun kisha** journalist.

shinchiku new building; **shinchiku no** newly built; **shinchiku suru** to build, rebuild.

shinchintaisha replacing the old with new; replacement; metabolism; **shinchintaisha suru** to be renewed; to be replaced.

shinchishiki new knowledge; advanced idea.

shincho books newly published.

shinchoo care; prudence; **shinchoo na** careful, cautious; **imi shinchoo** having deep meaning; to be of profound significance.

shinchoo height, stature; **shinchoo ga takai** to be tall.

shinchuu brass.

shinchuu true motive; mind; **shinchuu o sassuru** to share (someone's) feelings.

shindai sleeper (on a train).

shindai fortune, property.

shindan diagnosis; **shindan suru** to diagnose.

shinden sanctuary (in a Shinto shrine).

shindoo tremor, shock, vibration; oscillation; **shindoo suru** to shake, vibrate (from an earthquake or collision); to swing, oscillate, move to and fro.

shingai infringement, encroachment; **shingai suru** to infringe; to make an attack upon.

shingaku theology.

shingari rear; rearguard; **shingari o tsutomeru** to bring up the rear.

shingata new style; new design.

shingenchi seismic center; center of disturbance.

shingetsu new moon.

shingi genuineness, authenticity; **shingi o tashikameru** to ascertain the truth.

shingi consideration, discussion, investigation; **shingi suru** to consider, to investigate.

shingoo signal; **kiken shingoo** danger signal; **shingoo suru** to signal, give a signal.

shingu bedding and bedclothes.

shin'i real intentions; true meaning.

shinikakatta dying; at the point of death.

shinime moment of death.

shinimonogurui death struggle; desperation; **shinimonogurui de** desperately; **shinimonogurui no** desperate; **shinimonogurui ni naru** to make a desperate effort.

shinin dead person.

shinitaeru to die out.

shiniwakareru to be parted by death.

shinja believer; faithful (person).

shinjin divine worship; devotion; **shinjin bukai** pious, devout; **shinjin suru** to worship; to regard with adoration.

shinjiru See **shinzuru**.

shinjitsu truth; reality; **shinjitsu na** true, real; **shinjitsu ni** truly, really.

shinjitsu sincerity; faithfulness; **shinjitsu na** sincere; faithful.

shinjoo article of faith; creed; (one's) true feelings.

shinju pearl.

shinjuu double suicide; suicide for love.

shinka real value, true worth; **shinka o mitomeru** to appreciate the true value.

shinka evolution; **shinka suru** to evolve.

shinkaichi newly developed district.

shinkan, shinkansho new publication; new book.

shinkei nerves; **shinkei kabin** nervousness; being overly sensitive; **shinkei no** nervous; **shinkeishitsu** nervous temperament; **shinkeishitsu no** nervous; **shinkei suijaku** nervous breakdown; **shinkeitsuu** neuralgia; **shinkei seishin anteizai** tranquilizer.

shinken na earnest; **shinken ni naru** to be earnest; to become earnest.

shinkijiku new device; originality; **shinkijiku o dasu** to introduce a new method.

shinkoku declaration; report (tax return, etc.); **shinkoku suru** to state; to report.

shinkoku na deep, serious.

shinkon new marriage; **shinkon no** newly married; **shinkon ryokoo** honeymoon; **shinkon ryokoo o suru** to go on a honeymoon.

shinkoo faith; belief; **shinkoo no jiyuu** freedom of faith; **shinkoo no nai** unbelieving; **shinkoo suru** to believe in.

shinkoo advance, progress; **shinkoo suru** to advance, to progress.

shinkoo friendship, cordiality.

shinku hardship; tribulation; **shinku suru** to suffer hardship.

shinkuukan vacuum tube.

shinkyuu promotion; **shinkyuu suru** to win a promotion; to be promoted.

shinme sprout, shoot; **shinme o dasu** to bud, sprout.

shinmi blood relation; **shinmi ni natte sewa o suru** to look after with great kindness.

shinmiri heart to heart; earnestly; **shinmiri hanasu** to have a heart-to-heart talk.

shinmitsu intimacy; familiarity; close friendship; **shinmitsu na** intimate; familiar; **shinmitsu na aidagara de aru** to have a strong friendship.

shinmotsu present, gift.

shinmyoo na fair; commendable, conscientious; docile; **shinmyoo ni** commendably; quietly; meekly; fairly.

shinnen new year. **Shinnen omedetoo.** I wish you a Happy New Year.

shinnen faith, belief; deeply rooted conviction.

shinnin confidence, trust; **shinnin suru** to confide in, believe in.

shinninjoo credentials.

shinnyuu invasion; inroad; trespass; intrusion; **shinnyuu suru** to invade; to intrude into; **shinnyuusha** invader; trespasser.

shinnyuusei new student; freshman.

shinobi stealthy movement; going in disguise.

shinobu to bear, endure; to conceal; to hide oneself; to steal along one's way; **fujiyuu o shinobu** to suffer privation; **hitome o shinobu** to elude observation; **yo o shinobu** to live in concealment.

shinogiyoi genial; nice; mild.

shinogu to endure, bear; to rise above.

shinonde patiently; meekly; secretly.

SHINPAI uneasiness; apprehension; anxiety; worry; care; fear; **shinpai na koto** trouble, difficulty; **shinpai no amari** overcome with anxiety; **shinpai suru** to fear; to be anxious.

shinpan judgment; **shinpan suru** to judge; to umpire; **shinpansha** umpire; judge.

shinpan new edition, new publication; **shinpan no** newly edited, newly published.

shinpi mystery; **shinpi na** mysterious, mystic.

shinpo progress, advance, improvement. **shinpo suru** to make progress.

shinpu Catholic priest.

shinpu bride.

shinpuku admiration and devotion, honest submission; **shinpuku suru** to acknowledge another's superiority; to obey faithfully.

shinrai trust, reliance; confidence; **shinrai suru** to trust, to place confidence in.

shinratsu severity; poignance; **shinratsu na** severe; poignant.

shinreki new calendar; Gregorian calendar, solar calendar (as distinguished from the lunar calendar used in the past).

shinri examination, trial; **shinri suru** to try, to examine.

shinri truth, truism; **shinri o motomeru** to seek truth.

shinri psychic state; **shinrigaku** psychology.

shinrin forest, wood.

shinroo bridegroom.

SHINRUI relation, relative.

shinryaku aggression; invasion; **shinryaku suru** to invade.

shinryoku fresh green.

shinsa examination, investigation, inspection; **shinsa suru** to examine, inquire into; **shinsain** jury, committee of inquiry.

shinsai disaster caused by earthquake.

shinsatsu medical examination; **shinsatsu o ukeru** to consult a physician; **shinsatsu suru** to examine a patient.

shinsei sacredness, sanctity; **shinsei na** holy, sacred, hallowed; **shinsei ni suru** to make holy; **shinsei o kegasu** to defile the sacredness.

shinsei application, petition; **shinsei suru** to apply; **shinseinin** applicant, petitioner, claimant.

shinseki relative.

shinsen na fresh, new.

SHINSETSU kindness; goodness; friendliness; **shinsetsu na** kind, good, cordial; **shinsetsu o suru** to do a kindness.

shinsetsu new establishment; **shinsetsu no** newly organized, newly formed; **shinsetsu suru** to establish newly.

shinshaku consideration, allowance; **nan no shinshaku mo naku** without any consideration; **shinshaku suru** to take into consideration.

shinshi gentleman; man of position; **shinshi kyooyaku** gentleman's agreement; **shinshirashii** gentlemanlike.

shinshiki new style; new system; **shinshiki no** of a new style; modern.

shinshin no rising.

shinshitsu bedchamber, bedroom.

shinshoku food and sleep; **shinshoku o wasurete** forgetful of sleep and other comforts; regardless of oneself.

shinshoku erosion; **shinshoku suru** to erode.

shinshuku expansion and contraction; elasticity; **shinshuku suru** to expand and contract; **shinshuku jizai** elasticity; **shinshuku jizai no** elastic.

shinshutsu marching out; emergence; **shinshutsu suru** to march out; emerge.

shinsoo true state; **shinsoo o akiraka ni suru** to disclose the real state of affairs; **shinsoo o kataru** to lay bare the truth of a matter.

shinsui launching; **shinsui suru** to launch; to be launched; **shinsuishiki** launching (ceremony).

shinsui fascination, infatuation; **shinsui suru** to be fascinated.

shinsui flooding, inundation; **shinsui suru** to be flooded.

shintai image of a god.

shintai body; person; constitution; **shintai kensa** physical examination; **shintai no** bodily, corporal.

shintai advance and retreat; movement; **shintai suru** to move, to act.

shintaku trust; **shintaku suru** to entrust with; to leave in trust (property, etc.); **shintaku gaisha** trust company; **shintaku shikin** trust fund.

shintei presentation; **shintei suru** to present, give.

shinten personal; confidential (written on the envelope of a letter); **shinten no** private, confidential; **shintensho** confidential letter.

shinto believer (religious).

shin to shita silent, still; deserted.

shin to suru prevailing silence.

shintsuu mental suffering; anxiety.

SHINU to die, pass away, expire; **shinu made** to the end; **shinu kakugo de** at the risk of one's life.

shinwa myth, mythology.

shin'ya dead of night, midnight; shin'ya ni late at night.

Shin'yaku Seisho New Testament.

shin'yoo confidence, trust; credit; shin'yoo ga aru to be trusted by; shin'yoo o eru to have credit with; shin'yoo suru to trust; to credit; shin'yoojoo letter of credit; shin'yoo kumiai credit association, credit union.

shin'yuu intimate friend.

shinzen amity, goodwill; shinzen shisetsu goodwill mission.

shinzoku relation, relative.

SHINZOO heart; shinzoobyoo heart disease; shinzoomahi heart failure.

shinzui essence.

shinzuru, shinjiru to believe in; to accept (something) as true; to trust.

SHIO salt (often used with the prefix o-); shiokarai salty; shio de aji o tsukeru to season with salt; shio ni tsukeru to salt; to pickle in salt.

shioki punishment; execution; shioki o suru to punish; to execute.

shiokuri supply; allowance; shiokuri o suru to furnish a person with money (for living expenses, schooling, etc.).

shiorashii moving, touching; plausible; shiorashii koto o iu to say pretty things.

shioreru to wither, droop; to be in low spirits.

shippai failure; defeat; shippai suru to fail; to be unsuccessful.

shippi useless expenses.

shippitsu writing; shippitsu suru to write.

shippo tail; shippo o dasu to give (someone) away; to disclose (someone's) identity; shippo o maku to acknowledge defeat; shippo o osaeru to find fault (with someone).

shippuu violent wind; gale.

shirabakkureru (colloq.) to dissemble; to pretend not to understand.

SHIRABERU to investigate; to examine; to prepare a lesson for.

shirafu soberness; sobriety; state of not being drunk.

shirakeru to become chilled; to be spoiled. Ano hito ga kuru to itsumo za ga shirakemasu He is always a wet blanket.

shiranu unknown, unfamiliar; shiranu kao o suru to look on with indifference.

shirase information; news; sign; notice.

SHIRASERU to notify; to send a notice; kekkon o shiraseru to send a notice of marriage.

shirazu shirazu unawares; unconsciously.

shirei instructions; order, notice.

shiren trial, test; shiren ni taeru to stand the test; shiren o ukeru to be tried, be tested.

shireru to become known.

shiri private gain; self-interest; shiri o hakaru to look to one's own interests.

shiri buttocks; rump; bottom; shiri ga nagai to wear out one's welcome; shiri ga wareru to be brought to light; to be found out; shiri o mukeru to turn one's back upon.

shirikon silicon.

shirime contemptuous glance; shirime ni kakeru to look disdainfully at.

shirioshi backing, support; shirioshi o suru to back, support.

shiritsu private establishment (school, welfare agency, etc.); shiritsu no (adj.) private.

shiritsu municipal establishment; shiritsu no municipal, city.

shirizokeru to refuse; to reject; to repel, to drive back.

shirizoku to retreat, retire, withdraw; to leave; ippo shirizoku to take a step backward.

shiro fortress; castle.

shiro (n.) white.

SHIROI (adj.) white; shiroku suru to whiten.

shirooto amateur.

shirozatoo white sugar, granulated sugar.

SHIRU to learn; to become acquainted with; shitte iru to know. Nihongo mo Chuugokugo mo shitte imasu. He knows both Japanese and Chinese.

shiru juice, sap; fluid; soup, broth; shiru no ooi juicy, succulent.

shirushi sign, mark, symbol, badge; shirushi o tsukeru to mark, to tick.

shirusu to write down; to describe.

shiryo consideration; thought; shiryo no aru thoughtful; shiryo no nai thoughtless.

shiryoku desperate effort; shiryoku o tsukushite with desperate courage.

shiryoku funds, resources, means.

shiryoku eyesight, sight, vision.

shiryoo materials, data.

shiryuu branch stream.

shisai reason; circumstances; details, particulars; shisai no minute, detailed; shisai ni minutely, in detail.

shisaku speculation; meditation; shisaku ni fukeru to be engrossed in thought; shisaku suru to think; to speculate.

shisaku trial production; shisaku suru to manufacture on a trial (experimental) basis.

shisan property; fortune; assets.

shisatsu inspection; examination; shisatsu shite aruku to make a tour of inspection; shisatsu suru to visit; to inspect.

shisei carriage, posture, pose; **shisei o tadasu** to hold oneself up.

shisei municipal organization; **shisei choosa** municipal census.

shiseiji illegitimate child.

shiseki place of historical interest.

shisen line of vision (sight); **shisen o sakeru** to avoid the public gaze.

shisen branch line.

shisetsu institution; institute; **shisetsu suru** to institute; to equip.

shisetsu mission; envoy.

shisha dead person.

shisha branch office.

shisha preview; **shisha o okonau** to hold a preview.

shishokan post office box.

shishoo teacher, master (of traditional arts and sports).

shishoo casualties; number of killed and wounded; **shishoosha** dead and injured.

shishunki adolescence, puberty; **shishunki no** adolescent.

shishutsu expenditure; payment; **shishutsu suru** to pay; to disburse.

shishuu collection of poems.

shishuu embroidery; **shishuu suru** to embroider.

shisoo thought, idea.

shissaku error, mistake; **shissaku suru** to do (anything) amiss; to make a mistake.

shisseki reproof, reprimand; **shisseki suru** to reprove.

shisshoku unemployment; **shisshoku suru** to become unemployed.

shisso simplicity, plainness, frugality; **shisso na** simple, plain; **shisso ni kurasu** to live a simple life; to live plainly.

shissoo running fast; going at full speed; **shissoo suru** to run away; to run at full speed.

shissoo disappearance (of a person); **shissoo suru** to disappear.

SHITA tongue; **shita o dasu** to put out one's tongue; **shita o maku** to be astonished.

SHITA foot; bottom; lower place; **-no shita de** under, below; **-no shita ni** under, below; **shita e** down, downward; **shita kara** from below, from the bottom; **shita no** lower; downward, subordinate; inferior.

shitabi burning with less intensity; **shitabi ni naru** to reach a low mark, to wane.

shitagaeru to be attended by, to bring under subjection.

shitagaki rough copy, draft; **shitagaki o suru** to draft; to make a rough copy.

SHITAGATTE accordingly, consequently; correspondingly.

shitagau to follow; to accompany; to obey.

shitageiko preparation; rehearsal; **shitageiko o suru** to prepare.

SHITAGI underwear, undergarment.

shitagokoro secret desire, intention; **shitagokoro ga aru** to have a secret desire.

shitagoshirae preparation, arrangement.

shitai dead body.

shitaji ground; groundwork, preparation.

shitakensa previous examination.

SHITAKU preparation; arrangement; **shitaku o suru** to prepare.

shitamachi downtown.

shitami preliminary inspection.

shitamuki downward look, downward tendency; **shitamuki no** downward; prone; **shitamuki ni naru** to look down.

shitanuri undercoating, prime; **shitanuri o suru** to put on the first coat (of paint).

SHITASHII intimate; familiar; **shitashii aidagara de aru** to be on intimate terms; **shitashiku** intimately; personally; **shitashiku suru** to be great friends.

shitashimi friendship, friendly feeling; **shitashimi no aru** familiar, close, affectionate; **shitashimi no nai** unfamiliar; strange; cold.

shitashimu to become friendly with; to become a great friend of.

shitashirabe preliminary inquiry; preparation; doing homework; **shitashirabe o suru** to inquire beforehand.

shitataru to drip; to drop.

shitate cut; tailoring; getting ready; **shitate no yoi** well-tailored; **shitatemono** sewing; tailoring; **shitateya** dressmaker; tailor.

shitate ni deru to treat (someone) with deference; to behave humbly.

shitateru to make (clothes); to train for a trade.

shitatsuzumi smacking one's lips; **shitatsuzumi o utsu** to smack one's lips; **shitatsuzumi o utte taberu** to eat with much relish.

shitau to yearn after; to long for.

shitauchi tut.

shitauke subcontract; **shitauke ni dasu** to sublet.

shitayaku subordinate employee.

shitayomi preparation of one's lessons; rehearsal; **shitayomi o suru** to prepare one's lessons.

shitazumi being in the lower layer of something; **shitazumi ni naru** to be in the lower layer; to be placed under something; **shitazumi no seikatsu o suru** to be low in the social scale.

shitchi swampy land; damp ground.

shitei designation; **shitei no** recognized; appointed; **shitei suru** to designate; to name; to appoint.

shitei private mansion.

shiteki pointing out; **shiteki suru** to point out; to show; to indicate.

shiteki poetic.

shiteki private, personal.

shiten branch store.

shitogeru to bring about; to complete.

shitoo na right and proper; fair; reasonable.

shitoshito gently; softly; damp; wet.

shitoyaka na gentle, graceful.

SHITSU nature, character; quality.

-shitsu suffix denoting: room, chamber; **kyooshitsu** classroom; **shinshitsu** bedroom.

shitsuboku na simpleminded.

shitsuboo disappointment; despair; **shitsuboo shite** disappointedly; **shitsuboo saseru** to disappoint; **shitsuboo suru** to be disappointed at.

shitsugen slip of the tongue; blunder in speech.

shitsugyoo unemployment; **shitsugyoo suru** to be thrown out of work.

shitsuji steward; manager; butler.

shitsuke discipline; breeding; training; **shitsuke no yoi** disciplined, well-bred.

shitsukeru to train, bring up.

shitsukkoi, shitsukoi obstinate, persistent.

shitsumei loss of eyesight; **shitsumei suru** to lose one's sight.

SHITSUMON question; interrogation; **shitsumon suru** to question.

shitsumu attending to one's business.

shitsunai interior of a room; **shitsunai de** in a room; **shitsunai sooshoku** interior decoration.

SHITSUREI breach of etiquette, discourtesy; **shitsurei na** impolite; **shitsurei na koto o iu** to say rude things.

shitsuren broken heart; disappointment in love; **shitsuren suru** to be crossed in love; to become heartbroken.

shittakaburi pretension to knowledge; **shittakaburi o suru** to pretend to know.

SHITTE IRU See **SHIRU.**

shitto jealousy; **shitto suru** to be jealous.

shiwa wrinkles; lines on one's face; creases; rumples; **shiwa ga yoru** to become wrinkled; **shiwa ni naru** to be crumpled; **shiwa o nobasu** to smooth the creases.

shiwaza act, action, deed.

shiyoo use, employ; **shiyoo suru** to use; to make use of; **shiyoohoo** directions for use; **shiyoonin** employee.

shiyoo private business, private use; **shiyoo de** for private use, on private business; **shiyoo suru** to turn to private use.

shizai private fortune, money; **shizai o toojite** out of one's own purse, at one's own expense.

shizen nature; **shizen no** natural, instinctive; **shizen ni** naturally, spontaneously.

SHIZUKA NA silent, quiet, still, peaceful; **shizuka ni kurasu** to live in peace; **shizuka ni naru** to become still, get calm.

shizuku drop; **shizuku ga tareru** to drip.

shizumaru to become quiet.

shizumeru to quiet, calm, pacify; to quell; to subdue; to sink, send to the bottom.

shizumu to sink; to go to the bottom; to feel depressed.

sho writing; document; calligraphy, penmanship; book.

-sho suffix denoting: public office; **keisatsusho** police station; **Zeimusho** Office of Internal Revenue.

shobatsu punishment; **shobatsu suru** to punish; to impose a punishment.

shobun disposition; management; punishment; **shobun suru** to dispose of; to punish.

shochi management, action; **shochi suru** to manage; to dispose of; to deal with.

shochuu kyuuka summer vacation.

shoen first public performance of a play.

shoga pictures and writings.

shogen preface, introduction.

shogeru to be dejected, cast down.

shohan first edition of a book.

shoho first step; elements; **shoho no** elementary, rudimentary.

shohoo prescription.

shojo (n.) virgin, maiden; **shojo no** (adj.) virgin.

shoka early summer.

shokan letter; **shokansen** letter paper.

shokatsu jurisdiction.

shokei punishment.

shoki expectation, anticipation; **shoki no** expected.

shoki heat, hot weather; **shoki ni ataru** to be affected by the heat.

shoki first stage, beginning.

shoki clerk.

shokikan secretary.

shokken authority; official power; **shokken o ran'yoo suru** to abuse one's official authority.

shokki tableware.

shokkoo workman.

shoku office; situation, position; occupation, employment, job; **shoku ni tsuku** to take a post; **shoku o motomeru** to look for employment.

shoku eating; food; appetite; **shoku ga susumu** to have a good appetite.

shokuatari attack of indigestion, food poisoning.

shokuba workshop; place of work.

shokubutsu plant; shokubutsugaku botany; shokubutsuen botanical garden.

shokudai candle-stand.

SHOKUDOO dining room; shokudoosha dining car.

SHOKUEN table salt.

shokugo after a meal.

shokugyoo occupation, employment.

shokuhi charge for boarding; board.

shukuin staff; personnel.

SHOKUJI meal; diet; shokuji o suru to eat; shokujidoki mealtime.

shokuji typesetting; typography; composition; shokuji o suru to compose; shokujikoo typesetter.

shokumin colonization, settlement; colonists; shokumin suru to colonize; to found a colony; shokuminchi colony; shokuminchi no colonial.

shokumotsu food.

shokumu duties, functions; shokumu o hatasu to discharge a duty; shokumujoo officially, in the line of duty; shokumujoo no official.

shokun Ladies and gentlemen! (used in a speech).

shokunin workman; artisan.

shokupan bread; loaf of bread.

shokuryoohin articles of food, foodstuffs.

shokushi, hitosashiyubi forefinger; index finger; shokushi o ugokasu to be desirous of.

shokutaku person with nonofficial status; person employed without tenure.

shokutaku dinner table; shokutaku ni tsuku to take one's seat at the table.

shokuyoku appetite; relish; shokuyoku ga nai to have no appetite; shokuyoku o susumaseru to stimulate one's appetite.

shokuyoo no used for food; shokuyoo ni teki suru to be fit for the table.

shomei signature; shomei suru to sign.

shomen document; letter.

shomotsu book.

shonbori lonely, solitarily.

shonichi first day; opening day.

shoo nature, disposition; character; quality; shoo no yoi of good quality; shoo ga au to be congenial; shoo ga awanai to be incompatible.

shoo chapter, section.

shoo prize, reward; shoo o ataeru to give a prize; shoo o eru to get a prize.

shoo quotient (math).

shoo ministry.

SHOOBAI trade, business; shoobai ni narana not to be paying; shoobai o suru to do business; shoobainin merchant.

shoobatsu rewards (honors) and punishment.

Gakkoo de shoobatsu o uketa koto wa arimasen. I have received no honors or punishment in my school days.

shooben urine; shooben o suru to urinate.

shoobi admiration; appreciation; shoobi suru to praise; to applaud.

shooboo prevention and extinction of fires; shoobooshi fireman; shoobuoosho firehouse; shoobootai fire company. (See also hi.)

shoobu match, contest; game; shoobu o kimeru to fight to a finish; shoobu o suru to have a match (game, sport).

shoobun innate disposition, temperament.

shoochi consent, acceptance; shoochi no ue de by mutual agreement; shoochi suru to consent; to agree to; to understand, to know.

shoochoo symbol; symbolism.

shoodaku consent, acceptance; shoodaku suru to consent to; to comply with.

shoodoku disinfection, sterilization; shoodoku suru to disinfect; shoodokuzai disinfectant; antidote.

shoodoo impulse; impetus.

shoofuda price tag; shoofuda tsuki no marked with a price tag; genuine.

SHOOGAI life; lifetime; all one's days; to the end of one's life; shoogai no lifelong; shoogai o oeru to end one's days.

shoogai injury, harm.

shoogaibutsu obstacle.

SHOOGAKKOO grade school, elementary school.

shoogaku small sum.

shoogakukin scholarship.

SHOOGATSU New Year; January.

shoogen testimony, evidence; shoogen suru to testify to.

shoogi game of Japanese chess; shoogi o sasu to play chess.

shoogidaoshi falling in rapid succession one after another; shoogidaoshi ni naru to fall forward, one upon another as when a train makes a sudden stop; to fall like ninepins.

SHOOGO noon, midday.

shoogyoo commerce, trade; shoogyoo no commercial.

shoohai prize cup; medal.

shoohai victory or defeat; shoohai o arasou to contend for victory.

shoohei engagement (for a position); employment; shoohei suru to engage; to employ.

shoohi consumption; spending; shoohi suru to consume; to spend; shoohisha consumer.

shoohin short piece; sketch.

shoohin goods; commodity; shoohinken gift certificate (issued by retail stores).

shoohyoo trademark.

shooji paper sliding door.

shoojiki honesty, uprightness; **shoojiki na** honest, upright; **shoojiki ni** honestly, frankly.

shoojin devotion; aspiration; religious purification; abstinence from animal food; vegetable diet; **shoojin suru** to devote oneself to.

shoojiru See **shoozuru.**

shoojo young girl; little girl.

shoojoo certificate of merit; honorary certificate.

shoojoo condition of illness; symptom.

shooka digestion; **shooka furyoo** indigestion; **shooka suru** to digest; **shookaki** digestive organ.

SHOOKAI introduction; recommendation; **shookai suru** to introduce, recommend; **shookaijoo** a letter of introduction; **shookaisha** introducer.

shookai minute explanation.

shookai company, firm.

shookai inquiry, reference; **shookai suru** to inquire.

shookaki fire extinguisher.

shookaku raising to a higher status; **shookaku suru** to be raised to higher ranks.

shookan summons; call to appear; **shookan suru** to summon, call up; **shookanjoo** summons; a written summons.

shookaryoku digestion.

shookasen fireplug, hydrant.

shooken securities; bond.

shooki soberness; **shooki ni kaeru** to come to one's senses; **shooki o ushinau** to lose one's senses; to faint.

shookibo small scale.

shookin prize (in money); **shookin o kakeru** to offer a cash prize.

shookizuku to come to one's senses.

shooko proof, evidence; **shookohin** evidence (thing).

shookodateru to prove; to testify.

shookoo brief tranquility; temporary ease.

shookoogyoo commerce and industry.

Shookoo Kaigisho Chamber of Commerce and Industry.

shookyokuteki negative; passive.

shookyuu promotion; **shookyuu suru** to be promoted.

shookyuu raise in wages.

shoomei proof; certification; **shoomei suru** to prove; to certify; **shoomeisho** certificate; **mimoto shoomeisho** identification card (or other document).

shoomei illumination, lighting.

shoomen front; **shoomen kara miru** to take a front view; **shoomen shoototsu** head-on collision.

shoometsu extinction; disappearance; **shoometsu suru** to disappear; to be extinguished.

shoomi net; **shoomi gokiro aru** to weigh five kilograms net.

shoomon bond; deed; **shoomon o ireru** to give bond; to sign a written agreement.

shoomoo consumption; waste; **shoomoo suru** to consume; to waste; to tire out.

shoonen youth, boy; boyhood.

shooni infant, baby; **shoonika** pediatrics.

shoonin recognition; acknowledgment; witness; surety; **shoonin suru** to recognize; to admit; **shoonin ni tatsu** to be a witness to.

shoonin merchant, trader; **shoonin ni naru** to become a merchant.

shoorai (n.) future; (adj.) **shoorai no** future; prospective.

shoorei encouragement; promotion; **shoorei suru** to encourage; to promote; to urge.

shoori victory, triumph; **shoori o eru** to win a victory.

shooryaku abbreviation, omission; **shooryaku suru** to eliminate; to omit.

shooryoo small quantity.

shoosai details, particulars; **shoosai ni** in detail; **shoosai no** minute, detailed.

shoosan praise; admiration; **shoosan suru** to praise; to admire.

shoosen merchant vessel.

shoosetsu fiction; romance; novel; **shoosetsuka** novelist; novel writer; **shoosetsuteki** fictitious, romantic.

shooshi death by fire.

shooshin promotion, advancement; **shooshin suru** to rise in rank.

shooshin prudence, caution, timidity; **shooshin na** timid, cautious, prudent.

shoosho bond; document; certificate; diploma.

shooshoku light eating; **shooshokuka** light eater.

shooshoo little, few; in a small degree.

shooshuu calling out; summons; convocation; draft (into military service); **shooshuu suru** to call out; to summon; to assemble.

shoosoku news; **shoosoku o kiku** to hear from; to have news of (someone); **shoosoku ni tsuujiru** to be well informed; **shoosokutsuu** well-informed person.

shoosoo irritation, fretfulness; impatience; **shoosoo suru** to fret; to fidget, be impatient.

shoosui emaciation, haggardness; **shoosui suru** to become emaciated.

shoosuru to call; to name.

shoosuu decimal, fraction; small number; minority; **shoosuu de aru** to be very few.

shootai true character; **shootai naku** out of one's senses; **shootai o arawasu** to reveal one's true character; **shootai o tsukamu** to get at the bottom of an affair.

shootai invitation; **shootai suru** to invite.

shooten focus; **shooten o awaseru** to focus; to bring into focus.

shooten shop, store.

shootoo putting out lights; **shootoo suru** to put out the light; **shootoorei** curfew.

shoototsu collision, crash; conflict; **iken no shoototsu** conflict of opinions; **shoototsu suru** to run into; to collide.

shoouindoo show window.

shooyo reward; giving a reward; **shooyo o ataeru** to give a reward.

shooyoo commerce, business; **shooyoo no** commercial; pertaining to business.

SHOOYU soy sauce.

shoozen sadly, sorrowfully; **shoozen to** with a heavy heart, sadly.

shoozoo portrait; likeness; **shoozoo o kakeru** to have one's portrait painted.

shoozuru to produce; to yield; to grow; to arise; to spring up.

shori management; transaction; treatment; **shori suru** to manage; to treat.

shoron preface, introduction.

shorui documents, papers.

shosai study, library.

shoseki, HON books.

shosen in the end; after all.

shoshin belief, conviction.

shoshinsha beginner, novice.

shosuru to conduct oneself; to deal with; to condemn, sentence.

shotai household; **shotaidoogu** household necessities; **shotaijimiru** to be sobered down by household cares; **shotaimochi** family person; **shotaimochi ga ii** to be a good housekeeper; **shotainushi** head of a household.

shotaimen first interview; **shotaimen no hito** a stranger.

SHOTCHUU (*colloq.*) always; often; all the time. **Shotchuu kaze o hikimasu.** I catch cold often.

shoten bookshop.

shotoku income; earnings; **shotokuzei** income tax.

shotoo elementary.

shou to carry on the back.

shoyoo no necessary, requisite, needed.

shoyuu possession; **shoyuu suru** to have; to possess; **shoyuuchi** one's land; one's estate; **shoyuuhin** belongings; **shoyuuken** property; proprietorship, ownership; **shoyuusha** proprietor.

shozai whereabouts; site, position; situation. **shozai o hakken suru** to discover (someone's) whereabouts; **shozai o kuramasu** to conceal (one's own) whereabouts.

shozaichi site, locality.

shozaifumei no missing.

shozoku one's post, one's attachment; **shozoku no** attached to, belonging to, **shozoku saseru** to attach; to put under the control of.

shozon opinion; view; intention; **shozon o akasu** to tell one's real intention; **shozon o tazuneru** to ask (someone's) opinion about.

shu lord; chief; principal; master; **shu to shite** mainly, chiefly.

shubi course of an event; **shubi yoku** successfully; luckily.

shuchoo assertion; maintenance; opinion; **shuchoo o toosu** to impose one's opinion on someone else; **shuchoo suru** to assert, to maintain; to advocate; to insist upon.

shudai subject, theme.

SHUDAN means, way; measures, steps. **shudan o miidasu** to find the means to; **shudan o toru** to take means.

shuei guard; **shuei suru** to keep guard.

shuen feast, banquet; cocktail party; **shuen o moyoosu** to hold a cocktail party.

shuen starring, playing the leading part.

SHUFU housewife.

shufu capital, metropolis.

shugei manual arts; handicraft.

shugi principle; ism; **shugi o mamoru** to stick to one's principles.

shugo protection, guard; **shugo suru** to protect, watch over.

shuhitsu chief editor.

shuisho prospectus.

SHUJIN master; employer; one's husband.

shujinkoo hero, heroine (in a novel).

shujin'yaku host, hostess.

shuju no various, several, sundry.

shujutsu surgical operation.

shukan subjectivity; subjective view; **shukanteki** subjective.

shukei paymaster; accountant.

shuken sovereignty; **shukensha** supreme ruler; chief of state.

shuki memorandum, note; **shuki o kaku** to make a memorandum of.

shukka outbreak of fire; **shukka suru** to start a fire.

shukke (Buddhist) priest.

shukketsu bleeding, hemorrhage; **shukketsu**

suru to bleed; **shukketsu o tomeru** to stop bleeding.

shukkin attendance (at the office); **shukkin suru** to go to work; **shukkinbo** attendance record, time book; **shukkin jikan** office-going hour.

shukkoo departure of a ship from a port; **shukkoo suru** to sail.

shukoo plan, idea, contrivance; **shukoo o korasu** to devise a plan.

shukoo handiwork, handicraft, manual work.

shukuboo cherished desire.

shukuboo o tassuru to attain a cherished desire.

shukuchoku night duty; **shukuchoku suru** to keep night watch; to be on night duty; **shukuchokuin** person on night duty.

shukudai homework; **shukadai ni suru** to reserve for future discussion; to keep in abeyance.

shukuden congratulatory telegram.

shukufuku blessing; **shukufuku sareta** blessed, happy; **shukufuku suru** to bless.

shukuhai toast (congratulatory cup); **shukuhai o ageru** to drink a toast.

shukuhaku lodging, accommodation; **shukuhaku suru** to put up for the night; to lodge; **shukuhakunin** lodger; **shukuhakuryoo** room and board; lodging charge; hotel bill.

shukujitsu holiday.

shukumei fate, destiny; predestination; **shukumei no** predestined; **shukumeiron** fatalism; **shukumerion sha** fatalist.

shukun distinguished service; meritorious deeds.

shukusatsuban pocket-sized edition of a book; monthly bound edition of newspapers.

shukusha residence; lodging house; billet.

shukusha drawing on a small scale.

shukushoo reduction, curtailment; **shukushoo suru** to reduce; to retrench; to curtail.

shukusuru to congratulate.

shukuten celebration; commemoration; **shukuten o ageru** to celebrate.

shukutoo benediction.

shukuzu reduced drawing; reduced copy.

SHUMI taste; interest; **shumi no aru** tasteful; **shumi no nai** tasteless, dull; **shumi o motsu** to have taste for; to like.

shumoku items; article.

shun season; **shun no yasai** vegetables in season.

shunin person in charge; responsible official.

shunkan moment, instant; **shunkan ni** in a moment; **shunkan no** momentary, instantaneous.

shunoo brains; soul; leader. **Tanaka-san wa sono jigyoo no shunoo to natte iru.** Mr. Tanaka is the driving force of that enterprise.

shunretsu na unrelenting; rigorous; drastic.

shuppan publication; **shuppan suru** to publish, issue; **shuppansha** publisher.

shuppan sailing; **shuppan suru** to sail, to set sail.

shuppatsu departure; starting; **shuppatsu suru** to depart; to leave; to start; **shuppatsuten** starting point.

shuppei dispatch of troops.

shuren dexterity.

shurui kind, sort, variety; **arayuru shurui no** all kinds of; **onaji shurui no** of the same kind.

shuryoku main force; main body.

shuryoo hunting; shooting; **shuryooka** hunter.

shusai sponsorship; **-no shusai de** under the auspices of.

SHUU week.

shuukyoku end, conclusion; **shuukyoku no** last, final; **shuukyoku o tsugeru** to come to an end.

shuunyuu income; receipts; revenue; **shuunyuu ga ooi** to enjoy a comfortable income.

shuuressha last train.

shuuri repair; **shuuri suru** to repair, mend.

shuuryoo completion; **shuuryoo suru** to complete the course of.

shuusai genius; talented person.

shuusaku study.

shuusan gathering and dispersion.

shuusanchi distributing center.

shuusei amendment; revision; modification; **shuusei suru** to amend; to revise; to modify; **shuuseian** amendment (to a bill).

shuusen recommendation; mediation; **shuusen suru** to recommend; to mediate.

shuusen end of war; **shuusen ni naru** to come to the end of a war.

shuusengyoo brokerage; commission agency; **shuusenryoo** commission; brokerage; **shuusenya** broker, commission agent; real estate agency; employment agency.

shuusennin go-between; middleman.

shuushi religion; sect, denomination.

shuushi income and expenditure. **Shuushi ga tsugunawanai.** We cannot make ends meet.

shuushi from beginning to end.

shuushin morality, ethics.

shuushin lifetime; all one's life; **shuushin chooeki** penal servitude for life; **shuushin kaiin** life member.

shuushoku securing employment; **shuushoku**

suru to secure a position in an office; to enter into service.

shuushuku contraction, shrinking; **shuushuku suru** to contract; to shrink.

shuushuu collection; **shuushuu suru** to collect; to gather.

shuutai unseemly sight; shameful conduct; scandalous condition; **shuutai o enzuru** to behave disgracefully.

shuuten terminal point.

SHUUTO father-in-law; **SHUUTOME** mother-in-law.

shuutoo na cautious; scrupulous, thorough; **shuutoo na chuui** scrupulous (meticulous) care.

shuuu shower; **shuuu ni au** to be caught in a shower.

shuuwai acceptance of a bribe; graft; **shuuwai suru** to take a bribe.

shuuya all night; whole night through; **shuuya unten** all-night service (for trolley cars, buses).

shuuyoo culture; cultivation; **shuuyoo o tsumu** to make a constant effort to improve oneself; **shuuyoo suru** to cultivate.

shuuyoo accommodation, reception; **shuuyoo suru** to take in; to quarter.

shuuyooryoku capacity.

shuuzei collection of taxes; **shuuzei suru** to collect taxes; **shuuzeiri** tax collector.

shuuzen repair; mending; **shuuzen suru** to repair; to mend.

shuwan ability, skill, talent; **shuwan no aru** able, capable, talented.

shuyoo na chief; important; essential.

shuzoku race; family; class.

shuzooka sake brewer.

soaku na crude, coarse; inferior.

SOBA buckwheat; dark buckwheat noodles; **kake soba** buckwheat noodles served in soup; **mori soba** buckwheat noodles served with soup but in a separate container.

SOBA side; neighborhood, proximity; **soba ni, soba de** at hand, beside; **soba no** neighboring.

sobadateru to prick up one's ears; **mimi o sobadatete kiku** to strain one's ears to listen.

sobieru to rise; to tower; to soar. **Yama ga takaku sobieru.** The mountain towers.

SOBO grandmother.

soboku simplicity, artlessness; **soboku na** simple, artless.

soburi behavior; bearing, manner; **soburi o suru** to behave oneself; to assume the air of.

sobyoo rough sketch.

sochi management; disposal; dealing.

SOCHIRA, SOTCHI there; that way.

sodachi breeding, bringing up; **sodachi no warui** ill-bred; of slow growth; **sodachi no yoi** well-bred; of good social background.

SODATERU to bring up, raise; to train; **hana o sodateru** to grow flowers; **kodomo o sodateru** to bring up a child.

SODATSU to grow; to be brought up.

SODE sleeve; **sode ni sugaru** to hang on a person's sleeve; to beg for mercy; **sode o hiku** to pull (someone) by the sleeve.

soen long negligence; **soen ni naru** to neglect to visit.

soeru to add; to affix, attach; **chikara o soeru** to give a person assistance; **kyoo o soeru** to liven up the entertainment.

SOFU grandfather; **SOFUBO** grandparents.

sogai check; obstruction, impediment; **sogai suru** to check; to obstruct, impede.

sogeki sniping; **sogeki suru** to aim and shoot; to fire at; to snipe.

sogo discrepancy; disappointment, failure; **sogo suru** to go wrong; to be in disagreement.

sogu to chip; to cut aslant; to diminish, reduce; **kyoomi o sogu** to spoil the pleasure.

sokkenai cold; blunt; dry; curt; **sokkenai aisatsu** curt salutation.

sokki shorthand, stenography; **sokkiroku** shorthand records; stenographic transcript; **sokkisha** stenographer.

sokkin spot cash; **sokkin de harau** to pay cash.

sokkoojo meteorological station, weather bureau.

SOKKURI whole; just as it is; altogether; **jitsubutsu sokkuri** to be true to life.

sokkyookyoku improvisation (in music).

SOKO that place, there; **soko e** there, to that place; **soko kara** from there; **soko ni, soko de**, in that place.

soko bottom, depth; sole (shoe); **sokoshirenu** bottomless, unpredictable; **kokoro no soko kara** from the bottom of one's heart.

sokode now; then; thereupon; accordingly.

sokoi underlying motive; true intention.

sokoiji spite, malice; **sokoiji no warui** malicious, spiteful.

sokojikara latent (potential) energy; reserve of force; **sokojikara no aru** strong; energetic **sokojikara no aru koe** deep (tone of) voice.

sokoku one's native land; **sokokuai** love of the native land.

sokonau to harm, hurt, injure, damage, spoil, ruin.

sokonuke sawagi boisterous merrymaking.

sokoo conduct, behavior; **sokoo ga osamaranai** to conduct oneself improperly.

SOKORA, SOKORA ATARI thereabouts; about there.

soko soko ni hastily, hurriedly.

sokotsu carelessness, heedlessness; **sokotsu na** careless, heedless.

-SOKU counter denoting: pair (for shoes, socks, and stockings); **kutsu issoku** one pair of shoes.

sokubai suru to sell on the spot.

sokubaku restriction, restraint; **sokubaku sareru** to be restricted; **sokubaku suru** to restrict.

sokudo speed, velocity.

sokui accession to the throne.

sokuji at once, immediately.

sokujitsu same day; on the very same day.

sokumen side, flank; **sokumen no** lateral, flanking.

sokuryoku speed, velocity; **sokuryoku o choosetsu suru** to regulate the speed.

sokuryoo land survey; **sokuryoo suru** to measure; to survey; **sokuryooshi** surveyor.

sokusei rapid completion; quick mastery; **sokusei kooza** intensive course.

sokuseki footprint.

sokushi instantaneous death; **sokushi suru** to die instantly.

sokushin promotion; acceleration, hastening; **sokushin suru** to promote; to further; **shokuyoku o sokushin suru** to stimulate the appetite.

sokutatsu, sokutatsu yuubin special delivery; **sokutatsu de** by special delivery; **sokutatsu de dasu** to send by special delivery.

sokutei measurement; **sokutei suru** to measure.

sokutoo prompt answer, ready reply; **sokutoo suru** to reply at once.

SOKUZA NI at once, immediately, instantly.

somaru to be dyed, be colored; to be infected with.

SOMATSU crudeness, coarseness; **somatsu na** crude; coarse; poor; **somatsu ni suru** to treat lightly; to handle roughly.

some dye; dyeing; **some ga yoi** to be well dyed, **someko** dyestuff, dye.

someru to dye; to stain.

sometsuke dyeing; printing; blue-and-white porcelain.

SOMOSOMO in the first place.

somukeru to turn away, avert; **kao o somukeru** to turn one's face away.

SOMUKU to revolt against; to rise against; to act contrary to; to disobey; to violate;

ryooshin ni somuku to go against one's principles.

son loss, damage; disadvantage; **son na** disadvantageous; **son ni naru** to be disadvantageous to; **son o suru** to suffer a loss.

sonaeru to prepare; to provide for; **igen o sonaeru** to possess great dignity; **man'ichi ni sonaeru** to prepare for the worst.

sonaeru to offer (to the altar).

sonaetsukeru to provide with; to equip with.

sonawaru to be furnished with, be supplied with.

sonboo existence; life or death fate; **sonboo ni kansuru mondai** a question of life or death; **sonboo ni kansuru** to decide the fate.

sonchoo esteem, respect; appreciation; **sonchoo suru** to esteem, respect.

sonchoo village headman; mayor.

sondai haughtiness, arrogance; **sondai na** arrogant, haughty; **sondai ni kamaeru** to have a haughty bearing.

son'eki profit and loss; loss and gain; **son'eki o keisan suru** to calculate profit and loss.

songai damage, injury; loss; **songai baishoo** compensation for damages; **songai baishoo o yookyuu suru** to sue for damages; **songai o ataeru** to do damage; **songai o koomuru** to suffer a loss.

sonjiru See **sonzuru.**

sonkai village assembly.

SONKEI respect; high regard; honor; **sonkei suru** to respect, esteem, honor; **sonkei sareru** to be respected.

sonmin villagers.

SONNA that sort of, such; of the kind, of the sort; **sonna hito** such a person; a person like that; **sonna ni** so; in that way; so much; particularly.

SONO that, those; **sono ba** that place; **sono ba de** then and there; on the spot; **sono go** after that, afterward; from that time on; **sono go no** later; **sono hen** about, thereabouts; **sono hoka** besides, beyond, moreover; **sono hoka no** other, another; **sono hoka wa** the rest, the others; **sono koro** around that time; in those days; **sono koro no** of that time; **sono kuse** and yet, notwithstanding; **sono mama** as it is, in that condition; **sono mama ni shite oku** to leave as it is; **sono ta** besides, moreover; beyond; **sono te** that trick [that hand]; that device; **sono toori** just so; exactly in that way; **sono uchi ni** before long; by and by; in the meantime; **SONO UE** in addition; moreover. **Sono te wa kuwanu.** None of your games! I'm not so easily cheated. **Sono ue no koto wa yakusoku**

dekimasen. I can't promise any more than that.

sonryoo hire, rent (tools, articles); **sonryoo de kariru** to hire; **sonryoo de kasu** to hire out; to rent out.

sonshitsu loss, damage; disadvantage.

sonshoo injury, damage, casualty; **sonshoo o koomuru** to be damaged; **sonshoo suru** to injure, damage.

sonsuru to exist; to remain.

sontoku loss and gain, profit and loss; **sontoku no mondai de wa nai** not to be a question of money.

sonzai existence; **sonzai suru** to exist; to remain.

sonzoku continuance; **sonzoku suru** to continue; to last.

sonzuru to be worn out, be damaged.

SOO that way; so; idea; **soo iu** that sort of; **soo iu wake de** for that reason. **Soo desu.** That is so. **Soo shite kudasai.** Please do so.

soo thought, conception; **soo o neru** to meditate, to work on a plan.

soo bonze; priest, monk.

soo layer, stratum, seam.

sooan draft; rough cast.

sooba current price; quotation; speculation; **sooba ni te o dasu** to engage in speculation; **soobashi** speculator.

sooban sooner or later; by and by.

soobetsukai farewell meeting; farewell dinner.

soochi arrangement, equipment; **soochi suru** to equip with; to arrange.

soochoo university president.

soochoo early morning; **soochoo ni** early in the morning.

soochoo na solemn; sublime.

sooda soda; bicarbonate of soda.

soodai representative; deputy; **soodai ni naru** to represent.

soodan consultation, conference; **soodan no ue** after consultation; **soodan suru** to consult, confer; **soodan ni noru** to take part in a consultation.

soodasui soda water.

soodoo confusion, disorder; disturbance; **soodoo o okosu** to raise a disturbance.

soodooin general mobilization.

soofu sending; **soofu suru** to send; to forward.

soogakari de full force; with a united force; everybody participating.

soogaku musical performance; music.

soogaku total amount; sum total.

soogankyoo binoculars.

soogawa whole leather.

soogei sending off and welcoming (people).

soogi funeral service; **soogi o okonau** to hold a funeral service; **soogisha, soogiya** undertaker.

soogi dispute; quarrel; conflict; (labor) strike; **soogidan** strikers.

soogo reciprocity; **soogo no** mutual, reciprocal.

soogon grandeur; solemnity; **soogon na** magnificent; grand; solemn.

soogoo looks, features; **soogoo o kuzushite warau** to smile gleefully; to be radiant with joy.

soogoo synthesis; putting together; **soogoo suru** to put together.

soogoo daigaku university.

soogyoo start of an enterprise.

soohaku paleness; **soohaku na** deadly pale.

soohoo both parties; both sides; each side; **soohoo no** either; both; mutual.

sooi difference, disparity; **-ni sooi nai** must be, it is certain that; **sooi naku** certainly; without fail; **-to sooi suru** to differ; to disagree; to be contrary to.

sooi new device; novel idea; originality.

SOOJI cleaning; sweeping; **sooji o suru** to clean; to sweep.

soojishoku general resignation; **soojishoku o suru** to resign in a body.

soojite generally; in general; for the most part.

soojuku premature growth, precocity; **soojuku no** precocious.

soojuu management; control; manipulation; **soojuu suru** to manage; to handle; to control; **kikai o soojuu suru** to operate a machine; **otto o soojuu suru** to manage one's husband; **soojuushi** pilot; manipulator.

sookai freshness; exhilaration; **sookai na** refreshing, enlivening; **sookai ni suru** to refresh; to exhilarate, enliven; **sookai ni naru** to be refreshed.

sookai general meeting; general assembly.

sookan first publication (of a new magazine, paper, etc.); **sookangoo** initial number (issue) of a magazine.

sookan deportation; **sookan suru** to send back; to deport.

sookan grand sight.

sookatsu summary; **sookatsu suru** to sum up; to summarize.

SOOKEI total; sum total; **sookei de** in all, as a total; **sookei suru** to sum up; to total.

sooken healthiness; **sooken na** healthy, sound, stout.

sookin remittance; **sookin suru** to remit money; to send money.

sooko warehouse; **sooko ni azukeru** to store in a warehouse; **sooko ni hokan suru** to store.

sookon early marriage.

sookoo manuscript; copy; **sookoo o tsukuru** to draft; to make a draft.

SOO KOO SURU UCHI NI in the meantime; meanwhile.

sookutsu den, lair; nest; **dooroboo no sookutsu** den of thieves.

sookuzure collapse, complete rout; **sookuzure ni naru** to be routed.

sookyo daring enterprise.

soomei wisdom, sagacity; **soomei na** wise, clearheaded.

soomen Japanese noodle (popular in summer).

soomoku plants and trees.

soomokuroku general table of contents.

soomu general affairs; director; manager.

soonan meeting with an accident; mishap. **soonan suru** to meet with an accident; **soonansha** victim of an accident; **soonan shingoo** signal of distress.

soonen prime of life.

soonyuu insertion; **sooyuu suru** to insert, put in.

sooon noise, hubbub.

soooo fitness, suitability; **soooo na** appropriate, adequate; **soooo suru** to be suitable, to be fitting.

sooran superintendence, control; **sooran suru** to superintend, manage.

soorei splendor, magnificence; **soorei na** magnificent, splendid.

sooretsu funeral procession.

sooretsu na heroic, tragic; **sooretsu na saigo o togeru** to die a heroic death.

sooritsu establishment, foundation; institution; organization; **sooritsu suru** to establish, institute, found; **sooritsusha** founder.

sooron introduction; general remarks; quarrel, dispute; **sooron suru** to quarrel; to argue.

sooryo priest, monk, bonze.

sooryooji consul-general; **sooryoojikan** consulate-general.

soosa search, investigation; **soosa suru** to search, look for, hunt for.

soosa process, operation, management.

soosai general manager; president; governor.

soosaku creation; original work; **soosaku suru** to create; to originate; to write an original work; **soosakuka** person of originality; fiction writer; **soosakuteki** creative, original.

soosaku search, investigation; **soosaku suru** to search, to look for, to hunt for; **soosakutai** search party.

soosenkyo general election.

sooshihainin general manager.

sooshiki funeral; funeral services.

sooshin transmission of a message; telegraphic service.

sooshingu personal ornaments, furnishings.

SOOSHITE, SOSHITE and then; and in addition.

sooshitsu loss; forfeiture; **sooshitsu suru** to lose; to be lost.

soosho series (of books); collected works.

sooshoku ornamentation, decoration, adornment; **sooshoku no nai** plain, unadorned; **sooshoku suru** to ornament, adorn, decorate.

sooshuunyuu total income.

soosoo early; as soon as possible; without delay.

soosu Worcestershire sauce.

soosuu total number.

sootaiteki relative; correlative.

sootatsu conveyance; delivery; **sootatsu suru** to send; to forward; to convey.

sootei binding; design; **sootei suru** to bind; to design.

sooto daring enterprise.

sootoku governor-general; viceroy.

SOOTOO fitness, suitability; **sootoo na, sootoo no** suitable; respectable; reasonable; moderate; considerable; **sootoo ni kurashite iru** to be comfortably off; **sootoo suru** to be fit for.

sootoo sweeping away; **sootoo suru** to sweep away.

soowa episode.

soozai daily dishes.

soozen noisily; uproariously; **soozen to** in a noisy manner.

soozoku succession; inheritance; **soozoku suru** to inherit; to succeed; **zaisan o soozoku suru** to inherit an estate.

soozokunin heir, heiress.

soozoo creation; **soozoo suru** to create.

soozoo imagination; fancy; **soozoo ni tomu** imaginative; **soozoo suru** to imagine, fancy; **soozooryoku** power of imagination.

soozooshii noisy, full of noise.

sopurano soprano.

SORA! there! **Sora miro!** There! You see! I told you so *(colloq.)*!

SORA sky; air; heavens; **sora de** by heart, by memory; **sora takaku** high up in the sky; **sora de oboeru** to learn by heart; **sora de yomu** to recite from memory.

soradanomi hoping against hope; vain hope.

sorairo sky blue, azure.

soramoyoo look of the sky; weather; situation.

sorasu to evade, elude, dodge; to turn aside; to draw off; **hanashi o waki ni sorasu** to turn the talk away; **me o sorasu** to look away;

to avert one's eyes from; **shitsumon o sorasu** to parry a question.

sorasu to bend, to curve; to turn backward.

sorazorashii feigned; false; hypocritical; **sorazorashiku** in obvious dissimulation, hypocritically.

SORE it, that; **sore da kara** therefore, accordingly; **sore dake** that much, so much; **sore na noni** yet, in spite of that; **sore demo** still, yet; **sore hodo** so much, so; **sore kara** and then, after that; **sore made** till that time; **sore nara** then, if so; **sore ni** besides that; **sore tomo** or else.

soreru to stray; to glance off.

sori warp; curve; bend; **sori ga au** to get along (with each other) very well; **sori ga awanai** not to be on good terms (with someone).

sorimi straightening oneself up; holding one's head high; **sorimi ni naru** to throw back one's head.

soroban abacus; finance; **soroban ga toreru** to pay; to be profitable; **soroban o hajiku** to move counters of an abacus; to calculate. **Soroban ga awanai.** The accounts do not square.

soroeru to put in order, arrange in order.

soroi set; suit; **soroi mo sorotte** without exception; **soroi no** of the same pattern, uniform.

SOROSORO slowly, gradually; gently.

sorou to become complete; to be arranged in order; to gather, assemble; to agree, be in accord.

soru to bend; to warp; to bend backward. **Hi ni atatte ita ga sorimashita.** The sun has warped the board.

soru to shave; **kao o soru** to shave oneself.

soryaku roughness; **soryaku no** rough, cursory; **soryaku ni** roughly.

sosei resuscitation; reanimation; revival; **sosei suru** to revive, come to life again; **sosei no omoi o suru** to feel revived, to feel a great relief.

soseihin article of inferior quality.

sosen ancestor.

soshaku chewing, mastication; **soshaku suru** to chew, masticate.

soshakuchi leased ground.

soshakuken lease.

soshi obstruction; check, prevention; **soshi suru** to check; to hold in check; to hinder, impede.

soshiki system; organization; formation; composition; **soshiki suru** to form; to organize; to constitute; **soshikiteki** systematic; methodical; **soshikiteki ni suru** to systematize.

soshiru to slander; to blame, speak ill of.

SOSHITE See **SOOSHITE.**

soshitsu predisposition; nature; makings. **Ano hito ni wa shijin no soshitsu ga aru.** He is very poetic. (He has the poet in him.)

soshoku plain diet; **soshoku suru** to eat poorly (live on poor fare).

soshoo lawsuit; action; case; **soshoo o okosu** to sue; **soshoo suru** to sue; to start a lawsuit; to go to law.

sosogu to pour into; to pour on; to water; to pour (itself) into.

sosokkashii hasty; careless; heedless; **sosokkashii koto o suru** to act carelessly; to make a stupid mistake.

sosonokasu to tempt, entice; to stir up.

sosoru to incite, stir up, to excite.

sossen suru to take the lead; to take the initiative.

sosui drainage.

SOTCHI, SOCHIRA there; that way.

sotchinoke laying aside; neglecting; **sotchinoke ni suru** to neglect; to leave out in the cold.

sotchoku plainness, frankness, candidness; **sotchoku na** simple and honest; **sotchoku ni hanasu** to speak frankly.

SOTO out of doors, outside; **soto e iku** go outside.

sotobori outer moat (around Japanese castles).

sotogawa outer side; outside.

sotoumi open sea.

sotsu waste; bungling; fault; **sotsu ga nai** to be faultless.

sotsugyoo graduation; completion of a course of study; **sotsugyoo suru** to complete a course; to graduate from; **sotsugyoosei** graduate, alumnus; **sotsugyoo shiki** graduation ceremony; commencement; **sotsugyoo shoosho** certificate; diploma.

sotsuu understanding; **sotsuu suru** to understand (each other); **ishi ga sotsuu suru** to come to a good mutual understanding.

SOTTO quietly; softly; gently; secretly; **sotto shite oku** to leave it as it is.

sottoo fainting; **sottoo suru** to faint.

sowasowa nervously; restlessly; **sowasowa suru** to be restless; to be nervous.

soyogu to rustle; to wave.

soyoo grounding; elementary knowledge; culture; **soyoo ga aru** to be well grounded in.

soyosoyo to softly, gently (said only of the blowing of the wind); **soyosoyo fuku kaze** gentle breeze.

sozei taxes; taxation.

su sandbank; shallow; **su ni noriageru** to run aground.

su vinegar.

su nest; den; **su ni tsuku** to brood, incubate; **su o tsukuru** to build a nest.

suashi barefoot; **suashi de** barefoot(ed).

subarashii splendid, magnificent.

subashikkoi, subayai nimble; active, smart; quick-witted.

subayai See **subashikkoi.**

subekkoi smooth; slippery; velvety.

suberikomu to slide into; to slip into.

suberu to slide; to slip; to glide.

subesube shita smooth; velvety.

SUBETE whole, all; altogether; **subete no** all; whole; every.

sudare bamboo blind; **sudare o kakeru** to hang a bamboo blind; **sudare o maku** to roll up a bamboo blind.

sude empty hand; **sude de** unarmed, empty-handed.

SUDENI already.

sudoori passing by without calling; **sudoori suru** to pass by without calling (at someone's house).

SUE end; future; **sue ni wa** in the long run, **sue no** last; final; youngest; **sue no aru wakamono** a promising youth.

suekko youngest son, youngest daughter.

sueru to set, place, lay.

suetsuke fitting up; installation; **suetsuke no** fixed, stationary.

suetsukeru to fit up; to set, place in position.

sugao unpainted face.

sugaru to cling to; to lean on.

sugata form, figure, shape; **sugata o kaeru** to disguise oneself; **sugata o kakusu** to disappear.

sugenai cold; rough; flat; **sugenaku** coldly, roughly; flatly; **sugenaku kotowaru** to refuse flatly.

sugi cryptomeria; Japanese cedar.

-SUGIRU suffix denoting: be excessively, do (something) excessively; **omosugiru** to be too heavy; **tabesugiru** to eat excessively.

sugiru to pass by; to go too far.

SUGOI uncanny, weird; ghastly, lurid; **sugoi hikari** lurid light.

sugosu to pass, spend (time); to take too much.

sugosugo dejectedly; disconsolately; with a heavy heart.

SUGU soon; immediately; close by; near; **sugu hana no saki ni** just under one's nose; **sugu ni** immediately, instantly.

sugureru to surpass, excel; to be excellent; to be strong.

sugurete eminently; conspicuously; by far.

suhada bare skin; **suhada ni naru** to bare oneself; **suhada ni kiru** to wear next to the skin.

suhadaka nudity; state of being stark naked; **suhadaka de** stark naked.

sui essence; pith; elegance; fashion; **sui na** fashionable; refined, tasteful; **sui o kikasu** to pardon (someone else's) folly.

sui sour, acid; **sui mo amai mo shirinuita hito** person who has tasted the bitter and the sweet of life.

suiageru to suck up.

suichoku no perpendicular, vertical.

suichuu (*n.*) being in the water; **suichuu no** (*adj.*) underwater; **suichuu ni** (*adv.*) underwater.

suidasu to suck out.

suiden paddy field, rice field.

SUIDOO water service; waterworks; city water; channel; **suidoo o hiku** to have water pipes laid; to have water supplied; **suidookan** water pipe.

suiei swimming; **suieigi** bathing suit; **suieijoo** swimming place.

suifu sailor, seaman; **suifu ni naru** to become a sailor.

suigai damage by flood; flood disaster; **suigaichi** flooded district.

suigen, suigenchi source of a river; fountainhead.

suihei water level; horizon; **suihei no** level, horizontal; **suihei ni** horizontally.

suihei sailor (in the navy); **suiheifuku** seaman's uniform.

suiheisen horizon; sealine; horizontal line.

suihen waterside.

suijaku emaciation, debility; **suijaku suru** to be weakened; to grow weak.

suiji cooking, cookery; **suiji gakari** person in charge of cooking; cook; **suiji suru** to cook; **suijiba** kitchen.

suijooki vapor, steam.

suijun water level.

suika watermelon.

suikan drunken fellow.

suiki moisture, humidity; dropsy; **suiki no aru** moist, humid; **suiki ga dekiru** to become dropsical.

suikomu to inhale; to draw in; to absorb; to suck in.

suikoo execution; **suikoo suru** to execute, carry out.

suikuchi mouthpiece; cigar holder.

suikyo recommendation; **suikyo ni yotte** through (someone's) recommendation. **suikyo suru** to recommend.

suikyoo drunken frenzy; whim, vagary; **suikyoo de** out of mere pique; just for kicks; **suikyoo na** frenzied with drink.

suimen water surface; **suimen kara ichi meetoru ue** one meter above the water; **suimen ni ukabu** to rise to the surface.

SUIMIN sleep; **suiminbusoku** want of sleep.
suimon floodgate.
SUIMONO soup (Japanese style); **suimono wan** soup bowl. (See also **suupu.**)
suinan calamity by water; casualty at sea.
suiri reasoning; induction; **suiri suru** to reason; to induce.
suiro waterway; watercourse.
suiron reasoning; **suiron suru** to reason; to deduce.
suiryoku hydraulic power; **suiryoku denki** hydroelectricity.
suiryoo guess, conjecture; **suiryoo suru** to guess; to presume; to consider.
suiryoo quantity of water, volume of water.
suiryuu stream; water current.
suisaiga watercolor painting; **suisaigaka** watercolor painter.
suisanbutsu marine products: fish, crabs, lobsters, clams, oysters, seaweeds.
suisangyoo fishery; marine products industry. (See also **suisanbutsu.**)
suisatsu guess, conjecture; sympathy; **suisatsu suru** to conjecture, to guess, to infer from.
suisentoire flush toilet.
suisen recommendation; **suisen suru** to recommend; **suisenjoo** letter of recommendation.
suisen daffodil.
suisha water mill, water wheel.
suishin depth of water.
suishinki propeller; screw.
suishoo recommendation; approval; praise; **suishoo suru** to recommend; to praise.
suishoo crystal; **suishoo no yoo na** crystalline, crystal-like.
suisoku conjecture, supposition; inference; **suisoku suru** to conjecture; to suppose.
suisoo water tank, cistern.
Suisu Switzerland; **Suisu no** *(adj.)* Swiss; **Suisujin** Swiss (person).
suitai decline; decay; **suitai suru** to decline; to decay; to fall.
suitchi switch.
suitei presumption; conclusion; **suitei suru** to presume; to conclude.
suitoo canteen.
suitoo gakari cashier, teller.
suitorigami blotting paper, blotter.
suitoru to suck up; to absorb.
suitsuku to stick fast to, adhere.
suiun transportation by water; **suiun no ben** facilities for transportation by water. **Oosaka wa suiun no ben ga ii desu.** Osaka City has very good facilities for marine transportation.
suiyaku liquid medicine.
suiyoku cold water bath.
SUIYOOBI Wednesday.

suizokukan aquarium.
SUJI line; strips; muscle; sinew, tendon; fiber; plot; source, quarter.
sujigaki plot of a play.
sujimukai no See **sujimukoo no.**
sujimukoo no diagonally opposite; **sujimukoo no ie** a house diagonally across the street.
sujoo past career; one's past; birth; blood; origin; **sujoo no iyashii** of low birth; **sujoo no shirenai** of unknown character; **sujoo no yoi** of good family; of good birth.
sukaafu scarf.
sukaato skirt.
sukashi watermark; transparency; openwork; **sukashi no** watermarked.
sukasu to look through; to hold to the light; to thin out; to leave an opening.
SUKEETO skating; pair of skates; **sukeeto o suru** to skate.
suketchi sketch, sketching; **suketchi ni iku** to go sketching; **suketchi suru** to make a sketch.
SUKI fondness; love; fancy; taste; **suki na** *(adj.)* favorite, pet; **suki ni** as one pleases; at one's pleasure; **suki ni naru** to become fond of; **suki ni saseru** to let (someone) do as he or she pleases. **Suki desu.** I like it.
suki opening; crack; chance, opportunity; leisure; unguarded point; **suki ga nai** to find no chance; **suki o nerau** to watch for a chance.
suki spade, plow.
sukihara empty stomach.
sukii ski.
sukikirai likes and dislikes; **sukikirai no ooi** squeamish; finical, finicky, too particular.
sukima space; crevice; intermission; **sukima naku** leaving no space; compactly.
sukitooru to be transparent, be clear; **sukitootta** clear, transparent.
SUKIYAKI Japanese dish of meat and vegetables usually cooked on the table.
sukizuki taste, liking, fondness; matter of taste; **sukizuki ga aru** each to one's own taste. **Sore wa sukizuki desu.** It is a matter of taste.
SUKKARI completely, entirely.
sukoburu very, highly, extremely, awfully.
SUKOSHI little, few, bit; **sukoshi demo** any, even a little; **sukoshi no** a little, a few, slight; **sukoshi mo** not in the least *(used with a negative verb);* **sukoshi zutsu** little by little.
Sukottorando Scotland; **Sukottorando no** *(adj.)* Scots; of Scotland; **Sukottorandojin** Scot (person).
SUKU become empty; become sparse; **aida ga suku** to become separated; **te ga suku**

to be disengaged. **Onaka ga sukimashita.**
I'm hungry. **Kono densha wa suite imasu.**
This streetcar isn't crowded.

sukui help, rescue, relief, salvation; **sukui o
motomeru** to ask for help, call for help; to
seek salvation; **sukuinushi** savior, deliverer.

sukuidasu to help (someone) out of; to rescue.

sukumu to be cramped; to be paralyzed with
fear.

SUKUNAI to be few, little, scanty, scarce.
Shuunyuu ga sukunai desu. Her income
is small.

sukunakaranu not a little; not small;
considerable; much; **sukunakaranu
meiwaku** considerable inconvenience;
much trouble.

SUKUNAKUTOMO at least, to say the least.

sukuramu scrimmage; **sukuramu o kumu** to
line up for a scrimmage.

sukurin movie screen.

SUKUU to help, save, rescue; to relieve;
sukuu koto no dekinai hopeless.

sukuu to scoop, to ladle; to trip up.

sumai dwelling, residence, abode.

sumanai to be sorry for; to have no excuse
for.

sumaseru to bring to an end.

sumashita affected, stuck-up; indifferent.

SUMASU to finish, conclude, get through.
Gohan wa sumasemashita. We have
finished our meal.

sumasu to clear, to clarify; to look demure, to
be affected.

sumau to live, dwell.

SUMI India ink; ink stick (cake of ink used to
prepare ink for brush writing); **sumi o
suru** to rub an ink stick; **sumi o tsukeru**
to dip in ink; to smear with ink.

SUMI charcoal; **sumiya** charcoal dealer.

sumi corner, nook; **sumi kara sumi made**
every nook and corner; **sumi ni oku** to put
in the corner.

sumika dwelling, residence.

sumikomu to live in an employer's house.

SUMIMASEN pardon me; I'm sorry.
**Sumimasen ga enpitsu o kashite
kudasai.** Pardon me—may I borrow your
pencil?

sumiyaka na quick, rapid, swift, speedy,
prompt.

sumizumi all the corners; every nook and
corner. **Kono hen wa sumizumi made
shitte imasu.** I know every nook and
corner of this neighborhood.

sumoo Japanese wrestling; **sumoo o toru** to
wrestle.

SUMU to reside, live. **Kono machi ni sunde
imasu.** I live in this town. **Doko ni sunde
imasu ka?** Where do you live?

sumu to end; to come to an end.

sumu to become clear (liquid).

sun Japanese inch (corresponds to 1.193
American inches). (No longer used.)

SUNA sand; **suna de migaku** to polish with
sand; **suna o maku** to scatter sand.

sunao meekness, gentleness; **sunao ni**
obediently, meekly; **sunao na** meek,
gentle; **sunao ni suru** to obey; to be
obedient.

SUNAWACHI namely, that is to say; nothing
but; neither more nor less; thereupon.

sune leg; shin; **sune ni kizu o motsu mi**
someone having a guilty conscience; **oya
no sune o kajiru** to sponge off one's
parents.

suneru to be peevish; to sulk; to be in a snit.

sunka moment's leisure; little time to spare;
sunka mo nai to have no time to spare.

su no mono vinegary dish; vegetables
seasoned with vinegar.

sunpoo measure, dimensions; **sunpoo o toru**
to take measurements (for a new suit);
sunpoo no toori ni according to the
measurements; **sunpoogaki** measurement,
specification.

Supein Spain; **Supeingo** Spanish (language);
Supeinjin Spaniard.

supootsu sports; **supootsubangumi** sports
program.

suppadaka nudity, nakedness.

SUPPAI sour, acid, tart. **Kono miruku wa
suppaku natte imasu.** This milk has
turned sour.

suppanuku to expose; to disclose.

suppokasu to leave undone; to neglect.

suppon snapping turtle.

SUPUUN spoon.

-sura particle denoting: even, so much as.
Kodomo sura shitte imasu. Even a child
knows it.

surari to shita slender, graceful.

surasura smoothly; without a hitch.

surechigau to pass by each other.

surekkarashi pert person.

sureru to rub; to graze; to be worn out.

suri pickpocket, cutpurse.

suriherasu to wear down; to wear away.

surikireru to get worn out; to become
threadbare.

surikomu to rub in.

surimono printed matter; **surimono ni suru** to
print.

surimuku to rub off; to chafe.

surippu slip (woman's undergarment).

suriru thrill.

suritsubusu to grind down; to rub out of
shape; to dissipate one's fortune.

SURU to do; to play; to practice; to make; to

change one thing into another; to act as, officiate as. **Suru koto ga nai desu.** I have nothing to do. **Nihongo no benkyoo o shimashita.** I have studied Japanese. **Kyooto e iku koto ni shimashita.** I have decided to go to Kyoto. **Ano hito wa kyooshi o shite imasu.** He is a teacher. **Sore wa sen en shimasu.** It costs one thousand yen.

suru to print; to duplicate. **Meishi o sutte moraitai desu.** I would like to have visiting cards printed.

suru to pick (someone's) pocket.

suru to grind, to bray.

suru to rub, to file.

suru to lose one's fortune. **Kabu de okame o surimashita.** She lost her fortune on the stock market.

surudoi sharp, acute, keen, cutting.

SURUTO whereupon, just then; then, well. **Suruto minna de goman en desu ne?** Then the total will be fifty thousand yen, won't it?

susamajii alarming, dreadful, fearful, terrible.

susamu to grow in intensity or violence; to go to ruin; to grow wild; to be addicted to.

susanda ruined, desolate, dreary. **Susanda seikatsu o shite imasu.** He is living a wild life.

suso skirt (of a dress); bottom (of a mountain); **zubon no suso** trouser cuff.

susu soot; **susu darake no** sooty.

susugu to rinse; to wash.

susukeru to be stained with soot; **susuboketa, susuketa** smutty.

susumeru to promote; to advance, put forward; to put on (a watch); **kooshoo o susumeru** to proceed with the negotiations.

susumeru to recommend; to advise, to counsel; to encourage, to present, to offer.

susumu to progress, advance, go forward.

susunde of one's own accord; willingly.

susurinaki sobbing; **susurinaki o suru** to sob.

susurinaku to sob; to whimper.

sutaa star (of movies or stage).

sutaato (n.) start (in a sport); **sutaato o kiru** to start.

sutajio studio (for movies, broadcasting).

sutanpu stamp; datemark.

sutareru to fall into disuse; to go out of use or fashion.

sutasuta to quickly, hurriedly.

sutebachi despair; self-abandonment; **sutebachi ni naru** to abandon oneself to despair.

sutebasho dumping ground.

sutego deserted child; foundling.

SUTEKI NA splendid, brilliant, fine, remarkable, superb; **SUTEKI NI** exceedingly, remarkably; **suteki na gochisoo** a fine dinner.

sutekki walking stick, cane.

sutemi disregard of one's life; desperation; **sutemi ni naru** to abandon oneself to despair.

sutene bargain price; **sutene no** ridiculously cheap; **sutene de uru** to sell at a sacrifice; to sell dirt cheap.

SUTERU to throw away, abandon; to give up.

suteuri sacrifice sale; a less-than-cost bargain; **suteuri ni suru** to sell at a sacrifice.

sutezerifu menace; parting shot; **sutezerifu o nokosu** to leave with a parting remark.

suto See **sutoraiki.**

sutoobu stove.

sutoraiki, suto strike (walkout of labor).

sutoraiku strike (baseball).

sutoroo (beverage) straw.

SUU to breathe; to inhale; to sip; to absorb; to smoke; **iki o suu** to breathe the air; **tabako o suu** to smoke a cigarette.

SUU- prefix denoting: several; **suujitsu** several days; **suunin** several persons.

suu number, figure; **daitasuu** majority.

suugaku mathematics; **suugaku no** mathematical; **suugakusha** mathematician.

suuhai worship; adoration; **suuhai suru** to worship, venerate.

SUUJI figure, numeral; **suuji no** numerical; **suujijoo** numerically.

suukoo loftiness, sublimity; **suukoo na** lofty, sublime.

SUUPU soup (Occidental style); **suupu zara** soup plate. (See also **shiru** and **tsuyu.**)

suusei trend; drift; tendency; tide, current; **yo no suusei ni tomonatte** with the trend of the times.

suwari stability; **suwari ga yoi** to sit well; to be stable.

SUWARU to sit; to squat; to be set; **chan to suwaru** to sit straight; **raku ni suwaru** to sit comfortably.

suyaki unglazed pottery; **suyaki no** unglazed.

suyasuya to quietly, gently, peacefully; **suyasuya to nemuru** to sleep quietly.

suzu tin.

suzu bell, handbell; **suzu no oto** tinkle of a bell; **suzu o narasu** to ring a bell.

suzume sparrow.

suzumi enjoying the cool air; **suzumi ni iku** to go out to cool off.

suzumu to cool oneself; to enjoy the cool breeze.

suzunari cluster (of fruit); **suzunari ni natte iru** to hang in clusters.

suzuri ink stone (used in preparing ink for brush writing) (see also **sumi**); **suzuribako** ink-stone case.

SUZUSHII cool, refreshing; **suzushii kao o suru** to assume a nonchalant air; to appear calm and unconcerned.

T

ta rice field, paddy field; **ta o tagayasu** to till a rice field; **ta ni mizu o hiku** to irrigate a rice field.

ta others, rest; **ta no** other, another.

ta- prefix denoting: many, much; **tagaku no okane** large amount of money.

TABAKO cigarette; **tabako ire** cigarette case; **tabako o suu** to smoke a cigarette; **tabakoya** cigar store (stand).

tabaneru to bundle; to tie up in a bundle.

tabeakiru to become tired of (a food).

tabehajimeru to begin to eat.

tabekata how to eat. **Nihonshoku no tabekata o setsumei shite kudasai.** Please explain how to eat Japanese food.

TABEMONO food; provisions; edibles. **Nani ka tabemono wa arimasu ka?** Can we get something to eat? **Nihon de wa omo na tabemono wa okome desu.** In Japan, rice is the staple food.

TABERU to eat; to take; to live on; **gekkyuu de taberu** to live on the salary; **hitokuchi taberu** to have a mouthful (of food). **Yooshoku bakari tabete imasu.** I am eating only foreign (Occidental) food.

tabesugi overeating, surfeit.

tabesugiru to overeat.

tabetsukeru to be accustomed to eat. **Chuuka ryoori wa tabetsukete imasen.** I am not accustomed to Chinese food.

tabezu girai disliking (a food) without tasting; food prejudice.

tabi socks worn with kimono; **tabi issoku** pair of tabi; **tabi o haku** to put on socks; **tabihadashi** wearing socks but no shoes; **tabihadashi de** in one's socks.

tabi journey; **tabi o suru** to travel; **jinsei no tabi** life's journey.

-tabi times, occasion; **-tabi goto ni** whenever, every time now.

tabikoogyoo local performances (of a theatrical company); road performances.

tabisaki while on journey. **Sono tegami wa tabisaki de uketorimashita.** I received that letter while I was on a trip.

TABITABI often, many times, repeatedly. **Sono koto wa tabitabi hanashi ni demashita.** That subject came up often in our conversation.

taboo being fully occupied with; being busy; **taboo na** busy; **taboo ni torimagire** on account of the pressure of business; **taboo de aru** to be busy.

TABUN perhaps, probably. **Kon'ya tabun kuru deshoo.** He will probably come tonight.

tabun reaching (others') ears; **tabun o habakaru** to be afraid of publicity.

tabyoo being sickly; being weak and feeble.

TACHI nature, character, quality, disposition, **tachi no yoi** of good quality; **tachi no warui** of bad quality.

tachiagaru to stand up, rise to one's feet.

tachiai presence, attendance; **-ni tachiai o motomeru** to request (someone's) presence as a witness.

tachiau to stand by; to fight with; **-ni tachiau** to attend; **-to tachiau** to fight with.

tachibanashi o suru to talk standing; to stand chattering together.

tachidokoro ni on the spot, instantly. **Tachidokoro ni kesshin shimashita.** He made up his mind in an instant.

tachidomaru to stop short, to halt, stand still; **kyuu ni tachidomaru** to come to a sudden halt.

tachidooshi (n.) standing the whole way. **Ueno made tachidooshi deshita.** We had to stand the whole way to Ueno.

tachifusagaru to block (someone's) passage.

tachigie going out (said of a charcoal fire, etc.); being dropped (said of matters); half-burned. **Sono keikaku wa tachigie ni narimashita.** The plan has fallen through.

tachigiki eavesdropping, overhearing; **tachigiki o suru** to eavesdrop.

tachigui eating while standing; **tachigui o suru** to eat standing.

tachigusare dilapidation (of a building); **tachigusare ni naru** to fall into ruin.

tachiiru to enter; to penetrate; to interfere. **Shibafu ni tachiiranaide de kudasai.** Keep off the grass. **Tachiitta koto o otazune shimasu ga . . .** It might be too personal, but may I ask . . .

tachiki standing tree.

tachikomeru to screen, envelop. **Kasumi ga tachikomeru.** The mist envelops all things.

tachimachi at once; in an instant. **Nihon ni kuru to tachimachi yuumei ni narimashita.** As soon as he came to Japan, he became prominent.

tachimawaru to go round; to play one's part; to maneuver; **joozu ni tachimawaru** to

play one's part well; **zuruku
tachimawaru** to act in a cunning way.

tachimi seeing a play from the gallery (from
standing room).

tachimukau to fight against.

tachinaoru to regain one's footing; to recover.

tachinoki removal; vacation; evacuation; **-ni
tachinoki o meizuru** to order to vacate;
tachinoki meirei order for removal;
deportation order; an eviction order;
tachinokisaki refuge.

tachinoku to quit; to leave; to vacate.

tachiokure being late in getting started.

tachiokureru to be tardy, be behind time.

tachioojoo standstill, deadlock, being kept
standing; **tachioojoo o suru** to come to a
standstill; to be in a dilemma.

tachisukumu to stand petrified with fear.

tachiyoru to call at; **-no uchi ni tachiyoru** to
drop in.

tachizume being kept standing.

tada merely, only, simply; free of charge.

tadachi ni at once, immediately, directly;
without delay. **Tadachi ni kite kudasai.**
Please come immediately.

tadagoto trivial matter; commonplace (thing).
Tadagoto de nai. It is no trivial matter.

TADAIMA now, just now; I'm home
(greeting); **tadaima no tokoro** for the
present; **tadaima de wa** now, nowadays.

tadai no heavy, great; serious; **tadai no
songai** heavy loss; **tadai no eikyoo o
koomuru** to be seriously affected.

tadanori free ride; stealing a ride.

tadare sore; inflammation; **tadareru** to break
out in sores; to be inflamed.

TADASHI however; provided that. **Tadashi
kodomo wa hangaku desu.** (But) children
are (charged) half-price.

TADASHII right, proper.

tadasu to examine, investigate; to inquire into;
to question.

tadayou to drift about; to wander; **kao ni urei
o tadayowasete** with a worried look; **nami
ni tadayou fune** a boat drifting at the
mercy of the waves.

tadooshi transitive verb (one which can take
the particle o).

tadoru to go on wearily.

taedae brokenly; feebly, faintly.

taegatai intolerable, unbearable.

taema break; gap; pause.

taeru to bear; to bear up; **konku ni taeru** to
bear up under privation; **nin ni taeru** to be
equal to one's duty; **juunen no shiyoo ni
taeru** to be good for ten years.

taeru to become extinct; **onshin ga taeru** to
hear nothing from (someone). **Kyookyuu
ga taeru.** The supply is cut off.

taezu constantly; **taezu doryoku suru** to
make a constant effort.

taga hoop; **taga o hazushite sawaide iru** to
go on a spree.

tagaeru to break; to violate; **yakusoku o
tagaeru** to break a promise.

tagai ni with one another; with each other;
mutually.

tagaku large sum.

tagayasu to till, plow, cultivate; **hatake o
tagayasu** to farm; to work on a farm.

tagei varied accomplishments; **tagei na** highly
accomplished; **tagei na hito** versatile
person; **tagei no** many-sided.

tagon telling others; **tagon suru** to tell others.

tagui kind, class, sort; **tagui naki** matchless,
unique.

taguru to haul in (hand over hand); to follow
up; to trace to its source.

tahata farm; field; cultivated land.

tahoo another side; other side; **tahoo de wa**
on the other side; **tahoomen** many
directions; many sides; different subjects.

tai opposite; even, equal; versus, against; **-ni
tai suru** versus, against, toward, to; **san tai
go no seiseki** a score of 3 to 5; **tai Bei
booeki** trade with the U.S.A.

tai body, form; **tai o kawasu** to dodge; **tai o
nasanai** to be in bad form.

tai party, corps, band; **tai o kumu** to form in a
line, to form a party; **tai o toku** to disband.

tai- prefix denoting: great, large, grand;
general, main, principal; serious; **tainin**
important mission; **taiyaku** important task.

-tai suffix denoting: be desirous of, want to do
(something). **Tabetai desu.** I want to eat.
Mitai desu. I want to see it.

taibetsu general classification; **taibetsu suru**
to classify roughly.

taibu bulkiness; greater part; **taibu no**
voluminous.

taibyoo serious illness.

taida idleness, laziness; **taida na** idle, lazy.

taido attitude; **taido o ippen suru** to change
one's attitude completely.

taifuu gale, typhoon.

TAIGAI generally; almost; probably. **Doyoobi
wa taigai uchi ni imasu.** I am usually at
home on Saturdays.

taigaku, taikoo leaving school.

taigan opposite bank of a river.

taigen, taigen soogo bragging, boasting;
taigen soogo o suru to boast.

taigi toil, exertion, labor; **taigi sooni**
languidly; **taigi desu** to feel tired.

taigo ranks; **taigo o midashite** in confusion.

taigotettei spiritual awakening.

taigun large crowd (herd, flock, school, etc.);
kujira no taigun large school of whales.

taigun large force, great army.

taiguu treatment; service; rating; **taiguu ga warui** to treat coldly; to be paid poorly; **taiguu ga yoi** to treat well, be hospitable, pay well.

taigyoo slowdown strike.

taihai crushing defeat; **taihai suru** to meet with a crushing defeat.

taihai decay, corruption; **taihai suru** to be ruined.

taihan for the most part.

taihei peace, tranquility.

TAIHEIYOO Pacific Ocean.

TAIHEN very, extremely, remarkably; **taihen na** serious, dreadful; innumerable; **taihen ni** very. **Taihen omoshiroi desu.** It is very interesting.

taiho arrest; apprehension; **taihojoo** warrant of arrest.

taiho deterioration; retrogression, going backward.

taihoo gun; cannon; **taihoo o utsu** to fire a gun.

taii general idea; résumé; outline.

taii abdication.

taiiku physical education.

taiin suru to be released from (leave) a hospital.

taiji subjugation; wiping out; control.

taijoo leaving, exit; **-ni taijoo o meizuru** to order (a person) out of the room; **taijoo suru** to leave.

taijuu weight (of the body); **taijuu ga masu** to gain weight.

taika authority, distinguished person (in any circle, i.e., master painter, great musician, eminent scholar, etc.).

taika great fire.

taika degeneration.

taika fireproof; **taika kenchiku** fireproof building.

taikai withdrawal of membership (from an association or society).

taikau, taiku physique; **taikaku kensa** physical examination.

taikan high official.

taikanshiki coronation.

taika renga firebrick.

taikei system; **taikei o tateru** to systematize.

taiken personal experience; **taiken suru** to experience.

taiketsu confrontation; **-to . . . o taiketsu saseru** to confront (someone) with (another).

taiki standing by; being ready; **taiki no shisei** in a position of readiness.

taiki atmosphere.

taikin large sum of money.

taiko drum.

taikobara potbelly, paunch, bay window.

taikoo opposition; rivalry, confrontation; **taikoo undoo** a countermovement; **taikoo suru** to oppose; to face; to counteract; **taikoosaku** counterplan, countermeasures; **taikoosha** rival, antagonist.

taikoo fundamental principle, code.

taikoo See **taigaku.**

taiku See **taikaku.**

taikutsu ennui; dullness; **-ni taikutsu suru** to be bored; to become weary of; **taikutsu saseru** to bore.

taikyaku retreat; **taikyaku suru** to retreat.

taikyo, taishutsu leaving, quitting; **taikyo suru** to leave, quit; **taikyo meirei o dasu** to issue an order for departure.

taikyoku general state; general situation; **taikyoku ni me o tsukeru** to take a large view of things.

taikyoo leaving the capital.

taikyuuryoku durability; endurance.

taiman negligence.

taimen dignity, honor, reputation; **-no taimen o sonjiru** to bring disgrace on; **taimen o omonzuru** to have a sense of honor; to make much of one's dignity; **taimen o tamotsu** to keep one's reputation.

taimen interview, meeting; **taimen suru** to interview, to meet.

taimoo great ambition; **taimoo o idaku** to harbor an ambition.

tainin important mission; **tainin o hatasu** to carry out an important mission.

tainoo nonpayment; **tainoo suru** to be delinquent in payment; **tainookin** arrears; **tainoosha** delinquent payer.

taion body temperature; **taion o hakaru** to take the (body) temperature; **taionkei** clinical thermometer.

taipisuto typist.

taipuraitaa typewriter.

taira evenness; level; flatness; **taira na** flat; **taira ni suru** to level, flatten.

tairageru to subdue; to subjugate.

tairiku continent; **tairiku no** continental.

tairitsu opposition; rivalry.

tairyaku outline; summary; **tairyaku o noberu** to give an outline.

tairyoo large quantity; **tairyoo seisan** mass production.

tairyoo big catch (of fish).

taisa great difference; **taisa o shoojiru** to make a great difference; **taisa ga aru** there is a great difference.

taisai grand festival; great fete.

taisan dispersion; **taisan saseru** to break up; **taisan suru** to take flight; to be dispersed.

taisei structure; system; organization; trend of affairs; general situation; **sekai no taisei**

international situation; **taisei ni tsuujiru** to be conversant with the trend.

taisei completion, accomplishment; **taisei suru** to complete.

TAISEIYOO Atlantic Ocean.

taiseki accumulation; heap; **taiseki suru** to accumulate.

taisen great war; **Dai niji sekai taisen** World War II.

TAISETSU NA important, precious. **Hakkiri kaku koto ga taisetsu desu.** It is important to write clearly. **Taisetsu ni shite kudasai.** Please take good care of it.

taishaku loan; **taishakuhyoo** balance sheet.

taishikan embassy; **taishikan'in** embassy attaché.

taishin kenchiku earthquake-proof building.

taishita great; important; remarkable.

taishite very, greatly; importantly; remarkably (used with negative expressions).

taishitsu physical constitution.

taishoku gluttony; **taishoku no** gluttonous, greedy; **taishoku suru** to eat (too) much.

taishoku resignation; **taishoku teate** retirement allowance; **-o taishoku suru** to resign from an office; to retire from service.

taishoo object.

taishoo title of the highest officers of the army and navy; general, admiral; leader; head.

taishuka heavy drinker.

taishutsu leaving; **taishutsu suru** to leave, retire from. (See also **taikyo**.)

TAISOO very; exceedingly; many; much. **Taisoo omoshiroi shibai desu.** It is an exceedingly enjoyable play.

TAISOO physical exercise, gymnastics; **taisoo o suru** to exercise.

taisuru to front; to oppose; to be opposite to; to correspond to.

TAITEI generally; usually; mostly; **taitei no hito** most people. **Taitei wa arukimasu.** Usually I walk. **Nichiyoobi wa taitei uchi ni imasu.** Generally I stay at home on Sundays.

taiteki powerful enemy. **Yudan taiteki.** False security is a great foe.

taitoku suru to master; to comprehend.

taitoo equality, equal footing; **taitoo ni** on equal terms; **taitoo no** equal.

taitoru title.

taiu heavy rain, downpour.

taiwa dialogue; conversation; **to taiwa suru** talk with.

TAIWAN Taiwan; **Taiwan no** Taiwanese.

taiya tire.

taiyaku important task; heavy role.

TAIYOO sun; **taiyooreki** the solar calendar; Gregorian calendar.

taiyoo summary; general principle; résumé.

taiyoo ocean; **taiyoo no** oceanic.

taizai stay; **taizai suru** to stay.

taizen calmness, composure; **taizen to shite** calmly, composedly.

tajitsu one day in the future; some day.

tajoo na amorous; wanton; of loose morals.

takaburu to be proud; to be haughty; to hold up one's head.

takadai height; upland.

takadaka at the height; **takadaka to** aloft, proudly.

TAKAI high, tall; **takai tatemono** tall building; **takai yama** tall mountain. **Nedan ga takai.** The price is high.

takai another world; **takai suru** to die.

takaibiki loud snore.

takamaru to rise; to swell; to be raised.

takara treasure.

takaru to swarm; to gather, assemble; to crowd.

takasa height.

takatobi high jump; running away; **takatobi suru** to run away (to avoid).

takawarai loud laugh; ringing laughter.

take bamboo.

take length; measure; height; **take ga takai** to be tall.

takenawa being at its height, being in full swing.

taki waterfall.

takibi bonfire; wood fire; **takibi o suru** to make a fire.

takidashi boiling rice for sufferers in an emergency.

takimono fuel; firewood.

takitsuke kindling wood.

takitsukeru to light, kindle; **kenka o takitsukeru** to fan a quarrel; to incite; **sutoobu ni hi o takitsukeru** to make a fire in the stove.

takkuru tackle; **takkuru suru** to tackle.

tako kite; **tako o ageru** to fly a kite.

takokujin foreigner.

TAKU to boil rice or other food.

takuchi house lot; residential land.

takuetsu excellence; superiority; **takuetsu suru** to be distinguished, exceed in.

takuhatsu religious begging.

takujisho day nursery.

takujoo denwa desk telephone.

takumashii robust, strong.

takumi skill, adroitness, cleverness; **takumi na** skillful, dexterous.

takuramu to scheme, plan; to play a trick; to design, devise; to invent; **muhon o takuramu** to conspire.

TAKUSAN much, many, a lot; **takusan no** numerous. **Moo takusan desu.** No, thank you (I've had enough). **Takusan tabemashita.** I ate a lot.

takusetsu excellent opinion; enlightened views.

TAKUSHII taxicab.

takusuru to trust; to entrust.

takuwae store, reserve, savings; **issen no takuwae mo nai** to have not a penny saved.

takuwaeru to save, amass, lay by, hoard; **hige o takuwaeru** to wear a mustache; **kane o takuwaeru** to save money.

TAMA rare; seldom, not often; **tama ni** rarely, once in a while.

tama ball; globe; bead; jewel; **tama no ase** beads of perspiration; **me no tama** eyeball; **teppoo no tama** bullets; **tama o nageru** to throw a ball.

TAMAGO egg; **tamago no kimi** yolk of an egg; **tamago no shiromi** white of an egg; **tamago o kaesu** to hatch an egg.

TAMANEGI onion.

tamaranai to be unbearable; cannot help; be dying for.

tamari pool; waiting room.

tamarimizu stagnant water.

tamaru to collect, accumulate, gather; **harai ga tamaru** to be in arrears; **shakkin ga tamaru** to run up debts.

tamashii soul; spirit; **tamashii o ubau** to enchant.

tamatama by chance. **Tamatama kare wa byooki deshita.** It so happened that he was ill.

tamatsuki billiards.

tamazan calculation on the **soroban** (an abacus).

TAME benefit; consequence; aim; reason; for the purpose of; for the sake of; because of; **hoomon shita tame ni** as a result of his visit; **tame ni naranai** to be of no good; **tame ni naru** to do good.

tameike irrigation pond; reservoir.

tameiki sigh; **tameiki o tsuku** to heave a sigh.

tamerau to hesitate, waver.

tameru to save, put by, store; to accumulate, collect.

tameshi experiment; attempt; **tameshi ni** by way of experiment.

tameshi example, precedent. **Sonna tameshi wa nai.** There is no precedent for this.

TAMESU to try, attempt; to make a trial of; to put to the test; **yuuki o tamesu** to put one's courage to test.

tamoto sleeve of Japanese dress; foot; **hashi no tamoto** foot of a bridge.

tan phlegm; **tan o haku** to expectorate; to spit out.

-tan measure of land (about .245 acres); roll of cloth (about 12 yards).

TANA shelf, rack; **jibun no koto wa tana ni ageru** to criticize others without recognizing one's own defects; **tana ni ageru** to put up on a shelf.

tanaoroshi inventory; stock-taking; fault-finding; **tanaoroshi suru** to take stock; to pick holes in (someone else's) character.

tanazarashi shopworn merchandise; secondhand merchandise; **tanazarashi ni naru** to be shopworn.

tanbe field, rice field.

tanchoo monotony, lack of variety; **tanchoo na** monotonous, dull.

tandoku being by oneself; **tandoku hikoo** solo flight.

tane seed; stone or pit of a fruit; breed; child; cause, sources; secret of a trick; **tane o maku, tanemaki o suru** to sow (seeds); **namida no tane** source of grief.

taneabura seed oil, canola oil (used in cooking).

tanegire being incapable of supplying something, being exhausted; **tanegire ni naru** to run short of (something).

tanen many years.

tangan entreaty, supplication, petition; **tangan suru** to entreat, supplicate, petition; appeal.

tan'i unit.

tani, tanima valley.

tanigawa stream running through a valley.

tanin stranger; (other) person.

tanin gyoogi standing on ceremony. **Tanin gyoogi ni naranaide kudasai.** Please don't stand on ceremony.

tanisoko bottom of a valley.

tan'itsu singleness; **tan'itsu no** single, sole, simple.

tan'itsuka unification.

TANJOO birth; **tanjoo o iwau** to celebrate a birth; **tanjoo suru** to be born; **TANJOOBI** birthday.

tanjun simplicity, plainness; **tanjun na** simple, naïve, unsophisticated.

tanjuu pistol; revolver.

tanka, waka Japanese verse of 31 syllables.

tanken exploration; expedition; **tanken suru** to explore; **tankenryokoo** an expedition.

tanki quick temper; **tanki na** irritable, quick-tempered; **tanki o okosu** to become impatient.

tankoo coal mine; **tankoofu** coal miner.

tankoobon separate volume; **tankoobon to shite shuppan suru** to publish in book form.

tanmei short life, early death.

tanmono cloth, piece goods, drapery.

tannin charge, duty; **tannin suru** to take charge of.

tanomi request; solicitation, reliance; **-o hito no tanomi de suru** to do something at the request of (someone else); **tanomi ni naranai** to be unreliable.

tanomoshii reliable, trusty; **sue tanomoshii wakamono** promising youngster.

TANOMU to ask; to beg, to desire; to trust to; to rely on (someone to do something); **isha o tanomu** to call a doctor; **kodomo o tanomu** to entrust someone with the care of a child. **Yamada-san ni tanonde kudasai.** Please ask Mr. Yamada to do it.

TANOSHII to be pleasant, delightful, enjoyable.

tanoshimi pleasure, enjoyment, amusement.

tanoshimu to take pleasure in; to enjoy oneself; to amuse oneself with; **jinsei o tanoshimu** to enjoy life.

tanpaku quality of being simple; frankness; **tanpaku na** simple, unaffected, plain (as a diet).

tanpen short piece; **tanpen shoosetsu** short story.

tanrei na graceful.

tanren temper; forge; training; **seinen no ishi o tanren suru** to train the mind of a young person; **tetsu o tanren suru** to temper metal; **tanren suru** to temper; to forge; to train.

tansei sigh; groan; lamentation; **tansei o morasu** to lament; to sigh deeply.

TANSHIN alone.

tansho weak point or defect (in personality); **tansho o oginau** to remedy a defect; **-ga tansho de aru** -is one's weak point.

tanshuku shortening, curtailment; **tanshuku suru** to shorten, cut off.

TANSU Japanese-style chest of drawers.

tantei detective, undercover person; **himitsu tantei** private detective; **tantei shoosetsu** detective story.

tantoo dagger.

tantoo suru to take charge of.

taoreru to fall; to fall down, tumble down; **taoreta ie** tumbledown house; **taorekakatta ginkoo** insecure financial institution.

TAORU towel.

taosu to throw down; to bring down; to beat; **ki o kiritaosu** to fell a tree; **shakkin o taosu** to fail to pay a debt.

tappitsu elegant penmanship.

TAPPURI much, great deal, plentifully, full. **Go fiito tappuri aru.** It is a good five feet.

-tara suffix denoting; if, when, in case; **ame ga futtara** if (in case) it rains; **Yamada-san ga kitara** if Mr. Yamada should come.

tarasu to drop; to let drop; to dribble; to let fall; to hang down; to suspend; **maku o tarasu** to hang a curtain; **yodare o tarasu** to drool; **yuka e mizu o tarasu** to spill water on the floor.

tarazu not enough, insufficient, short of; **ni man en tarazu de** for less than 20,000 yen.

tareru to drip, trickle down, fall in drops. **Amadare ga noki kara tareru.** The rain drops from the eaves. **Ki no eda ga hikuku tarete iru.** The branches of the tree are drooping low.

tariru, taru to be enough, be sufficient; **shinrai suru ni tariru** to be worthy; to be trusted.

taru barrel, cask.

tarumu to become slack, loose, lax. **Nawa ga tarunde imasu.** The rope is slackening.

tasatsu murder.

TASHIKA if I remember right; **tashika na** certain, sure. **Tashika desu.** It is certain. **Tashika soo iimashita.** I think (I'm pretty sure) he said so.

tashikameru to make certain, authenticate, verify.

tashinami circumspection; self-control; accomplishments secretly enjoyed; **tashinami ga nai** lack of self-control. **Ano hito wa e no tashinami ga aru.** She can paint.

TASHOO more or less; in some measure, a little; somewhat. **Tashoo no chigai wa aru deshoo.** There will be some difference, but not much.

tasogare evening, twilight.

TASSHA healthiness; **tassha na** healthy, strong; **tassha ni kurasu** to enjoy vigorous health; **tassha ni naru** to get well. **Otassha desu ka?** Are you well?

tassuru to reach, arrive at, get to, attain; **mokutekichi ni tassuru** to arrive at a destination; **sen en ni tassuru** to run into 1000 yen.

TASU to add; **ni ni san o tasu** two plus three; **moo sukoshi mizu o tasu** to add a little more water.

tasukaru to be saved, be rescued; to be of help; **fushigi ni tasukaru** to have a miraculous escape; **taihen tasukaru** to be greatly relieved.

tasuke salvation; preservation; deliverance; succor, help, aid, assistance; **kami no tasuke** help from God; **tasukebune** lifeboat.

TASUKERU to help, aid, assist; to reinforce; **komatte iru hito o tasukeru** to help a person in need.

tasuu large number, majority; **tasuu no**

many; **tasuu o shimeru** to command a majority; **tasuuketsu** decision by the majority.

tatakau to fight with; to fight against; to fight a battle; **yuuwaku to tatakau** to struggle with temptation.

tataki striking, beating, pounding, chopping fine; concrete.

tatakiau to scuffle.

tatakifuseru to knock down.

tatakikomu to strike into; to train hard.

tatakikowasu to knock to pieces.

tatakinomesu to knock down.

tatakiotosu to strike (fruit) from a tree; to attack (someone) so violently that s(he) is obliged to resign her/his post.

tatakitsukeru to throw a thing against something; to throw to.

TATAKU to strike, beat, hit; to knock; **taiko o tataku** to beat a drum; **to o tataku** to tap at the door.

TATAMI floor mat made of rice straw tightly bound together and covered on the upper surface with matting; **tatami o shiku** to lay down a **tatami.**

TATAMU to fold; to shut up; to wind up; to do away with; **ie o tatamu** to shut up one's house; **kami o yottsu ni tatamu** to fold a paper into four.

tatari evil consequence.

tataru to bring evil upon, to cast an evil spell on; to inflict a calamity on.

TATE length, height; **tate no** lengthwise.

tate shield; **-ni tate o tsuku** to set oneself against, oppose, defy (someone).

-tate suffix denoting: just; fresh from; **takitate** just boiled; **kitate** just arrived; **dekitate** just completed.

tatefuda sign, signboard.

tategu furnishings (of a house); fixture; **tategu o ireru** to furnish a house.

tateguya shop where house furnishings are made and sold.

tatekae defraying the expense for another person; **tatekaekin** the sum defrayed temporarily for another person; advance (payment).

tatekakeru to rest, stand, lean, set, place something against.

tatekomoru to shut oneself up, confine oneself, remain in seclusion.

tatekomu to be crowded (with people); to be pressed with business; to be crowded with buildings; **shigoto ga tatekonde iru** to be pressed (with business).

tatemae ceremony of putting the framework in a Japanese house or other building.

tatemae principle; policy; rule; **-o tatemae to suru** to make a point of.

tatemashi extension of a building.

TATEMONO building, house. **Nihonshiki no tatemono ni sunde imasu.** I live in a Japanese-style house.

tatenaosu to build again; to reconstruct.

TATERU to build, construct, erect, set up; to shut, close; **hata o tateru** to hoist a flag; **ie o tateru** to build a house; **kinenhi o tateru** to erect a monument; **to o tateru** to shut the door.

tatetsubo floor space of a building. **Kono uchi wa tatetsubo ga hyaku tsubo aru.** The floor space of this house is 100 **tsubo** (**tsubo**: about 6 feet by 6 feet).

tatetsuke opening and shutting of doors and windows. **Kono uchi wa tatetsuke ga yoi.** The doors and windows of this house open and shut smoothly.

tateyoko length and breadth; lengthwise and crosswise.

TATOE even if, even though; **tatoe donna koto ga atte mo** whatever may happen; **tatoe joodan ni mo sey o** even in jest.

tatoe simile, metaphor, example; **tatoe ni iu yooni** as the saying goes.

TATOEBA for instance, for example.

tatoeru to compare; to give an example.

TATSU to sever, cut off; to chop off; to break; **futatsu ni tatsu** to cut in two; **sake o tatsu** to abstain from sake.

TATSU to stand up, to rise, to get on one's feet; to leave; **asu Tookyoo o tatsu** to leave Tokyo tomorrow; **seki o tatsu** to leave the seat. **Kemuri ga tatsu.** The smoke rises.

tatsujin master; expert; one who is adept; **yumi no tatsujin** archery expert.

tatsumaki waterspout, sand pillar.

TATTA only, merely; **tatta ima** just now, a moment ago.

tatte earnestly; **tatte no negai** earnest request.

tattobu to value; to set a value on.

tattoi noble, august, high (in rank); valuable.

taue rice transplantation; **taue doki** the rice-planting season; **taue uta** the rice-planting song; **taue o suru** to transplant rice.

tawagoto silly talk, nonsense.

tawainai easy; innocent; droll.

tawamureru to play; to frolic; to jest; to dally; **onna ni tawamureru** to flirt with a woman.

tawara straw bag for rice; bale.

tawashi scrubbing brush.

tayasu to exterminate; to eradicate; to put an end to.

TAYASUI easy, simple. **Tayasui goyoo desu.** It's an easy thing. I'll be glad to do it for you.

tayoo pressure of business; many things to do.

tayori intelligence, news, tidings; letter; **tayori ga nai** to hear nothing from; **tayori o suru** to write a letter.

tayori reliance, dependence; **tayori to naru hito** one's second self, a reliable person.

tayoru to rely on, depend on.

tayumu to flag, slacken one's efforts, relax one's attention.

tazei great number.

tazuna rein, bridle; **tazuna o shimeru** to tighten the reins; **tazuna o yurumeru** to slacken the reins.

TAZUNERU to look for, search for, hunt for; ask; **anpi o tazuneru** to inquire after a person; **michi o tazuneru** to ask the way to.

TE hand; arm; paw; helping hand, possession; handwriting; means, way, trick; hand (in card playing); **te ga aite iru** to be free; to have no work on hand; **te ga tarinai** to be shorthanded.

-te suffix denoting: one who performs; direction; **kamite** upper part; **shimote** lower part; **yarite** clever fellow, cunning fellow; **yomite** one who reads.

teaka dirt from the hands; **teaka ga tsuku** to become soiled from handling.

TEARAI, OTEARAI toilet, bathroom.

tearai rough, violent; **tearai koto o suru** to act violently.

teashi hand and foot. **Watakushi no teashi to natte hataraite kuremashita.** He was my right-hand man.

teatari shidai ni at random.

teate recompense; allowance; medical care; **rinji teate** temporary allowance; **kizu no teate o suru** to dress a wound; **teate o dasu** to give an allowance.

teatsui hospitable; courteous.

tebanashi de with the hands free; openly; broadly; **kodomo o tebanshi de asobaseru** to leave children by themselves; **tebanashi de jitensha ni noru** to ride a bicycle without using the handlebars.

tebanasu to let go of, release.

tebayaku quickly, rapidly.

tebikae note, memo.

tebikaeru to withhold from, hold off (buying goods, etc.).

tebiki leading another by the hand to show the way; guidance; guidebook; **Yamada-san no tebiki de** through Mr. Yamada's good offices.

tebiroi wide, roomy; on a large scale; **tebiroku shoobai o suru** to carry on a large trade, do a big business.

tebukuro gloves; **tebukuro o hameru** to put on gloves.

tebura empty hands; naked fist; **tubura de hoomon suru** to call on (someone) without bringing a present.

teburi gesture; customs.

tebusoku too short of helping hands.

techigai something amiss, something wrong; **techigai ni naru** to go wrong.

techoo notebook, memorandum book.

tedashi meddling; interference; **tedashi o suru** to poke one's nose into.

tedasuke aid, assistance; **tedasuke ni naru** to be of help to.

tedate means, measures, steps; method.

tedori net receipts; **tedori juuman en** to receive 100,000 yen net.

TEEBURU table (Occidental).

teepu tape; **teepu rekoodaa** tape recorder.

tefuki hand towel.

tegai no self-sustained, self-fed; **tegai no inu ni te o kamareru** to be bitten by a pet dog; to be betrayed by a favorite person.

tegakari hold; clue, trace; **tegakari o eru** to find a clue to.

tegakeru to engage in; to have experience in; to bring up.

TEGAMI letter, note, correspondence; **tegami o dasu** to send a letter, write to; **tegami o morau** to receive a letter.

tegara merit; achievement, distinguished service.

tegaru na easy (not difficult) to do; **tegaru na shokuji** light meal; **tegaru ni hoomon suru** to make an informal call.

tegata draft, bill, note; sign; **hyakuman en no tegata** draft for one million yen; **yakusoku tegata** promissory note.

tegatai safe; steady and honest, reliable; prudent; of good reputation (said of a shop).

tegawari substitute. **Watakushi wa tegawari o sagashite imasu.** I am looking for someone to relieve me. I am looking for someone to take my place.

tegiwa workmanship, skill (in doing or making); **tegiwa yoku** cleverly, skillfully; **tegiwa ga warui** unskillful.

tegokoro discretion, consideration; **tegokoro o kuwaeru** to use one's discretion.

tegoro handy; convenient; moderate (in price or size); just right. **Tegoro na uchi ga mitsukarimashita.** We've found a house just right for us.

tegotae reaction, response; resistance; **tegotae ga aru** to be responsive; to be effective.

tegowai strong; handy.

teguchi way, means.

tehai arrangement.

tehajime beginning; **tehajime ni** first, to begin with; **tehajime no** opening, first.

tehazu order, arrangement, plan; **tehazu o suru** to make arrangements.

tehodoki rudimentary lesson.

tehon model, pattern.

tei appearance, style; **tei yoku kotowaru** to decline politely.

teiboo dike; bank, embankment.

teichi lowland, low ground.

teiden power failure.

teido degree, standard, measure, extent; **teido no takai** of high standard; **teido no mondai** a question of degree.

TEIEN formal garden.

teigi definition.

teigi proposal; **teigi suru** to propose.

teihaku anchorage, mooring; **teihaku chuu no fune** vessels in the harbor; **teihaku suru** to be at anchor.

teihyoo settled opinion; reputation; **-to no teihyoo ga aru** to have the reputation of.

teiin regular staff; capacity (of a car); quorum.

TEIJIKA NA nearby; **teijika na tokoro** place nearby.

teijuu suru to live (at a permanent address).

teika fixed price, list price; **teikahyoo** price list.

teika suru to grow worse, deteriorate.

teikei cooperation; **teikei suru** to join hands with; to act in concert with.

teiken definite view, fixed opinion.

teiketsu conclusion, contract; **shakkan o teiketsu suru** to arrange a loan.

teiki fixed (regular) time, definite period; time; **teiki jooshaken** season ticket; commutation ticket; **teiki kankoobutsu** periodical; **teiki ni** periodically.

teikiatsu low atmospheric pressure.

teikoku fixed time, appointed time.

teikoku empire; **teikoku no** imperial.

teikoo resistance, opposition; **-ni teikoo suru** to resist, oppose, fight.

teikyoo offer; **teikyoo suru** to offer; to put at (someone's) disposal.

teikyuu, tenisu tennis; **teikyuu o suru** to play tennis.

teikyuubi periodic holiday observed by stores.

teikyuu na low; cheap; vulgar.

TEINEI NA polite, courteous; careful, scrupulous. **Teinei na taido de hanashimashita.** He spoke very courteously. **Teinei na shigoto o shimashita.** He did a very careful job.

teinen retirement age.

teinoo feeblemindedness, imbecility; **teinooji** imbecile child, idiot.

teippai one's utmost.

teiraku fall; depression; **teiraku suru** to fall, go down.

teire care; keeping; repairing; trimming (a garden); **teire no ikitodoita uchi** carefully kept house; **teire o suru** to repair, to renovate.

teiri low rate of interest.

teiryoo fixed quantity.

TEIRYUUJOO bus stop, streetcar stop.

teisai appearance, show; style; **teisai o tsukuru** to keep up appearances; **teisai ga yoi** pleasing in appearance.

teisatsu reconnaissance.

teisei correction; revision; **teisei suru** to correct, revise.

teisetsu faithfulness, constancy, devotion.

teisha stopping a vehicle (car, train, etc.); **hijoo teisha** emergency stop; **teisha suru** to stop at; **teisha o meizuru** to order a vehicle to stop.

teishaba, teishajoo, EKI railway station.

teishi stop, stoppage, suspension; **shiharai o teishi suru** to suspend payment; to stop payment.

teishoku regular occupation.

teishoo discourse; lecture.

teishu head of a family; husband; innkeeper.

teishuku virtue; **teishuku na** virtuous and refined (woman).

teishutsu presentation (in the formal, official sense); **teishutsusha** introducer, presenter.

teishuu regular income; **teishuu ga nai** to have no regular income.

teisoo chastity, faithfulness.

teisuru to present, offer; to pass; **ikan o teisuru** to be a grand sight.

teitai accumulation, piling up; indigestion; **teitai suru** to accumulate, pile up.

teitaku mansion.

teito metropolis; imperial capital.

teiton standstill; stagnation; **teiton suru** to come to a standstill.

teitoo mortgage, security; **teitoo ni toru** to hold (something) as security.

tejina parlor tricks, conjuring tricks; **tejinashi** juggler, magician.

tejoo handcuff.

tejun order; systematic plan; **tejun ga kuruu** to go out of order; **tejun o sadameru** to arrange for.

tekagen discretion, consideration; **tekagen ga wakaranai** to be little used to; **tekagen o suru** to use one's discretion; to make allowances.

tekazu trouble; **tekazu o kakeru** to give trouble.

teki enemy, opponent, antagonist; **teki mikata** friend and foe; **tekichi** enemy's land.

tekibishii severe, strict, stern, rigorous, intense.

tekichuu hit, hitting the mark.

tekigaishin hostile feeling.

tekigi suitability for an occasion; **tekigi na** suitable; **tekigi ni** suitably; **tekigi no shochi o suru** to act as one thinks fit.

tekigoo conformity, agreement; **tekigoo suru** to conform to.

tekihatsu disclosure, exposure; **tekihatsu suru** to disclose, expose; **fusei jiken o tekihatsu suru** expose.

tekihi fitness, suitability. **Tekihi wa wakarimasen.** I cannot tell whether it is suitable or not.

tekihoo proper method; legality.

tekihyoo apt remark; **tekihyoo o kudasu** to make a pertinent comment.

tekikaku, tekkaku exactness; acuteness; **tekikaku na** exact, acute.

TEKIMEN NI immediately.

tekin security (money), deposit; **tekin o utsu** to give a deposit.

tekinin competence, fitness.

tekioo fitness; adaptability.

tekipaki actively; briskly; promptly.

tekirei good example.

tekiryoo proper quantity.

tekisei kensa test for quality; aptitude test.

tekisetsu fitness, appropriateness; **tekisetsu na** appropriate.

tekishi, tekitai hostility, animosity.

tekishutsu extraction; quotation; **tekishutsu suru** to extract.

tekisuru to fit, suit, agree; **kenkoo ni tekisuru** to be good for one's health; **shokuyoo ni tekisuru** to be fit to eat.

tekisuto text, textbook.

tekitai (see **tekishi**) **ni tekitai suru** to stand against.

TEKITOO NA appropriate, suitable; **tekitoo ni** in an appropriate fashion. (See also **tekisetsu**.)

tekiyoo summary, résumé; application; **tekiyoo suru** to apply.

tekizai tekisho right person in the right place. **Kare wa tekizai tekisho desu.** He is the right man for that place.

tekizu wound; **tekizu o ou** to be wounded (in a fight).

tekkai withdrawal; **takkai suru** to withdraw.

tekkaku See **tekikaku**.

tekkan iron pipe.

tekken clenched fist.

tekkin konkuriito concrete reinforced with steel.

tekkiri surely, without doubt.

tekkoojo iron foundry, ironworks.

tekkotsu iron frame, steel skeleton.

tekkyoo iron bridge.

tekozuru to be at one's wit's end; to have much trouble with. **Ano hito ni wa zuibun tekozurimashita.** He was an awkward customer to deal with.

tekubari preparation.

TEKUBI wrist.

tekuse no warui light-fingered, thievish.

TEMA time; wages; **temachin** wages, service charge. **Kono shigoto wa tema ga kakaru.** This job takes a lot of time. **Tema wa ikura desu ka?** How much do I owe you (for your services)?

temae this side.

temaegatte willfulness, selfishness; **temaegatte na yatsu** selfish fellow.

temane gesture; **temane o suru** to gesticulate.

temaneki beckoning.

temawari one's personal effects.

temawashi preparation, arrangement; **temawashi ga yoi** to be fully prepared in advance; **temawashi suru** to get ready.

TEMIJIKA NI in short; **temijika ni ieba** in short, in brief.

temochibusata feeling awkward, or ill at ease.

temoto money on hand; **temoto ga kurushii** to be short of cash.

TEMPURA See **TENPURA**.

temukai resistance.

ten dot; mark; point; **ten no uchidokoro no nai** faultless; **ookisa no ten de** in point of size.

ten heaven, sky.

tenami skill; **tenami o miseru** to show one's skill.

tenboo view, observation; **tenboo suru** to view, look upon; **tenbookyoo** periscope; telescope; **tenboosha** observation car; parlor car.

tenbun natural endowment; **tenbun no yutaka na** highly gifted.

tenchi change of air; **tenchi suru** to go (to another place) for a change of air.

tenchi heaven and earth; universe; sphere.

TENDE (always used with a negative) at all; altogether; **tende hanashi ni naranai** to leave no room for negotiation. **Tende yoku nai.** It is no good at all.

tengoku heaven, paradise.

tengu long-nosed goblin in Japanese mythology.

tenimotsu luggage, hand baggage; **tenimotsu toriatsukaijo** baggage room.

ten'in store clerk.

tenioha grammatical particles such as **wa, ga, o, ni,** etc.

tenisu See **teikyuu**.

tenji braille (dots).

tenjoo ceiling.

tenka entire country.

tenkai development, expansion; **tenkai suru** to develop, expand.

tenkan conversion; **tenkan suru** to convert, divert, turn.

tenkei model, specimen; **tenkeiteki Amerikajin** typical American.

tenken inspection; **tenken suru** to inspect.

TENKI, tenkoo weather; humor; **TENKI YOHOO** weather forecast. **Kyoo wa tenki ga warui.** The weather is bad today. He is ill-tempered today.

tenki turning point.

tenkin change of office; **-ni tenkin ni naru** to be transferred to.

tenko roll call.

tenkoo weather (see also **tenki**); **tenkoo fujun** unseasonable weather.

tenkoo turn, shift; **tenkoo suru** to turn.

tenkyo change of residence; **-ni tenkyo suru** to move to.

tenmatsu details (of an event).

tenmei providence, fate; **tenmei o shiru** to resign oneself to fate.

tenmon astronomy; **tenmondai** astronomical observatory; **tenmongakusha** astronomer.

tennen nature; **tennen no bi** natural beauty; **tennen gasu** natural gas.

tennentoo smallpox.

tennin transfer; change of post.

tennoo emperor; **Tennoo Heika** His Majesty the Emperor.

tennyo heavenly maiden.

TENOHIRA palm of the hand.

tenpen chii natural disaster (earthquake, flood, typhoon, etc.).

tenpin gift of heaven; innate nature; **tenpin o hakki suru** to bring all one's talents into play.

tenpuku downfall; **tenpuku suru** to turn over, capsize.

TENPURA, TEMPURA deep-fried fish, shrimps, and vegetables.

tenrankai exhibition.

tensai genius; natural gift. **Tensai hada no hito desu.** He is something of a genius.

tensai calamity.

tensai reproduction of something which was once published.

tensaku correction (of a composition, poem, etc.).

tensei nature; by nature. **Tensei shoojiki desu.** He is honest by nature.

tenseki suru to transfer one's legal domicile. (See also **tentaku**.)

tensen dotted line.

tensha transcription; **tensha suru** to copy, transcribe.

tenshi angel.

tenshin ranman naïvete; artlessness, innocence.

tensho letter of introduction.

tenshu shopkeeper, storekeeper.

tenshukaku castle tower.

tensoo transmission; forwarding; **yuubinbutso o Kyooto ni tensoo suru** to forward mail to Kyoto.

tensui oke rainwater tank.

tentai heavenly bodies.

tentaku, tenseki change of residence.

tentan unselfishness.

tentekomai o suru to be in a business boom.

tentoo overturning; fall; **ki ga tentoo suru** to lose one's presence of mind; **tentoo suru** to fall; to overturn.

tentoo shop; **tentoo ni dasu** to put something on sale.

tenugui Japanese towel; **tenugui kake** towel rack.

tenukari fault; oversight.

tenurui slow, dilatory.

tenzai suru to be dotted with.

teochi fault; slip; omission.

teoke wooden pail.

teokure ni naru to be too late.

teppen top, summit; **atama no teppen** crown (of the head).

teppitsu stylus (for handwritten mimeograph work).

tera Buddhist temple.

terasu to shine on, shed light on; to refer to; **jijitsu ni terashite** in the light of the facts.

TEREBI television.

terekkusu telex.

terikaesu to reflect.

terikomu to shine into.

teritsukeru to shine down upon.

tero terrorism.

TERU to shine; to be fine; **tette mo futte mo** rain or shine. (See also **terasu**.)

teryoori homemade dish.

tesage handbag.

tesaguri groping; **tesaguri de iku** to grope (in the dark).

TESAKI hand; finger; agent; follower; tool; **tesaki no kiyoo na** dexterous.

tesei handmade; homemade.

teshita follower; agent, vassal. (See also **tesaki**.)

tesoo line in the palm; **tesoo o miru** to read a palm.

tessaku iron railing.

tessuru to pierce, penetrate.

tesuri handrail.

tesuu trouble, care; **tesuu ga kakaru** to require care, be troublesome.

tesuuryoo fee, commission.

tetsu iron; **tetsubin** iron kettle.

TETSUDAI help, assistance; assistant, helper.

TETSUDAU to help, assist, lend a hand; **shigoto o tetsudau** to help (someone) with work.

TETSUDOO railway, railroad.

tetsugaku philosophy; **tetsugaku joo** philosophically.

tetsujoomoo wire entanglements; barbed-wire entanglements.

tetsuke(kin) advance (money), deposit; **tetsukekin o utsu** to pay a deposit.

tetsuya all night through; **tetsuya suru** to be up all night.

tetsuzuki process, formalities, proceedings; **tetsuzuki o suru** to take steps.

tettei suru to get to the bottom; to be thorough.

tetteiteki na thoroughgoing.

tettoo tetsubi thoroughly (from beginning to end).

tettoribayai quick; rough and ready.

tewake o suru to divide work.

tewatashi handing over personally.

tezaiku handiwork.

tezema narrowness; smallness. **Koko wa tezema de komarimasu.** We are cramped for space here.

tezukami ni suru to take with the fingers.

tezuru connection; **tezuru o motomeru** to hunt up a connection.

tezuyoi firm, resolute.

TO particle denoting: and; with; along with; if, when; as soon as. **Asoko wa haru ni naru to komimasu.** That place gets very crowded in spring. **Kyooto e Yamada-san to ikimashita.** I went to Kyoto with Mr. Yamada. **Tookyoo to Kyooto e ikimashita.** I went to Tokyo and Kyoto.

TO door.

tobaku gambling.

tobasu to let fly; to omit; to hurry; **kaze ni booshi o tobasu** to have one's hat blown off by the wind.

tobiagaru to fly up; to take wing, take flight; to jump to one's feet.

tobiaruku to run about.

tobidasu to fly out; to take wing; to run out.

tobidoogu firearm.

tobihi flying sparks; leap of flames; chicken pox.

tobiiri open contest.

tobikakaru to spring (leap, jump) upon.

tobikiri extra fine; best, choicest; **tobikiri jooto no shina** top-grade article.

tobikomu to jump (spring) into; to rush; **heya ni tobikomu** to burst into the room; **mizu ni tobikomu** to dive into water.

tobikosu to jump over, leap over.

tobimawaru to fly about; to jump about.

tobinoku to jump back; to spring aside.

tobiokiru to jump out of bed; to start up; to jump for.

tobioriru to jump down, leap down.

tobira leaf of a gate (or door); title page of a book.

tobisaru to fly away.

TOBI TOBI NI here and there; at intervals; at random, without order; **tobi tobi no** sporadic.

tobitsuku to fly at, spring at, leap at.

tobokeru to pretend ignorance.

toboshii to be scarce; to be short.

TOBU to fly; to jump, leap, bound.

tochi ground, land; **tochi no mono** native, villager.

TOCHUU on the way; halfway; **tochuu de yameru** to give up halfway; **tochuu gesha suru** to stop over (on a train trip).

todaeru to cease, stop, end; to drop.

TODANA cupboard, closet.

TODOKERU to report; to send. **Okome o todokete kudasai.** Please send me the rice.

todokoori hitch, hindrance; being in arrears; **todokoori naku** duly, regularly; smoothly.

todokooru to be in arrears; to be left undone; to be stagnant. **Shigoto ga takusan todokootte imasu.** There is a good deal of work left undone.

todoku to reach, get to; to attain; **me no todoku kagiri** so far as (anyone) can see; **omoi ga todoku** to realize one's objective.

todomaru to stop, halt, stand still.

todome finishing stroke, *coup de grace*.

todomeru to stop, cease, put an end to.

togameru to censure, to rebuke; to disapprove; **ki ga togameru** to feel uneasy.

togarasu to sharpen; to point; to pout; **enpitsu o togarasu** to sharpen a pencil.

togaru to be pointed, come to a point; **togatta hana** hawk nose.

toge splinter; thorn; **toge ga aru kotoba** stinging words; **yubi ni toge ga sasaru** to get a splinter in one's finger.

togeru to accomplish, achieve; to attain, gain, realize; to commit; **yakusoku o togeru** to fulfill one's promise.

togireru to break; to pause; to be interrupted.

togu to whet, grind, sharpen; **naifu o togu** to sharpen a knife.

toguchi doorway.

toho going on foot.

tohoo ni kureru to be bewildered.

toiawaseru to inquire, to refer. **Taishikan de toiawasete kudasai.** Please inquire at the Embassy.

toitsumeru to press for an answer.

tojikomeru to confine, shut in; **ame ni tojikomerareru** to be housebound by rain.

tojikomoru to confine oneself to; to shut oneself up.

tojimari o suru to lock a door.

TOJIRU to bind; to file; to sew up.

TOJIRU to shut, close.

tokai city, town; **tokaijin** city people, townsfolk.

tokaku (to be) apt to; in one way or other; **tokaku suru uchi ni** in the meantime. **Wakai mono wa tokaku keisotsu de aru.** Young people are apt to act hastily.

tokasu to melt, liquefy; to fuse; **koori o takasu** to melt ice; **satoo o mizu ni tokasu** to dissolve sugar in water.

tokeau to be melted together; to come to a mutual understanding.

TOKEI clock, watch; **oki dokei** clock; **ude dokei** wristwatch; **tokeiya** a watchmaker.

tokeru to melt; dissolve; **mizu ni tokeru** to be soluble in water; **netsu de tokeru** to melt by heat.

tokeru to get loose, come untied. **Musubime ga toketa.** The knot has come untied.

TOKI time; hour; moment; time when; **toki hazure no** out of season; **toki o eta** seasonable, timely. **Kyooto e itta toki kaimashita.** I bought it when I went to Kyoto.

TOKIDOKI now and then; occasionally. **Tokidoki aimashita.** I met him occasionally.

tokifuseru to persuade; to convince; to argue down; to prevail upon.

tokitsukeru to persuade, prevail upon.

tokka special prices; **tokka hanbai** sale at reduced prices.

tokken exclusive right or privilege.

tokki projection; **tokki suru** to project.

tokkoo special virtue, efficacy.

tukkumiau to grapple with each other.

tokku ni (adv.) a long time ago.

tokku no (adj.) a long time ago; **tokku no mukashi** long ago, ages ago.

tokkuri sake bottle.

tokkyuu special express (train).

TOKO alcove; floor; bed; bedding; **toko no ma** guest room alcove in a Japanese house where hanging scrolls, flower arrangements, etc., are displayed; **toko o shiku** to spread out bedding, make a bed; **toko ni tsuite iru** to be in bed; **tokokazari** alcove ornament.

tokoage to leave a sickbed.

tokoo voyage, passage; **-e tokoo suru** to make a voyage to; **tokoosha** passenger, emigrant.

TOKORO address, place; **tokoro o eru** to find a right place.

tokorode then, well, now.

TOKOROGA but, however, on the contrary.

tokoya barbershop, barber.

toku profit, gain; **toku na** profitable, advantageous; **toku o suru** to gain, profit, benefit.

toku virtue, morality.

toku to untie, undo, unbind; to melt; to fuse; to smelt.

TOKUBETSU NO special, particular, exceptional; **TOKUBETSU NI** specially.

tokuchoo characteristic.

tokudane exclusive news, scoop (newspaper).

tokuden special telegram.

tokugi morality; **tokugijoo** morally; from the moral point of view.

tokuhain special representative, special correspondent (of a newspaper).

tokui pride, self-complacency; one's forte; customer, patron.

tokumei anonymity; **tokumei de** anonymously.

TOKU NI especially. **Ashita wa toku ni hayaku kite kudasai.** Please come especially early tomorrow.

tokusaku better way, wiser way.

tokusan specialty of a locality.

tokusei special make; deluxe.

tokusetsu specially set up, specially organized.

tokushi benevolence, charity; **tokushika** charitable or self-sacrificing person.

tokushi special envoy.

tokushoku special feature, specialty.

tokushu na special.

tokuten score (sports).

tokuto carefully, attentively.

tokutokuto proudly; with a triumphant air.

tokutooseki special seat.

tokuyaku special contract.

tokuyuu no peculiar; characteristic.

tomadoi suru to be bewildered.

TOMARU to stop (at or in). **Itami wa tomarimashita.** The pain is gone. **Kono densha wa shinagawa de tomarimasu ka?** Does this train stop at Shinagawa Station?

tomaru to lodge; **hitoban tomaru** to stay overnight.

tomasu to enrich, make wealthy.

TOMATO tomato.

tomeru to stop, bring to stop; **gasu o tomeru** to turn off the gas; **kuruma o tomeru** to stop a car.

tomeru to give lodging (to a person), give shelter.

-TOMO of course; even though; **donna koto ga okoroo tomo** whatever may happen. **Ikimasu tomo.** Of course I will go.

tomo attendant; suite; **tomo ni** together with; including; **tomo o suru** to follow (someone). **Daika sooryoo tomo ni sen en desu.** The price is 1000 yen, including postage.

TOMODACHI friend. **Tomodachi ni ai ni ikimasu.** I am going to see a friend.

tomodaore common ruin.

tomokaku at all events, at any rate.

tomokasegi suru to work (both husband and wife) for a living.

tomonau to accompany, go with; **heigai ga tomonau** to be attended with evil.

tomosu to burn, light, turn on (a lamp).

tomu to grow rich. **Ano hito wa keiken ni tonde imasu.** He has great experience.

tomurai funeral, burial.

tomurau to mourn for the dead.

ton ton, tonnage.

tonaeru to recite; to repeat; to chant.

TONARI neighboring house; next-door neighbor; **tonari no** adjoining, next; **tonari atte iru** to be next door to each other; **tonari no hito** next-door neighbor.

tonbo dragonfly.

tonda surprising; extraordinary; shocking, terrible; unexpected; **tonda me ni au** to meet with a misfortune.

tondemonai surprising; extraordinary; unexpected; awful; abused; **tondemonai koto ni naru** to become serious; to take an unexpected turn.

TONIKAKU in any case.

tonjaku care, heed, regard; **jikan ni tonjaku naku** regardless of time.

tonkatsu pork cutlet.

tonkyoo ludicrousness; wild screech or act (to scare or make others laugh); **tonkyoo na** freakish.

tonneru tunnel.

tonogata men, gentlemen; **tonogata no** men's, gentlemen's.

tonto not at all, not in the least; entirely. **Ano hito wa ton to konai.** She does not come at all.

tonton byooshi without a hitch. **Koto ga tonton byooshi ni hakonde imasu.** Things are going along swimmingly.

ton'ya wholesale shop, wholesale dealer.

TOO ten, ten years old.

too political party; **Shakaitoo** Socialist Party.

too counter for cattle (denoting: head); **ushi hattoo** eight cows.

too rightness, propriety, justness; this; **too no honnin** person in question; **toogetsu** this month.

-too tower, pagoda.

-too suffix denoting: grade, class; **ittoo** first class.

tooa East Asia.

tooben answer; explanation; defense.

tooboe howling; **inu no tooboe** the howling of dogs; **tooboe suru** to howl.

tooboo flight, desertion; **tooboo suru** to run away; **tooboosha** a fugitive.

TOOBUN for the time being. **Toobun ame wa furanai deshoo.** It won't rain for a while.

toobun sugar content; **toobun o fukunda** sugary.

toochaku arrival; **toochaku jun ni** in order of arrival; **toochaku shidai** immediately on arrival; **toochaku suru** to arrive.

toochi this place, here.

toochoku being on duty; on watch.

toodai lighthouse.

toodori president, director.

tooen distant (blood) relation.

tooge mountain pass, defile; crisis; **Hakone no tooge** Hakone Pass; **tooge o kosu** to pass the critical stage.

toogi debate, discussion; **toogi suru** to discuss, debate.

toogoku imprisonment.

Tooguu Crown Prince.

toogyo rule, management.

tooha party, faction; school; clique.

tooha suru to traverse; to travel on foot; to tramp.

tooheki thievishness; kleptomania.

toohi escape, flight; **toohi suru** to escape, fly.

toohyoo voting; poll; **-ni toohyoo suru** to vote for; **toohyoo de kimeru** to decide by vote; **toohyoo ni iku** to go to the polls.

TOOI far, far away. **Tanaka-san no uchi wa koko kara tooi desu.** Mr. Tanaka's house is far from here.

tooin party member.

tooitsu unification, uniformity; **tooitsuteki** unifying.

tooji at that time; at this time.

toojiru See **toozuru.**

toojisha person concerned; **toojisha ni kakeau** to negotiate with the persons concerned.

toojitsu day in question; appointed day; day of issue (for a ticket, etc.).

toojoo suru to get on board a ship or plane.

toojoo stage entrance; **toojoo suru** to go on the stage.

TOOKA ten days; tenth day of the month.

tookan mailing, posting; **tegami o tookan suru** to mail a letter.

tookarazu before long, in the near future.

tookei statistics; **tookei o toru** to make a survey.

tooki registration; **tooki suru** to register.

tooki earthenware.

tookoo suru to contribute to a periodical.

tookoo suru to go to school.

tookoo suru to surrender.

tooku a distant place; **ki ga tooku naru** to faint, swoon.

tookyokusha authorities concerned.

tookyori equal distance.

tookyuu class, grade; **tookyuu o tsukeru** to grade.

toomawari detour; roundabout way; **toomawari o suru** to detour.

toomawashi na roundabout, indirect; **toomawashi ni** indirectly; in a roundabout way.

toome distant view; **toome ga kiku** to be able to see a long way off.

toomei na transparent.

toomen no present; urgent; immediate; **toomen no mondai** matter in hand.

toomichi long way, great distance.

toonan robbery, burglary.

tooni long ago; already.

toonin person in question.

toonoku to recede; to get away. **Ashi ga toonoku.** Her visits are becoming rarer.

toonori long ride, long drive; **toonori o suru** to take a long drive; **jitensha no toonori o suru** to go on a long cycling excursion.

toorai suru to come, arrive; to occur; to come to hand. **Kikai ga toorai shita.** An opportunity presented itself.

toorei returning a salute; returning a call.

TOORI road, street; traffic; **toori o yoku suru** to clear a passage; **toori ippen no** casual; indifferent.

-TOORI like, as; **watakushi no iu toori** as I say.

-toori kinds. **Iku toori mo aru.** There are many kinds.

toorigakari passing, chance; **toorigakari no hito** passersby.

toorikakaru to happen to pass (come by).

toorikosu to go beyond; to walk past; to pass.

toorinuke passing through.

tooroku registration; **tooroku suru** to register.

tooron debate, discussion; **tooron suru** to debate; **tooronkai** forum.

tooroo fixed stone lantern, dedicatory lantern.

TOORU to go along; to pass; to go by the name of; to be admissible; to get through; **shiken ni tooru** to pass an examination; **sujimichi ga tootte iru** to be consistent; to be logical. **Kono basu wa Ginza o toorimasu.** This bus goes through Ginza.

tooryuu suru to stay at.

toosa exploration; survey.

toosei management, control; regulation; **toosei suru** to bring under government control; to regulate, govern.

toosen winning a prize; success in a lottery; **toosen bangoo** winning numbers; **toosensha** successful candidate.

tooshaban mimeograph, duplicator.

tooshi investment; **-ni tooshi suru** to invest in; **tooshika** investor.

toosho contribution; **tooshoran** letters-to-the-editor column.

tooshu present master; head of a family.

toosoo escape.

TOOSU to let (someone) pass through; to admit; to carry; to realize; to make; to usher in; **me o toosu** to run over, glance over; **mon o toosu** to admit a person within the gates.

toosutaa toaster.

toosuto toast (bread).

TOOTEI by no means (used with a negative); after all. **Sonna koto wa tootei dekimasen.** I can't possibly do such a thing.

tootoi precious, valuable; high; noble; sacred, holy. **Tootoi ojikan o saite kudasaimashite arigatoo gozaimashita.** Thank you for spending your precious time on me.

TOOTOO at last, at length, finally. **Tootoo sono shigoto o shite shimaimashita.** I've finally finished that work.

tootoo to flowing in torrents; eloquently; **tootoo to nagareru** to flow majestically (as a river); **tootoo to noberu** to speak fluently.

toowaku suru to be perplexed, be puzzled; to be embarrassed; to be at a loss.

TOOYOO Orient; **Tooyoo no** *(adj.)* Oriental; **Tooyoojin** *(n.)* Oriental.

tooyoo appointment, promotion; **tooyoo suru** to appoint, promote.

tooyoo kanji (ideographic) characters included in the official list of 1850 (**Tooyoo Kanji Hyoo**) designated by the Japanese Government as the basic symbols in writing (replaced by **jooyoo kanji** in 1981).

tooza present time; current deposit; **tooza no kozukai** pocket money adequate for the present.

toozakaru to become more distant; to go away; **akuyuu kara toozakaru** to keep away from bad companions.

toozakeru to keep clear of, away from; to keep at a distance.

toozen matter of course; naturally.

toozoku thief, robber, burglar.

toozuru to throw; to throw away, throw off; to abandon; **ippyoo o toozuru** to cast a vote.

toppatsu outbreak; **toppatsuteki** unexpected, sudden.

toppi na extravagant, fantastic, venturesome.

toppuu gust of wind.

tora tiger.

toraeru to catch, seize, take hold of; **erikubi o toraeru** to seize (someone) by the neck.

torahoomu trachoma.

torai suru to come over the sea; to visit (a country).

TORAKKU truck; track field.

toranpu playing cards; **toranpu o suru** to play cards.

TORI bird, fowl; **TORINIKU** chicken meat, poultry.

toriaezu in haste; for the time being.

toriageru to take up, take in one's hand; **fuhei o toriageru** to listen to a complaint.

toriatsukai handling (of a thing); arrangement (of a business); treatment (of a guest). **Toriatsukai chuui.** Handle with care.

toriau to hold each other; to struggle for; to take notice of.

toriawase assortment; combination.

torichigaeru to mistake; to misunderstand; to misapprehend.

torie worth, merit, useful (strong) point; **torie no aru** useful, valuable, worthy; **torie no nai** worthless, good for nothing.

torihakarau to manage; to arrange; to dispose of; to settle; to deal with.

toriharau to remove, take away, clear away; to clear by taking (things) away.

torihazusu to remove; to take to pieces.

torihiki transaction, dealing; **torihiki o suru** to do business with; **torihiki o hajimeru** to open an account with; **torihikisaki** customer; business connection.

torii open front gate of a shrine, often painted red.

toriire harvest, crop; **toriire doki** harvesttime.

toriireru to take in; to harvest, gather in; to accept; to adopt.

toriisogi in a hurry; with dispatch.

torikaeru to change, exchange; to renew.

torikaeshi recovery, retrieval; **torikaeshi ga tsukanai** irrevocable.

torikaesu to get back; to regain, recover; to recall.

torikakaru to begin, commence; to set about.

torikawasu to exchange.

torikesu to cancel, revoke; **chuumon o torikesu** to cancel an order; **zenhanketsu o torikesu** to revoke a former decision.

torikimeru to arrange; to agree upon, settle, decide upon.

toriko captive, prisoner of war.

torikomu to take in; to bring over; to be in confusion; to get in favor with; **sentakumono o torikomu** to take in washing. **Kyoo wa sukoshi torikonde imasu.** This place is upset today.

torikoshiguroo unnecessary worry; **torikoshiguroo o suru** to run to meet trouble; to be overanxious.

torikowasu to pull down; to take down; to break down; to break up.

torikumu to wrestle with; to grapple with; to be matched against.

torimagireru to be in confusion; **zatsumu ni torimagireru** to be under the pressure of routine business.

torimaku to surround, hem in, encircle, enclose; to fawn upon.

torimatomeru to gather all together; to collect; to pack; **kazai doogu o torimatomeru** to collect one's household goods.

torimidasu to disturb; to lose one's composure. **Heya wa torimidashite atta.** The room was in disorder.

torimodosu to take back; to regain, recover; to resume.

torimotsu to treat; to receive; to entertain.

torinaosu to recover; to mend; to alter.

torinashi mediation, intercession.

torinasu to plead for; to mediate; to recommend.

torinigasu to fail to catch; **kikai o torinigasu** to miss an opportunity.

torinokeru to remove, take away; to clear away, get rid of.

toriotosu to let fall, slip, drop; to miss one's hold.

torishimari management, supervision, control; **torishimariyaku** manager, director.

torishimaru to manage, control, superintend, oversee.

torisoroeru to put together; to gather; to assort.

toritate no fresh (from); **toritate no momo** fresh peaches; **toritate no sakana** fish fresh from the sea.

toritateru to collect; to promote; to patronize; **kashikin o toritateru** to collect loans; **yakunin ni toritateru** to appoint (someone) to a post.

toritomeru to ascertain, make sure; to make definite; **inochi o toritomeru** to have a narrow escape.

toritsugi intermediation; receiving a thing and handing it to another; agency; agent; answering a knock (or bell); usher; **toritsugi o suru** to act as an agent, to transmit; to convey.

toritsuke run on a bank.

toritsukeru to fit; to furnish; to install; to draw out (of the bank); **kikai o toritsukeru** to set up an apparatus.

toritsuku to hold fast to, cling to; to catch hold of; **toritsuku shima mo nai** to be left helpless.

toritsukurou to mend, repair, patch; **teisai o toritsukurou** to keep up appearances.

toriya bird fancier; poultry dealer.

toriyoseru to get, obtain, procure.

tororo grated yam.

torotoro suru to doze; to take a nap.

TORU to take; to take in one's hand, take hold of; to get; to fetch; to hand; to pass; to receive; to gain; to accept; to adopt; to choose; to buy; to gather; to pick; to eat; to charge; to manage; to interpret; to take away; to catch; to deprive a person of; to possess; to take possession of; to need, require; to preserve; to engage; to subscribe to; to insist; **eiyoobutsu o toru** to take nourishing food; **fude o toru** to take a pen in hand; to write; **jikan o toru** to take time; **jimu o toru** to do business; **ichiban chiisai no o toru** to pick the smallest one; **kane o torareru** to have one's money stolen; **ki no mi o toru** to pick fruit from trees; **kusa o toru** to weed; **hyaku man en no gekkyuu o toru** to receive a salary of one million yen; **rishi o toru** to charge interest; **sakana o toru** to catch fish; **shashin o toru** to have a picture taken; **shibai no seki o totte oku** to reserve a seat at a theater; **shinbun o toru** to subscribe to a newspaper; **tsuyoi taido o toru** to assume a fair attitude toward; **wairo o toru** to accept a bribe; **waruku toru** to take amiss. **Heya o totte okimashita.** I have engaged a room for you. **Kare wa kataku totte ugokanai.** He tries to carry his point and won't yield. **Shio o totte kudasai.** Will you pass me the salt? **Yasai wa ano mise kara torimasu.** We buy vegetables from that store.

Toruko Turkey; **Torukogo** Turkish (language); **Torukojin** Turk.

toryoo paints.

TOSHI year; age; **toshi to tomo ni** with age; **toshi o mukaeru** to welcome the New Year; **toshi o okuru** to pass the years; **toshi o toru** to grow old; **toshigoro** marriageable age; **onaji toshigoro no** of about the same age; **toshigoro no musume** daughter of marriageable age; **toshishita** younger; junior; **toshiue** senior; older; **TOSHIYORI** old person. **Tanaka-san yori mittsu toshi shita desu.** He is three years younger than Mr. Tanaka. **Yamada-san yori mittsu toshi ue desu.** He is three years older than Mr. Yamada.

toshi towns and cities; **toshi keikaku** city planning.

toshikoshi New Year's Eve.

toshimawari luck attending one's age. **Kotoshi wa toshimawari ga warui.** This year is an unlucky one for me.

-to shite as; for; in the capacity of; **orei to shite** as a token of thanks; **soodai to shite shusseki suru** to attend as a representative.

tosho books; **tosho gakari** librarian; **toshokan** library; **tosho etsuranshitsu** reading room.

TOSSA NO AIDA NI in a moment; quick as thought; on the spur of the moment.

tosshin suru to rush; to dash; to charge.

totan zinc.

totan'ita galvanized iron sheets.

-totan ni just as; in the act of. **Watakushi ga hairu totan ni kare wa dete itta.** He went out just as I entered.

TOTEMO very, awfully; extraordinarily.

totonoeru to prepare, get ready; to arrange.

totonou to be prepared; to be arranged; to be in good order; to be ready, be settled.

TOTSUZEN suddenly, abruptly; all of a sudden; **totsuzen no** sudden, abrupt. **Totsuzen jishoku shimashita.** She resigned without giving notice.

totte handle; knob; **totte o tsukeru** to fix a handle.

tottei jetty, breakwater.

TOU to ask, question.

tozan mountain climbing.

tozetsu stoppage, cessation; interruption; **tozetsu suru** to be stopped; to be interrupted.

tsuba saliva; **tsuba o kakeru** to spit at.

tsubasa wings.

tsubo land measure of six **shaku** (Japanese feet) square. **Kono niwa wa sanbyaku tsubo arimasu.** This garden has an area of three hundred **tsubo.**

tsubo jar; **tsubo ni ireru** to pot (plant).

tsubomeru to make narrow; to pucker up; **kasa o tsubomeru** to shut an umbrella; **kuchi o tsubomeru** to pucker up the lips.

tsubomi flower bud.

tsubu grain; drop (of liquid).

tsubureru to be crushed; to be smashed, be broken; to break; **menboku ga tsubureru** to be put out of countenance. **Ginkoo ga tsubureta.** The bank failed.

tsubusu to crush; to smash, break; **shindai o tsubusu** to dissipate one's fortune; **jikan o tsubusu** to kill time.

tsubuyaku to mutter, grumble; to murmur.

TSUCHI ground, earth; mud; clay.

tsuchikusai rustic; boorish.

tsue cane, walking stick; **tsue o tomeru** to make a stopover; **tsue o tsuku** to walk with a walking stick.

tsugeguchi talebearing; **tsugeguchi suru** to carry tales.

tsugeru to tell; to inform; to bid; **itoma o tsugeru** to bid farewell.

TSUGI next, succeeding, adjacent; **tsugi no ma** next room. **Kono tsugi wa dare desu ka?** Who comes next to her?

tsugi patch; **tsugi o ateru** to patch.

tsugime joint; seam; **tsugime nashi no** seamless.

TSUGOO circumstances; **tsugoo ni yori** for certain reasons; **tsugoo yoku** fortunately; **tsugoo ga yoi** to be convenient; **tsugoo suru** to arrange; to manage.

tsugoo in all; together.

tsugu to pour out; to fill; **ocha o ippai tsugu** to pour a cup of tea.

tsugu to join, to piece together; **ki ni take o tsugu** to graft bamboo onto a tree; to be incongruous.

tsugu to rank next to, to be next to, to rank second to.

tsugu to succeed, to accede; to inherit.

TSUI unintentionally; by mistake.

tsui pair, couple.

tsuide order, sequence; **tsuide ni** by way of, incidentally, when, as; **tsuide no setsu** at your convenience.

tsuihoo banishment, exile.

tsuika supplement, appendix; **tsuika suru** to add, supplement.

tsuikyuu investigation; **tsuikyuu suru** to inquire closely into (a matter).

TSUINI at last, finally; at length.

tsuiraku crash; fall; **tsuiraku suru** to fall; to crash.

tsuiseki pursuit, chase; **tsuiseki suru** to pursue.

TSUITACHI first day of the month.

tsuitate screen.

TSUITE (always used following **ni**) of, about, concerning; **kono ten ni tsuite** on this point. **Kono mondai ni tsuite doo omoimasu ka?** What do you think about this?

tsuitoo mourning; **tsuitoo suru** to mourn (a death); **tsuitoo no kotoba** memorial address; eulogy.

tsuitotsu bumping into the rear; **tsuitotsu suru** to collide (from behind).

tsuiyasu to spend, expend, lay out; **mono o mueki ni tsuiyasu** to be wasteful.

tsujitsuma consistency; **tsujitsuma no awanu** inconsistent.

tsukaeru to be clogged, be obstructed, be blocked; to be barred; **kotoba ga tsukaeru** to stammer, to stick in one's throat; **mune ga tsukaeru** to feel heavy in the stomach. **Kuda ga tsukaete iru.** The pipe is choked.

tsukai message; errand; messenger.

tsukaihatasu to squander, spend all (one's money).

tsukaikata usage, application. **Kono kikai no tsukaikata ga wakarimasen.** I don't know how to use this machine.

tsukaikomu to embezzle.

tsukaimichi employment, use.

tsukainareru to be accustomed to using.

tsukaisugiru to use excessively; to spend too much.

tsukamaeru to catch; to seize; to take hold of.

tsukamaru to be caught, be taken; to be arrested.

tsukamaseru to let (someone) grasp; to bribe.

tsukamiai grappling, fighting (without a weapon).

tsukamu to seize, catch, grasp, hold.

tsukare weariness, fatigue.

TSUKARERU to get tired, grow weary, become fatigued.

tsukaru to soak in; to be soaked in, be steeped in; **kaisui ni tsukaru** to take a dip (in the sea).

tsukasadoru to rule, govern, administer; to take charge of.

TSUKAU to use, put to use, employ; to take; to spend; **atama o tsukau** to use one's brain; **yu o tsukau** to take a hot bath. **Ano hito wa rippa na Nihongo o tsukaimasu.** He speaks good Japanese.

tsukeiru to take advantage of (someone); to presume on (someone's) good nature; to impose on (someone's) kindness.

tsukekomu to enter; to take advantage of another's weakness.

tsukemono pickles; pickled vegetables.

tsukenerau to prowl, to dog, shadow; to hang about.

TSUKERU to attach one thing to another, to set one thing on another, to stick on, to sew on; to wear, to make an entry (in a book); **kata o tsukeru** to make an end (of something); **ki o tsukeru** to take care; **mikomi o tsukeru** to form a judgment; **kusuri o tsukeru** to apply a medicine; **na o tsukeru** to name; **pan ni bataa o tsukeru** to spread butter on bread; **te o tsukeru** to put one's hand to a task; to eat.

tsukeru to soak in, steep in.

TSUKI moon; month; **mikazuki** crescent; **tsuki ni nikai** twice a month; **tsuki no de** rising of the moon.

-tsuki suffix denoting: assigned to; attached to; per. **Hitori ni tsuki gosen en desu.** The charge is 5000 yen per person.

tsukiageru to thrust up; to push up; to toss.

tsukiai keeping company; association; intercourse; **tsukiai no tame ni** for the sake of friendship; **tsukiai nikui** to be difficult to get along with; **tsukiai o suru** to keep company with.

tsukiatari dead end (street); collision, crash.

tsukiau to keep company with, associate with.

tsukidasu to thrust out, stick out, push out, stretch out.

tsukihajime beginning of a month.

tsukihi days and months; time; years; date.

tsukikaesu to thrust back.

tsukimatou to follow, shadow (someone); to hang on; to pursue.

tsukimono accessory, adjunct, appendage; part; anything which is attached to or is an indispensable part of something.

tsukinami na commonplace; conventional.

tsukinuku to thrust through, pierce, penetrate.

tsukiokure no of the previous month; **tsukiokure no zasshi** back numbers of a magazine.

tsukiotosu to throw or push (someone) down or off.

tsukiru to become exhausted; to be used up, be consumed. **Okane ga tsukimashita.** I ran out of money.

tsukisoi attendant; nurse; chaperon.

tsukisou to attend (someone); to accompany.

tsukitaosu to knock down.

tsukitomeru to ascertain, make sure of; to assure, convince, satisfy oneself of.

tsukitoosu to thrust, pierce.

tsukitsukeru to thrust before; to put (place) under (someone's) nose; to point at.

tsukiyo moonlit night.

tsukizue end of a month.

tsukizuki no monthly; **tsukizuki no teate** monthly allowance.

tsukkakaru to fall on, pick a quarrel with (someone).

tsukkakeru to slip on.

tsukkiru to cross; to go (run) across; to go through.

tsukkomu to thrust in; to plunge in; to poke into.

TSUKU to arrive at. **Fune wa ima tsukimashita.** The ship has just arrived. **Koobe ni tsukimashita.** He arrived at Kobe.

tsuku to adhere to, to stick to. **Te ni penki ga tsuite iru.** There is paint on her hand.

tsuku to pierce, to thrust, to stab; **tantoo de tsuku** to stab (someone) with a dagger.

TSUKUE table, desk.

TSUKURU to make, manufacture; to prepare, produce; to turn out; to frame; to build, erect; to form; to raise; to cultivate; to constitute; **ie o tsukuru** to build a house; **kane o tsukuru** to make a fortune; **rajio o tsukuru** to make a radio; **retsu o tsukuru** to form in line.

tsukusu to exhaust; to come to the end of; to serve (someone); to make efforts.

tsukuzuku thoroughly, utterly, quite; **tsukuzuku iya ni naru** to become utterly disgusted; **tsukuzuku kangaeru** to reflect carefully.

TSUMA wife.

tsumadatsu to stand on tiptoe.

tsumahajiki ni suru to flick; to disdain; to shun; to scorn.

tsumamidasu to pick out, drag out, turn out.

tsumamu to pick, pinch, take a pinch of.

TSUMARANAI trifling, worthless, commonplace; **tsumaranai koto** matter of no importance; **tsumaranai mono** trifling thing.

TSUMARI in the end; in the long run; finally; in a word.

tsumaru to be blocked up; to be full, be packed; to be shortened; **hentoo ni tsumaru** to be at a loss for a reply; **kane ni tsumaru** to be pressed for money; **ki ga tsumaru** to be oppressive.

tsumashii frugal, thrifty, economical.

tsumazuku to take a false step; to lose one's footing, stumble, fall.

TSUME nail; claw; hoof; hook; **tsume o kiru** to cut one's nails.

tsumekakeru to crowd (a house); to throng to (the door).

tsumekiri constant attendance; staying at one's post without a break.

tsumekomu to cram; to stuff; to jam; to pack; **heya ni hito o tsumekomu** to crowd people into a room.

tsumemono o suru to stuff, pack.

tsumeru to cram; to stuff; to fill; to pack; to charge; **kaban ni tsumeru** to pack a suitcase.

TSUMETAI cold (to the touch), chilly; icy; **tsumetai kokoro** cold heart; **tsumetai mizu** cold water.

tsumi crime, offense; sin; fault; **tsumi na** sinful, cruel, inhuman.

tsumiageru to heap up, make a pile; to accumulate.

tsumidasu to send off, ship off.

tsumihoroboshi atonement of sins, expiation.

tsumikaeru to reship.

tsumikomu to load; to put on board; to take in.

tsumini cargo, freight.

tsumitateru to save up (money); to lay by; to reserve, amass, accumulate.

TSUMORI intention; motive, expectation;

understanding. **Haratta tsumori desu.** I believe I've paid for it. **Iku tsumori desu.** I intend to go.

tsumorigaki written estimate; written measurement.

tsumoru to accumulate; to be piled up; to amount to. **Tsumoru hanashi ni yo o fukashita.** We had much to talk about and sat up far into the night. **Yuki ga tsumoru.** Snow is piled up on the ground.

tsumu to pile up, heap up; to load; to accumulate; to take on board; to pick; to pluck; to pull out.

tsumujikaze whirlwind, tornado.

tsuna cord, rope, line. **Tanomi no tsuna mo kireta.** The last ray of hope is gone.

tsunagi connection, link.

tsunagu to tie, fasten, chain, connect, join.

tsunami tidal waves.

tsune usual state; **tsune no** usual, ordinary, common; **tsune ni** always.

tsuneru to pinch.

tsuno horn; **tsuno o hayasu** to become jealous.

tsunoru to solicit (a subscription); to collect; to grow violent, severe, intense, fierce; to become worse.

tsunzaku to rend, break; to pierce; to split.

tsupparu to stretch (an arm or leg against something); to plant one's feet on the ground.

TSURAI hard; painful; bitter; **tsuraku** bitterly, harshly.

tsuranaru to range; to lie in a row; to be present at. **Matsuda-san no kekkonshiki ni tsuranatta.** I attended Mr. Matsuda's wedding.

tsuranuku to pierce; to pass through.

tsurara icicle.

tsurasa pain, painfulness.

tsure companion.

tsureai (*colloq.*) spouse, husband, wife.

tsuredatsu to go along with.

TSURERU to take (with). **Tomodachi o tsurete ikimashita.** I took a friend of mine with me.

tsuresou to be married, be husband and wife.

tsuri change. **Gohyaku en no tsuri o moraimashita.** I received change of 500 yen.

tsuri fishing (with a hook and line). **Tsuri o shi ni ikimashita.** I went fishing.

tsuriai balance, equilibrium; harmony; **tsurial o toru** to balance oneself.

tsurusu to hang, suspend; to swing.

tsutaeru to convey; to report; to deliver; to communicate.

tsutawaru to be handed down; to be transmitted.

tsute intermediary; good offices; **tsute o motomeru** to hunt up connections.

tsutomaru to be fit for; to be equal to (a position).

TSUTOME duty; service; **tsutome o hatasu** to discharge one's duties; **tsutomeguchi** place of employment.

TSUTOMERU to serve, to hold (fill) a post; to exert oneself; to make an effort; to endeavor; to labor, work; **tsutomesaki** one's place of employment. **Takagi-san wa ginkoo ni tsutomete imasu.** Takagi works for a bank.

tsutsu pipe, tube; gun barrel; gun.

tsutsuku to poke at; to pick at, to peck.

tsutsumashii modest, reserved.

TSUTSUMI package, parcel; **tsutsumigami** wrapping paper, packing sheet.

tsutsumi dike, embankment.

TSUTSUMU to wrap, to do up, to pack.

tsutsushimi prudence, discretion, caution; **tsutsushimi no nai** immodest, indiscreet; **tsutsushimi o wasureru** to lose one's self-control.

tsutsushimu to be discreet; to be careful, be prudent; to restrain oneself.

tsuttatsu to stand; to stand up straight.

tsuu connoisseur, authority, expert judge.

-tsuu counter for letters, telegrams; **tegami o ittsuu dasu** to send a letter.

tsuuchi information; **tsuuchi suru** to inform.

tsuuchoo official communication, notification.

tsuufuu ventilation.

tsuugaku suru to go to school.

tsuuji bowel movement; **tsuuji ga tomaru** to become constipated; **tsuuji o tsukeru** to loosen the bowels.

tsuujiru to pass; to run; to be opened (to traffic); to be understood.

tsuujoo usually; ordinarily; as a rule.

tsuukai na extremely delightful; pleasant; **tsuukai na otoko** a man of spirit. **Sore wa tsuukai de atta.** It was a delightful sensation.

tsuukan passing through customs.

tsuukan suru to feel keenly, feel acutely.

tsuukin suru to go to the office.

tsuukoku announcement, notice, information; **tsuukoku suru** to notify.

tsuukoo passing; transit; **tsuukoodome no** thoroughfare; **tsuukoodome ni suru** to close a road; to stop traffic.

TSUUREI as a rule; commonly.

tsuusan sum total.

tsuusetsu na keen, acute.

tsuushin correspondence, communication; **tsuushinsha** news agency.

tsuushoo common name.

tsuutatsu notification; **tsuutatsu suru** to notify.

tsuuun transportation, moving van; **tsuuun gaisha** mover.

-TSUUWA counter denoting: phone call unit. **Ittsuuwa wa sanpun desu.** One telephone call unit is based on three minutes' conversation.

tsuuwaryoo charge for a telephone call.

tsuuyaku interpretation, interpreter; **tsuuyaku suru** to interpret.

tsuuyoomon public gate; side gate.

tsuuyoo suru to pass for; to circulate; to be current; to hold good.

tsuya gloss, luster.

TSUYOI strong, powerful, robust, healthy.

tsuyoki firmness; **tsuyoki o shimesu** to show firmness.

tsuyomeru to strengthen; to invigorate; to intensify; **imi o tsuyomeru** to emphasize.

tsuyomi strength, power; strong point.

tsuyosa strength, power.

tsuyu rainy season (June–July); **tsuyu no iri** start of the rainy season; **tsuyu no ake** end of the rainy season.

tsuyu, otsuyu soup, broth; gravy (Japanese style).

tsuyu dew, dewdrop. **Tsuyu ga oriru.** The dew falls.

TSUZUKERU to continue; to keep on.

tsuzuki continuation; connection; succession.

TSUZUKU to go on; to follow, go in succession; to last. **Ame wa mikka tsuzukimashita.** The rain continued to fall for three days.

tsuzuri spelling.

tsuzuru to spell words; to compose (a tune); **bun o tsuzuru** to write.

U

uba wet nurse.

ubaguruma baby carriage.

ubau to take by force, snatch; to rob (someone of something).

ubu naïveté; greenness.

UCHI house; home; inside, interior; **sono hi no uchi ni** in the course of that day; **uchi no koto** household matters; **uchi de asobu** to play indoors.

uchiageru to shoot up; to send up; to set off.

uchiakeru to disclose, reveal; to confide (a secret); **himitsu o uchiakeru** to give secret information; to disclose secrets.

uchiau to exchange blows.

uchiawase previous arrangement; consultation; **uchiawase o suru** to make arrangements for.

uchiawaseru to strike (one thing against another); to make arrangements for something.

uchidasu to begin to beat; to strike out; to close.

uchideshi apprentice; private pupil.

uchigawa inside.

uchikaesu to strike, beat, hit back, return a blow.

uchikesu to deny; to negate; to contradict.

uchiki retiring disposition; shyness.

uchikiru to close; to discontinue; **kooshoo o uchikiru** to drop negotiations.

uchikomu to drive in; to strike into; to shoot into; to fall deeply in love with; to be absorbed in; **kugi o uchikomu** to drive a nail into; **tama o uchikomu** to send bullets into.

uchimaku real state of things; inside facts; **uchimaku o abaku** to see behind the scenes.

uchiotosu to strike down, knock down, floor; to shoot down.

uchitaosu to knock down, strike down, overthrow.

uchitokeru to open one's heart; to be frank, to be candid.

uchitomeru, uchitoru to kill, slay, shoot dead.

uchiumi inland sea.

uchiwa family circle; private circle (of friends); **uchiwa dooshi** those who are of the same party (or family, etc.); member of the inner circle.

uchiwake item breakdown (of an account); details.

uchooten ni naru to be in ecstasy.

uchuu universe, cosmos; **uchuu hikooshi** astronaut; **uchuu kaihatsu** space development; **uchuusen** spacecraft.

UDE arm; ability; **ude o furuu** to exercise a talent; **ude o kasu** to lend a helping hand; **ude o tamesu** to test one's ability; **udekiki** able man; man of ability.

udon noodle; **udonko** wheat flour; **udonya** restaurant where Japanese noodles are the specialty.

UE upper part, surface, topside; top, summit, head; after, on, upon; **ichiban ue no** uppermost; **shiken no ue de** on examination; **ue ni tatsu hito** one who stands in authority over others; **ue no** higher; upper; superior.

ue hunger; starvation; **uejini** death by starvation.

uekaeru to transplant, replant; **hoka no hachi ni uekaeru** to transplant into another pot.

ueki plant; potted plant; **uekiya** gardener.

uekomi thicket, shrubbery.

ueru to plant.

ueru to become hungry; to starve; to be famished; to hunger for.

ueshita up and down; shirts and trousers; **ueshita ni naru** to be upside down; **ueshita ni suru** to turn upside down.

uetsuke planting; transplanting.

ugai gargling, rinsing the mouth; **ugai suru** to gargle; **ugaigusuri** a gargle.

ugatsu to dig; to cut through; to pierce; **ugatta koto o iu** to make a pointed remark.

UGOKASU to move; to shift; to remove, to set in motion; **chooshuu o ugokasu** to move an audience; **hito no kokoro o ugokasu** to touch the heart.

ugoki movement, motion.

UGOKU to move; to shift; to sway; to work; to be transferred to another position. **Ugoite wa ikemasen.** Don't move.

ugomeku to wriggle, squirm.

uisukii whiskey.

ukaberu to float, keep afloat.

ukabu to float; to come to the surface, appear. **Ii kangae ga ukanda.** I hit upon a good idea.

UKAGAU to pay a visit; to inquire *(humble)*. **Sono koto wa Yamada-san ni ukagaimashita.** I asked Mr. Yamada about it. **Yamada-san no otaku ni ukagaimashita.** I visited Yamada's house.

ukagau to watch for, to look for, to be on the lookout for; **hito no kaoiro o ukagau** to study a person's face; **kikai o ukagau** to look for a chance.

ukareru to make merry; to be gay.

ukasareru to be carried away, be captivated; **netsu ni ukasareru** to be delirious with fever.

ukatsu carelessness, thoughtlessness; stupidity.

uke reputation, popularity; acceptance, assent, consent. **Ano hito wa uke ga ii.** She has a good reputation.

ukedasu, ukemodosu to redeem, take (something) out of pawn.

ukekotae reply, answer; **ukekotae o suru** to reply, answer.

ukemi acting on the defensive; passive (in grammar).

ukemochi charge.

ukemodosu See **ukedasu**.

ukenagasu to ward off, turn aside; **shitsumon o takumi ni ukenagasu** to ignore a question diplomatically.

ukeoi contract for work.

ukeou to undertake; to take upon oneself; to assume.

UKERU to receive; to accept; to have, to obtain; to take; **hoomon o ukeru** to receive a visit; **shujutsu o ukeru** to have an operation (surgical). (See also **uketoru**.)

uketomeru to stop; to catch; to ward off; **tama o uketomeru** to catch a ball.

UKETORI receipt; acceptance; **uketorinin** receiver, recipient.

UKETORU (see **UKERU**) to receive; to accept. **Tegami o uketorimashita.** I received a letter.

uketsugi succession; inheritance.

UKETSUKE receiving; accepting; reception desk; **uketsuke gakari** receptionist.

ukewatashi delivery, transfer; **ukewatashi o suru** to deliver, transfer.

uki float, buoy.

ukiagaru to rise to the surface; to float.

ukiashi unsteadiness; wavering, faltering; **ukiashi ni naru** to waver, become unsteady.

ukibukuro air bladder (of a fish), life buoy, life belt.

UKKARI vacantly; carelessly; without attention.

uku to float; to come to the surface; to be left over; to be saved; **ki ga uku** to be gay, to be exhilarated.

UMA horse, mount; **umakata** driver of a pack horse; **umaya** horse stable.

UMAI good; nice; tasty; skillful; successful; profitable; **umai mono** delicious, dainty food.

umami deliciousness, flavor; **umami no aru hanashi** a nice speech.

umare birth, lineage; **umare no yoi** to be well-born, be high-born.

UMARERU to be born; **hinka ni umareru** to come from a poor family; **umareru to sugu** at birth.

umaretsuki by nature; by temperament.

umaru to be filled up; to be hurried.

umeawase amends, compensation; **sonshitsu no umeawase o suru** to make up for a loss.

umeki moan, groan.

umeku to groan, moan.

umeru to bury; to reclaim; to fill up.

umetate reclamation; filling up; **umetatechi** reclaimed land; **umetate kooji** reclamation work.

UMI sea; ocean; **hi no umi** vast sheet of fire; sea of fire; **umi de oyogu** to swim in the ocean; **umibe** beach, seashore.

umi pus; **umi o motsu** to form pus.

umi no haha one's natural mother.

umitate fresh (said of an egg).

UMU to bear, give birth to, be delivered of. **Anzuru yori umu ga yasui.** Fear often exaggerates danger.

umu existence, presence; yes or no; **umu o iwasezu** forcibly; whether one will or not. **Ayamari no umu o shirasete kudasai.** Let me know whether there is any mistake.

umu to form pus, fester.

un fortune, lot, destiny, fate; **un no warui** unlucky; **un no yoi** lucky.

un (*colloq.*) yes; hmm; well; groan.

unadareru to hang one's head.

unagasu to urge, press, demand, to call upon; to stimulate.

unari groan; roar; humming.

unaru to groan; to roar; to howl, to hum.

unasareru to have a nightmare, have bad dreams.

unazuku to nod, bow one's head in assent.

unchin freight; portage; shipping expenses.

undei no sa all the difference in the world.

UNDOO movement, motion; physical exercise; **undoo suru** to move; to exercise; to walk; to campaign; **undooka** athlete.

une furrow.

uneru to wind; to undulate; **nami ga uneru** to swell.

unga canal; **ungachitai** canal zone.

unmei destiny, fate, fortune; doom.

unomi ni suru to gulp down.

unpan transportation; **unpan suru** to transport.

unsoo carrying, transport; **unsoo suru** to carry, transport; **unsooya** mover, forwarding agent.

UNTEN operation; driving; working; **unten suru** to drive, operate, work; **untenshu** engineer (operator of an engine); chauffeur; motorman; **unten menkyo** driver's license.

unto (*colloq.*) with great force; with all one's might; soundly; liberally; **kane ga unto aru** to have lots of money; **unto osu** to push with all one's might.

unubore self-conceit; **unubore ga tsuyoi** to be full of conceit.

unuboreru to be vain; to be conceited, to think highly of oneself.

un'yu traffic; transport.

unzan operation, calculation; **unzan suru** to calculate.

unzari suru to be disgusted with.

UO fish; **uogashi** fish market.

uppun resentment, grudge, enmity.

URA reverse side; back, sole of the foot; lining of clothes; hidden meaning of an expression; second half of baseball inning.

uradana house in an alley.

uradoori back street.

uragaki endorsement; **uragaki suru** to endorse.

uragiri treachery, perfidy.

uragiru to betray, turn traitor, go over to the enemy.

uraguchi back entrance.

uraji lining; cloth for lining.

urameshii reproachful; resentful; hateful.

urami resentment; grudge; hatred; malice; **urami o idaku** to bear a grudge.

uramichi byway; back road.

uramon back gate.

uramu to bear a grudge; to feel bitter against; to think ill of.

uranai fortune-telling; fortune-teller.

uranau to divine, forecast; **minoue o uranau** to tell (someone's) fortune.

uraniwa backyard; rear garden.

urate rear of a building.

URAYAMASHII enviable. **Anata ga urayamashii desu.** I envy you.

urayamu to envy, be envious of, be jealous of; **hito no koofuku o urayamu** to envy a person his good luck.

urekko popular person; social lion; **bundan no urekko** popular writer.

urekuchi market.

ureshigaru to be glad; to take delight in; to feel happy.

URESHII glad, joyous, delighted, happy. **Ome ni kakarete ureshii desu.** I'm glad to be able to see you.

uriage proceeds (returns) of a sale.

URIBA sales counter.

uribagakari sales clerk.

uridame proceeds, cash in a money box.

uridashi bargain sale; opening sale.

uridasu to offer for sale, place on the market, put on sale.

urikire sold out.

uriko salespeople.

urimono for sale; **urimono ni dasu** to put up for sale.

URINE sale price.

urioshimi holding (hoarding) goods for future sale; **urioshimi o suru** to hoard goods for future sale.

urotaeru to be confused, be thrown into confusion; to be upset.

urotsuku to loiter, hang about; to wander about.

URU to sell; to deal in; to offer for sale. **Sore wa doko de utte imasu ka?** Where is it sold?

uru to gain; to get.

urumu to be wet; to be moist; to be blurred; to be dimmed.

uruoi moisture, damp; enrichment; grace, charm; **uruoi no aru** moist; profitable; tasteful.

uruosu to wet, moisten; to dip; to be moistened, be wet; to benefit (someone).

URUSAI annoying, tiresome, harassing, irksome; noisy. **Urusai!** Pipe down!

uruudoshi leap year.

uruwashii beautiful, pretty; fine; **gokigen uruwashiku** in good humor; in excellent health.

uryoo rainfall; **uryookei** rain gauge.

usagi rabbit.

usankusai suspicious-looking; uncanny.

USHI cattle; cow; bull; ox.

USHINAU to lose; to miss; to part with; to be deprived of.

USHIRO (*n.*) back, rear; (*adj.*) **ushiro no** back, hind, rear; **ushiroashi** hind legs; **ushiro ni** behind; **ushiro e mawaru** to get behind.

ushirogurai shady; not aboveboard; **ushirogurai koto** underhanded, shady transaction.

ushiromuki standing with the back toward another.

ushiroyubi o sasu to point a finger of scorn at; **ushiroyubi o sasareru** to be talked about as an object of scorn.

uso lie, falsehood; **makka na uso** a pack of lies; **uso no** no false; **uso o tsuku** to lie; **uso happyaku o naraberu** to tell all sorts of lies.

usugurai gloomy, dim, dusky, dark.

USUI thin; light; weak; **ninjoo no usui hito** coldhearted person.

usukimi warui dismal; weird, eerie.

usuppera na thin; flimsy; superficial.

usuragu to thin; to fade, grow pale; to be toned down; to become dim.

usurasamui chilly; rather cold.

UTA ode, poem; song; **uta o utau** to sing a song; **uta o yomu** to compose a poem.

utagai doubt; **utagai naku** beyond doubt; **utagai o harasu** to clear away suspicion; **utagai o idaku** to harbor suspicion; **utagai o toku** to clear up all doubts.

utagau to doubt; to be doubtful of. **Utagau yochi ga nai.** There is no room for doubt.

UTAU to sing, chant, carol; to recite; **hanauta o utau** to hum a song.

uten rainy weather; rainy day.

utouto suru to doze off, to slumber.

UTSU to strike, hit, beat; to fire, shoot; to drive in; to give a performance; to attack, assault; to send a telegram; **denpoo o utsu** to send a telegram; **fui o utsu** to make a sudden attack; **kugi o utsu** to drive in a nail; **pisutoru de utsu** to shoot with a revolver; **shibai o utsu** to give a play; to play a trick. **Tokei ga niji o utta.** The clock struck two.

utsubuse ni on one's face.

UTSUKUSHII beautiful, fair; **utsukushii hanashi** a beautiful story; **utsukushii keshiki** beautiful scenery.

utsumuku to look down; to stoop; **utsumuite aruku** to walk with one's head bent.

utsurigi caprice, whim; **utsurigi no** capricious, changeable.

utsuru to be reflected; to fall upon; to be becoming; to be taken; **kagami ni utsuru** to be reflected in a mirror; **shashin ni utsuru** to be photographed. **Ano kata ni wa ano kimono ga yoku utsuru.** That dress is very becoming to her.

utsuru to remove; to change, shift; to be infectious.

utsushi copy.

UTSUSU to remove; to transfer; to pour; to carry; to turn; to direct; **jimusho o utsusu** to move the office; **miruku o hoka no bin ni utsusu** to pour milk from one bottle into another.

utsusu to copy, to transcribe; to describe, to picture; to photograph; **sashin o uteusu** to have one's picture taken.

utsuwa vessel; caliber; **sono utsuwa de nai** to be by no means qualified.

uttae accusation, charge; lawsuit; complaint; petition; **uttae o kiku** to hear a case.

uttaeru to sue; to complain to; **hootei ni uttaeru** to take legal proceedings against someone; **risei ni uttaeru** to appeal to reason; **yoron ni uttaeru** to appeal to public opinion.

uttooshii depressing, oppressive, gloomy.

uwabe surface, exterior.

UWAGI upper or outer garment; coat; jacket.

uwagoto o iu to be delirious.

uwaki fickleness, inconstancy; flirtation; **uwaki na** fickle, flirtatious; **uwakimono** licentious man, wanton woman.

uwame upward glance.

uwamuki upward trend. **Sooba ga uwamuki de aru.** Prices show an upward trend.

uwamuku to look up, to turn one's face upward.

uwanosora absentmindedness; **uwanosora de kiku** to listen absently.

uwanuri final coating (of plaster or paint); **son no uwanuri o suru** to add to one's loss; to suffer loss upon loss.

uwasa rumor, report, talk; **uwasa o suru** to spread a rumor.

uwate better hand; **uwate ni deru** to get the upper hand.

uwayaku superior official.

uyamau to respect; to honor.

uyamuya ambiguity; vagueness; **uyamuya ni suru** to obscure an issue; **uyamuya ni hoomuru** to suppress a matter.

uyauyashiku respectfully.

uyoku right wing; right field (in baseball).

uyo kyokusetsu much meandering; **uyo kyokusetsu o hete** after aimless wandering.

uzoo muzoo rabble; all sorts and conditions of men.

uzukumaru to crouch, squat down.

uzumaki eddy, whirlpool.

uzumaku to whirl, swirl; to flow in whirls; to curl.

uzumaru to be filled up; to be buried.

uzumeru to bury.

uzumoreru to be covered with; to live in obscurity.

W

WA particle denoting: sentence topic: = as for. **Doitsugo wa benkyoo shimashita.** [As far as German is concerned] I studied German. **Kinoo wa ikimashita.** I went yesterday (but not today). **Watakushi wa ikimasen.** As for me, I'm not going.

wa circle; ring; wheel; **wa ni wa o kakeru** to exaggerate.

waapuro word processor.

wabiru to apologize for; to make an excuse; to beg pardon.

wabishii miserable, poor, wretched; **wabishii kurashi o suru** to lead a lonely life.

wabun text in Japanese; **wabun eiyaku** translating into English from Japanese; **wabun denpoo** telegram in Japanese.

wadachi rut, wheel track.

wadai topic, subject; **wadai ni noboru** to be talked about.

wadakamari ill feeling; reserve; **wadakamari ga aru** to be vexed at something.

wadakamaru to be coiled up (as a snake); to be rooted; to be harbored.

Wa-Ei jisho, Wa-Ei jiten Japanese-English dictionary.

wafuku Japanese clothes; kimono.

wagamama willfulness; waywardness; **wagamama na** willful, wayward; **wagamama o suru** to have one's own way; **wagamamamono** self-willed person.

wagoo suru to harmonize with; to agree with each other.

wairo bribery, bribe; **wairo o tsukau** to bribe, corrupt; **wairo o toru** to be bribed, to take a bribe.

waishatsu man's dress shirt.

waiwai noisily, clamorously.

waka, tanka Japanese verse of 31 syllables; Japanese verse.

wakagaeri rejuvenation.

wakage youthful spirit.

WAKAI young, youthful; **wakai hito** young person; **wakakatta toki** when she was young; **wakamono** young man.

wakai suru to make up, settle amicably; to accommodate with.

wakarazuya blockhead; incorrigible person.

WAKARE farewell, parting; division; branch; **wakare no sakazuki** a parting cup; **wakare o oshimu** to be reluctant to part; **wakare o tsugeru** to say good-bye.

WAKARERU to branch off, split, part; to break up, be divided; to get separated; **eikyuu ni wakareru** to part forever.

wakari understanding; **wakari no yoi** intelligent, sensible; **wakari no warui** slow to understand.

wakarikitta well-known; obvious.

WAKARU to understand, realize, comprehend; **wakari nikui** hard to understand.

wakasu to boil; to heat; **cha o wakasu** to make tea; **yu o wakasu** to boil water.

WAKE reason; ground; meaning; circumstance; **wake no wakaranai hanashi** a strange story; senseless talk; **wake no wakatta hito** a person amenable to reason; **wake o tazuneru** to ask the reason. **Sore wa doo iu wake desu ka.** What do you mean by that?

wakehedate partiality, favoritism; **wakehedate no nai** impartial, fair; **wakehedate o suru** to be partial, to discriminate.

wakemae share, portion.

wakeme dividing line, decisive event.

WAKERU to divide, separate; to distribute; to distinguish; **itsutsu ni wakeru** to divide into five parts. **Tochi o kodomo ni wakemashita.** He divided his estate among his children.

waki side; other way; supporting role; **waki no** other, another; side, lateral; **waki ni yoru** to step aside; **waki e oku** to lay aside; **waki o tsutomeru** to support the leading actor (in a No play).

wakimae discernment, discrimination; judgment; understanding; **wakimae no nai** thoughtless, indiscreet.

wakime sidelong glance; **wakime mo furazu** without looking aside, devoting oneself entirely to.

wakimi o suru to look aside; to look off.

WAKU to boil. **Furo ga wakimashita.** The

bath is ready. **Yu ga waite imasu.** The water is boiling.

waku to gush out; to spring; to grow.

waku frame, embroidery frame.

wameku to cry; to scream, yell, shriek.

wan bay; inlet; gulf.

wanpaku kozoo spoiled child; naughty boy.

wanpaku na willful; naughty.

wanryoku physical strength.

warai laughter; smile; ridicule; **waraigao** smiling face; smile; **waraigusa** laughingstock, butt of ridicule; **warai joogo** ticklish person.

waraji straw sandals; **waraji o haku** to put on straw sandals; to fly from (official) pursuit; **waraji o nugu** to take off straw sandals; to settle down.

WARAU to laugh; to smile; to chuckle; to deride, jeer.

wareme crack, crevice, fissure.

wari rate, proportion, percentage; 10%; **wari no yoi** profitable; **wari ni** comparatively; **nen ichiwari no risoku** interest of 10 percent annually.

wariai rate, proportion; **wariai ni** comparatively.

waribiki discount, price reduction; **waribiki suru** to allow a discount.

waridasu to calculate, compute; to deduce from, conclude from.

warikireru to be divisible. **Sanjuuku wa juusan de warikireru.** Thirty-nine can be divided by 13.

WARU to split; to crush; to divide; to get lower than; to dilute; to open one's heart; to cut; to halve; to cleave; to rend; **juuni o roku de waru** to divide 12 by 6; **maki o waru** to split wood for fuel. **Kono sake wa mizu de watte aru.** This sake is mixed with water.

warubireru to act timidly; to fear; **warubirezu** with good grace; without fear.

warudakumi evil design, machination; **warudakumi o suru** to conspire.

warugashikoi cunning, artful.

warugi ill will; **warugi no nai** without malice; **warugi no nai hito** good-natured person. **Watashi wa warugi de shita no de wa arimasen.** I meant no offense at all.

WARUI bad, ill, evil; unlucky; wormy, rotten; wrong; defective; detrimental, slanderous; **waruku natta tabemono** spoiled food; **warui koto o suru** to do wrong; to commit a sin, commit a crime; **karada ni warui** to be injurious to the health; **waruku suru** to make a thing worse; **waruku suru to** if things go wrong; **waruku toru** to take amiss. **Ano hito wa me ga warui.** He has poor eyesight.

warujie (n.) craftiness, cunning; **warujie no aru** (adj.) cunning; **hito ni warujie o tsukeru** to put a person up to mischief.

warukuchi abuse, abusive language; **kage de warukuchi o iu** to backbite; **warukuchi o iu** to speak ill of.

warumono bad fellow; rogue.

warusa mischief; trick.

wasei of Japanese make.

wasen Japanese rowboat.

washizukami grasping, clutching; **washizukami ni suru** to grasp, clutch.

wasuregachi na forgetful.

wasuremono thing left behind; **wasuremono o suru** to leave (something) behind.

wasureppoi to have a poor memory.

WASURERU to forget; to lose sight of; to leave behind; **shinshoku o wasureru** to forget sleep and food, be devoted to.

WATA cotton; cotton wool; **wata ire** padded clothes; **wata no ki** a cotton plant; **wata no yoo ni tsukareru** to get dog tired.

WATAKUSHI I; secrecy; privacy; **watakushi no** my; private; personal; **watakushi no nai** disinterested, unselfish; **watakushitachi** we.

watari passing; crossing; **watari ni fune** timely help/offer; **watari o tsukeru** to pave the way; to establish some connection.

watariau to cross swords with; to quarrel with.

wataru to go over; to go; **Chuugoku kara Nippon ni wataru** to come from China to Japan; **hashi o wataru** to cross a bridge; **umi o wataru** to sail across the sea.

WATASHI I (more informal than **WATAKUSHI**).

watashi ferry; place where passengers take a ferryboat; **watashibune** ferryboat.

WATASU to pass (a person) over; to carry across; to take over; to ferry over; to hand deliver; to transfer; to make over; to pay; **kyuuryoo o watasu** to pay wages; **mukoogawa ni watasu** to take over to the other side (of the river).

watto with a sudden outcry; **watto nakidasu** to burst into tears.

wayaku suru to translate into Japanese.

waza to purposely, on purpose; **wazatorashii** artificial, unnatural; studied; **wazatorashiku** artificially.

wazawai misfortune, adversity, calamity.

WAZAWAZA intentionally, on purpose; **wazawaza iku** to take the trouble to go.

WAZUKA NA small (quantity); few (in number); slight.

wazurawashii vexatious, troublesome; wearisome; **yononaka ga wazurawashii** to be weary of life.

wazurawasu to trouble; to keep a person busy; to exercise; to cause inconvenience.

Y

-YA particle denoting: and (used when a list is incomplete); or; as soon as; **are ya kore ya de** with one thing or another; **tori ya kemono** birds and beasts; **Tookyoo ni tsuku ya** as soon as I got to Tokyo.

-ya suffix denoting: store, dealer; **sakanaya** fish market; fishmonger.

yaa oh; hallo.

yaado yard.

yabo boorishness; want of taste; **yabo na** uncouth, vulgar, unrefined; senseless; rusty; **yabo na otoko** boor, silly fellow.

yabuisha quack doctor.

yabun evening, nighttime. **Yabun ni demashite osoreirimasu.** I must apologize for calling on you so late at night.

yabunirami squint; cross-eye; **yabunirami no** cross-eyed.

yabure rupture, breach; rent, tear; **kimono no yabure** tear in a garment; **yabure kabure** desperation, self-abandonment.

yabureru to be torn, be rent; to be broken; to be beaten; to fail in one's design. **Kare no keikaku wa yabureta.** His attempt had failed. **Kimono ga yaburete iru.** The clothes are torn.

YABURU to tear, rend; to break, destroy, crush; **heiwa o yaburu** to disturb the peace; **kami o yaburu** to tear a sheet of paper.

yachin house rent; **yachin no todokoori** rent arrears. **Yachin ga agarimashita.** The rent has been raised.

yado, yadoya hotel, inn, lodging; **ichiya no yado o kasu** to give a night's lodging; **yado o kou** to ask for lodging; **yado o toru** to stay at an inn for the night.

yadonashi homelessness; homeless person, vagrant.

yadoya, yado inn, hotel; **yadoya ni tomaru** to stay at an inn; **yadoya no hiyoo** hotel expenses.

yagai field; **yagai undoo** outdoor exercise; **yagai no** open air, outdoors.

yagaku night study; evening school; **yagakkoo** night school.

yagate presently, soon; before long.

yagoo shop name; firm name.

yagu bedclothes, bedding.

yagura tower, turret; **hinomiyagura** fire tower.

yagyoo night work; **yagyoo teate** overtime (for night work); **yagyoo o suru** to work at night.

YAHARI too, also; as well; still; all the same; after all. **Demo yahari yamemashoo.** I won't do it, notwithstanding your persuasion. **Yahari dame desu.** That won't do, either.

yaiyai hey!; hard; pressingly; **yaiyai itte saisoku suru** to press (someone) for.

yaji heckling; cheering; rooting.

yajiru to cheer; to support; to disturb; to heckle; to interrupt; to obstruct. **Benshi o yajiritaoshita.** The speaker was hissed down.

yajiuma mob, busybodies, bystander.

yakai evening party; ball; **yakai o moyoosu** to give a party.

YAKAMASHII noisy, uproarious; rigorous, strict. **Ano heya wa taihen yakamashii desu.** That room is very noisy.

yakan night, nighttime.

yakan kettle.

yake despair, desperation.

yakeato ruins left after a fire.

yakedo scald, burn.

yakei night view; **Koobe no yakei** the view by night of Kobe.

yakei night watch.

YAKERU to burn; to be burned; to be destroyed; to be roasted; to be broiled; to be scorched; **hi ni yaketa kao** sunburned face; **yakeru yoo na atsusa** burning heat of day; **mune ga yakeru** to have heartburn.

yakeshinu to perish by fire.

yaketsuku to scorch, burn; **yaketsuku yoo na taiyoo** burning sun.

yaki baking, roasting; firing of porcelain; tempering of a sword. **Kono tooki wa yaki ga ii desu.** This porcelain is well fired.

yakimashi further copies (prints) of a photograph.

yakimochi toasted *mochi* (rice cake); jealousy; **yakimochi yaki** jealous person; **yakimochi o yaku** to be jealous.

yakimoki suru to be impatient; to be nervous.

yakimono ceramic ware, pottery; broiled, baked, or roasted dish.

yakin night duty, night work; **yakin o suru** to be on night duty.

yakinaoshi warming (of cooked food); literary rehash, adaptation; **yakinaoshi suru** to adapt from, to rehash. **Kore wa furui Nihon no shoosetsu no yakinaoshi desu.** This is an adaptation from an old Japanese story.

yakinaosu to bake for the second time; to roast again; to imitate.

yakiniku roast meat.

yakitori roast fowl.

yakizakana broiled fish.

yakkai trouble; support; dependence; **yakkai o kakeru** to give trouble; to be under the care of; to be welcomed by; **yakkai na** troublesome, difficult, annoying; **yakkaimono** burden, drag, nuisance. **Yakkaibarai.** Good riddance to bad rubbish.

yakki to naru to get warm; to become excited.

YAKKYOKU pharmacy; dispensary.

yakoo ressha night train.

YAKU to burn; to set something on fire; to broil; to roast; **imo o yaku** to bake potatoes; **niku o yaku** to roast meat; **sakana o yaku** to broil fish; **sumi o yaku** to make charcoal; **te o yaku** to burn one's fingers or hand; to be at a loss.

YAKU translation, version; **yakusha** translator; **yakusu, yaku suru** to translate.

YAKU about, approximately.

yaku office; duty; part in a drama; **yakuba** public office; **yakume** duty; business; mission; **yakume o hatasu** to discharge one's duties; **yakunin** government official; **yakusha** actor, actress; **yakusho** public office; **yaku ni tatsu** to be of use; **yaku o tsutomeru** to play the part of.

yakuhin drugs, chemicals.

yakusoku promise; engagement; appointment; **yakusoku suru** to promise.

yakyuu baseball; **yakyuu o suru** to play baseball.

YAMA mountain; hill; mine; crown (of a hat); pile; speculation; climax (of a drama); **yama no yoo na** mountainous; **yamakuzure** landslide; **yamamichi** mountain road; **yamanobori** mountain climbing; **yamabiraki** the opening of a mountain to pilgrims or climbers for the year; **yamadera** temple in the mountains; **yamaguni** mountainous country. **Koko ga kono shoosetsu no yama desu.** Here is the climax of this novel. **Yama ga atatta.** The speculation has turned out well.

yamadashi bumpkin, rustic.

yamai illness; **yamai ni kakaru** to become ill.

yamakaji forest fire.

yamamori heap; heaping up anything in measuring; heaping full; **yamamori ni suru** to heap up; to fill to overflowing.

yamashii to feel ashamed; to have qualms of conscience.

yamawake ni suru to divide equally into two parts.

yame end, conclusion, finish; abolition, stop, discontinuance; **yame ni suru** to be discontinued.

YAMERU to stop; to break; to give up, abandon; to resign; to discontinue; **gakkoo o yameru** to leave school; **hanashi o yameru** to cease talking; **shoku o yameru** to retire from office; **torihiki o yameru** to close an account.

yamiagari convalescence; **yamiagari no** convalescent.

yamitsuki infatuation; feeling ill; **yamitsuki ni naru** (colloq.) to develop into a passion; to be wholly given up to.

yamitsuku (colloq.) to be taken ill; to be wholly given up to; to run madly after.

yamiyo dark night.

yamome widow.

YAMU to stop, cease, abate; to clamp down; to drop down; **yamu o enai** unavoidable; necessary; **yamu o ezu** unavoidably. **Ame ga yamimashita.** The rain has stopped.

yanami row of houses.

yane roof; **yaneura** attic.

yanushi owner of a house; landlord.

yanwari softly; gently.

YAOYA fruit and vegetable market; greengrocer.

-YARA and so on; and the like; **nani yara ka yara de** with one thing or other.

yariba disposal place; **yariba ga nai** to be at a loss as to where to put (something); **yariba ni komaru** to be at a loss as to what to do with (something).

yaridasu to begin to do.

yarikake half-done, half-finished.

yarikakeru to begin; to set about; to proceed to make.

yarikaneru to hesitate to do. **Ano hito wa donna koto demo yarikanenai otoko da.** He is up to all sorts of things. He will go to any extreme.

yarikata manner of doing; **yarikata ga ii** to go about one's task in the right way. **Sore wa yarikata shidai desu.** It depends on how you do it.

yarikomeru to silence; to snub; to put down; to argue down.

yarikuchi manner of acting; policy. **Yarikuchi ga shaku da.** I am displeased with his way of doing things.

yarikuri to make shift; **yarikuri o suru** to live by one's wits.

yarinaosu to do over again; to try again; to start over again; to resume.

yarippanashi ni suru to neglect; to leave in disorder.

yarisokonai failure.

yarisugiru to overdo; to go too far; to do too much.

yarisugosu to go past.

yaritogeru to accomplish, perform, achieve; to finish.

yaritori exchange; **yaritori suru** to exchange.

YARU to give, present (something to someone in one's in group). **Inu ni mizu o yatta.** I gave water to the dog.

yaru to do, to undertake.

YASAI vegetables.

YASASHII gentle, tender; easy, simple; **yasashii mondai** easy question; **yasashii kotoba o kakeru** to speak kindly (words) to (someone).

yasegaman suru to endure (anything) because of pride.

yasei wildness; **yasei suru** to grow wild (without being cultivated).

YASERU to become lean (thin); to lose freshness.

yashiki mansion; premises; grounds; home site.

yashin ambition, aspiration; schemes; **yashin manman** highly ambitious; **yashin o idaku** to be ambitious; **yashinka** ambitious person.

yashinai nutrition; bringing up; **karada no yashinai ni naru** to be nutritious.

yashinau to bring up; to support; to subsist; to maintain; to feed.

yashinaioya foster father; foster mother.

yashiro, oyashiro Shinto shrine.

yasuagari (*n.*) inexpensiveness, cheapness, economy.

yasubushin flimsily constructed building.

YASUI cheap, inexpensive; **yasui hon** cheap book; **yasumono** low priced (cheaply made) article. **Bukka ga yasuku narimashita.** Prices have come down. **Yasumonokai no zeni ushinai.** Penny wise and pound foolish.

-YASUI suffix denoting: easy to, simple to; **kowareyasui** to be easy to break; **yomiyasui** to be easy to read.

yasumaru to be rested; to feel at rest; **karada no yasumaru toki ga nai** to be too busy to relax for a moment.

yasumeru to rest (oneself); to give rest; to ease; **karada o yasumeru** to rest from work; **ki o yasumeru** to set (one's mind) at ease.

YASUMI rest; recess; holiday; vacation: **natsuyasumi** summer vacation.

YASUMU to rest; to go to bed; to take a vacation; **gakkoo o yasumu** to be absent from school; **yoru hayaku yasumu** to go to bed early in the evening.

yasuppoi cheap, flashy; mean; **yasuppoku mieru** to look cheap.

yasuraka na peaceful, calm; **yasuraka ni** peacefully, at rest.

yasuri file, rasp; **yasuri o kakeru** to file.

yasuukeai ready promise; irresponsible promise; **yasuukeai o suru** to promise readily; to promise without due consideration.

yasuuri bargain sale; **yasuuri o suru** to sell at a bargain price.

yasuyado lodging house; cheap inn.

yasuyasu easily, with ease.

yatai float (in a festival); one's fortune; **yatai mise** open-air stall (or booth).

yatara na careless; indiscriminate.

YATOI employment; employee; **yatoi gaikokujin** foreign employees; **yatoiire** employment, hire; **yatoinin** employee; servant; **yatoinushi** employer.

yatou to engage, employ, hire.

yatsuatari ni indiscriminately, recklessly.

yatsugibaya ni in rapid succession.

yatsureru to get thin; to be worn out, to waste away; **miru kage mo naku yatsurete iru** to be a mere shadow of one's former self.

yatte miru to try, attempt.

YATTO at last; with difficulty; **yatto kurashite iku** to have great difficulty making both ends meet. **Yatto kippu ga kaeta.** I could buy a ticket only with difficulty.

yattoko pincers; nippers; wrench.

YATTSU, HACHI eight. (See also **yooka, hachigatsu.**)

yattsukeru to attack.

yawarageru to soften, lessen, lighten; to moderate; to relax; **koe o yawarageru** to speak softly; **kotoba o yawarageru** to speak gently (with soft words).

yawaragu to soften; to be softened; to become mild, become moderate. **Arashi ga yawaragimashita.** The storm has abated.

YAWARAKAI soft, gentle, tender, mild; **yawarakai niku** tender meat.

yaya to some degree, somewhat. **Yaya shina ga ochiru.** It is somewhat inferior in quality.

YAYAKOSHII difficult, complicated, intricate. **Yayakoshii hanashi desu.** It is a complicated story.

yayamo sureba to be apt to, be liable to.

YO night; **yo o akasu** to pass a night without sleep. **Yo ga akeru.** The day is breaking.

YO world, age, times; **yo ni deru** to see the light, to rise in the world; **yo o itou** to be weary of life; **yo o saru** to depart this life, to die.

-yo above, over; more; **san mairu yo** over three miles; three miles plus.

yoakashi sitting up all night.

YOAKE dawn, daybreak; **yoake ni** at dawn, at daybreak.

yobawari calling (someone) by name; **doroboo yobawari suru** to brand as a thief.

yobi reserve; preparation; **yobi no** reserve, spare; **yobihin** spare store, reserve supply; **yobikin** reserve fund, emergency fund.

yobiageru to call out, call up; **namae o yobiageru** to call out (someone's) name.

yobiatsumeru to call together, assemble, summon.

yobidashi subpoena; calling out; summoning.

yobidasu to call out; to call up.

yobigoe cry; cry of street hucksters.

yobiireru to call (someone) in; to hail (someone) into.

yobikakeru to call (out) to; to speak to, address.

yobiko whistle; birdcall; **yobikobue** (police) whistle.

yobikomu to call a person in.

yobimono chief attraction; feature attraction; **kyoogi chuu no yobimono** feature attraction of the tournament.

yobiokosu to wake, rouse; to call; **kioku o yobiokosu** to call to mind.

yobirin (call) bell; buzzer.

yobitateru to call out; to call to; to ask to come.

yobitomeru to call and stop; to call to (someone) to stop; to call (someone) back.

yobiuri hawking.

yobiyoseru to call, summon, send for; to call together, assemble.

yoboo prevention, precaution; **yoboo chuusha** preventive injection, inoculation; **yoboo suru** to prevent; to keep as a precaution against.

yoboyobo tottering.

YOBU to call; to call out to; to call after; to send for; to invite; **isha o yobu** to send for a doctor.

yobun (n.) surplus, extra; **yobun no** (adj.) surplus, extra, remaining.

yobyoo complication.

yochi foresight; **yochi suru** to know beforehand.

yochi room, space.

yodan digression; **yodan ni wataru** to digress; **yodan wa shibaraku oki** to return to the main subject.

yodare saliva; **yodare o tarasu** to slobber.

yodooshi all night, all night through.

yofukashi o suru to keep late hours; to sit up late at night.

yofuke late hours; **yofuke ni** late at night.

yogen prediction, prophecy; **yogen suru** to foretell, predict.

yogi bedcover.

yogi nai unavoidable.

yogisha night train.

yogore dirt, filth, soil; **yogoreme** visible stain.

yogoreru to become dirty, become filthy; to be stained; **yogoreppoi** easily soiled; liable to be soiled.

YOGOSU to make unclean; to stain; to soil, foul.

yoha aftermath; tail end; **taifuu no yoha** the end of a typhoon.

yohaku space; margin.

YOHODO to a great degree; very greatly; for a good while; **yohodo mae** quite a while ago; **yohodo no** large number of, great deal of.

yohoo forecast, prediction; **tenki yohoo** weather forecast; **yohoo suru** to forecast, predict.

YOI, II good, right, fine; **yoi kangae** a good idea. **Sore de yoi.** That will do. **Itte yoi.** You may go.

yoi evening; **yoi no kuchi ni** in the early evening; **yoi no myoojoo** evening star; Venus.

yoi intoxication; **yoi ga deru** to become intoxicated; **yoi ga mawaru** to get tipsy; **yoi ga sameru** to sober up; **yoidore** drunkard; **yoidore ni naru** to be drunk.

yoigoshi overnight.

yoin trailing note, reverberation; agreeable aftertaste, suggestion; **yoin no aru** trailing; suggestive; pregnant.

yoippari sitting (staying) up very late; **yoippari no asaneboo** late to bed and late to rise.

yoizame sobering up.

yojireru to be twisted, be contorted.

yojiru to twist.

yoka spare time; **yoka ni** in spare time; **yoka ga aru** to have leisure; **yoka o riyoo suru** to take advantage of spare time.

yokan presentiment, premonition; **yokan ga suru** to have a premonition.

yokan chill in the air (early spring).

yokare ashikare right or wrong; rightly or wrongly.

yokaze night wind.

-yoke suffix denoting: shelter, screen; **hiyoke** sunshade.

YOKEI NA extra; unnecessary; enough and then some; superfluous; **yokei na mono** unnecessary (thing); **yokei na hiyoo** extra expenses. **Yokei na osewa desu.** Mind your own business.

yokeru to avoid, shun; to keep off from; to keep aloof.

yoki expectation, anticipation; **yoki ni hanshite** contrary to expectation; **yoki shinai** unlooked for; **yoki suru** to expect, anticipate.

yokin money deposited; **yokin suru** to deposit money in the bank.

YOKKA four days, fourth day of the month.

yokkaku bathers; visitors at a spa (or hot spring).

yokkyuu craving, desire.

YOKO width; side; flank; **yoko no** sidelong; horizontal; **yoko ni** across, crossways; **yoko kara kuchi o dasu** to cut in; to put in a word; **yoko ni naru** to be down; **yokobai ni naru** to lie on one's side.

yokochoo lane; side street.

yokodori suru to snatch.

yokogiru to cross, traverse; to sail across; **toori o mukoo e yokogiru** to go across the street.

yokoku notice, announcement; **yokoku nashi ni** without warning; **yokoku no toori** as previously announced; **yokoku suru** to give notice in advance.

yokome sidelong glance; **yokome de miru** to look askance at; **yokome o tsukau** to cast a sidelong glance.

yokomichi byroad; wrong direction; digression; **yokomichi ni hairu** to deviate from.

yokomoji Occidental script or letters.

yokoo rehearsal; preliminary exercise.

yokoppara side (of the body).

yokoshima wickedness; **yokoshima na** wicked.

YOKOSU to send; to forward; to hand over, give over, deliver.

yokotaeru to lay down; **mi o byooshoo ni yokotaeru** to become ill; to lie down in a sickbed.

yokotaoshi ni naru to fall sideways.

yokotawaru to lie down; to lie across; **nagaisu ni yokotawaru** to lie on a sofa.

yokoyari interruption (of conversation); **-ni yokoyari o ireru** to break in; to cut in.

yokozuke ni suru to bring alongside (a pier, etc.).

YOKU well; often; thoroughly. **Kono hon wa yoku kakete iru.** This book is written well.

yoku greed, desire; **yoku no fukai** avaricious, greedy; **yoku o hanarete** without ulterior motive; **yoku toku zuku de** for gain; for self-interest; **yokubari** greedy person.

YOKUASA following (next) morning.

YOKUBAN following (next) evening.

yokubaru to be avaricious, be greedy.

yokuboo desire, ambition.

YOKUCHOO next morning.

YOKUGETSU next month.

YOKUJITSU next day.

yokujoo public bath.

yokume partiality, prejudice; **yokume de miru** to show prejudice. **Ikura yokume de mite mo.** Even if I give it the benefit of the doubt.

YOKUNEN next year.

yokusei control, suppression; **yokusei dekinai** uncontrollable; **yokusei suru** to control; to suppress.

YOKUSHITSU bathroom.

YOKUSOO bathtub.

yokusuru to bathe; to take a bath; **onkei ni yokusuru** to be favored with; **onten ni yokusuru** to receive a special favor.

yokuyoku very, extremely; carefully; **yokuyoku iya ni natta** being quite sick of; **yokuyoku no koto de nakereba** unless driven to extremes; **yokuyoku no riyuu** a very strong reason.

yokuyokujitsu next day but one; two days later.

yokuyokunen next year but one; two years later.

yokuyoo intonation, modulation; **yokuyoo no aru** modulated; **yokuyoo no nai** monotonous; **yokuyoo o tsukeru** to modulate.

yokyoo entertainment; extra show, side show.

yomawari night watch; night watchmen.

yomei remainder of one's life; **yomei ikubaku mo nai** to have only a few years left (to live).

yomeru to be able to read; to read well; to see; to understand; to see through. **Kono shoosetsu wa chotto yomeru.** This novel is rather interesting (reading).

yomi reading, Japanese reading of a Chinese character (**kun** reading).

yomiageru to read out, read aloud; to finish reading, read through; **hon o yomiageru** to read through a book.

yomiayamari misreading; mispronunciation.

yomiayamaru to misread; to mispronounce.

yomichi night journey; **yomichi o iku** to go by night.

yomigaeru to come to one's senses; to be freshened; to be brought to life; to rise from the dead. **Yomigaetta yoo na kokochi ga suru.** I feel like myself again (a new man).

yomikaki reading and writing; **yomikaki ga dekiru** to be able to read and write.

yomikata reading, pronunciation; reading lesson.

yomikikaseru to read (a book) to (someone).

yomikonasu to digest what one reads.

yomimono reading, reading matter; **kodomo no yomimono** children's books; juvenile literature.

yominaosu to reread.

yominikui illegible; difficult to read; **yominikui ji** illegible handwriting.

yomiotosu to overlook (miss) in reading; to skip (over).

yomiowaru to read through; to finish reading.

yomite poet; reader.

yomiyoi easy to read; legible; **yomiyoi ji** legible handwriting.

YOMU to read; to recite; to understand; to see; **hito no kaoiro o yomu** to read (someone's) face; **hito no shinchuu o yomu** to guess what a person means; **musabori yomu** to devour (a book); **uta o yomu** to recite a poem; to compose a poem; **zatto yomu** to run one's eyes over; to scan.

YON, YOTTSU, SHI four; **juuyon** fourteen; **yonjuu** forty.

yonabe night work; **yonabe o suru** to do night work.

YONAKA midnight; **yonaka ni** in the dead of night; in the middle of the night.

yonareru to get used to the world; to grow accustomed to the ways of the world; to grow worldly; **yonarenu** inexperienced; green; **yonareta hito** man (woman) of the world. **Kare wa mada yonarenai.** He has seen little of life.

yondokoronai unavoidable; urgent, pressing; necessary; **yondokoronaku** unavoidably; out of necessity; unwillingly.

yonen nai wholly engrossed; earnest; eager; **kenkyuu ni yonen nai** to be absorbed in study.

yononaka world; public; times; **yononaka e deru** to start life; **yononaka ga iya ni naru** to be sick of the world.

-YOO manner, style, way, appearance; **-no yoo na** of the manner of, like; **-no yoo ni** in the manner of; **-no yoo desu** it's like. **Kuru yoo desu.** It appears that he is coming.

yoo main point; essence; **yoo wa** in brief.

yoo business; task; use; service; **yoo ga aru** to have business on hand; **yoo o tasu** to go to the bathroom.

yoobo foster mother.

yooboo expectation; urgent request; **yooboo suru** to demand.

YOOCHIEN kindergarten.

yoodan business talk.

yoodateru to lend, advance (money); to accommodate.

yoodo iodine.

yoofubo foster parents.

YOOFUKU Western-style clothes.

yoogisha suspect, suspected person.

yoogo protection, safeguard; **yoogo suru** to protect, defend.

yoogo wording; terms.

yoogu tools, implements.

yooguruto yogurt.

yoohinten haberdashery.

yoohoo directions for use; uses.

YOOI easiness, simplicity; **yooi de nai** difficult; **yooi na** easy, simple.

yooi preparation, provision; prudence; **man'ichi no yooi o suru** to prepare for an emergency; **yooi suru** to get ready.

yooiku suru to bring up; to rear.

YOOJI, YOO business. (See also **yooken**.)

yooji infant, baby.

yoojin care, prudence; **yoojin bukai** careful; **yoojin no tame** as a precaution; **yoojin suru** to be careful; **yoojinboo** bodyguard.

yoojin high official.

yoojo adopted daughter.

yoojoo suru to take care of one's health.

YOOKA eight days; eighth day of the month.

yooka adoptive family.

yookai dissolution; melting, smelting, fusion; **yookai suru** to dissolve; melt; to smelt; to fuse.

yookan Occidental-style building.

yookan bittersweet jelly of beans (popular snack or dessert item).

yooken, YOOJI business; matter of business. **Nani ka goyooken ga arimasu ka?** Do you have any business to transact?

yooki weather; gaiety; **yooki na** bright; cheerful (of disposition); **yooki ni atarareru** to be affected by the weather; **yooki ni naru** to be merry, become lively.

yooki receptacle; vessel.

yookoo traveling abroad; **yookoo suru** to go abroad.

yookyuu claim; demand; request; **yookyuu suru** to claim; to demand; **yookyuusha** claimant.

yoomu important mission.

yoomuki business; mission; errand; **yoomuki o tazuneru** to inquire into (someone's) business; to ask (someone) his or her business.

yoorei example.

yooro important position; high office; **yooro ni tatsu** to occupy an important position.

yoorooin old-age home, nursing home.

yoorookin old-age pension.

YOOROPPA Europe; **Yooroppajin** European.

yoosen letter paper.

yoosha naku without ceremony; mercilessly.

yooshi point, gist; essential (important) points;

summary; blank printed forms; **denpoo yooshi** telegraph form.

yooshi adopted son; **yooshi ni suru** to adopt a child.

yooshiki mode; form; style.

yoosho Western books.

yooshoku Western food; **yooshokuya** restaurant serving Western food.

yooshoku shinju cultured pearl.

yooshu Western wine.

yooso essential element; important factor.

yoosoo Western-style books, clothes, dress; **yoosoo suru** to be dressed in European style.

YOOSU condition; circumstances; appearance; **-no yoosu o suru** to show signs of; **yoosu o ukagau** to observe; to see how things stand.

yoosuru require; need.

yootashi transacting business; **yootashi ni iku** to go out on an errand.

yooten gist; main point.

yooto use; **yooto ga hiroi** to have various (many) uses.

YOOYAKU at last; at length; gradually; narrowly; **yooyaku ma ni au** to be barely on time. **Yooyaku ame ga yanda.** At last the rain stopped.

yopparai drunkard, drunk.

yoreru to be twisted, get twisted.

yoreyore no worn out; seedy; threadbare.

-YORI from; out of; at; in; since; than; before; **umi no kanata yori** from beyond the sea. **A wa B yori se ga takai.** A is taller than B. **Kai wa gogo yoji yori hajimaru.** The party is to begin at four in the afternoon.

yori twist, ply; **yori ito** twisted thread; **yori o kakeru** to give a twist.

yoriai meeting; gathering.

yoridasu to pick out, single out; to sort out.

yoridokoro ground; source; authority; reliance; **yoridokoro no aru** sure, reliable, authentic; **yoridokoro no nai** groundless, unfounded, unreliable.

yorikakaru to lean (stand) against.

yorimichi stop (on the way); **yorimichi o suru** to visit on the way; to break a journey.

yorinuki no (*adj.*) choice, select.

yorinuku to choose, select, pick out; **tasuu no uchi kara yorinuku** to pick (a few) out of a large number.

yorisou to draw close, draw near; to nestle.

yoritoru to choose.

yoriwakeru to sort out, assort, classify; to pick out; to separate.

yorokeru to totter; to stagger.

yorokobashii glad, joyous, delighted. **Konna**

yorokobashii koto wa arimasen. Nothing gives me as much pleasure.

yorokobasu to delight, rejoice; to bring joy, gladden.

YOROKOBI joy, delight; congratulations; **yorokobi o noberu** to congratulate.

YOROKOBU to be glad; to rejoice; to be delighted (at). **Yorokonde.** Gladly. With pleasure.

yoron public opinion.

YOROSHII to be good; to be permissible; to be acceptable.

YOROSHIKU well; properly; in an appropriate way; best regards. **Aoki-san ni yoroshiku.** Please remember me to Aoki.

yoroyoro unsteadily; **yoroyoro to aruku** to walk unsteadily (feebly or drunkenly).

yorozuya general store.

YORU night.

yoru to depend on; to hang on; to be based upon, be founded on; **goirai ni yori** at your request; **saikin no choosa ni yoreba** according to the latest information.

yoseru to let approach, let come near; to bring near; to draw near; to add; **isu o yoseru** to draw up one's chair; **-ni mi o yoseru** to become dependent on.

yoshi all right; well; good; now; even if, though; **yoshi nanigoto ga okoroo tomo** whatever may happen. **Yoshi boku ga yatte miyoo.** Now I'll try.

-no yoshi I hear . . .

yoshin preliminary tremors.

yoshin preliminary examination.

yoshuu preparation; rehearsal; **yoshuu suru** to prepare lessons; to rehearse.

YOSO somewhere else; another place; **yoso de** elsewhere, somewhere else; **yoso goto** another's affair; **yoso mi** looking off, aside, away.

yosoku estimation, estimate; forecast; **yosoku suru** to estimate, to forecast, predict.

yosoo anticipation, expectation; **yosoo suru** to expect, anticipate; **yosoogai ni** unexpectedly; **yosoogai no** unexpected.

yosoou to dress (attire, equip) oneself in.

YOSU to stop, to drop; to leave off; to give up; to cut off; **tabako o yosu** to stop smoking. **Joodan wa yose.** None of your jokes.

yosutebito hermit; monk.

yotayota unsteadily.

yotei plan; schedule; **yotei no toori** as prearranged.

yotsugi heir; heiress.

yotsukado crossroads; corner of the street.

YOTTE and so, consequently, therefore.

yotto yacht.

YOTTSU, YON, SHI four. **Yottsu kaimashita.** I bought four of them.

you to get drunk; to feel sick (from motion); **fune ni you** to get seasick; **hikooki ni you** to get airsick; **sake ni you** to get drunk.

YOWAI weak; feeble (in body); poor-spirited; delicate (things); mild, gentle; **ki no yowai** fainthearted; softhearted, limited; **karada ga yowai** to have a weak constitution; to be in poor health.

yowaki (stock market term) bears; shorts; selling spirit.

yowami weakness, feebleness; **yowami ni tsukekomu** to take advantage of (someone's) weak point; **yowami o miseru** to display cowardice.

yowamushi weak person; crybaby.

yowane weakness; confession of weakness; **yowane o haku** to betray weakness; to complain.

yowatari going through the world; living; **yowatari no heta na** dull-witted, shiftless; **yowatari no joozu na** shrewd, hardheaded.

yoyaku reservation; advance booking; **yoyaku suru** to book in advance; to subscribe to; **yoyaku mooshikomikin** subscription (money); initial installment; **yoyakusha** subscriber.

yoyuu spare, reserve (money, time, etc.); **yoyuu shakushaku** to have a good deal in reserve.

YU, OYU hot water; **yu ni hairu** to take a bath; **yu o tsukawaseru** to bathe (a child or invalid); **yu o sasu** to pour hot water; **yu o wakasu** to boil water.

YUBI finger, toe; **yubi o kuwaeru** to look with envy; **yubiwa o yubi ni hameru** to put a ring on a finger.

YUBUNE bathtub.

yudan negligence; inattention; carelessness; imprudence; unguarded moment; **sukoshi mo yudan ga nai** to be always on one's guard; **yudan suru** to be negligent. **Yudan taiteki.** Danger comes soonest when it is despised.

YUDAYAJIN Jew, Jewish person.

yuderu to boil; to seethe.

yudono bathroom (for bathing only).

yuen lampsoot, lampblack; **yuen ga tatsu** to smoke.

yugameru to distort; to contort; to crook, bend; to curve; to warp; **kao o yugameru** to make a wry face.

yugamu to warp; to swerve, deflect; to be crooked, be distorted.

yuge jet of stream, vapor; **yuge o tatete okoru** to fume (with anger).

yuigon testament, will; one's dying wish,

yuigon o kaku to make a will; **yuigon o sezu ni shinu** to die intestate; **yuigon suru** to leave a will.

yuiitsu only, sole; unique.

yuisho lineage, blood; history.

YUKA floor; **yuka o haku** to sweep the floor; **yukaita** floorboard.

yukai pleasure; happiness; merriment; **yukai na** pleasant, happy, merry, joyful.

yukashii attractive, amiable; winning, engaging.

yukata light, unlined cotton garment worn in summer.

yuketsu blood transfusion.

YUKI, IKI going; bound for; **Oosaka yuki no densha** the Osaka train.

YUKI snow; **yuki o itadaku** snowcapped; **yuki o kaku** to shovel away the snow; **yukidoke** thawing (of ice and snow); **yukidoke suru** to thaw; **yuki ga furu** to snow. **Yuki ga tsumoru.** The snow covers the ground.

yukiatari battari rashly; impetuously; on the spur of the moment; **yukiatari battari ni yaru** to take chances, to act impetuously.

yukichigai crossing. **Kimi no tegami wa boku no to yukichigai ni natta.** Your letter crossed mine.

yukidomari blind alley; dead end (of a street); impasse.

yukigakari circumstances; convention.

yukigake ni on one's way to.

yukiki going and coming; traffic; **yukiki no hito** passersby; acquaintances; **yukiki suru** to come and go; to associate.

yukisaki one's destination.

yukitodoku to be scrupulous; to be prudent; be careful; to be attentive.

yukitsuke no favorite; regular; **yukitsuke no mise** one's favorite shop.

yukiwataru to extend; to prevail; to spread; to penetrate; to pervade.

yukizumaru to stand still; to arrive at a deadlock; **kotoba ga yukizumaru** to be at a loss for words.

YUKKURI slowly, at leisure, leisurely; **yukkuri suru** to enjoy one's free time. **Yukkuri nasai.** Stay as long as you can.

YUKU, IKU to go, proceed; to travel; **kisha de yuku** to go by train; **umaku yuku** to go well; to be successful.

yukue whereabouts; **yukue fumei** missing; **yukue o kuramasu** to conceal oneself; **yukue o sagasu** to trace (someone).

yukusaki destination; future.

yukusue future.

yukute way; path; **yukute o saegiru** to stand in the way; **yukute o terasu** to light the way.

yukuyuku on the way; **yukuyuku wa** in the end, in the course of time.

yume dream; **yume no yo** dream world; **-o yume ni miru** to see in a dream; **yume kara sameru** to wake from a dream; to be disillusioned; **yume o miru** to dream.

YUNOMI mug, cup.

YUNYUUHIN imports, imported goods.

yurai origin; history; **yurai suru** to originate.

yure shake, sway, rock, jolt, roll, pitch.

yureru to shake, rock, pitch; to tremble.

yuriokosu to shake up; to wake up by shaking.

yuru to shake; to swing; to joggle.

yurui relaxed, loosening, slack.

yurumeru to loosen, unloose; to unbend, relax; **te o yurumeru** to loosen one's hold of.

yurumu to loosen, become (get) loose; to abate. **Ki ga yurunde iru.** His attention is wandering.

yurushi permission, leave; license; initiation; pardon, forgiveness; **yurushi o ete** with permission; **yurushi o kou** to ask permission.

YURUSU to permit, allow; to approve; **jikan no yurusu kagiri** so far as time permits.

yuruyaka na lenient; mild; **yuruyaka na saka** gentle slope.

yuruyuru slowly, leisurely.

YUSHUTSU export, exportation; **yushutsu suru** to export; **yushutsuhin** exports.

yusoo transportation, conveyance; **yusoo suru** to convey, transport.

yusuburu to shake; to swing.

YUSUGU to wash out; to rinse.

yusuri extortion, blackmail; blackmailer; **yusuru** to extort (money), blackmail; to squeeze.

yutaka na abundant, plentiful, copious; **yutaka na seikatsu** rich living.

yutanpo hot water bottle. **Yutanpo o irete oyasuminasai.** Get into bed with a hot water bottle.

yutori room, margin; elbow room; spare (money, time); **yutori o toru** to leave some room for.

yuttari shita easy; composed; **yuttari shita kimochi ni naru** to feel easy; to feel at home.

YUU, IU to speak, talk; to mention.

yuu to tie; to dress; to arrange; **kami o yuu** to dress one's hair.

YUUBE last night; yesterday evening. (See also **sakuban.**)

yuuben eloquence; **yuuben na** eloquent, fluent; **yuuben o furuu** to speak eloquently; **yuubenka** eloquent speaker.

yuubi grace, elegance; refinement; **yuubi na** graceful, elegant.

YUUBIN mail, post; **gaikoku yuubin** foreign mail; **yuubin chokin** postal savings; **yuubin haitatsunin** letter carrier; **yuubin kawase** money order; **YUUBIN KITTE** postage stamp; **sokutatsu yuubin** special delivery; **yuubin o dasu** to send a letter by mail; **YUUBINBAKO** mailbox, letter box; **yuubinbutsu** mail, postal matter; **dai isshu yuubinbutsu** first-class mail; **dai nishu yuubinbutsu** second-class mail; **YUUBINKYOKU** post office. (See also **yuusooryoo.**)

yuuboo hopefulness; **yuuboo na** hopeful, promising; **zento yuuboo na seinen** a promising youth.

yuuchoo na sedate, calm, composed; tedious, wearisome, slow.

YUUDACHI shower; **yuudachi ga kuru** to have a shower; **yuudachi ni au** to be caught in a shower.

yuudai na magnificent, imposing.

yuudoku na poisonous, venomous.

yuudoo inducement; **yuudoo suru** to draw, lure, lead.

yuueki usefulness; benefit, advantage, instructiveness; **yuueki na** useful, advantageous; **yuueki desu** to be useful; to be beneficial; **yuueki ni tsukau** to make the best use of.

yuuenchi recreation ground, public playground.

yuuetsu superiority, supremacy; **yuuetsu suru** to be superior to, to surpass; **yuuetsukan** sense of superiority.

yuugai na bad, harmful, injurious; **kenkoo ni yuugai de aru** to be bad for the health.

YUUGATA evening.

yuugi play, game, amusement; **yuugi o suru** to play a game.

yuugoo melting, fusion, union, harmony; **yuugoo suru** to melt down, to harmonize; to fuse, unite.

yuuguu warm treatment; **-ni yuuguu sareru** to be received cordially by; **-o yuuguu suru** to give a warm reception to.

YUUHAN supper, evening meal.

yuuhi setting sun.

yuui na capable, able, efficient; **shoorai yuui na** promising.

YUUJIN friend, companion.

yuujoo friendliness; friendly feelings.

yuujuufudan irresolution, indecision; **yuujuufudan no** irresolute.

yuukai abduction, kidnapping; **yuukai suru** to kidnap; **yuukaisha** kidnapper.

yuukan evening issue, evening paper.

yuukan na brave, courageous, daring; **yuukan ni** courageously.

yuukensha elector, voter.

yuuki courage, valor; **yuuki rinrin** spiritedly, bravely; **yuuki o dasu** to gather one's courage; **yuuki o ushinau** to lose courage.

yuukoo na efficient; meritorious, **yuukoo de aru** to be effective, to hold good; **yuukoo ni tsukau** to make good use of.

yuukyuu no salaried.

yuumei na famous, noted, celebrated; **yuumei ni naru** to become famous.

yuumoa humor; **yuumoa ni tomu** to have a sense of humor.

YUURANBASU sight-seeing bus.

yuuretsu superiority; inferiority; merits; difference; **yuuretsu ga nai** to be equal; **yuuretsu o arasou** to strive for superiority.

yuuri profitable; profitability.

yuuryo anxiety, concern; **yuuryo subeki** serious, grave; **yuuryo suru** to become anxious about, become troubled.

yuuryoku na powerful, influential; controlling; **yuuryokusha** influential person.

yuuryoo na superior, excellent, choice; **yuuryoo na seiseki** excellent result.

yuusenken priority, first claim.

yuushi volunteer; supporter; interested person.

yuushoo victory; superiority.

yuushuu superiority; sublimity, excellence; **yuushuu na** superior, best, excellent.

yuusooryoo postage. (See also **yuubin, yuuzei.**)

yuutai generous treatment; hospitality, welcome; **yuutai o ukeru** to be welcomed at.

yuutai voluntary resignation, voluntary retirement; **-o yuutai suru** to resign or retire voluntarily from . . .

yuutoo superiority; excellency; top grade; **yuutoo no** high-grade, superior, excellent, first-rate; **yuutoo de sotsugyoo suru** to graduate with honors.

yuuutsu na melancholy, cheerless, gloomy.

yuuwa suru to melt; to soften; to soothe; to conciliate, placate, propitiate; to be reconciled with.

yuuwaku temptation, enticement; **yuuwaku suru** to tempt, entice; **yuuwaku to tatakau** to resist temptation.

yuuyake evening glow; afterglow.

yuuyami twilight, dusk; **yuuyami semaru koro** in the gathering dusk.

yuuyo delay; hesitation; extension of time, grace, reprieve; **yuuyo naku** without delay; without allowing an extension; **yuuyo o ataeru** to give an extension; **yuuyo suru** to hesitate, give time.

yuuyoo usefulness; **yuuyoo na** useful, serviceable; **yuuyoo ni** usefully, effectively.

yuuyuu leisurely; deliberately; serenely, placidly, calmly.

yuuzai guiltiness; conviction; culpability; **yuuzai no** guilty.

yuuzei postage. (See also **yuubin, yuusooryoo.**)

yuuzuu circulation (of a bill or note); accommodation; versatility; adaptability; **yuuzuu o kikasu** to adapt oneself; **yuuzuu suru** to advance money.

yuzuriau to compromise, concede mutually, meet halfway.

yuzuriukeru to obtain by transfer; to take over; to inherit.

yuzuriwatashi alienation; conveyance; transfer.

yuzuru to make over; to hand over; to transfer; to part with; **hito ni seki o yuzuru** to make room for; **ippo mo yuzuranai** not to yield a step.

Z

zaazaa plenty, freely, profusely (said of rain or water); **zaazaa mizu o nagasu** to let water run freely. **Ame ga zaazaa futte iru.** It is pouring.

ZABUTON cushion to sit on; **zabuton o shiku** to seat oneself on a cushion.

zadan familiar conversation, table talk; **zadankai** (discussion) meeting.

zaiaku sin, transgression, offense, crime; **zaiaku o okasu** to commit a sin; to commit a crime.

zaibatsu powerful financial group.

zaichuu containing. **Insatsubutsu zaichuu.** Printed matter only.

zaidan foundation; financial group.

zaigai abroad, overseas; **zaigai nipponjin** Japanese residents abroad.

zaigaku in school; **zaigaku chuu** while in school; **zaigaku suru** to be in school, at school.

zaigen source of revenue; resources; **zaigen ni toboshii** to lack financial resources.

zaigoo sins, sinful acts; **zaigoo no fukai** sinful.

ZAIJUU residence; **Nyuuyooku zaijuu no Nipponjin** Japanese residents in New York.

zaikyoo being in the capital; staying in Tokyo; **zaikyoo no yuujin** a friend in the capital (in Tokyo).

zaimoku wood, timber, lumber.

zainin criminal, offender, malefactor.

zairai existing hitherto; **zairai no** usual, ordinary, conventional.

zairyoku financial status.

zairyoo raw material; data.

zairyuu residing, dwelling; **-ni zairyuu suru** to reside in.

zaisan property; fortune; **zaisan o tsukuru** to make a fortune; **zaisanka** wealthy person.

zaisei finance; financial affairs; **zaisei joo** financially, from a financial point of view; **zaisei joo no** fiscal.

zaishoku service; tenure (of office); **zaishoku chuu** during one's term of office.

ZAITAKU being at home. **Myoonichi wa gozaitaku deshoo ka?** Will you be at home tomorrow?

zakka miscellaneous goods; **zakkashoo** grocer; general dealer.

zakkubaran na frank, plain, outspoken; **zakkubaran ni** frankly, plainly; **zakkubaran ni hanasu** to speak plainly.

zanbu remainder, rest, balance.

zanbu to with a great splash.

zange repentence; penitence; confession of sins; **zange suru** to repent, be penitent.

zangen slander; false charge.

zankoku cruelty, brutality; harshness, coldheartedness; inhumanity; **zankoku na** cruel, brutal, merciless, harsh; **zánkoku ni atsukau** to treat cruelly.

zanmu remaining business; **zanmu o seiri suru** to wind up affairs.

zannen regret, chagrin; mortification; **zannen na** regrettable; mortifying; **zannen ni omou** to regret; to be sorry for.

zannin brutality, cruelty; coldheartedness; **zannin na** brutal, cruel; **zannin ni mo** brutally, cruelly; **zanninsei** cruel nature.

zanpai rout, crushing defeat; **zanpai suru** to be routed, be beaten to the ground.

zanshi suru to be killed in an accident.

zansho heat of late summer, lingering summer, Indian summer.

zansonsha survivor.

zanson suru to survive; to subsist; to remain, be left.

zappi miscellaneous expense; incidental expense.

zappoo general news; **zappooran** news columns.

ZARA NI in plenty; plentifully; everywhere; **zara ni aru** to be very common; to be found everywhere.

zarazara rough feeling; **zarazara suru** to feel rough.

ZASEKI seat; room.

zasetsu breakdown; setback; collapse; discouragement; **zasetsu suru** to break down, receive a setback; to become discouraged; to collapse. **Keikaku wa**

chuuto de zasetsu shita. The plan collapsed before it was completed.

ZASHIKI room; living room in a Japanese house; **kyaku o zashiki e toosu** to show a visitor into the living room.

zashoo suru to run ashore, run aground; to be stranded.

ZASSHI magazine, periodical, journal; **zasshi o toru** to subscribe to a magazine.

zasshu crossbreed, hybrid; variety; various kinds; **zasshu no** mixed, crossbred, hybrid; **zasshu o tsukuru** to cross, interbreed.

zatsudan chatting, gossiping; **zatsudan suru** to gossip, chat.

zatsuji miscellaneous affairs.

zatsumu routine work; miscellaneous business; **zatsumu ni owareru** to be kept busy with miscellaneous business.

zatsu na rough, coarse; miscellaneous; **zatsu ni kaku** to write carelessly, scribble; to draw roughly; **zatsu na kotoba o tsukau** to speak roughly; **zatsu na tatekata** crude (flimsy) construction.

zatsuon hubbub; murmur; static (on the radio).

zatsuyoo miscellaneous business.

zatsuzen disorder, confusion; indiscriminately, desultorily; **zatsuzen to shita** disorderly; desultory; indiscriminate. **Zatsuzen to tsumikasanete aru.** They are heaped in disorderly fashion.

zatta no sundry, miscellaneous, various, diverse; all sorts of; **zatta no mono** all sorts of things.

ZATTO roughly; hastily; briefly; approximately; **zatto shita** rough, cursory, coarse; **zatto shita mitsumori** rough estimate; **zatto me o toosu** to glance cursorily through (a book); **zatto setsumei suru** to explain briefly.

zattoo bustle; congestion; confusion; **zattoo shita machi** busy street; **zattoo suru** to bustle; to be crowded (with).

zawameki to be noisy; to rustle.

zawatsuku to be noisy; to rustle; to murmur, to be agitated.

zawazawa murmuringly, rustlingly; noisily; **zawazawa suru** to be noisy; to be agitated.

ze ga hi demo whether right or wrong; by hook or by crook; by all means. **Ze ga hi demo sore o te ni irenakereba naranai.** By hook or by crook, I must get it.

ZEHI by all means; under any circumstance.

ZEI tax, duty; rate; **zei o chooshuu suru** to collect taxes; **zei o kasuru** to impose a tax (on); to levy a tax; **zei o osameru** to pay taxes; **zeikan** customs, customhouse.

zeitaku, zeitakuhin luxury; extravagance; **zeitaku na** luxuriant, extravagant; **zeitaku**

ni luxuriantly, extravagantly; **zeitaku ni kurasu** to live in luxury; **zeitaku o iu** to ask too much; **zeitaku o suru** to indulge in luxury.

zekkoo severance of a friendship or acquaintanceship.

zekkoo no finest, best; capital, splendid; **zekkoo no kikai** splendid opportunity, golden opportunity.

zekkyoo exclamation, ejaculation; **zekkyoo suru** to exclaim; to shout, yell.

zen Buddhist sect emphasizing religious meditation.

zen'aku good and bad; right and wrong.

ZENBU all parts, whole, entire lot; **zenbu de** altogether; in all.

zenbu first part; front; forepart.

zenbun complete sentence; full text.

zenchi complete recovery; perfect cure; **zenchi suru** to be completely cured or recovered.

zenchoo presage, omen; sign, symptom.

zendai mimon no unprecedented, unheard of, record-breaking.

ZENGAKU total amount, sum total.

ZENGO before and after; order; thereabouts, somewhere about; **zengo no kankei** context (of a sentence); **zengo o tsuujite** from the first to the last.

zengo fukaku being unconscious; **zengo fukaku ni** quite unconsciously.

zengosaku remedial measures; **zengosaku o koozuru** to consider the remedies.

zen'i good intention; good faith; **zen'i no** well-meant, well-intentioned, in good faith.

zenin approval; **zenin suru** to approve.

zen'in everybody present; all members.

ZENJITSU previous day, day before.

zenjutsu no previously mentioned, above mentioned.

zenka previous criminal record; **zenkamono** ex-convict.

zenkai complete recovery of health.

zenkai last occasion; previous installment; **zenkai ni** last time, previously; **zenkai no** last, previous.

zenkan whole volume, entire book.

zenkei whole view; panoramic view; bird's-eye view.

zenken full power; full authority; **zenken o inin suru** to entrust a person with full power (or authority).

zenki previous period; first term; first half of the year.

zenki no aforementioned, above mentioned; **zenki no toori** as mentioned above.

zenkoku whole country, whole land; **zenkoku**

ni throughout the country; **zenkokuteki no** national, country-wide.

zenkoo good conduct, good deed.

zenkoo whole school; **zenkoo seito** the whole student body.

zenmai spring (of clocks, etc.).

zenmai flowering fern.

zenmetsu annihilation, extermination; **-o zenmetsu saseru** to annihilate.

zennan zennyo pious men and women, pious people.

zennin virtuous person.

zennoo advance payment; **zennoo suru** to pay in advance.

zenpai complete defeat, crushing defeat; **zenpai suru** to suffer a crushing defeat.

zenpai total abolition; **zenpai suru** to abolish, to make a clean sweep of.

zenpan first half.

ZENPOO front; **zenpoo ni** ahead, in front; **zenpoo no** front, forward.

zenpuku no utmost, greatest; wholehearted; **zenpuku no doryoku o suru** to exert oneself to the utmost.

zenrei precedent; previous example; **zenrei no nai** unprecedented.

zenretsu front rank.

zenryoku all one's energy (strength, power); **zenryoku o tsukusu** to do one's best.

zenryoo goodness, integrity; **zenryoo na** good, virtuous, honest.

zensei height of prosperity; zenith of power; **zensei jidai** golden age; age of prosperity; **zensei o kiwameru** to be at the height of prosperity.

zensekai whole world; world at large; **zensekai ni** all over the world.

zensha no former, prior.

zenshi whole city; all over the city; **zenshi itaru tokoro ni** everywhere in the city; **zenshimin** all the citizens; all the residents of the city.

zenshin whole body; full-length photo (of the body); all over the body; **zenshin fuzui** total paralysis; **zenshin fuzui ni naru** to become paralyzed.

zenshin advance, progress; **zenshin suru** to advance.

zenshin gradual (slow but steady) advance; **zenshin suru** to move step by step.

zenshin antecedents; (one's) past.

zenshin one's whole heart; **zenshin o komete** with all of one's heart.

zensho taking proper measures; **zensho suru** to manage tactfully.

zenshoo complete destruction by fire; **zenshoo suru** to be entirely destroyed by fire.

zenshoo complete victory, unbroken series of

victories; **zenshoo suru** to win a complete victory.

zenshoogai one's whole life; **zenshoogai o tsuujite** throughout one's life.

zensokuryoku full speed, top speed; **zensokuryoku o dasu** to go at full speed.

ZENTAI whole body; entirety; naturally; as a matter of course; on earth; **zentai de** in all, altogether; **zentai to shite** in general; **zentai ni** wholly, entirely, generally; **zentai no** whole, entire, complete.

zento future; prospect; future career; **zento ni nozomi o kakeru** to pin one's hopes on one's future; **zento ryooen** distant goal.

ZEN'YA previous night; **sono zen'ya** night before.

zen'yaku complete translation.

ZENZEN entirely, completely, wholly; thoroughly; exactly; at all. **Zenzen shiranai.** I don't know at all.

zeppan out of print.

zeppeki precipice, cliff.

zero zero, nought, nothing.

zessei matchless, peerless.

zesshoku fasting, abstention from food; **zesshoku suru** to go without food.

zessoku cessation of breathing; expiration; **zessoku suru** to die, expire.

zessuru to go out of existence, become extinct; to exceed, be beyond (something).

zetchoo highest point, summit, zenith; **zetchoo ni tassuru** to reach the summit.

zetsuboo despair, hopelessness; **zetsubooteki no** hopeless, desperate; **mattaku zetsuboo de aru** to be utterly hopeless; **zetsuboo suru** to despair, give up hope.

zetsudai no gigantic, colossal, enormous; **zetsudai no doryoku o suru** to make a supreme effort.

zetsuen isolation; insulation; **zetsuen suru** to sever connections with; to insulate; **zetsuensen** insulated wire.

zetsumei death; **zetsumei suru** to die, expire.

zetsumetsu extermination; extinction; **zetsumetsu suru** to exterminate, stamp out; to die out.

zetsumu nil, nought, nothing; **-wa zetsumu de aru** there can be no such.

ZETTAI absoluteness, positiveness; **zettai ni** decidedly, absolutely; **zettai no** absolute, positive; **zettai zetsumei** desperation, last extremity.

zokkai world; life; laity; **zokkoo no** worldly, mundane.

zokkoku dependency; subject state, tributary.

zokkoo continuation; **zokko suru** to continue, proceed with.

zokuaku na being coarse, vulgar, gross, unrefined.

zokuhatsu, zokushutsu successive occurrence; **zokuhatsu suru** to occur in succession.

zokuhen sequel.

zoku na worldly; popular; common; vulgar; **zoku ni** commonly, popularly.

zokusetsu common saying; popular view; tradition.

zokushoo popular designation; popular name.

zoku suru to belong to; to pertain to; to come under. **Beikoku ni zoku suru.** It belongs to the United States.

zokuzoku successively, in rapid succession.

zokuzoku suru to feel chilly; to shiver; to thrill.

zonbun to the full; to one's heart's content; **omou zonbun naku** to cry to one's heart's content.

zonjiru See zonzuru.

zonmei living, being alive; existence; **zonmei chuu ni** during one's lifetime; **zonmeisha** survivor.

zonzai na careless, inattentive; rough; rude; **zonzai ni** roughly, crudely, carelessly; **zonzai na mono no iikata o suru** to be rough spoken; **zonzai ni kaku** to write carelessly.

zonzuru to know; to be aware of, be conscious of; to think; to be acquainted with. **Kono fukin wa yoku zonjite imasu.** I know this neighborhood well. **Sono hito o go-zonji desu ka?** Are you acquainted with him?

zoo image, statue, statuette; figure.

zoo elephant.

zoochiku extension; addition; **zoochiku suru** to enlarge; to build an extension.

zoochoo presumption; **zoochoo suru** to become arrogant.

zooen reinforcements; **zooen suru** to reinforce.

zoofuku ki amplifier.

zoogaku increase, augmentation; **zoogaku o suru** to increase, raise (money, salary, etc.).

zoogen increase and/or decrease.

zooheikyoku mint (for money).

zooho supplement, enlargement; **-o zooho suru** to enlarge, supplement.

zooin increase in personnel; increased staff.

zooka increase, augmentation; **zooka suru** to increase, augment; **zookaritsu** the rate of increase.

ZOOKIN cleaning rag; mop.

zookyuu wage increase, pay increase; **zookyuu suru** to increase wages.

zooo hatred, spite, antipathy.

ZOORI sandals; **zoori o haku** to wear sandals.

zoosaku fittings; furniture; alterations, features; **zoosaku no sorotta kao** regular features, comely face; **zoosaku o suru** to make alterations in a house. **Zoosakuzuki kashiya.** Furnished house to let.

ZOOSA NAI not difficult, easy, simple; **zoosa naku** easily, without difficulty.

zoosen shipbuilding; **zoosenjo** shipyard, dockyard.

zooshi increase in capital; **zooshi suru** to increase the capital.

zooshin promotion; betterment, increase; **zooshin suru** to promote; to increase; to be conducive to; **nooritsu o zooshin suru** to increase efficiency.

zoosho collection of books.

zooshuu additional income, increase of receipts.

zoosui rise (swelling) of a river.

zootei presentation, offer; **zootei suru** to present; to give a present; **zooteihin** gift, present; **zooteisha** giver.

zootoo exchange of presents; **zootoo suru** to exchange presents; **zootoohin** presents, gifts.

zoowai bribery, corruption; **zoowai suru** to bribe; to offer a bribe; **zoowai jiken** bribery case; **zoowaisha** briber.

zooyo presentation; donation, present; **zooyo suru** to present; to donate; **zooyosha** donor.

zoozei increase in taxation, tax increase; **zoozei an** bill for an increase in taxation; **ichiwari no zoozei** a 10 percent increase in taxation; **zoozei suru** to increase taxes.

zorozoro dragging along, trailing along, going with many followers. **Minna ga zorozoro tsuite aruku.** They follow at her heels.

zotto suru to shudder, shiver, to feel shocked; **hito o zotto saseru** to make (someone) shudder; **kangaete mo zotto suru** to shudder at the thought of.

zu drawing, picture; diagram; map; **zu de setsumei suru** to illustrate by a diagram; **zu ni noru** to be puffed up; **zu o hiku** to draw a diagram.

-zu a negative ending denoting: not, without. **Gohan o tabezu ni ikimashita.** She went there without eating.

zuan plan, design; sketch; **zuan o tsukuru** to prepare a design; **zuanka** designer, draftsperson.

zubazuba (colloq.) frankly, candidly; **zubazuba itte shimau** to speak frankly.

ZUBON trousers, pants.

zubora negligence; nonchalance; slovenliness; **zubora na** negligent, slovenly; **zubora ni** negligently; with nonchalance; **zubora ni naru** to become negligent.

zuboshi bull's-eye, mark; **zuboshi o sasu** to hit the mark.

zubunure ni naru to become soaked (drenched) to the skin.

zubutoi bold, daring, audacious; impudent; **zubutoi hito** bold fellow; **zubutoi koto o suru** to do a bold thing.

zudon to with a bang, with a thud. **Zudon to teppoo no oto ga shita.** Bang! went the gun.

zugayooshi drawing paper.

ZUIBUN fairly, pretty, tolerably; extremely; **zuibun na** awful, nasty, very disagreeable; **zuibun samui** very cold.

zuihitsu stray notes; essay; jottings; miscellaneous writings.

ZUII liberty, freedom; absence of restraint; **zuii ni** freely, voluntarily; **zuii no** free, voluntary, optional. **Gozuii ni meshiagatte kudasai.** Please help yourself.

zuiichi (n.) best; foremost; **Nippon zuiichi no sakura no meisho** the most famous place for cherry blossoms in Japan. **Sekai zuiichi desu.** It is the largest in the world.

zuiji at any time; as occasion demands.

zuikoo accompanying; attendance on a journey; **zuikoo suru** to accompany (someone); **zuikooin** staff (personnel), attendants.

zujoo overhead; over one's head; **zujoo ni ochite kuru** to fall on one's head; **zujoo o tobu** to fly overhead.

zukai illustration, graphic representation; **zukai suru** to illustrate; **zukai shite setsumei suru** to illustrate with a diagram.

zukazuka straightly, directly.

zukizuki itamu, zukizuki suru to throb with pain.

zumen drawing, plan, map.

-zumi suffix denoting: maximum weight capacity of; shipment by; **kisenzumi** shipment by freight; **kyuutonzumi kasha** nine-ton freight car.

zunguri shita dumpy, stocky.

ZUNOO head, brains; **zunoo meiseki no** clearheaded; **zunoo o yoosuru shigoto** brain work.

zunukete exceptionally, extraordinarily; far above the average; **zunukete se no takai kodomo** an exceptionally tall child.

zunzun rapidly; apace; in leaps and bounds; **zunzun saki e iku** to go ahead at a rapid pace; **zunzun susumu** to proceed rapidly.

zurari to all in a row; in a long row; **zurari to narabu** to stand in a long row; to sit in a long row.

zureru to slip down; to slip off.

zuru to slip down. **Zubon ga zuru.** His trousers are slipping.

zuru cheating.

zurui sly, crafty; unfair; **zurui otoko** foxy fellow; **zurui koto o suru** to do a tricky thing.

zurukeru to shirk (neglect) one's duty; to be tardy; to be idle; **gakkoo o zurukeru** to play truant from school.

zushin to with a thud; with a heavy sound.

zutazuta pieces; **zutazuta ni** in pieces, stripes; **zutazuta ni hikisaku** to tear to shreds; **zutazuta ni kiru** to cut to pieces.

-ZUTSU each, apiece; **hi ni sankai zutsu** three times a day; **hitori ni mittsu zutsu** three pieces to each person; **ni sannin**
zutsu by twos and threes; **sukoshi zutsu** little by little, bit by bit.

ZUTSUU headache; **wareru yoo na zutsuu** a splitting headache; **zutsuu no tane** a cause of worry; **zutsuu ga suru** to have a headache.

ZUTTO directly to the point; straight to the spot; very much; by far; all the time; **zutto ii** very much better; **zutto izen** long time ago; **zutto tsuzuite** all the time. **Zutto massugu itte kudasai.** Keep straight on.

zuutai body, frame, physique.

zuuzuuben dialect spoken in the northeastern part of Japan.

zuuzuushii impudent, audacious; shameless; **zuuzuushiku** impudently, audaciously, shamelessly; **zuuzuushiku naru** to become impudent; **zuuzuushisa** impudence, audacity, effrontery; shamelessness. **Zuuzuushii otoko da.** He is impudent.

GLOSSARY OF
GEOGRAPHICAL NAMES

Afurika Africa.
Ajia Asia.
Airurando Ireland.
Aisurando Iceland.
Amerika America.
Amerika Gasshuukoku U.S.A.
Arasuka Alaska.
Arujeria Algeria.
Arupusu Alps.
Aruzenchin Argentina.
Beikoku America/U.S.A.
Biruma Burma.
Bonbei Bombay.
Burajiru Brazil.
Chiri Chile.
Chuubei Central America.
Chuugoku China.
Chuuoo Amerika Central America.
Denmaaku Denmark.
Doitsu Germany.
Eikoku England.
Ejiputo Egypt.
Firipin Phillippines.
Furansu France.
Gasshuukoku United States.
Girisha Greece.
Hangarii Hungary.
Hawai Hawaii.
Hokkaidoo Hokkaido.
Hokubei North America.
Honkon Hong Kong.
Igirisu England/Great Britain.
Indo India.
Indoneshia Indonesia.
Indo shina Indochina.
Iraku Iraq.
Iran Iran.
Isuraeru Israel.
Itaria Italy.
Juneebu Geneva.
Kanada Canada.
Kankoku South Korea.
Kita Amerika North America.

Kita Choosen North Korea.
Koobe Kobe.
Kyooto Kyoto.
Kyuuba Cuba.
Kyuushuu Kyushu.
Manira Manila.
Maree Malaya.
Mekishiko Mexico.
Minami Afurika South Africa.
Minami Amerika South America.
Mosukuwa Moscow.
Nanbei South America.
Nihon Japan.
Nihonkai Japan Sea.
Nippon Japan.
Noruee Norway.
Nyuu Jirando New Zealand.
Nyuu Yooku New York.
Oosaka Osaka.
Ooshuu Europe.
Oosutorariya Australia.
Oosutoria Austria.
Oranda Holland/Netherlands.
Pakisutan Pakistan.
Pekin Beijing.
Perushawan Persian Gulf.
Poorando Poland.
Porutogaru Portugal.
Rondon London.
Roshia Russia.
San Furanshisuko San Francisco.
Shiberia Siberia.
Shingapooru Singapore.
Sueeden Sweden.
Suisu Switzerland.
Supein Spain.
Suriranka Sri Lanka.
Tai Thailand.
Taiheiyoo Pacific Ocean.
Taipee Taipei.
Taiseiyoo Atlantic Ocean.
Taiwan Taiwan.
Tookyoo Tokyo.
Toonan-Ajia Southeast Asia.
Toruko Turkey.
Washinton Washington, DC.
Yooroppa Europe.

English-Japanese

A

a, an hitotsu, ichi (but no word is usually used for this).
　　There is a man. Otoko no hito ga imasu.
　　He is a policeman. Junsa desu.
abandon (to) suteru *(give up)*; misuteru *(forsake, desert)*; yameru *(relinquish)*.
abbreviate (to) ryaku suru *(simplify)*; shooryaku suru *(omit, cut out)*.
abbreviation ryaku, ryakugo.
ability shuwan *(capacity)*; giryoo *(skill)*; nooryoku, sainoo *(talent)*.
able dekiru; binwan na, yuunoo na.
able (to be) dekiru.
abolish (to) haishi suru.
abortion datai.
about goro *(point in time)*; kurai, gurai, hodo, bakari *(quantity)*; mawari *(nearness of a place)*; -ni tsuite *(concerning)*.
above -no ue *(higher than, over)*; -ijoo *(more than)*.
abroad kaigai ni *(overseas)*.
absence rusu *(from home, from the office)*; kesseki *(from school, from a meeting)*.
absent rusu no, kesseki no.
absolute zettaiteki.
absorb (to) suiageru *(suck up)*; suitoru *(take in)*.
abstain (to) kiken suru *(from voting)*.
abstract chuushooteki.
absurd okashii, baka na.
abundant takusan no.
abuse akuyoo.
abuse (to) akuyoo suru.
academy akademii, gakkai.
accent akusento.
accent (to) kyoochoo suru *(emphasize)*.
accept (to) ukeru, osameru *(take in)*; shoodaku suru *(agree to)*.
acceptance shoodaku.
accident jiko.
　　by accident guuzen ni.
accidental guuzen no.
accidentally guuzen ni; omoi gake naku *(unexpectedly)*.
accommodate (to) tekioo saseru *(adapt, adjust)*; shuuyoo suru *(take in)*.
accommodation tekioo *(adaptation)*; shisetsu *(facilities)*.
accompany (to) isshoni tsuite iku.
accomplish (to) shitogeru, kansei suru.
accord itchi, choowa *(harmony)*; ishi *(choice, will)*.
according to -ni yoreba; -ni yotte *(depending on)*.
account kanjoo *(statement of money)*; hanashi *(narration)*.

accountant kaikei gakari.
accrue (to) rishi o **shoozuru.**
accuracy seikaku sa.
accurate seikaku na.
accuse (to) hinan suru.
accustom (to) narasu; shuukan o tsukeru *(habituate)*.
ache itami
ache (to) itamu
achieve (to) shitogeru *(accomplish)*.
achievement kooseki.
acid *adj.* suppai. *-n.* san.
acknowledge (to) mitomeru.
acknowledgment uketori *(receipt)*.
acquaintance shirai.
acquire (to) eru *(gain)*; te ni ireru *(acquire property or rights)*.
across mukoogawa *(across the street)*.
　　go across yokogiru.
　　come across mitsukeru *(happen to find)*.
act maku *(of a play)*; okonai *(deed)*.
act (to) suru *(do)*; furumau *(behave)*.
active katsudooteki, sakan na.
activity katsudoo.
actor yakusha; eiga haiyuu *(movie actor)*.
actress joyuu.
actual hontoo no.
actually hontoo ni.
acute surudoi *(sharp)*; kyuusei no *(opp. of chronic)*.
adapt (to) tekigoo saseru *(make fit)*.
add (to) kuwaeru.
addition tashizan *(math.)*; kuwaeta mono *(thing added)*.
address juusho *(of a place)*; hanashi *(speech)*.
address (to) hanashikakeru *(speak to)*.
　　to address a letter tegami ni atena o kaku.
adequate tekitoo na.
adjective keiyooshi.
adjoining tonari no.
administer (to) kanri suru.
admiral kaigun taishoo.
admiration kanpuku, kanshin.
admire (to) kanshin suru, uyamau.
admission nyuujooryoo *(charge)*.
admit (to) mitomeru *(recognize)*; ireru *(let in)*.
admittance nyuujoo *(entrance)*.
　　No admittance. Tachiiri kinshi.
adopt (to) toriireru.
adult otona.
advance (to) susumeru.
advanced technology sentan gijutsu.
advantage rieki *(benefit)*.
adventure booken.
adverb fukushi.
advertise (to) kookoku suru.
advertisement kookoku.

classified ad sangyoo kookoku.
advertising kookoku.
  agency kookoku dairi ten.
  campaign kookoku sen.
  research kookoku choosa.
advice chuukoku.
advise (to) chuukoku suru.
affair koto, kotogara.
affect (to) eikyoo suru *(influence)*.
affected kidotta *(in manner)*.
affection aijoo.
affectionate aijoo no aru.
affirm (to) dangen suru *(state as a fact)*.
affirmation dangen.
afloat (to be) ukabiagaru.
afraid kowai.
after ato de *(later)*; ato *(next to)*; sorekara *(and then)*.
afternoon gogo.
afterward sono go.
again mata, moo ichido.
against -ni taishite.
age (to) toshi o toru *(said of a person)*; furuku naru *(said of a thing)*.
agency dairiten *(office of an agent)*.
agent dairinin *(person)*.
aggravate (to) motto waruku suru *(make worse)*.
ago mae.
agree (to) sansei suru.
agreeable kokoroyoi *(pleasing)*.
agreement keiyaku, kyootei, dooi.
agricultural noogyoo no.
agriculture noogyoo.
ahead mae ni *(in front of)*; saki ni *(of time or place)*.
aid enjo.
  first aid ookyuu teate.
  first-aid station ookyuu teatesho.
aid (to) enjo suru.
aim mokuteki *(purpose)*.
aim at (to) nerau.
air kuuki.
airfield hikoojoo.
air force kuugun.
airmail kookuubin.
airplane hikooki.
airport kuukoo.
aisle toorimichi.
alarm odoroki *(sudden fear)*; keihoo *(warning)*.
  alarm clock mezamashi-dokei.
alcohol arukooru.
alike onaji yoo ni *(in a similar way)*.
all minna, subete, zenbu.
alliance doomei.
allow (to) yurusu *(permit)*; ataeru *(give)*.
ally mikata.

almost taitei, hotondo.
alone hitori de; tandoku de.
along -ni sotte *(parallel to)*; issho ni *(together with)*.
already sude ni, moo.
also yahari, mata, -mo.
altar saidan.
alter (to) kaeru.
alternate *adj.* hitotsu oki no. -*n.* kawari no hito *(person)*; kawari no mono *(thing)*.
alternate (to) hitotsu oki ni suru; koogo ni suru.
although keredomo.
altitude takasa.
altogether mina de *(in all)*, mattaku *(completely)*.
  It's five hundred yen altogether. Mina de gohyaku en desu.
always itsu mo *(at all times)*; itsu demo *(at any time)*.
amaze (to) odorokaseru.
amazement odoroki.
ambassador taishi.
ambitious haki no aru, yashin no aru.
amend (to) teisei suru.
America Beikoku, Amerika.
  American Beikokujin, Amerikajin *(person)*; Amerika no *(pertaining to the U.S.A.)*.
among -no naka no, -no naka ni, -no naka de.
amount gaku; soogaku *(total)*.
ample juubun na.
amplifier zoofuku ki; anpu.
amuse (to) tanoshimaseru, omoshirogaraseru.
amusement goraku.
amusing omoshiroi.
analyze (to) bunseki suru, kentoo suru.
ancestor sosen.
anchor ikari.
ancient furui, mukashi no.
and to, ya, soshite.
anecdote itsuwa.
angel tenshi.
anger ikari.
anger (to) okoru, okoraseru.
angry (to be) okotte iru.
  to get angry okoru.
animal doobutsu.
animate (to) kappatsu ni suru.
annex bekkan *(building)*.
annihilate (to) zenmetsu saseru.
anniversary kinenbi.
announce (to) koohyoo suru *(publish)*; seimei suru *(declare)*.
annoy (to) komaraseru.
annual maitoshi no.
annul (to) torikesu.
anonymous tokumei no.

another hoka no.

answer henji, kotae.

answer (to) kotaeru, henji o suru.

antenna antena.

anticipate (to) yosoo suru.

antique kottoohin.

anxiety shinpai.

anxious (to get) shinpai suru.

any nani ka, dare ka; sukoshi mo *(not even a little)*.

anybody dare ka, dare demo.

anyhow tomokaku, tonikaku.

anything nani ka, nan demo.

anywhere doko demo.

apart betsu, betsu ni.

apartment apaato.

apiece -zutsu.

apologize (to) ayamaru.

apparent akiraka na *(obvious)*.

appeal (to) uttaeru.

appear (to) arawareru *(make an appearance)*.

appearance mikake *(mien)*.

appease (to) nadameru.

appendix furoku *(of a book)*; moochoo *(of the body)*.

appetite shokuyoku.

applaud (to) hakushu kassai suru.

applause kassai.

apple ringo.

application mooshikomi *(request)*.

apply (to) mooshikomu.

appoint (to) ninmei suru.

appointment ninmei *(assignment to office)*; yakusoku *(engagement)*.

appreciate (to) kansha suru *(thank)*; arigataku omou *(feel gratified)*.

appreciation kansha.

appropriate *adj.* tekitoo na.

approve (to) sansei suru *(agree)*; yoi to omou *(think well of)*.

April Shigatsu.

apron epuron, maekake.

arbitrary dokudanteki na.

arcade aakeedo.

architect kenchikuka.

architecture kenchiku.

ardent nesshin na.

area akichi *(open space)*; chiiki *(region)*.

argue (to) iiarasou; giron suru.

argument iiarasoi, ronsoo.

arithmetic sanjutsu.

arm ude *(of the body)*; buki *(weapon)*.
　　armaments buki.
　　arms reduction gunshuku.

arm (to) *v.t.* busoo saseru; *v.i.* busoo suru.

army rikugun.

around -no mawari ni.

arouse (to) me o samasaseru *(awaken)*; sawagaseru *(stir up)*.

arrange (to) seiton suru *(set in order)*; uchiawaseru *(make an arrangement)*.

arrangement uchiawase *(plan)*.

arrest taiho.

arrest (to) taiho suru, tsukamaeru.

arrival toochaku.

arrive (to) toochaku suru, tsuku.

art geijutsu *(art in general)*; bijutsu *(fine arts)*.

article shinamono *(commodity)*; kiji *(writing)*.

artificial jinzoo no *(not natural)*.

artist geijutsuka, geinoojin *(performing artist)*; bijutsuka *(person skilled in one of the fine arts)*.

artistic geijutsuteki.

as -to shite *(in the capacity of)*; -no yoo ni *(in such a manner)*; -hodo *(as . . . as)*.

ascertain (to) tashikameru, kakutei suru *(determine)*.

ash hai.

ashamed (to feel) hazukashiku omou.

aside soba ni; waki e *(nearby)*.

ask (to) kiku, tazuneru.

asleep (to be) nemutte iru.

aspire (to) netsuboo suru.

aspirin asupirin.

assault shuugeki, bookoo.

assemble (to) atsumeru *(bring together)*; atsumaru *(come together)*.

assembly shuukai, kumitate.

asset shisan.

assign (to) ategau *(allot)*; shitei suru *(designate)*.

assist (to) tetsudau, tasukeru.

assistant tetsudai, joshu.

associate (to) koosai suru *(mingle with)*; rensoo suru *(relate in thinking)*.

assume (to) hikiukeru *(undertake)*; katei suru *(suppose)*.

assurance hoshoo, ukeai.

assure (to) hoshoo suru.

astonish (to) odorokasu, bikkuri saseru.

astound (to) bikkuri gyooten saseru.

astronaut uchuu hikooshi.

asylum seishin byooin.

at ni, de.

athlete undooka.

athletics undoo.

atmosphere fun'iki.

attach (to) tsukeru.

attack (to) koogeki suru, semeru, osou.

attain (to) tassuru *(gain)*; toochaku suru *(reach)*.

attempt (to) kokoromiru.

attend (to) -ni shusseki suru *(be present at)*.

attention chuui.
attic yane ura.
attitude taido.
attorney bengoshi *(lawyer).*
   power of attorney ininken, dairinin.
attract (to) chuui o hiku *(draw attention);* miwaku suru *(entice).*
attraction miwaku.
attractive miryokuteki, aikyoo ga aru.
audience choshuu.
audit kaikei kansa suru.
August Hachigatsu.
aunt oba, obasan.
author chosha *(writer of a book).*
authority taika *(great expert);* tookyokusha *(government).*
authorize (to) kengen o ataeru.
automatic jidooteki.
automobile jidoosha.
autumn aki.
average heikin.
avoid (to) sakeru.
awake (to be) me ga samete iru.
awaken (to) okosu *(arouse).*
award shoohin, shooyo.
award (to) shooyo a dasu.
aware (to be) shoochi shite iru.
away achira ni, atchi ni.
   Go away. Atchi e itte.
awful osoroshii, taihen na.
awkward fuben na, bukiyoo na.

baby akanboo.
back senaka *(of the body);* ura *(of a house, etc.).*
background haikei.
backward ushiro ni *(toward the back);* gyaku ni *(in a reverse direction).*
bacon beekon.
bad warui.
badge kishoo.
bag fukuro.
baggage nimotsu *(heavy, such as trunks);* tenimotsu *(hand luggage).*
bake (to) yaku.
baker pan'ya.
bakery pan'ya.
balance tsuriai; nokori *(remainder).*
balcony barukonii.
ball tama *(sphere);* mari, booru *(for a game).*
balloon keikikyuu *(aircraft);* fuusen *(toy).*
banana banana.
band bando, gakudan.
bandage hootai.

banister tesuri.
bank ginkoo *(financial institution);* dote *(of a river).*
   bank account ginkoo yokin kooza.
   bank balance ginkoo yokin zandaka.
   bank charge ginkoo tesuu ryoo.
   bank check ginkoo kogitte.
   bank letter of credit ginkoo shin-yoo joo.
   bank loan ginkoo kashitsuke.
   bank note satsu.
   bank statement ginkoo kanjoo hookoku sho.
banker ginkooka.
bankruptcy hasan.
banquet enkai.
bar baa *(for drinks);* kanaboo *(rod).*
barber rihatsushi, tokoya.
barbershop rihatsuten.
bare hadaka no.
barefoot suashi no.
barn ushigoya.
barrel taru.
barren ko o umanai *(sterile);* fumoo no *(land).*
basin tarai.
basis kiso, konkyo.
basket kago.
   wastepaper basket kuzu-kago.
bath o-furo *(hot);* mizu-buro *(cold).*
   to take a bath furo ni hairu.
bathe (to) kaisuiyoku o suru *(in the sea);* mizu o abiru *(in running water).*
bathroom furoba; tearai *(toilet),* toire.
battle ikusa, sensoo.
bay wan.
be (to) iru, oru *(there is: animate);* aru *(there is: inanimate);* da *(it is—).*
beach umibe, kaigan.
bean mame.
bear kuma.
bear (to) gaman suru *(endure);* umu *(give birth to).*
beard hige.
beat (to) utsu.
beautiful utsukushii, kirei na.
beauty utsukushisa; bijin *(beautiful woman).*
beauty parlor biyooin.
because kara, node *(used after a sentence or clause).*
become (to) -ni naru.
becoming (be) niau *(befitting).*
bed nedoko, beddo; shindai *(berth).*
beef gyuuniku.
beer biiru.
beet biitsu, kabu.
before mae, mae ni.

beg (to) tanomu.

beggar kojiki.

begin (to) *v.t.* hajimeru; *v.i.* hajimaru.

beginning hajime.

behave (to) furumau.

behavior furumai.

behind ushiro ni, ato ni.

belief kakushin *(conviction);* shinkoo *(faith);* iken *(opinion).*

believe (to) shinjiru.

bell kane, beru.

belong to -ni zokusuru.

below shita ni.

belt beruto; obi *(sash);* kawa-obi *(leather).*

bench benchi.

bend (to) *v.t.* mageru; *v.i.* magaru.

beneath shita ni.

benefit rieki *(good advantage);* onkei *(favor).*

bequest izoo.

beside -no soba ni, -no soba de.

besides -no hoka ni, sono ue *(moreover).*

best ichiban ii.

bet kake.

bet (to) kakeru.

betray (to) uragiru *(act treacherously).*

better motto ii.
　　better than yori ii.

between -no aida ni.

beware (to) yoojin suru.

beyond -no mukoo ni.

bicycle jitensha.

bid (to) ne o tsukeru *(offer a price);* nyuusatsu suru *(make a bid).*

big ookii, ooki na.

bill denpyoo *(grocer's bill, restaurant bill of fare).*

billion juu-oku.

bind (to) yuwaeru, shibaru *(tie).*

bird tori.

birth tanjoo.
　　to give birth umu.

birthday tanjoobi.

biscuit bisuketto *(tea biscuit, cookie).*

bishop kantoku *(Protestant);* shikyoo *(Catholic).*

bit sukoshi.

bite kamikizu *(dog bite);* sashikizu *(mosquito bite).*

bite (to) kamu *(chew);* sasu *(said of insects).*

bitter nigai.

bitterness nigami.

black kuroi.

black person kokujin.

blade ha.

blame seme *(censure);* tsumi *(crime, sin).*

blame (to) semeru; hihan suru *(criticize).*

blank hakushi *(blank sheet of paper).*

　　fill in a blank form yooshi.

blanket moofu.

bleed (to) shukketsu suru.

bless (to) kiyomeru *(consecrate);* agameru *(praise, glorify).*

blessing shukufuku *(benediction);* kami no megumi *(God's blessing).*

blind *adj.* moomoku no.

blindness moomoku.

block katamari *(bulky piece);* kukaku *(row of houses).*

block (to) fusagu, samatageru.

blood chi.

bloom (to) saku.
　　hana ga saku the flowers are blooming.

blossom hana.

blotter suitorigami.

blouse burausu.

blow (to) fuku *(wind).*

blue aoi.

blush (to) sekimen suru, akaku naru.

board ita *(plank);* makanai *(food).*

boardinghouse geshukuya.

boarding pass toojooken.

boast (to) jiman suru.

boat booto *(rowboat);* fune *(powered by motor).*

body karada *(living or dead person);* shigai *(corpse).*

boil (to) wakasu *(water);* yuderu *(cook in water).*

boiler boiraa.

bold daitan na.

bomb bakudan.

bomb (to) bakugeki suru.

bond shooken *(document).*

bone hone.

book hon.
　　textbook kyookasho.

bookseller hon'ya.

bookstore hon'ya.

border kokkyoo *(frontier of a country);* kyookai *(boundary, limit).*

boring omoshiroku nai *(uninteresting).*

born (to be) umareru.

borrow (to) kariru.

boss uwayaku.

both futari tomo *(people);* ryoohoo *(things).*

bother (to) nayamasu *(annoy);* jama suru *(trouble).*

bottle bin.

bottom soko.

bounce (to) hanekaeru.

bowl donburi, booru.

box hako.

boy shoonen, otoko no ko.

bracelet udewa.

braid uchihimo, amigami.

brain noo; atama *(intellectual ability)*.
brake bureeki.
branch eda *(of tree)*; shiten *(office, etc.)*.
brassière burajaa.
brave yuukan na.
bread pan.
break (to) kowasu *(destroy)*; yaburu *(tear, rip)*.
breakfast asagohan.
breast mune *(human)*.
breath iki.
breathe (to) iki o suru.
breeze soyokaze.
bribe wairo.
    to take a bribe wairo o toru.
brick renga.
bride hanayome.
bridegroom hanamuko.
bridge hashi.
brief mijikai *(short)*.
bright akarui *(with light)*; hade na *(of color)*.
brighten (to) akaruku suru *(with light)*.
brilliant migoto na.
bring (to) motte kuru.
    to bring up sodateru *(a child)*; mochidasu *(for discussion)*.
Britain Eikoku, Igirisu. (See also **English**.)
    British Eikoku no, Igirisu no.
broad hiroi.
broadcast hoosoo.
broadcast (to) hoosoo suru.
broil (to) yaku.
broken kowareta.
brook ogawa.
broom hooki.
brother niisan, oniisan, ani *(older)*; otooto *(younger)*.
brother-in-law gi-kei, giri no ani *(older)*; gitei, giri no otooto *(younger)*.
brown chairo.
bruise uchikizu.
bruise (to) *v.t.* uchikizu o ukeru.
brush fude *(for writing)*; hake, burashi *(for sweeping)*.
bubble awa.
buckle bakkuru, bijoo.
bud tsubomi.
Buddha Hotoke.
    statue of the Buddha Butsuzoo.
Buddhism Bukkyoo.
budget yosan.
build (to) tateru.
building tatemono.
bulletin keiji *(pinned on a board)*; kaihoo *(publication)*.
    bulletin board keijiban.
bundle tsutsumi.
burn (to) yaku; moyasu *(throw into a fire)*.

burst (to) sakeru *(pipes, etc.)*.
bus basu.
bush shigemi.
business yooji *(errand)*; shigoto *(work)*; shoobai *(profession)*.
businessperson kaishain.
busy isogashii.
but ga, shikashi, keredomo *(however)*.
butcher nikuya.
butcher shop nikuya.
butter bataa.
button botan.
buy (to) kau.
buyer kaite, baiyaa.
by soba ni *(nearby)*; de *(by means of)*.

C

cab takushii *(taxi)*.
cabbage kyabetsu.
cable keeburu *(rope, wire)*; kaigai denshin *(cablegram)*.
cage tori kago *(for birds)*; ori *(for animals)*.
cake keeki.
calculator keisanki.
calendar karendaa, koyomi.
calf koushi.
call (to) hoomon suru *(to make a call, visit)*; yobu *(to summon)*.
calm shizuka na, odayaka na.
calm (to) shizuka ni suru.
camera kamera.
camp kyanpu.
camp (to) kyanpu suru.
can kan.
can (be able) dekiru *(can do)*; -koto ga dekiru *(can—)*.
can opener kan-kiri.
cancel (to) torikesu *(revoke)*; sakujo suru *(delete)*.
candidate koohosha.
candle roosoku.
candy kyandii, ame.
cap booshi *(hat)*; futa *(lid)*.
capital shuto *(city)*; shihon *(money)*.
    capital punishment shikei.
capricious kimagure na.
captain rikugun taii *(army)*; senchoo *(merchant ship)*; kaigun taisa *(navy)*.
captive toriko.
capture (to) toriko ni suru, tsukamaeru.
car kuruma *(vehicle)*; jidoosha *(automobile)*.
carbon paper kaabon peepaa.
card hagaki *(postcard)*; e-hagaki *(illustrated postcard)*; toranpu *(playing card)*.
care (to) kamau *(be concerned)*; sewa o suru *(care for a child)*.

    to take care daiji ni suru.
careful chuuibukai.
careless fuchuui na.
caress aibu; hooyoo.
carpenter daiku.
carpet juutan.
carry (to) motte iku *(take to);* hakobu *(transport).*
carve (to) kiru *(meat);* chookoku suru *(sculpture).*
case hako *(box);* jiken *(matter).*
cash genkin.
    to cash a check kogitte o genkin ni kaeru.
cashier genkin gakari, genkin suitoo gakari.
cassette kasetto.
castle shiro.
cat neko.
catch (to) toraeru.
    I have caught a cold. Kaze o hikimashita.
    I could not catch the train. Densha ni ma ni aimasen deshita.
category shurui *(kind);* burui *(class).*
cathedral jiin.
Catholic Kyuukyoo, Katorikku.
cattle ushi *(cow, ox);* kachiku *(livestock).*
cause gen'in.
    without cause gen'in nashi ni.
cause (to) gen'in to naru *(bring about);* -saseru *(cause a person to do . . .).*
cease (to) yamu, owaru *(come to an end).*
ceiling tenjoo.
celebrate (to) iwau.
cellar chikashitsu.
cement semento.
cemetery bochi, hakaba.
censorship ken'etsu.
center chuushin *(of a circle).*
central chuushin no, chuuoo no.
    central heating danboo-soochi *(heating system).*
century seiki.
ceremony shiki.
certain tashika na *(without doubt);* aru *(a certain).*
certainty tashika na koto.
certificate shoomeisho.
chain kusari.
chair isu, koshikake.
chairperson gichoo.
chalk hakuboku, chooku.
challenge choosen.
challenge (to) choosen suru.
champion chanpion, senshu *(athletic);* tooshi *(fighter);* yoogosha *(defender).*
chance chansu *(opportunity);* guuzen *(coincidence);* unmei *(luck, fortune).*
    to take a chance chansu o toru.

change henka, kawari *(alteration);* komakai okane *(small change);* otsuri *(money returned as change).*
change (to) kaeru *(make different);* kawaru *(become different).*
chapel reihaidoo *(place of worship).*
chapter shoo.
character tokuchoo *(unique feature, distinctive mark);* seishitsu *(disposition).*
characteristic *adj.* dokutoku no.
charge (to) tsumu *(load);* kokuhatsu suru *(accuse);* tsuke ni suru *(charge to an account).*
charitable omoiyari no aru *(sympathetic).*
charity jizen.
charming miwakuteki na *(fascinating);* taihen utsukushii *(very attractive);* aikyoo no aru *(engaging).*
chase (to) oikakeru.
chat (to) shaberu, uchikutsuroide hanasu.
cheap yasui.
cheat (to) damasu.
check chikki *(claim check);* kogitte *(bank check).*
check (to) kuitomeru *(hold back, hamper).*
cheer (to) nagusameru *(comfort);* genkizukeru *(enliven).*
cheerful akarui *(disposition);* genki na *(lively).*
cheese chiizu.
chemical *n.* kagaku seihin. *-adj.* kagaku no.
chemistry kagaku.
cherish (to) daiji ni suru.
cherry sakura no hana *(blossom);* sakura no ki *(tree);* sakuranbo *(fruit).*
chest mune *(of the body);* hako *(box).*
chestnut kuri.
chew (to) kamu.
chicken niwatori, chikin.
chief *n.* shunin *(head person). -adj.* omo na.
chimney entotsu.
chin ago.
China Chuugoku.
    Communist China Chuukyoo.
    Chinese Chuugokujin *(person);* Chuugoku no *(pertaining to the country).*
chip kirehashi, kakera.
chocolate chokoreeto.
choice sentaku *(selection);* yorigonomi *(preference).*
choke (to) *v.t.* chissoku saseru *(suffocate); v.i.* chissoku suru.
choose (to) erabu *(make a choice of);* yoru *(pick out).*
chop (to) kizamu *(mince).*
chopsticks hashi.
Christian Kirisutokyoo-shinja *(person).*
    Christianity Kirisutokyoo.
Christmas Kurisumasu.

church kyookai.
cigar hamaki, shigaa.
    cigar store tabakoya.
cigarette makitabako, shigaretto.
circle maru; enshuu *(circumference)*.
circular *adj.* marui. *-n.* kaijoo.
circulate (to) kubaru *(distribute)*.
circumstances jijoo *(conditions)*; baai
    (case).
citizen shimin.
city shi.
city hall kookaidoo.
civilization bunmei.
civilize (to) bunmeika suru.
claim seikyuu *(demand)*; yookyuu *(request)*;
    shuchoo *(insistence)*.
claim (to) seikyuu suru *(demand)*; shuchoo
    suru *(insist)*.
clamor sawagi *(loud noise)*.
clap (to) hakushu suru *(applaud)*.
class shurui *(kind)*; kaikyuu *(social status)*;
    kurasu *(school)*.
    first class ittoo *(in plane, etc.)*.
classic koten.
classify (to) bunrui suru.
    classified ad sangyoo kookoku.
clause jookoo, setsu *(grammar)*.
clean kirei na.
clean (to) sooji suru *(rooms, etc.)*.
    to make clean kirei ni suru.
cleaner kuriininguya *(laundry)*.
cleanliness seiketsu sa.
clear kirei na.
    The sky is clear today. Kyoo wa sora ga
    harete imasu.
    This is clear. Kore wa kirei desu.
    clear soup osumashi.
clerk jimuin *(office)*; ginkooin *(bank)*.
clever rikoo na *(intelligent)*; joozu na
    (dexterous); kayoo na *(skillful)*.
climate kikoo.
climb (to) noboru.
clip kurippu.
clip (to) karu.
clock tokei.
    alarm clock mezamashi dokei.
close -no soba ni *(nearby)*; no chikaku ni
    (close to); kinjo ni *(in the
    neighborhood)*.
close (to) *v.t.* shimeru; *v.i.* shimaru.
closed kyuugyoo *(business)*; heiten *(store)*.
closet todana *(cupboard)*; oshiire *(for storage)*.
cloth kire, nuno *(general term)*.
    cotton cloth momen mono.
    silk cloth kinu mono.
clothes kimono *(Japanese)*; yoofuku
    (Occidental).
cloud kumo.

cloudy kumotte iru.
clover kuroobaa.
club boo *(heavy stick)*; kurabu *(association)*.
coal sekitan.
coarse arai, somatsu na *(roughly made)*; katoo
    na *(rude)*.
coast kaigan *(beach)*; engan *(shore)*.
coat kooto *(Japanese)*; uwagi *(Occidental-
    style jacket)*.
cocktail kakuteru.
code kisoku *(set of rules)*.
coffee koohii.
coffin hitsugi, kan'oke.
coin kahei.
cold samui *(weather)*; tsumetai *(to the
    touch)*.
    to catch a cold kaze o hiku.
    It is cold. Samui desu.
    I am cold. Watashi wa samui desu.
coldness samusa, tsumetasa.
collaborate (to) kyoodoo de hataraku *(work
    together)*.
collar karaa *(for men)*; kubiwa *(for animals)*,
    eri.
collect (to) *v.t.* atsumeru *(gather, get together)*;
    v.i. atsumaru *(come together)*.
collection shuushuu *(of stamps, etc.)*; kashikin
    chooshuu *(of debts)*.
college daigaku *(university)*.
colonial shokuminchi no.
colony shokuminchi.
color iro.
color (to) iro o tsukeru *(add color)*.
column enchuu *(pillar)*; ran *(newspaper)*.
comb kushi.
comb (to) kushi de toku, kushi o kakeru
    (one's hair).
combination kumiawase.
combine (to) kumiawaseru *(join together)*.
come (to) kuru.
    to come around yatte kuru.
    to come back kaette kuru.
    to come in hairu.
comedy kigeki.
comet suisei.
comfort nagusame *(consolation)*.
comfort (to) nagusameru *(console)*.
comfortable kokochi yoi, raku na.
comma konma, kuten.
command shiki *(military direction)*; meirei
    (order).
command (to) meizuru *(direct)*; shihai suru
    (control); meirei suru *(give orders)*.
commander shikisha.
commercial *adj.* shoobai no, shoogyoo no; *n.*
    komaasharu *(advertisement)*.
commission ninmu *(charge, duty)*; toritsugi
    (agency); tesuuryoo *(for service)*.

commit (to) okasu *(a crime).*
common futsuu no *(ordinary);* atarimae no *(usual).*
   common sense jooshiki.
communicate (to) renraku suru *(contact);* tsuushin suru *(correspond with).*
communication renraku, tsuushin; shomen *(written message).*
   mass communication masukomi.
community shakai *(society).*
compact disk konpakuto disaku.
companion nakama *(comrade);* aite *(partner);* tsure *(traveling).*
company kyaku *(social);* kaisha *(firm).*
compare (to) hikaku suru, kuraberu.
comparison hikaku.
compete (to) kyoosoo suru, kisou.
competition kyoosoo *(rivalry);* shiai *(contest).*
complain (to) fuhei o iu *(make a complaint).*
complaint fuhei, kujoo.
complete zenbu no *(entire);* kanzen na *(perfect).*
complex fukuzatsu na *(complicated).*
complexion kaoiro.
complicate (to) fukuzatsu ni suru.
   to get complicated fukuzatsu ni naru.
compliment sanji *(praise);* oseji *(flattering speech).*
compose (to) sakkyoku suru *(music);* shi o tsukuru *(poetry).*
composer sakkyokuka *(of music).*
composition sakubun *(as a school subject);* sakuhin *(prose or poetry);* sakkyoku *(music);* haigoo *(arrangement).*
comprise naritatsu, fukumu.
compromise jooho *(concession);* dakyoo *(agreement).*
compromise (to) dakyoo suru.
computer konpyuutaa.
   computer language konpyuutaa gengo.
   computer program konpyuutaa puroguramu.
   digital computer dejitaru konpyuutaa.
   personal computer pasokon.
conceit unubore *(overweening, excessive self-importance).*
conceited unuboreta.
conceive (to) jutai suru *(become pregnant);* kokoro ni idaku *(form a conception of, imagine).*
concentrate (to) shuuchuu suru.
concern jigyoo *(enterprise);* shinpai *(anxiety).*
   a matter of great concern juudai na mondai.
   to be concerned shinpai suru.

concerning -ni tsuite.
concert ongakukai.
concrete konkuriito *(for building).*
condemn (to) hinan suru *(censure);* senkoku suru *(sentence).*
condense (to) asshuku suru *(compress);* mijikaku suru *(shorten).*
condition jootai *(aspect);* jooken *(terms).*
   critical condition kiken jootai.
   on condition that -no jooken de.
conduct furumai *(behavior);* okonai *(deed).*
   bad conduct warui okonai.
   good conduct yoi okonai.
conduct (to) okonau *(perform).*
   to conduct a business shoobai o keiei suru.
   to conduct an orchestra ookesutora o shiki suru.
conductor shashoo *(of trains, etc.);* shikisha *(of an orchestra).*
confess (to) jinin suru *(acknowledge);* mitomeru *(admit);* hakujoo suru *(make a confession).*
confession kokuhaku, hakujoo.
confidence shin'yoo, shinrai *(trust);* jishin *(self-confidence).*
confident jishin no aru.
confidential himitsu no.
confirm (to) tashikameru *(establish firmly);* kakushoo suru *(verify).*
confirmation kakunin *(corroboration);* kakushoo *(proof).*
congratulate (to) iwau, shukusu.
congratulations omedetoo gozaimasu.
connect (to) tsunagu *(join).*
connection kankei *(relation);* tsunagari *(link).*
conquer (to) seifuku suru.
conquest seifuku.
conscience ryooshin.
conscientious ryooshinteki na.
conscious kizuite iru *(aware).*
consent dooi *(assent);* itchi *(unanimity).*
conservative hoshuteki na.
consider (to) yoku kangaete miru *(contemplate);* kooryo ni ireru *(to take into account);* kangaeru *(think).*
considerable kanari no *(much).*
consideration kooryo *(careful thought);* omoiyari *(thoughtful regard).*
consistent shubi ikkan shita.
consist of (to) -kara naru *(be composed of).*
constant kawaranai *(unchanging);* chuujitsu na *(faithful).*
constitution kenpoo *(of a state);* taikaku *(of the body).*
constitutional kenpoojoo no.
consul ryooji.

consulate ryoojikan.
contagious densensei no.
  a contagious disease densenbyoo.
contain (to) ireru *(include)*; haitte iru *(have within)*; fukurude.
container iremono.
contemporary gendai no *(of the day)*; doojidai no *(existing at the same time)*.
contented manzoku shita.
contentment manzoku *(satisfaction)*.
contents naiyoo.
continent *n.* tairiku.
continual taema no nai *(unceasing)*.
continue (to) *v.t.* tsuzukeru; *v.i.* tsuzuku.
contraception hinin *(birth control)*.
contract keiyaku *(agreement)*; keiyakusho *(written document of an agreement)*.
contractor keiyakunin, ukeoinin.
contradict (to) hanbaku suru *(rebut)*; mujun suru *(conflict with)*.
contradiction hanbaku *(rebuttal)*; mujun *(inconsistency)*.
contradictory mujun shite iru.
contrary hantai no.
  on the contrary hantai ni, kaette.
contrast taishoo.
contrast (to) taishoo suru.
contribute (to) kifu suru *(money, etc.)*; kikoo suru *(to a publication)*.
contribution kifu *(donation)*; kikoo *(something written for a publication)*.
control toosei *(government)*; yokusei *(restraint)*.
  birth control sanji seigen.
control (to) toogyo suru *(govern)*; toosei suru *(regulate)*.
controversy ronsoo, giron *(dispute)*.
convenience benri, tsugoo.
convenient tsugoo no yoi, benri na.
convent shuudooin.
convention kyoogikai, kaigi, shuukai.
conversation kaiwa *(dialogue)*; hanashi *(talk)*.
converse (to) hanasu.
convert (to) *v.t.* kaeru *(change into)*; kaishuu saseru *(to a religion)*.
convict (to) yuuzai to senkoku suru *(declare guilty)*.
conviction kakushin *(firm belief)*; yuuzai hanketsu *(verdict of guilty)*.
cook ryoorinin *(of Japanese or any other kind of food)*; kokku *(for other than Japanese food)*.
cook (to) ryoori suru, ryoori o tsukuru.
cool suzushii *(temperature)*; tsumetai *(to the touch)*; reisei na *(unexcited)*; reitan na *(lacking in zeal)*.
cool (to) tsumetaku suru.
copy utsushi, kopii *(of a letter, etc.)*; mosha *(of a picture)*.

corporation kaisha *(firm)*; shadan-hoojin *(corporate body)*.
correct tadashii *(right)*; tashika na *(sure)*; seikaku na *(accurate)*; machigai no nai *(without error)*.
correct (to) naosu; koosei suru *(proofread)*, tensaku suru *(school papers)*.
correction teisei *(of an error)*; koosei *(in proofreading)*; tensaku *(of a school composition)*.
correspond (to) buntsuu suru, tsuushin suru *(exchange letters)*; itchi suru *(agree)*.
correspondence tsuushin; buntsuu.
correspondent tsuushin'in *(of a periodical)*; tokuhain *(mass media)*.
corrupt (to) fuhai suru *(rot)*; daraku suru *(morally)*.
corruption daraku *(moral deterioration)*.
cost nedan *(price)*; hiyoo *(expense)*.
costume fukusoo, kimono; yoofuku *(Western)*; ishoo *(fancy dress)*.
cotton wata *(raw)*; momen *(woven)*.
cough seki.
count keisan *(reckoning)*.
count (to) kazoeru.
counter kauntaa *(restaurant, etc.)*; chooba *(in Japanese-style hotel)*.
countless kazoekirenai.
country inaka *(rural region)*; kuni *(nation)*.
countryman inaka mono *(a rustic)*; dookokujin *(compatriot)*.
couple futatsu *(of things)*; futari *(of people)*; futsuka *(of days)*; fuufu *(husband and wife)*.
courage yuuki.
  to have courage yuuki ga aru.
course kamoku, katei *(of study)*; koosu, michi *(road followed)*; yarikata *(line of conduct or action)*.
court saibansho *(tribunal)*.
  law court hootei.
courteous teinei na; teichoo na *(polite)*.
courtesy teinei *(politeness)*; kooi *(favor)*; reigi *(civility)*.
courtyard nakaniwa.
cousin itoko
  second cousin mata itoko.
cover futa, kabaa.
cow meushi.
co-worker shigoto nakama.
crack wareme *(split)*; sukima *(chink)*; hibi *(flaw)*.
crack (to) *v.t.* waru; *v.i.* wareru; hibi ga hairu *(break without separating)*.
  to crack a nut kurumi o waru.
  to crack a joke joodan o tobasu.
  a hard nut to crack nan mondai.
cradle yurikago.

crash shoototsu *(collision)*.
crash (to) shoototsu suru.
crazy kichigai jimita *(half-crazed)*.
   crazy about muchuu ni natta.
cream kuriimu.
create (to) tsukuru *(bring into being)*; soosaku suru *(produce)*.
creature ikimono *(living thing)*.
credit kurejitto, shin'yoo *(trust)*.
creditor kashi nushi, saikensha.
crime tsumi.
   to commit a crime hanzai o okasu.
crisis kiki *(crucial time)*; tooge *(of a sickness, etc.)*.
   political crisis seiji no kiki.
   financial crisis keizai no kiki.
critic hihyooka *(reviewer)*.
critical hihyooteki *(inclined to criticize)*; kiki no *(serious)*.
criticism hihyoo, hihan.
criticize (to) hihyoo suru *(discuss critically)*; hinan suru *(find fault with)*.
crooked magatte iru *(bent)*; nejireta *(twisted)*; fushoojiki na *(dishonest)*.
crop shuukaku *(yield)*; toriire *(harvest)*.
cross juuji *(lines that intersect)*; juujika *(religious symbol)*.
crossing tokoo *(ocean)*; koosaten *(intersection)*.
crossroads koosaten; yotsukado.
crouch (to) kagamu.
crow karasu.
crowd hito gomi.
   to be crowded konde iru.
crown kanmuri.
crown (to) eikan o sazukeru *(reward or honor)*.
cruel zankoku na.
cruelty zangyaku.
crumb pan kuzu.
crumble (to) kuzureru *(collapse)*; mu ni kisuru *(come to nothing)*; kona ni suru *(break into crumbs)*.
crust pan no kawa.
crutch matsubazue.
cry sakebi goe *(shout)*; naki goe *(weeping)*.
cry (to) sakebu *(shout)*; naku *(weep)*.
cunning warugashikoi *(sly)*; zurui *(crafty)*.
cup yunomi *(teacup)*; koppu *(glass)*; kappu *(trophy)*.
   a cup of coffee koohii ippai.
   a cup of tea o-cha ippai.
cure (to) naosu.
   to be cured of naoru.
curiosity kookishin.
curious kookishin ga tsuyoi *(inquisitive)*; kimyoo na *(strange)*.
curl kaaru *(of hair)*.
current *adj.* genzai no *(present)*; ryuutsuu

shite iru *(in general circulation)*. *-n.* nagare *(stream)*.
curtain mado kake, kaaten *(for a window)*; maku *(theater)*.
curve yumi nari *(arched shape)*; kyokusen *(curved line)*.
curve (to) *v.t.* mageru; *v.i.* magaru.
cushion kusshon; zabuton *(for sitting)*.
custom shuukan *(habit)*; fuuzoku *(convention)*.
customary futsuu no *(ordinary)*.
customer kyaku.
customhouse zeikan.
customs official zeikanri.
cut kirikizu *(wound)*; kirehashi *(a piece of something)*.
cut (to) *v.t.* kiru; *v.i.* kireru.

dagger tantoo.
daily mainichi no.
   daily newspaper nikkan shinbun.
dainty kyasha na.
dam damu, seki.
damage songai *(loss)*; higai *(injury, harm)*.
damage (to) dame ni suru.
damp shimeppoi *(of things)*; shikki no ooi *(of atmosphere)*.
dance dansu *(foreign)*; odori *(Japanese)*.
dance (to) odoru.
danger kiken.
dangerous abunai.
dark kurai *(little light)*; koi *(color)*; kuroi *(person)*.
dash (to) tosshin suru *(rush)*.
data deeta.
   data processor deeta purosessa.
date yakusoku *(appointment)*; hizuke *(on a letter)*.
daughter musume *(plain form)*; ojoosan *(respect form)*.
dawn yoake.
day hi, hiru *(daytime)*.
   day after tomorrow asatte.
   day before yesterday ototoi.
   yesterday kinoo.
   today kyoo.
dazzle (to) me o kuramasu.
dead shinda *(lacking life)*.
   dead leaves kareha.
deaf mimi no kikoenai.
deal torihiki *(business)*.
   a great deal hijoo ni takusan.
deal (to) torihiki suru *(trade)*; tsukiau *(associate with)*.
dealer shoonin.

dear takai *(price)*; kawaii *(beloved)*.
death shi *(loss of life)*; shiboo *(act or fact of dying)*.
debate ronsoo.
debit karigata.
debt shakkin *(sum due)*; saimu *(liability)*.
debtor karinushi.
decanter tokkuri.
decay fuhai *(rot)*.
decay (to) kusaru *(rot)*; otoroeru *(decline)*; taika suru *(deteriorate)*.
deceased shiboo.
deceit azamuki.
deceive (to) damasu *(cheat)*; azamuku *(delude)*.
December Juunigatsu.
decent ontoo na *(proper)*; joohin na *(modest)*; kanari rippa na *(respectable)*.
decide (to) kimeru.
decision kettei.
decisive ketteiteki.
deck kanpan, dekki *(of a ship)*; hito kumi *(of playing cards)*.
declare (to) shinkoku suru *(report)*; mooshitateru *(state)*.
decline jitai *(refuse)*.
decline (to) jitai suru.
decrease genshoo.
decrease (to) *v.t.* herasu, sukunaku suru; *v.i.* heru.
decree hanketsu *(judicial decision)*; hoorei *(ordinance)*.
dedicate (to) sasageru *(consecrate)*; yudaneru *(devote oneself to one's work)*.
deed kooi *(action)*; jikkoo *(performance)*; okonai *(act)*; shoosho *(document)*.
deep fukai *(opp. of shallow)*; koi *(color)*.
deer shika.
defeat haisen *(military)*; shippai *(failure)*.
defeat (to) *v.t.* makasu;
  to be defeated *v.i.* makeru.
defect ketten.
defend (to) mamoru.
defense booei.
defiance choosen *(challenge)*; mushi *(disregarding)*.
define (to) teigi suru.
definite hakkiri shita.
defy (to) choosen suru *(challenge)*; mushi suru *(disregard)*.
degree do *(on a thermometer, etc.)*; gakui *(diploma)*.
  by degrees dandan.
delay chien.
delay (to) *v.i.* okureru.
delegate daihyoo *(representative)*.
delegate (to) haken suru *(depute)*; inin suru *(entrust)*; daihyoo suru *(represent)*.

deliberate (to) shian suru *(consider)*; shingi suru *(discuss)*.
deliberately shinchoo ni, yuuyuu to.
delicacy bimyoosa *(of coloring, etc.)*.
delicate yowai *(in health)*; kowareyasui *(fragile)*.
  a delicate situation muzukashii tachiba.
delicious oishii.
delight ureshisa.
deliver (to) todokeru *(goods)*; watasu *(hand over)*.
deliverance kyuushutsu *(from bondage, etc.)*; sukui dasu koto.
delivery haitatsu *(forwarding)*.
demand yookyuu, motome *(request)*; juyoo *(for goods)*.
  to be in demand juyoo ga aru.
democracy minshushugi, demokurashii.
demonstrate (to) jitsuen suru.
demonstration jitsuen *(exhibition)*; jii undoo, demo *(mass meeting, protest parade)*.
denial hitei *(negation)*; hinin *(disavowal)*; kyohi *(refusal)*.
denounce (to) kokuhatsu suru *(inform against)*; haki suru *(repudiate)*.
dense fukai *(as fog)*; oishigetta *(as forest)*; konda *(crowded)*.
density mitsudo.
dentist haisha.
deny (to) uchikesu.
depart (to) deru.
department bumon *(section)*; depaato *(department store)*.
departure shuppatsu.
depend (to) tayoru *(for support)*; tanomi ni suru *(rely on)*.
dependent tayotte iru *(on one's parents, etc.)*.
deplore (to) nageku *(lament)*.
deposit tetsukekin *(as a binder)*; yokin *(in a bank)*.
depreciation genka shookyaku.
depress (to) kiochi suru.
depression fukeiki *(in business)*; yuuutsu *(of mind)*.
deprive (to) ubaitoru.
depth fukasa.
deride (to) azakeru.
descend (to) kudaru *(go down)*; oriru *(alight from)*; kudari ni naru *(slope down)*.
descendant shison.
describe (to) setsumei suru, noberu *(give an account of)*.
description setsumei, jojutsu *(of a person)*.
desert sabaku.
desert (to) suteru *(one's family or friend)*; dassoo suru *(from the army or prison)*.
deserve (to) shikaku ga aru *(be entitled to)*; kachi ga aru *(be worthy of)*.

design zuan *(sketch)*; kooan *(idea, scheme)*; dezdin *(dress, etc.)*.

designer zuanka *(of patterns)*; kooansha *(of ideas)*; dezainaa *(of dresses)*.

desirable nozomashii.

desire yokuboo *(craving)*; nozomi *(wish, hope)*.

desire (to) nozomu *(long for)*; kiboo suru *(wish)*.

desk tsukue, desuku.

desolate wabishii, sabishii.

despair zetsuboo, rakutan *(despondency)*.

despair (to) zetsuboo suru *(lose hope)*; rakutan suru *(be disappointed)*.

desperate zetsuboo teki na *(beyond hope)*; kiken na *(dangerous)*; hisshi no *(frantic)*; mukoomizu no *(reckless)*.

despise (to) misageru.

despite akui *(malice)*; bujoku *(insult)*; keibetsu *(scorn)*.

    despite -ni mo kakawarazu.

dessert dezaato.

destiny unmei.

destroy (to) kowasu; hakai suru *(demolish)*; dainashi ni suru *(ruin)*; zenmetsu saseru *(annihilate)*.

destruction hakai.

detach (to) hikihanasu *(unfasten, separate)*.

detail saimoku *(item)*; kuwashii koto, shoosai *(particulars)*.

    in detail kuwashiku.

detain (to) hikitomeru.

detect (to) tantei suru.

detective tantei.

    detective story tantei shoosetsu.

determination saiketsu *(decision)*; kesshin *(resolution)*; ketsudan ryoku *(firmness of purpose)*.

determine (to) kakutei suru *(ascertain)*; kimeru *(decide)*.

detest (to) kirau.

detour mawari michi.

detrimental furieki na, yoku nai.

develop (to) hatten saseru *(cause to grow)*; keihatsu suru *(unfold)*; genzoo suru *(photo negatives)*.

development seichoo *(growth)*; hatten *(gradual progress)*; kakuchoo *(expansion)*.

device kufuu.

devil oni, akuma.

devise (to) kufuu suru.

devoid kakete iru *(lacking in)*.

devote (to) sasageru *(give up, direct)*.

devour gatsugatsu taberu *(eat hungrily and greedily)*; horobosu *(destroy)*.

    devour a book musabori yomu.

dew tsuyu.

dial daiyaru, mojiban.

    telephone dial daiyaru.

dial (to) diayaru o mawasu.

dialect hoogen.

dialogue kaiwa, taiwa.

diameter chokkei.

diamond daiyamondo.

diary nikki.

    to keep a diary nikki o tsukeru.

dictate (to) kakitoraseru *(a letter)*.

dictation kakitori *(practice in spelling)*; koojutsu *(business)*.

dictionary jisho, jiten, jibiki *(lexicon)*.

    English-Japanese dictionary Ei-Wa jiten.

    Japanese-English dictionary Wa-Ei jiten.

die (to) shinu.

diesel diizeru.

Diet gikai *(Japanese Parliament)*.

diet shokuji ryoohoo *(prescribed allowance of food)*; daietto *(for weight loss)*.

difference chigai *(dissimilarity)*; sabetsu *(distinction)*; iken no sooi *(disagreement)*.

different (be) chigau.

differ from (to) chigau.

difficult muzukashii.

difficulty konnan, mendoo.

dig (to) horu.

digest (to) shooka suru *(food)*; kanryaku ni suru *(abbreviate)*.

dignity igen *(of bearing)*.

dim usugurai.

dimension menseki *(area)*; ookisa *(size)*.

diminish (to) *v.i.* chiisaku naru *(in size)*; sukunaku naru *(in number)*.

dine (to) shokuji o suru.

dining room shokudoo.

dinner hiru no shokuji, hirugohan *(noon meal)*; ban no shokuji, yuuhan *(evening meal)*.

dip (to) tsukeru, hitasu.

diplomacy gaikoo *(between nations)*; kakehiki *(tactful dealing)*.

diplomat gaikookan.

direct massugu na *(straight)*; jika no *(direct rays, etc.)*.

direct (to) shiiji suru *(point the way)*; sashizu suru *(order)*.

direction hoogaku *(way)*; shidoo *(guidance)*; kanri *(control)*; sashizu *(instruction)*.

director shihainin *(manager)*; juuyaku *(of a company)*; shunin *(chief)*.

directory juushoroku.

    telephone directory denwachoo.

dirt obutsu *(filth)*; doro *(mud)*; hokori *(dust)*.

dirty kitanai.
disability muryoku.
disabled muryoku ni natta.
disadvantage furi.
disagree (to) itchi shinai.
disagreeable fuyukai na.
disagreement fuitchi *(discord);* fuchoowa
   (disharmony); iken no sooi *(dissent);* fuwa
   (quarrel).
disappear (to) mienaku naru.
disappearance mienaku naru koto,
   shooshitsu.
disappoint (to) shitsuboo saseru.
disapprove (to) sansei shinai.
disaster tensai *(calamity).*
disastrous hisan na, saigai no ookii *(flood,*
   etc.).
discharge kaiko *(release from duty);* jotai
   (army).
discharge (to) funaoroshi o suru *(cargo);*
   hassha suru *(a gun);* hima o dasu
   (dismiss).
discipline kunren *(drill);* kiritsu *(order).*
disclaim (to) hooki suru.
disclose (to) arawasu *(expose);* abaku *(reveal);*
   happyoo suru *(make known).*
disclosure bakuro.
discomfort fukai.
disconnect (to) kiru *(sever a connection).*
discontent fumanzoku na.
discontinue (to) chuushi suru.
discord fuwa.
discotheque disuko.
discount waribiki.
discount (to) waribiki suru.
discourage (to) rakutan saseru
   to be discouraged gakkari suru.
discouragement rakutan.
discover (to) mitsukeru *(find small things);*
   hakken suru *(find more important things).*
discovery hakken.
discreet shiryo no aru *(judicious);* shinchoo na
   (prudent); yoojinbukai *(wary).*
discretion shiryo *(prudence).*
discuss (to) toogi suru *(talk over);* tooron suru
   (argue).
discussion toogi *(debate);* tooron
   (argument).
disdain keibetsu.
disdain (to) keibetsu suru.
disease byooki.
disgrace fumeiyo *(dishonor);* haji *(shame).*
disguise hensoo.
   in disguise hensoo shite.
disguise (to) hensoo suru.
disgust iyake.
disgust (to) mune o waruku suru *(nauseate);*
   kimochi waruku saseru *(create an*
   aversion).

   be disgusted unzari suru.
dish sara.
dishonest fushoojiki na.
disk enban.
dislike kirai.
dislike (to) kirau.
dismiss (to) ikaseru *(allow to go);* menshoku
   suru *(expel);* hima o dasu *(discharge).*
dismissal hima.
disobey (to) somuku.
disorder ranzatsu *(lack of order);* konzatsu
   (confusion).
dispense with (to) shobun suru *(dispose of).*
display chinretsu *(show);* hyoogen
   (manifestation); misebirakashi
   (ostentation).
displease (to) ki ni sawaraseru *(offend).*
displeasure fuman *(dissatisfaction).*
disposal shobun.
dispose (to) naraberu *(arrange);* -ki ni naru
   (be inclined to).
   to dispose of shobun suru.
dispute kooron *(debate);* soogi *(controversy);*
   kenka *(altercation).*
dispute (to) toogi suru *(argue about);*
   hanbaku suru *(contest);* teikoo suru
   (oppose).
dissolve (to) tokasu *(melt);* torikesu *(annul).*
distance kyori.
distant tooi *(far off).*
distinct hakkiri shita *(clear);* tokushu na
   (different).
distinction tokuchoo *(individuality).*
distinguish (to) miwakeru *(visually);*
   kikiwakeru *(by sound).*
distort (to) yugameru *(twist);* kojitsukeru
   (pervert).
distract (to) ki o torareru.
distress nayami *(worry);* nageki *(grief);*
   kutsuu *(pain).*
distribute (to) wariateru *(allot);* makichirasu
   (spread out); bunpai suru *(apportion);*
   kubaru *(deal out).*
district chihoo *(region);* ku *(city ward).*
distrust fushin'yoo.
distrust (to) shinjinai.
disturb (to) jama suru.
disturbance jama.
ditch mizo.
dive (to) tobikomu.
divide (to) wakeru *(separate, part);* waru *(by*
   cutting); shikiru *(by partition).*
divine shinsei na.
   divine being kami.
   divine service reihaishiki.
division warizan *(math.);* bunkatsu
   (separation).
divorce (to) rikon suru.
   divorced rikon shita hito.

dizziness memai.

dizzy memai ga suru.

do (to) suru *(act)*; tsukuru *(make)*.

dock hatoba, dokku.

doctor isha *(medical)*; hakase *(academic)*.

doctrine shugi.

document shorui *(papers)*; shoosho *(deed)*; bunsho *(official letter)*.

dog inu.

doll ningyoo.

dome maru tenjoo, doomu.

domestic katei no *(household)*; kainarasareta *(domesticated, tame)*; kokunai no *(native, pertaining to one's country)*.
  domestic affairs kaji *(of a household)*.
  domestic animal kachiku.

dominate (to) shihai suru *(govern)*.

door to, doa *(Western-style)*.
  Japanese sliding door shooji.
  entrance door genkan no doa.
  back door uraguchi no doa.

dose fukuyooryoo *(medicine)*.

dot ten.

double nibai.

double (to) nibai ni suru.

doubt utagai *(lack of certainty)*; fushin *(misgiving)*.

doubt (to) utagau *(disbelieve)*; fushin ni omou *(question)*.

doubtful tashika de nai *(uncertain)*; hakkiri shinai *(ambiguous)*; utagawashii *(questionable)*.

doubtless utagai nai.

down shita.

dozen daasu.

draft kawase tegata *(bank order)*; shitae *(sketch)*; shitagaki *(of a plan)*.
  draft (draught) of wind sukima kaze.

drag (to) hiku *(draw forcibly)*; hikizuru *(pull)*.

drain (to) haisui suru *(carry away water)*; nomihosu *(drink up)*.

drama engeki, dorama *(a play)*; gekiteki jiken *(event)*.

draw (to) kaku *(pictures)*; hikitsukeru *(attention)*.
  to draw back shirizoku.

drawer hikidashi *(of a table, etc.)*.

drawing room zashiki.

dread osore.

dread (to) osoreru.

dreadful osoroshii.

dream yume.

dream (to) yume o miru.

dreamer kuusooka, musooka.

dress kimono *(Japanese)*; doresu, yoofuku *(Western)*.

dress (to) *v.t.* kimono o kiseru; *v.i.* kimono o kiru.

dressmaker yoofukuya, yoosaishi *(of Western clothes)*; shitateya.

drink nomimono.
  drinking water nomimizu.

drink (to) nomu.

drip (to) shitataru.

drive (to) unten suru.

driver untenshu.

drop itteki *(of liquid)*.

drop (to) *v.t.* otosu *(let fall)*; *v.i.* ochiru *(from a height)*.

drown (to) oboreru.

drug kusuri *(medicine)*; mayaku *(narcotics)*.

drugstore kusuriya.

drum taiko; doramu *(Occidental-style)*.

drunk yotte iru.
  drunken person yopparai.

dry kawaita *(of things)*; kansoo shita *(of climate)*.

dry (to) kawakasu *(make dry)*; nuguu *(wipe one's eyes, etc.)*; kawaku *(become dry)*.

dryness kawaki *(thirst)*.

duck ahiru *(domestic)*; kamo *(wild)*.

due manki *(payable)*; toozen no *(fit, proper)*.
  due to -no tame ni.

dull nibui *(blunt)*; bonyari shita *(stupid)*; omoshiroku nai *(uninteresting)*.

during -no aida, -kan, -chuu (juu).
  during ten years juunen kan.
  during one's absence rusu no aida, rusu chuu.

dust chiri; hokori *(a finer dust than* chiri*)*.

dust (to) sooji suru, hokori o harau.

dusty hokori no ooi.

Dutch Oranda no.

duty tsutome *(work to be done)*; gimu *(moral or legal obligation)*; kanzei *(on imported goods)*.

duty free muzei no.

dwarf kobito *(person)*; kogata no *(undersized)*.
  dwarf trees bonsai no ki.

dwell (to) sumu.

dye senryoo.

dye (to) someru.

E

each kaku-: *(prefix)* -zutsu: *(suffix)*.
  each person meimei; kakuji
  each person or thing sorezore *(of several)*.
  each other otagai ni.
  each time -tabi ni.

eager nesshin na *(ardent)*.

eagle washi.

ear mimi.

early *adj.* hayai. *-adv.* hayaku.

earn (to) kasegu *(by labor)*.

earnest majime na *(serious)*; nesshin na *(intense)*.

earth tsuchi *(soil)*; chikyuu *(world)*.

ease raku, kiraku.

ease (to) raku ni suru.

easily yasashiku; tegaru ni *(readily)*; surasura to *(smoothly)*.

east higashi.
    the East Tooyoo.
    East Asia Higashi Ajia.

Easter fukkatsusai, iisutaa.

eastern higashi no.

easy yasashii.

eat (to) taberu; meshiagaru *(honorific: respect)*.

echo yamabiko *(a phenomenon of nature)*; hankyoo *(in other cases)*.

echo (to) hankyoo suru.

economical keizaijoo no, keizaiteki na.

economize (to) setsuyaku suru *(use economically)*.

economy class ekonomii kurasu.

edge ha *(of blade)*; hashi *(of cloth)*; kishi *(of cliff, etc.)*.

edition han.
    first edition shohan.
    new edition shinpan.
    revised edition kaiteiban.

editor henshuusha *(of books or magazines)*; shuhitsu *(of newspaper)*.

editorial shasetsu.

education kyooiku.
    to receive an education kyooiku o ukeru.

effect kekka *(consequence)*.

effective yuukoo na *(operative)*; yuunoo na *(efficient)*.

efficiency nooritsu.

effort doryoku *(strenuous attempt)*; honeori *(exertion)*; rooku *(strain)*.
    with an effort hone otte.
    without any effort doryoku sezu ni.

egg tamago.

egoism jiko chuushin shugi.

eight yattsu, hachi.

eighteen juuhachi.

eighteenth juuhachi ban.

eighth dai hachi.

eightieth hachijuu ban.

eighty hachijuu.

either dochiraka no *(one of the two)*; dochira mo *(each of two)*.
    either . . . or -ka . . . ka, -ka aruiwa . . . ka

elastic shinshukusei no aru, shinayaka na *(flexible)*.

elbow hiji.

elder toshiue no.

elderly nenpai no.

eldest ichiban toshi ue no.

elect (to) erabu *(choose)*; senkyo suru *(by vote)*.

election senkyo.

electric denki no.

electrical denki no.

electricity denki.

elegant yuuga na *(graceful)*; joohin na *(tasteful)*.

element yooso *(component part)*.

elementary shoho no.

elephant zoo.

elevator erebeetaa.

eleven juuichi.

eleventh dai juuichi.

eliminate (to) nozoku *(exclude)*; sakujo suru *(get rid of)*; habuku *(omit)*.

eloquence yuuben.

eloquent yuuben na.

else hoka ni.
    anyone else hoka ni dare ka.
    something else hoka ni nani ka.

elsewhere hoka ni doko ka.

elude (to) nogareru *(evade)*; sakeru *(escape adroitly from)*.

embark (to) joosen suru *(board a ship)*; shuppan suru *(depart)*.

embarrass (to) komaraseru.
    I was embarrassed. Komarimashita.

embarrassing toowaku saseru.

embarrassment toowaku *(perplexity)*.

embassy taishikan.

embody gutaika suru *(make concrete)*.

embrace (to) daku *(a person)*; torimaku *(encircle)*; hoogan suru *(contain)*.

embroidery nuitori, shisuu.

emerge (to) arawareru *(come out into view)*.

emergency hijooji.

eminent kencho na *(distinguished)*.

emotion kanjoo *(feeling)*.
    appeal to the emotions kanjoo ni uttaeru.
    with emotion kandoo shite.

emperor tennoo.

emphasis kyoochoo.

emphasize (to) kyoochoo suru.

emphatic tsuyoi.

empire teikoku.

employee yatoinin, shiyoonin, juugyoo in.

employer yatoinushi.

employment shokugyoo *(occupation)*; shigoto *(work)*; koyoo.

empty kara no.

enable (to) -ga dekiru.

enamel enameru.

enclose (to) kakomu *(surround)*; kakou *(shut in)*, doofuu suru *(in a letter)*.

enclosure kakoi *(fence)*; doofuubutsu *(enclosed materials)*.

encourage (to) genki zukeru *(hearten)*; yuuki zukeru *(put courage into)*.

encouragement hagemashi.

end sue *(latter part)*; owari *(the close)*; ketsumatsu *(conclusion)*; shimai *(finish)*.

end (to) owaru, shimau.

endeavor jinryoku, doryoku.

endeavor (to) doryoku suru *(try hard)*; kokoromiru *(attempt)*.

endorse (to) uragaki suru.

endure (to) gaman suru *(bear bravely)*; mochikotaeru *(hold out)*.

enemy teki.

energy chikara *(power)*; genki *(vigor)*.
    atomic energy genshiryoku.
    energy crisis nenryoo kiki.
    mental energy seishin nooryoku.
    solar energy taiyoo enerugii.

enforce (to) shiiru *(press)*.

engage (to) yatou *(hire)*.

engaged isogashii *(busy)*; kon'yaku shite iru *(betrothed)*.

engagement yakusoku *(formal promise)*; kon'yaku *(betrothal)*; yooji *(business)*.

engine kikai *(machine)*; kikan *(boiler)*, enjin *(of car, etc.)*.

engineer gishi *(of factory)*.

English eigo *(pertaining to the language)*; Igirisu (Eikoku) no *(pertaining to the country)*; Igirisujin (Eikokujin) *(pertaining to the people)*.

engrave (to) horu; insatsu suru *(print)*.

enjoy (to) tanoshimu.

enjoyment tanoshimi.

enlarge (to) ookiku suru *(make bigger)*; hikinobasu *(a photograph, etc.)*.

enlist (to) guntai ni hairu *(in the army)*; hito no shiji o eru *(secure one's support)*.

enormous kyodai na.

enough juubun.

enter (to) hairu.

entertain (to) tanoshimaseru *(amuse)*; motenasu *(guests)*.

entertainment goraku *(amusement)*; yokyoo *(public show)*.

enthusiasm nesshin.

enthusiastic nesshin na.

entire kanzen na *(complete)*; zentai no *(whole)*.

entitle (to) na o tsukeru.

entrance iriguchi.

entrust (to) makaseru *(a duty, etc.)*; azukeru *(a thing to another person)*.

enumerate (to) kazoeru *(count)*.

envelope fuutoo *(for letters)*.

envious urayamashii.

envy urayami, shitto *(jealousy)*.

envy (to) urayamu *(feel envy of)*; shitto suru *(begrudge)*.

episode soowa, episoodo.

equal onaji *(the same)*; byoodoo no *(equitable)*.

equal (to) -ni hitoshii.
    A equals B. A wa B desu.

equality byoodoo.

equator sekidoo.

equilibrium tsuriai.

equip (to) yooi suru *(supply)*; soobi suru *(fit)*; mijitaku suru *(array)*.

equipment shitaku, junbi, soochi.

era jidai.

erase (to) kesu nuguikesu *(wipe out)*.

eraser keshi gomu.

erect (to) tateru *(set up)*.

err (to) machigaeru.

errand tsukai.

error machigai.

escalator esukareetaa.

escape toosoo *(running away)*; datsugoku *(from prison)*.

escape (to) nigeru *(get free)*; nogareru *(get off safely)*.

escort (to) goei suru *(with military)*; tsukisou *(accompany)*.

especially tokuni.

essay ronbun, zuihitsu.

essence yooten *(main points)*; hontai *(a thing in itself)*; yooso *(element)*.

essential kanarazu iru, nakute wa naranai *(necessary)*; honshitsuteki no *(of essential character)*.

establish tateru, setsuritsu suru *(found)*; kakutei suru *(ascertain)*; seitei suru *(prove)*.

establishment setsuritsu *(business firm)*.

estate shoyuuchi *(property)*; jisho *(ground)*.

esteem sonkei *(respect form)*.

esteem (to) sonkei suru.

esthetic fuuryuu na, biteki na.

estimate mitsumori *(of the cost)*; hyooka *(of the value)*.

estimate (to) hyooka suru *(appraise)*; mitsumoru *(compute)*; handan suru *(judge)*.

estimation mitsumori, hyooka.

eternal eikyuu no *(everlasting)*; huhen no *(immutable)*.

eternity eikyuu, eien *(infinite time)*; fumetsu *(immortality)*.

ether eeteru.

European Yoorappajin *(people)*; Yooroppa no *(pertaining to Europe)*.

evade sakeru.

evasion kaihi.

eve yuugata *(evening)*; zenya *(the evening or day before a festival)*.

even mo, demo *(also)*; taira na *(level)*; choodo *(just)*.

evening ban, yoru, yuugata.

Good evening! Konban wa.

yesterday evening sakuban, yuube.

tomorrow evening myooban, ashita no ban.

event dekigoto, jiken.

ever itsu demo *(always)*; taezu *(incessantly)*; ima made ni *(up to now)*; itsu ka *(on any occasion)*.

every mai-, donna -demo; zenbu *(all)*.

everyday mainichi.

every year maitoshi.

everybody dare mo *(referring to members of a group)*; dare demo *(no matter who)*; minna *(all)*.

everything nan demo *(no matter what)*; zenbu, minna *(all things)*.

everywhere doko de mo *(no matter where)*; hooboo *(all over)*.

evidence shooko *(proof)*.

evident akiraka na *(obvious)*.

evil *adj.* warui, akushitsu na *(wicked)*; fukitsu na *(unlucky)*. -*n.* aku *(vice)*; jaaku *(wickedness)*; warui koto *(bad thing)*.

evoke (to) hikiokosu *(draw forth)*.

evolve (to) tenkai suru *(unfold, unroll)*; hatten suru *(develop)*.

exact seikaku na *(accurate)*; genmitsu na *(precise)*; genkaku na *(rigorous)*.

exaggerate (to) kochoo suru, oogesa ni iu.

exaggeration kochoo, oogesa.

exalt (to) takameru *(raise high)*; homesoyasu *(extol)*.

exaltation takameru koto.

examination kensa *(inspection)*; choosa *(investigation)*; koosatsu *(consideration)*; shiken *(test)*.

examine (to) shiraberu *(inspect)*; shiken suru *(give a test)*.

example rei *(illustration)*; tehon *(model, pattern)*.

exceed sugiru, kosu *(go over)*.

excel (to) sugureru.

She excels in English. Eigo ni sugurete iru.

excellence subarashisa, kesshutsu *(superiority)*; choosho *(great merit)*.

excellent sugureta.

except -no hoka wa.

except (to) nozoku *(omit)*.

exception reigai.

exceptional reigaiteki na.

exceptionally reigaiteki ni *(unusually)*; hijoo ni *(very)*.

excess yobun.

excessive yobun no *(surplus)*; hoogai na *(exorbitant)*.

exchange kookan *(of things in general)*; ryoogae *(of coins)*.

exchange (to) torikaeru, kookan suru *(barter)*.

exchange rate kawase sooba.

excite (to) *v.i.* sawagu *(a body of people)*; *v.t.* ugokasu *(arouse a feeling)*.

to get excited koofun suru.

excitement koofun.

exclaim sakebu *(cry out)*; zekkyoo suru *(speak vehemently)*.

exclamation zekkyoo *(outcry)*; kantanshi *(an interjection)*.

exclamation mark kantanfu.

exclude (to) nozoku.

exclusive dokusenteki *(monopolistic)*; -o nozoite *(not including)*.

excursion ensoku *(picnic)*; yuuran ryokoo *(pleasure tour)*.

excuse koojitsu *(bad)*; iiwake *(apology)*.

excuse (to) yurusu *(forgive)*; benkai suru *(vindicate)*.

Excuse me. Gomen nasai.

execute (to) jikkoo suru *(carry out)*; suikoo suru *(perform)*.

execution shikkoo, suikoo.

exempt (to) menzuru *(free)*.

exercise undoo *(of the body)*; renshuu *(lesson)*.

exercise (to) undoo suru *(engage in athletics)*; renshuu suru *(practice)*.

exert (to) tsukusu *(put forth)*; mochiiru *(use)*.

exertion doryoku, jinryoku *(vigorous effort)*.

exhaust (to) kara ni suru *(empty)*; tsukai tsukusu *(use up)*; tsukarehatesaseru *(tire out)*.

exhaustion hiroo *(extreme fatigue)*.

exhibit (to) tenji suru *(show publicly)*.

exhibition hakurankai *(exposition)*; tenjikai *(show)*.

exile tsuihoo *(banishment)*; tsuihoonin *(person in exile)*.

exile (to) tsuihoo suru.

exist sonzai suru, aru *(be)*.

existence sonzai *(being)*; seizon *(life)*.

exit deguchi.

expand hirogeru *(spread out)*; kakuchoo suru *(extend)*; kakudai saseru *(amplify)*.

expansion kakuchoo *(dilation)*; hirogari *(expanse)*.

expansive koodai na *(extensive)*; kokoro no hiroi *(comprehensive)*.

expect (to) kitai suru *(look forward to)*; -to omou *(suppose)*.

expectation kitai *(anticipation)*; yosoo *(probability)*.

expedition tanken *(for exploration)*.
expel (to) oiharau *(drive out)*; menshoku suru *(dismiss)*.
expense hiyoo.
expensive takai, kooka na *(costly)*.
experience keiken *(personal observation)*.
experience (to) keiken suru *(undergo)*.
experiment (to) shiken suru *(test)*, tamesu *(try out)*.
expert *adj.* kurooto *(in doing something)*. *-n.* senmonka *(specialist)*.
expire (to) kikan ga kireru *(come to an end)*, iki o hikitoru *(breathe one's last)*; kieru *(die out)*; shoometsu suru *(become extinct)*.
explain (to) setsumei suru *(give an explanation)*; kaishaku suru *(interpret)*; benmei suru *(justify by an explanation)*.
explanation setsumei.
explanatory setsumeiteki, setsumei no.
explode (to) bakuhatsu suru.
exploit tegara *(brilliant achievement)*.
exploit (to) kuimono ni suru *(take advantage of for one's own ends)*.
explore (to) tanken suru *(search through)*; choosa suru *(inquire into)*.
explosion bakuhatsu.
export yushutsu.
export (to) yushutsu suru.
expose (to) sarasu *(leave unprotected)*; chinretsu suru *(exhibit)*; roshutsu suru *(in photography)*; abaku *(disclose, reveal)*.
express sokutatsu *(special delivery)*; kyuukoo *(train)*.
express (to) iiarawasu *(state)*.
expression hyoojoo *(facial)*; hyoogen *(verbal)*.
expressive hyoojoo ni tomu.
expulsion hoochiku.
exquisite sensai na *(delicate)*.
extend (to) nobasu *(in length or term)*; hirogeru *(in breadth)*; okuru *(invitation, greetings)*.
extensive koodai na *(far-reaching)*.
extent han'i *(space, scope, degree)*.
to some extent aru teido.
exterior soto, hyoomen *(surface)*.
exterminate (to) tayasu.
external gaibu no *(outside)*.
extinct horobite shimatta.
extinction shoometsu.
extinguish kesu *(put out)*; tayasu *(put an end to)*.
extra betsu no; googai *(edition of a newspaper)*.
extract bassui *(excerpt)*.
extract (to) nuku *(pull out)*; nuki-toru *(pull out with difficulty)*; tekishutsu suru *(draw forth)*.

extraordinary futsuu de nai *(exceptional)*; hibon na *(uncommon)*; ichijirushii *(remarkable)*.
extravagance zeitaku *(lavish wastefulness)*; hoojuu *(unrestrained excess)*.
extravagant zeitaku na *(profuse, wasteful)*; mucha na *(unreasonable)*; hoogai na *(exorbitant, excessive)*.
extreme kyokutan na *(utmost)*; ichiban tooi *(outermost)*.
extremely taihen, hijoo ni.
extremity hashi *(extreme point)*.
eye me.
eyebrow mayuge.
eyeglasses megane.
eyelid mabuta.

F

fable otogibanashi, guuwa.
face kao.
face (to) mukau.
facilitate raku ni suru.
facility yooi *(ease)*; bengi *(convenience)*.
fact koto; shidai *(of an occurrence)*; jikoo *(particulars)*.
in fact jitsu wa.
factory kooba, koojoo.
faculty shuwan *(aptitude)*; gakubu *(of a university)*.
fade iro ga sameru.
fail (to) shippai suru *(be unsuccessful)*; hasan suru *(become bankrupt)*.
without fail machigai naku, kitto, zehi.
faint usui *(of color)*; yowai *(wanting in courage)*; kasuka na *(of sound, etc.)*.
faint (to) kizetsu suru.
fair *adj.* kirei na *(pretty)*; iro no shiroi *(of complexion)*; koohei na *(impartial)*. *-n.* ichi *(market)*; jizen ichi *(bazaar)*.
faith shinkoo *(belief)*; shinjoo *(creed)*; kyoogi *(religious doctrine)*; shinrai *(trust)*.
faithful chuujitsu na.
fall tsuiraku *(drop)*; taki *(cascade)*; aki *(autumn)*; kanraku *(surrender)*; gakai *(of a government)*.
fall (to) ochiru *(drop)*; furu *(rain, snow)*; sagaru *(prices)*.
fall down korobu.
false uso no, hontoo de nai *(not true)*; fujitsu na *(not faithful)*; sorazorashii *(feigned)*; nise *(counterfeit)*.
fame meisei.
familiar yoku shirarete iru *(well known)*; kikinareta *(to the ear)*; minareta *(to the*

eye); arifureta *(common);* shitashii
(intimate).
family kazoku.
   family name myooji.
famine busshi no ketsuboo *(scarcity of food);*
   kikin *(failure of crops);* kiga *(starvation).*
famous yuumei na.
fan sensu *(folding);* uchiwa *(nonfolding).*
   electric fan senpuuki.
fancy soozooryoku *(imagination);* kangae
   (idea).
fantastic kuusooteki na *(extravagant);* iyoo na
   (grotesque); soozoojoo no *(imaginary),*
   subarashii *(wonderful).*
far tooi.
   as far as made.
   so far ima made *(up to now).*
fare ryookin *(cost of transportation).*
   one-way fare katamichi ryookin.
farm hatake *(field);* noojoo *(ranch).*
farmer noofu, hyakushoo.
farming noogyoo *(agriculture).*
farther motto tooi.
farthest ichiban tooi.
fashion tsukuri kata *(shape);* ryuukoo, fasshon
   (style).
fashionable (to become) ryuukoo suru.
fast hayai.
fasten (to) shikkari tomeru *(make fast);* kukuri
   tsukeru *(attach securely).*
fat *adj.* futotta. *-n.* abura.
fatal inochi ni kakawaru.
   fatal accident chimeiteki jiko.
   fatal disease fuji no yamai.
   fatal wound chimeishoo.
fate unmei *(destiny);* un *(appointed lot).*
father otoosan *(respect);* chichi *(plain).*
faucet jaguchi.
fault ketten *(defect);* tansho *(weak point);*
   machigai *(mistake).*
favor onegai *(request).*
   Could (will) you do me a favor? Onegai
   dekimasu ka?
favor (to) ekohiiki o suru *(be partial to);* shiji
   suru *(support).*
favorable kooi aru *(well disposed);* shoodaku
   no *(consenting).*
favorite *adj.* ki ni iri no *(preferred);* daisuki
   na *(liked greatly). -n.* ninkimono *(person).*
fax fakkusu.
fear osore *(dread);* shinpai *(anxiety).*
fear (to) osoreru.
fearless daitan na.
feather hane.
feature tokuchoo *(characteristic);* yooten
   (striking point); kaodachi *(appearance).*
February Nigatsu.
federal chuuoo seifu no *(pertaining to the
   central government).*

fee gessha *(monthly);* shinsatsuryoo
   (doctor's).
feeble yowai *(weak);* bonyari shita
   (indistinct).
feed (to) tabesaseru.
feel (to) sawaru *(touch);* kanjiru *(perceive a
   sensation).*
feeling kankaku *(sense);* kimochi *(sensation);*
   kanjoo *(emotion).*
fellow *adj.* nakama no. *-n.* nakama
   (associate).
fellowship shoogakukin *(grant);* shinboku
   (friendliness).
female onna *(woman).*
   female sex josei.
feminine onna no.
fence kakine *(enclosure for garden);* kakoi
   (for other purposes); hei.
fencing kendoo *(Japanese-style);* fenshingu
   (foreign).
ferocious kyooboo na *(fierce);* yaban na
   (savage).
ferry watashibune *(ferryboat);* renrakusen
   (connected with trains).
fertile koeta *(productive).*
fertilize (to) hiryoo o hodokosu.
fertilizer hiryoo *(manure);* kagaku hiryoo
   (chemical).
fervent netsuretsu na *(ardent).*
fervor netsu joo *(ardor).*
festival saijitsu *(feast day);* omatsuri, matsuri
   (of shrine or temple).
fetch motte kuru.
fever netsu.
few ni san *(two or three);* sukoshi *(not
   many).*
fiber sen'i.
fiberoptic communication hikari tsuushin.
fiction shoosetsu, fikushon.
field nohara *(open country);* bokusoochi
   (meadow).
   rice field ta.
fierce araarashii *(ferocious);* mooretsu na
   (violent); hageshii *(furious).*
fiery hi no yoo na *(glowing).*
fifteen juugo.
fifteenth dai juugo; juugo nichi *(of the
   month);* juugo ban.
fifth dai go.
fiftieth dai gojuu.
fifty gojuu.
fig ichijiku.
fight kenka *(brawl);* sensoo *(battle).*
fight (to) sensoo suru *(wage war);* doryoku
   suru *(struggle for);* kenka suru *(quarrel).*
figure suuji *(number);* katachi *(form);* sugata
   (body); moyoo *(design, pattern).*
file yasuri *(tool);* retsu *(row);* fairu *(official
   file);* tojikomi *(for letters).*

fill (to) v.t. ippai ni suru; v.i. ippai ni naru (become full).

film fuirumu (for camera); eiga (motion picture).

filthy kitanai (unclean); gehin na (obscene).

final saigo no (last); shuukyoku no (conclusive).
    finally tootoo.

finance zaisei.

finance (to) kane o dasu.

financial zaiseijoo no.

find (to) mitsukeru.

fine adj. komakai (small); hosoi (slender); usui (thin); utsukushii (beautiful); ii (good); genki na (healthy).

fine n. bakkin (penalty).

finger yubi.

finish (to) shimau, oeru; dekiagaru (complete a piece of work); shiageru (get a thing done).

fire hi; kaji (conflagration).

fireworks hanabi.

firm adj. katai (compact); shikkari shita (rigid).

firm n. shookai, kaisha (commercial).

first adj. dai ichi no, ichi ban no (ordinal number). -adv. hajime.
    at first hajime wa.
    for the first time hajimete.

fish sakana, uo; sashimi (slices of raw fish).
    raw fish namazakana.

fish (to) tsuri o suru.
    go out fishing tsuri ni iku.

fisherman ryooshi.

fist nigiri kobushi.

fit adj. tekitoo na (appropriate); datoo na (proper, right). -n. hossa (convulsion).

fit (to) tekigoo suru (be fit for); awaseru (make to suit); junbi suru (qualify); au (be adjusted to fit).

fitness tekitoo.

five itsutsu, go.

fix (to) kimeru (determine); toritsukeru (arrange); naosu (mend).

flag hata.

flame honoo.

flank sokumen (side).

flank (to) sokumen o mamoru.

flash hirameki (lightning).

flat hiratai (level); kin'itsu no (unvarying); ki no nuketa (stale).

flatter oseji o iu.

flattery oseji (insincere compliment).

flavor aji (taste); kaori (smell).

fleet kantai (navy).

flesh niku (meat for eating); nikutai (of the human body).

flexibility shinayakasa.

flexible shinayaka na (pliable).

flight hikoo (trip by air); tooboo (fleeing); kaidan (of stairs).

fling (to) tosshin suru (dash, rush); nagetsukeru (hurl, toss).

flint hiuchi ishi.

float (to) uku (on water); ukabu (on water or in air).

flood oomizu, koozui.

flood (to) shinsui saseru (inundate); shinsui suru (be inundated); hanran suru (overflow).

floor yuka (of a room).

floppy disk furoppii disuku.

flourish (to) sakaeru (thrive).

flow nagareru.

flower hana.
    flower arrangement ikebana, kadoo.

fluid ekitai.

fly hae.

fly (to) tobu.

foam awa.

foam (to) awa ga tatsu.

fog kiri (mist); moya (haze).
    thick fog noomu.

fold hida (in a garment).

fold (to) tatamu, oru.

foliage ha.

follow (to) -ni shitagau (go or come after); -ni tsuite kuru (come traveling with someone); -ni tsuite iku (go accompanying someone); issho ni iku (accompany).

following sono tsugi no (next).
    the following day akuru hi.

fond (be) konomu.

fondness suki.

food tabemono.

fool baka.

foolish baka na (silly); bakarashii (nonsensical); bakageta (ridiculous).

foot ashi (of the body); fiito (measure).

football futtobooru, shuukyuu.

footstep ashidori (tread); ashiato (footprint).

for -no kawari ni (in place of); -o daihyoo shite (representing); -ni taishite (in return for, in contrast with); -no tsugunai ni (in compensation for); -no tame ni (on behalf of, in support of, for the purpose of, because of); -ni mukatte (in the direction of); -no wari ni wa (in respect of).
    for example tatoeba.
    for the first time hajimete.
    for the most part daibubun.
    for the present ima no tokoro.

forbid kinjiru.

force chikara (strength); guntai (troops).
    by force muri ni.

force (to) bookoo suru (use force upon); kojiakeru (break open); oshiyaru (impel);

    muri ni, shiite *(when followed by a causative verb)*.
    I forced her to go. Muri ni ikaseta.
ford (to) asase o wataru *(wade across)*.
foreground zenkei.
forehead hitai.
foreign gaikoku no *(pertaining to foreign countries in general)*; seiyoo no *(of the West)*.
foreigner gaikokujin, gaijin *(foreigners in general)*; oobeijin *(Western)*.
forest hayashi, mori *(grove)*; shinrin *(dense growth)*.
forget (to) wasureru.
forgetfulness wasureppoi koto.
forgive yurusu.
forgiveness yurushi.
fork fooku *(for eating)*; wakaremichi *(parting of the ways)*; shiryuu *(of a river)*; mata *(of a tree)*.
form katachi *(shape)*; keishiki *(formality)*; yooshi *(blank)*.
form (to) katachizukuru *(shape)*; tsukuru *(organize)*; -ni naru *(constitute)*; tsukuriageru *(build up)*.
formal seishiki no.
formation soshiki.
former mae no, saki no *(previous)*.
formerly mae ni *(previously)*; moto *(originally)*.
formula hooshiki, yarikata *(method)*.
forsake (to) misuteru *(abandon)*.
fort yoosai.
fortieth yonjuu ban me no; dai yonjuu.
fortunate un ga ii.
fortunately un yoku, shiawase ni mo *(luckily)*.
fortune shiawase *(good luck)*; zaisan *(wealth)*; unsei *(fate)*.
forty shijuu, yonjuu.
forward zenpoo e *(onward)*.
    move forward zenshin suru.
forward (to) okuru *(goods)*; kaisoo suru, tensoo suru *(letters)*.
foster yoo—.
    foster daughter yoojo.
    foster father yoofu.
    foster mother yoobo.
    foster son yooshi.
found (to) setsuritsu suru *(establish, start)*; kiso o oku *(lay the base of)*.
foundation dodai *(groundwork)*; konkyo *(basis)*; shuppatsuten *(beginning)*; zaidan *(endowed institution)*.
founder sooritsusha *(one who establishes or lays a foundation)*.
fountain funsui.
four yottsu, shi, yon.

fourteen juushi, juuyon.
fourteenth juuyon ban me no *(place)*; juuyokka *(of the month)*.
fourth yottsu me, dai shi, dai yon; yokka *(of the month)*.
fowl tori *(bird)*.
fox kitsune.
fragment kakera, kirehashi.
fragrance yoi nioi.
fragrant nioi no ii.
frail yowayowashii.
frame gakubuchi.
frame (to) e o gaku ni ireru *(a picture)*.
frank sotchoku na *(openhearted)*; koozen no, akarasama na *(without guile)*.
frankness sotchoku.
free tada *(gratis)*; jiyuu na *(liberated)*; muzei *(without tax)*.
free (to) v.t. hanasu *(let go free)*; v.i. jiyuu ni naru *(be set free)*.
freedom jiyuu *(liberty)*; dokuritsu *(independence)*.
freeze (to) v.t. kooraseru; v.i. kooru.
freight kamotsu *(goods)*.
French furansu no *(pertaining to France)*; furansugo *(language)*; furansujin *(people)*.
frequent tabitabi no *(recurring often)*.
frequent (to) yoku iku *(visit often)*.
frequently tabitabi *(often)*; yoku *(at short intervals)*.
fresh mizumizushii *(newly grown)*; dekitate no *(just made)*; shinsen na, atarashii *(said of foods)*.
friction masatsu, atsureki.
Friday Kin'yoobi.
friend tomodachi; yuujin.
friendly aiso no ii.
friendship yuujoo *(friendly attachment)*; yuugi *(intimacy)*.
frighten (to) odorokasu;
    be frightened bikkuri suru, odoroku.
frightening kowai.
fringe fusa *(tuft)*; heri *(border)*.
frivolity fumajime.
frivolous fumajime na.
frog kaeru.
from -kara.
    from now on ima kara.
front mae, zenmen *(forward part)*; zenpoo *(forward place)*; shoomen *(of a building)*; sensen *(line of battle)*.
frost shimo.
fruit kudamono.
fry (to) furai ni suru, ageru.
frying pan furai pan, age nabe.
fuel nenryoo.
fugitive *n.* toosoosha *(runaway)*; boomeisha *(political refugee)*.

fulfill (to) hatasu *(perform);* jikkoo suru *(execute).*

full ippai no *(filled to capacity).*

fully mattaku.

fun tanoshimi *(amusement).*

function hataraki.

function (to) hataraku.

fund kikin.

fundamental kisoteki na.

funds shikin *(sum of money).*

funny kokkei na.

fur kegawa.

furious okotte iru *(angry).*

furnace ro.

furnish (to) kyookyuu suru *(provide);* sonaeru *(equip).*

furniture kagu.

furrow ato *(track);* wadachi *(rut);* fukai shiwa *(deep wrinkle).*

furrow (to) kao o shikameru *(make a wrinkle in the face).*

further sono ue *(besides).*
    further away motto saki.
    further on motto saki e.

fury gekido *(wild anger);* kyooboo *(violence).*

future *adj.* mirai no. *-n.* mirai *(time to come);* shoorai *(prospect).*
    in the future mirai ni, shoorai.

G

gaiety nigiyakasa *(mirth).*

gain rieki *(opposite of loss);* mooke *(earnings);* zooka *(increase).*

gain (to) te ni ireru, eru *(obtain);* masu *(increase).*

gallant isamashii.

gallery gyaraii *(of fine arts);* tachimi-seki *(standing room in a theater).*

gamble (to) kakegoto o suru, kakeru.

game yuugi *(amusement);* kyoogi *(sporting contest);* shoobugoto *(of chance).*

garage gareeji.

garden niwa.
    public garden kooen.

gardener uekiya, niwashi.

garlic ninniku.

gas gasu.

gasoline gasorin.

gate mon.

gather *v.t.* yoseatsumeru *(bring together);* atsumeru *(collect);* saishuu suru *(pick up);* tsumu *(as flowers); v.i.* atsumaru *(assemble).*

gay yooki na *(said of people);* hade na *(said of colors).*

gem hooseki *(jewel).*

gender sei.

general *adj.* ippan no, ippanteki no *(belonging to the whole);* taitei no *(common to many).*
    in general, generally ippan ni.

general *n.* taishoo *(military).*

generalize (to) ippanka shite kangaeru.

generation sedai *(used when referring to people, as in "young generation");* jidai *(period of time).*

generosity kandaisa, kimae no yosa.

generous ki no ookii, kandai na.

genius tensai.

gentle otonashii *(said of people);* yasashii *(said of manners);* odayaka na *(quiet).*

gentleman shinshi.

genuine honmono no *(authentic);* senjitsu na *(sincere).*

geographical chiriteki no.

geography chiri.

germ baikin.

German doitsu no *(pertaining to Germany);* doitsugo *(language);* doitsujin *(people).*

gesture miburi.

get (to) naru *(become, turn);* te ni ireru *(get hold of).*

ghastly zotto suru.

giant *adj.* ooki na, ookii. *-n.* oootoko *(big man).*

gift miyage *(souvenir);* okurimono, purezento *(present);* sainoo *(talent).*

gifted sainoo no aru *(talented).*

girl onna no ko.

give (to) sashiageru *(to others: humble);* ageru *(to others);* yaru *(to others: fam.);* watasu *(hand over);* kudasaru *(from others: respect);* kureru *(from others: fam.).*
    give back kaesu.

glad ureshii *(delighted, happy).*
    be glad yorokobu.

gladly yorokonde.

glance hitome.
    at a glance hitome de.

glance (to) chiratto miru *(look rapidly);* zatto me o toosu *(read rapidly).*

glass garasu *(material).*
    looking glass kagami.
    drinking glass koppu.

gleam kagayaki *(shine);* hirameki *(of intelligence).*

gleam (to) kagayaku.

glitter kagayaki.

glitter (to) pikapika hikaru.

globe tama *(round object);* chikyuu *(the earth).*

gloomy kurai *(dark);* usugurai *(somber);* inki na *(depressed).*

glorious kooei aru *(illustrious);* soogon na *(majestic);* subarashii *(delightful).*

glory kooei *(honor);* sookan *(splendor).*

glove tebukuro.

   a pair of gloves tebukuro hitokumi.

go (to) yuku, iku; mairu *(honorific: humble);* irassharu *(honorific: respect).*

   to go away itte shimau.

   to go back kaeru.

   to go down oriru *(stairs, etc.);* kudaru *(mountains, etc.).*

   to go into hairu.

   to go out deru.

   to go up noboru, agaru.

god kami *(deity);* guuzoo *(idol).*

gold kin.

golden kin'iro no.

good ii, yoi.

   Good afternoon! Konnichi wa.

   Good evening! Konban wa.

   Good morning! Ohayoo gozaimasu.

   Good night! Oyasumi nasai *(said when going to bed).*

good-bye sayonara.

goods shinamono.

goodwill kooi.

goose gachoo.

gossip goshippu, uwasabanashi.

gossip (to) uwasabanashi o suru, hito no uwasa o suru.

govern (to) osameru *(rule);* kanri suru *(control).*

government seiji *(politics);* seitai *(form of government);* kanri *(management);* toochi kikan *(governing body).*

grace shitoyakasa.

graceful shitoyaka na.

grain kokumotsu.

grammar bunpoo.

grand subarashii *(magnificent);* rippa na *(splendid).*

   Grand! migoto desu.

grandchild mago.

granddaughter mago musume.

grandfather ojiisan, sofu.

grandmother obaasan, sobo.

grandson mago musuko.

grant kyoka *(permission);* joseikin *(funds).*

grant (to) kikitodokeru *(consent to);* ataeru *(give);* juyo suru *(bestow);* yurusu *(allow, permit).*

grape budoo.

grapefruit gureepu furuutsu.

grasp (to) nigiru *(in the hand);* tsukamu *(with the hand or mind).*

grass kusa.

grasshopper inago.

grateful arigatai.

gratitude kansha.

grave *adj.* juudai na *(serious).*

grave *n.* haka *(place of burial).*

gravel jari.

gray nezumi iro, hai iro.

grease abura.

great ookii *(large);* idai na *(much above the average).*

greatness idaisa.

greedy kuishinboo na *(for food);* yokufukai *(for gain).*

green midori.

greet (to) aisatsu suru.

greeting aisatsu.

grief fukai kanashimi *(deep sorrow);* shintsuu *(distress).*

grieve (to) *v.t.* fukaku kanashimaseru *(cause grief to);* kurushimaseru *(distress); v.i.* fukaku kanashimu *(feel grief);* nageku *(lament).*

grin (to) niyatto warau.

grind surikudaku.

groan unari goe.

groan (to) unaru, umeku.

grocer shokuryoohin'ya.

grocery store shokuryoohin'ya.

grope tesaguri suru.

gross juuni daasu *(12 doz.).*

ground jimen *(surface of earth);* dodai *(foundation).*

group guruupu; shuudan *(assemblage).*

group (to) matomeru.

grow (to) hattatsu suru *(develop);* seichoo suru *(said of animate things);* haeru *(flourish in earth).*

growth seichoo.

grudge urami.

   hold a grudge against uramu.

gruff bukkiraboo na.

guard hoshoo *(sentry);* shashoo *(of a train);* bannin *(watchman).*

guard (to) mamoru.

guardian kookennin *(legal);* hogosha *(keeper).*

guess suiryoo, ate zuiryoo.

guess (to) soozoo suru.

   guess right iiateru.

guide annaisha *(tourist);* michi annaisha *(one who shows the way);* shidoosha *(leader).*

guide (to) annai suru *(lead the way).*

guilt tsumi.

gum nori, gomu.

   chewing gum chuuingamu.

gun juu *(firearm);* teppoo *(rifle, shotgun);* kenjuu *(revolver).*

gush (to) fukideru.

H

habit shuukan.

habitual shuukanteki na *(customary);* jooshuuteki *(regular).*

hail arare *(small hailstone);* hyoo *(large hailstone).*

hail (to) arare ga furu.

hair ke *(in general);* kami *(of the head).*

hairdo heya sutairu.

hairdresser biyooshi.

half hanbun.

   half-hour hanjikan, sanjippun.

hall hiroma, hooru.

ham hamu.

hammer kanazuchi.

hand te.

hand (to) watasu *(hand over).*

handbag handobaggu, tesage.

handful te ippai.

handkerchief hankachi.

handle te, hikite *(of a door);* e, te *(of a tool).*

handle (to) atsukau.

handsome tanrei na *(good-looking);* yooboo no utsukushii *(beautiful).*

handy kiyoo na *(said of persons);* choohoo na, benri na *(said of things).*

hang *v.t.* kakeru *(something);* kubi o kukuru *(a person);* *v.i.* sagaru *(hang down).*

happen (to) furikakaru *(befall);* okoru *(occur).*

happening dekigoto *(event);* jiken *(incident).*

happiness koofuku *(well-being);* shiawase *(fortune, luck).*

happy ureshii, koofuku na *(felicitous, joyous);* shiawase na *(favored by luck).*

harbor minato.

hard katai *(solid, as opposed to soft);* muzukashii *(difficult).*

   to study hard isshookenmei benkyoo suru.

harden (to) *v.t.* katameru, kataku suru *(solidify);* katamaru *(become solid).*

hardly hotondo *(used with a negative expression).*

hardness kenroo.

hardship konnan.

hardware kanamono.

   hardware store kanamonoya.

hardy joobu na.

hare no-usagi.

harm gai *(damage);* songai *(loss);* sonshoo *(injury).*

harm (to) gaisuru.

harmful warui.

harmless gai no nai.

harmonious tsuriai no toreta *(balanced).*

harmony waon *(musical);* haigoo *(of colors);* enman, choowa *(between persons).*

harsh soaku na *(coarse);* fuchoowa na *(discordant);* kibishii *(stern).*

harvest shuukaku.

haste isogi.

hasten (to) isogu *(hurry);* isogaseru *(hurry a person);* hayameru *(a result);* isoide suru *(hurry to).*

hat booshi.

hate nikumi.

hate (to) nikumu, kirau.

hateful nikurashii.

hatred nikushimi.

haughty gooman na.

have (to) motsu *(possess, hold);* nomu *(drink);* taberu *(eat);* uketoru *(receive).*

haven minato, hinansho.

hay karekusa.

he kare, ano hito.

head atama *(of the body);* kashiro *(leader),* shunin *(chief).*

headache zutsuu.

heal *v.t.* naosu *(mend);* *v.i.* naoru *(be mended).*

health kenkoo.

healthy kenkoo na, joobu na.

heap yama.

   to heap up tsumu.

hear (to) kiku.

hearing kiku chikara, chooryoku.

   hard of hearing mimi ga tooi.

heart shinzoo *(organ of the body);* kokoro *(as seat of the emotions).*

heat (to) atatameru, atsuku suru.

heaven tengoku *(Christian);* gokuraku *(Buddhist).*

   Heavens! oya maa!

heavy omoi.

hedge ike gaki.

heed (to) shitagau.

heel kakato.

height takasa.

heir soozokunin.

heiress soozokunin.

helm kaji.

help tetsudai.

help (to) tetsudau *(give a helping hand);* sewa o suru *(take care of);* tasukeru *(rescue).*

helper tetsudai.

helpful yaku ni tatsu.

hem fuchi *(margin);* heri *(edge);* sakai *(border).*

hen mendori.

henceforth kore kara.

her, hers kanojo no. (See also **him.**)

herb yakusoo *(medical).*

herd mure.

here koko *(this place)*; kotchi, kochira *(this side)*.

herewith koko ni.

hero eiyuu *(of a battle)*; shujinkoo *(of a novel)*.

heroic eiyuuteki.

heroine jojoofu *(person of great deeds)*; onna shujinkoo *(of a novel)*.

herring nishin.

herself jibun *(self, same word is used for both male and female)*.

  by herself hitori de, jibun de.

hesitate (to) tamerau, chuucho suru.

hide (to) kakusu *(conceal)*; himitsu ni suru *(keep secret)*; kakureru *(conceal oneself)*.

hideous zotto suru yoo na.

high takai.

higher -yori mo takai.

hill oka *(small mountain)*; saka (on a road).

him ano kata ni, ano hito ni *(to him)*; ano kata o, ano hito o *(as object of sentence)*.

himself jibun *(same word used also for "herself")*.

  by himself jibun de.

hind ushiro no.

hinder (to) jama suru, samatageru.

hinge chootsugai.

hint hinto, honomekashi *(allusion)*; atekosuri *(insinuation)*.

hint (to) honomekasu *(allude to)*; atekosuru *(insinuate)*.

hip oshiri, koshi.

hire (to) yatou *(servants, etc.)*; kariru *(cars)*.

his ano hito no, kare no.

historian rekishika.

historic rekishijoo no, rekishiteki no.

history rekishi.

hit (to) utsu, tataku, naguru.

  to hit against butsukeru.

hoarse shagare goe no.

hoe kuwa.

hold (to) motsu *(have)*; okonau *(a ceremony)*; kaisai suru *(an exhibition or conference)*; tamotsu *(maintain)*.

hole ana.

holiday yasumi *(period of recreation or rest)*; matsuri *(festival)*; saijitsu *(national holiday)*.

hollow *adj.* kara no *(empty)*. *-n.* kubomi *(cavity)*.

holy shinsei na *(sacred)*; koogooshii *(divine)*; shinkooshin no fukai *(deeply pious)*.

homage keii *(respect)*.

home uchi, katei *(family)*.

  hometown kokyoo, kuni, furusato.

honest shoojiki na *(truthful)*; seijitsu na *(sincere)*; sotchoku na *(frank)*.

honesty seijitsu.

honey hachimitsu.

honor meiyo *(fame)*; shin'yoo *(credit)*; sonkei *(esteem)*.

honor (to) meiyo o ataeru *(exalt)*; hijoo ni sonkei suru *(venerate)*.

honorable tootoi, sonkei subeki.

hood zukin *(garment)*.

hoof hizume.

hook kugi *(to hang things on)*.

hope kiboo *(opp. of despair)*; kitai *(confident anticipation)*; mikomi *(probability)*.

hope (to) nozomi o kakeru *(count on)*; nozomu *(desire)*.

hopeful kiboo ni michite iru, ate ni shite iru.

hopeless nozomi no nai.

horizon chiheisen *(of land)*; suiheisen *(of sea)*.

horizontal yoko no.

horn tsuno *(of animals)*; tsuno bue *(wind instrument)*, horun *(English horn)*.

horrible osoroshii *(terrible)*; monosugoi *(ghastly)*.

horror kyoofu.

horse uma.

horseback (on) uma ni notte iru.

hosiery kutsushita.

hospitable motenashi no yoi.

hospital byooin.

host shujin *(one who entertains another, hotel keeper)*.

hostess hosutesu, onna shujin *(in a hotel or restaurant)*; okami *(in an inn)*; shujin *(at home)*.

hostile tekii no aru.

hot atsui.

hotel hoteru *(Western-style)*; yadoya, ryokan *(Japanese-style)*.

hot spring onsen.

hour jikan.

  two hours ni jikan.

house ie *(the structure)*; uchi *(home, one's abode)*.

household shotai, katei *(home)*.

housekeeper kaseifu.

how doo, donna ni.

  How are you? Ogenki desu ka?

  How beautiful! Maa kirei desu ne.

  how long dono kurai nagaku.

  how many dono kurai, ikutsu.

  how much ikura.

  how often nando kurai.

however ga, keredomo; donna ni -mo, ikura -mo *(in whatever way, to whatever degree)*.

howl (to) hoeru *(said of animals)*; unaru *(said of the wind)*.

human *adj.* ningen no *(characteristic of people)*. *-n.* ningen, hito.

  human being ningen.

  human nature ningensei.

human race jinrui.
humane ninjoo no aru *(compassionate)*; jihibukai *(merciful)*.
humanity jindoo.
humble kenson na *(modest)*; hikaeme na *(not pretentious)*.
humid shimeppoi *(damp)*; shikki no takai *(of high humidity)*.
humiliate jisonshin o kizutsukeru, haji o kakaseru *(mortify)*.
humility kenson *(humbleness)*.
humor kishitsu *(disposition)*; kibun *(mood)*; kimagure *(caprice)*; kokkei, yuumoa *(jocularity)*.
   in good humor jookigen.
hundred hyaku.
hundredth hyakubanme no.
hunger ue *(famine)*; kuufuku *(craving for food)*.
hungry (be) onaka ga suita.
hunt kari ryoo *(hunting)*.
hunt (to) kari o suru *(shoot animals)*; sagasu *(look for)*.
hunter ryooshi.
hurry *n.* isogu koto, isogi.
   be in a hurry isoide iru.
hurry (to) isogu.
hurt (to) *v.i.* itamu; *v.t.* itameru.
husband otto.
hush (to) shizuka ni saseru *(quiet)*; damaraseru *(silence)*; osaeru *(restrain)*.
hyphen haifun.
hypocrisy gizen.
hypocrite gizensha.
hypothesis kasetsu.

I

I watakushi, watashi, boku *(used by men among friends)*.
ice koori.
icy koori de tsurutsuru shita.
idea kangae *(thought)*; chishiki *(knowledge)*; inshoo *(impression)*; shinnen *(belief)*; omoitsuki *(intention)*.
ideal *n.* risoo. *-adj.* risooteki na.
idealism risooshugi.
idealist risooka.
identical dooitsu no.
idiot hakuchi.
idle shigoto no nai *(unemployed)*; hima de aru *(not active)*; namaketa *(lazy)*.
idleness namakeru koto.
if moshi.
ignoble iyashii, gehin na.
ignorance mugaku *(lack of education)*; muchi *(lack of knowledge)*.

ignorant mugaku na *(without education)*; muchi na *(unthinking, uninformed)*; fuannai no *(unaware)*.
ignore (to) mushi suru.
ill kagen ga warui, byooki no *(sick, unwell)*; warui *(bad, evil)*.
illness byooki.
illusion sakkaku *(optical)*; moosoo *(delusion)*.
illustrate (to) sashie o ireru *(pictures and diagrams)*; rei o shimesu *(give examples)*.
illustration sashie *(picture)*; rei, tatoe *(example)*.
image sugata *(form)*; chookokuzoo *(carved statue)*; guuzoo *(idol)*.
imaginary soozoo no.
imagination soozoo.
imagine (to) soozoo suru *(form a mental picture)*; omou *(think)*; kangaeru *(suppose)*.
imitate (to) maneru, mane o suru.
imitation mane *(copy)*; magaimono, nisemono *(fake)*.
immediate sugu no, chokusetsu no.
immediately sugu ni.
imminent sashisematta *(impending)*.
immobility fudoosei.
immoral fudootoku na.
immorality fudootoku.
immortal fujimi no, shinu koto no nai.
immortality fushi, fukutsusei.
impartial koohei na.
impatience tanki.
impatient (be) ki ga hayai *(of character)*; tanki na *(quick tempered)*.
imperfect fukanzen na *(incomplete)*; kekkan no aru *(faulty)*.
impertinence shitsurei.
impertinent shitsurei na *(rude)*; namaiki na *(insolent)*.
impetuosity sekkachi.
impetuous gekiretsu na, nesshin na.
impious fushinjin na.
import yunyuuhin *(goods)*.
import (to) yunyuu suru.
importance juuyoosei.
important daiji na *(of consequence)*; kan'yoo na *(essential)*; chomei na *(eminent)*.
impossible fukanoo na.
impress (to) osu *(imprint)*; inshoo zukeru *(produce a vivid impression)*; kandoo saseru *(move deeply)*.
impression inshoo
   be under the impression that -to omotte iru, ki ga suru.
imprison (to) keimusho ni ireru.
improve (to) *v.t.* jootatsu saseru *(ameliorate)*; yoku suru *(better)*; kairyoo suru *(reform)*; *v.i.* jootatsu suru *(become better)*.

improvement kairyoo *(reform).*
improvise (to) sokkyoo de suru.
imprudence fukinshin.
imprudent fukinshin na.
impulse shoodoo *(propulsion);* shigeki *(impetus).*
impure fujun na *(adulterated).*
in ni, de; -no nakani *(inside);* -no uchi ni *(within).*
   in order to tame ni.
inadequate fujuubun na, futekitoo na.
inaugurate *v.t.* hajimeru *(begin); v.i.* hajimaru *(be inaugurated).*
incapable -ga dekinai, muryoku na.
incapacity munoo, futekitoo.
inch inchi *(American measure).*
incident dekigoto *(occurrence).*
include fukumu, fukumeru
   to be included haitte iru.
income shuunyuu *(earnings).*
incomparable hikaku no dekinai.
incompatible ki no awanai *(inharmonious);* itchi shinai *(inconsistent);* ryooritsu shinai *(not able to coexist).*
incompetent chikara no nai, munoo na.
incomplete fukanzen na.
incomprehensible ryookai dekinai.
inconvenience fuben.
inconvenient fuben na *(not suitable);* tsugoo ga warui *(troublesome).*
incorrect machigatte iru *(inaccurate);* datoo de nai *(improper).*
increase zooka.
increase (to) *v.t.* fuyasu *(quantity);* ookiku suru *(size);* ageru *(price); v.i.* fueru *(in quantity);* ookiku naru *(in size);* takaku naru *(in price).*
incredible shinjirarenai.
incur ukeru *(meet with);* au *(run into).*
indebted kari no aru *(owing money);* sewa ni natte iru *(obliged).*
indecision fuketsudan.
indecisive niekiranai.
indeed hontoo ni *(in fact).*
independence dokuritsu *(self-government).*
independent dokuritsu no.
index sakuin *(of books).*
index finger hitosashi yubi.
indicate (to) shimesu.
indicative -o shimesu *(giving an indication of);* -o honomekasu *(giving a hint).*
indifference mukanshin.
indifferent reitan na *(pertaining to feelings);* mutonjaku na *(pertaining to appearance).*
indignant fungai shita *(angered).*
indignation fungai.
indirect toomawashi no *(devious);* kansetsu no *(not straightforward).*
   indirect answer kansetsu no henji.

indirectly kansetsu ni.
indiscretion shiryo no nai koto *(imprudence).*
indispensable zettai hitsuyoo na *(absolutely necessary);* sakerarenai *(unavoidable).*
individual *adj.* koko no *(separate);* dokutoku no *(peculiar).* *-n.* kojin.
indivisible wakeru koto no dekinai *(entity).*
indolence bushoo *(sloth, idleness).*
indolent bushoo na *(idle, lazy, slothful);* mukatsudoo no *(inactive).*
indoors okunai.
   to go indoors naka e hairu.
induce (to) sasoikomu *(attract).*
induct (to) hikiireru *(introduce into a place).*
indulge (in) -ni fukeru.
indulgence kimama, wagamama.
indulgent tenurui *(not severe).*
   indulgent (parent) yasashii.
industrial sangyoo no.
industrious kinben na *(hardworking).*
industry sangyoo.
inexhaustible tsukinai *(limitless);* taenai *(unfailing);* tsukarenai *(unwearied).*
inexplicable fukakai na *(incomprehensible).*
inexpressible iiarawasenai *(indescribable).*
infallible zenzen ayamari no nai *(free from error);* kesshite machigawanai *(never mistaken).*
infamous hyooban no warui *(notorious);* fumenboku na *(shameful).*
infancy akanboo no toki *(babyhood);* shoki *(beginning of existence).*
infant *n.* akanboo, chiisai kodomo *(very young baby).* *-adj.* akanboo no *(pertaining to a baby).*
infantry hohei.
infection kansen *(contagion).*
infer (to) suiri suru *(conclude by reasoning);* ketsuron o hikidasu *(draw conclusions).*
inference ketsuron *(conclusion);* suiron *(deduction).*
inferior *adj.* shita no *(less important);* somatsu na *(poor quality).* *-n.* shita no kaikyuu *(lower in rank).*
infernal meido no, jigoku no *(hellish);* hidoo no *(inhuman, devilish).*
infinite kagiri no nai *(endless);* hijoo na *(very great).*
infinity mugen *(boundlessness).*
inflation infure.
inflict (to) ataeru *(impose).*
influence eikyoo *(effect);* seiryoku *(personal).*
influence (to) eikyoo suru.
inform (to) shiraseru.
information shirase *(news);* hoochi *(report);* chishiki, joohoo *(knowledge).*
ingenious rikoo na *(clever);* kiyoo na *(skillful);* koomyoo na *(cleverly contrived).*

ingenuity rikoosa *(cleverness)*.

ingratitude onshirazu.

inhabit kyojuu suru *(reside)*; sumu, yadoru *(live in)*.

inhabitant kyojuusha.

inherit (to) soozoku suru.

inheritance isan *(thing inherited)*; soozoku *(an inheriting)*.

inhuman zannin na.

initial *adj.* hajime no *(beginning)*. *-n.* kashira mo ji *(letter)*.

   initial stage shoki.

initiate (to) hajimeru *(begin)*; seishiki ni kanyuu saseru *(admit)*.

initiative dokusooryoku *(originality)*.

injurious yuugai na *(harmful, hurtful)*.

injury kega *(wound)*; songai *(damage)*.

injustice fuhoo, fusei *(iniquity)*, fukoohei *(unjust act)*.

ink sumi *(Japanese only)*; inki, inku *(other)*.

inkwell inkitsubo.

inland kokunai no *(domestic)*.

inn yadoya, ryokan.

innate umaretsuki no *(inborn)*.

innkeeper ryokan no shujin, yadoya no shujin.

innocence mujaki *(freedom from wrong)*.

innocent muzai no *(not guilty)*; mujaki na *(guileless)*.

inquire tazuneru.

inquiry toiawase.

inscription kaite aru koto.

insect mushi.

insensitive mukankaku na *(not able to feel)*; heiki na *(callous)*.

inseparable hanasu koto ga dekinai.

inside naka.

insight kenshiki.

   person of insight kenshiki aru hito.

insignificant tsumaranai *(unimportant)*; muimi na *(meaningless)*.

insincere seii no nai.

insinuate (to) sore to naku iu *(hint)*.

insist (to) kyoochoo suru; iiharu.

   He insisted on this point. Kare wa kono ten o kyoochoo shita.

insistence kyoochoo; shuchoo.

inspect (to) shiraberu *(examine)*; ken'etsu suru *(view officially)*.

inspection ken'etsu *(official viewing)*; choosa *(critical examination)*.

install (to) ninmei suru *(place a person in office)*; soochi suru, toritsukeru *(put in position for use)*.

installment bunkatsubarai *(a portion of money paid at stated times)*.

instance rei *(example)*; baai *(occasion)*.

instant *adj.* kyuu na. *-n.* sokuji *(precise moment)*; shunkan *(moment)*.

instantaneous sokuza no.

   instantaneous death sokushi.

instantly sokuza ni, sugu.

instead (of) kawari ni.

instigate (to) sosonokasu *(incite)*.

instinct honnoo.

instinctive honnooteki na.

institute kyookai, gakkai *(institution, society)*.

institute (to) setsuritsu suru *(establish)*.

institution setsuritsu *(establishment)*; seitei *(of law)*; seido *(system)*; kanrei *(custom)*; gakkai *(learned society)*.

instruct (to) oshieru *(teach)*; kyooju suru *(educate)*.

instruction jugyoo *(a lesson)*; yoohoo *(a teaching or precept)*.

instructor kyooshi.

instrument doogu *(for work or means)*; gakki *(musical)*.

insufficiency fujuubun *(inadequacy)*; futekitoo *(incompetency)*.

insufficient fujuubun na *(not sufficient)*; futekitoo na *(inadequate)*.

insult bujoku *(insolence)*; burei *(impoliteness)*.

insult (to) bujoku suru.

insuperable uchikatenai *(insurmountable)*.

insurance hoken.

   life insurance seimei hoken.

insure (to) hoken o kakeru.

integral kanzen na.

intellect chishiki.

intellectual *adj.* chishiki no. *-n.* chishikijin.

intelligence chiryoku *(mental ability)*; chisei *(mentality)*; joohoo *(information)*.

intelligent kashikoi.

intend (to) -tsumori.

   I intend to marry her. Ano hito to kekkon suru tsumori desu.

   I intend to go. Iku tsumori desu.

intense nesshin na.

intensity kyoodo.

intention kangae.

interest kyoomi *(pleasurable concern)*; kanshin *(intellectual curiosity)*; riken *(pecuniary concern)*; rishi *(rate)*.

   compound interest fukuri.

   have an interest in kyoomi o motsu.

interest (to) kyoomi o okosaseru *(attract attention)*; kookishin o hiku *(excite the curiosity of)*; doojoo o hiku *(excite sympathy)*.

interesting omoshiroi.

interfere (to) kanshoo suru *(meddle)*; chootei suru *(mediate)*; jama suru *(interrupt)*.

interference boogai, jama.

interior naka, naibu.

intermediate chuukan no.

international kokusaiteki, kokusai.

international relations kokusai kankei.

interpose (to) -no aida ni ireru.

interpret (to) kaishaku suru, handan suru (construe).

interpretation kaishaku, setsumei (explanation); handan (judgment); tsuuyaku (translation).

interpreter tsuuyaku.

interrupt (to) saegiru (break in upon); jama o suru (hinder); chuushi saseru (break the continuity of).

interruption chuushi, jama.

interval kankaku.

interview menkai (meeting); mensetsu, intabyuu (job interview), kaiken (with reporters).

interview (to) menkai suru.

intimacy shinmitsu.

intimate shinmitsu na (very friendly); kojinteki no (personal); shitashii (friendly).

intimidate (to) obiyakasu.

into ni, no naka e.

intolerable gaman no dekinai.

intolerance kyooryoo.

intolerant kyooryoo na (bigoted).

intonation koe no taka hiku, intoneeshon.

introduce (to) shookai suru (a person).

introduction shookai (of a person); jobun (of a book).

intuition chokkan.

invade (to) shinnyuu suru (overrun); shinryaku suru (aggress); oshiyoseru (rush into).

invariable kawaranai.

invasion shinryaku.

invent (to) hatsumei suru (method, etc.); kangaedasu (a story).

invention hatsumei (something discovered after experimentation); tsukurigoto (a falsehood).

inventor hatsumeika.

invert (to) hantai ni suru (reverse).

invest (to) tooshi suru.

investment tooshi.

invisible me ni tsukanai.

invitation shootai.

invite (to) shootai suru, maneku.

invoice okurijoo, inboisu.

invoke (to) kami ni inoru.

involuntary muishiki no.

involve (to) hikikomu.

iron tetsu (metal); airon (for pressing).

iron (to) airon o kakeru (clothes).

irony hiniku.

irregular fukisoku na.

irreparable torikaeshi ga tsukanai.

irresistible tomeru koto no dekinai.

irritate (to) iraira saseru.

irritation shigeki (medical term); okoraseru koto (exasperation, annoyance).

island shima.

isolate (to) kakuri suru.

Israel Isuraeru.

issue hakkoo (of a newspaper or other publication); mondai ten (problem).

issue (to) hakkoo suru.

it sore (often omitted in Japanese).

    It's here. Koko ni arimasu.

    It's late. Osoi desu.

Italian adj. Itarii no. -n. Itariijin (people).

item koomoku.

its sono.

itself hitoride ni (by, of itself).

ivy tsuta.

J

jacket uwagi; jaketto (sweater).

jam jamu.

January Ichigatsu.

Japan Nippon, Nihon.

Japanese adj. -Nippon no, Nihon no, Nipponjin, Nihonjin (person); Nippongo, Nihongo (language).

jar tsubo, kame.

jaw ago.

jealous shittobukai.

jealousy yakimochi, shitto.

jelly jerii.

jewel hooseki.

job shigoto (work); shokugyoo (occupation); chii (position).

join (to) awaseru (put together); kuttsukeru (fasten); renketsu saseru (connect, link); issho ni naru (become united).

joint n. kansetsu (of the body); awaseme (seam); tsugime (junction). -adj. kyoodoo no (common).

joke joodan.

joke (to) joodan o iu (jest); fuzakeru (be humorous).

jolly yukai na.

journal nikki (diary); nikkan shinbun (daily newspaper); zasshi (magazine).

journalism jaanarizumu (practice of); shinbungaku (study of).

journalist jaanarisuto, shinbunkisha (reporter).

journey ryokoo.

joy yorokobi.

joyous ureshii.

judge saibankan (public officer in a court of justice); shinpan (umpire); kanteika (connoisseur).

judge (to) handan suru (estimate, conclude); saiban suru (at court).

judgment handan (adjudication); hanketsu

(court decision); hihan *(criticism);*
handanryoku *(powers of
discrimination).*
judicial saibanjoo no.
juice shiru, juusu.
July Shichigatsu.
jump tobiagari.
jump (to) tobu, janpu suru.
June Rokugatsu.
junior *adj.* toshishita no. *(opp. to senior).*
just *adj.* tadashii *(upright);* koosei na
(impartial); seitoo na *(lawful);* tekitoo na
(proper); jissai no *(actual). -adv.* choodo
(exactly); hon no *(only);* yatto *(hardly).*
justice seigi *(righteousness);* kooketsu
(integrity); koosei *(fairness).*
justify seitooka suru.

K

keen eibin na *(acute).*
keep kau *(animals);* motsu *(hold);* totte oku
(hold on to).
    keep in mind oboete oku.
    keep quiet shizuka ni suru.
    Keep still! Oshizuka ni.
kettle yakan.
key kagi.
kick (to) keru.
kill (to) korosu.
kin miyori.
kind *adj.* shinsetsu na *(gentle); -n.* shurui
(class, variety, sort).
kindly *adv.* shinsetsu ni.
kindness shinsetsu *(benevolence);* aijoo
(love); kooi *(goodwill).*
king oo.
kingdom ookoku *(monarchical state);* kuni
(realm).
kiss kisu, seppun.
kiss (to) kisu suru, seppun suru.
kitchen daidokoro.
kite tako.
knee hizagashira.
kneel (to) hizamazuku.
knife naifu.
knit (to) amu.
    knitting amimono.
knock (to) tataku.
    knock against -ni butsukaru.
    knock at the door to o tataku.
knot musubime.
know (to) shitte iru, zonjite iru *(humble).*
knowledge chishiki *(information);* gakumon
(learning).
known yuumei na.
    make known shiraseru.

Korean *adj.* Kankoku no, Choosen no. *-n.*
Choosenjin *(people);* Choosengo
(language).

L

label fuda; raberu, retteru.
labor *n.* roodoo, shigoto.
laboratory jikkenjo.
lace reesu *(fabric);* himo *(of shoe).*
lack (to) fusoku suru.
lacquer urushi.
    lacquerware nuri mono.
lady fujin.
    Ladies Fujin tearaijo *(toilet).*
lake mizuumi; -ko *(in compound names).*
    Lake Biwa Biwako.
lamb kohitsuji.
lame bikko.
lamp dentoo *(electric).*
land riku *(solid part of the earth's surface);*
jimen *(ground).*
land (to) jooriku saseru, jooriku suru
(disembark); oriru *(alight).*
landscape keshiki.
language kotoba, gengo; -go *(in
compounds).*
    Japanese language Nihongo.
lantern choochin *(paper);* tooroo *(metal or
stone);* ishi dooroo *(stone).*
large ookii, ookina.
laser reezaa.
last *n.* ichiban ato *(end of something). -adj.*
saikin no *(most recent);* saigo no *(final). -
adv.* owari ni *(after all others);* saikin
(most lately).
    last night yuube, sakuban.
last (to) tsuzuku *(continue);* mochikotaeru
(endure); nagamochi suru *(wear well).*
lasting eizoku suru *(durable);* fuhen no,
eikyuu no *(permanent).*
latch kannuki.
late osoi *(opp. to early);* ko- *(prefixed to the
name of someone deceased).*
lately saikin.
latter ato no, koosha no.
laugh warai.
laugh (to) warau.
laughter warai.
lavish kimae no yoi.
law hooritsu.
lawful hooritsu ni kanatta.
lawn shibafu.
lay (to) oku *(put);* umu *(eggs).*
layer soo.
lazy namaketa; bushoo na.
lead namari *(mineral);* shidoo *(guidance).*

lead (to) annai suru *(guide)*.
leader shidoosha *(guide)*.
leadership shidooryoku.
leaf ha.
leak (to) moru.
lean (to) katamuku *(incline)*; yorikakaru *(lean against)*.
leap hiyaku.
leap (to) tobikoeru *(pass over)*; tobu *(jump)*.
learn narau, benkyoo suru *(study)*; kioku suru *(memorize)*.
learned hakugaku na, gakumon no aru.
learning gakumon *(knowledge)*; hakushiki *(erudition)*.
least ichiban chiisai *(in size)*; ichiban sukunai *(in number or amount)*.
   at least sukunaku tomo.
leather kawa.
leave yasumi *(holiday)*.
leave (to) deru *(depart)*; tatsu *(depart for a long trip)*; azukeru *(on deposit)*.
lecture koogi *(in classroom)*; kooen *(in public)*; setsuyu *(admonition)*.
left *n.* hidari.
leg ashi.
legal hooritsujoo no.
legend densetsu.
legislation hooritsu seitei *(enacting of laws)*; hooritsu *(laws)*.
legislator rippoosha.
legislature rippoobu.
legitimate goohoo no *(lawful)*, doori ni kanatta *(reasonable)*.
leisure hima.
lemon remon.
   lemonade remoneedo.
lend (to) kasu.
length nagasa.
lengthen (to) nagaku suru *(make longer)*; nobasu *(prolong)*.
less chiisai *(in size)*; sukoshi no, sukunai *(in quantity)*; yori chiisai *(smaller than)*; yori sukunai *(fewer than)*.
lesson jugyoo *(schoolwork)*; gakka *(subject)*; ka *(chapter)*.
let (to) saseru *(allow)*; kasu *(loan)*.
   house for let kashiya.
letter tegami *(epistle)*; ji *(in alphabet)*.
level *n.* heimen *(flat surface)*; heichi *(flat ground)*. *-adj.* taira na *(even)*; suihei no *(horizontal)*.
   (at) the same level onaji takasa *(said of height)*; onaji teido *(said of degree)*.
liability saimu.
liable seme o oubeki *(responsible)*; fukusubeki *(subject to)*; kakariyasui *(exposed to)*.
liar usotsuki.
liberal hoofu na, takusan no *(abundant)*; kechi

kechi shinai *(not sparing)*; kimae ga ii *(generous)*; shinpoteki na *(progressive)*.
liberty jiyuu.
library toshokan *(public)*; shosai, toshoshitsu *(private, home)*.
license kyoka *(permission)*; ninka *(authorization)*; kyokasho, menjoo *(certification)*.
   driver's license unten menkyo.
lick (to) nameru.
lie uso.
   tell a lie uso o tsuku.
lie (to) yoko ni naru *(rest)*.
lieutenant rikugun chuui *(army)*; kaigun taii *(navy)*.
life inochi *(animate existence)*; genki *(energy)*.
lift (to) ageru *(raise)*; mochiageru *(hold up)*.
light *adj.* karui *(weight)*; usui *(color)*; yasashii *(work)*. *-n.* hikari *(beam)*; akari *(of lamp, flame)*; kootaku *(brightness)*.
   sunlight hi no hikari.
light (to) hi o tsukeru.
   light the fire hi o tsukeru.
   light the lamp akari o tsukeru.
lighten (to) akaruku suru *(make bright)*; karuku suru *(diminish in weight)*.
lighthouse toodai.
lighting shoomei *(illumination)*.
lightning inabikari *(from cloud to cloud)*.
   flash of lightning denkoo.
light up terasu.
like *adj.* onajiyoo na *(similar)*; nite iru *(alike)*.
like (to) konomu, suku.
   Would you like to go? Ikitai desu ka?
likely tabun *(probably)*; tekitoo na *(suitable)*; tanomoshii *(promising)*; mottomo rashii *(credible)*.
likewise dooyoo ni *(similarly)*; mata *(too, also)*; nao mata *(moreover)*.
liking *n.* konomi.
limb te ashi *(hand or foot)*; eda *(branch)*.
limit seigen *(in the abstract sense)*; kyookai, sakai *(boundary)*.
limit (to) seigen suru.
limp bikko o hiku.
line kei, sen, ito *(thread)*; retsu *(row)*; kakei *(lineage)*; iegara *(family)*; michi *(course, route)*; -sen *(suffixed to the name of railroad)*, shoobai *(trade)*.
   Tokaido Line Tookaidoosen *(The Tokaido Railroad)*.
line (to) sen o hiku *(mark with lines)*; rinkaku o toru *(outline)*; ichiretsu ni suru *(align)*; ura o tsukeru *(cover with lining)*; retsu o tsukuru *(line up)*.
   lining ura *(of dresses)*.
linen rinneru.

linger (to) urouro suru; nagabiku.

link tsunagime.

link (to) tsunagu.

lion raion, shishi.

lip kuchibiru.

liquid ekitai.

liquor sake (*Japanese rice wine*); yooshu (*foreign*).

list mokuroku (*catalogue*); kakakuhyoo (*price*).

list (to) kakinaraberu.

listen kiku.

literary bungaku no.

literature bungaku.

little chiisai, chiisa na (*not big*); sukoshi (*quantity*); tsumaranai (*trivial*); kechi na (*mean, petty*).

live *adj.* ikite iru.

live (to) sumu (*dwell*); ikiru (*exist*); ikite iru (*be living*); ikinagaraeru (*remain alive*); kurasu (*spend one's days*).

lively genki no yoi (*spirited*); yooki na (*cheerful*); kappatsu na (*brisk*).

liver kanzoo (*organ of body*); kimo, rebaa (*food*).

load omoni (*burden*); nimotsu (*on a conveyance*).

load (to) tsumu.

loan kashikin (*money that is lent*); shakkin (*borrowed money*).

loan (to) kasu (*lend*); kariru (*borrow*).

local chihooteki na, chihoo no.

locate (to) mitsukeru.

location basho.

lock kagi.

lock (to) kagi o kakeru.

locomotive kikansha.

log maruta.

logic ronri.

logical ronriteki na.

loneliness sabishisa.

lonely kodoku no (*isolated*); sabishii (*lonesome*).

long nagai (*lengthy*); hosonagai (*elongated*); takai (*tall*).

     a long time nagai aida.

     before long mamonaku.

     long ago mukashi.

longing akogare.

look ichi moku (*glance*); yooboo (*aspect*); yoosu (*deportment*); kaotsuki (*countenance*).

look (to) miru (*oneself*); goran nasaru (*respect: used in speaking of a person outside one's in group*); mieru (*have the appearance, seem*).

     Look out! Abunai.

loose yurui (*not tight*); darashi no nai (*lax*);

fumimochi na (*wanton*); fuseikaku na (*inexact*).

loosen (to) toku (*undo*); yurumeru (*slacken*).

lord shihaisha (*ruler*); shujin (*master*); shu (*Christ*).

lose (to) ushinau; nakusu (*cease to have*); otosu (*by dropping*); makeru (*be beaten*).

loss son, sonshitsu.

lost nakushita (*gone out of one's possession*); yukue fumei no (*missing*).

lot *adv.* takusan (*great deal*); oozei (*multitude*).

     a lot of people oozei no hito.

loud *adj.* oogoe no, ookina koe no (*said of a voice*); ookina oto (*loud sound*); soozooshii (*noisy*); kebakebashii (*gaudy*).

love ai (*parental fraternal*); ren'ai (*between man and woman*).

love (to) aisuru (*as a parent*); koi suru, ren'ai suru (*one of the opposite sex*).

     fall in love koi ni ochiiru.

lovely utsukushii (*beautiful*); kawairashii (*charming*); subarashii (*wonderful*).

low hikui (*not high*); yowai (*weak*); iyashii (*in society*).

lower (to) sageru, orosu (*haul down*); ichidan to sageru (*make less elevated*).

loyal chuujitsu na; chuugi na.

loyalty chuusetsu; chuugi.

luck un, kooun.

     bad luck un ga warui.

     good luck un ga ii.

lucky un ga ii, kooun na.

luggage nimotsu.

luminous hikaru.

lump katamari.

lunch hirugohan, ranchi.

lung hai.

luxurious zeitaku na.

luxury zeitaku.

M

machine kikai.

mad ki no kurutta, kichigai (*insane*); muchuu no (*infatuated*); okotta (*angry*).

madam okusama.

madness kichigai.

magazine zasshi.

magistrate hanji.

magnificent rippa na (*grand, stately*); subarashii (*splendid*).

maid musume (*girl*); otetsudai (*servant*).

mail yuubin.

main omo na.

     mainland hondo.

main road hondoo.

main street hondoori.

maintain (to) tamotsu, fji suru.

majesty igen *(dignity)*.

    His Majesty heika.

major *adj.* omo na.

majority daibubun *(opp. of minority);* kahansuu *(plurality);* daitasuu *(most of, greater part).*

make (to) tsukuru; koshiraeru *(construct, manufacture).*

male osu *(animal);* otoko *(human).*

malice tekii.

man otoko *(male human).*

manage (to) keiei suru *(a business).*

management toriatsukai *(handling);* soojuu, toogyo *(control);* keiei *(direction).*

manager shihainin, maneejaa.

mankind jinrui *(human race).*

manner gyoogi *(deportment);* taido *(attitude);* yarikata *(method).*

manners sahoo.

manufacture seizoo.

manufacture (to) seizoo suru.

manufacturer seizoosha; seisakusha, seizoogyoosha.

manuscript genkoo.

many *adj.* takusan no, oozei no.

map chizu.

maple momiji.

March Sangatsu.

march kooshin *(parade);* kooshin kyoku *(music).*

march (to) kooshin suru *(in a parade);* susumu *(proceed).*

marine umi no *(oceanic);* kookaijoo no *(nautical).*

mark shirushi, maaku; ato *(impression);* shimi *(stain);* kizuato *(scar);* kizu *(scratch).*

mark (to) maaku o tsukeru.

    to make a mark shirushi o tsukeru.

market ichiba, maaketto.

    bear market uri sooba.

    bull market kai sooba.

    buyer's market kaite shijoo.

    market forces shijoo no jissei.

    market index shijoo shisuu.

    marketing maaketingu.

    market position shikyoo.

    market price shika.

    market share shijoo sen-yuu ritsu.

    market trends shijoo dookoo.

    market value shijoo kakaku.

marriage kekkon.

marry (to) kekkon suru.

marvel fushigi.

marvelous fushigi na.

masculine otoko no.

mask men, masuku.

mask (to) men o kaburu.

mason ishiya.

mass *n.* taishuu.

    mass communication masukomi.

    mass production tairyoo seisan.

mast masuto, hobashira.

master shujin *(of the house);* shujin *(employer);* sensei *(teacher).*

master (to) joozu ni naru *(become skillful);* yoku oboeru *(learn well).*

masterpiece meisaku, kessaku.

mat tatami *(for floor of Japanese house).*

match matchi *(for fire);* shiai *(contest);* kyoogi *(game).*

match (to) niau *(be suitably associated, fit together).*

material *n.* zairyoo *(cloth, etc.).*

maternal haha kata no.

mathematics suugaku.

matter mondai *(problem);* jiken *(event);* koto *(thing).*

matter (to) kamau, mondai ni suru.

mattress mattoresu.

mature (to) otona ni naru *(reach adulthood);* jukusuru *(as a fruit).*

maximum saidaigen.

May Gogatsu.

may -ka mo shiremasen *(possibility).*

    It may rain. Ame ga furu ka mo shiremasen. -te mo ii desu *(have my permission to).*

    You may go. Itte mo ii desu. *(You have my permission to go.)*

mayor shichoo.

me watashi ni *(to me);* watashi o *(as obj. of verb).*

meadow bokujoo.

meal shokuji, gohan.

mean *adj.* iji no warui, hiretsu na *(base).*

mean (to) imi suru.

    What does it mean? Sore no imi wa nan desu ka?

meaning imi.

meantime, meanwhile sono aida ni.

    in the meantime soo shite iru uchi ni.

measure sunpoo *(dimension);* monosashi *(yardstick).*

measure (to) sunpoo o toru *(length),* hakaru *(reckon).*

meat niku.

mechanic kikaikoo *(worker in a factory).*

mechanical kikaiteki no; kikai no.

mechanically kikaiteki ni.

medal medaru, kunshoo *(military).*

meddle (to) kanshoo suru *(interfere).*

mediate (to) chootei suru *(arbitrate);* chuukai suru *(act as an intermediary);* tonnasu *(intercede).*

medical igakuteki no.

medicine kusuri *(a drug);* igaku *(the science).*

mediocre nami no, taishita koto no nai.

mediocrity heibon.

meditate (to) mokusoo suru.

meditation mokusoo *(contemplation).*

medium *adj.* chuu kurai no. *-n.* chuu kurai.

meet (to) au, o me ni kakaru *(respect).*

meeting kai *(assembly).*

melt (to) *v.t.* tokasu; *v.i.* tokeru.

member kaiin *(of an association).*

memorize (to) oboeru.

memory kioku.

mend (to) naosu *(repair);* tsugu *(darn);* tsukurou *(patch up).*

mental seishin no.

mention genkyuu.

    honorable mention hoojoo.

mention (to) iu, hanasu *(in speaking);* kaku *(in writing).*

    Don't mention it. Doo itashimashite.

merchandise shoohin.

merchant shoonin.

merciful jihibukai *(compassionate).*

merciless mujihi na.

mercury suigin.

mercy jihi *(compassion).*

merit *n.* kachi *(worth);* tegara *(deed).*

merry yukai na; tanoshii *(joyous).*

message kotozuke *(verbal).*

messenger tsukai.

metal kane.

metallic kane no, kanamono no.

method hoohoo.

metropolis shuto *(capital);* chuushin-chi *(central place).*

microphone maikurohon, maiku.

microscope kenbikyoo.

microwave oven denshi renji.

midday hiru.

middle naka no, chuukan no *(intermediate);* chuui no *(medium).*

    in the middle of mannaka ni.

    Middle Ages Chuusei.

    middle class chuusan kaikyuu.

midnight mayonaka.

might *n.* chikara *(strength).*

mighty chikara no tsuyoi, taishita.

mild otonashii *(gentle);* kandai na *(not severe).*

mildness odayakasa.

military rikugun no.

milk gyuunyuu *(cow's),* miruku.

milkman gyuunyuu ya.

mill suisha *(water);* fuusha *(wind);* seifunjoo *(flour).*

million hyakuman.

    one hundred million ichioku.

millionaire hyakuman chooja.

mind kokoro *(intention);* kangae *(thought);* atama *(brain, head).*

    frame of mind kimochi.

mind (to) ki ni kakeru *(bear in mind);* sewa o suru *(take care of).*

mine *pron.* watashi no, watashi no mono; *-n.* koozan *(for minerals).*

miner koofu.

mineral *n.* koobutsu. *-adj.* koobutsu no.

minimum saishoogen no.

minister daijin *(of state);* kooshi *(diplomatic);* bokushi *(of religion).*

ministry -shoo *(suffix);* seishoku *(of church).*

    Ministry of Foreign Affairs Gaimushoo.

mink ten, minku.

minor miseinensha *(legal: less than 20 years old).*

minority shoosuu *(smaller number);* shoosuu too *(opp. of majority);* miseinen *(legal infancy).*

minute fun *(time).*

    Any minute now. Moo sugu desu.

    Wait a minute! Chotto matte kudasai.

miracle kiseki *(religious).*

mirror kagami.

miscellaneous iroiro na.

mischief itazura.

mischievous itazurazuki na.

misdemeanor fugyooseki.

miser kechinboo.

miserable fukoo na *(unfortunate);* hisan na *(wretched);* aware na *(pitiable).*

miserably mijime ni.

misery komatte iru koto *(a state of being in distress).*

misfortune fukoo *(unhappiness);* sainan *(calamity).*

mishap omoigakenai dekigoto.

misprint insatsu chigai, misupurinto.

Miss -san *(same suffix as for Mr. and Mrs.).*

    Miss Yamada. Yamada-san.

miss (to) ma ni awanai *(fail to get on time);* nakusuru *(lose);* kizukanai *(fail to perceive).*

mission dendoo kai, misshon *(religious);* shisetsu *(official).*

missionary senkyooshi, dendooshi.

mist kasumi.

mistake machigai.

mistake (to) machigau.

Mister -san. See **Miss.**

    Mr. Yamada. Yamada-san.

mistrust fushin'yoo.

mistrust (to) shinyoo shinai, ayashimu.

mistrustful utagaibukai.

misunderstand (to) gokai suru.

misunderstanding gokai *(mistake);* iken no sooi *(disagreement).*

misuse machigatte tsukau koto.

misuse (to) machigatte tsukau.

mix (to) *v.t.* mazeru *(put together); v.i.* mazaru, majiwaru *(associate).*

mixture mazeta mono.

mob gunshuu *(crowd).*

mobilization dooin.

mobilize (to) dooin suru.

mock (to) baka ni suru *(ridicule);* maneru *(mimic).*

mockery baka ni suru koto.

mode ryuukoo, moodo.

model moderu *(photography, fashion);* mokei *(copy);* tehon *(example);* hinagata *(miniature).*

model (to) katadoru *(to copy).*

moderate onken na *(temperate);* tegoro no *(medium).*

moderate (to) setsudo o mamoru *(keep within bounds);* yawarageru *(one's temper).*

moderation tekido, sessei.

modern kindai no; kindaiteki *(of the present time);* gendai no *(contemporary);* modan na *(new in fashion).*

modest kenson no *(unassuming);* shitoyaka na *(moderate, unaggressive).*

modesty kenson.

modification henkoo.

modify (to) aratameru *(alter);* kanwa suru *(lessen);* keigen suru *(tone down).*

moist *adj.* shikketa, shimeppoi. *-n.* shikke.

moisten (to) shimesu *(dampen);* shimeru *(become moist).*

moment shunkan.

   Any moment now. Moo sugu desu.

   Just a moment! Chotto matte kudasai.

monarchy kunshu seitai *(system);* kunshukoku *(nation).*

monastery shuudooin.

Monday Getsuyoobi.

money kane, okane.

   money order yuubin gawase.

   paper money satsu.

monk shuudoosoo.

monkey saru.

monologue hitorigoto.

   to talk to oneself hitorigoto o iu.

monopoly dokusen; senbai.

monorail monoreeru.

monotonous tanchoo na.

monotony tanchoo.

monster kaibutsu *(dragon, etc.).*

monstrosity kikai na koto.

monstrous kikai na.

month tsuki.

   this month kongetsu.

   last month sengetsu.

   next month raigetsu.

monthly *adj.* maigetsu no. *-adv.* maigetsu. *-n.* gekkanzasshi *(monthly magazine).*

monument kinenhi.

monumental kinen no.

mood kibun *(feeling);* kigen *(temper).*

moody muttsuri shita.

moon tsuki.

   full moon mangetsu.

moonlight tsuki no hikari.

mop moppu.

moral *adj.* dootokuteki na *(virtuous). -n.* kyookun *(maxim).*

morale shiki.

moralist dootoku shugisha.

morality dootoku.

more motto.

morning asa.

morsel hito kire *(a little piece).*

mortal *adj.* kanarazu shinu *(subject to death).*

mortgage teitoo.

mortgage (to) teitoo ni suru.

mosquito ka.

most *adj.* taitei no *(greatest number);* daitai *(the majority of);* ichiban *(used for the superlative).*

   most numerous ichiban ooi.

mostly taitei.

moth ga.

mother okaasan, okaasama *(respect);* haha.

motion undoo *(opp. of rest);* teburi, miburi *(gesture).*

motionless ugokanai.

motive dooki.

motor hatsudooki, mootaa.

motor (to) unten suru *(drive a car).*

mount yama *(mountain).*

mount (to) daishi ni haru *(pictures);* noboru *(ascend).*

   mount a horse uma ni noru.

mountain yama.

mountainous yama no ooi.

mourn (to) nageku, kanashimu *(lament).*

mournful kanashimi ni shizunda.

mourning mo.

mouse nezumi.

mouth kuchi.

movable ugokasu koto no dekiru.

move ugoki, idoo.

move (to) *v.t.* ugokasu; *v.i.* ugoku, hikkosu *(change one's dwelling).*

   move back hikkomeru, hikkomu.

   move forward *v.t.* mae e dasu; *v.i.* mae e deru.

movement koodoo *(action).*

movies eiga.

moving ugokasu, kandoo saseru *(evoking emotion);* hikkoshi *(changing one's dwelling).*

much takusan, takusan no.

   much better zutto ii.

mud doro.

muddy doro no ooi; doro darake no *(covered with mud)*.

mule raba.

multiple tasuu no.

multiply kakeru; masu *(increase)*.

multitude oozei, gunshuu.

mumble (to) butsu butsu iu.

municipal shi no, toshi no.

municipality jichiku, shi tookyoku.

munitions gunjuhin.

murder hitogoroshi, satsujin.

   to commit a murder hitogoroshi o suru.

murder (to) hito o korosu.

murmur zawameki, sasayaki.

murmur (to) sasayaku.

muscle kinniku.

museum hakubutsukan.

   art museum bijutsukan.

mushroom kinoko.

music ongaku.

musical *adj.* ongaku no. *-n.* myuujikaru.

musician ongakka.

must -nakereba naranai, -nakereba ikenai *(have to)*; -ni chigai nai *(in the sense of an obvious inference)*.

   I must go. Ikanakereba naranai. Ikanakereba ikenai.

   You must have said so. Soo itta ni chigai nai.

mustard karashi.

mute oshi no *(unable to speak)*.

mutter (to) butsu butsu iu *(mumble)*; sasayaku *(murmur)*.

mutton hitsuji no niku.

my watashi no *(of or relating to me)*; uchi no *(pertaining to things or persons of one's home or workplace)*.

myself jibun, watakushi jishin.

mysterious fushigi na *(strange)*; fukakai na *(inexplicable)*.

mystery shinpi; fukakai na koto.

myth shinwa.

N

nail tsume *(of a finger or toe)*; kugi *(fastener)*.

nail (to) kugi o utsu.

naïve mujaki na *(innocent)*; adokenai *(unsophisticated)*.

naked hadaka no.

name namae *(designation)*; hyooban *(fame)*.

   first name namae.

   last name myooji.

   My name is . . . Namae wa . . . to iimasu.

   What is your name? Onamae wa?

name (to) namae o tsukeru.

nameless na no nai.

namely sunawachi.

nap keba *(of wool)*; hirune *(short sleep)*.

napkin napukin.

narrow semai.

narrow (to) *v.t.* sebameru; *v.i.* semaku naru.

nasty iji no warui.

nation kokumin *(people)*; kuni *(country)*.

national kokumin no, kuni no.

nationality kokuseki.

nationalization kokkateki ni suru koto, kokueika.

nationalize (to) kokuei ni suru *(to have the state operate)*.

native *adj.* naikoku no *(opp. of foreign)*; dochaku no *(aboriginal)*. *-n.* naikokujin *(opp. of foreigner)*; dojin *(aborigine)*.

natural shizen no, shizen no mama no *(nonartificial)*; mikaikon no *(uncultivated)*.

naturalness kazarike no nai koto.

nature seishitsu *(character)*; shizen *(the physical universe)*.

naughty itazura na.

naval kaigun no.

navy kaigun.

near soba no, chikai *(not far)*; kinjo no *(around the corner)*.

nearly hotondo *(almost)*; kare kore *(about)*.

neat kichinto shita *(tidy, orderly)*; kozappari shita *(smart, dapper)*; shumi no ii *(trim)*; seizen to shita *(orderly)*.

neatness sappari shite iru koto.

necessarily yamu naku, hitsuyoo ni kararete.

necessary hitsuyoo na.

necessity hitsuyoo.

neck kubi.

necklace kubi kazari, nekkuresu.

necktie nekutai.

need iriyoo *(want)*; hitsuyoo *(necessity)*; nyuuyoo *(demand)*; kyuuboo *(destitution)*.

   be in need of iriyoo desu.

need (to) iru *(want)*; hoshii desu *(wish to have)*.

needle hari.

needless fuhitsuyoo na.

needy konkyuu shite iru.

negative *n.* uchikeshi *(expression)*; nega *(photograph)*. *-adj.* insei no *(opp. of positive)*; hantai no *(contrary)*.

neglect kamawanai koto *(want of attention)*; mushi *(disregard)*.

neglect (to) namakeru, mushi suru.

negotiate kooshoo suru, danpan suru.

negotiation kooshoo, danpan.

neighbor tonari.

neighborhood kinjo.

neither dochira mo *(negative);* mo-mo . . . *(negative).*
Neither apples nor oranges are expensive. Ringo mo mikan mo takaku nai.
Neither is delicious. Dochira mo oishiku nai.

nephew oi.

nerve shinkei *(in anatomy);* daitan *(pluck);* yuuki *(courage).*

nervous shinkeishitsu na *(behavior);* shinkei no *(pertaining to nerves);* kurooshoo no *(apprehensive).*

nest su.

net ami.

neuter chuusei.

neutral chuuritsu no *(not involved in hostilities);* kooheimushi no *(impartial).*

never kesshite *(with a negative verb).*

nevertheless -ni mo kakawarazu.

new kondo no *(recently appointed);* atarashii *(recently acquired).*

news tayori *(tidings);* nyuusu, hoodoo *(newspaper news).*

newspaper shinbun.

next tsugi no, ichiban chikai *(nearest);* tonari no *(neighboring);* kondo *(after this).*

nice ii, yoi *(agreeable);* shinsetsu na *(kind).*

nickname adana.

niece mei.

night yoru.

nightmare warui yume, akumu.

nine kokonotsu, ku, kyuu.

no iie.
Note that when answering a question in the negative, the usage of yes and no in Japanese is opposite to their usage in English.
Didn't you see it?
No, I didn't. Hai, mimasen deshita.
Yes, I did. Iie, mimashita.

nobility kazoku, kizoku *(titled group).*

noble *adj.* kooketsu na *(high-minded);* yuudai na *(imposing);* kedakai *(dignified);* mibun no takai *(aristocratic).*

nobody dare mo, donata mo *(followed by a negative verb).*

noise oto *(sound);* urusai oto *(unpleasant sound).*

noisy soozooshii; urusai.

nominate (to) shimei suru.

nomination shimei.

none dare mo, donata mo *(of persons);* dore mo *(of things) (followed by a negative verb).*

nonsense bakageta koto, bakarashii koto.

noon hiru, shoogo.

normal *adj.* atarimae no *(not strange);*
hyoojunteki na *(standard);* futsuu no *(regular);* heikin no *(average).*

north kita.

northeast hokutoo, toohuko.

northern kita no.

northwest seihoku, hokusei.

nose hana.

nostril hana no ana.

not -nai, -masen.
I do not go. Ikimasen *(polite).* Ikanai *(plain).*
It is not a station. Eki de wa arimasen (ja arimasen).
It is not expensive. Takaku arimasen.

note tegami *(a letter);* kiroku *(for later reference);* satsu *(paper money).*

note (to) shirusu *(mark down);* hikki suru *(take note of).*
note down kakitomeru.

nothing nani mo *(with a negative verb).*

notice shirase, kokuchi *(public notice);* chuumoku *(observation).*

notice (to) ki o tsukeru, chuui suru *(pay attention to).*

notify (to) tsuuchi suru *(inform);* happyoo suru *(announce).*

notion ippanteki gainen *(general conception);* kangae *(idea);* iken *(opinion);* ikoo *(intention).*

noun meishi *(substantive).*

nourish jiyoo ga aru.

nourishment jiyoo, jiyoobutsu *(nutriment);* shokumotsu *(food).*

novel *adj.* atarashii *(new);* kawatta *(strange).* -n. shoosetsu.

novelty kawatta mono *(thing);* kawatta koto *(event).*

November Juuichigatsu.

now ima.
now and then toki doki.

nowadays konogoro; chikagoro.

nowhere doko ni mo *(with a negative verb).*

nuclear kaka no.
nuclear energy genshiryoku.
nuclear reactor genshiro.

nude *adj.* hadaka no *(naked).* -n. nuudo, rataiga *(in art).*

nuisance meiwaku *(action);* yakkai na hito *(person).*

nullify (to) mukoo ni suru *(make invalid);* yameru *(cancel);* dame ni suru *(make useless).*

numb (to become) kogoeru *(from cold);* shibireru *(from pressure).*

number suuji *(numeral);* banchi *(indicating location);* ban *(turn);* bangoo *(for telephone or room);* -goo *(issue of a periodical).*

number (to) kazoeru *(count)*.
numerous takusan no.
nun ama.
nurse kangofu.
nursery kodomo beya *(for children);* uekiya *(for plants).*
nut kurumi.

O

oak kashi.
oar kai.
oat karasu mugi.
oath chikai.
   to take an oath chikai o tateru.
obedience fukujuu *(submission);* juujun *(dutifulness).*
obedient juujun na, sunao na.
obey shitagau, iu koto o kiku.
object mono *(article);* mokuteki *(aim).*
object (to) hantai suru.
objection hantai *(adverse reason).*
   I have no objection to it. Hantai shimasen.
objectionable iya na *(offensive);* monku no desoo na *(open to objection);* omoshiroku nai *(unpleasant).*
objective *n.* mokuteki *(purpose).* *-adj.* kyakkanteki na.
objectively kyakkanteki ni.
objectivity kyakkansei.
obligation gimu *(duty);* on *(debt of gratitude);* giri *(sense of duty).*
obligatory gimuteki, hitsuyoo na.
oblige (to) muri ni saseru *(compel).*
   be much obliged arigatoo zonjimasu.
obliging shinsetsu na.
oblique katamuita, aimai na.
obscure *adj.* bonyari shita.
obscurity aimaisa.
observation kansatsu *(notice);* kanshi *(watching).*
observatory tenmondai *(astronomical);* sokkoojo *(meteorological).*
observe (to) mokugeki suru *(catch sight of);* miru *(see);* ki ga tsuku *(notice).*
observer bookansha; obuzaabaa *(at a conference).*
obstacle shoogai *(hindrance);* jama *(impediment).*
obstinacy goojoo *(stubbornness);* gankyoo *(persistence).*
obstinate ganko na *(stubborn);* gankyoo na *(persistent).*
obvious akiraka na.
obviously akiraka ni.

occasion ori, kikai.
occasionally tama ni *(at times).*
occupation shigoto *(employment);* shokugyoo *(calling);* gyoomu *(business);* shoobai *(trade);* senryoo *(military).*
occupy (to) senryoo suru *(by force of arms);* sumu *(live in);* te ga fusagaru *(take up space).*
   to be occupied fusagatte iru.
occur (to) okoru.
occurrence dekigoto.
ocean umi.
   Indian Ocean Indoyoo.
October Juugatsu.
odd hen na *(strange);* hanpa no *(not paired).*
   odd number kisuu.
odor kaori *(fragrance);* nioi *(smell).*
of no
   roof of the house ie no yane.
off *(usually expressed by verbs).*
   She cut it off. Kirihanashite shimaimashita.
   The button is off. Botan ga hazurete imasu.
   The train is off. Densha wa dete shimaimashita.
offend (to) *v.i.* ki ni sawaru *(displease);* *v.t.* okoraseru *(make angry).*
offense hansoku *(transgression);* tsumi *(crime);* bujoku *(insult).*
offensive *adj.* fuyukai na *(unpleasant);* burei na *(insolent);* iya na *(disgusting);* kooseiteki *(aggressive).* *-n.* koogeki
offer mooshikomi, mooshiide.
offer (to) sonaeru *(as act of worship);* sashiageru *(as a present);* mooshideru *(make an offer);* teikyoo suru *(propose to give);* susumeru *(proffer).*
offering sonaemono *(to a deity);* kenkin *(gift of money to a church).*
office jimusho *(in general);* yakusho *(of govt.).*
   branch office shiten.
   head office honsha, honten.
officer yakunin *(civil);* shookoo *(military).*
official *adj.* seishiki no *(formal);* omote muki no *(public).* *-n.* yakunin.
often tabi tabi, yoku.
oil abura.
old furui *(of things);* toshiyori *(of persons).*
old age roonen
old man ojiisan.
old woman obaasan.
older toshiue no.
   older brother niisan, oniisan; ani.
   older sister neesan, oneesan; ane.
oldest nenchoo no.
   oldest daughter *(among daughters)* choojo.

oldest son *(among sons)* choonan.
olive oriibu.
  olive oil oriibu oiru.
ominous fukitsu na *(inauspicious);* yochi
  suru *(prognostic);* ken'aku na
  (threatening).
on -no ue ni, -no ue de, -no ue no.
  It is on the desk. Tsukue no ue ni aru.
once ichi do *(one time);* moto *(formerly);* mae
  ni *(before).*
  at once sugu ni.
  all at once kyuu ni, totsuzen.
  once in a while tokidoki.
  once a year ichinen ni ichido.
  once more moo ichido.
one hitotsu, ichi *(a single person or thing);*
  katahoo *(one of a pair);* kata *(in paired
  compounds, such as;* kata me = *one eye);*
  pron. hito, jibun.
oneself jishin, jibun.
onion tamanegi.
only tada *(merely, but);* tatta *(emphatic);*
  honno *(nothing but).*
open *adj.* hiraita, hirobiro shita.
open (to) *v.t.* akeru; *v.i.* aku.
opening kuchi *(gap);* ana *(hole);* hajime
  (beginning); kuchi, kikai, chansu
  (opportunity).
opera opera, kageki.
operate *v.i.* ugoku *(function);* *v.t.* soojuu suru
  (work); kanri suru *(superintend).*
operation shujutsu *(surgical);* sagyoo
  (working); unten *(of a mechanism).*
opinion kangae, kenkai *(notion).*
opponent hantaisha *(in debate);* aite *(in
  sport);* kyoosoosha *(in business).*
opportune kootsugoo no.
opportunity kikai.
oppose (to) hantai suru.
opposite *adj.* -no mukoo no, -no mukai no
  (facing). -*n.* mukoogawa *(the other side).*
opposition hantai.
oppress shiitageru, osaeru.
oppression appaku *(tyranny);* konnan
  (hardship).
optimism rakutenshugi.
optimistic rakutenteki.
oral kootoo no, kuchi de iu, kuchi no.
  oral examination kootoo shiken.
orange *n.* mikan *(tangerine);* orenji.
orator enzetsusha.
oratory yuuben, enzetsu.
orchard kudamono batake, kajuen.
orchestra kangengaku, ookesutora.
ordeal shiren *(severe trial).*
order iitsuke, meirei *(injunction);* kunrei
  (instruction); jun *(regular arrangement);*
  chuumon *(commission to supply).*
  in order to -tame ni.

  put in order seiri suru.
order (to) iitsukeru *(command);* chuumon
  suru *(give an order for).*
ordinary futsuu no *(common);* atarimae no
  (not special).
organ orugan *(musical instrument).*
organization koosei *(formation);* soshiki
  (system); dantai *(body).*
organize (to) soshiki suru *(to form);* sooritsu
  suru *(to institute).*
Orient Tooyoo.
oriental *adj.* tooyoo no. -*n.* Tooyoojin.
origin moto, kigen.
originality dokusoosei.
originate (to) hajimeru, soosaku suru
  (invent).
ornament kazari.
orphan koji.
other hoka no *(not the same);* moo hitotsu no
  (additional).
ought -beki *(obligation).*
  You ought to go to a doctor. Isha e iku
  beki desu.
ounce onsu.
our, ours watashitachi no, watashidomo no.
out soto e *(outside).*
outcome kekka.
outdo (to) dashinuku.
outer soto no, sotogawa no.
outlast (to) -yori mochi ga ii.
  This outlasts that one. Kore wa sore yori
  mochi ga ii desu.
outlay keihi *(expenses);* shuppi
  (expenditure).
outlet deguchi.
outline rinkaku *(contour);* aramashi *(essential
  points).*
outline (to) aramashi o noberu *(state the gist);*
  autorain o kaku *(write).*
outlook mikomi.
output sangaku *(product, yield).*
outrage ranboo.
outrageous ranboo na, hidoi.
outside soto, omote.
oval daen no, daenkei no.
oven obun.
overcoat oobaa, oobaakooto.
overcome (to) -ni uchikatsu; -ni makeru *(be
  overcome).*
overflow (to) hanran suru *(said of a river);*
  koboreru *(water in a vessel).*
overlook (to) miotosu *(omit seeing);* miwatasu
  (view from a high place); minogasu
  (refrain from seeing).
overpower (to) makasu, attoo suru.
overrule (to) iatsu suru, kyakka suru *(reject,
  decide against).*
overrun (to) habikoru, afureru.
overseas kaigai no.

oversight miotoshi *(failure to notice)*; shissaku *(mistake)*.

overtake (to) oitsuku.

overthrow (to) hikkurikaesu *(upset)*; uchitaosu *(knock down)*; seifuku suru *(vanquish)*; kutsugaesu *(subvert)*.

overwhelm (to) attoo suru *(crush)*; seifuku suru *(defeat)*.

owe (to) -ni kari ga aru *(be financially indebted to a person)*.

own *adj.* jibun no.

own (to) motsu, shoyuu suru.

owner mochinushi *(proprietor)*; ninushi *(of goods)*.

ox ushi.

oxygen sanso.

oyster kaki.

pace -ho, -po *(suffix: step)*.
    She took two paces. Niho arukimashita.

pace (to) aruite hakaru.

pacific odayaka na *(quiet, calm)*; shizuka na *(still, as water; placid, as the sea; serene, as the mind; peaceful, as sleep)*; heiwateki na *(not warlike)*.

Pacific Ocean Taiheiyoo.

pack (to) tsutsumu, nizukuri suru.

page *n.* peeji.

pagoda too.

pain kurushimi *(distress)*; nayami *(suffering)*; itami *(ache)*; fuan *(uneasiness)*.

pain (to) *v.t.* kurushimeru *(cause pain to)*; *v.i.* itamu *(ache, smart)*.

painful itai.

paint penki.

paint (to) penki o nuru *(a house, etc.)*; e o kaku *(a picture)*.

painter penkiya *(for houses)*; ekaki *(artist)*.

painting e o kaku koto *(art, hobby, vocation)*; e *(that which is painted)*.

pair ittsui *(of objects)*; fuufu *(married couple)*; hitokumi *(a set)*.

pair (to) kumiawaseru.

pale usui *(of color)*; aoi *(of the face)*.

palm tenohira *(of the hand)*.

pamphlet panfuretto.

pan nabe.

pancake pankeeki.

pane garasu ita.
    windowpane mado no garasu ita.

pang sashikomi *(sudden sharp pain)*; uzuki *(twinge)*.

panic kyookoo.

panorama panorama.

pants zubon.

paper kami.

parachute parashuuto, rakkasan.

parade kanpeishiki *(military)*; pareedo, gyooretsu, kooshin *(for popular celebrations)*.

parade (to) kooshin suru.

paragraph paragurafu.

parallel *adj.* heikoo no.

parallel (to) heikoo suru.

paralysis mahi.

paralyze mahi suru.

parcel tsutsumi *(package)*; kozutsumi *(for mail)*.
    parcel post kozutsumi yuubin.

pardon yurushi.

pardon (to) yoosha suru *(forgive)*; yurusu *(excuse)*.
    Pardon me! Shitsurei.

parenthesis kakko.

parents ryooshin.

park kooen.

park (to) chuusha suru.

parliament gikai.

part bun, bubun *(portion, piece)*; bu *(of a book)*; hen *(district)*.
    the greater part daibubun.

part (to) wareru *(separate, divide, split)*; kireru *(as a cable)*; wakareru *(take leave)*.
    to part from hanareru.
    to part with tebanasu.

partial hiiki na *(biased, not fair)*; ichi bubun no *(not total)*.

partially ichibubun.

particular *adj.* sore zore no, meimei no *(individual)*; betsudan no, tokubetsu no *(special)*; kichoomen na *(precise)*. *-n.* kuwashii koto *(a detail)*.

particularly toku ni, tokubetsu ni.

party seitoo *(political)*; enkai, paatii *(entertainment)*.

pass tooge *(over a mountain)*; pasu, kippu *(ticket)*; nyuujooken *(of admission)*.

pass (to) tooru *(go beyond)*; tatsu *(time)*.

passage fune no ryokoo *(on a ship)*; watashi *(across a river)*; rooka *(corridor)*.

passenger jookyaku *(train, etc.)*; senkyaku *(ship)*.

passing *adj.* ichijiteki no *(temporary)*. *-n.* tsuuka *(passage)*.

passion joonetsu *(emotion)*, netsujoo *(intense emotion)*; nekkyoo *(fervid devotion)*; kanshaku *(fury)*.

passive *adj.* ukemi no. *-n.* ukemi *(grammatical verb form)*.

past *n.* kako *(time gone by)*; rireki *(past life or career)*. *adj.* kako no *(gone by)*; sugita bakari no *(just passed)*; izen no *(ago)*.
    half-past seven shichiji han.
    the past year sakunen.

paste *n.* nori.

patch tsugi.

patch (to) tsugu.

patent tokkyo.

paternal chichi no, chichikata no.

path komichi.

pathetic kanashii.

patience gaman *(forbearance)*; shinboo *(perseverance)*.

patient *adj.* gaman zuyoi, shinboo zuyoi. *-n.* kanja *(sick person)*.

patriot aikokusha.

patriotism aikokushin *(nationalism)*.

patron hogosha *(protector)*; kooensha, patoron *(backer)*; hiiki kyaku *(regular customer)*.

patronize (to) hiiki ni suru.

pattern gara, moyoo *(of fabric)*; tehon *(model)*; mihon *(sample)*.

pause kyuushi *(short stop)*.

pause (to) *v.i.* tomaru.

pave (to) hosoo suru.

pavement hodoo.

pay kyuuryoo *(salary)*; chingin *(wages)*.

pay (to) harau.

payment shiharai *(paying)*; shiharaikin *(sum paid)*.

pea endoomame.

    green peas guriin piisu.

peace heiwa *(opp. of war)*.

peaceful heiwa na.

peach momo.

peak itadaki.

pear nashi.

pearl shinju.

peasant hyakushoo *(farmer)*; inakamono *(rustic)*.

pebble jari.

peculiar tokushu na *(characteristic)*; hen na *(strange)*.

pecuniary kinsenjoo no.

pedal pedaru.

pedal (to) pedaru o fumu.

pedestrian hokoosha.

peel kawa.

peel (to) kawa o muku.

pen pen *(for writing)*; ori *(sty)*.

    fountain pen mannenhitsu.

penalty bakkin *(fine)*; kei *(punishment)*.

pencil enpitsu.

penetrate (to) *v.t.* hairikomu *v.i.* tsukiiru.

peninsula hantoo.

penitence kookai *(repentance)*.

pension onkyuu *(government)*; nenkin *(annuity)*.

people hitobito, hito, hitotachi *(individuals collectively)*; kokumin *(a nation)*.

pepper koshoo.

perceive (to) ryookai suru *(apprehend)*; shikibetsu suru *(discern)*; wakaru *(grasp)*.

percentage hyakubun ritsu, paasenteeji.

perfect kanzen na.

perfect (to) kansei suru.

perfection kansei *(completion)*; kanzen *(being unblemished)*; jukutatsu *(proficiency)*.

perfectly kanzen ni.

perform (to) suru *(do)*; nashitogeru *(accomplish)*; enjiru *(act, as in a play)*.

performance suru koto *(doing)*; jikkoo *(execution)*; engeki *(of a drama)*; yokyoo *(entertainment)*.

perfume koosui.

perfume (to) koosui o tsukeru.

perhaps tabun *(probably)*; hyotto suru to *(maybe)*.

peril kiken.

period jidai *(era)*; shuushifu *(in punctuation)*.

periodical zasshi *(magazine)*.

perish (to) horobiru *(suffer destruction)*; kusaru *(spoil, decay)*; shinu *(die)*.

permanent eikyuu no *(lasting)*; eikyuuteki na *(perpetual)*; fuhen no *(unchanging)*.

permission kyoka *(permitting)*; menkyo *(license)*; dooi *(consent)*.

permit menkyo *(license)*; menkyojoo *(written permission)*.

permit (to) kyoka suru *(allow)*.

perplex (to) *v.t.* komaraseru *(throw into confusion)*; *v.i.* komaru *(be perplexed)*.

persecute (to) hakugai suru.

persecution hakugai.

perseverance nintai.

persist (to) ganbaru *(insist on)*; jizoku suru *(last)*.

person hito; -nin *(suffix)*.

    three persons sannin.

personal kojin no *(individual)*; jibun no *(one's own)*; shiyoo no *(private)*.

personality jinkaku *(character)*; kosei *(distinctive personal quality)*.

perspective mikomi *(prospect)*.

persuade (to) tokifuseru, settoku suru.

pertaining to -ni kan shite.

petty chiisai *(small in size)*; sasai na *(trifling)*; kechi na *(mean)*.

pharmacist kusuriya.

pharmacy kusuriya.

phenomenal hijoo na.

phenomenon genshoo.

philosopher tetsugakusha.

philosophical tetsugakuteki.

philosophy tetsugaku.

photograph shashin.

take a photograph shashin o toru.
photograph (to) utsusu.
phrase ku.
physical shizen no *(natural)*; nikutai no *(bodily)*.
physician isha.
physics butsurigaku.
piano piano.
pick (to) tsumu *(flowers, grass)*; erabu *(select)*.
  to pick up hirou.
picnic pikunikku, ensoku.
picture shashin *(photo)*; e *(painting)*.
picture (to) egaku.
picturesque e no yoo na.
pie pai.
piece kire *(obtained by cutting)*; kakera *(broken piece)*.
pig buta.
pigeon hato.
pile yama *(heap)*.
pile (to) tsumu.
  to pile up tsumiageru.
pill gan'yaku.
pillar hashira.
pillow makura.
pilot mizusaki annai *(of a ship)*; soojuushi *(of a plane)*.
pin pin.
pin (to) pin o sasu.
pinch (to) tsuneru.
pine matsu.
pink pinku.
pious keiken na *(devout)*; shinjinbukai *(religious)*.
pipe kiseru, paipu *(for smoking)*; tekkan *(of iron)*.
pitiful kawaisoo na *(touching)*; mijime na *(miserable)*.
pity doojoo.
pity (to) doojoo suru.
place tokoro.
place (to) oku.
  to take place okoru.
plain *adj.* akiraka na *(evident)*; karui *(said of food)*; jimi na *(unadorned)*; futsuu no *(ordinary)*. -*n.* heichi *(level ground)*.
plan zumen *(drawing)*; keikaku *(project)*.
plan (to) keikaku suru *(devise a method or course)*.
plane hikooki *(airplane)*; heimen *(level surface)*.
plant shokubutsu.
plant (to) ueru.
plaster kooyaku *(medical)*; kabe *(mud)*; shikkui *(sand and lime)*.
plate sara *(for eating)*; ita *(of metal)*.
platform purattohoomu, hoomu *(for trains)*; endan *(stage)*.

platter oozara.
play asobi *(children's play)*; shibai, engeki *(dramatic performance)*.
play (to) asobu *(for amusement)*; hiku *(a string or keyboard instrument)*; fuku *(a wind instrument)*.
plea negai.
plead (to) uttaeru.
pleasant kokoromochi no yoi *(giving pleasure)*; yukai na *(cheerful)*.
please (to) yorokobasu *(delight)*; tanoshimaseru *(give pleasure to)*.
  Please. Doozo.
pleasure tanoshimi *(delight)*; yorokobi *(enjoyment)*.
pledge yakusoku *(promise)*; shirushi *(guarantee)*.
pledge (to) teitoo ni ireru *(give as a pledge)*; yakusoku suru *(promise)*.
plenty takusan *(much)*; juubun *(enough)*.
plot jisho *(land)*; inboo *(conspiracy)*.
plot (to) takuramu *(scheme secretly)*; inboo o megurasu *(conspire)*.
plow suki.
plow (to) tagayasu.
plum ume.
plunder (to) ryakudatsu suru.
plural fukusuu.
plus purasu, tasu.
pocket poketto.
  pocket money kozukai.
poem shi; uta.
poet shijin.
poetic shiteki no.
poetry shi, uta.
point saki *(tapering end)*; kangae *(opinion)*; ten *(dot)*; pointo *(prominent feature)*.
point (to) togarasu.
  to point out yubi sasu *(with the hand)*; chuui o hiku *(draw attention)*.
pointed togatta.
poison doku.
poison (to) doku o ireru *(infect with poison)*; dokusatsu suru *(kill with poison)*.
poisoning chuudoku.
polar kyokuchi no.
pole sao.
policeman junsa, keikan.
policy shudan *(method)*; hooshin *(guiding principle)*; seisaku *(course of action in govt.)*.
  insurance policy hoken shoosho.
Polish Poorandojin *(people)*; Poorando no *(country)*.
polish tsuya.
  shoe polish kutsuzumi.
polish (to) migaku.
polite teinei na.

politeness teinei.
political seijijoo no, seijiteki na.
    political party seitoo.
politics seiji.
pollution osen.
    air pollution kuuki osen.
pond ike.
poor binboo na *(opp. of rich)*; warui *(in quality)*; kawaisoo na *(worthy of pity)*.
popular ninki no aru *(liked)*; hyooban no ii *(famous, talked of)*; taishuuteki na *(in general favor)*.
population jinkoo.
pork butaniku.
port minato.
porter monban *(gatekeeper)*; akaboo *(at railway stations)*; booi *(at hotels)*.
portrait shoozooga.
position tsutomeguchi *(employment)*; tachiba *(circumstances)*; oki dokoro *(place)*.
positive *adj.* tashika na *(sure)*; meikaku na *(definite)*; utagai no nai *(unquestionable)*; jishin no aru *(convinced)*. *-n.* poji *(in photography)*.
possess (to) motsu.
possession mochimono *(thing held)*.
possibility kanoosei.
possible dekiru.
post hashira *(pillar)*; kui *(stake)*; yuubinbutsu *(mail)*; posuto *(mailbox)*.
postage yuubinryoo.
    postage stamp kitte.
postcard hagaki *(plain)*; ehagaki *(picture)*.
poster posutaa.
posterity shison.
post office yuubinkyoku.
pot nabe *(pan)*; tsubo *(jar)*; hachi *(bowl)*.
potato jagaimo.
pound pondo.
pour (to) tsugu *(into glass)*; hidoku furu *(said of rain)*.
poverty binboo.
powder kona.
power chikara.
powerful tsuyoi *(strong)*; yuuryoku na *(influential)*.
practical jissaiteki na *(opp. of theoretical)*; jitsuyooteki na *(useful)*.
practice jitsuyoo *(opp. of theory)*; keiko *(exercise)*.
practice (to) jikkoo suru *(carry out)*; keiko suru *(exercise)*.
praise shoosan *(commendation)*.
praise (to) homeru.
prank itazura.
pray (to) inoru.
prayer inori.
preach (to) sekkyoo suru.
precaution yoojin.

precede (to) sakidatsu.
preceding mae no.
precept kyookun.
precious kooka na *(costly)*; taisetsu na *(highly esteemed)*.
precise seikaku na *(exact)*; kuwashii *(detailed)*; kichoomen na *(regular)*.
precision seikaku *(accuracy)*; seimitsu *(exactitude)*.
predecessor zenninsha.
preface jobun.
prefer -hoo ga suki desu *(one thing to another)*.
    I prefer this. Kono hoo ga suki desu.
pregnant ninshin shite iru.
prejudice henken *(bias)*.
prejudice (to) henken o motaseru.
preliminary kari no, yobiteki no.
prepare (to) shitaku o suru, junbi o suru.
prescribe (to) sashizu suru *(dictate)*; shohoo o kaku *(medicine)*.
presence shusseki *(at a meeting, etc.)*.
present *adj.* shusseki shite iru *(opp. of absent)*; ima no, genzai no *(now existing)*. *-n.* genzai *(the present time)*; ima *(now)*; okurimono, purezento *(gift)*.
    to make a present okurimono o suru.
    for the present toobun.
present (to) ageru, sashiageru *(a gift)*; shookai suru *(introduce a person)*; miseru *(exhibit)*; teishutsu suru *(offer)*; noberu *(state)*.
preserve (to) hozon suru *(maintain)*; satoozuke ni suru *(in sugar)*; suzuke ni suru *(in vinegar)*.
preside (to) shikai suru.
president shachoo *(of a company)*; toodori *(of a bank)*; daitooryoo *(of a country)*; gakuchoo *(of a university)*.
press shinbun *(newspaper)*; assakuki *(machine)*.
press (to) susumeru *(urge)*; shimeru *(squeeze)*; puresu suru *(iron)*; osu *(push)*.
pressing puresu.
pressure atsuryoku *(compulsion)*.
prestige meisei *(fame)*; ishin *(dignity)*.
presume (to) suitei suru *(assume)*; katei suru *(suppose)*; omou *(guess)*.
pretend (to) misekakeru *(lay claim)*; -furi o suru *(make believe)*.
pretext koojitsu *(pretense)*; benkai *(excuse)*.
pretty *adj.* kirei na *(beautiful)*. *-adv.* kanari *(fairly)*.
prevail (to) katsu *(be victorious)*; yuusei de aru *(be predominant)*; ryuukoo suru *(be prevalent)*.
prevent (to) samatageru *(hinder)*; mamoru *(guard against)*; jama o suru *(stand in one's way)*.

prevention booshi, yoboo.

previous saki no *(former)*; mae no *(prior to)*.
the previous year mae no toshi.

prey gisei *(victim)*.

price nedan *(charge)*; daika *(cost)*; bukka *(of commodities)*.
price index bukka shisuu.

pride hokori *(in something or someone)*; unubore *(self-conceit)*; kooman *(haughtiness)*.

priest sooryo *(Buddhist)*; kannushi *(Shinto)*; bokushi *(Protestant)*; shinpu *(Catholic)*.

principal *adj.* dai ichi no *(first)*; omo na *(main, most important)*. -n. gankin *(money)*; koochoo *(of a school)*.

principle gensoku *(fundamental rule)*; shugi *(doctrine, an -ism)*.

print (to) shuppan suru *(publish)*; insatsu suru *(to put into print)*.

prison keimusho.

prisoner shuujin *(criminal)*; horyo *(of war)*.

private *adj.* watakushi no, shiyoo no *(opp. of public)*; shiei no *(privately operated)*; kojin no *(personal)*.

privilege tokken *(prerogative)*; tokuten *(peculiar right)*.

prize shoohin.

prize (to) omonjiru *(esteem)*; daiji ni suru *(value highly)*.

probable arisoo na *(likely to be)*; yuuboo na *(promising)*.

probably tabun *(perhaps)*; taitei *(most likely)*.

problem mondai.

procedure tetsuzuki *(steps)*; junjo *(way of proceeding)*.

proceed (to) susumu *(move on)*; hajimeru *(begin)*; tsuzukeru *(continue)*.

process hoohoo *(method)*; katei *(course)*.

procession gyooretsu.

proclaim (to) koohyoo suru *(publish)*; fukoku suru *(promulgate)*; sengen suru *(declare officially)*.

produce (to) seisan suru *(yield)*; enshutsu suru *(as plays)*.

product sanbutsu *(agricultural produce)*; seisakuhin *(of industrial manufacture)*.

production seisaku *(through manufacture)*.

productive hoofu na *(producing abundantly)*; yoku tsukuridasu *(bringing forth)*.

profess to hakujoo suru.

profession shokugyoo *(a calling)*; koogen *(avowal)*; sengen *(declaration)*.

professional shokugyoo joo no *(pertaining to work)*; senmonteki *(technical)*.

professor kyooju *(of a university)*.

profile yokogao.

profit rieki *(pecuniary gain)*; eki *(advantage)*.

profit (to) eki o eru; toku o suru.

program puroguramu *(theatrical, computer, etc.)*; keikaku *(plan)*.
programming puroguramingu.

progress zenshin *(movement forward)*.

progress (to) shinpo suru *(improve)*; zenshin suru *(advance)*; tsugoo yoku iku *(get on well)*; hattatsu suru *(develop)*.

prohibit kinjiru *(forbid)*.

prohibition kinshi *(order forbidding)*.

project keikaku *(plan)*; kigyoo *(industrial)*.

project (to) keikaku suru *(devise)*; tsukidasu *(protrude)*.

promise yakusoku *(engagement)*; keiyaku *(contract)*; mikomi *(hope)*.

promise (to) yakusoku o suru.
to keep a promise yakusoku o mamoru.

prompt hayai, subayai *(quick)*; sumiyaka na *(speedy)*; sassoku no *(done quickly)*.

prompt (to) unagasu.

promptness binsoku.

pronounce (to) hatsuon suru *(articulate)*; senkoku suru *(announce formally)*; sengen suru *(declare)*.

proof shoomei *(demonstration)*; shooko *(evidence)*; kooseizuri *(printing)*.

proper tekitoo na *(appropriate)*; joohin na *(respectable)*; dokutoku no *(particular)*; tadashii *(correct)*.

property zaisan *(assets)*; jisho *(land)*.

proportion wari, wariai *(ratio)*; warimae *(share)*; tsuriai *(balance)*.

proposal mooshikomi, teian.

propose (to) teian suru *(propound)*; mooshikomu *(offer)*.

prosaic sanbun no *(of prose)*; omoshiroku nai *(dull, commonplace)*.

prose sanbun.

prospect mikomi *(outlook)*; nagame *(view)*; mitooshi *(mental view)*; yosoo *(expectation)*.

prosper (to) sakaeru, han'ei suru.

prosperity hanjoo *(of a business)*; ryuusei *(state of thriving)*; seikoo *(success)*.

prosperous sakan na *(thriving)*; rieki no aru *(profitable)*.

protect (to) hogo suru *(keep safe)*; fusegu *(defend)*.

protection hogo *(guarding from harm)*; kooen *(patronage)*.

protector hogosha.

protest koogi *(dissent)*; fufuku *(disapproval)*.

protest (to) koogi suru *(make a protest)*; hantai suru *(oppose)*; genmei suru *(declare formally)*.

Protestant Purotesutanto, Shinkyoo.

proud tokui na.

prove (to) shoomei suru *(demonstrate);* tashikameru *(make certain);* jikken suru *(experiment).*

proverb kotowaza.

provide yooi suru *(supply).*

   provide with kyookyuu suru.

province chihoo *(place at a distance from the capital);* han'i *(sphere or scope).*

provision chozoohin *(of food, etc.);* shokuryoohin *(supplies);* kitei *(stipulation);* junbi *(preparation);* yobi *(reserve).*

provoke (to) kanjoo o okosaseru *(call forth);* okoraseru *(rouse to anger);* fungai saseru *(exasperate);* okosu *(stimulate).*

proximity chikai koto; kinsetsu.

prudence yoojin, shinchoo na koto.

prune sumomo.

psychological shinrigaku joo no.

psychology shinrigaku.

public *adj.* ooyake no *(opp. of personal);* kookai no *(open to all).* -*n.* kokumin *(the people).*

   to make public koohyoo suru.

publication happyoo *(public notification);* shuppan *(publishing);* shuppanbutsu *(published materials).*

publish (to) shuppan suru *(books, etc.);* happyoo suru *(make known).*

publisher shuppansha.

pull (to) hiku.

pulpit koodan.

pulse myaku.

pump ponpu.

punish (to) bassuru.

punishment batsu *(act of punishing);* keibatsu *(penalty imposed by court).*

pupil seito *(school);* deshi *(disciple);* hitomi *(of the eye).*

purchase kaimono *(that which is bought);* torihiki *(act of buying).*

purchase (to) kau, koonyuu suru.

pure junsui no *(unmixed);* seijun na *(uncontaminated);* kirei na *(unsullied),* junketsu na *(chaste);* keppaku na *(guiltless).*

purity junketsu *(chastity).*

purpose mokuteki *(object);* -tsumori *(intention).*

purse saifu.

pursue (to) oikakeru *(chase);* tsukimatou *(follow closely);* jikkoo suru *(carry on).*

pursuit tsuiseki *(chase).*

push (to) osu *(opp. to pull);* oshiugokasu *(move by pushing);* tsukidasu *(thrust);* shiiru *(force).*

put *v.t.* oku.

   put away shimau.

   put off nobasu, enki suru.

   put on kaburu *(hat);* kiru *(dress);* haku *(shoes).*

puzzle nazo *(enigma);* pazuru *(quiz);* nandai *(difficult problem).*

puzzle (to) toowaku saseru *(perplex).*

   be puzzled toowaku suru.

quaint fuugawari na.

qualify (to) tekioo saseru *(fit);* shikaku o eru *(have the qualifications for).*

   be qualified for shikaku ga aru.

quality hinshitsu *(degree of excellence);* seishitsu *(property).*

quantity ryoo, bunryoo *(amount);* suuryoo *(numbers).*

quarrel (to) kenka suru.

quarter yon bun no ichi *(one-fourth part);* hen *(district).*

queen jooo.

queer hen na, myoo na *(strange);* okashii *(funny);* okashi na *(unusual).*

quench (to) iyasu *(one's thirst);* kesu *(extinguish).*

question shitsumon *(interrogation);* koto *(matter);* mondai *(problem).*

question (to) shitsumon suru, tazuneru *(inquire);* tou *(ask);* gimon o okosu *(raise a doubt);* utagau *(doubt).*

quick hayai.

quickly hayaku.

   Come quickly! Hayaku kite kudasai.

quiet *adj.* shizuka na *(calm);* otonashii *(of character);* ochitsuita *(not showy).* -*n.* shizukesa *(stillness);* kyuusoku *(repose);* ochitsuki *(peace of mind).*

   Keep quiet! Shizuka ni shite kudasai!

quiet (to) *v.t.* shizuka ni saseru; *v.i.* shizuka ni naru.

quit (to) hanasu *(let go);* hooki suru *(abandon);* yameru *(cease).*

quite sukkari *(completely);* jijitsujoo *(actually);* kanari *(somewhat);* tashoo wa *(to a certain extent);* taihen *(very).*

   quite good totemo yoroshii.

quote (to) in'yoo suru *(cite);* hikiai ni dasu *(refer to);* mitsumoru *(estimate).*

rabbit usagi.

race kyoosoo *(contest);* jinshu *(of human beings).*

race (to) kyoosoo suru.

radio rajio.

rag boro.

rage ikari.

ragged boro boro no.

rail reeru *(of railway)*; tesuri *(of a fence)*.

railroad tetsudoo.

    railroad station eki.

    railroad train kisha, densha.

rain ame.

rain (to) ame ga furu.

rainbow niji.

rainy ame furi no.

    rainy season baiu, tsuyu.

    rainy weather uten.

raise (to) ageru *(move upward)*; mochiageru *(lift up)*; kakageru *(hoist)*; saibai suru *(grow)*.

raisin hoshibudoo.

rake kumade.

range han'i *(scope)*; narabi *(row)*; dennetsuki *(electric cookstove)*; gasu konro *(gas stove)*.

range (to) *v.t.* naraberu.

rank retsu *(row)*; kaikyuu *(military)*.

ransom minoshirokin *(money demanded)*; kaihoo *(release from captivity)*.

rapid *adj.* hayai. *-n.* kyuuryuu *(swift current)*.

rapidity sokudo.

rapidly kyuu ni, hayaku.

rapture uchooten.

rash *adj.* sekkachi na.

rat nezumi.

rate wariai *(proportion)*; sooba *(of exchange)*; sokudo *(speed)*.

rate (to) nedan o tsukeru, mitsumoru *(estimate)*.

rather kanari *(tolerably, fairly)*; mushiro *(instead of)*; sukoshi *(somewhat)*.

    I'd rather go. Watakushi wa dochira ka to ieba ikitai desu.

    rather good kanari yoi.

    rather than -yori mo.

ration haikyuu shokuryoohin.

rational rikutsu no aru.

rave (to) tawagoto o iu *(talk wildly)*; donaru *(talk furiously)*.

raw nama no *(uncooked)*.

ray koosen, hikari.

razor kamisori.

reach (to) todoku *(come to)*; oitsuku *(overtake)*; -ni tassuru *(attain to)*.

react (to) *v.i.* hannoo suru *(act in response)*.

reaction handoo *(against)*; hanpatsu *(repulsion)*.

read (to) yomu.

reading dokusho.

ready yooi no totonotta *(completely prepared)*; yorokonde . . . suru *(willing)*; kakugo no tsuita *(mentally prepared for)*; tejika na *(handy)*.

real hontoo no *(true)*; jitsuzai suru *(actually existing)*; jissai no *(opp. of imaginary)*; honmono no *(genuine)*.

reality shinjitsu *(opp. of fantasy)*; genjitsu *(actuality)*.

realization jitsugen.

realize (to) jitsugen suru *(effectuate)*; ki ga tsuku *(come to understand)*.

really hontoo ni.

    Really! Soo nan desu ka!

rear ushiro.

rear (to) *v.t.* sodateru *(bring up)*.

reason risei ryoku *(intellectual faculty)*; doori *(explanation)*; riyuu *(cause)*; dooki *(motive)*; wake *(ground)*; iiwake *(excuse)*.

reason (to) suiri suru *(draw a conclusion)*; handan o kudasu *(form a judgment)*; kentoo suru *(examine critically)*.

    by reason of -no tame ni.

reasonable risei no aru *(endowed with reason)*; muri ga nai *(justifiable)*; koohei na *(fair-minded)*; gooriteki na *(rational)*.

reasoning riron, ronkyuu.

reassure (to) anshin saseru.

rebel muhonnin *(person)*.

rebel (to) boodo o okosu *(take up arms against)*; shitagawanai *(disobey)*; somuku *(act against)*.

rebellion hanran *(revolt)*; boodoo *(riot)*; hankoo *(resistance)*; muhon *(treason)*.

recall torikeshi *(act of revoking)*; kaisoo *(recollection)*.

recall (to) omoidasu *(recollect)*; torikesu *(revoke)*; yobikaesu *(call back)*.

receipt uketori.

receive (to) uketoru.

receiver reshiibaa *(radio)*; uketorinin *(person)*.

recent chikagoro no *(modern)*; atarashii *(new)*; saikin no *(the latest)*.

reception kangei *(welcoming)*; kangeikai, resepushon *(social entertainment)*.

recess kyuuka *(vacation)*; yasumi jikan *(school)*; kyuukei *(conference)*.

reciprocal soogo no *(mutual)*; okaeshi no *(done in return)*.

recite (to) anshoo suru *(repeat from memory)*; roogin suru *(as a poem, etc.)*; monogataru *(recount)*.

recognize (to) wakaru, mitomeru.

recoil (to) handoo *(as a gun)*; hanekaeri *(spring back)*.

recollect (to) omoidasu.

recollection oboe *(reminiscence)*; kaisoo *(remembrance)*; tsuioku *(retrospection)*; omoide *(that which is recollected)*.

recommend (to) suisen suru.

recommendation suisen.

reconcile (to) wakai saseru.

record kiroku *(written note);* rireki *(career);* rekoodo *(phonograph).*

record (to) kiroku suru *(in writing);* rokuon suru *(in sound).*

recover (to) torimodosu *(get back);* zenkai suru *(from sickness).*

recruit shinpei.

rectangle choohookei.

red *adj.* akai. *-n.* aka.

redeem (to) shookan suru.

redouble (to) issoo tsuyomeru.

reduce (to) *v.t.* -ni suru *(convert);* herasu *(make small).*

reduction waribiki *(discount).*

reed ashi.

refer (to) sankoo ni suru *(consult);* makaseru *(a matter to a person).*

reference mimoto shoomeisho *(a statement of qualifications for someone);* kikiawase *(inquiry);* kankei *(relation).*

refine (to) seisei suru *(oil, etc.).*

refinement seisei *(of oil, etc.);* joohinsa *(elegance).*

reflect (to) hansha suru *(throw back light, etc.);* arawasu *(show);* kangaeru *(ponder).*

reflection hansha.

reform kaikaku *(political);* kanka *(of persons).*

reform (to) kaizen suru *(amend);* aratameru *(make better);* kaikaku suru *(renovate).*

refrain orikaeshi.

refrain (to) sashihikaeru *(abstain from);* gaman suru *(forbear).*

refresh (to) arata ni suru *(make new).*

refreshment tabemono *(food);* karui nomimono *(drink).*

refuge hinan *(shelter);* hinanjo *(place of retreat);* hogo *(protection).*
  to take refuge hinan suru.

refund harai modoshi.

refund (to) harai modosu.

refusal kotowari.

refuse kotowaru *(decline);* jitai suru *(decline to receive);* shoodaku shinai *(reject).*

refute (to) hanbaku suru.

regard kooryo *(consideration);* sonkei *(respect).*
  in regard to -ni tsuite.

regime toochi *(administration);* kanri *(control);* seiken *(political power).*

regiment rentai.

register choomen *(record book);* meibo *(of names).*

register (to) kaku *(a name);* kakitome ni suru *(a letter).*
  registered letter kakitome.

regret kookai *(repentance);* shitsuboo *(disappointment);* zannen *(remorse).*

regret (to) zannen ni omou *(be sorry for);* ki no doku ni omou *(deplore);* ikan ni omou *(lament);* kookai suru *(repent);* oshiku omou *(be sorry for the loss of).*

regular kimatta *(according to rule);* futsuu no *(usual);* teiki no *(at intervals).*

regulate (to) choosetsu suru.

regulation kisoku.

rehearsal shitageiko, renshuu, rihaasaru.

rehearse (to) shitageiko suru, renshuu suru.

reign jidai *(period).*

reign (to) osameru.

reinforce (to) hokyoo suru.

reject (to) kotowaru.

rejoice (to) yorokobu.

relapse burikaeshi *(recurrence of illness).*

relate (to) hanasu *(narrate);* kankei o tsukeru *(connect).*

relation kankei *(connection);* shinrui *(kinsman).*

relationship kankei.

relative *adj.* hikakuteki, kankei aru. *n.* shinrui, shinseki *(kinsman).*

relax (to) kitsurogu *(take one's ease);* ochitsuku *(calm down);* yurumu *(become loose);* yawaragu *(become less strict).*

relaxation kibarashi *(recreation);* kyuuyoo *(rest);* yurumi *(of muscles);* tegokoro *(of regulations).*

release (to) hanasu *(let go free);* tooka suru *(let fall from);* happyoo suru *(make public).*

relent (to) yawaragu, kandai ni naru.

relentless mujihi na.

relevant kankei no aru.

reliable tashika na.

reliance shinrai *(trust);* shin'yoo *(confidence).*

relic ibutsu.

relief kyuujo *(help);* keigen *(alleviation);* anraku *(comfort).*

relieve (to) tasukeru *(raid);* raku ni suru *(give comfort).*

religion shuukyoo.
  Buddhist religion Bukkyoo.
  Shintoism Shintoo.

religious shuukyooteki na *(of religion);* shinkoo no *(devout);* shinjin bukai, keikan na *(pious).*

relinquish (to) suteru, hooki suru.

relish aji *(taste);* kaori *(flavor);* fuumi *(good taste).*

relish (to) ajiwatte miru *(savor);* oishiku taberu *(eat with pleasure);* tanoshimu *(enjoy).*

reluctance chuucho.

reluctant iyagaru, fushoo bushoo no.

rely upon tayoru *(depend upon).*

remain todomaru, taizai suru *(stay)*.

remainder nokori *(remaining part)*; zanryuusha *(remaining person)*.

remark itta kotoba *(anything said)*; iken *(comment)*.

remark (to) -ni chuumoku suru *(take notice of)*; hihyoo suru *(comment)*.

remarkable chuumoku subeki *(noteworthy)*; sugureta *(exceptional)*; subarashii *(striking)*.

remedy kusuri *(medicine)*; chiryoo *(treatment)*.

remember (to) oboeru; omoidasu *(recollect)*.

remembrance omoide *(recollection)*; kiokuryoku *(memory)*; kinen *(commemoration)*.

remind (to) omoidasaseru *(bring something to mind)*.

remorse kookai *(regret)*; ryooshin no togame *(pangs of conscience)*.

remote tooi, hanareta.
   remote control rimokon.

removal iten *(of or from house)*; kaishoku *(position)*.

remove (to) dokeru, torinozoku.

renew atarashiku suru *(make new again)*; irekaeru *(replace)*; kurikaesu *(repeat)*.

rent yachin *(for a house)*.

rent (to) kasu *(to somebody)*; kariru *(from somebody)*.

repair shuuzen *(act of repairing)*; kaifuku *(restoration to a sound state)*.

repair (to) naosu *(mend)*; kaifuku suru *(restore)*; teisei suru *(remedy)*.

repeat (to) kurikaesu *(do once more)*; sono mama tsutaeru *(tell to another)*; kurikaeshite okonau *(do over again)*.

repent (to) kuiru, kookai suru.

repetition kurikaeshi, hanpuku.

reply henji.

reply (to) henji suru.

report hookoku, shirase *(account)*.

report (to) hookoku suru.

represent (to) dairi suru *(persons, etc.)*; arawasu *(as a symbol)*; egakidasu *(portray)*.

representation daihyoo *(delegate)*; mooshitate *(petition)*.

representative dairinin; daihyoo *(delegate)*.

repress (to) yokuatsu suru *(suppress)*; yokusei suru *(keep under control)*.

reprimand shisseki.

reprimand (to) shikaru, hinan suru.

reprisal shikaeshi, fukushuu.

reproach shisseki *(upbraiding)*; togame *(censure)*.

reproach (to) shikaru.

reproduce (to) fukusha suru *(make a copy)*; saisei suru *(remake)*.

reputation hyooban, meisei.

request negai, seikyuu.

request (to) negau *(beg)*; tanomu *(ask)*.

require (to) iru *(need)*.

rescue sukuidashi, kyuujo.

rescue (to) sukuidasu *(deliver from)*; kaihoo suru *(set free)*.

research (to) kenkyuu suru, shiraberu.

resent (to) okoru, hankan o motsu.

resentment urami *(animosity)*; fungai *(indignation)*.

reservation yoyaku *(at a hotel)*.

reserve junbi *(readiness)*; yobihin *(stock)*.
   without reserve fukuzoonaku *(freely)*.

reserve (to) totte oku *(set apart, keep in store)*.

reside (to) sumu.

residence sumai; juusho.

resign (to) yameru *(relinquish)*; dannen suru *(abandon)*; jishoku suru *(give up office)*; taishoku suru *(retire)*.
   to resign oneself shitagau, akirameru *(accept one's fate)*.

resignation jishoku.

resist (to) teikoo suru *(withstand)*; gekitai suru *(repel)*; hantai suru *(oppose)*.

resistance teikoo, hantai.

resolute shikkari shita.

resolution ketsudan *(firmness)*; kesshin *(formed purpose)*.

resolve (to) kesshin suru *(determine)*; kaiketsu suru *(settle)*.

resort hoyoochi *(for health)*.
   summer resort hishochi.

resort (to) -ni uttaeru.

resources shigen.

respect sonkei *(esteem)*; kankei *(relation)*.
   in respect to -ni kanshite.

respect (to) kooryo suru *(heed)*; sonchoo suru *(treat with deference)*; uyamau *(revere)*.

respectful teinei na, reigi tadashii *(well mannered)*.

respective kakuji no, sorezore no.

respite yuuyo *(delay)*; shikei no shikkoo yuuyo *(reprieve)*; ichijiteki chuushi *(temporary cessation)*.

responsibility sekinin.

responsible sekinin ga aru.

rest nokori *(remainder)*; yasumi *(repose)*; suimin *(sleep)*; teishi *(cessation of motion)*.

rest (to) yasumu; suimin o toru *(have some sleep)*.

restaurant ryooriya *(Japanese)*; resutoran *(Western-style)*.

restless ochitsukanai.

restoration fukkoo *(revival)*; kaifuku *(recovery)*.

restore (to) moto ni modosu *(bring back)*; kaesu *(give back)*; fukushoku saseru *(reinstate);* fukkoo suru *(reestablish);* naosu *(reconstruct).*

restrain (to) yokusei suru.

restraint yokusei.

   without restraint enryo naku.

restrict seigen suru, kagiru.

restriction seigen *(limitation).*

result kekka.

result (to) -ni owaru *(end up in).*

resume (to) futatabi hajimeru.

retail kouri.

retail (to) kouri suru.

retain (to) hoji suru *(keep);* kioku suru *(memorize).*

retaliate (to) shikaeshi suru.

retaliation shikaeshi, fukushuu.

retire (to) intai suru *(from work);* yasumu *(rest).*

retirement intai.

retract torikesu.

retreat taikyaku *(military).*

retreat (to) taikyaku suru.

retrieve (to) torimodosu *(recover);* sukuidasu *(rescue).*

return (to) kaeru *(come back);* kaesu *(give back).*

reveal (to) shimesu *(disclose);* shiraseru *(make known);* bakuro suru *(divulge).*

revelation happyoo *(disclosure);* Mokushiroku *(Book of the Bible).*

revenge fukushuu.

revenue shotoku *(income of an individual);* sainyuu *(of the state).*

reverence suuhai *(veneration);* sonkei *(esteem).*

reverend bokushi *(Protestant clergyman);* shinpu *(Catholic clergyman).*

reverse abekobe, hantai.

reverse (to) abekobe ni suru.

revert (to) moto ni modoru.

review hihyoo *(critical);* fukushuu *(study).*

review (to) saichoosa suru *(view again);* kansatsu suru *(survey);* kaisoo suru *(reconsider);* hihyoo o kaku *(books).*

revise (to) teisei suru *(correct).*

revision kaisei, kaitei.

revive (to) fukkatsu suru.

revoke (to) torikesu *(annul);* haishi suru *(abolish).*

revolt hanran.

revolt (to) hanran o okosu *(rebel).*

revolution kakumei.

revolve (to) mawaru, kaiten suru.

reward hoobi, hooshuu.

reward (to) -ni mukuiru *(repay);* hoobi o ataeru *(give a reward to).*

   be rewarded mukuirareru.

rhyme in.

rib abara bone.

ribbon ribon.

rice ine *(plant);* kome *(raw grain);* gohan *(cooked).*

rich kanemochi no *(wealthy);* yutaka na *(abundant).*

richness yuufuku.

rid (get) torinozoku.

riddle nazo.

ride noru koto.

ride (to) -ni noru.

ridiculous bakarashii.

rifle shoojuu.

right *adj.* tadashii *(correct);* mottomo na *(reasonable);* machigai no nai *(not wrong);* migi no *(direction).* *-n.* kenri *(privilege);* migi *(direction).*

   have a right to kenri ga aru.

   to the right migigawa ni.

righteous koohei na, tadashii.

righteousness seigi, koohei.

rightful tadashii.

rigid kyuukutsu na *(not flexible);* genkaku na *(strict).*

rigor genkaku.

rigorous genkaku na.

ring wa *(circle, link, wheel);* yubiwa *(for finger).*

ring (to) *v.t.* narasu; *v.i.* naru.

rinse (to) yusugu.

riot soodoo, boodoo.

riot (to) soodoo o okosu.

ripe jukushita.

ripen (to) jukusu *(become ripe);* jukusaseru *(make ripe).*

rise agari, shusse *(getting ahead).*

rise (to) agaru *(go up);* okiru *(from bed, etc.);* deru *(said of the sun).*

risk booken *(hazard);* kiken *(peril).*

   run a risk booken o suru.

risk (to) kiken ni sarasu *(expose to peril);* kakeru *(venture);* ichi ka bachi ka yatte miru *(take the chance of).*

rite gishiki.

ritual gishiki *(rite);* shikiten *(ceremony).*

rival kyoosoosha *(competitor);* teki *(enemy);* aite *(in sport).*

rivalry kyoosoo.

river kawa.

road michi, dooro.

   main road oodoori.

   middle of the road michi no mannaka.

roar unari *(of an animal);* todoroki *(of waves, etc.).*

roar (to) unaru *(of animals);* todoroku *(of waves, etc.);* donaru *(vociferate).*

roast roosuto.

roast (to) roosuto ni suru.

   roast beef roosuto biifu.

rob (to) nusumu.

robber doroboo, gootoo.

robbery nusumi.

robe gaun *(gown)*; yukata *(Japanese bathrobe)*.

robot robotto.

robust ganjoo na.

rock iwa.

rock (to) *v.t.* yusuru; *v.i.* yureru.

rocky iwa no ooi.

rod boo, sao.

roll maki gami *(of paper)*; rooru pan *(bread)*.

roll (to) korobasu *(roll over)*; maku *(wind)*; tsutsumu *(enwrap)*; sayuu ni yusuru *(shake from side to side)*; korobu *(tumble down)*.

romantic romanchikku na.

romanticism roomanshugi.

roof yane.

room heya *(of a house)*; basho *(space)*.

   make room for basho o tsukuru.

   There's no room. Basho ga arimasen.

root ne.

rope nawa, tsuna.

rose bara.

rot (to) kusaru *(decay)*.

rough zara zara shita *(opp. of smooth)*; deko boko no *(opp. of level)*; arai *(said of the sea)*; ranboo na *(riotous)*; gekiretsu na *(violent)*; arappoi *(rude)*.

round *adj.* marui. *-adv.* maruku. *-n.* maru, en *(circle)*.

round off (to) shiageru.

rouse me o samasu.

rout (to) haisoo suru.

route tsuuro, ruuto.

routine kimatta junjo *(fixed procedure)*.

rove (to) urotsuku.

row narabi *(line)*; sawagi *(disturbance)*.

   be in a row narande iru.

   place in a row ichiretsu ni oku.

row (to) kogu *(a boat)*.

royal kooshitsu no.

rub (to) kosuru *(any object)*; sasuru *(the body)*.

rubber gomu.

rubbish garakuta, gomi.

rude busahoo na *(unmannerly)*; soya na *(uncivil)*; shitsurei na, burei na *(impolite)*; ranboo na *(rough)*.

ruin haikyo *(remains)*; koseki *(historical site)*; hakai *(destruction)*; metsuboo *(decay)*.

ruin (to) waruku suru *(damage)*; dame ni suru *(make useless)*.

rule monosashi *(measure)*; joogi *(ruler for lines)*; kisoku *(principle)*.

   as a rule ippan ni.

rule (to) suji o hiku *(mark with lines)*; osameru *(govern)*.

ruler shihaisha *(sovereign)*; joogi *(for drawing lines)*.

rumor uwasa.

run (to) hashiru, kakeru.

   run away nigeru.

rural inaka no.

rush ooisogi *(great haste)*; kyuugeki na zooka *(sudden increase)*.

rush (to) isogu.

   rush hour rasshu awaa.

   rush into tobikomu.

   rush out tobidasu.

   rush toward hashitte iku.

Russian Roshiya no *(pertaining to Russia)*; Roshiyajin *(person)*; Roshiyago *(language)*; Roshiya *(country)*.

rust sabi.

rust (to) *v.t.* sabisaseru; *v.i.* sabiru.

rustic inaka no; inaka mono no *(person)*.

rusty sabita.

rye raimugi.

sacred shinsei na *(hallowed)*.

sacrifice gisei *(surrender of a desirable thing)*.

sacrifice (to) gisei ni suru *(renounce something)*.

sacrilege bootoku.

sad kanashii.

sadden (to) kanashimaseru.

saddle kura.

sadness kanashimi.

safe *adj.* buji na, anzen na *(free from danger)*; tashika na *(reliable)*. *-n.* kinko *(strongbox)*.

safely buji ni.

safety buji, anzen.

sail ho.

sail (to) shuppan suru *(depart)*; fune de iku *(go by boat)*; kookai suru *(navigate)*.

saint seija, seijin.

sake tame; mokuteki *(purpose)*.

   for the sake of -no tame ni.

salad sarada.

salary gekkyuu *(monthly)*; nenkyuu *(annual)*; sarari.

sale uridashi *(bargain)*; hanbai *(selling)*.

   sales analysis hanbai bunseki.

   sales estimate yosoo uriage daka.

   sales force hanbai in.

   sales promotion hanbai sokushin.

   sales quota hanbai wariate.

   sales territory hanbai chiiki.

   sales volume hanbai ryoo.

salt shio, shokuen *(for the table)*.

salt (to) shio de aji o tsukeru.

salute eshaku (*nod*); aisatsu (*greeting*); keirei (*military*).
salute (to) aisatsu suru.
salvation sukui.
same onaji.
    all the same mattaku onaji.
sample mihon, sanpuru.
sanctuary reihaidoo (*in a church*); shinden (*Shinto shrine*).
sand suna.
sandal sandaru (*Occidental-style*); zoori (*Japanese-style*).
sandwich sandoitchi.
sandy suna no (*pertaining to sand*); sunachi no (*land*); usuchairo no (*in color*).
sane shooki no.
sanitary eiseitekina.
sap jueki (*of trees*); genki (*vitality*).
sap (to) yowaraseru.
sarcasm hiniku, fuushi.
sarcastic hiniku na.
sardine iwashi.
sash obi.
satellite eisei.
satiate (to) akisaseru.
satin shusu.
satisfaction manzoku.
satisfactory manzoka na (*contented*); juubun na (*sufficient*); yoi (*adequate, good*).
satisfy (to) manzoku saseru (*gratify*); zenbu hensai suru (*discharge*); baishoo suru (*recompense*).
saturate (to) hitasu.
Saturday Doyoobi.
sauce soosu (*Worcestershire*); shooyu (*soy sauce*).
saucer koohii zara (*for coffee cup*); chataku (*for Japanese teacups*).
sausage sooseeji.
savage *adj.* yaban na. *-n.* yabanjin.
save (to) sukuu (*rescue*); takuwaeru (*hoard*); setsuyaku suru (*economize*); tasukeru (*from injury*); tameru (*put by*).
    be saved tasukaru.
    save time jikan o setsuyaku suru.
savings chokin, ginkoo yokin (*bank*).
savior sukuinushi.
say (to) iu, ossharu (*honorific; respect*).
    Say! Chotto!
scales hakari (*weighing instrument*); uroko (*of fish*).
scan (to) kuwashiku shiraberu.
scandal shuubun, gigoku, oshoku.
scanty sukunai, toboshii.
scar kizu ato.
scarce sukunai, fusoku na; mare na.
scarcely karoojite (*with difficulty*); yatto (*barely*); hotondo (*with a negative verb; almost, not*).

scarcely know hotondo zonjimasen (*honorific: humble*).
scare (to) *v.t.* odokasu.
    get scared odoroku.
scarf sukaafu, erimaki.
scatter *v.t.* makichirasu (*strew*); oichirasu (*disperse*).
scene keshiki (*landscape*); bamen (*movie, etc.*).
scenery keshiki; kookei (*sight, spectacle*).
schedule jikanhyoo (*timetable*); ichiranhyoo (*catalogue*).
scheme keikaku (*in a good sense*); takurami (*in a bad sense*).
scholar seito (*student*); gakusha (*learned person*).
school gakkoo.
    go to school tsuugaku suru.
    junior high school chuugakkoo.
    leave school taigaku suru.
    primary school shoogakkoo.
    senior high school kootoogakkoo.
science kagaku.
scientific kagakuteki.
scientist kagakusha.
scissors hasami.
scold (to) shikaru.
scope han'i.
scorn keibetsu.
scorn (to) keibetsu suru.
scornful keibetsuteki na.
scrape (to) kezuru, kaku.
scratch kakikizu (*made by nail or claw*); kasurikizu (*wound*).
scratch (to) kaku (*an itchy place*); hikkaku (*cause a wound*).
scream sakebigoe.
scream (to) sakebu (*cry out*).
screen shikiri (*partition*); maku (*curtain*).
    folding screen byoobu.
    paper screen shooji (*in a Japanese house*).
screw neji.
    screwdriver nejimawashi.
scribble (to) nagurigaki suru.
scroll makimono.
scruple chuucho, tamerai.
scrupulous ryooshin teki na.
scrutinize (to) sensaku suru.
sculpture chookoku.
sea umi.
seal han, in, fuuin (*impression*); azarashi (*animal*).
seal (to) han o osu; fuujiru (*close up*).
seam nuime.
search soosaku (*quest*); sensaku (*inquiry*); tsuikyuu (*close inquiry*); ginmi (*scrutiny*).
search (to) sagasu (*explore*); jitto mitsumeru

(scrutinize carefully); saguru *(probe);*
shiraberu *(examine).*
seashore kaigan.
seasickness funayoi.
season kisetsu.
    rainy season baiu, tsuyu.
season (to) aji o tsukeru.
seat koshikake *(anything to sit on);* isu
(chair); benchi *(bench);* seki *(place where
one sits).*
seat (to) koshikakeru.
second *n.* dai ni *(in succession);* byoo *(in
time);* futsuka *(of the month). -adj.* ni
banme no.
second (to) sansei suru *(support).*
secondary dai ni no.
secret *adj.* himitsu no. *-n.* himitsu.
secretary hisho *(in a business office);* shoki
(recording officer; as a title).
sect shuuha, ha.
section bun *(part);* kuiki *(area, zone).*
secure anshin na *(free from care);* buji na
(safe); daijoobu na *(sure).*
secure (to) shikkari to suru *(make fast);* eru
(obtain); hoshoo suru *(guarantee).*
security tanpo *(for debts);* teitoo *(deposited as
a pledge);* anzen *(safety).*
see miru *(look at);* miseru *(show). -ni au (meet
face to face);* wakaru *(comprehend);*
tamesu *(try out).*
    I see. Wakarimashita.
seed tane.
seek (to) sagasu *(look for);* sagashimotomeru
(try to obtain).
seem (to) mieru.
    She seems not to know it. Shiranai
rashii.
seize (to) tsukamaeru.
seldom metta ni *(with negative).*
    I seldom go. Metta ni ikimasen.
select (to) erabu.
selection sentei.
self jibun, jishin.
    by itself shizen ni.
    by oneself hitori de.
    myself watashi jishin.
selfish migatte na *(concerned unduly with
oneself);* rikoteki na *(egoistic).*
selfishness wagamama.
self service serufu saabisu
sell (to) uru.
semicolon semikoron.
senate jooin *(U.S.);* sangiin *(Japan).*
senator jooingiin *(U.S.);* sangiingiin
(Japanese).
send (to) okuru *(to a distant place);* todokeru
(nearby); dasu *(by mail).*
senior toshiue *(in age);* senpai *(old-timer).*
sensation kankaku *(perception by the senses);*

kimochi *(feeling);* kandoo *(excited
feeling);* koofun *(excitement);* hyooban *(of
gossip, etc.).*
sense chikaku *(perception);* ishiki
(consciousness); kanji *(sensation);* kannen
(mental discernment); funbetsu *(practical
judgment);* imi *(meaning).*
senseless mukankaku na *(thoughtless);*
bakageta *(foolish).*
sensibility kankaku.
sensible kenmei na *(wise);* kashikoi
(sagacious); shiryo no aru *(thoughtful).*
sensitive kanjiyasui *(delicate);* shinkei kabin
na *(overly sensitive);* sugu ki ni suru
(touchy).
sensitivity shinkei kabin.
sentence bunshoo *(in writing);* bun *(gram.);*
senkoku *(judgment).*
sentiment kanji, joosoo.
sentimental senchimentaru na; kanshooteki
na.
separate wakareta *(disconnected);* betsu no
(distinct); koko no *(individual);* hitori
hitori no *(single);* kakuri shita *(isolated).*
separate (to) hanasu; wakeru; setsudan suru
(sever); hikihanasu *(disconnect);* hanareru
(disunite); bekkyo suru *(live apart, part
company).*
separately betsu betsu ni, tandoku ni.
separation bunri, datsuri.
September Kugatsu.
serene ochitsuita *(tranquil);* hareta
(unclouded); uraraka na *(bright and clear);*
odayaka na *(placid).*
sergeant gunsoo *(army);* keibu *(in a police
force).*
series shiriizu, renzoku.
serious majime na *(solemn);* juudai na
(important); kitoku no *(dying, critically
ill).*
seriously majime ni.
sermon sekkyoo.
servant meshitsukai.
    maidservant otetsudai.
serve (to) hookoo suru *(act as a servant);*
kyuuji o suru *(wait on table);* yaku ni tatsu
(be of use); tsugoo ga yoi *(be suitable);*
-no tame ni hataraku *(give service to).*
service sewa *(assistance rendered);* hookoo
(servant's occupation); saabisu *(treatment
in hotels, etc.);* reihai *(religious).*
session kaiki *(period);* kaitei *(sitting of law
court);* gakki *(school term).*
set *adj.* kimatta, kitei no. *-n.* kumi *(things of
the same kind).*
    complete set hito kumi.
set (to) *v.t.* oku *(place);* tateru *(erect);*
hajimeru *(begin);* totonoeru; kimeru *(fix);*
v.i. shizumu *(as the sun).*

settle (to) kimeru *(fix)*; kaiketsu suru *(solve)*; ochitsuku *(settle down)*; imin suru *(colonize)*.

settlement kaiketsu *(of an affair)*; jidan *(agreement)*; seisan *(liquidation)*; setsurumento *(social service)*.

seven nanatsu, shichi.

seventeen juunana, juushichi.

seventeenth dai juunana; juushichi nichi *(of the month)*.

seventh dai shichi; nanoka *(of the month)*.

seventieth dai nanajuu.

seventy nanajuu, shichijuu.

several iro iro no *(diverse)*; ikutsuka no *(various)*.

    several times suukai.

severe hidoi *(harsh)*; kibishii *(strict)*; genkaku na *(stern)*; gensei na *(rigidly accurate)*; mooretsu na *(intense)*.

severity gekiretsu *(harshness)*; genkaku *(strictness)*.

sew (to) nuu.

sewer gesui.

sex sei.

    female sex mesu *(animals)*; josei *(humans)*.

    male sex osu *(animals)*; dansei *(humans)*.

sexual seiteki na.

shabby misuborashii.

shade hikage *(of sun)*; kage *(of trees, etc.)*.

shade (to) kage ni suru *(cast shade upon)*; hikari ga ataranai yoo ni suru *(protect from light)*; kakusu *(screen from view)*.

shadow kage.

shady kage no ooi.

shake (to) *v.t.* yusuru *(rock, swing)*; furu *(by holding)*; *v.i.* furueru *(tremble)*.

shallow asai.

sham *adj.* nise no. -*n.* nise.

sham (to) -no furi o suru.

shame haji *(disgrace)*; hazukashisa *(consciousness of shortcoming)*; fumenboku *(ignominy)*; fumeiyo *(dishonor)*.

shame (to) haji saseru.

shameful hazukashii.

shameless haji shirazu no.

shape katachi *(form)*; keijoo *(configuration)*; sugata *(guise)*.

shape (to) katachi o tsukeru.

shapeless katachi no nai.

share bun *(part)*; wakemae *(portion)*; kabu *(finance)*.

share (to) wakeru *(divide)*; buntan suru *(partake)*.

shareholder kabunushi.

sharp *adj.* surudoi *(as blades, needles)*; yoku kireru *(as edge for cutting)*; saki no togatta *(pointed)*; nukeme no nai *(shrewd)*.

sharpen (to) togu *(an edge)*; togarasu *(a point)*; kezuru *(a pencil)*.

shatter (to) konagona ni kowasu *(break in pieces)*; kujiku *(hope)*.

shave (to) soru *(blade)*; kezuru *(plane)*.

she ano onna no hito, kanojo.

shed koya.

shed tears (to) namida o nagasu.

sheep hitsuji.

sheer kewashii *(steep)*; mattaku no *(utter)*.

sheet shikifu *(for a bed)*; ichi mai no kami *(of paper)*.

shelf tana.

shell kara *(of mollusks)*; koo *(of lobster, crab, etc.)*.

shelter hinanjo *(refuge)*; hinangoya *(shed)*; hogo *(protection)*.

shelter (to) *v.t.* hogo suru *(protect)*; yadorasu *(lodge)*; kakumau *(give refuge)*; *v.i.* hinan suru *(take refuge)*.

shepherd hitsuijikai.

shield tate.

shield (to) hogo suru.

shift kootai *(act of taking a turn)*.

shift (to) *v.t.* utsusu, kaeru.

shine (to) hikaru *(glitter)*; teru *(as sun or moon)*; kagayaku *(sun)*.

ship fune.

    steamship kisen.

ship (to) fune de okuru *(send by ship)*; okuru *(send by any means)*.

shipment funazumi *(ship's load)*; ni *(cargo)*; tsumini *(the goods shipped)*.

shirt shatsu, waishatsu *(Western-style)*; juban *(Japanese)*.

shiver miburui.

shiver (to) furueru, miburui suru.

shock shokku, shoogeki *(impact)*; shoototsu *(collision)*; shindoo *(by earthquake)*; kandoo *(of the mind)*.

    have a shock bikkuri suru.

shock (to) odorokasu *(with fear)*; odoroku *(be shocked)*.

shoe kutsu.

shoemaker kutsuya.

shoot utsu *(as a gun)*.

shooting shageki.

shop mise; -ya *(in compounds)*.

    butcher shop nikuya.

shopping kaimono.

shore kaigan.

short mijikai *(not long)*; hikui *(not tall)*.

    short distance shookyori, tan kyori.

shorten (to) *v.t.* mijikaku suru *(make shorter)*; tsumeru *(curtail)*; *v.i.* mijikaku naru *(become shorter)*; tsumaru *(be curtailed)*.

shorthand sokki.

shot happoo *(of a gun)*; chuusha *(injection)*.
shoulder kata.
shout oogoe *(loud voice)*.
shout (to) oogoe de yobu *(call out)*; oogoe o
  dasu *(utter a loud cry)*; sakebu, donaru
  (utter with a shout).
  to shout at donari tsukeru.
shove (to) oshiwakeru.
shovel shaberu.
show shibai, misemono *(public show)*.
show (to) miseru *(let see)*; oshieru *(point
  out)*.
shower niwaka ame *(of rain)*; yuudachi *(in
  summer)*.
shrill kandakai.
shrimp ebi.
shrine jinja *(Shinto)*.
shrink (to) chijimu.
shrub kanboku.
shun (to) sakeru.
shut *adj.* shimatta, tojita.
shut (to) *v.t.* shimeru *(a door, etc.)*; tojiru
  (things with lids); *v.i.* shimaru *(be shut)*.
shy hazukashii *(bashful)*; uchiki na *(timid)*;
  kimari ga warui *(embarrassed)*.
sick (be) guai ga warui *(unwell)*.
  She got sick. Byooki ni narimashita.
sickness byooki.
side kawa (gawa).
sidewalk hodoo, jindoo.
siege kakomi.
sigh tameiki.
sigh (to) tameiki o tsuku.
sight shiryoku *(power of seeing)*; nagame
  (view, scene); keshiki *(scenery)*.
  out of sight mienai.
sign sain *(signature)*; shirushi *(indication)*;
  chookoo *(symptom)*; zenchoo *(omen)*;
  fugoo *(mark)*; kanban *(signboard)*; miburi
  (gesture).
sign (to) shomei suru *(one's name)*.
signal shingoo, keihoo.
signal (to) shingoo o okuru.
signature shomei, sain.
significance imi *(meaning)*; juuyoosei
  (importance).
significant juuyoo na.
signify (to) -o imi suru.
silence seishuku, chinmoku.
silence (to) damaraseru.
silent shizuka na.
silicon keiso.
silicone shirikon.
silk kinu.
  silk cloth kenpu.
silken kinu no.
silkworm kaiko.
silly baka na.

silver gin.
silvery gin'iro no.
similar nite iru *(resembling)*; onaji yoo na
  (same kind); ruiji shita *(alike)*.
similarity ruiji.
simple kantan na *(not complicated)*; tanjun na
  (not combined); wake no nai, yasashii
  (easy).
simplicity tanjun, kantan.
simply tan ni.
simulate (to) -no mane o suru.
simultaneous dooji no.
sin tsumi.
sin (to) tsumi o okasu.
since -kara *(because)*; -te kara *(after, follows
  verb in -te form)*.
sincere seijitsu na.
sincerely hontoo ni *(truly)*; seijitsu ni.
sincerity seijitsu.
sinew suji.
sing utau; naku *(birds)*.
  sing a song uta o utau.
singer kashu; utaite.
single tada hitotsu no *(one only)*; kokono
  (individual); dokushin no *(unmarried)*.
singular mezurashii *(uncommon, rare)*; hen na
  (strange); fushigi na *(wondrous)*.
sinister ninsoo no waruii *(person)*.
sink nagashi *(in a kitchen)*.
sink (to) *v.i.* shizumu *(be submerged)*; *v.t.*
  shizumeru *(submerge, go down)*.
sinner tsumibito.
sip (to) susuru.
sir sensei *(teacher, lawyer, title of respect)*.
  Thank you, sir. Arigatoo gozaimasu.
sister neesan, oneesan, ane *(older)*; imooto
  (younger).
sister-in-law gi-shi, giri no ane *(older)*; gimai,
  giru no imooto *(younger)*.
sit (to) koshikakeru *(on a chair)*; suwaru.
site basho *(place)*; shikichi *(for a building)*.
situation tsutome guchi *(employment)*; jijoo
  (circumstance).
six muttsu, roku.
sixteen juuroku.
sixteenth dai juuroku, juurokunichi *(of the
  month)*.
sixth dai roku; muika *(the sixth of the
  month)*.
sixtieth dai rokujuu.
sixty rokujuu.
size ookisa, saizu *(dimension)*; sunpoo
  (measure).
skate (to) sukeeto o suru.
skates sukeeto.
skeleton gaikotsu.
skeptic *n.* utagai bukai hito.
sketch suketchi *(rough drawing)*; shitagaki

(rough draft); gaiyoo *(outline);* shasei *(from nature).*

ski, (skiing) sukii.
    a pair of skis sukii hitokumi.

skill gijutsu.

skillful joozu na.

skin hifu *(human, animal);* kawa *(of animals or fruit).*

skirt sukaato *(Western dress);* suso, hakama *(Japanese kimono).*

skull zugaikotsu.

sky sora.
    blue sky aozora.

slander (to) waruku iu; chuushoo suru.

slap hirate uchi.
    to slap (someone's) face kao o hirate de utsu.

slate *n.* sekiban.

slaughter tosatsu *(butchering);* gyakusatsu *(massacre).*

slave dorei.

slavery dorei seido.

sled sori.

sleep nemuri.

sleep (to) nemuru *(slumber);* yasumu *(rest, doze);* neru.

sleeve sode.

slender hossori shita *(slim, opp. of stout);* kabosoi *(slight);* yowai *(weak, feeble);* hinjaku na *(meager).*

slice kire.

slice (to) usuku kiru.

slide (to) suberu.

slight kyasha na *(slender);* karui *(not severe);* sukoshi no *(small, not great).*

slight (to) keibetsu suru.

slip surippu *(article of woman's clothing).*

slip (to) subette korobu *(trip);* tsumazuku *(stumble);* fumihazusu *(miss one's footing).*

slipper surippa.

slippery suberiyasui, tsuru tsuru shita.

slope keisha *(slant);* koobai *(incline);* saka *(hill);* shamen *(inclined plane);* keisachi *(sloping ground).*

slot hosonagai ana.

slovenly bushoo na.

slow osoi.

slow (to be) okureru *(fall behind).*

slowly yukkuri.

slowness osoi koto.

slumber karui nemuri, madoromi.

slumber *v.i.* utouto suru *(sleep lightly);* nemuru *(sleep);* utatane suru *(doze);* inemuri suru *(drowse).*

sly zurui.

small chiisai *(not big);* hosoi *(slender).*

smart kashikoi *(clever);* haikara na, sumaato na *(elegant in dress).*

smash (to) kowasu.

to be smashed kowareru.

smear (to) nasuritsukeru.

smell nioi *(odor);* kaori *(scent);* akushuu *(stink).*

smell (to) kagu *(get the odor of, exercise the sense of smell);* nioi ga suru *(emit an odor);* warui nioi ga aru *(be rank);* hijoo ni kusai *(stink).*

smile bishoo, hohoemi.

smile (to) niko niko suru, hohoemu.

smoke kemuri.

smoke (to) kemuri o haku *(emit smoke);* tabako o suu *(cigarettes).*

smooth sube sube shita *(not rough);* taira na *(level, even);* odayaka na *(not ruffled);* dekoboko no nai *(not jagged).*

smooth (to) nobasu, nadaraka ni suru.

smother chissoku saseru *(suffocate);* akubi o kamikorosu *(a yawn);* kanjoo o osaeru *(an emotion);* kakusu *(conceal);* momikesu *(stifle).*

smuggle (to) mitsuyunyuu suru.

snake hebi.

snapshot sunappu shashin.

snatch (to) hittakuru *(grab);* nusumu *(steal).*

sneer (to) reishoo suru.

sneeze (to) kushami o suru.

snore (to) ibiki o kaku.

snow yuki.
    snowfall yukifuri.

snow (to) yuki ga furu.

snowstorm fubuki.

so (thus) desu kara.
    and so on -nado, -too.
    It is so. Soo desu.
    I think so. Soo omoimasu.

soak (to) shimitooru *(permeate);* nurasu *(drench).*

soap sekken.

sob susuri naki.

sob (to) susuri naku.

sober yotte inai *(not intoxicated);* majime na *(serious).*

sociable shakooteki na *(fond of company);* koosai joozu na *(companionable).*

social shakai no, shakaiteki na.

society shakai *(community);* jooryuu shakai *(upper class);* tsukiai *(companionship);* dooseki *(company);* kai *(association).*

sock(s) kutsushita *(Western);* tabi *(Japanese).*

socket soketto *(electric).*

soft yawarakai *(not hard);* yasashii *(not harsh).*

soften (to) yawarakaku suru *(as an object);* yawarageru *(in feeling).*

soil tsuchi *(earth);* tochi *(ground).*

soil (to) yogosu.

soldier heitai.

sole *adj.* tatta hitori no *(one and only; pertaining to persons);* tatta hitotsu no *(pertaining to inanimate things);* tandoku no *(exclusive to one);* dokutoku no *(unique).* -*n.* soko *(of a shoe);* ashi no ura *(of the foot).*

solemn genshuku na.

solemnity genshuku, soogon.

solicit segamu *(ask earnestly of);* kongan suru *(importune);* konsei suru *(entreat).*

solid joobu na *(strong);* katai *(hard).*

solitary hitori de kurasu *(living alone);* tsure nashi no *(without companions);* sabishii *(lonely);* hitodoori no mare na *(unfrequented).*

solitude kodoku *(being alone);* sabishisa *(loneliness).*

soluble tokeru.

solution kaishaku *(a solving);* setsumei *(explanation);* kaiketsu *(settlement).*

solve (to) kaiketsu suru *(clear up);* setsumei suru *(explain);* kaitoo suru *(find an answer);* toku *(a problem).*

some *(often omitted in Japanese)* ikuraka no *(an indefinite quantity);* sukoshi *(a little, a few);* ni-san *(two or three).*

    Give me some water, please. Mizu o kudasai.

somebody donata ka *(honorific: respect);* dare ka.

somehow doo ni ka *(in some way or other);* nan to ka shite *(in one way or another);* doomo *(for some reason or other).*

someone donata ka *(honorific: respect);* dare ka.

something nani ka.

sometime itsuka *(at an indefinite time);* sono uchi ni *(at a time hereafter);* shibaraku *(for a certain period).*

sometimes toki ni wa *(at times);* toki doki *(occasionally);* tama ni *(now and then).*

somewhat ikuraka *(in some measure);* sukoshi *(a little);* ikubun *(to some extent).*

somewhere doko ka ni, doko ka de *(in or at someplace);* doko ka e *(to someplace);* aru tokoro *(a certain place).*

son musuko.

song uta.

    popular song ryuukooka.

soon sugu.

soot susu.

soothe (to) nadameru *(calm down);* nagusameru *(comfort);* shizumeru *(assuage).*

sore *adj.* tadareta *(inflamed);* itamu *(painful to the touch).* -*n.* odeki *(boil);* tadare *(a festering).*

sorrow kanashimi, nageki.

sorry (be) kinodoku ni omou.

    Excuse me. Okinodoku desu *(I am sorry for you).*

    I am sorry Sumimasen. Gomen nasai.

sort shurui *(kind, class);* hinshitsu *(character, nature).*

sort out (to) yoriwakeru.

soul tamashii.

sound *adj.* kenkoo na, kenzen na *(of healthy mind);* itande inai *(undamaged);* tashika na *(reliable);* ronriteki na *(logical).* -*n.* oto *(that which is heard);* hibiki *(reverberation).*

sound (to) fuku *(a wind instrument);* narasu *(other musical instroments);* aizu suru *(give a signal);* oto o saseru *(make a sound).*

soup suupu *(Western style);* suimono *(Japanese).*

sour suppai.

source moto *(origin);* minamoto *(of a river).*

south minami.

southeast toonan.

    Southeast Asia Toonan Ajia.

southern minami no.

southwest nansei.

sovereign kunshu.

sow (to) maku *(scatter);* makichirasu *(disseminate);* hiromeru *(propagate).*

space aita basho *(room);* supeesu; tokoro *(place);* kankaku *(interval);* kyori *(distance).*

space (to) kankaku o oku.

spacecraft uchuusen.

spacious hirobiro to shita *(vast, broad);* ookii *(large).*

spade suki.

spare *adj.* yobi no *(held in reserve);* yobun no *(superfluous);* fuyoo no *(not required);* hinjaku na *(scanty);* kiritsumeta *(stinted).* -*n.* yobi *(reserve).*

spare (to) oshimu *(use grudgingly);* ken'yaku suru *(economize);* yurusu *(forbear);* sashi hikaeru *(refrain from);* tebanasu *(release).*

spark hi no ko, hibana *(of fire);* kirameki *(gleam);* kakki *(animating principle).*

sparkle (to) kagayaku.

sparrow suzume.

speak (to) hanasu *(narrate);* iu *(mention).*

speaker hanashite, enzetsusha *(one who delivers a speech);* kooensha, kooshi *(lecturer);* supiikaa *(radio loudspeaker).*

special tokubetsu no *(of a particular kind);* sen'yoo no *(private);* tokutei no *(definite);* namihazure no *(extraordinary);* tokushu no *(particular).*

specialty tokusanhin *(special product);* meisan *(famous product);* tokushoku *(special feature).*

specific tokushu na, tokutei na.

specify (to) shitei suru.

spectacle kookei *(sight)*; sookan *(noteworthy scene)*; misemono *(public show)*.

spectator kenbutsunin *(onlooker)*; bookansha *(bystander)*.

speculate (to) kangaeru *(consider)*; shisaku suru *(meditate)*; suisoku suru *(conjecture)*; tooshi suru *(invest)*.

speech hanashi *(talk)*; hanasu nooryoku *(faculty of speaking)*; kotoba *(language)*; enzetsu *(public address)*.

speed sokuryoku *(velocity)*; hayasa *(swiftness)*.

speedy sokuryoku no hayai.

spell majinai *(charm)*.

spell (to) tsuzuri.

spelling tsuzuri.

spend (to) tsukau *(pay out)*; kurasu *(time)*.

sphere tama *(globe)*; kyuumen *(spherical surface)*; tentai *(heavenly body)*.

spice yakumi *(condiment)*; kaori *(fragrance)*; kooryoo *(aromatic vegetable flavoring)*.

spider kumo.

spill (to) kobosu.

to get spilled koboreru.

spin (to) tsumugu *(yarn)*; kakeru *(a web)*; mawasu *(a top)*; mayu o tsukuru *(silk; by a silkworm)*.

spirit tamashii *(as distinct from matter)*; seishin *(disposition of mind)*; kakki *(vigor)*; netsui *(ardor)*.

spiritual seishinteki na *(concerned with things of the mind or soul)*; kami no *(divine)*; shinsei na *(sacred)*; shuukyoojoo no *(religious)*.

spit (to) tsuba o haku.

spite ijiwaru *(malice)*; urami *(grudge)*.

in spite of -ni mo kakawarazu.

spite (to) ijiwaru o suru.

spiteful ijiwarui.

splash (to) hanekakeru, haneageru.

splendid rippa na *(imposing)*; subarashii *(magnificent)*; migoto na *(admirable)*.

splendor kagayaki, migoto.

split (to) *v.t.* saku *(crack)*; waru *(divide)*; sogu *(cleave)*; *v.i.* wareru.

spoil (to) itameru *(damage)*; dame ni suru *(render useless by injury)*; waruku suru *(make bad)*.

sponge *n.* kaimen, suponji.

spontaneous shizen na *(natural)*; jihatsuteki no *(voluntary)*; jidooteki na *(self-acting)*.

spoon saji.

spoonful saji ippai no.

sport undoo, supootsu *(recreation)*; tanoshimi *(pastime)*; joodan *(jest)*.

spot tokoro *(place)*; ten *(speck)*; shimi *(stain)*.

spread (to) *v.t.* hirogeru *(in length and breadth)*; nuru *(butter)*; hiromaru *(news)*; *v.i.* hirogaru *(to be disseminated)*.

spring haru *(season)*; bane *(of machinery)*; onsen *(of hot water)*; izumi *(of cold water)*.

spring (to) tobu *(leap)*; shoojiru *(proceed, originate)*.

sprinkle (to) maku *(with water)*; furikakeru *(with powder, etc.)*.

sprout (to) me o fuku *(put forth shoots)*; haete kuru *(spring up)*.

spry subashikoi.

spur (to) hakusha o kakeru *(a horse)*.

spurn (to) hanetsukeru.

spy supai, kanchoo.

spy (to) saguru.

squadron kantai.

squander (to) mudazukai suru.

square seihookei *(geom.)*; hiroba *(in a town)*.

squeeze (to) hasamu *(between two things)*; nigiri shimeru *(in one's hand)*; shiboru *(press out liquids)*.

squirrel risu.

stable *n.* umagoya. *-adj.* shikkari shita *(firm)*; antei shita *(steady)*; kyooko na *(steadfast)*.

stack shoka *(library)*.

stack (to) tsumi kasaneru.

stadium kyoogijoo, sutajiamu.

staff sao *(pole)*; boo *(rod)*; shokuin *(of a business)*.

staff (to) shokuin o soroeru.

stage butai, suteeji *(theatrical)*; endan *(elevated platform)*.

stain shimi, yogore.

stain (to) *v.t.* yogosu; *v.i.* yogoreru *(get stained)*.

stair(s) dan, kaidan.

stammer (to) domoru.

stamp kitte *(postage stamp)*; han *(rubber stamp, etc.)*; keshiin *(postmark)*.

stamp (to) sutanpu o osu.

stand dai *(to set things on)*; hankoo *(resistance)*; boogyo *(defense)*; uriba *(booth)*.

stand (to) tatsu *(get up)*; tachitsuzukeru *(remain standing)*; tatte iru *(be in a standing position)*; oite aru *(be placed; speaking of an inanimate thing)*; aru *(be located)*; tachiagaru *(stand up)*; tateru *(erect)*.

star hoshi *(celestial)*; sutaa, hanagata *(theatrical)*.

stare (to) -o mitsumeru.

start hajime *(beginning)*; shuppatsuten *(starting point)*; odoroki *(shock)*.

start (to) *v.t.* hajimeru *(begin)*; *v.i.* hajimaru *(begin)*; shuppatsu suru *(depart)*; deru *(of trains, etc.)*.

starve (to) ueru.

state kokka *(political body)*; jootai *(condition)*.

state (to) iu *(say)*; hanasu *(tell)*; noberu *(express in speech)*; chinjutsu suru *(express in writing)*.

stately doodoo to shita.

statement seimei.

station eki.

statistic tookei.

statue zoo.

    bronze statue doozoo.

statute kisoku *(rule, regulation)*.

stay taizai.

stay (to) *v.t.* tomaru *(stop)*; *v.i.* okuraseru *(delay)*.

steady shikkari shita.

steak bifuteki.

steal nusumu.

steam jooki, suchiimu.

steam (to) musu.

steamer kisen *(steamship)*.

steel hagane, kootetsu.

steep *adj.* kyuu na, kewashii *(precipitous)*; kyuukoobai no *(high-pitched)*.

steer (to) kaji o toru.

stem kuki.

stenographer sokkisha.

stenography sokki.

step dan *(of a staircase)*; ashi oto *(sound of a footstep)*; ashi ato *(footprint)*; dankai *(successive stage)*.

step (to) aruku *(walk)*; fumu *(tread on)*.

sterile ko o umanai *(barren)*; fumoo no *(not fertile)*; minori no nai *(unproductive)*.

stern *adj.* genkaku na *(severe)*; kakoku na *(harsh)*.

stew shichuu.

stew (to) torobi de niru.

stick boo.

stick (to) sasu *(pierce)*; tsuku *(adhere)*.

stiff kowabatta *(rigid)*; katai *(hard)*; ugokanai *(not moving freely)*.

stiffen (to) kowabaru.

still *adj.* shizuka na *(quiet)*. *-adv.* mada *(more)*; yahari *(after all)*; sore demo *(nevertheless)*; ima made *(yet)*.

    Keep still! Jitto shite! Ugokanaide!

stimulate (to) shigeki suru.

stimulus shigeki.

sting hari *(of an animal)*; toge *(of a plant)*.

sting (to) sasu, piri piri suru.

stinginess kechi.

stingy kechi na.

stir (to) ugokasu *(move, shake)*; kakimawasu *(liquids)*.

stitch (to) nuu *(sew)*; kagaru *(darn)*.

stock zaikohin *(goods)*; shihon *(capital)*; kabuken *(shares)*.

stock (to) takuwaeru.

stock exchange kabushiki torihikisho.

stocking kutsushita.

stomach i, onaka.

stone ishi.

stool koshikake.

stop teiryuujo *(stopping place for buses, etc.)*; shuushi *(end)*.

stop (to) yameru *(discontinue)*; tomeru *(cause to cease)*; teishi suru *(suspend)*; jama suru *(interrupt)*; yokusei suru *(restrain)*; soshi suru *(prevent)*; owaraseru *(put an end to)*; fusagu *(block)*; tomaru *(come to rest)*.

store mise.

    department store depaato.

stork koonotori.

storm arashi.

story hanashi *(speech)*; uwasa *(gossip)*; monogatari *(tale)*; itsuwa *(anecdote)*; densetsu *(legend)*.

stove sutoobu.

straight massugu na *(opp. of crooked)*; itchokusen no *(in a straight line)*.

straighten (to) massugu ni suru.

strain kinchoo *(tension)*; hijoo na doryoku *(excessive effort)*; karoo *(overexertion)*.

strain (to) muri o suru.

strange mezurashii *(rare)*; fushigi na *(wondrous)*; kimyoo na *(odd)*.

stranger shiranai hito *(unknown person)*; yoso no hito *(outsider)*.

strap himo.

straw wara.

strawberry ichigo.

stream nagare *(current)*; ogawa *(small river)*.

stream (to) nagareru.

street machi *(with houses, etc.)*; michi *(road, way)*.

strength tsuyosa *(vigor)*; tairyoku *(bodily)*.

strengthen (to) tsuyoku suru *(make stronger)*; zookyoo suru *(reinforce)*; tsuyoku naru *(become stronger)*.

strenuous hone no oreru.

stress kyoochoo *(emphasis)*; appaku *(pressure)*; kinpaku *(strain)*.

stress (to) kyoochoo suru.

stretch (to) nobasu *(extend in length)*; hirogeru *(extend in breadth)*; dasu *(reach out)*; nobiru *(lengthen)*.

strict kibishii.

stride kappo.

stride (to) kappo suru.

strife arasoi *(conflict)*.

strike sutoraiki, higyoo, suto *(work)*; storaiku *(baseball)*.

strike (to) butsu *(beat)*; tataku *(rap, knock)*; shoototsu suru *(collide)*; sutoraiki o suru, higyoo suru *(quit work)*; kokoro o utsu *(impress)*.

string himo.

strip (to) hadaka ni suru *(lay bare)*; toriharau *(divest)*; kimono o nugu *(undress)*.

stripe shima.

strive (to) honeoru *(try hard)*; doryoku suru *(endeavor)*; funtoo suru *(struggle vigorously)*.

stroke dageki *(blow)*; suji *(line)*; kaku *(of a Japanese character)*.

stroll sanpo.

stroll (to) sanpo suru.

strong tsuyoi *(having strength)*; joobu na *(not easily broken)*; kenkoo na *(healthy)*; daijoobu na *(reliable)*.

structure koosei *(construction)*; kumitate *(framework)*; kenchiku *(building)*; soshiki *(organization)*.

struggle kumiuchi *(body to body)*; arasoi *(strife)*; honeori *(violent effort)*.

struggle (to) doryoku suru *(make great efforts)*; mogaku *(writhe)*; tatakau *(fight)*; arasou *(contend)*.

stubborn ganko na *(hardheaded)*; goojoo na *(obstinate)*; shibutoi *(perverse)*; te ni oenai *(intractable)*; fukutsu no *(unyielding)*.

student seito, gakusei.

studious yoku benkyoo suru *(assiduous in study)*; gakumonzuki no *(given to study)*; nesshin na *(zealous)*.

study benkyoo *(application of the mind)*; kenkyuu *(research, investigation, etc.)*.

study (to) benkyoo suru, narau *(learn)*.

stuff shina *(material, goods)*; mono *(substance, matter)*; garakuta *(rubbish)*; tawagoto *(nonsense)*.

stuff (to) tsumekomu *(fill with something)*; tsumemono o suru *(cooking)*.

stumble (to) tsumazuku *(trip up)*; yoromeku *(miss one's footing)*; yoro yoro aruku *(walk unsteadily)*.

stump kirikabu.

stun (to) me o mawasaseru.

stunt kyokugei *(tricks)*.

stupendous tohoo mo nai.

stupid oroka na, baka na.

stupidity baka sa, oroka sa.

stupor mahi.

sturdy shikkari shita.

stutter (to) domoru.

style ryuukoo, sutairu *(mode of fashion)*; hanashiburi *(mode of speaking)*.

subdue seifuku suru *(conquer)*; uchikatsu *(overcome)*; iatsu suru *(render submissive)*; yokusei suru *(repress)*.

subject shinmin *(of a country)*; mondai *(theme of discussion)*; gakka *(of study)*.

subject (to) shitagaeru *(subdue)*.

subjective shukanteki.

subjugate (to) seifuku suru *(subdue)*.

sublime suukoo na.

submission fukujuu *(subjection)*; koofuku *(surrender)*.

submissive juujun na.

submit (to) teishutsu suru *(turn in)*; shitagawaseru *(yield)*.

subordinate buka, haika.

subordinate (to) shita ni oku.

subscribe (to) yoyaku suru *(to newspapers, etc.)*; sansei suru *(give assent)*.

subscription yoyaku.

subside (to) shizumaru *(become tranquil)*; hekomu *(dent)*.

subsidy hojokin *(grant of money)*.

subsist (to) kurashite iku.

substance honshitsu, hontai.

substantial jitsuzai suru *(actual)*; hontoo no *(real)*; oohaba no *(major)*.

substantiate (to) shoomei suru.

substitute kawari *(a person)*; daiyoohin *(a thing representing another)*.

substitute (to) dairi suru *(person)*; daiyoo suru *(thing)*.

substitution daiyoo.

subtle bimyoo na.

subtract (to) hiku *(take out or away)*.

subtraction hikizan.

suburb koogai.

succeed (to) ato o tsugu *(be a successor to)*; seikoo suru *(effect one's purpose)*.

success seikoo *(favorable termination)*; kooun *(good fortune)*.

successful seikoo shita.

succession renzoku *(sequence)*; keishoo *(to a position, throne, etc.)*.

successor soozokusha.

such konna *(like this, of this sort)*; sonna *(like that, of that sort)*.

sudden kyuu na.

suddenly kyuu ni *(abruptly)*; fui ni *(unexpectedly)*.

sue (to) soshoo o okosu *(take legal action)*; uttaeru *(bring suit)*.

suffer (to) kurushimu *(be in pain)*; gaman suru *(endure patiently)*; songai o koomuru *(a loss)*.

suffering kurushimi *(pain)*; songai *(loss)*.

sufficient takusan no *(plenty)*; juubun na *(enough)*.

sugar satoo, osatoo.

suggest (to) omoidasaseru *(hint)*; iidasu *(propose)*.

suggestion kangae, anji, hinto *(hint)*; teigi *(proposal)*.

suicide jisatsu.

    to commit suicide jisatsu suru.

suit yoofuku, suutsu *(of clothes);* kokuso *(legal proceedings).*

suit (to) niau *(fit);* tsugoo ga ii *(be convenient).*

suitable choodo ii *(fitting, proper);* niau *(becoming).*

sulk (to) mutto suru *(be offended);* suneru *(pout).*

sullen fukigen na *(in a bad mood);* inki na *(gloomy).*

sum gaku *(quantity);* gookei *(total amount);* kingaku *(amount of money).*

summary tekiyoo sho *(brief account);* gaiyoo *(synopsis).*

summer natsu.

summit choojoo *(top).*

summon (to) shookan suru.

summons shookanjoo.

sumptuous zeitaku na.

sum up (to) gaikatsu suru.

sun hi, taiyoo.

    rising sun asahi.

    setting sun yuuhi.

sunbeam nikkoo.

sunburn hiyake.

Sunday Nichiyoobi.

sundry iroiro no.

    sundry expenses zappi.

    sundry goods zakka.

sunny urarakana.

sunrise hi no de.

sunset hi no iri.

sunshine hinata.

superb subarashii.

superconductor choo dendoo tai.

superficial uwabe dake no *(outward);* senpaku na *(shallow; said of persons).*

superfluous yokei na.

superintendent kantoku *(supervisor);* kanrisha *(manager);* koochoo *(of school).*

superior sugureta *(better);* jootoo no *(of great excellence);* yuusei na *(larger);* kookyuu no *(of higher rank).*

    to be superior sugurete iru.

superiority yuushuu.

superstition meishin.

supervise (to) kantoku suru.

supper yuuhan.

supplement bessatsu *(of a book);* furoku *(of a magazine).*

supplement (to) oginau.

supplementary furoku no.

supply kyookyuu *(process of supplying);* kyookyuuhin *(thing supplied).*

supply (to) kyookyuu suru.

support sasaemono *(prop);* shiji *(moral support);* fuyoo *(maintenance).*

support (to) shiji suru *(hold up);* motaseru *(maintain);* genkizukeru *(encourage);* tasukeru *(assist).*

suppose (to) soozoo suru *(imagine);* omou *(think);* katei suru *(assume tentatively);* suitei suru *(presume).*

suppress shizumeru *(subdue);* kinshi suru *(stop);* osaeru *(restrain);* kamikorosu *(smother).*

supreme saikoo no.

sure tashika na *(certain);* ate ni naru *(reliable);* hontoo no *(true);* joobu na *(stable).*

surely tashika ni.

surety tanpo *(pledge);* hoshoonin *(sponsor).*

surf yose nami *(on the shore);* uchinami *(on rocks).*

surface hyoomen.

surgeon gekai.

surgery geka *(treatment);* shujutsu *(operation).*

surmount (to) noboru *(climb);* uchikatsu *(overcome).*

surname myooji.

surpass (to) sugureru *(be better than);* shinogu *(outdo);* sugiru *(exceed);* amaru *(be beyond).*

surplus yojoo *(the remainder);* amari *(the rest).*

surprise odoroki *(amazement);* omoigakenai koto *(something unexpected).*

surprise (to) bikkuri saseru *(strike with wonder);* odorokasu *(cause surprise);* fui uchi suru *(take unawares).*

surrender hikiwatashi *(of a thing);* koosan *(of a person);* koofuku *(of an army).*

surrender (to) tewatasu *(hand over);* hooki suru *(give up something);* koofuku suru *(submit).*

surround (to) torimaku.

surroundings kankyoo.

survey sokuryoo *(land measurement);* kenchi *(land surveying);* tsuuran *(comprehensive view).*

survey (to) miwatasu *(look over);* ippanteki ni miru *(take a general view);* kenbun suru *(inspect);* choosa suru *(examine).*

survive (to) ikinokoru *(pertaining to people);* nokoru *(pertaining to other cases).*

susceptibility kanjusei.

susceptible takan na, kanjooteki na.

suspect utagawashii hito *(suspected person).*

suspect (to) kanzuku *(have an inkling);* -de wa nai ka to omou *(half-believe);* soozoo suru *(surmise);* utagau *(doubt).*

suspense fuan *(feeling of);* mitei.

suspension chuuburarin.

suspicion kengi *(distrust);* utagai *(doubt).*

suspicious utagai bukai *(distrustful)*; ayashii *(doubtful)*.
sustain (to) sasaeru.
swallow tsubame *(bird)*.
swallow (to) nomikomu.
swamp numa.
swan hakuchoo, suwan.
sway (to) yureru.
swear (to) chikau *(take an oath)*; akutai o tsuku *(curse)*.
sweat ase.
sweat (to) ase ga deru.
sweep (to) haku *(with a broom)*; sooji suru *(clean up)*.
sweet amai *(of taste)*; kawairashii *(of face)*; yasashii *(of disposition)*.
sweetness airashisa *(of person)*; amasa *(of food)*.
swell (to) fukureru *(bulge out)*; hareru *(become swollen)*; ookiku naru *(expand)*.
swift hayai.
swim (to) oyogu.
swindler sagishi.
swing (to) yureru, bura-bura ugoku *(as a pendulum)*; fureru *(use as a swing)*.
switch *n.* suitchi *(electric)*
   to switch on suitchi o ireru.
   to switch off suitchi o kiru.
sword katana.
syllable onsetsu.
symbol shoochoo *(emblem)*; fugoo *(mark, sign)*.
symbolic shoochooteki.
symbolize (to) shoochoo suru *(be a symbol of)*; fugoo de arawasu *(represent by symbols)*.
symmetrical tsuriai no toreta.
symmetry tsuriai, kinsei.
sympathetic omoiyari no aru *(compassionate)*; ki no atta *(congenial)*.
sympathize (to) ki no doku ni omou *(feel sympathy)*; sansei suru *(agree with)*; nagusameru *(condole)*.
sympathy doojoo.
symptom chookoo.
syrup shiroppu.
system shoshiki *(organization)*; hoohoo *(method)*; chitsujo *(order)*.

T

table teeburu *(European)*; chabudai *(Japanese low table)*.
tablecloth teeburukurosu, teeburukake.
tablespoon teeburu supuun; oosaji.
tacit anmoku no.
tacitly soreto naku, anmoku ni.

taciturn mukuchi na.
tack (to) byoo de tomeru.
tact josai nasa, kiten.
tactfully josai naku, umaku.
tag fuda.
tail o, shippo.
tailor yoofukuya *(for Western clothes)*; shitateya *(for Japanese clothes)*.
take (to) toru *(get, lay hold of)*; motte iku *(carry or take to)*; tsukamu *(grasp)*; uketoru *(receive)*; tsurete iku *(take to, lead to)*.
tale hanashi; monogatari *(old story)*.
talent sainoo *(special faculty)*; shuwan *(natural ability)*.
talk hanashi; oshaberi *(chattering)*; danwa *(conversation)*.
talk (to) hanasu.
talkative oshaberi na.
tall takai.
   She is tall. Se ga takai desu.
tame nareta *(domesticated)*; sunao na *(docile)*; juujun na *(submissive)*; mukiryoku na *(dull)*.
tangerine mikan.
tangle (to) motsuresaseru *(entangle)*; karamaseru *(confuse)*.
tank suisoo, tanku *(for water, etc.)*; tanku, sensha *(vehicle of war)*.
tape teepu.
   tape recorder teepu rekoodaa.
   videotape bideo teepu.
tar koorutaaru.
tardy guzuguzu shita, jikan ni okureru.
target mato.
tarnish henshoku.
   to be tarnished kumotte iru.
tarry (to) nagai suru.
task shigoto *(piece of work)*; hone no oreru shigoto *(toil)*; tsutome *(duty)*.
taste aji *(of food)*; shumi *(for art)*.
taste (to) aji o miru.
tax zei, zeikin.
   export tax yushutsu hin zei.
   import tax yunyuu hin zei.
   sales tax uriage zei.
   tax allowance zei koojo.
   taxation kazei.
   tax base kazei hyoojun.
   tax deduction zei koojo.
   tax evasion datsu zei.
   tax-free income hibazei shotoku.
   tax shelter zeikin hinan shudan.
taxi takushii.
tea ocha *(Japanese)*; koocha *(black tea)*.
teach oshieru *(give instruction)*; shitsukeru *(train)*.
teacher sensei.
team chiimu.

tear namida *(teardrop);* kagizaki *(a rip in clothing).*

tear (to) yaburu *(rip);* mushiri toru *(pull violently away);* yabureru *(become torn);* hagasu *(tear off).*

tease (to) nayamasu *(annoy);* ijimeru *(torment).*

teaspoon chasaji.

technical gijutsuteki no.

technique gijutsu, tekunikku.

tedious kudoi, nagatarashii.

telecommunications denki tsuushin.

telegram denpoo.

telegraph denshin.

telegraph (to) denpoo o utsu.

telephone denwa.
    car phone jidoosha denwa.
    cordless phone koodoresu hon.

telephone (to) denwa o kakeru.

telex terekkusu.

tell (to) hanasu *(relate);* iu *(say);* oshieru *(instruct).*

temper umare tsuki *(disposition);* seishitsu *(temperament);* kidate *(personality);* kigen *(mood).*

temperance sessei, kinshu *(moderation).*

temperate odayaka na *(mild);* tekido no *(moderate).*

temperature ondo *(of the air);* taion *(of the body).*

tempest ooarashi.

temple miya, omiya *(Shinto);* tera, otera *(Buddhist);* komekami *(of the forehead).*

temporary hakanai *(transient);* kari no.

tempt (to) yuuwaku suru *(seduce);* sosoru *(incite);* izanau *(induce);* unagasu *(persuade).*

temptation yuuwaku *(seduction);* tameshi *(trial).*

ten too, juu.
    ten days tooka.
    ten o'clock juuji.

tenacious shinboozuyoi *(unyielding);* nebarizuyoi *(tough).*

tenacity kyoojin-sei, gankyoo.

tenant shakuyanin *(of a house);* shakuchinin *(of land).*

tend (to) mukau *(be directed toward);* keikoo ga aru *(have a tendency);* kooken suru *(serve);* ki o tsukeru *(attend to);* kaihoo suru *(watch over).*

tendency keikoo *(trend);* seiheki *(inclination);* fuuchoo *(drift).*

tender *adj.* yawarakai.

tennis tenisu, teikyuu.

tense katakurushii *(stiff);* jisei *(grammar).*
    future tense mirai.
    past tense kako.
    present tense genzai.

tension kinchoo.

tent tento.

tenth dai juu, juu banme, juu ban.
    tenth of the month tooka.

tepid nurui.

term kigen *(limited period);* jooken *(condition);* gakki *(of school).*

terrace takadai *(raised ground);* terasu *(of a house).*

terrible osoroshii *(dreadful);* hidoi *(awful);* hisan na *(wretched).*

terrify (to) odorokasu.
    be terrified at -ni odoroku.

territory ryoodo *(as a colony);* ryoochi *(possession of a state or individual).*

terror kyoofu.

test tameshi *(experiment);* shiken *(probe);* shikinseki *(touchstone).*

test (to) kensa suru.

testify (to) shoogen suru *(give evidence);* shookodateru *(attest).*

testimony shoomei *(law);* shooko *(evidence).*

text shudai; tekisuto *(of a document).*

textbook kyookasho.

than yori, yorimo.
    less than ika.
    more than ijoo.

thank (to) rei o iu.
    Thank you. Arigatoo.
    Thank you very much. Doomo arigatoo gozaimasu.

thanks kansha *(gratitude).*

that *adj.* sono, ano. *-pron.* sore, are.
    that person ano hito.
    That's it! Soo da!

thaw yukidoke.

theater gekijoo.

their, theirs karerano, ano katagata no, ano katatachi no, ano hitotachi no.

theme daimoku, shudai *(subject);* wadai *(topic).*

themselves ano katagata jishin.

then sono toki, sono toki ni *(at that time);* sore kara *(after that);* sore de *(at that point);* sono baai *(in that case).*

theoretical rironteki.

theoretically rironjoo.

theory gakuri *(scientific principle);* riron *(opp. of practice);* gakusetsu *(doctrine).*

there asoko, achira *(places outside of immediate reach);* soko, sochira *(places near the conversation partner).*

thereafter sore irai.

therefore sore desu kara.

there is (are) iru *(for animate beings);* aru *(for inanimate beings).*

thereupon sokode.

thermometer kandankei *(weather);* taionkei *(clinical).*

these kono, kore.

thesis ronbun.

they karera, ano katagata, ano katatachi, ano hitotachi *(pertaining to people);* are *(pertaining to things).*

thick atsui *(flat things);* futoi *(approximately cylindrical things);* koi *(liquids, hair, etc.).*

thicken (to) atsuku suru, koku suru.

thickness atsusa; kosa.

thief doroboo.

thigh momo.

thimble yubinuki.

thin usui *(flat things, liquids);* hosoi *(approximately cylindrical things);* yaseta *(persons).*

thing mono *(in concrete sense);* koto *(abstract).*

think kangaeru *(conceive);* omou *(suppose);* jukkoo suru *(ponder);* soozoo suru *(imagine);* shian suru *(meditate).*

third *n.* dai san, sanbanme. *-adj.* dai san no, sanbanme no.

   third of the month mikka.

thirst nodo no kawaki.

   to quench one's thirst nodo no kawaki o iyasu.

thirsty (be) nodo ga kawaite iru.

thirteen juusan.

thirty sanjuu.

this *adj.* kono. *-pron.* kore.

   this one kore.

thorn toge.

thorough kanzen na *(complete);* tetteiteki na *(utter);* mattaku no *(out and out).*

though ga *(but, however).*

   Though it was raining . . . Ame ga futte ita ga . . .

thought kangae, shisoo *(that which is thought);* shisaku *(cogitation);* shian *(meditation);* an *(idea).*

thoughtful shinsetsu na *(kind).*

thoughtless karuhazumi na *(careless);* fushinsetsu na *(inconsiderate).*

thousand sen.

   ten thousand man, ichiman.

   three thousand sanzen.

thrash (to) muchiutsu.

thread ito.

thread (to) ito o toosu.

   thread a needle hari ni ito o toosu.

threat kyoohaku.

threaten (to) kyoohaku suru.

three mittsu, san.

threshold iriguchi *(entrance);* shikii *(door sill).*

thrift ken'yaku.

thrifty ken'yaku na.

thrill suriru, senritsu.

thrill (to) kandoo suru; suriru o kanjiru.

thrilling wakuwaku saseru yoo na.

thrive (to) hanjoo suru.

thriving hanjoo shite iru.

throat nodo.

throb (to) dooki ga suru, doki doki suru.

throne gyokuza.

throng gunshuu.

through *prep.* -o tooshite *(by the medium of);* tsuranuite *(across);* -no naka ni *(in the midst of);* -juu *(during the whole period).* *-adv.* hajime kara owari made *(from beginning to end);* zutto *(all the way).*

throughout *prep.* -juu *(periods of time).* *-adv.* sukkari, doko mo ka mo *(everywhere).*

throw (to) nageru *(fling);* hooru *(hurl).*

thumb oyayubi.

thunder (to) kaminari ga naru.

thunderbolt kaminari.

Thursday Mokuyoobi.

thus kono yoo ni, koo iu fuu ni *(in this manner);* desu kara *(so, therefore);* shitagatte *(accordingly).*

thwart (to) jama suru.

ticket kippu, ken.

   ticket of admission nyuujooken.

   ticket window kippu uriba.

tickle (to) kusuguru.

ticklish kusuguttai.

tide shio, chooryuu.

tidy kichin to shita *(arranged in good order);* kogirei na *(neat).*

tie musubime *(knot);* tsunagari *(connection).*

tie (to) shibaru *(tie roughly);* yuwaeru *(tie up).*

   tie a knot musubu.

tiger tora.

tight katai *(close);* kataku musunda *(compact);* harikitta *(taut);* kitchiri atta *(close-fitting).*

tile kawara, tairu.

till made.

   till now ima made.

   till then sono toki made.

tilt (to) katamuku.

timber zaimoku.

time toki; jiki *(opportunity);* jikan *(hour);* kikan *(period);* jidai *(era).*

   from time to time tokidoki.

   in time ma ni au yoo ni.

   time sharing taimu shearingu.

   time zone jikan tai.

   What time is it? Nanji desu ka?

timid uchiki na.

timidity uchiki.

tin suzu.

   tin can kan, kanzume no kan.

tinkle (to) chirin chirin naru.

tiny chiisana.

tip saki *(end);* kokorozuke, chippu *(gratuity);* chadai *(gratuity given in Japanese inns).*

tip over (to) hikkurikaesu.

tire taiya *(for wheels)*.

tire (to) *v.t.* tsukaresaseru; *v.i.* tsukareru *(get tired)*.

tired tsukareta.

tireless tsukare o shiranai.

tiresome taikutsu na.

title dai, taitoru, daimoku; shomei *(of a book)*; katagaki *(rank)*; kengen *(business)*.

to e *(toward)*; made *(until, up to)*.
    Tell him to come. Kuru yoo ni itte kudasai.
    I went to buy. Kai ni ikimashita.
    to him sono hito ni.

toad hikigaeru.

toast toosuto *(bread)*; kanpai *(proposing a health)*.

toast (to) **(bread)** pan o yaku.

tobacco tabako.

today kyoo.

toe ashi no yubi.

together issho ni, minna de *(all together)*.

toil honeori.

toil (to) roodoo suru; kuroo suru.

toilet toire, otearai, benjo *(washroom)*.

token shirushi *(sign)*; kinenhin *(souvenir)*; katami *(keepsake)*.

tolerable gaman dekiru.

tolerance kandai.

tolerant kandai na.

tolerate (to) oome ni miru *(permit)*; gaman suru *(endure)*; kandai ni toriatsukau *(be broad-minded)*.

toll zeikin *(tax)*; tsuukooryoo *(passage money)*; shishoosha no kazu *(casualties)*.

tomato tomato.

tomb haka *(grave)*; nookotsujo *(vault)*.

tomorrow ashita, myoonichi.

ton ton.

tone oto; kuchoo *(of speech)*; iroai *(color)*.

tongs hibashi.

tongue shita.

tonight kon'ya.

too mo *(also)*; -sugiru *(excessively)*.
    too expensive takasugiru.

tool doogu.

tooth ha.

toothache haita.

toothbrush haburashi.

toothpaste hamigaki.

toothpick tsumayooji.

tooth powder hamigakiko.

top ue *(summit)*; koma *(toy)*.

top (to) ue ni naru.

topic topikku; shudai *(subject)*; wadai *(of conversation)*.

torch taimatsu.

torment kashaku *(torture)*.

torment (to) kurushimeru.

torture *n.* goomon *(for forced confession)*; kurushimi *(anguish)*.

toss (to) nageru.

total *adj.* sookei no *(entire)*; kanzen na *(complete)*. *-n.* gookei *(total amount)*.

totally kanzen ni.

touch (to) sawaru.

touching aware na.

touchy shinkei kabin na.

tough tsuyoi *(strong)*; ganjoo na *(robust)*; goojoo na *(stubborn)*; hidoi *(laborious)*; katai *(hard)*.

tour ryokoo, tabi *(travel)*; kankooryokoo *(pleasure trip)*.

tour (to) ryokoo suru.

tourist kankookyaku, yuuransha, tsuurisuto.
    Tourist Agency Ryokooannaijo.

tournament shiai.

toward -no hoo e *(direction)*; goro *(about: in point of time)*.

towel tenugui *(Japanese)*; taoru *(Western)*.

tower too.

town machi, tokai *(city)*.

toy omocha.

trace ato *(remains)*; keiseki *(vestige)*; kekka *(evidence)*.

trace (to) toosha suru *(through paper)*; tsuiseki suru *(track down)*.

track senro *(railroad)*.

trade shoobai *(domestic)*; booeki *(with foreign countries)*.
    trade union roodoo kumiai.

tradition shikitari, dentoo.

traditional dentooteki na.

traffic torihiki *(commerce)*; kootsuu *(movement of people, vehicles, etc.)*.

tragedy higeki *(opp. of comedy)*; kanashii dekigoto *(sad event)*.

tragic higekiteki na.

trail komichi *(mountain path)*; ato *(trace)*.

trail (to) ato o tsukeru *(pursue)*.

train kisha *(steam- or diesel-powered)*; densha *(electric)*.

train (to) kyooiku suru *(educate)*; shikomu *(animals)*.

training kunren.

traitor uragirimono *(betrayer)*; kokuzoku *(rebel)*.

trample (to) fumiarasu.

tranquil shizuka na.

tranquility heian.

tranquilizer chinseizai, seishin'anteizai, torankiraizaa.

transaction torihiki.
    business transaction shoogyoo torihiki.

transfer norikae kippu *(ticket)*.

transfer (to) norikaeru *(change cars)*; utsusu *(shift)*; ugokasu *(move)*; yuzuru *(hand over)*.

transformer hengatsu ki.

transistor toranjisutaa.

    portable transistor radio keitai yoo toranjisutaa rajio.

transition hensen, suii *(change)*.

translate (to) hon'yaku suru.

translation hon'yaku, yaku.

translator hon'yakusha.

transmission dentatsu.

transmit (to) watasu *(hand over)*; tsutaeru *(pass on)*.

transparent sukitootta.

transport *n.* unsoo.

transport (to) unpan suru *(carry)*; unsoo suru *(by ship or railroad)*.

transportation yusoo *(conveyance)*; unsoo *(shipping)*; kootsuu no ben *(means of travel)*.

trap wana.

trap (to) wana de toru.

trash gomi, kuzu *(rubbish)*; garakuta *(odds and ends)*.

travel ryokoo, tabi.

travel (to) ryokoo suru.

traveler ryokoosha.

tray bon, obon.

treacherous uragiru yoo na, fuchuujitsu no *(disloyal)*.

treachery uragiri.

treason muhon.

treasure takara.

treasure (to) daiji ni suru.

treasurer kaikeigakari.

treasury shikin.

treat gochisoo.

treat (to) motenasu *(entertain)*; atsukau *(deal with)*; chiryoo suru *(give medical treatment)*; ogoru *(treat a person to)*.

treatment toriatsukai *(conduct toward)*; chiryoo *(medical)*.

treaty jooyaku.

    commercial treaty tsuushoo'jooyaku.

tree ki.

    evergreen tokiwagi.

tremble (to) furueru.

trembling *adj.* furuete iru. *-n.* miburui.

tremendous taihen na.

trench mizo *(ditch)*; zangoo *(military)*.

trend keikoo *(general tendency)*; hookoo, muki *(general direction)*.

trial saiban *(law)*; shiren *(hardship)*; kokoromi *(experiment)*.

triangle sankaku.

tribe shuzoku.

tribulation kannan.

tribunal saibansho *(a court of justice)*; saiban *(that which judges)*.

trick itazura, torikku *(mischief)*; sakuryaku *(stratagem)*.

trick (to) damasu.

trifle tsumaranai mono *(negligible thing)*; kudaranai koto *(insignificant matter)*.

trifle (to) tsumaranai koto ni jikan o tsubusu.

trifling tsumaranai *(uninteresting)*; kudaranai *(trivial)*.

trim (to) karikomu.

trimming kazari.

trip ryokoo.

    to take a trip ryokoo ni iku.

trip (to) tsumazuku *(take a false step)*; tsumazukaseru *(trip up)*.

triple sanbai no.

triumph shoori *(victory)*; daiseikoo *(success)*.

triumph (to) shoori o eru.

triumphant shoori o eta.

trivial kudaranai.

troop guntai.

trophy kappu, torofii.

trot (to) hayaashi de kakeru.

trouble konnan *(difficulty)*; mendoo *(bother)*; shinpai *(anxiety)*; nangi *(distress)*.

trouble (to) mendoo o kakeru *(put to inconvenience)*; komaraseru *(perplex)*; jama suru *(disturb)*.

    Don't trouble yourself! Shinpai shinai de kudasai.

trousers zubon.

truck torakku.

true hontoo no *(opp. of false)*; makoto no *(true-hearted)*; shin no *(real)*; jijitsu no *(actual)*; seikaku na *(exact)*.

truly hontoo ni *(correctly)*; chuujitsu ni *(faithfully)*; jitsu ni *(really)*; mattaku *(indeed)*.

trump kirifuda.

trumpet toranpetto.

trunk miki *(of tree)*; toranku *(baggage)*.

trust shin'yoo *(faith)*; gimu *(responsibility)*; shinrai *(reliance)*; kakushin *(confidence)*.

trust (to) shin'yoo suru *(give credit to)*; shinrai suru *(rely on)*.

trusting shinzuru.

trustworthy ate ni naru.

truth hontoo no koto *(correspondence to reality)*; jijitsu *(fact)*.

truthful shoojiki na *(veracious)*; jitchoku na *(upright)*.

truthfully shoojiki ni.

truthfulness seijitsu, seikakusa.

try (to) tamesu, kokoromiru *(prove by experiment)*; yatte miru *(attempt)*.

    to try to go ikoo to suru.

tube kuda, chuubu.

Tuesday Kayoobi.

tumble (to) korobu *(of persons)*; taoreru *(of things)*; ochiru *(roll over)*.

tumult oosawagi *(uproar)*.

tune senritsu, shirabe, fushi *(melody)*.

tune (to) chooshi o awaseru *(adjust)*; choowa suru *(be in harmony)*.

tunnel tonneru.

turf shiba, shibafu.

turkey shichimenchoo.

turmoil soodoo.

turn junban *(place in line, order, etc.)*; kaiten *(rotation)*; kaabu *(curve)*; hookoo tenkan *(change in direction)*.

turn (to) mawasu *(cause to revolve)*; mawaru *(revolve)*; magaru *(swerve)*.

    Turn left. Hidari e magatte kudasai.

    turn on a light tsukeru.

turnip kabu.

twelfth dai juuni.

    twelfth of the month juuninichi.

twelve juuni.

twentieth dai nijuu.

    twentieth of the month hatsuka.

twenty nijuu.

    twenty years of age hatachi.

twice nido.

twilight yuugata, tasogare *(poetic)*.

twin futago.

twist (to) nejiru *(distort)*; yoriawaseru *(intertwine)*; orikomu *(interweave)*.

two futatsu, ni.

type kata *(specimen)*; moderu *(model)*; tenkei *(pattern)*; taipu, katsuji *(printing)*.

type (to) taipu suru.

typewriter taipuraitaa.

tyranny ooboo, gyakusei.

tyrant hookun.

U

ugliness migurushii koto.

ugly mittomonai.

ulcer kaiyoo.

ulterior hyoomen no, sotogawa no.

ultimate saigo no.

ultimately saigo ni.

umbrella kasa.

umpire shinpankan, anpaiya.

umpire (to) shinpan suru.

unable dekinai.

    I'm unable to do it. Suru koto ga dekimasen.

unanimity manjoo itchi.

unanimous onaji kangae no *(agreeing in opinion)*; manjoo itchi no *(consent of all)*.

unanimously iku doon ni *(with one voice)*; manjoo itchi de *(with a unanimous voice)*.

unaware kizukanai.

unbearable tamaranai *(unendurable)*; gaman dekinai *(not able to be borne)*.

unbelievable shinjirarenai.

unbutton botan o hazusu.

uncertain fukakutei na *(undecided)*; gura gura shita *(unsteady)*; tashika de nai *(not sure)*; abunai *(risky)*; hakkiri shinai *(not settled)*.

uncertainty hakkiri shinai koto.

unchangeable fuhen no.

uncle oji, ojisan.

uncomfortable kokochi no warui, raku de nai.

uncommon metta ni nai *(infrequent)*; hijoo na *(extraordinary)*; mezurashii *(rare)*; fushigi na *(strange)*.

unconscious kizetsu shita *(having lost consciousness)*; kizukanai *(unaware)*.

unconsciously shirazu ni.

uncover (to) futa o toru *(take off a lid)*; ooi o toru *(take off a covering)*.

undecided kimatte inai.

undeniable hitei dekinai, mooshibun no nai.

under -no shita ni, -no shita de, -no shita no.

underdeveloped country teikaihatsukoku.

undergo ukeru; shujutsu o ukeru *(undergo an operation)*.

underground chika *(subterranean)*; himitsu no *(secret)*.

underline (to) shita ni sen o hiku *(underscore)*; kyoochoo suru *(emphasize)*.

underneath -no shita ni, -no shita de, -no shita no.

understand (to) wakaru; rikai suru.

understanding *adj.* wakari no yoi. *-n.* rikai.

undertake (to) hikiukeru *(take upon oneself)*; kuwadateru *(attempt)*.

undertaking shigoto *(task)*; jigyoo *(enterprise)*.

undesirable nozomashikunai.

undignified omomi no nai, hin no nai, fukinshin na.

undo (to) moto ni kaesu *(reverse)*; torikesu *(annul)*; hazusu *(unfasten)*; toku *(a knot)*; akeru *(open, as a parcel)*; nugu *(take off)*; muda ni suru *(bring to naught)*; tokeru *(come undone)*.

undress (to) kimono o nugu *(oneself)*; kimono o nugaseru *(make someone else undress)*.

uneasiness fuan.

uneasy fuan na; ochitsukanai *(restless)*.

unemployed shigoto no nai *(out of work)*; shitsugyooshita.

unequal fukoohei na, fubyoodoo na.

uneven fusoroi na *(not in line)*; deko boko na *(rough)*.

uneventful buji heion na.

unexpected omoigakenai *(not expected)*; yoki

shinai *(unforeseen);* totsuzen na *(sudden);* igai na *(surprising).*

unexpectedly igai ni, fui ni *(abruptly).*

unfailing tsukinai *(inexhaustible);* shinrai no dekiru *(sure).*

unfair fukoohei na *(biased);* tadashiku nai *(not right).*

unfaithful fuchuujitsu na.

unfamiliar yoku shiranai *(not well known);* shirarenai *(unknown);* keiken ga nai *(inexperienced).*

unfavorable yoku nai *(not good);* furi na *(not satisfactory);* tsugoo no warui *(inconvenient).*

unfit tekishinai *(unsuitable);* funiai na *(unbecoming).*

unfold (to) hirogeru.

unforeseen fui no, omoigakenai.

unforgettable wasurerarenai.

unfortunate fukoo na.

unfortunately ainiku *(unluckily);* zannen nagara *(regrettably).*

ungrateful arigataku omotte inai.

unhappily fushiawase ni.

unhappiness fushiawase.

unhappy fushiawase na.

unharmed buji na.

unhealthy karada no yowai *(sickly);* doku ni naru *(harmful to the health).*

unheard of mada kiita koto no nai.

unhesitatingly chuucho sezu ni.

unhoped for boogai no, kitai shinakatta.

unhurt kega no nai.

uniform *adj.* onaji yoo na *(about the same);* soroi no *(of the same pattern).* -*n.* yunifoomu, seifuku.

uniformity kin'itsu, kakuitsu.

uniformly dooyoo ni.

unify (to) tooitsu suru.

unimportant daiji de nai, tsumaranai *(worthless).*

unintentional koi de nai.

unintentionally koi de naku, muishiki ni.

uninviting ki no susumanai.

union kumiai *(association);* gappei *(combination);* engumi *(marriage).*

    labor union roodoo kumiai.

unique hitotsu kiri no *(single, sole);* dokutoku no *(peerless);* subarashii *(wonderful).*

union itchi, kyoodoo.

unit tan'i.

    unit price tanka.

unite (to) awaseru *(join into one);* ketsugoo suru *(combine);* gappei suru *(amalgamate);* gattai suru *(coalesce).*

united rengoo shita.

United Nations Kokuren.

United States Amerika Gasshuukoku.

unity tooitsu, itchi.

universal zen sekai no *(covering all the world);* ippan ni okonawareru *(widely practiced).*

universe uchuu.

university daigaku.

unjust fukoohei na.

unjustifiable iiwake no tatanai, too o enai.

unkempt darashi no nai.

unkind fushinsetsu na.

unknown shirarete inai.

unlawful fuhoo no, hooritsu ni hansuru.

unless -nakereba *(if not).*

    Unless you come . . . Anata ga konakereba . . .

unlikely arisoo de nai, hontoorashiku nai.

unlimited saigen no nai, seigen no nai.

unload (to) tsumini o ageru *(a ship's cargo);* ni o orosu *(take down from a truck or train).*

unlucky un no warui.

unmask (to) bakuro suru.

unmistakably machigai naku.

unnecessary yokei na *(superfluous);* mueki na *(useless);* muda na *(of no use);* fuhitsuyoo na *(not necessary).*

unoccupied aite iru *(untenanted);* yooji ga nai *(disengaged).*

unofficial hikooshiki no *(informal).*

unpack (to) ni o toku, nimotsu o hiraku.

unpleasant fuyukai na *(disagreeable);* iya na *(offensive).*

unpublished shuppan sarete inai.

unquestionably tashika ni.

unravel (to) toku, hodoku *(disentangle);* kaiketsu suru *(solve).*

unreal higenjitsuteki na.

unreasonable wake no wakaranai *(not governed by reason);* hoogai na *(exorbitant).*

unrecognizable wakari kaneru, mitomegatai.

unreliable ate ni naranai.

unrest fuon, fuanjootai.

unrestrained kimama na, yokusei no nai.

unrestricted museigen no.

unroll (to) toku, hirogeru.

unsafe abunai *(dangerous);* anzen de nai *(not safe).*

unsatisfactory fumanzoku na *(not satisfactory);* fujuubun na *(inadequate).*

unsatisfied fumanzoku na, manzoku shite inai.

unscrupulous buenryo na, mukoo mizu no.

unseemly mittomonai.

unseen kakurete iru, mienai.

unselfish rikoteki de nai, jibun o wasureta.

unspeakable iiyoo no nai.

unstable fuantei na.

unsteady shikkari shinai.

unsuccessful seikoo shinai, fuseikoo no.

unsuitable futekitoo na *(inappropriate)*; niawanai *(not becoming)*.

unthinkable kangaerarenai.

untidy darashi ga nai.

untie (to) hodoku.

until made.

    until now ima made.

untiring tsukarenai.

untrue uso no, hontoo de nai.

untrustworthy ate ni naranai.

untruth uso.

unusual ijoo na *(uncommon)*; mare na *(rare)*; metta ni nai *(not frequent)*; narete inai *(unfamiliar)*; mezurashii *(strange)*; reigai no *(exceptional)*.

unwarranted hoshoo no nai, fukakujitsu na.

unwell guai ga warui.

unwholesome kenkoo ni yoku nai, kenzen de nai.

unwilling fuhon'i no *(disinclined)*; ki ga susumanai *(reluctant)*.

unwise oroka na, kashikoku nai.

unworthy kudaranai *(wanting merit)*; fusawashiku nai *(unsuitable)*.

unyielding ganko na.

up ue, ue ni.

    eat up tabete shimau.

    give up akirameru.

upheaval dooran.

uphold (to) saseru, shiji suru *(support)*; kakunin suru *(court decision)*.

upkeep ijihi *(expense)*; iji *(maintenance)*.

upon -no ue ni, -no ue de, -no ue no.

upper ue no.

upright tatte iru *(erect)*; shoojiki na *(honest)*.

uprising boodoo *(revolt)*; ikki *(riot)*.

uproar oosawagi *(disturbance)*; soozooshii koe *(clamor)*.

upset (to) kutsugaesu *(overturn)*; taosu *(overthrow)*; shippai saseru *(frustrate)*; awatesaseru *(make nervous)*.

    to be upset roobai suru.

upside down sakasama *(topsy turvy)*; abekobe *(reverse)*.

upstairs nikai.

upward uwamuki no.

uranium uranyuumu.

urge (to) susumeru *(incite)*; isogaseru *(hasten)*; karitateru *(press)*; hagemasu *(exhort)*.

urgency seppaku, kinkyuu.

urgent isogi no, kinkyuu no.

urinate (to) shooyoo o suru, shooben suru.

us watashitachi.

U.S.A. Amerika Gasshuukoku.

use tsukaikata *(manner of using)*.

    to be of use yaku ni tatsu.

use (to) tsukau.

used to -mono da *(habitual in the past)*; -ni narete iru *(accustomed)*.

    I am used to dangerous places. Abunai basho ni narete iru.

    She used to go there every day. Mainichi itta mono da.

useful yaku ni tatsu *(serviceable)*; choohoo na *(handy)*; yuuyoo na *(good for something)*.

useless muyoo na *(of no service)*; dame na *(fruitless)*; muda na *(futile)*.

usher annai, annainin.

usher (to) annai suru.

usual futsuu no *(commonplace)*; itsu mo no *(habitual)*.

usually itsu mo, taitei.

usurp (to) ooryoo suru, shingai suru.

utensil doogu.

utility jitsuyoo, yuuyoo *(usefulness)*; kooeki jigyoo *(public utility)*.

    The rent includes utilities. Yachin ni wa suidoo-gasu-denki ga haitte imasu.

utilize riyoo suru.

utmost *adj.* sei ippai no *(maximum effort)*; kyokudo no *(extreme)*.

utter tetteiteki na *(total)*; kanzen na *(complete)*; mattaku no *(entire)*; mujooken no *(unconditional)*.

utter (to) iu *(say)*; hanasu *(speak)*; iiarawasu *(express)*.

utterly zenzen *(absolutely)*; mattaku *(totally)*; sukkari *(completely)*.

V

vacant kara no *(empty)*; aite iru *(unoccupied)*; karite no nai *(untenanted)*.

vacation yasumi.

vague hakkirai shinai *(indefinite)*; aimai na *(ambiguous)*.

vain yaku ni tatanai *(useless)*; muda na *(fruitless)*; unbore no tsuyoi, kyoeishin no tsuyoi *(conceited)*.

    in vain muda ni.

valiant isamashii *(brave)*; yuuki no aru *(courageous)*.

valid tashika na *(well founded)*; yuukoo na *(effective)*.

validity seitoo sa, kakujitsu sa.

valley tani.

valuable kooka na *(precious)*; neuchi no aru *(in terms of money, materially)*.

    valuables kichoohin.

value neuchi *(worth)*; atai *(cost)*.

value (to) nebumi suru *(appraise)*; sonchoo suru *(rate highly)*; daiji ni suru *(think important)*.

valued kichoo na.

valve ben, barubu.

vanilla banira.

vanish (to) kieuseru *(disappear)*; usureru *(fade away)*; nakunaru *(cease to exist)*.

vanity kyoeishin, unubore *(conceit)*.

vanquish seifuku suru *(conquer)*; makasu *(defeat)*.

vapor yuge *(of water)*; kitai *(gaseous state of liquid or solid)*.

variable kawariyasui.

variance fuwa *(antagonism)*; hendoo *(deviation, discord)*; fuitchi, chigai *(divergence)*.

variation henka, chigai *(modification, change)*.

varied samazama no.

variety henka ni tomu koto *(diversity)*; kuichigai *(difference)*; shurui *(kinds)*.

various iroiro no.

varnish (to) urushi o nuru.

vary (to) kaeru, chigaeru *(alter)*; henka o soeru *(diversity)*.

vase tsubo.

    flower vase kabin.

vast hiroi.

vault kinko *(safe)*.

veal koushi no niku.

vegetable yasai.

vehemence hageshisa.

vehement hageshii, nesshin na.

vehicle norimono.

veil maku *(curtain)*; beeru *(for face)*.

veil (to) beeru o kakeru.

vein joomyaku *(blood vessel)*.

velocity sokuryoku, hayasa *(speed)*.

velvet biroodo, berubetto.

venerable sonkei subeki, rippa na *(respected)*.

venerate (to) uyamau.

veneration sonkei.

vengeance fukushuu.

venom doku *(poison)*; urami *(ill will)*.

venomous doku no aru.

ventilation kazetooshi, tsuufuu.

ventilator tsuufuuki.

venture kiken na kuwadate.

venture (to) kiken ni sarasu *(risk)*; omoikitte yaru *(brave danger)*.

verb dooshi.

verdict hyooketsu *(of law)*; handan *(judgment)*; kettei *(decision)*.

verge hashi *(edge)*; heri *(brink)*; kyookai *(borderline)*.

    on the verge of -ni hinsuru.

verge (to) chikazuku.

verification kakunin.

verify (to) shoomei suru *(prove)*; tashikameru *(ascertain)*.

versatile tagei no, bannoo no.

verse shi *(poem)*; ku *(line of a poem)*.

version hanashi *(of a story)*; hon'yaku *(translation)*; iken *(opinion)*.

vertical suichoku no, tate no *(perpendicular)*.

very taihen, taisoo, hijoo ni, hanahadashiku, totemo.

vessel fune *(ship)*; iremono *(receptacle)*.

vest chokki.

vex (to) urusagaraseru *(annoy)*; okoraseru *(provoke)*; nayamasu *(distress)*.

via -keiyu.

vibrate (to) yureru *(oscillate)*; furueru *(quiver)*.

vice fudootoku *(depravity)*; akuheki *(evil habit)*.

vice president fuku daitooryoo *(of a country)*; fuku kaichoo *(of a society)*; fuku shachoo *(of a firm)*.

vice versa abekobe, hantai.

vicinity kinjo *(neighborhood)*; chikai koto *(nearness)*.

victim higaisha *(injured one)*; soonansha *(sufferer)*; giseisha *(one who is a sacrifice)*.

victor shoorisha.

victorious shoori o eta, katta.

victory shoori

video bideo.

    VCR bii-sii-aaru.

    video camera bideo kamera.

    video disc bideo disuku.

    video game bideo geemu.

vie (with) (to) kisou.

view keshiki *(prospect)*; iken *(opinion)*.

view (to) miru; yuuran suru *(sightseeing)*.

vigor seiryoku *(vitality)*; genki *(energy)*.

vigorous genki na *(energetic)*; tsuyoi *(strong)*; kappatsu na *(active)*.

vile katoo na.

village mura.

villain warumono.

vindicate (to) bengo suru.

vindictive shuunen bukai.

vine tsuru.

vinegar su.

violence bookoo *(outrage)*; booryoku *(exertion of physical force)*.

violent hageshii, hidoi *(wild)*.

violet *n.* sumire *(flower)*; murasaki iro *(color)*.

violin baiorin.

virtue toku *(moral excellence)*; zenkoo *(opp. of vice)*; misao *(chastity)*; kooketsu *(uprightness)*.

virtuous dootoku no takai *(morally good)*; kooketsu na *(honorable)*; dootokuteki na *(moral)*.

visibility shikai.

visible me ni mieru.

visibly me ni miete.

vision shiryoku *(eyesight).*

visit hoomon *(call on someone);* omimai *(to sick people).*

visit (to) tazuneru, hoomon suru *(a person);* kenbutsu suru *(museums, etc.).*

visitor okyakusama *(guest).*

visual shikaku no.

visual education shikaku kyooiku.

visualize (to) kokoro ni egaku.

vital seimei no *(of life);* hijoo ni juudai na *(very important);* kan'yoo na *(indispensable).*

vitality tairyoku.

vivacious kaikatsu na *(jovial);* yooki na *(lively);* genki na *(spirited).*

vivid hakkiri shita.

vocabulary tango *(individual words);* goi *(list of words).*

vocal koe no.

vocation shokugyoo *(profession);* shoobai *(business);* teishoku *(regular employment).*

vogue hayari, ryuukoo.

voice koe.

voice (to) koe o dasu *(utter);* iken o haku *(give expression to).*

void kooryoku no nai *(not binding);* mukoo no *(nullified).*

void (to) dasu *(throw, send out, empty).*

volume yooseki *(of a solid);* ryoo *(quantity);* -kan, -satsu *(counter for books and magazines).*

one volume issatsu.

voluminous kasabaru.

voluntary jihatsuteki.

volunteer shiboosha.

vomit (to) haku.

vote hyoo.

vote (to) toohyoo suru.

voucher uketori *(receipt).*

vouch for (to) hoshoo suru *(guarantee);* hoshoonin ni naru *(stand sponsor for).*

vow seiyaku *(promise);* chikai *(oath).*

vow (to) seiyaku suru *(promise);* dangen suru *(assert);* chikau *(pledge).*

vowel boin.

voyage kookai.

vulgar gehin na.

vulnerable yowami no aru.

W

wade (to) wataru.

waffle waffuru.

wag (to) furu.

wage chingin.

wager kakegoto *(act of betting);* kake *(bet).*

wager (to) kakegoto o suru.

wages chingin *(pay);* kyuuryoo *(salary, payroll).*

wagon kuruma.

waist koshi.

wait matsu koto *(act of waiting).*

wait (to) matsu.

waiter weetaa.

wake (to) okosu.

be awakened okosareru.

walk sanpo.

Go for a walk (take a walk). Sanpo suru.

walk (to) aruku.

wall kabe.

wallet saifu *(purse);* satsu-ire *(for paper money).*

walnut kurumi.

waltz warutsu.

wander (to) aruki mawaru.

want ketsuboo.

want (to) iru *(need);* hoshii desu *(want to have a thing).*

want to go ikitai.

war sensoo.

war (to) sensoo o suru.

warble (to) saezuru.

ward boogo *(guard);* mihari *(watch);* kyoodoo byooshitsu *(in a hospital);* ku *(division of a city, borough).*

wardrobe tansu.

ware, wares shinamono; saikumono *(handicraft);* toojiki *(chinaware).*

warehouse sooko.

warfare sensoo *(war).*

warm atatakai.

warm (to) atatakaku suru *(keep warm).*

warmth atatakasa.

warn (to) chuui suru *(caution);* imashimeru *(admonish).*

warning chuui, kunkai *(admonition);* yokoku *(notice).*

warrant hoshoo *(guarantee);* shoomeisho *(certificate).*

warrant (to) hoshoo suru.

warrior heishi *(soldier);* yuushi *(distinguished soldier).*

wary yoojinbukai.

wash sentaku *(washing).*

wash (to) arau.

washroom otearai, toire.

waste amarimono *(waste material);* kuzu *(refuse).*

wastepaper kamikuzu.

waste (to) muda ni suru.

watch tokei *(timepiece).*

wristwatch udedokei.

watch (to) ban o suru *(guard);* ki o tsukeru *(pay attention).*

watchful yoojinbukai *(cautious).*

water mizu.

water (to) mizu o yaru *(plants)*.

waterfall taki.

waterproof *adj.* mizu no tooranai. *-n.* boosui, taisui.

watt watto.

wave nami.

wave (to) yureru *(sway)*; hirugaeru *(flutter)*; furimawasu *(brandish)*.

waver (to) tamerau *(hesitate)*.

wax roo, wakkusu.

way michi *(road)*; toori *(street)*; hoohoo *(method)*.

we watashitachi, watakushidomo.

weak yowai.

weaken (to) yowaku suru *(make weak)*; yowaku naru *(get weak)*.

weakly yowayowashii, byooshin na *(sickly)*.

weakness ketten *(weak points)*.

wealth zaisan *(riches)*; tomi *(fortune)*.

wealthy kanemochi no *(rich)*; yutaka na *(well off)*.

weapon buki.

wear (to) kiru *(coat, dress)*; haku *(pants, shoes)*; shimeru *(girdle)*; kaburu *(hat)*; hameru *(ring, gloves)*; kakeru *(spectacles)*.

weariness hiroo *(fatigue)*; taikutsu *(tedium)*.

weary tsukareta *(tired)*; akita *(bored)*; taikutsu na *(tedious)*.

weather tenki.

    rainy weather ame, uten.

    cloudy weather kumori.

weave (to) oru.

wedding kekkonshiki *(ceremony)*.

wedge kusabi.

Wednesday Suiyoobi.

weed zassoo.

weed (to) zassoo o nuku.

week shuu *(counter for weeks)*.

    next week raishuu.

    this week konshuu.

    two weeks nishuukan.

weekend *n.* shuumatsu, wiikuendo.

weekly shuukan zasshi *(periodical)*.

weep (to) naku.

weigh (to) mekata o hakaru.

weight mekata.

welcome kangei.

    You're welcome. Yoku irasshaimashita. *(Glad that you've come.)* Doo itashimashite. *(It was nothing. Don't mention it.)*

welfare fukushi *(well-being)*; han'ei *(prosperity)*.

well ido *(for water)*.

west nishi.

western nishi no.

wet nureta, nurete iru.

wet (to) nurasu.

whale kujira.

what *pron.* nan, nani. *-adj.* dono *(which)*.

    what he said itta koto *(that which he said)*.

    What is it? Nan desu ka?

whatever nan de mo.

    whatever he heard nan de mo kiita koto.

    whatever he saw nan de mo mita mono.

wheat komugi.

wheel kuruma, wa.

when itsu *(interrogative)*; -toki, toki ni *(at the particular time that)*; -tara *(if, when)*; -to *(whenever)*.

    When I asked Mr. Yamada . . . Yamada-san ni kiitara . . .

    When I have a headache . . . Atama ga itai to . . .

    When I went to Kyoto . . . Kyooto e itta toki . . .

whenever -to, tabi ni *(every time)*; itsu mo *(always)*; itsu de mo *(at all times)*.

where doko ni, doko de, doko e *(in what place)*; dochira *(polite, used like doko)*; doko e *(whither)*.

wherever doko—demo; doko—temo.

    Wherever we go, there are many people. Doko e itte mo hito ga ooi.

whether ka, ka doo ka. -mo -mo.

    I don't know whether the library is open today. Toshokan wa kyoo aite iru ka doo ka shiranai.

    I intend to go whether it rains or snows. Ame ga futtemo, yuki ga futtemo iku tsumori desu.

which *pron.* dore *(of several)*; dochira *(of two)*. *-adj.* dono.

while -uchi ni; -aida ni.

    Wait a while. Chotto matte kudasai.

whim kimagure.

whimper (to) shikushiku naku.

whine (to) nakigoe o dasu.

whip muchi.

whip (to) muchi de utsu *(lash)*; sekkan suru *(flog)*.

whisper sasayaki.

whisper (to) sasayaku *(speak softly or under the breath)*; naisho banashi o suru *(speak in secret)*.

whistle fue *(instrument)*; kuchibue *(made with the mouth)*.

whistle (to) kuchibue o fuku.

white *adj.* shiroi. *-n.* shiro.

who *n.* donata, dare *(interrogative)*.

whoever dare de mo.

whole *adj.* zen- *(prefix)*; -juu *(suffix)*; zenbu no. *-n.* zenbu.

wholesale oroshi, oroshiuri.

wholesome kenkoo ni yoi *(salubrious)*; kenzen na *(sound)*.

whom dare ni, donata ni *(as indirect object)*; dare o, donata o *(as direct object)*.

whose donata no, dare no.

why naze, doo shite.

wicked warui *(bad)*; yokoshima na *(sinful)*; ijiwaru na *(ill-tempered)*.

wide hiroi.

widen *v.t.* hirogeru; *v.i.* hirogaru.

widow miboojin.

widower otoko yamome.

width haba.

wife tsuma; okusama *(your wife)*; kanai *(my wife)*.

wig katsura.

wild yasei no *(opp. of domestic)*; arehateta *(uncultivated)*; arai *(untamed)*; ranboo na *(lawless)*; kyooki no *(frantic)*.

wilderness arano.

wildness ranboo sa.

will ishi *(the faculty)*; ishi no chikara *(willpower)*; ketsui *(determination)*; negai *(wish)*; kiboo *(desire)*; yuigonjoo *(testament)*.

will (to) yuigon o nokosu *(bequeath)*.

willful koi no.

willing yorokonde . . . suru.

I'm willing to go. Yorokonde ikimasu.

willingly yorokonde.

win shoori, kachi.

win (to) toru *(prizes)*; katsu *(races)*; hakusuru *(fame, etc.)*.

wind kaze.

wind (to) maku.

window mado.

windy kaze ga fuku.

wine budooshu, wain *(grape)*; sake *(Japanese; made from rice)*.

wing hane *(of birds)*; yoku *(airplane)*.

wink mekubase, mabataki *(blink)*; isshunkan *(instant)*.

winner shoorisha *(victory)*; jushoosha *(recipient of an award)*.

winter fuyu.

wipe (to) fuku.

wire harigane *(metal)*; denpoo *(telegram)*.

wire (to) denpoo o utsu *(send a telegram)*.

wisdom funbetsu *(prudence)*; chie *(intelligence)*.

wise kashikoi *(sagacious)*; shiryo no aru *(sensible)*; hakushiki na *(learned)*.

wish negai *(longing)*; nozomi *(hope)*.

wish (to) -ga hoshii *(wish for something)*; nozomu *(hope)*.

wit kichi *(smart utterance)*; richi *(intelligence)*; funbetsu *(sense)*.

witch miko, majo.

with -to, -to issho ni *(together with)*; de *(by means of)*.

withdraw (to) hikisageru *(take back)*; saru *(remove)*; hikiageru *(evacuate)*.

withdrawal hikisage, tekkai; hikidashi *(bank)*.

wither (to) kareru.

within -no uchi ni, naka ni *(internally)*; ie no naka ni *(in the house)*; okunai ni *(indoors)*.

without -nashi *(not with)*; -nai de *(without -ing)*.

I went out without any money. Okane nashi de gaishutsu shita.

I went to school without having breakfast. Asagohan o tabenai de gakkoo e itta.

witness shooko *(testimony)*; shoogen *(verbal evidence)*; mokugekisha *(eyewitness)*; shoonin *(legal)*.

witness (to) mokugeki suru *(be a spectator)*; shimesu *(show)*; shoonin to shite shomei suru *(sign as a witness)*.

witty ki no kiita, kashikoi *(clever)*.

woe kunoo *(affliction)*.

wolf ookami.

woman onna, onna no hito, fujin *(lady)*.

wonder odoroki *(feeling)*; fushigi *(cause of)*; kiseki *(miracle)*.

wonder (to) odoroku *(be surprised)*; fushigi ni omou *(take as strange)*.

wonderful fushigi na *(strange)*; subarashii *(splendid)*.

wood ki; zaimoku *(lumber)*.

woods hayashi.

woodwork kizaiku.

wool yoomoo *(coat of sheep)*; keito *(yarn)*; ke *(material)*.

woolen keori no.

word kotoba *(speech)*; yakusoku *(promise)*; tayori *(news)*.

word for word ichiji ichiji.

word processor waapuro.

work roodoo *(manual labor)*; shigoto *(mission, job)*; shoku *(employment, occupation)*; chosaku *(literary work)*.

work (to) shigoto o suru, hataraku.

worker roodoosha *(wage earner)*; shokunin *(craftsman)*.

work of art geijutsu sakuhin.

workshop shigotoba, seisakujo.

world sekai *(earth)*; chikyuu *(the globe)*; seken *(society)*.

worldliness zokushuu.

worldly kono yo teki na.

worm mushi.

worry shinpai *(care)*; kuroo *(trouble)*; mendoo *(difficulty)*.

worry (to) *v.i.* shinpai suru; *v.t.* shinpai saseru *(make one worry)*.

Don't worry! Shinpai shinaide kudasai.

worse -yori mo warui, sara ni warui.

worship reihai *(religion)*; suuhai *(admiration)*.

worship (to) reihai suru, ogamu.
worst ichiban warui.
worth *adj.* neuchi ga aru, kai ga aru
  (worthwhile). *-n.* kachi, neuchi.
worthless neuchi no nai.
worthy kachi no aru *(good enough for);* -ni
  fusawashii *(deserving).*
wound kega *(injury);* kizu *(scratch).*
wound (to) kizutsukeru *(injure);* kega o saseru
  (hurt).
  get wounded kega o suru.
wounded kega o shita.
wrap (to) tsutsumu.
wrathful ikidootte iru.
wreath hanawa.
wreck nanpa *(of a ship).*
  a wrecked ship nanpasen.
wreck (to) hakai suru *(demolish);* kowasu
  (bring disaster on).
  to be shipwrecked nanpa suru.
wrestle (to) sumoo o toru *(Japanese-style);*
  resuringu o suru *(Western-style);* kutoo
  suru *(struggle with).*
wrestler sumootori *(Japanese-style);* resuraa
  (Western-style).
wrestling sumoo *(Japanese-style);* resuringu
  (Western-style).
wretched mijime na.
wring shiboru.
wrinkle shiwa.
wrinkle (to) hitai ni shiwa o yoseru *(one's
  forehead).*
  to wrinkle with age toshi o totte shiwa ga
  yoru.
wrist tekubi.
  wristband udewa.
write (to) kaku.
writer chosha *(author);* sakka *(novelist);*
  shoki *(clerk);* kaita hito *(one who wrote).*
writing hisseki *(handwriting);* kaita mono
  (that which is written).
  to state it in writing kaita mono de noberu.
  to put in writing shomen ni suru.
written kaite aru, kakareta.
wrong *adj.* warui, yoku nai *(bad);* ayamatta,
  machigatta *(mistaken);* fusei na *(not
  moral).* *-n.* fusei, fugi.
wrong (to) fusei o okonau.

Y

yacht yotto.
Yankee yankii.

yard niwa *(garden);* yaado, yaaru *(measure).*
yarn ito.
  wool yarn keito.
yawn akubi.
yawn (to) akubi o suru.
year toshi, -nen.
  per year nen ni.
  ten years junnen.
  this year konne, kotoshi.
yearly mainen no *(every year);* nen ni ichido
  no *(once a year).*
yearn for (to) -ni kogareru.
yearning akogare.
yeast iisuto, kooji.
yell sakebigoe.
yell (to) sakebu.
yellow *n.* kiiro. *-adj.* kiiroi.
yen en *(Japanese currency).*
yes hai, ee, soo de gozaimasu *(extra
  polite).*
yesterday kinoo, sakujitsu.
yet mada *(still);* soredemo *(nevertheless).*
  and yet sore na noni.
yield (to) sansuru *(produce);* yurusu *(grant);*
  ataeru *(give over);* shitagau *(follow).*
yielding juujun na *(compliant).*
yoke kubiki.
yolk tamago no kimi.
you anata *(sing.);* anatagata *(pl.);* kimi *(used
  by men to close male friends).*
young wakai.
your anata no *(sing.);* anatagata no *(pl.).*
yours anata no, anata no mono *(sing.),*
  anatatachi no, anatatachi no mono *(pl.).*
yourself jishin, jibun.
youth wakai toki *(the period);* wakai otoko
  (young man).
youthful wakawakashii.
youthfulness wakawakashisa.

Z

zeal nesshin.
zealous nesshin na.
zero zero, rei.
zipper zippaa, jippaa.
zone chitai, chiiki *(area);* -tai *(in
  compounds).*
  safety zone anzen chitai.
  temperate zone ontai.
zone (to) chiiki o kugiru.
zoo doobutsuen.
zoology doobutsugaku.

GLOSSARY OF
GEOGRAPHICAL NAMES

Africa Afurika.
Alaska Arasuka.
Algeria Arujeria.
Alps Arupusu.
America Amerika, Beikoku.
   Central America Chuuoo Amerika,
   Chuubei.
   North America Kita Amerika, Hokubei.
   South America Minami Amerika,
   Nanbei.
Argentina Aruzenchin.
Asia Ajia.
Atlantic Ocean Taiseiyoo.
Australia Oosutorariya.
Austria Oosutoria.
Beijing Pekin.
Bombay Bonbei.
Brazil Burajiru.
Burma Biruma.
Canada Kanada.
Chile Chiri.
China Chuugoku.
Cuba Kyuuba.
Denmark Denmaaku.
Egypt Ejiputo.
England Igirisu, Eikoku.
Europe Yooroppa, Ooshuu.
France Furansu.
Geneva Juneebu.
Germany Doitsu.
Great Britain Igirisu.
Greece Girisha.
Hawaii Hawai.
Hokkaido Hokkaidoo.
Hong Kong Honkon.
Hungary Hangarii.
Iceland Aisurando.
India Indo.
Indochina Indo shina.
Indonesia Indoneshia.
Iran Iran.

Iraq Iraku.
Ireland Airurando.
Israel Isuraeru.
Italy Itaria.
Japan Nippon, Nihon.
   Japan Sea Nihonkai.
Kobe Koobe.
Korea Kankoku *(South); * Kita Choosen
   (North).
Kyoto Kyooto.
Kyushu Kyuushuu.
London Rondon.
Malaya Maree.
Manila Manira.
Mexico Mekishiko.
Moscow Mosukuwa.
Netherlands Oranda.
New York Nyuu Yooku.
New Zealand Nyuu Jiirando.
Norway Noruuee.
Osaka Oosaka.
Pacific Ocean Taiheiyoo.
Pakistan Pakisutan.
Persian Gulf Perusha wan.
Philippines Firipin.
Poland Poorando.
Portugal Porutogaru.
Russia Roshia.
San Francisco San Furanshisuko.
Siberia Shiberia.
Singapore Shingapooru.
South Africa Minami Afurika.
Southeast Asia Toonan-Ajia.
Spain Supein.
Sri Lanka Suriranka.
Sweden Sueeden.
Switzerland Suisu.
Taipei Taipee.
Taiwan Taiwan.
Thailand Tai.
Tokyo Tookyoo.
Turkey Toruko.
United States Gasshuukoku.
   U.S.A. Amerika Gasshuukoku, Beikoku.
Washington D.C. Washinton.